I0754617

JOSÉ RODRIGUEZ GASPAR FRANCIA.—*See note, p.* 223.

THE

HISTORY OF PARAGUAY,

WITH

Notes of Personal Observations,

AND

REMINISCENCES OF DIPLOMACY UNDER DIFFICULTIES.

BY

CHARLES A. WASHBURN,

COMMISSIONER AND MINISTER RESIDENT OF THE UNITED STATES AT ASUNCION FROM 1861 TO 1868.

IN TWO VOLUMES.

VOL. I.

BOSTON:
LEE AND SHEPARD, PUBLISHERS.
NEW YORK:
LEE, SHEPARD, AND DILLINGHAM.
1871.

University Press: Welch, Bigelow, & Co.,
Cambridge.

CONTENTS.

CHAPTER I.

1526-1537.

CHAPTER II.

1537-1542.

CHAPTER III.

1542-1545.

CHAPTER VII.

CHAPTER VIII.

CHAPTER IX.

CHAPTER X.

CHAPTER XI.

CHAPTER XII.

CHAPTER XIII.

CHAPTER XIV.

CHAPTER XV.

CHAPTER XVI.

CHAPTER XVII.

CHAPTER XVIII.

CHAPTER XIX.

CHAPTER XX.

CHAPTER XXI.

CHAPTER XXII.

CHAPTER XXIII.

CHAPTER XXIV.

CHAPTER XXV.

CHAPTER XXVI.

CHAPTER XXVII.

CHAPTER XXVIII.

CHAPTER XXIX.

CHAPTER XXX.

CHAPTER XXXI.

CHAPTER XXXII.

CHAPTER XXXIII.

CHAPTER XXXIV.

CHAPTER XXXV.

CHAPTER XXXVI.

CHAPTER XXXVII.

HISTORY OF PARAGUAY.

PARAGUAY.

CHAPTER I.

1526-1537.

Introductory. — Discovery of Paraguay by Sebastian Cabot. — Antecedents of Cabot. — Origin of the Name Rio de la Plata. — San Espiritu. — The City of the Cesars. — Cabot returns to Spain, 1530. — His Character and Death. — Expedition of Don Pedro de Mendoza in 1534. — Unpopularity of Mendoza. — Buenos Aires. — Difficulties with the Natives. — Famine and Pestilence. — Corpus Cristi. — Efforts to establish Communication with Peru. — Death of Mendoza. — Domingo Martinez de Irala. — First Settlement of Asuncion. — Plague of Locusts. — Ruiz de Galan. — Internal Dissensions. — Battle with the Payaguas. — Treachery. — Battle with the Guaranis. — Miraculous Interference. — Irala chosen Governor. — Arrival of Emigrants. — Colonists united in Asuncion. — Favorable Prospects.

TILL within a few years the country of which I propose to write was so little known that but few people could tell anything more of it than that a region called Paraguay existed, and was to be found on all the maps of South America. Of the general aspect of this country and its history the popular knowledge was limited to traditions of its settlement by Spanish colonists, of the establishment of a religious order within its borders, which flourished for a time and was then expelled, to be succeeded by the reign of a gloomy despot, who made the land one vast prison-house, over which he ruled with a rod of iron. In these early traditions the land was always represented as of surpassing beauty and fertility, and the people as of exceeding gentleness and hospitality, who received the weary traveller and the war-worn soldier in a manner so simple and kind that they soon forgot their distant homes and friends, and resigned themselves to a life of idleness and sensuous enjoyment, which they were as unwilling to relinquish as were the companions of Ulysses to leave the Syrtes after having once eaten of the lotus fruit. By many persons the land was classed with that fatuous city so long said to exist in some part of Central America, to which many travellers had gone, but whence none had returned. Connected with these stories of Paraguay were others based on the accounts of Spanish and Portuguese voyagers and discoverers in South America, concerning a country which the companions of the great navigator, Sebastian Cabot, found somewhere in the interior of the continent, and which proved to be only a death mirage to many an unfortunate expedition.

But these vague traditions of the past, which gave such a romantic coloring to all that was known of Paraguay that it seemed to be suspended, like the flying island, between the domains of fiction and reality, have recently been dispelled, and the lurid light of a war which only terminated when the nation and race were virtually extinct has drawn the eyes of the world to this secluded region, which has been the scene of the darkest tragedy of modern times.

The historical account of the country where these tragic events occurred requires neither to be overdrawn nor highly colored to trespass hard on the limits of human credulity. A plain narrative of facts will be as much as the reader can believe. The naked history of the country has been so remarkable, the character of the people so peculiar, the government so anomalous, the prominent historic figures so strange, and the last scene of the long tragedy of personal government, which, while it lasted, held an entire people submissive to a despotism of unexampled severity, has in all its aspects been so terrible, that the writer who attempts to describe them must omit much, and tone down more, if he would be fully credited. The materials exist for a strange book, and as little is known of the country or its traditions, even by those most intelligent and most familiar with the history of the rest of the world, it must be entirely the fault of the writer if his work shall not be interesting. It will embrace the history of a people and nation during their whole existence, — a people the like of which never existed before and never can exist again.

PARAGUAY is situate between the parallels of 21° 20′ and 27° 32′ south latitude, and between 18° 16′ and 22° 39′ east of Washington. Its area is about once and three-fourths that of the State of Pennsylvania, being a little over eighty-two thousand square miles. This is the Paraguay known and acknowledged by the adjacent nations. But from the time when its independence was first asserted, it has always had disputes in regard to boundaries with every country whose territory adjoins it, and this area would be doubled were the questions of limits all decided in its favor. The disputed territory, however, being almost destitute of population, it matters little what may be the rightful and legal boundaries as affecting the history of the country or the character and habits of the people.

Paraguay, of which so little is generally known that it is usually spoken of as a new country, was one of the first in America settled by Europeans, and its capital, Asuncion, was a thriving colony long before the landing of the Pilgrims of Plymouth Rock, and even before John Smith made the traditional acquaintance of Pocahontas. The credit of the discovery of this country is generally, and I believe correctly, ascribed to Sebastian Cabot, the son of John Cabot the famous navigator, who was the first European that ever set foot in North America.

The adventures of Sebastian Cabot concern this work only so far as they relate to Paraguay. But as he was the first European who ever ascended the river Plata, it is proper to remark of him, that the place of his birth has been a matter of much doubt and dispute, though the preponderance of testimony goes to prove that he was born in England. John Cabot was, like Columbus, a native of Genoa, though he married and resided for years in Venice, where several of his children were born. He afterwards moved to England, and took up his residence in Bristol, where, it is claimed by many,

Sebastian was born. He there entered into the service of the English government, and under a contract with King Henry VII. he made several voyages to the West, and was the first to discover the continent of North America. In some of these voyages he was accompanied by his son Sebastian, who, after his father's death, entered into the service of the King of Spain, and under his patronage became a famous and successful navigator, and the discoverer of countries before unknown.

The discoveries of John Cabot in North America, and while in the English service, though vastly more important in their results than those subsequently made by Sebastian, were in themselves less meritorious, and for a long time excited far less attention. The difference in the results, however, is to be ascribed to difference in the character, habits, and religion of the people of the two nations which he served, and the different objects had in view by the respective emigrants. The Spanish adventurers cared little for countries whose wealth was only in their soil, and to be extracted by patient labor. They were eager and enterprising in the search for regions rich in gold, silver, spices, and precious stones. The countries discovered in North America by the elder Cabot, which gave England the pretext for claiming not only them but the vast regions adjoining, offered little to tempt the cupidity of the Spaniards; and they were left to those colonists who went there to remain and enjoy the fruits of their own toil, rather than grow rich on the spoil of a conquered race. On the other hand, the countries to which Spanish avarice and superstition were directed were abounding in wealth, and the invaders had little thought of benefiting themselves, except by despoiling the rightful possessors of their treasures. They went to rob the natives of their gold and silver, and to force them to be their slaves and drudge for more. At the same time that they enslaved them, they tortured them into the profession of the religion they had imported; and as they had seen that in the Old World the love of money was the root of all evil, and the cares of this world and the deceitfulness of riches were ever in the way of conversion to the true faith, they piously relieved the Indians of these snares of the soul, even going so far in the discharge of their painful duty as to relieve them of life at the same time, if necessary to get their possessions into their own hands. They came with the sword of rapine in one hand and the torch of the Inquisition in the other. The seeds sown by them have given forth such fruits of anarchy, superstition, revolution, and barbarism as have marked the history of Mexico, Central America, and the South-American states ever since. On the other hand, that country where first landed the Pilgrim fathers, who came not to rob the Indians, but to labor and earn their bread as God ordained of old, — not to persecute others into their belief, but to enjoy their own in peace, and who there first set the seal of their faith and the impress of their form of government, — that country is now the home of liberty and law, national strength, and advanced civilization. In view of these results that have followed from the early discoveries of John and Sebastian Cabot, we may well pay a passing tribute to their memory, and be grateful to that Providence that gave their great talents and virtues to England before they were secured to the service of Spain.

It was in the month of April, 1526, that Cabot, with three small vessels and one private caravel, and three hundred and fifty men, left Spain with the object of reaching the Moluccas, or Spice Islands. It was his purpose to reach them by passing through the Straits of Magellan, that had been discovered, as early as 1519, by that famous navigator whose name they bear. But, like Columbus and many others of the early explorers, Cabot, in seeking for one thing, found another. Having been compelled from the smallness of his vessels and scanty supplies to abandon his project of following the route of Magellan, he turned northward, and, entering the broad bay that forms the mouth of the Rio de la Plata, he ascended it, under the illusion that he had discovered another channel by which he could pass through to the Pacific. He soon learned, however, that the river was not a channel to the Pacific, and his vessels had already suffered so much since he left Spain, that he was obliged to abandon his idea of reaching the Moluccas until he could obtain large reinforcements of both men and ships. He therefore set about the exploration of the country, where his apparent ill fortune had cast him. Fifteen years before, in 1511, Juan Diaz de Solis had, with a similar object, — that of finding a western passage to the Indies, — entered the same broad estuary whence he was never to return. Going ashore on the island of Martin Garcia, he was murdered by the savages and his expedition broken up. The river, however, received, and was known by, the name of the Rio de Solis until some time after the advent of Cabot, who, deluded by the reports of the Indians whom he encountered on the banks of what is now called the Paraguay, gave that affluent the name of the Rio de la Plata (River of Silver). And as the marvellous accounts of vast quantities of gold and silver near its head-waters reached Europe at the same time with the news of its discovery, the alluring name of Rio de la Plata was soon applied to the whole river below, thus superseding entirely the name of Rio de Solis.

The great navigator lived to learn, however, that the silver, of which he heard such marvellous accounts, all came from a land which he was never to see, and that the valley of the River of Silver was almost destitute of the precious metals.

The Rio de la Plata, or River Plate, or what passes for that at present, can hardly be considered a river. The name is used vaguely and with different meanings as it is applied to the river or the valley ; as by the latter is included the whole vast territory drained by all those great rivers that find their outlet to the ocean through the broad estuary that is strictly the Rio de la Plata. Above the confluence of the Uruguay and the Parana, those rivers are always called by their respective names ; and hence the Plata only extends from that point to the ocean, a distance of less than two hundred and fifty miles.

Entering this broad estuary, Cabot with his small fleet skirted along its banks past where Buenos Aires now stands, making observations as he went, until he arrived at the mouth of the Uruguay. This river he first undertook to explore, but after various disasters and losses he divided his forces, and, leaving his two larger vessels, he entered the Parana with only a small brig and the caravel. As he passed up the river, the Indians came in large numbers to the river-banks, being greatly astonished at the sight of the vessels. He proceeded up the river to the mouth of the Carcarañа, or Tercero as it is now called, where he landed and commenced building a fort. This was the first Spanish settlement in this part of the world, and was named, by Cabot, San Espiritu. Here he left seventy men to guard the place, and then pursued his voyage. Before departing, however, he strictly enjoined those left in charge of the fort to cultivate the most friendly relations possible with the Indians, and to improve the time of his absence by explorations of the adjacent country. The neighboring Indians appeared very friendly and harmless, and after the departure of the commander small parties were sent out to make observations on the character and productions of the country. One of these parties, consisting of five persons under the command of a person named Cesar, never returned; and from the adventures of the party, real or imaginary, originated the tradition of a great inland city, near the foot of the Andes, far away to the southwest of all regions then known or explored by Europeans. It is certain that these men never returned, and what became of them is not known. But the tradition was current, many years later, that after long wandering they came to a finely cultivated and fertile country, inhabited by a race of people highly civilized and living in refinement and luxury. They were said to be possessed of great stores of gold and silver, and cattle and horses in vast numbers. The capital of this marvellous country was said to be an immense city, in which were to be found all the splendors and refinement of the most luxurious cities of the East. The architecture was elegant and grand; the streets wide, regular, and clean, and the torrents from the Andes were carried in immense aqueducts to all parts of the city, where health, comfort, or utility might require. The stories of the wonderful wealth of this fabled land grew more and more extravagant as time passed, and one expedition after another set out in search of it. As none ever returned, it was supposed they had found the El Dorado so delightful that they would not leave it, even for so short a time as was necessary to notify their fellow-adventurers of their good fortune. After many years, however, the report got currency that Cesar and his followers had been detained by the king of the country they had discovered; that he had treated them with great kindness, but for a long time refused them permission to leave his dominions; but that after many years he relented and allowed them to depart, not, however, till so long a period had elapsed, that, on returning to the site of the colony of San Espiritu founded by Cabot, they found it had long since disappeared and themselves abandoned in a sea of forest. At last, however, they struck the trail that led to the Pacific, and, following the tide of the gold-seekers to Peru, it was there that one of the party related his adventures to somebody else, who in turn related them to Ruy Diaz de Guzman, the first historian of Paraguay.

From a source so misty and mythical came this legend or tradition, and for several generations the belief in that region of fabulous wealth was so strong that repeated expeditions were formed, both in Chili and Buenos Aires, to search for the "City of the Cesars," as it was called, until subsequent explorations satisfied all searchers for it that there was not, and never had been, any such place.

After leaving San Espiritu, the passage of Cabot and his party up the river was slow and difficult. The channel is so tortuous, that, for a sailing-vessel to make continuous headway against the stream, the wind must blow from all points of the compass during the twenty-four hours. Besides, the river is in some parts so broad and full of islands that it appears more like a succession of lakes than a flowing stream, and for the first explorers it was a work of tedious labor and trial to find the channel. To avoid the delays caused by adverse winds, and a current running in every direction within the space of a few miles, Cabot resolved to clear away the decks, and razee the sides of his vessels, and then fit them with row-locks and oars, so as to be able to double the short bends in the river when the wind was unfavorable.

At length, however, he arrived with his little force of one hundred and twenty men at the confluence of the Parana and Paraguay, about three hundred and fifty miles above Fort San Espiritu. Here the Parana appearing to be the larger river, they followed it up about one hundred and fifty miles; but finding the volume of water rapidly diminishing, and the navigation difficult, by reason of the frequent rapids, they stopped at a place near the island of Apipé, where they remained some thirty days, exploring the neighboring country and trafficking with the Guarani Indians, whom they met there. These Indians, having some trinkets of gold and silver, were asked where they obtained them. They replied that they came from the west. The party thereupon returned to the mouth of the Paraguay, for they could see nothing to tempt them to remain in a country which promised no spoils of gold and silver to be taken from the heretic and heathen. The spoils of Mexico and Peru had dazzled the eyes of the Spanish adventurers, and Paradise itself would not have satisfied them without a plentiful supply of the precious metals. Cabot's aspirations were those of a good, great, and wisely ambitious man, and he looked for fame as a discoverer. But nothing would satisfy the great monarch whom he served, Charles V., except gold, and his followers and companions knew no motive but greed.

Returning to the mouth of the Paraguay, the little party began the ascent of the river, which above its confluence with the Parana flows between well-defined banks, and is consequently of easy navigation. They met with no incident of importance till they reached a point called Angostura, some eight leagues below Asuncion, where the little river Cañabé unites with the Paraguay. Here they were attacked by a large force of Payagua Indians, and a fierce battle was fought. The accounts of this battle are conflicting, — one of them saying that the Indians attacked the intruders in great force, having as many as three hundred canoes, each with its complement of warriors; that the Spaniards made fearful havoc among them with their cannon and small arms, losing only two of their own force, who were taken prisoners. This account is contradicted by other writers, who state that the Spaniards lost heavily, and, among others, the officer second in command of the expedition. Whatever their losses, however, the party continued their voyage up the river, passing by the site of the present capital, Asuncion. Wherever they stopped they cultivated friendly relations with the Indians, and exchanged with them such things as they could spare for those products of the country required for food, and for their trinkets of gold and silver. The latter were the great object of their desire, and they eagerly inquired whence they came. The answer was always the same, — from a country far to the west. Cabot now believed that he was near the rich mines of Peru, and was strengthened in his conviction that he had discovered a new route to that land of untold wealth, much more available and easy of passage than the one by the Isthmus of Darien. He now believed that the wealth of the Indies must find its way to Europe by the river he was the first to discover, and it was not till he had passed a long distance above the mouth of the Parana that he fixed on the name Rio de la Plata as the title of the Paraguay. But this name soon came to be regarded as that of the entire river to its mouth, and now that which Cabot thus denominated the River of Silver is seven hundred miles from the body of water which to-day bears the name.

In order to prosecute his discoveries, and establish this line of communication with Peru, Cabot soon found that an increase of force was indispensable; and so, after making various expeditions into the interior of the country, and informing himself of the great natural resources of Paraguay, notwithstanding its lack of mineral wealth, he returned to the fort at San Espiritu, whence he despatched two of his most trusted followers to Spain, in order to obtain the needed reinforcements and the royal authority to continue his expedition into a different region from that he had set out to explore. They took with them several Guarani Indians and an assortment of the productions of Paraguay; and the accounts they gave of the fertility of the soil, the salubrity of the climate, the general aspect and beauty of the country, the gentle and docile character of the predominant class of Indians, would at another time have secured to them an enthusiastic reception and a ready compliance of the government with their request. But at that time the spoils of Peru were pouring into Spain, and government and people were all mad for gold. Hence the story of a land of surpassing beauty and agricultural wealth attracted but little attention. The country promised no rich spoils to military invaders, and no large military force ever entered Paraguay. Hence the subjugation to the Spanish rule was gradual, and the people became subjects, rather than slaves, of the superior race.

The causes that, according to the late Mr. Buckle, had developed the civilization of Peru and Mexico, had never existed in the countries of the Plata. In those countries only of the New World had there been that combination of the elements that lead to the accumulation of wealth, and consequently to the existence of classes. The class having wealth naturally had leisure for the cultivation of such arts and sciences as had ever chanced to dawn on their unenlightened intellects; and to preserve the advantages of their wealth they had in the course of ages wrought out the governments and civilization that existed at the time of the Spanish invasion. Wealth had brought luxury, and luxury had brought in its train the pomp and pride of power, to be supported by heavy taxes on the poor and by large standing armies. But in the other parts of America, where Nature was less prolific and spontaneous in her bounties, the native Indians had never advanced beyond their nomadic character. It was the same in the regions of the Plata as in that part of North America now constituting the United States. There were many tribes, more or less numerous and powerful, but none worthy to be called nations, or having sufficient wealth to tempt the cupidity of European monarchs to undertake large and expensive expeditions to effect their subjugation or conversion. Hence it was that small colonies, usually fitted out at private expense, were sent out to get possession of such sections of country as might be desirable for trade or agriculture, and which they would be able to hold against the neighboring savages. These colonies, to a considerable extent, went forth with similar ideas to those who first peopled those parts of North America south of New England. That the pioneers of civilization in the North experienced cruel hardships is well known; and were we to pursue the early history of the regions of the Plata, we should find it made up of adventure and danger on one side, and treachery and hate on the other. The exceptions of the Puritans and the Quakers do not disprove the fact, that the art, cunning, and fraud of the European were as a rule met with treachery, hate, and cruelty by the savage.

More fortunate than Columbus, Raleigh, and others of the most meritorious discoverers of the New World, Sebastian Cabot realized something more than envy and misrepresentation for his services. His messengers not having succeeded in obtaining the reinforcements he had asked for, he determined, in 1530, to return himself to Spain, to impress upon the king the importance of his discoveries. But the great monarch was too much occupied in fighting heretics in Europe, and robbing the heathen in Mexico and Peru, to spend time or money on a new country that did not promise immediate returns. Cabot resumed his old position of Piloto Mayor, which he had held before his last expedition to America. This position, as the chief director of all foreign expeditions of Spain, was perhaps the one for which at his time of life he was best adapted. He was now an old man, and his name and fame as a navigator excelled that of any person living; and though he remained in Europe, he could still pursue his studies as a geographer, and plan and execute other projects of discovery. He lived some thirty years after returning from

America, and after a life of vicissitudes and adventures of the most extraordinary character, with a name unblemished and unstained by any of the excesses or cruelties that have blackened the memory of nearly every one of the early American discoverers, he at last returned to England, "to die at home at last."

It was four years after Cabot's return to Spain — that is, in 1534 — before another expedition was fitted out for the Rio de la Plata. The projector of this expedition was Don Pedro de Mendoza, a member of the royal household and a gentleman of large fortune, who had seen service under the Emperor in his Italian wars. He offered to do at his own expense what Cabot could do only with the assistance of the crown. He asked and obtained permission to fit out an expedition at his own cost to take possession of the countries discovered by Cabot, and establish settlements at such points as he might select. In return for this service he was to be appointed Governor, with the title of Adelantado, and was to enjoy certain privileges, supposed to be of great value, on the sole condition that the Emperor was not to be called upon to defray any part of the expenses. The extraordinary privileges granted by the crown consisted of the right to rob the Indians and retain an unusual part of the spoils, paying less than the customary percentage of the treasure so stolen into the royal treasury. As marking the moral character of the period and of the great monarch who regarded it as his peculiar mission to exterminate heresy from the earth, it should be observed, that the atrocious conduct of Pizarro in his treatment of the Inca was so far regarded as legitimate and proper, that in the contract, or *Asiento*, with Mendoza, Charles V. expressly stipulated that the ransom of any other foreign sovereign who might be captured, though by law all belonging to the Emperor, should be divided among the conquerors, reserving to the crown only the royal fifth.

According to the Asiento, the Adelantado was to take out one thousand men, fully armed and equipped, with supplies sufficient for a year. He was also to take out a number of missionaries to convert the Indians as fast as they robbed and enslaved them. The fate of this expedition, conceived in such a spirit of iniquity, was such as it deserved.

The favorable terms granted to Mendoza being made public, people came forward in great numbers, eager to join the expedition. Many men of rank and position offered to join, and so popular was the enterprise, that instead of one thousand men, as had been agreed upon, it was found at the first muster, after they had got started, that there were two thousand six hundred and fifty men, besides the crews of the fourteen ships, bound for the River of Silver.

As is usually the case in such enterprises, there were several turbulent spirits in the party, and, unfortunately, Mendoza was not the man to command their obedience or respect. Several disgraceful incidents occurred before the expedition reached the Plata. The military commander of the troops was Don Juan de Osorio, an officer of high repute, who had distinguished himself under the "Great Captain." The Adelantado soon became very unpopular, while Osorio was greatly beloved. This excited the jealousy of Mendoza, and while the fleet was at Rio de Janeiro he ordered Osorio to be put under arrest. Osorio requested to be brought before the Adelantado, that he might clear himself of the charges that had been made against him. But on coming into the presence of the Adelantado, that high official fell into a great passion, and used most violent and insulting language to his lieutenant. As Osorio was leaving, the Adelantado made some brutal remark, which the Alguazil Mayor, or chief constable, Juan de Ayolas, understood to be an order to despatch him, when he drew a dagger and plunged it into his heart.

Thus fell the man of most importance for the success of the expedition, through the bad temper and arrogance of the chief in command. The event rendered Mendoza more unpopular than ever, and caused many misgivings as to the success of the expedition. Indeed, the subsequent fate of both the Adelantado and the Alguazil might well lead them to suppose that they were pursued by the avenging spirit of Osorio.

It was in the month of January, 1535, that the expedition first entered the Rio de la Plata. With a perversity of judgment that seemed to characterize all the acts of Mendoza, he moved up the broad and noble estuary, passing by the most suitable places for a town site, until he came to a place that combined all the inconveniences that could possibly exist on the banks of a large navigable river. The point thus selected, and where now stands the principal city of the Plata, has probably the worst harbor in the world for a large commercial town. Large vessels must always lie off some two or three leagues from the shore, and those of lighter draft that venture within the inner roads are liable to be left high and dry on the hard bottom, or *tosca,* when a *pampero,* or strong wind, from the west sets in. But if the wind blows strongly from the southeast, then they are liable to drag their anchors and be carried up so high inland, that, when the wind veers again, they are left many rods from the water, and can only be broken up for firewood. The cost of lightering a vessel of her cargo is much more than the freight of it from New York or Liverpool. The country in the vicinity, for as far as the eye could reach, was a dead level plain, without bush or tree ; the air in the hot, dry season being frequently so full of dust as to be almost insupportable, and the soil of that sticky, clayey character that a slight rain would render it almost impassable for man or animal. And this place was selected by Mendoza as the site of the first Spanish settlement in South America ; and its history illustrates the fact, confirmed by a thousand instances, that where the pioneers of a country first fix their abiding-place, there will be the principal town of the vicinity, even though other points near by possess greater advantages. And as if to be in harmony with the paradoxical and illusive name of River of Silver, this first settlement was called Buenos Aires. The tradition is, that the first person of Mendoza's party who landed exclaimed as he touched the shore, "*Que buenos aires son estos!*" This exclamation was accepted as a good augury by the commander, and the name of the place was, with true Spanish brevity and piety, declared to be Santa Maria de Buenos Aires.*

In his dealings with the Indians, Mendoza showed the same want of sense and tact as in everything else. On landing at Buenos Aires and examining the stock of provisions remaining, it was found that instead of a supply for twelve months, as had been stipulated, so little was left that the men had to be put at once on short allowance. The Querandi Indians whom they met, prompted by curiosity, came around in great numbers, and brought them some small supplies of game and fish; but as they did not bring sufficient for so large an army, Mendoza thought to intimidate and compel them. Greater folly it is impossible to conceive; for however sad havoc he might make in their number, and at however small loss to himself, it was clear that after having defeated them he would get no more provisions from that source, and his men were at the point of starvation. Undeterred by any such prudential considerations, the Adelantado ordered out a body of three hundred troops with a small cavalry force, which he placed under the command of his brother, Don Diego de Mendoza, who was the admiral of the squadron, and sent it out to chastise the Indians and teach them to show more hospitality. They soon encountered a large body of the natives, who lured them into an attack in the midst of a morass, where, though the Spanish veterans made fearful havoc among the savages, killing more than a thousand, the larger half of their own party was killed, including the admiral himself.

After this the Indians kept aloof for a time, contenting themselves with hovering about and sweeping down on any small parties that might be sent out in quest of food.

The Spaniards were now reduced to the greatest distress. To protect themselves, they erected a large fort, within which they put up some thatched mud houses to shelter themselves from the sun and rain. To the famine succeeded pestilence,

* The name given to the city on its *second* foundation was still longer: Ciudad de la Santisima Trinidad, Puerto de Santa Maria de Buenos Aires.

and there, shut up within their mud walls, the twenty-five hundred Spaniards yet left, who had come out to the River of Silver confident of speedy fortunes, saw no prospect before them but utter annihilation. Vessels had been despatched up and down the coast to look for a supply of food, but without obtaining any. Another, commanded by Ayolas, had been sent up the river, and he had not been heard from. The soldiers were reduced to eat their horses, dogs, cats, rats, and anything that would support life. One incident will suffice to illustrate their desperate condition. Three men were hung for stealing a horse, and the next morning it was found that they had been cut down and eaten by their companions. In this awful condition they were attacked by a force estimated by early writers at no less than twenty thousand. The Querandis, after the fatal battle against Diego de Mendoza, had called in the neighboring tribes to assist in the extirpation of the common enemy. Their principal weapon was the *bolas*. This consisted of several pieces of cord tied together at one end, with balls or weights attached to the loose strands at the other. A practised hand may throw this instrument with great accuracy to a long distance. It was the chief weapon used by the natives to bring down birds on the wing, and break or entangle the legs of the wild animals of the *pampas*. On this occasion, the Indians in vast hordes surrounded the fort of the Spaniards, and threw their *bolas*, to which they had attached burning matches. These falling on the roofs of the thatched hovels, they were soon all in a blaze, while three of the small vessels in the little river called the Riachuelo were set on fire in the same way. But the guns of the other vessels were now brought to bear on the savages, and made such havoc that they quickly dispersed. Nevertheless, though the savages had been driven back, the prospect was no less gloomy than before. But, fortunately, at this time a gleam of light breaks in on the ill-starred expedition. Ayolas's party, that had been sent up the river, returned with a supply of maize, which they had obtained from the Timbu Indians, the same with whom Cabot had been wise enough to establish friendly relations some seven years before. Ayolas, finding the Timbus so friendly and well disposed, left one hundred of his men with them, having first made a plan for a new fort, which he named Corpus Cristi, at a short distance from Cabot's former settlement of San Espiritu, that had been abandoned soon after the departure of the great navigator for Spain.

The favorable report brought by Ayolas of the friendly character of the Timbus induced Mendoza to abandon Buenos Aires, with his shattered forces, for the more hospitable regions of the interior. Of the two thousand six hundred and fifty men, besides the crews of the vessels, who had left Spain a year before, there remained but five hundred and sixty at Buenos Aires, and of these sixty died from exhaustion ere they reached the new fort.

From Corpus Cristi the Adelantado despatched Ayolas, with three hundred men, to explore the river above, and learn if it were practicable to carry into effect the original plan of the enterprise, which was to open easier communication with Peru. The Alguazil set forth on this forlorn undertaking, leaving his chief to await his return, as on his success now depended the last hope of the Adelantado. But Ayolas never reached Peru, and never returned to Corpus Cristi ; and Mendoza, discouraged and broken-hearted, and worn out with disease and grief, after waiting a year, and hearing nothing of him, resolved to return to Spain. The multitude of disasters he had encountered, and the misery and destruction brought upon his companions through his incapacity, were too much for a mind no stronger than his. He died on the passage home, a raving maniac.

Before leaving for Spain, the Adelantado having received no news of Ayolas, and seeing no other means of obtaining succor for his companions, despatched a near relative of his — Don Gonzalo de Mendoza — to Spain, to bring the necessary relief. But Gonzalo, greatly to the surprise and joy of all, soon returned, having obtained a good supply of provisions on the coast of Brazil. This happy turn of affairs induced the Adelantado to send Don Gonzalo and Don Salazar de Espinosa on another expedition, this time up the river, and in search of Ayolas. Before departing, the Adelantado appointed Ayolas his lieutenant, to succeed, on his return, to the command of the colony. Months before he had seen all his own bright prospects vanish, and had asked for the appointment of a successor. The successor named by the crown was Ayolas. Ayolas, however, was away on his expedition to the North, and it was known to the Spanish government that he had been absent a year from the colony, and it was doubtful whether or not he would ever return. He had not been heard of since his departure, though his orders at setting out were to be back in four months at the furthest. But though his return was extremely doubtful, Mendoza determined not to appoint another to serve in his stead, as he feared the conflict of authority that might arise if Ayolas were to come back and find another holding a commission from himself. Ayolas, however, was never to hear of the honors which his king had intended for him.

One good, however, resulted to the colony from the uncertainty regarding the fate of Ayolas. At the same time that his commission was sent out, an instrument, or letters-patent, was issued, providing for the choice of a successor by the colonists, should Ayolas not have previously come back. This act of confidence in the popular choice, so at variance with the general usage of the Spanish government, in this case at least had a favorable result. There chanced to be one man among the companions of Pedro de Mendoza gifted by nature with all those qualities required in a leader and founder of a colony, one of those rare individuals who by sheer force of character, by their courage, tact, energy, and justice, leave the impress of their genius on their age and generation. This man, Domingo Martinez de Irala, then holding the rank of captain, had been sent with Ayolas to establish communication with Peru. His position was that of admiral of the small fleet of three vessels that conveyed the expedition up the river. The party proceeded on their voyage, and, like Cabot before them, on reaching the confluence of the Parana and Paraguay, they first ascended the former, though it flows from the eastward, and from the direction opposite to which they were to look for those regions that had given the name to the river. They soon returned, and followed the Paraguay as far as what is now known as Fort Olimpo, 21° 2′ S., and some two hundred and forty miles above the site of the present capital, Asuncion. From this point Ayolas, with two hundred men, leaving but one hundred with Irala to guard the vessels and wait his return, marched into the interior to the west, in search of the fields of gold and rivers of silver that were luring him to destruction. Not one of the party ever saw the face of a white man afterwards.

Irala remained at Olimpo, or, as it was then named in the verbose piety of the Spaniards, Nuestra Señora de la Candelaria (Our Lady of the Candlemas), where he busily employed himself in exploring the country, and in cultivating friendly relations with the Payagua Indians who dwelt in the vicinity. While engaged in this laudable work, the expedition that had been sent by the Adelantado, under command of Gonzalo de Mendoza and Salazar de Espinosa, in search of Ayolas, arrived at Candelaria. From this point many parties were sent out to look for the long-absent Alguazil and his companions, but as no trace of them could be found, Mendoza and Espinosa insisted on returning to Corpus Cristi. But Irala still refused to abandon all hope of finding and saving his former chief, and therefore the commanders of the expedition sent in search of him and Ayolas returned, leaving him but a single vessel and his former force of one hundred men.

In descending the river from Candelaria, Mendoza observed that the place where Asuncion now stands had, from its topographical situation, peculiar advantages as a port or trading-post on the imaginary route to Peru. The river there makes an elbow, turning to the right, with an abrupt bluff just below on the left bank, forming thus a harbor of deep water close to the shore in front of where the city now stands. From the top of the bluff the river can be distinctly seen for leagues, and the whole country for miles in every direction is distinctly visible. Mendoza saw the advantages the place offered both for commercial purposes and for defence against hostile attacks, and he therefore resolved to remain there with a small body of men and erect a fort, while his companion, Espinoza, should proceed to Corpus Cristi or Buenos Aires and make a report of the attractions they had found up the river. The Indians they here encountered were the mild and tractable Guaranis, whose gentle manners and hospitable character contrasted strangely with the savage ferocity of the warlike Querandis, who had waged such vindictive war against them while at Buenos Aires. Mild and peaceable as these natives appeared, Mendoza knew enough of the Indian character to realize that a fortified post was the first essential among savages. He therefore immediately commenced building a fort; and as the day on which he begun this work chanced to be the 15th of August (1537), which in the Catholic calendar is the day of the Assumption of the Virgin, he gave to the place the name La Asuncion.*

Espinosa returned to Corpus Cristi, and thence to Buenos Aires, where a small force had always remained, to receive, welcome, and warn any arrivals subsequent to the departure of the main forces under Pedro de Mendoza for Corpus Cristi. The favorable reports given by him of the fine climate and fertile soil of Paraguay, as well as of the friendly reception they had met with from the Guaranis, were enough to make his

* In giving the names of places, I follow the spelling of the people who inhabit them. The early Spanish discoverers generally gave names having some peculiar signification, which, translated into another language, would be spelt differently. Thus Asuncion, in Spanish, is in meaning equivalent to Assumption in English, to Assomption in French, and to Assumpçao in Portuguese. Buenos Aires, translated into English, would be Good Airs, and Santa Fé would be Holy Faith. But no writer pretends to give the names of places uniformly as they would read if translated to the idiom in which he writes. I know not by what right, or according to what rule, an author changes some and allows others to stand as in the original. As it is considered the right of every man to spell his own name after his own fashion, and to require at least as a courtesy that others shall spell it in the same way, I see no good reason why the same rule should not obtain among writers when giving the names of places in countries where a different language from their own is spoken.

comrades, and others who had since arrived, eager to quit a region where they had suffered so terribly. They gladly left a place where they had experienced nothing but suffering and disappointment, where they were surrounded by savages bearing an implacable hatred towards them, and where death from starvation was ever threatening those whom the savages could not reach.

They therefore embarked for Asuncion, leaving only a small force sufficient to hold the fort, and reached their destination without any important incident. But instead of escaping from a land of famine to one of plenty, they found, on reaching the desired haven, that a plague of locusts had passed over the country but a short time before, consuming every green thing, leaving myriads of their numbers dead as they passed, filling the wells and springs and many other places with their bodies, to infect the air and breed a pestilence.

Thus it seemed that the companions of Mendoza were pursued by a relentless fate, not only while they remained at Buenos Aires, but until they had made an expiation by suffering in other parts. The visitation of the locusts, however, is a thing of rare occurrence, and when they do appear their ravages are generally confined to a strip of country of but few leagues in width, passing from west to east for a long distance; and though destructive of every leaf and plant in their course, the region they infest is not sufficient in extent to create anything like a general famine.

The fertile soil of Paraguay and the quick spontaneous growth soon repaired the ravages made by the locusts, and the colony from its commencement had every promise of uninterrupted prosperity. But the ambitious schemes of some of the leaders, whose object it was, not to found colonies, but to get gold, soon marred all their bright prospects. Irala, after waiting nine months at Olimpo and the vicinity, and having made every possible effort to learn something of his chief, Ayolas, reluctantly abandoned the search, and set out with his party to descend the river. The colony at this time was under the command of Ruiz de Galan, who had arrived subsequent to the first settlement of the place, and who, ranking Gonzalo de Mendoza, had assumed the authority as Governor. On the arrival of Irala, a dispute arose between him and Galan regarding the right to the chief command. It was quickly settled, however, by Galan making a close prisoner of his competitor. But Irala was not one to allow personal feelings or interests to interfere with the welfare of the colony, and it was arranged that he should be set at liberty, when he would return to Olimpo.

On returning to his former camping-ground he found the Payagua Indians, with whom he had previously cultivated friendly relations, were preparing to make an utter extermination of all trespassers on their ancient domain. Irala discovered their intention without their being aware of it, and when they thought to surprise him they met with both a surprise and a terrible defeat. Irala united the greatest courage and energy with herculean strength, and on this occasion he had need for each. The Payaguas are generally large and powerful men, much above the average of the South-American savages, and in this battle twelve of the strongest set upon him at once. Seven of the twelve he killed with his own hand. Some of the best authorities have it that he killed them all.

While Irala was thus engaged in the fruitless search for Ayolas, Galan left his post to return to Buenos Aires. He reached Çorpus Cristi about the 1st of January, 1538, and there, in conjunction with the forces then guarding that station, he committed an act of such gross and cowardly treachery on the unoffending natives as has few parallels in the catalogue of wrongs inflicted by civilized Christians on the savage heathen. The unsuspecting Timbus had been in the habit of supplying the fort at Corpus Cristi with such provisions as it was in their power to obtain, and in return they had been treated with kindness by the Spaniards, till they were disarmed of all suspicion, and had taken no precautions against surprise, nor made any preparations for defence. Thus exposed, Galan fell upon one of their little villages one morning at daybreak, burnt their houses, massacred the men, and made prisoners of the women and children, whom he allotted to the soldiers. After this feat Galan pursued his way to Buenos Aires, leaving Antonio de Mendoza in command at Corpus Cristi, with only one hundred men. The neighboring Indians did not wait long for their revenge. The Spaniards had killed the goose that laid the golden egg. They had destroyed some and outraged others of the Indians who had supplied them with food, and now they could not venture beyond the fort to obtain it except in considerable numbers. One day, when full one half of their whole body had gone out for this purpose, and were at a good distance from the fort, the Indians, who had watched their opportunity, fell upon them so furiously that scarcely a single one escaped. The fort was next attacked, and all within it would doubtless have shared the same fate but for the timely arrival of two vessels with troops from Buenos Aires, which had been despatched from there for its relief, in anticipation that the Indians would avenge themselves for the treachery of Galan on the small party left to guard the little settlement.

With this opportune reinforcement the Indians were finally defeated, but not without the loss of many Spaniards, among whom was Antonio de Mendoza, the commander of the fort. In this action first appears the name of a person who subsequently figured notably in the history of Paraguay. This was Don Diego de Abreu, at that time holding the rank of captain.

It was in this battle, that, according to the writers of the time, a miracle occurred, the account of which is implicitly believed in by most Paraguayans to this day. According to the tradition, while the battle was fiercest, there appeared on the top of the principal tower of the fort the figure of a man dressed in white, with a drawn sword in his hand, which flamed so resplendent that at the sight of it the Indians fell, blinded and astonished, to the ground. This miraculous intervention gave the victory to the Spaniards, and as it occurred on the 3d of

February, the day, according to the calendar, of San Blas, it was taken for granted that that saint had appeared in person to rescue the faithful and confound the heathen. From that time to this, San Blas has been regarded as the patron saint of Paraguay. Whether Galan regarded the appearance of the saint as an approval of his treacherous massacre of the Indians, the record does not say.

After this event at Corpus Cristi, Ruiz de Galan, Salazar de Espinosa, and several other persons of note in the history of the times, returned to Paraguay, taking with them nearly all of those who had remained in the fortress at Buenos Aires, or had arrived from Europe subsequent to the general evacuation of the place by Pedro de Mendoza. On reaching Asuncion, they found that Irala had returned from his second expedition after Ayolas, but that no Ayolas was to be found.

The emergency provided for in the royal letters-patent, that in case of the non-return of Ayolas the colonists should choose a governor from among themselves, had now arrived. This privilege was wisely exercised, for by this time Irala had had opportunity to display his great courage, energy, and disinterestedness, and though San Blas had testified in favor of Galan, yet the colonists with great unanimity elected the conqueror of the Payaguas in preference to the hero of Corpus Cristi.

The first important act of Irala after his election as Governor was to order the complete evacuation of Buenos Aires, and all the colonists to unite at Asuncion. About the same time that the last of the unfortunate Spaniards who had tried to found a colony at Buenos Aires took their departure for Paraguay, there arrived at the mouth of the river an Italian vessel, with emigrants who had left their country with the intention of going to Peru by way of the Straits of Magellan ; but the vessel, being unable to make its way through that dangerous and then little known channel, turned back and entered the Plata, where the whole party disposed of their effects, and joined their fortunes to the Spaniards, and with them moved up the river to Asuncion.

Thus the remnants of all the different expeditions to the

Plata, as well as many straggling emigrants, speculators, and priests, were found united in Asuncion, in the heart of a most prolific country, having a mild and salubrious climate, and inhabited by a race of Indians well affected towards them. It was far inland, nearly a thousand miles from tide-water, and everything seemed to promise rest and plenty to the pioneers who had been so long buffeted by adverse fortune.

The date of these events was as early as 1537,* eighty-three years before the landing of the Pilgrim fathers at Plymouth, and seventy years before the first settlement at Jamestown. Thus Asuncion is older than any town in the United States, and one of the oldest founded by Europeans in America.

* Azara fixes the date a year earlier; but this author, though generally very accurate, is believed to be in error here.

CHAPTER II.

1537-1542.

Wise Administration of Irala. — Union of the Spanish and Indian Races. — Conversion of the Indians. — The Guarani Language. — Its Preservation a Doubtful Blessing. — Character of Irala. — His Justice towards the Indians. — Plot of the Indians for the Destruction of the Colony. — Its Discovery. — Execution of the Leaders. — The Colonists abandon all Hope of returning to Spain. — Condition of the Different Tribes previous to the Arrival of the Spaniards. — Manners and Customs. — The Guaicurus. — Their Character and Habits. — The Mbayas. — Infanticide. — Final Extinction. — The Payaguas. — Origin of the Name "Paraguay." — Other Tribes of the Guarani Family. — The Guaranis compared with other Indian Nations. — Theory of Naturalists respecting the Origin of the Human Race. — The Guaranis only capable of Improvement and Religious Impressions.

NO sooner was Irala established in authority, than the colony began to experience the benefits of his energy and judgment. His first efforts were to conciliate the Indians in the vicinity, who were beginning to doubt the advantages of having such neighbors. But at the same time that he refused to permit injustice towards them by his followers, and labored to win their confidence by kindness and fair dealing, he took prompt measures to guard against treachery or surprise, by creating strong palisades, within which the colony could defend themselves in any sudden attack.

On entering upon his duties as governor of the new colony, two courses were open to him: one was that usually pursued by colonial governors in the New World, to rob and exterminate the native race; the other, to Christianize, elevate, and assimilate it to the European. Irala chose the latter, and though the results were not very successful, yet the effort to improve and elevate, rather than to rob and destroy, was worthy a Christian and a philanthropist.

The impress of Irala's government was thus permanently fixed on the character, social and political, of the people. During his administration they had entered on that road towards the peculiar civilization which produced the Paraguayan nation as it afterwards became. To assimilate the two races so that one should not become the slaves of the other was a difficult task; but Irala undertook to accomplish it, and succeeded. Yet these two races, that were made to live on terms approaching equality, were as different almost in their habits and nature as it is possible for two branches of the human family to be. This was the time of Spain's greatest power and splendor; and among the colonists were veterans who had fought through half Europe under the great Emperor. Then there were ambitious, aspiring young officers, who had borne his banners or spent their early manhood around his brilliant court. Beside these were many private individuals of good family and fortune, who, fired with the spirit of romance and adventure, had gone to the New World. These people, with their various tastes and projects, had formed connections with the Guarani women, to whom they were attached by no religious, legal, or moral bonds. Irala endeavored to impress upon his followers the duty of fidelity in such connections, and the obligations of paternity.

Among the accessions to the colony, after the abandonment of Buenos Aires, were two priests of the order of St. Francis, who at once commenced the work of converting the simple Guaranis to the Roman Catholic religion, the forms and ceremonies of which had a great charm for their unsuspecting nature. In this they were encouraged and assisted in every way by Irala. He saw that if the Spaniards were to mingle with the natives on any terms approaching equality, or if the priests would exercise effectually their spiritual functions, the two races must speak the same language. That the existing generation of natives should learn Spanish was out of the question, but the Spaniards might learn the Guarani. In fact, the soldiers, all of whom had already formed connections more or less regular and permanent with the native women, were fast learning their idiom. The priests applied themselves to acquire it and to make it a written language, that they might preach in that tongue. Thus it came about that the Guarani continued to be, and is yet, the language of the country. At present it is seldom written, and is so mixed with Spanish as to be very different from what it was at that time. The Spanish is the only language taught in the schools; but still most Paraguayans, from the highest to the lowest, prefer their native Guarani.

Whether or not it was wise policy to preserve the native dialect may be a question. It doubtless served the purposes of the early fathers, and enabled them to gain and retain an influence over the natives otherwise impossible. It may also be a question whether it were wise policy to encourage the Spaniards to take Indian women for wives and treat their natural progeny as children, instead of leaving them to follow the ways of their mothers. That both measures were most efficient for missionary, proselyting purposes, there can be no question. But if we judge from the result on the welfare of the country, we must come to a different conclusion, as to their wisdom, from what we shall if we regard them as measures of abstract right and justice. It is to these measures that the strange history and present condition of the country may be traced. The same unwritten language is still the common dialect of the country, and the mixed race, after more than three hundred years, is but a few removes from its primitive barbarism. Though the Guarani language and race were thus preserved, the condition of the people and their subsequent fate at the hands of an unnatural ruler, the offspring of this admixture of races, prove that their preservation was a doubtful blessing to the world. Nevertheless, the policy of Irala was humane and well intentioned, and showed that he at least desired to respect the rights of the possessors of the soil, and no further to change or violate their customs and prejudices than was required for the security and protection of his own people. His dealings with the Indians were in marked contrast with those of all other Spanish adventurers to the New World; and no European of any race or nation, not even William Penn, deserves so high credit for justice towards them as Irala. Penn only professed to deal with them honestly, but Irala labored incessantly to raise them from barbarism to civilization and Christianity. The Indians with whom Penn had to deal have disappeared from the earth, but the race that Irala undertook to elevate yet exists, is recognized as a nation, and has carried on a longer war against greater odds than was ever known before. And yet it is probable that only a small proportion of the readers of this history, all of whom know the story of Penn by heart, ever heard of Domingo Martinez de Irala.

But though the Guaranis were docile and peaceable as compared with the other Indians of the Plata, they had still much of that peculiar cunning and treachery in their character which have always rendered the aborigines of America unsafe neighbors. At first they appeared highly pleased at the advent of the Spaniards, but they soon began to suspect that their presence boded no good to them as a people, and with great secrecy arranged a plot for the surprise and destruction of the entire colony. The Governor, having observed how much impressed the natives had been at beholding the religious functions and ceremonies, had given orders for a procession and festival of extraordinary magnificence, to take place on Holy Thursday (1539). The Indians were invited to assemble for the occasion; but instead of the usual number at such festivals, it was noticed that they were several times more numerous than ever before, Irala suspected there was some cause for this not apparent, but he could detect nothing; and the plot was revealed, almost at the last hour, by an Indian girl, the servant and friend of Salazar de Espinosa, whose Indian lover had revealed to her the plan of the conspiracy. But the girl, thinking more of the white lover than of the tawny one, hastened to inform him of his danger, and gave him the names of the principal conspirators. The Governor took instant measures to have his whole force under arms and ready for action, but without giving the Indians the least sign that their plot was discovered. Just before the time fixed upon by the savages for the havoc to commence, and in the presence of the multitude, the leaders were suddenly seized, and their treacherous plot proclaimed aloud. Struck with astonishment and a sense of guilt, they confessed their crime, when, prompt as the decrees of fate, the ringleaders were executed in presence of their fellow-conspirators. Such energy struck terror into the hearts of the Indians, who confessed their complicity with the plot of assassination, but protested that for the future they would not only abandon all such designs, but would ever after be good and faithful friends and allies of the Spaniards.

Beyond this, the caciques and other principal Indians, who had held aloof hitherto from intimacy with the Spaniards, now offered to give up their daughters and sisters to them to be their servants, or rather, like the Sabine women, to become the means of forming a common bond of affection and dependence between the two races. The Spaniards, who had left their own country thinking to achieve fame and fortune in the New World and then return to claim the hands of the daughters of the old hidalgos of Castile or Aragon, soon gave up all thought or hope of ever seeing their native land again. Their early experience and hardships had made them long for rest, and when they reached Paraguay they forgot friends and home, and took to themselves the brown daughters of the wilderness instead of the proud beauties for whose smiles they had braved the perils of the deep and the hardships of the pioneer. "We will return no more" was the refrain of their hearts, and their actions, if not their lips, said, —

> "Let what is broken so remain, —
> The gods are hard to reconcile;
> 'T is hard to settle order once again.
> There *is* confusion worse than death,
> Trouble on trouble, pain on pain,
> Long labor unto aged breath,
> Sore task to hearts worn out with many wars,
> And eyes grown dim with gazing on the pilot stars."

The admixture of the Spanish and Indian races for the first two or three generations resulted, if we credit the earliest and one of the most reliable historians of the country (Ruy Diaz de Guzman), in the improvement of both. At least they had many quiet and domestic virtues which in that age were not consistent with the character of the Spanish cavalier. As Guzman was a Spaniard of pure blood, and certainly not prejudiced in favor of the Indians, the following testimony to the credit of the progeny of the mixed races may be fairly regarded as impartial: —

"They are generally good soldiers, of great spirit and valor; expert in the use of arms, especially in that of the musket, — so much so that when they go on long journeys, they are accustomed to live on the game which they kill with it. It is common for them to kill birds on the wing, and he is accounted unfit for a soldier who cannot bring down the pigeon or the sparrow. They are such excellent horsemen that there is no one who is not able to tame and ride the unbroken colt. The women, generally, are of an elevated and honest character; virtuous, beautiful, and of gentle disposition; endowed with discretion and industry, and expert with the needle, in which employment they are continually engaged; from all of which there has resulted to that colony so much increase and prosperity."

Irala was chosen Governor only for the short term of three years. In that time he had laid the foundation for results such as those described by Guzman. He had both awed and conciliated the Indians, and bound them to the Spaniards by the strongest ties that could be devised; he had founded various other settlements, besides Asuncion, that exist as villages to this day; he had caused a church and other public buildings to be erected, and, as far as human foresight could provide, had laid the foundation of a colony that promised to be the nucleus of a great and powerful nation. Every physical feature of the country conspired to this end, — a climate warm, but of wonderful salubrity; a soil of such exceptional fertility as to produce not only most of the cereals, roots, and fruits of other countries, but to yield spontaneously more kinds of valuable plants and herbs, more varieties of the best wood, and more fruit of various kinds, than any other known part of the world ; besides this, it had the negative merit — more important than all to the permanent prosperity of an infantile state — of an utter lack of silver and gold.

There are other reasons, however, besides those already given, why the Paraguayan colony should have had an experience and history different from any other in America. These are to be found mainly in the peculiar character and habits of the Indian tribe or nation among which this colony was founded, or rather on which it was grafted. A brief description of them would therefore seem to be in place before proceeding further.

The Guaranis were, at the time of the discovery of the Plata by Juan Diaz de Solis, much the most numerous Indian nation in South America. The savage and fierce Querandis and Charruas that he first met were branches of the same family. But having for many generations been exposed to a harder climate, where nature produced spontaneously but little of what was required for their sustenance, they developed into the hardy race that so bravely and successfully disputed with the troops of Charles V. the right to the possession of the lower regions of the Plata. Other tribes, like the Timbus, the Caracarás, Aomas, Chiriguanos, and many more, are supposed, from the similarity of language and other resemblances, to have originally descended from the same stock.

But the Guaranis of Paraguay were not of a temper or spirit to successfully oppose the invasion of the foreigner. They were neither vindictive nor warlike. As compared with the Querandis they were indolent, amiable, and without spirit or ambition. Their character and habits, before they had been seriously changed by contact with the Spaniards, may be learned from the following extract from Azara, whose great work on Paraguay and the adjacent countries is, and ever has been, regarded as a classic of the highest authority in all matters relating to the early history of that country, the character of its people, its physical features, and its animal and vegetable productions.*

Of the Guaranis in their primitive state he thus speaks: —

"This nation is the most numerous, and occupies more territory than all the others I have encountered, since up to the time of the discovery of America they inhabited all the country now possessed by the Portuguese. But within the limits of my description it extends to the north from the country of the Charruas, Bohanes, and

* Felix de Azara was born in Catalonia in the year 1746. He belonged to one of the most distinguished and influential families of Spain. His brother, Don Nicholas de Azara, was one of the ablest diplomatists of his time, having been for many years the Spanish Ambassador at Rome, and afterwards at Paris. He was a member of the Congress of Amiens, and was one of the signers of that famous treaty. In the year 1777, Spain and Portugal entered into a treaty called the treaty of San Ildefonso, in which it was stipulated that the two governments should send commissioners to run the boundary lines between the Spanish and Portuguese possessions throughout South America. Felix de Azara was appointed, on the part of Spain, as commissioner for the section comprising the northeastern limits between Paraguay and Brazil. He proceeded to Paraguay, and awaited the coming of his Portuguese colleagues; but they never arrived, and Azara remained twenty years in the country, repeatedly asking to be recalled, but never getting permission from his government to leave the country. Thus in enforced exile he passed the best years of his life in gathering and collating facts in regard to the plants, the forests, the peculiar animals with their habits, the birds, the fishes, and the insects of the country. With no theory to advance, no proselyting object in view, but animated with the sole desire to add to the world's knowledge of a vast, fertile, and unknown region, and with a jealous desire to give nothing but the exact truth, his book is now justly regarded as incomparably better than any that has since appeared. This work was dedicated to his brother Nicholas, and as nothing can better show the tender simplicity and fidelity of the man than this dedication, I give a translation of it here: —

"DEAR NICHOLAS, — Scarcely were we born when our parents separated us. During our lives we have never seen or conversed with each other but for the short space of two days in Barcelona, where I met you by accident. You have lived in the great world, and by your dignity, talents, virtues, and works you have made yourself illustrious in Spain and throughout all Europe; but I, without ever having arrived at any notable employment, without having had opportunity to know either you or others, have passed the best twenty years of my life in the extremes of the earth, forgotten by my friends, without books or anything written capable of instructing me; continually occupied in travelling through deserts or through immense and tremendous forests, almost without society other than that of the birds and wild animals, I have written the history of these; I send it and dedicate it to you, that through it you may know me and form an idea of my labors."

Minuanes to the parallel of sixteen degrees, without passing to the western side of the Paraguay River, except at the two extremities; that is, at the south they inhabited the islands of the Parana, and the western bank cf the Rio de la Plata, about Buenos Aires, while to the north they were found as far west as the Andes, where a large number of them resided, bearing the name of Chiriguanos. . . . . It should be observed, that, within the time here mentioned, there are other nations shut up in the midst of it, such as the Tupis, the Guayanás, the Nuaras, the Nalicuégos, and the Guasarapos. All these nations differ as much from each other as each differs from the Guaranis, as will be shown. The Guarani nation occupies the great extent of country of which I have spoken, without forming any political body, and without recognizing any common chief. . . . . The Guarani nation, throughout its whole extent, was divided into little societies or hordes, independent of each other, and each one with a different name, taken from their cacique, or captain, or from the place they inhabited. Sometimes all the tribes that lived on the bank of a certain river or in a certain district were comprehended under one name. This is the origin of the multitude of names that the conquerors gave to the different tribes that made up the Guarani nation. For example, without going out of the country now under description, they called the Guaranis by the names, Mbayas, Caracarás, Timbus, Tucaques, Carios, Mangolas, and many others. The habits of this nation were not in all parts the same. All the tribes that inhabited the immense tract possessed by the Portuguese were taken and held as slaves, and as they mixed with negroes brought from Africa, the race, as a race, is almost extinct. Beside this, the Portuguese of San Pablo, commonly called Mamelukes, did not content themselves with what I have just indicated; they made great and repeated raids into this country, and carried off, not only all the Guaranis they found at liberty, but as many as eight settlements (*pueblos*) that had been founded and established by the Spaniards in Paraguay.

"The conduct of the Spaniards has been very different. They have never sold a single Guarani, and preserve even now, in the Jesuit and other pueblos, thousands in a state of entire freedom, since there exists in the country I am describing a multitude of tribes beside Guaranis as free as before the arrival of the Spaniards. In the proper place I shall speak of the Guaranis, the subjects of Spain, that form the Christian pueblos. But now I only speak of this nation in a state of freedom, and as those who live in this state now dwell in the great forests, where I have not had opportunity to enter, my description will be proved from the perusal of ancient manuscripts and from personal information derived from those who had seen such Indians in their native freedom; to this I will add what I myself have observed whenever I have met any of these savages, and what I have noted among their converts to Christianity. In general, the Guaranis (unmixed) all live on the skirts of the forest, or in little openings that are found among the hills. And if they sometimes are located in the open plains, it is where there is no other tribe living near by. They feed upon honey, wild fruit, monkeys, etc., though their principal resource is derived from the cultivation of maize, beans, onions, ground-nuts, sweet potatoes, and mandioca. If they dwell near the rivers, they catch fish with arrows, or with fish-hooks made of wood, and some of them have little canoes. When they have made a harvest, they hoard it up for the rest of the year, as they do not find so many birds or quadrupeds for their sustenance as those do who live upon the plains. Wherefore they never go to the chase or to collect wild fruits but when they are not occupied in agriculture, and they never go so far away but that they may be at hand for the harvest; for this reason they are fixed, and not migratory, like the other nations of which I have spoken. Their language is very different from any other, but it is the same among all the tribes of this nation, so that speaking it you may travel all through Brazil, pass through Paraguay, and go through to Peru. This language is considered the most copious of all the savage idioms of America. Notwithstanding, it lacks for many expressions. It has only four numerals, and it is not possible in it to express five or six. The pronunciation is nasal and guttural. The padre Luis Bolaños has translated our catechism into this language, and the Jesuits have invented signs to express its nasal and guttural sounds, and they have even printed a dictionary and grammar of this language. But notwithstanding such aids it is very difficult to learn it, and requires more than a year to do it.

"The medium stature of this nation appears to me to be two inches less than that of the Spaniards, and consequently is much less than that of some other nations of South America. They are also more squat and ugly; they are not so dark as some others, but have a reddish tint; the women have small feet and hands, and other peculiarities. The men, in some instances, have a little beard and a little down on the body, which distinguishes them from other Indians, though in this they are very different from Europeans. . . . . The fecundity of this nation is not equal to that of ours, as I have never found but one Indian who was the father of more than ten children. The average number, one with another, is four to one family. The number of women is always greater than that of the men in the proportion of fifteen to fourteen. Their physiognomy is sombre, sad, and subdued. They speak little, and without ever crying out or complaining. Their voices are never hoarse, nor are they sonorous; they never laugh loudly, and the face never shows any signs of passion. They are very dirty, they recognize no Divinity, neither recompense, laws, punishment, nor obligation, and they never look a person in the face with whom they are conversing. In their marriages and amours they show the greatest coldness. The union of the sexes is neither followed nor preceded by any preparation or demonstration. They know no such thing as jealousy. It is well known with what frankness and pleasure they gave up their daughters and women to the conquerors, and they even do the same now, though converted to Christianity. The women marry very young, commonly at ten or twelve; the men a little later, after which they form a separate family. I have never found among the ancient manuscripts any allusion to music or dancing among the Guaranis. . . . . Each division or tribe has its captain, or cacique, whose dignity is commonly hereditary, and to whom some consideration is paid, though no reason can be given for it. There is never any difference between the cacique and others in his lodgings, dress, decoration, nor any distinct marks; he is obliged to labor like the others, without receiving tribute, service, or obedience."

These were the Guaranis, among whom the Spaniards landed when they came to Asuncion, of whom Azara thus speaks. The Spanish race grafted on this has produced the present Paraguayan nation. As they were the most numerous, so they were the most intelligent and docile, of all the South American Indians east of the Andes. And yet so low were they in the scale of human intelligence, that Azara says of them, "to compare the Peruvians with the savage nations of Paraguay and the Rio de la Plata would be to make a parallel between debasement of body and mind, and elegance, grandeur, strength, valor, and pride."

Of this great Guarani family, composed of so many tribes, and differing so much from each other, one of the most important, formerly, was the Mbayas.* This once powerful tribe regarded themselves as the natural enemies of all other tribes, nations, or people. In some respects they were greatly superior to those Guaranis whom the Spaniards met at Asuncion, and among whom they domiciled themselves. They were of larger stature, more active and courageous. But they were addicted to some barbarous practices of the most disgusting and horrible character. These practices, so destructive of their race, must have been of recent invention, or the tribe could never have become so numerous as it was at the time of the arrival of the Europeans. But they had no tradition of prophet or spirit that had taught them their abominations. Of them, their practices and their faith, the same author says: —

"As in their stature, strength, beauty, and elegance they are far superior to the Spaniards, they regard the European race as quite inferior to their own. As regards religion, they adore nothing, neither do they observe anything that makes the least allusion to this subject or to the future life. To explain their first origin, they express themselves in the following terms. 'In the beginning God created all nations as numerous as they now are, not contenting himself with the creation of one man and one woman; and he distributed them over all the face of the earth. Afterwards it occurred to him to create a Mbaya with his own particular woman, and as he had given away all the lands to other nations, so that there remained no more to allot, he ordered the bird called the caracara to go tell them that for his part he was very sorry there was no more land to give them; that therefore he had not created more than two Mbayas; but to remedy this inconvenience he had com-

* Though so classified by Azara, it is asserted by others that the Mbayas did not belong to the family of the Guaranis. Their language and habits are certainly so different as to lead to that conclusion.

manded that they should always wander through the territory of other nations, making war upon all, killing all adult men, and adopting the children and women to augment their number.' Never were divine precepts more faithfully observed, as the only occupation of the Mbayas is to wander about hunting and fishing to support themselves, and making war on the whole human race, killing or preserving alive their enemies, conformably with the order of the caracara. They make an exception of the Guanas, with whom they maintain close friendship. Indeed, the Mbayas always have a multitude of Guanas that serve them voluntarily as slaves, and gratuitously cultivate their lands and render other services. Besides these the Mbayas have other slaves, being the children and women which they capture, who are not only of the Indian, but of the Spanish race. The Mbayas have great affection for their slaves. They never command them with imperious tone, nor censure nor punish them, nor sell them, even though they may be prisoners of war. They trust to the good faith of the slave, and are content with what he is willing to do, and share with them all they have. Thus it happens that no prisoner, though a slave, desires to leave them; it is the same with the Spanish women they have with them, notwithstanding some of them were grown to womanhood, and had children, before being taken. What a contrast to the treatment that Europeans give to their African slaves!"

The Mbayas were brave and expert warriors, showing great courage and strategy in time of battle. But they were always content with a single success, and, that achieved, they left the field. But for this peculiarity of their tactics, says Azara, not a Spaniard or Portuguese would have been left on the confluents of the Plata. In their customs as regards polygamy and divorce, they were like the other Indian nations, the marriage being a union only so long as it might suit the two parties. But they had one custom so abhorrent to all natural instincts that few savages would follow it. This was the practice of killing at its birth every child born of a woman, save one. The first children of a couple were always killed off without the least remorse or compunction, and only when the mother apprehended that from her age or infirmities she would not bear another did she attempt to rear her infant. If, after this, another was born, it was instantly killed. Not only had they this horrible custom, but women would subject themselves to the most terrible beatings about the stomach and bowels, in order, as they said, that they might not lose their form and comeliness by too frequent child-bearing. The effect of this practice was necessarily to cause the population to decrease; and as no tribe or nation that adhered to it could long exist, it was probably adopted some time after the arrival of the Spaniards in the Plata. At least, no mention is made of it by their earliest writers. The race, numerous and powerful as it had been, soon became extinct, as did that of the Guaicurus, another tribe living on the right bank of the river, and which had been once even more powerful and proud than the Mbayas. These two, for some time previous to their extinction, had the same execrable custom of murdering all new-born children save one to a family.

Of this tribe (the Guaicurus) Azara remarks: —

> "It was one of the most numerous, and in my judgment was the most valiant, the strongest, the most warlike, and having the most lofty stature. They dwelt in the Chaco, almost in front of Asuncion. . . . . Of this nation, once so proud and considerable, there exists now but a single person, and he is the finest formed man in the world, being six feet seven inches in height. He has three wives, and not to be too much alone he has joined the tribe of the Tobas, and adopted their dress and style of painting themselves."

The only other tribe of Indians that had sufficient strength to oppose themselves to the Spaniards and to seriously molest them, and whose warfare enters into the history of the country, was the Payaguas. The name of the river, and subsequently of the country, was probably derived from this nation. The Payaguas were they who first encountered the expedition of Cabot and gave battle, and it was a branch of the same tribe that Irala found near Candelaria or Olimpo. Hence the name which the Indians of the lower country had already given it, — the "Rio de los Payaguas." The Spaniards, by a corruption of spelling, called it Paraguá or Paraguay, and thus the name of the country is derived from the name of a race now extinct.

THE LAST OF THE PAYAGUAS.

The Payaguas were a brave and warlike people, and from the first looked with distrust and suspicion on the Spaniards, regarding them much as the Puritans of New England were regarded by Philip of Pokanoket and his followers. For a long time they were the constant and implacable enemies of the foreigners, and many thousands of the early Spaniards perished at their hands; so that at various times they threatened the extinction, not only of the Spanish colonies, but of the Portuguese settlements to the north. But their incessant wars told heavily on their numbers, till at last they made peace with the colony at Asuncion, and from that time became dependent on their former enemies. Instead of warring upon them, they were so reduced in numbers that they were willing to render any service to the foreigners, like catching fish, taking care of their horses, and laboring in any menial capacity. But they never amalgamated with the Spaniards, nor with other Indians. Poor menial dependants, they retained all their former pride and undisguised contempt for everybody who was not a Payagua. Even to the time of the commencement of the late war, when the last man was taken for a soldier and the women to perform the drudgery of the camp, although the nation was reduced to some fifty persons dwelling on the bank of the river near the capital, they regarded themselves, as indeed do most nations and sects, as the chosen and elect of earth and heaven.

The early writers give the names of many other tribes which were said to belong to the great Guarani family. They differed very much from each other, however, in character, habits, and appearance. The Guaranis proper, who were known by no other name, — those who belonged to the same tribe or nation that was first met at Asuncion, — were the only natives the Spaniards could or would unite with, and from the union with them is the Paraguayan nation descended. They were less warlike, less active, inferior in stature, and more ugly in appearance than some, and not so completely debased and barbarous as others. In fact, some of the smaller tribes were but a little removed from the wild brutes of their own jungles. The lowest in the scale, perhaps, were the Guatos, who dwelt to the north of the Rio Apa, on some islands in a lake called the Lake of Jarayes. This tribe consisted of less than one hundred persons, and they were as unapproachable as wild beasts. No other person, Indian or foreigner, could ever come near, but that they would fly and hide in impenetrable jungles. For many generations they had held the same marshy fastnesses without increase or diminution, so far as their neighbors knew of their number. The tradition among the other tribes was that they had a language of their own; that they lived like unreasoning animals, without laws, religion, or chiefs. As compared with the Guatos the Guaranis were a civilized nation, but to compare the latter with the Peruvians that Pizarro encountered would be, as remarked by Azara, "to make a parallel between debasement of body and mind, and elegance, grandeur, strength, valor, and pride."

These smaller tribes may now be said to be extinct. There are still Indians to the north of Paraguay called Guatos. But they are entitled to that appellation only because of their low and debased condition. And yet they are greatly superior to the Guatos described by Azara. There are also many Indians, remnants of tribes, still living in what is called the Gran Chaco, on the right or west bank of the Paraguay, all of whom are now incorrectly called Guaicurus. But the Guaicurus nation has long been extinct, and the miserable wretches who inhabit that vast wilderness are so low in the scale of reasoning beings that one might doubt whether or not they have human souls.

It is alleged by naturalists that animals of the same genus will breed upon each other, and that when such is not the case, and that they will not, or do not, cross the one species with another, they must have had a different origin, and could not have descended from the same first progenitors; that the horse cannot be an improved ass, or the ass a degenerate variety of the horse, for though the mule is the fruit of the union of the two, yet there the power of reproduction ceases; that the wild goose and the tame goose could not have descended from the same original stock, since the mongrel of the two cannot continue his generation; whereas it is known that other species of animals having greater difference in appearance and habits — like the bull-dog and the King Charles spaniel, or the Cochin China hen and the little bantam — cross and mix, and the progeny of these cross again indiscriminately with other breeds, and this continually to any degree of relationship, and that all the shades of breed or blood may be found in the same animal. If this theory be correct, then the inference is strong that the

Guaranis and the other Indians of Paraguay had not a common origin or progenitors. The Spaniards in Paraguay never crossed with any but the Guaranis. There may have been instances of issue from a union of a Guaicuru or Payagua and a European. But if there were, there the cross must have stopped; for such a thing as a Payagua or Guaicuru with a tint of white blood was, to the best of my knowledge, never heard of. These and several other tribes of this region neither had, nor could be made to have, any ideas of a future state, or that they had immortal souls. The description of

> ". . . . the poor Indian! whose untutor'd mind
> Sees God in clouds, or hears him in the wind,"

would never apply to them. The missionaries found it labor lost to preach to them. They might tell of life and immortality beyond the grave, but the savage instinct told them that it did not apply to them, and so we never hear of a Guaicuru or Mbaya Christian or convert. For some inscrutable and wise purpose they were created to live and die in the primeval forest, and to become extinct from the earth. They never could be improved. They had two qualities, to a high degree, in common with the wild beast and the most civilized men, — physical courage and strength. Their only care was to get wherewith to eat, and then, like the hog or alligator, to lie in the sun for it to digest. During the several months of the author's detention in Corrientes, during the late war, he saw much of the Chaco Indians. The large military camp there rendered necessary the slaughter of many beef cattle to supply the troops and hospitals. Many Indians would come over from the Chaco in their canoes to dispute with the buzzards and the cur dogs for the offal of the slaughter pens. With this they would stuff themselves to repletion, and then sleep till they could repeat the unctuous feast. The habits of the different tribes varied accordingly as they lived on the bank of a river, in the open plains, or in the forest; but they nearly all cultivated little patches of maize, sugar-cane, and mandioca. They depended, more or less, according as they were situated, on the chase or on fishing for their supply of food. In a word, the native was the savage Indian of the New World, and, when that is said, his character, his habits, his laziness, are all pretty well understood. According to the development theory of the most eminent naturalists, it would appear that the Guaranis were of the lowest grade of human beings, and that the surrounding tribes were just at that stage of development below the line of humanity. The one race would cross with the Europeans, but not with the Payaguas or Guaicurus. They also were susceptible of religious impressions, and had an instinctive sense of a future life. But no religious impression could ever be made on the surrounding tribes, who were a degree lower in intelligence than the Guaranis. They could never be made to realize that there was a future state, and if "instinct," as Pope says, "must be right," then none of the tribes of the Plata save the Guaranis had human souls. It is from the different branches of this family, and from them alone, that all the people of the Plata, of mixed Indian and European blood, have descended. There was a great difference, however, between the Querandis and the Charruas near the mouth of the river, and the Guaranis of Paraguay, though all are from the same original stock. The Guaranis, among whom the Spaniards first pitched their tents, took more kindly to improvement than the tribes around them; they had more gentleness, and were more susceptible of religious impressions. They had houses of mud and thatch, such as could be made without tools of iron or steel, of which they were ignorant. In many respects they were similar to the inhabitants of the Marquesas and Omoo Islands, as described by Mr. Herman Melville. But they had not, like the Typees, the vice of cannibalism. Some writers have attempted to fasten this charge upon them. But no one, it is believed, having personal knowledge on the subject, has ever accused the Paraguayan tribes of any such practice. They either deny it; or make no allusion to it, as they would naturally do of a thing unknown or unthought of. With this brief digression on the character and habits of the native race, the direct history is now resumed.

CHAPTER III.

1542–1545.

Expedition of Alvar Nuñez de Vera Cabeza de Vaca. — Changes his Route. — Overland Journey. — Arrives in Asuncion, 1542. — His Reception. — Takes Possession of the Government. — His Instructions from the Emperor. — Difficulties in administering the Government. — Disaffection among the Officers. — Difficulties with the Indians. — His Magnanimous Course towards them. — Peace concluded. — Conspiracy formed against Cabeza de Vaca. — He is seized and imprisoned. — Irala proclaimed Governor. — Cabeza de Vaca sent a Prisoner to Spain. — Unjust Treatment of him by the Emperor. — He is finally tried and acquitted.

THE abandonment of Buenos Aires and the removal of the colony to Asuncion had not been foreseen by the Spanish government. It was known that Ayolas and his party had disappeared, and, naturally, there was much anxiety to learn the fate of his companions who had remained behind him. In the mean while, the colonists having wisely improved their privilege of electing their own Governor *ad interim*, in the event of the non-return of Ayolas, by choosing Irala, had, under his wise guidance, made great progress in consolidating their own power, at the same time that they had attached to them by interest and domestic ties the largest tribe of Indians. But of the success of the policy initiated by Irala little was known at the court of Charles V., and it was considered a matter of the first necessity to send additional forces to sustain the colonists, and also an executive officer duly accredited from the crown to command obedience, and by his prestige and judgment advance the imperial pretensions.

But where was such a man to be found? Certainly not among the courtiers or statesmen who flattered or counselled the Emperor. They might be able advisers in war, cunning to manage an intrigue, swift in devising taxes, and sharp on the scent of victims for an *auto-de-fe;* but such qualities could not satisfy the requirements of the mighty champion of the Holy Inquisition. Cruel and remorseless as was the bigotry of the great Emperor, it did not obliterate his practical sense. To all appearance he had found the right man for the unpromising position.

The person selected for the post was Alvar Nuñez de Vera Cabeza de Vaca, a man whose life seemed a romance stranger than fiction. He had already passed through the most trying vicissitudes imaginable, and under all circumstances had ever united strict integrity with sound judgment and practical sense. Connected with an influential family, he had filled various important posts at home until, in the year 1528, he accompanied the expedition sent to conquer Florida, as treasurer. This expedition was probably the most unfortunate that ever set sail from Europe. The ships that bore the party were nearly all lost in a hurricane, though that which carried Cabeza de Vaca reached the Florida coast, when every soul perished at the hands of the savages, save only Cabeza de Vaca and his slave. He made his captors believe he was rarely skilled in the healing art, and so effectually made good his pretensions by some cures he wrought, that the Indians regarded them as miracles, and from a slave promoted him to be their chief, or cacique. In this capacity he passed ten years, until the news reached him of the great events that were enacting in Mexico, when so great was his influence, and so entirely had he gained the confidence and regard of his people, he was permitted, in 1540, to go and join his countrymen, taking with him a considerable number of Florida Indians. The strange account of his adventures, with the proofs he brought of its truth, seemed little less miraculous to his own people than had his wonderful skill in medicine to the credulous Indians.

Cabeza de Vaca had not only the personal qualities and prestige of adventure that the position required, but he was possessed of a considerable fortune, which he was ready to embark in another expedition to the Plata. This latter was a great consideration with the government; for though at that time Spain was despoiling Mexico and Peru of their treasures, these were insufficient to support the magnificence of the court, and carry on the gigantic wars which his most catholic Majesty was waging against half of Europe. Hence it was an object to intrust the command of foreign expeditions to men of wealth, who would fit them out wholly or in part at their own expense, and who would trust to find their recompense in what they might obtain in the invaded countries.

The nomination of Alvar Nuñez de Vera Cabeza de Vaca — a name too long to be often repeated, and having so many words that some writers speak of him as Alvar Nuñez, and others as Cabeza de Vaca, and which, translated, would read *Alvar Nuñez de Vera cow's head* — was enough to awaken great interest in the enterprise, and he soon found more persons eager to follow his fortunes and share the dangers and rewards of adventure than he could take with him. Among them were several destined to fill important positions in the future history of Paraguay.

This expedition consisted of four ships, with their crews, and four hundred soldiers. From long experience, Cabeza de Vaca had learned the wants of a savage people, and from this could infer the necessities of a new colony. He accordingly laid in a stock of seeds and plants not known in the New World, and took with him a variety of domestic animals. He was the first to carry horned cattle to the valley of the Plata, from which have descended the innumerable herds that for so many generations furnished the most important articles of commerce in those vast regions.

Like many of the early expeditions to America, that of Cabeza de Vaca suffered terribly in the voyage across the Atlantic. The vessels of that day were small and badly constructed, and a sea voyage in one of them was a very different thing from a trip in a clipper ship of modern times. So seriously did this small fleet suffer, that on reaching the island of Santa Catalina, some nine hundred miles to the north of the mouth of the Plata, Cabeza de Vaca determined to cross from there to the main-land, and thence proceed directly to Paraguay. Before setting out on this difficult journey, he had learned of the general prosperity of the colony, of the election of Irala as Governor, and of the difficulties he was having in repressing some of his turbulent companions, who were greedy for gain by injustice to the Indians, and who thought that, as the Governor was elected by them, he ought to permit them to rob and oppress the natives without restraint. With a disregard of danger and toil characteristic of the man, he therefore left his ships to make their way as best they could to the mouth of the river, and thence to Asuncion, while he, with the larger part of his troops, set out for the same destination through the unknown forests. This journey of so large a force, through an unbroken wilderness, for some two thousand miles, has no parallel in the early history of America. The party reached Asuncion on March 11, 1542, having been four months and nine days on the route. Not a man had been lost on the whole journey, except one, who was accidentally drowned in crossing a river. Cabeza de Vaca's knowledge of the Indian character was such, that he made friends of all the natives through whose countries he passed. His men therefore scarcely wanted for anything on the route, and arrived in Paraguay in better health and condition than when they left the sea-coast. Before reaching his destination, he sent couriers in advance to announce his approach, and on nearing Asuncion he was met by a large concourse of people to welcome him as their new Governor, or Adelantado. Irala took the initiative in giving a cordial reception to his successor, and immediately resigned all authority into his hands, and the universal joy gave promise of harmony and prosperity.

The new Governor had come under very peculiar instructions from the King. They were very minute, and related to details that should have been left to the discretion of the Adelantado. Some of these instructions were sufficiently curious to be noted here. One was, that no lawyer or solicitor was to be permitted to exercise his calling. Nobody was to be denied permission to return to Spain whenever he might desire, and every one was to have the privilege of appealing directly to the home government, and even to the King. No one was to be prosecuted for debt for the first four years of the new administration. The estates of persons deceased intestate were to be strictly administered upon, and the rights of property of individuals made secure against the avarice of officials.

These instructions Cabeza de Vaca endeavored to execute faithfully and literally. But it was a task beyond his power or that of any man. Few of the Spanish officials were satisfied with the returns that honesty and faithful service would command. Irala, by his great activity and enthusiasm, by holding out hopes and visions of yet opening the way to Peru, had been able to restrain their cupidity and enforce obedience. But Cabeza de Vaca held out no such hopes, and the adventurers who had left home to rob and convert the heathen saw their "castles in Spain" vanishing into thin air. The stern morals and strict justice of Alvar Nuñez did not accord with the practices or hopes of many of the leading colonists. In consequence, there arose a party in opposition to him and his government, — a thing as impossible in Irala's administration as another leader than Napoleon would have been under the First Empire, or another than Cromwell in the time of the Commonwealth. But his severe discipline, as it limited the power of extortion of the officers, rendered him popular with the soldiers and the people generally; and in spite of disaffection among the former he inflicted a severe chastisement on the Payaguas, who, while professing friendship for the Europeans, were discovered in a plot for their utter extermination. He sent overtures of peace and amity to the Guaicurus, who attacked his ambassadors and obliged them to fly. He therefore sent a strong force against them, and though they pursued their usual mode of warfare, falling back and fighting behind ambushes, they were followed to their hiding-places, where many were killed and a large number taken prisoners. With these trophies he returned to Asuncion, where he gave orders for his prisoners to be treated with the greatest kindness. Having convinced them that the Spaniards wished to live in peace with the Indians, he selected some of the most intelligent of them and sent them back to their own people to offer terms of peace. The Guaicuru chiefs were greatly astonished to see their subjects return, not only alive and well, but full of admiration for their captors, and especially for their magnanimous Governor. This generous confidence on the part of Cabeza de Vaca had its desired effect. Twenty of the principal Guaicurus were sent to arrange the terms, and thus a peace was concluded that lasted for many years.

Alvar Nuñez continued with great activity in the work of conciliating the Indians by kindness when possible, by force when kindness would not avail, and by good faith always. The limits of this work will not allow of a complete account of the labors and difficulties of this faithful, energetic servant of the crown. But faithful and energetic though he was, he was not precisely the man for the position he was called to fill. In integrity, in energy, in purity of purpose, and in knowledge of the Indian character, his superior was not to be found ; but with all these qualities he had not the tact to overawe and control his own countrymen. His rules of conduct were so tight that his subordinates would not bear their tension. He might be considered as a sort of Spanish Catholic Puritan ; but his associates and subjects knew nothing of Puritan abnegation and self-control. With such different ideas and motives of conduct, it was impossible but that there should arise an opposing party composed of leading and influential members of the colony. With the common soldiers and the natives he was popular ; for they regarded him as their protector against the petty tyranny of the subordinate officers. The latter, for the same reason, determined to be rid of his presence. Taking advantage, therefore, of his being sick and confined to his bed, and of the absence of Irala, who as chief in command of the military had been sent into the Cordilleras to chastise the natives that had been causing much trouble, a large number of the disaffected officers assembled on some pretext near his house, and, no guard being ready to repel them, they entered, dragged him from his bed, sick as he was, and, loading him with fetters, cast him into prison and subjected him to most cruel indignities. The next day the people were called together, and the chief conspirators read a declaration to the effect that Alvar Nuñez de Vera Cabeza de Vaca having been guilty of the greatest crimes, and having the evident purpose of despoiling the colonists of their riches, was therefore deposed from his authority, and Domingo Martinez de Irala was proclaimed a second time, by the popular voice, Governor of the colony. It was also declared in this proclamation of the populace, that Nuñez should be sent to answer to the King for his misconduct.

When Irala returned from the Cordilleras he found everything in the greatest confusion. Even the best friends of Cabeza de Vaca were alarmed at the opposition he had provoked, and their alarm was much increased by the ill-timed efforts of some of his partisans to get up a counter-revolution. The conduct of Irala at this crisis has been very much criticised, and very differently estimated by different writers. That as lieutenant to Alvar Nuñez he had not acted with the same energy and good faith as when he was himself at the head of the government no one denies; but that he was in any way privy to the conspiracy, or that he approved it after its work was done, there exists no other evidence than the fact that he accepted the post from which Nuñez had been evicted. This in itself is a strong presumption against him, but it is not conclusive. On his return to the capital, it was the all but unanimous voice, even of the friends of the fallen Governor, that Irala should accept the offered position. They knew, and he knew, that if he refused to accept the post, and Cabeza de Vaca were released and restored to power, there existed such animosities as would lead to anarchy; that the colony would probably be ruined. There was no other man to be thought of for the position but one of these two. Under these circumstances Irala accepted the position, and Cabeza de Vaca was sent to Spain, that the government there might decide on the merits of the unhappy quarrel that had arisen between the two Governors. As the distinguished prisoner was being taken on board the vessel that was to bear him to Spain, he availed himself of his undoubted right to name his successor. Knowing that his arrest was illegal, and that it was for himself, and not for his subordinates, to name a substitute in case he must leave, he, at the moment of embarking, proclaimed aloud, that, in the name of the King, he appointed Juan de Salazar y Espinosa as the lawful and legitimate Governor. Little or no respect, however, was given to this verbal appointment, as Salazar had neither prestige nor talents to command it.

The services and sacrifices of Alvar Nuñez were but illy requited by his sovereign. He had too rigidly obeyed his instructions, and the great Emperor, like an Emperor later and greater than he, was as severe on those who erred from obedience as those who erred from disregard of his orders. With Charles V., as with Napoleon, it was a crime to fail. To bring the faithful Adelantado to trial was sure to fix the responsibility of his failure on those who had given him his instructions. This the government was not disposed to do, and though a neglect to do so was calculated to work the greatest injustice to both Cabeza de Vaca and to Irala, it refused for eight years to give a hearing to the former, and its approval of the latter was in such a way as to leave the charge of insubordination and schism hanging over him. Both had a right to complain, not so much of each other as of the crown; but as Alvar Nuñez had most implicitly obeyed instructions, he experienced most of that gratitude in which princes excel, — neglect. At last, after years of waiting, and long after Irala had been formally appointed Governor of the colony at Asuncion, Cabeza de Vaca was able to obtain an official investigation into his administration. Of course he was acquitted of every charge that had been brought against him. As if to make a mockery of his vindication, he was declared to be rehabilitated in his authority ; but he was destined never to return to Paraguay. In the long time that had intervened between his seizure and deportation and his rehabilitation, events had occurred that rendered his vindication an aggravation and his obedience a reproach. While waiting for the charges against him to be investigated, the government had indirectly pronounced against him by continuing to recognize Irala as Governor, and when at last he was declared acquitted of every charge against him, the government would not carry into effect the decree of the Council of the Indies. Irala was governing with great success, and the colony was in a flourishing condition, and it was not thought expedient to endanger its prosperity in order to do justice to a faithful public servant. The political life of Alvar Nuñez de Vera Cabeza de Vaca was at an end.

CHAPTER IV.

1545-1557.

Prosperity of the Colony. — New Towns built. — Results of the Admixture of the two Races. — Expeditions against the Indians. — Irala succeeds in opening Communication with Peru. — Political Affairs of that Country. — Irala returns to Asuncion. — Expedition under Captain Nuño de Chaves sent to explore the Region of the Upper Paraguay. — Consequences resulting from the Failure of that Expedition. — Death of Irala. — His Character and Public Services. — Influence of the Jesuits upon the Character of the Paraguayan People. — Paraguay constituted a Bishopric, 1547.

THE reports that reached Spain of the fine climate and soil of Paraguay, its beautiful diversity of hills and valleys, plains and woodlands, of a native race gentle and friendly to the foreigner, were sufficient to divert many emigrants from the more civilized countries of Peru and Mexico, where, though larger rewards were promised, the labors and dangers were correspondingly increased. The colony prospered greatly. Many towns were built more or less distant from Asuncion, each having an established municipal government in imitation of that at the capital, and to which the Indians as well as the Spaniards were to look for protection and justice. It was the constant endeavor of Irala to level all distinctions between the Europeans and the natives, and this he effected in a great measure by encouraging his countrymen to take the brown daughters of the forest for wives, to learn their language and conform to their customs in matters not of essential importance. This policy led to a very rapid increase of the colony, not so much, however, in his own lifetime as afterwards, when the sons and daughters of the mestizos grew up to maturity, and the lines of distinction between the two races became less marked, until at last the whole Guarani nation became, as it were, a Spanish colony.

Thus the government and policy of Irala permanently fixed the character, social and political, of the people. During his long administration they had entered so far on the road marked out for them by him, that they must continue to pursue it indefinitely. The singular combination of the Spanish cavalier and the Indian produced that form of civilization, the fruit of which was eventually the Paraguayan nation. From a union of such opposites there necessarily resulted a people of strange contradictions; a mixture of refinement and barbarism, civilization and ignorance. The cavaliers of Spain, high-spirited, punctilious, proud, and arrogant, took to themselves the dusky maids of Paraguay with their simple, rustic habits, their ignorance of domestic duties, their rude tastes, their simple innocence; and the result to their posterity has been what a philosopher might have foreseen, — the two extremes of refined courtesy and primitive barbarism. The Paraguayans descended from this cross are as punctilious, as courteous in deportment, as observant of the little amenities of civilized life, as were the courtiers of Charles V.; but in the houses of the richest of them is an absence of everything like comfort almost as great as among the Chaco Indians. A young lady who at a ball would be dressed with taste, and even elegance, and who would dance as gracefully as the belle of "our first society," the next day in her own house would be found barefooted, dressed with nothing but a chemise and petticoat, and invariably smoking a cigar; while in the two or three rooms of the house the furniture required by absolute necessity for eating, drinking, and sleeping would be so scanty as to be of less cost and value than that of the ball-dress of one of the daughters the evening before. Civilization is a plant whose growth is so slow as to be almost imperceptible. How many centuries has it taken for the present most enlightened nations to reach their as yet far from perfect development! Examples such as the history of Paraguay furnishes would seem to indicate that there is an innate barbarism in the human race that cannot be changed by education or custom till generation after generation has been exposed to the civilizing process. The very nature of the savage must be changed before he will take kindly to civilization; and it is as certain that an Indian child taken in infancy from its parents, and brought up with all the care that the most humane and refined căn bestow upon it, will still be a savage in many of its tastes and habits, as that the young partridge hatched by the domestic hen will at the first opportunity flee to the woods. The contact with the Europeans, and the mixture of the blue blood (*sangré azul*) of Spain, in three hundred years only produced a semi-civilization. The race of 1860 still had the peculiar qualities and characteristics of both branches of the original stock. It was an anomalous people, and the like had never been seen in any other country of America. The reason of this may be found in the fact, that in no other colony did the early colonists in large numbers adopt the native language and take the Indian women as wives.

The colonists continued to prosper so long as Irala was at their head, notwithstanding he was compelled to make many expeditions against unfriendly Indians, who were ever plotting their destruction. In one of these, that occurred soon after his restoration to power, as many as two thousand of the savages were slain, and more than that number taken prisoners. These last were distributed among the soldiers as prisoners of war (1545).

Many of the Spanish officers and soldiers under Irala's command were impatient at not finding any of the gold for which they had left their homes, and were anxious to make another effort to effect a passage through to Peru, notwithstanding the disastrous results of all previous attempts. Their Governor shared in this feeling, though from motives different from those of his followers. He therefore determined to lead an expedition himself; when this fact was known, no one doubted of its success. Naming Francisco de Mendoza as

Acting Governor during his absence, he set out with three hundred and fifty soldiers, nearly half of whom were cavalry, and two thousand Guarani Indians. It is, perhaps, needless to say that, after immense hardships and numerous engagements with the savages, Irala and his party were successful, and reached the confines of Peru. There they learned of great changes in the affairs of that country since their last information respecting it. They were informed of the civil war between Almagro and Pizarro, and the subsequent assassination of the latter. They also learned of the rebellion of Gonzalo de Pizarro, and its overthrow by that wonderful man of peace, La Gasca. Irala sent forward a deputation to advise La Gasca of his approach, and to offer the service of himself and followers in support of the royal authority. La Gasca received the messengers of Irala with kindness, though they were as unwelcome as unexpected. Many of the defeated partisans of Gonzalo Pizarro were lurking about, and he feared that they would try and enlist the soldiers of Irala to unite with them, and make another attempt at revolution. La Gasca, it seems, too, did not put full confidence in the professions and loyalty of Irala, and, being the direct representative of the crown, he removed him from the governorship of Paraguay, and appointed Diego Centeno in his place. But Centeno was an old man, and at the time of his appointment was on his death-bed at Chuquisaca. No one else was appointed by La Gasca in place of his old friend and devoted follower, and Irala, still Governor, returned to Asuncion.

Irala and his party were absent a year and a half on this expedition. During this time he had fought many battles with the Indians, and on his return brought, instead of gold and silver, twelve thousand captives, mostly women and children, who were allotted out to his followers as slaves. His long absence had caused many to believe he had shared the fate of Ayolas, and would never return. His lieutenant, Mendoza, had been killed in an insurrection against his authority, headed by Diego de Abreu. The insurrection was suppressed, and its leader executed. In the absence of a controlling mind there had appeared several ambitious of leadership. But Irala arranged all these disputes and rivalries, conciliating two of the most formidable and able of the malecontents, Francisco Ortiz de Vergara, and Alonzo Riqueline de Guzman, father of the historian Ruy Diaz de Guzman, by giving them his daughters in marriage.

The conduct of Irala in carrying off his prisoners to be treated as slaves does not appear in keeping with his general character. He is to be judged, however, by the moral code that prevailed in the sixteenth, and not by that of the nineteenth century. In his day, few questioned the right of the civilized invader to enslave or destroy the savage heretic. Yet Irala, though he distributed his captives among his own people as slaves, did not condemn them to perpetual bondage. He made provision, that, after one or two lives, their descendants should be enfranchised and become citizens; and thus, though coming far short of modern ideas of natural right and justice, he showed himself far in advance of his times.

The experience of Irala in the upper waters of the Paraguay had impressed upon him the importance of having a Spanish colony in that vicinity, whether that was to be the route of the great highway to Peru or not. He therefore despatched a party consisting of two hundred Spaniards and fifteen hundred Guaranis, under command of Captain Nuño de Chaves, to found a town at some point above Olimpo, wherever the situation might appear to be most eligible. Chaves was a man of energy, but vain and ambitious, and when once away from the control of his chief, he thought to strike off and found a colony on his own account. He accordingly ascended the river to a point above where Curumba now stands, and thence struck inland to the west, intending to go so far into the interior as to be beyond the reach or power of Irala or the government of Paraguay. He had to encounter many tribes of Indians, and had many battles with them, till his men, seeing that his conduct and plans were in direct violation of his orders, demanded that he should return to carry out his instructions, and make a settlement on the Upper

Paraguay. But he refused to yield to their demands, and the larger part of his troops deserted, and returned to Asuncion. Thus the expedition failed of its object, and from this failure the whole history of all the countries of the Plata has been changed. Had a Spanish settlement been established at that time on the upper waters of the Paraguay, the vast regions of Matto Grosso and Alta Amazonas would have continued a Spanish possession as long as Spain held dominion over any part of South America. Another colony than that at Asuncion, some three or four hundred miles higher up the river, would have rendered impossible the dark and gloomy reign of Francia; nor could the late war, that has made a desert of Paraguay, ever have taken place. By the failure of this expedition, the country was left to be taken possession of by the Portuguese, and is now a part of the Brazilian Empire. To that it has always been a source of expense and danger. It is so far distant from the more thickly settled parts of the empire, that it is next to impossible to reach it by land; and to approach it by water, rivers must be ascended that are controlled by three distinct powers. It gives no revenue to the crown, but has long been a constant tax on the national treasury, and at last was the occasion of a war that, while it almost depopulated Paraguay, wellnigh bankrupted the three powers allied against it.

A continuous narrative of the great and important events of Irala's life cannot be given in this work. From his first landing in the New World to his death, his career was a romance of activity, adventure, danger, and toil, all devoted to a conscientious discharge of his duty alike to his sovereign, his fellow-adventurers, and the defenceless natives. He was always active, now going forth to chastise some troublesome Indians, and now hurrying back to arrange disturbances and rivalries at the capital. Then he is busily engaged in assisting the missionaries in the work of Christianizing, instructing, and civilizing the Guaranis, and in establishing subordinate colonies at different points more or less distant; and suffice to say, that, to the day of his death, he continued to be the head and soul of the colony. He died in 1557, at the village of Ita, some twenty-five miles from Asuncion, whither he had gone to superintend the cutting of some timber for a cathedral in the capital. There, at the age of seventy years, he was seized with a sudden and violent fever, and expired, lamented alike, strange as it may seem, by his own countrymen, the Guaranis he had subdued, and the captured Indians of other tribes that he had enslaved. He was buried in the cathedral which he was engaged in building at the time of his death, — the first and the last great man ever known by the countries of the Plata.

Irala had lived long enough to see his policy vindicated by its success. The colony under his administration had grown rich, numerous, and strong, as no other colony in the New World had ever done with the same assistance from the mother country. That the results of his plans subsequent to his death were so different from what he anticipated may be ascribed to one of two natural causes, of which he had neither knowledge nor experience, — to the mixture of two races so incongruous that a hopeless inferiority should result from their amalgamation; or to adventitious circumstances that intervened, and perverted into evils measures in themselves good, just, and humane. To sustain the former hypothesis is scarcely possible; but there are many reasons for believing the latter.

The mixed character of the Paraguayan nation had been fixed by Irala, and for two hundred and fifty years after his death there was no violent revolution within, nor influx of foreign elements from without, to affect or change the national character. But it did change, until we have seen the whole people the mere passive instruments of their own destruction, — machines without will, and without the consciousness of power or self-assertion, mere material for war that could be directed as if insensate.

Before dying, Irala had named as his successor the original founder of Asuncion, Gonzalo de Mendoza. The nomination was approved, as the people then thought that whatever had been done by Irala must be right, as at a later period our people have thought that whatever was done by George Washington or Abraham Lincoln must necessarily have been right. But Mendoza died within a year of his nomination, and was succeeded by the son-in-law of Irala, Francisco Ortiz de Vergara. After the death of the founder of Paraguay, however, it was no longer a question of the stability of the colony. The Guarani Indians, more docile than any others in that part of the world, and more intelligent than the most, had, after some feeble attempts to destroy the uninvited Spaniards, ere this given up all hope of throwing off their dominion, and accepted them as the dominant race. The half-breeds, now coming of age, formed a connecting link between the two races; and as the brown señoritas of the country looked more kindly on the gallant Spaniards than on the dusky natives, the morality of the country being then, as ever since, of a most easy character, the succeeding generations showed an astonishing number having the blood of the two races in their veins.

It is beyond the purpose of this work to follow chronologically or treat historically many events that, though in themselves interesting, had no permanent influence on the general character and condition of the Paraguayan nation. The frequent skirmishes with the Indians, the perpetual jealousies and contentions for power, were matters of course, and can have no interest except for the people of the country. But for two hundred years after the death of Irala there was no event of sufficient influence or importance, either of a warlike or a political nature, to seriously affect or change the national character. The change that came over the people was wrought by other means. Early in the history of the colony the disciples of Ignatius Loyola fixed upon Paraguay as a field for their operations; and after they once were domiciled there, the history of the Jesuits was the history of Paraguay. The intrigues and conspiracies for the civil power were of little importance, for they left no permanent impression. There were some sixty different governors during the colonial period of the country, but little more than the names of most of them is known. Their descendants have atoned with their lives for the eminence their forefathers enjoyed. The conduct of the prince that took the hint from his courtier who cut off the heads of the tallest poppies, and served his ablest men in the same way, has been so closely imitated for the past fifty years, that nearly every family that could boast of gentle blood was extinct long before the termination of the great war in which all were indiscriminately sacrificed. The colony, in spite of petty jealousies and rivalries, was growing richer and stronger; the people in their unambitious way were prosperous; many thousand cattle and sheep grazed upon the open plains; the earth yielded its fruits so profusely that the necessities of life were had with very little labor, and nature had done all that was possible to tempt the people to a life of indolence and arcadian simplicity.

After the first dangers and toils of the pioneers were over, and the comforts of civilized life were procurable in the colony, many of the emigrants from Spain took with them their wives and children. The proud dames of Castile looked with a natural contempt on the Guarani women with whom their countrymen had consorted, and those who could boast the blue blood (*sangré azul*) of Spain affected great superiority to their darker neighbors. This pride of blood was long maintained among those families who could boast of it, especially by the female portion; the men being more indifferent to it, as they very likely would have, in addition to the legitimate family of the pure stock, several others of a mixed nature. Alas! could the aristocratic and proud Spaniards have foreseen the persecutions and disabilities, the tortures, imprisonment, and death, that were to be visited on their descendants for no crime but that of unmixed blood, they would have shuddered at its possession and claimed affinity with the Guarani.

The peculiar character of the Paraguayan people, however, as it has appeared during the last half-century, is not to be ascribed solely, nor even mainly, to the incongruous mixture of races from which it sprung. In the earlier periods of its existence there was as much independence and individuality of character as among any of the Spanish American colonies. This seems evident from the insubordination to authority that showed itself whenever power was grossly abused; and it was only after the influence of the Jesuits had emasculated the general mind of all sense of responsibility and every feeling of personal reliance, that the whole race became the willing forgers of their own fetters. It was through their system and polity that the national character was so thoroughly changed; and only by carefully tracing the course of their history can we find a solution of the peculiar development and formation of a people so extraordinary as the Paraguayans. The impress left by this brotherhood on the mind and habits of the people was so deeply fixed, that the expulsion of the order has not yet liberated them from the superstition, the moral and mental thraldom, to which they had become addicted, and which rendered it possible for the history of the country in later times to be little else than a tale of horrors.

As early as 1547 the Spanish court had asked from the Pope that the colony of Paraguay should be constituted a bishopric. The request was granted. The papal bull was issued, and the Friar Juan de Barrios, of Toledo, was named bishop. But owing to age and infirmities he never left Europe. In 1555 another bishop, Pedro de la Torre, was nominated to the place, and immediately embarked for Paraguay. Previous to this the whole of the South American possessions claimed by Spain were considered a part of the viceroyalty of Peru. The Viceroy of Peru and the *Audiencia* of Charcas had authority from the crown to administer the government of the Paraguayan colony, and all others that had been established in the valley of the Plata; but as an appeal to the King might result in a reversal of the action both of Viceroy and Council, Paraguay gradually became independent of her occidental neighbor, to which the establishment of a separate bishopric largely contributed. This bishopric included within its domain the whole valley of the Plata. But the great influx of population into the lower provinces soon rendered them too powerful and populous to remain in any respect tributary to Paraguay. It had been felt, soon after the breaking up of the colony at Buenos Aires and the final transfer of all its remnants to Asuncion, that there should be a town near the mouth of the river of sufficient strength to defend itself against the Indians, where vessels to and from Europe might load or discharge their cargoes and obtain supplies for their crews. Buenos Aires, therefore, was founded a second time, in 1580; and, notwithstanding its incommodious and unsafe harbor, it soon became a flourishing colony, and within a quarter of a century had as large a population as Asuncion. In 1620 the crown of Spain declared it, with all the regions of the Plata below the confluence of the Paraguay and Parana, to be a separate colony; and the Pope, at the request of the King, established a new bishopric, to hold spiritual dominion over it.

CHAPTER V.

1560-1636.

Buenos Aires founded a Second Time, 1580; declared to be a Separate Colony, 1620. — Saavedra appointed Governor. — Arrival of Jesuit Missionaries. — Pedro de la Torre, First Bishop of Paraguay; his Efforts in Behalf of the Indians. — Labors of the Jesuits. — Fraud and Deceit employed to cheat the Indians into Christianity. — Superstition. — The Virgin of Caacupé, and other Miracle-Workers. — Conflicting Opinions respecting the Influence of the Jesuits on the Indians. — Towns founded by the Jesuits. — Destruction of the Reductions of Guayrá. — Opposition of the Spanish Government to the Enslavement of the Indians. — Don Luis de Cespedes Jaray. — Expulsion of the Jesuits. — Destruction of the Spanish Settlements in Guayrá. — It becomes a Part of the Brazilian Empire.

THOUGH in point of time Paraguay had precedence of all the colonies of the Plata, and for a while was in strength and numbers the most important of all the Spanish dependencies east of the Andes, it gradually lost its relative rank after the second settlement at Buenos Aires, in 1580. This place, notwithstanding the inconveniences of its harbor, was to be the site of a great city, and after the Indians in the neighborhood had ceased to be dangerous, it soon became the metropolitan port of the entire valley. Other colonies were formed in the interior, all of which were dependent on it as the commercial *entrepôt*, so that, in time, Paraguay became a place of secondary importance. The colony of Tucuman had been founded as early as 1564, but as it did not have the advantages of river communication with the ocean like Paraguay, and in its early settlement had no master spirit like Irala to convert the natives into peaceable subjects, it did not flourish and grow strong and rich like its rival. Notwithstanding this, however, the jurisdiction of the Governor of Tucuman, Ramirez de Velazco, was in 1596 extended over Paraguay, and thus the older and more numerous colony was assigned a secondary position. Velazco, however, did not choose to take upon himself the increased responsibility, and by his wise choice of a substitute completely allayed any feelings of jealousy that his own appointment might have caused. The man to whom he delegated his authority was Hernando Arias de Saavedra, a native of Paraguay, who in his capacity of Governor displayed an ability and administrative capacity that had never been equalled by any of the governors from Spain save the great Irala. He made expeditions in various directions, even going down to Buenos Aires, where he embarked on a voyage of discovery along the coast, to the south of the mouth of the river. He cruised along the coast of Patagonia for some six hundred miles, and, after incredible hardships at the hands of the treacherous savages of these regions, was taken prisoner, with all his command. He succeeded, however, in escaping, and afterwards in rescuing all his companions. The results of his numerous expeditions served to convince him that there was a better way to subdue the Indians than to exterminate them, and that, as it would be a hard task to kill them all, it would be well to try and convert them. He therefore appealed to the court of Spain to aid him in this new plan of conquest, and, in 1608, King Philip III. issued the royal letters-patent to the Order of Jesus, for the conversion of the Indians of the province of Guayrá. This district of Guayrá comprised both banks of the Upper Parana, and is nearly east of Asuncion. In this region the towns of Ontéveros, Ciudad Real, and Villa Rica had been founded as early as 1554 by Don Ruy Diaz de Melgarejo. The first of the Jesuit priests who embarked on this mission were two Italians, Simon Maceta and Jose Cataldino. They reached Asuncion in 1610; but, on their arrival, Saavedra was no longer in power, having been superseded by Don Diego Marin Negron. The two padres, however, applied themselves with zeal to their pious work, and commenced forming the first Jesuit *reduction** on the banks of the Upper

* *Reduction* is the term used to express a town or settlement founded by the Jesuits, to which the Indians were invited to resort to receive instruction and become members of the community that was entirely under Jesuit control.

Parana, and in the vicinity of the towns founded by Melgarejo. The first reduction was called Loreto. Others of the same character were soon founded, as more of the Jesuit fathers soon found their way to this region, which had been selected for the field of their missionary labor in the New World. After the death of Negron, in 1615, Gonzales de Santa Cruz was named Governor by the Viceroy of Peru, but the court of Spain had by this time come to realize that Saavedra was the ruling spirit of the colony. He was therefore again appointed Governor, and held the office till 1620, when having succeeded in his two great projects, one of separating the government of the lower provinces from that of Paraguay, and the other of enlisting the Order of Jesus to undertake the conversion of the Indians, he retired from public life, to enjoy his honors free from the cares and responsibilities of office.

The first Jesuits that came to America landed at Bahia de Todos los Santos (Bay of All Saints) within ten years after the establishment of their order. The character of Ignatius Loyala the founder of this religious body, the principles of the order, the tendency and morality of their teachings, have been too often discussed and criticised to require here anything more than a plain historical statement of their work in Paraguay and the results which followed. As has always been the case with the first devotees of a new religious faith, a new system of government, or new schools of morality, the disciples of Loyola embraced his doctrines with great enthusiasm. In that age of superstition, or "age of faith," as it has since been called by those who mourn its departure, with its Holy Inquisition and machinery of torture, the Church was the great lever of power to which the military was often subordinate. To advance the cause of the Church and exterminate heresy was the chief duty of man, and no means were too cruel, no fraud too gross, no perfidy too scandalous, no torture too refined, to increase the power of those who professed to be followers of the Prince of Peace. Torquemada with his Holy Inquisition, and Alva with his hosts, had burned and slain their thousands of victims, to the infinite delight of their master, Philip II., and yet heresy would still abound, in spite of "pious combustion" or ruthless slaughter. It was at this time, when Spain, then the most powerful nation in the world, had been overtaxed in her wars against the infidels, — who, nevertheless, would not be convinced of their errors, but had waxed strong and numerous under persecution, — that Loyola conceived his idea of a universal regeneration by different means than those which had been employed by popes and kings for so many generations and with such unsatisfactory results. It was a pious and humane work that he proposed to his followers, and one that required the most entire abnegation and self-sacrifice. The world was to be renounced, and all its temporal blessings. The members of the order were to know no other duty or life than that of bringing the pagan and the infidel within the pale of the true Church. Wherever their presence was required, there were they to go without question. They were to brave toil, danger, and death, to cross oceans, travel across trackless deserts or through deep, dense forests, with no weapons but the symbols of their Church and the faith and doctrines they proclaimed. By these means they hoped to reach the heart and conscience of the savage and compel the respect and admiration of the enlightened.

The first followers of Loyola embraced his views with enthusiasm and entered on their work in the true spirit of gospel missionaries. They looked for no earthly recompense; they aspired only to bring the lost millions of the world into the fold of the Church, looking for their reward in the life to come. It was at that period in the existence of this order when its members were in the heat of enthusiasm and faith, that the first of the Jesuit fathers were despatched to the wilds of America on their sublime mission. They entered on their work with fervor and alacrity, and adhered to the principles of their order. The forms and ceremonies of the Roman Catholic Church were well calculated to make an impression on the minds of the ignorant and unsuspecting natives, and the story of Christ, his death and resurrection, and of the miracles wrought by saints and apostles, were accepted with little hesitation by these children of the wilderness. And when the natives saw that they came not to rob them of their gold or silver, nor to despoil them of their women, nor to drag them away and sell them into slavery, they eagerly conformed in all things essential to the rules and doctrines of the fathers.

The Jesuit fathers, on reaching Asuncion, found the colony very much distracted by the controversies and rivalries existing between the secular and spiritual authorities. The arrival of the Jesuits was calculated to aggravate, rather than allay, this discord. The first bishop, Pedro de la Torre, was a Franciscan, and his coming had been hailed with great joy by all parties. He had arrived in the time of Irala, who was so thoroughly the governor, that the bishop could do little else than second his efforts.

After the death of Irala, the policy which he had initiated, of incorporating the Indians into the body politic until the natives and the foreigners should become a homogeneous nation, was not followed by his successors with the same regard for the rights of the aborigines that he had always enforced. As has been seen, the prisoners taken by him in his wars with the Indians were usually allotted to their captors as slaves. The larger number were assigned to officers of note who had distinguished themselves at their capture, and who were under very stringent obligations to treat them well, and give them spiritual instruction. But in cases where whole tribes surrendered there was no allotment, and they were established by themselves in separate villages, under the general laws of the colony, to be administered by their own chiefs. A part of the males, however, were compelled to give one sixth of their time in labor to the colonists, but this could be exacted only for two lives, after which term the whole tribe were to be forever free. During Irala's lifetime these regulations were rigidly enforced; but when the government fell into weaker hands, and when priests and civil and military officers were struggling for the right and power to oppress, it frequently fared hard with the poor Indians. In truth, the treatment of the Indians in Paraguay, though far more indulgent than what had been inflicted on the natives of Peru, Mexico, or Brazil, was nevertheless very severe, and disgraceful to their oppressors. They were not slaves, for they could never be bought or sold ; but they were subjected to labor for those who had no interest in their lives, and who were under no responsibility to care for them and support them when sick. The abuses to which they were subjected were carried to so great an extent as to call for remonstrance and intervention from abroad. They were treated much worse in Peru than in Paraguay, and indeed so notorious was the cruelty practised on them there, that the padre Diego de Torres, with several assistants, was despatched from Rome as Provincial, with special orders to investigate the wrongs of the Indians and correct the abuses of which they were the victims. But the Spaniards wanted nobody to come between them and their greedy rule. The fathers, however, though unable to effect much, succeeded to some extent in alleviating the miseries of the unhappy natives, and in making it more respectable to treat them as human beings. Afterwards Torres went to Paraguay, but as his reputation had preceded him he was badly received by the Spaniards, who did not relish the idea that they were to be interfered with in their rights of living on the compelled labor of others. The arrival of the Jesuits, therefore, whose professed object was the redemption of the oppressed natives, was not welcomed by those who were living on their unrecompensed toil.

But the first labors of the Jesuits were not, and were not intended to be, exercised in the colony of Asuncion or any of its nearer branches. They first cast their eyes towards the province of Guayrá, situate some three hundred miles to the northeast of Asuncion, on the upper waters of the Parana, and near the Great Falls, or Salto de Guayrá, where, some years before, Ruy Diaz de Melgarejo had established the three towns, Ciudad Real, Ontéveros, and Villa Rica.

It was beyond these settlements, some sixty leagues to the east, on the Ibai, a tributary of the Parana, that the Jesuits established their first reduction, Loreto. Scarcely a vestige or trace of either of these villages or of the reduction now remain. The first settlers, after suffering incredible hardships from the Indians and the more savage Portuguese, were compelled to abandon the province. Twice was the site of Villa Rica changed, and it was not till 1678 that the present town known by that name was founded. The Jesuits, when compelled to abandon their first settlement at Loreto, descended the river, and established themselves in what is now known as the *Misiones*, on the left bank of the Parana, giving the same name to the place as they had given to that which they had abandoned.

But the Jesuits, notwithstanding the sublime devotion to duty that moved the early members of the order, recognized, in practice at least, if not in theory and principle, the idea that the end justifies the means; that, as their ends were pure and holy, they might employ fraud and deceit in their attainment. Though it is generally believed that the labors of this order in the countries of the Plata reflect more credit on it than any other portion of its history, yet the same fatal moral heresy that has made the very name of Jesuit a byword and a reproach — a synonyme for deceit and treachery — here, too, bore its legitimate fruits. The early fathers who came to Paraguay did not scruple to employ fraud to cheat the Indians into Christianity; they resorted to deceit as freely as did their brethren who hung around the courts of Europe, and swindled and robbed and cheated princes and potentates for the benefit of their holy order.

The early fathers, both the Franciscans and Jesuits, claimed to themselves the possession of miraculous powers. The Jesuits pretended to be descendants of St. Thomas, with a commission direct from Heaven to forgive sins, and to promise to all who would acknowledge the authority of the Roman Church, and enter within its pale, the reward of eternal felicity. The simple Indians accepted as true the words of the fathers, as they were supported by what seemed to them miraculous deeds. The spirit of St. Thomas was good enough to appear on certain convenient occasions, to impress them with the ocular proof of his presence; and so thoroughly convinced were the natives of being under the special protection of this saint, that a person in this age who should doubt it would be accounted as "little better than one of the wicked." It is known to this day, by proof as unquestionable to a Paraguayan mind as that the seasons succeed each other in their order, that the cross of St. Thomas is still miraculously borne about from one place to another, to the great comfort of believers and the confounding of sceptics. Its most fixed abiding-place on earth before the late war, or rather where it was most often to be seen, was in a small cave or fissure near the village of Paraguari, to which many pilgrims were wont to resort.

There was until recently another, miraculous agency in the country, having even more efficacy than that of St. Thomas. This was the image of the Virgin, in the church of the village, or *capilla*, of Caacupé, situated some twelve leagues from the capital. The miraculous character of this image was discovered a little less than a century ago, when the wife of the chief of the district, having a sick daughter, made a vow that if the child should recover she would give a valuable bracelet to the Virgin. The child did recover, and the mother told her neighbors of the circumstance, and when they had sick children they resorted to the Virgin, and made similar vows of jewels, and met with a similar return. At length the news of the miraculous cures came to the knowledge of the Bishop of Paraguay, and, to test the matter, he made a pilgrimage to the place, to see if the Virgin would work a miracle for him. She graciously complied, and the bishop formally inaugurated the worship of the Virgin of Caacupé, sending forth an episcopal letter accrediting the practice, and promising indulgence to the pilgrims who should visit the shrine. Thus the worship became legal and orthodox, and, according to the reports of those who have visited it, this is as good a miracle-worker as any country in the world can boast. For more than eighty years multitudes of people have been in the habit of visiting it, always carrying offerings of valuable jewels. There are several well-authenticated cases of persons whose offerings were of inferior quality being overtaken, soon after making them, with some terrible calamity. What became of all those jewels will be shown in one of the later chapters of this work.

There is also a miraculous cross in Corrientes that has wrought wonders on various occasions, and in fact every place or town of much importance in that part of the world has something of a miraculous character to save the people from everything but their sins.

The first success of the Jesuits in the conversion of the Indians was so wonderful that the fathers thought themselves specially favored of Heaven. The natives not only embraced their faith, but entered their reductions and accepted the mild rule of the spiritual traders. The name of a foreigner had before been as terrible as that of a destroying angel. The Spaniards had come to the country to get gold, and, disappointed in that, they had taken possession of the territory and forced the natives of that vicinity to most cruel, unrequited drudgery, while the Portuguese of Brazil had dragged off thousands of them to be sold into hopeless slavery. But the Jesuits had come to live and die among them. They sought not earthly possessions for themselves, but said to the trusting Indians, "Come and live with us; we will teach you to live in greater ease and comfort; we will instruct you in the ways of peace, security, and bliss; and we will show you how, when this brief life is past, you may live with us in Paradise, where the maize is sweeter, the fruits more juicy, maté more abundant, the women more numerous and amiable, than it ever entered into your hearts to conceive." This contrast between the promises of the Jesuits and the practices of both Spanish and Portuguese colonists naturally won the confidence of the Indians. They flocked to the reductions for the double purpose of securing the promised blessings, and also for the protection that beings, thus acting under the direct inspiration of Heaven, might be able to afford them. Nor were the confiding natives disappointed in their reception and treatment. They were to enjoy not only spiritual blessings, but temporal exemptions; for it had been made a preliminary condition between the crown and the founders of the reductions, that they were to be forever free from all control by the colonial civil or military authorities. It was also one of the primary and cardinal principles in the organization of the order that the natives should not be enslaved or subjected to unrecompensed labor.

The conduct of the Jesuits towards the Indians has been variously judged by different writers. But they have had the advantage of telling their own story, and none, of their own knowledge, to contradict them. They have had almost a complete monopoly of the means for making known their doings to the rest of the world. They always represented the success of their system as marvellous, and themselves as saints specially favored of Heaven, and that their success proved it. But *they* wrote the books, and not the Indians. Had the latter been able to tell their story, it might have been very different. When the man and lion, in the fable, had a dispute as to which was superior to the other, the man took the lion to a piece of statuary where the lion was represented as crouched at the feet of the man. At this the lion said, that, when lions became sculptors, the man would be represented at the feet of the lion. In the case of the Jesuits, *they* were the men and the natives were the lions, and they have given their own history so that it should be as creditable as possible to their own order. The most read, quoted, and credited of their historians is Charlevoix. But he was never in Paraguay, or near the reductions. His voluminous work was made from the writings of the fathers, and he had not even the advantage of knowing anything of his subject from personal observation, or of learning anything from the Indians themselves, of their condition or treatment. His work, therefore, should be styled "A Defence of the Jesuits in Paraguay, by a Member of their Order," rather than "A History," etc.* Whenever a lay writer has ventured to question incidentally the policy or conduct of the Jesuits, he has always called down on himself the most furious attacks of their defenders. Even Azara, who in everything else is admitted to have been a model of patience, truth, and impartiality, is accused of prejudice and partiality whenever he alludes to the Jesuits. Nor in these

* To show the character of Charlevoix's work, nothing can be more conclusive of its unreliable character than extracts from it. The following will show both the credulity of the man and the mendacity of his authorities. As it is not easy to disprove his accounts of marvellous and miraculous deeds of the fathers, I limit myself to his descriptions of some of the animals they encountered, — animals, it need not be said, that were never seen except by Jesuit fathers.

"Many of these reptiles live upon fish; and Father Montoya informs us that he one day happened to spy a huge snake whose head was as big as a calf's, fishing on the banks of a river; the first thing the monster did was to discharge by its mouth a great quantity of foam into the river; he then thrust his head into the water, and kept it very quiet till a great many small fishes, attracted by the foam, had gathered about it, when, suddenly opening his jaws, he laid about him and swallowed in great numbers all those who were unhappy enough to lie within his reach. . . . . This monstrous species of reptiles never quit the water; and in the rapids, which are pretty common in the Parana, they are often seen swimming with a huge tail, and their head, which is likewise very large, above water. . . . . It is certain that this great river swarms with sharks, much larger than those of other rivers; and that they lie in wait for oxen that come to drink its waters, seize them by the muzzle, and stifle them.

"In some parts of this country there are chameleons from five to six feet long, that carry their young ones about with them, and always keep their mouths open on that side from whence the wind blows. They are a very mild, but a very stupid animal. The monkeys here are in size almost equal to the human species, have great beards, and long tails. . . . . The ravens here are white. . . . . Among the fish found in the rivers and lakes there is one which differs in nothing from a hog, but that it has no teeth; and a water dog which barks like the land dogs of Europe. A missionary one day spied one of these animals on the banks of a river, when, having been wounded with an arrow, he fell to barking with all his might, till several others immediately came to his assistance and transported him to the other shore." — *The History of Paraguay: containing amongst many other New, Curious, and Interesting Particulars of the Country, a full and authentic Account of the Establishments formed there by the Jesuits, from among the Savage Natives; in the very Centre of Barbarism; Establishments allowed to have realized the Sublime Ideas of Fenelon, Sir Thomas More, and Plato.* Written originally in French, by the celebrated FATHER CHARLEVOIX; in Two Volumes. London: Printed for Lockyer Davis, in Holborn, Printer to the Royal Society. MDCCLXIX.

contradictory opinions does sectarian prejudice have much to do. The Protestant writers generally speak of them and their labors in Paraguay with almost unqualified praise, while their bitterest assailants are Roman Catholics, of whom the Franciscans were the most hostile and censorious. In these conflicting opinions it is but justice that the Jesuits should be judged by that test which must be final against all theories and disputed facts: "By their fruits ye shall know them." *

That the Jesuit fathers, who first undertook the conversion of the Paraguayan Indians, were actuated and moved by entire disinterestedness has never been questioned; and from the fact that they were not actuated by self-interest, it is to be inferred that their rule was just and mild compared with that of the gold-seeking Spaniards and Portuguese. But the pioneers who had caught the enthusiasm of Loyola from his own lips, and entered on the work of conversion from no hope of earthly reward, but expecting to be exposed to toils, dangers, and death in the performance of their duty, were succeeded by men of a very different stamp, — by men who found that a

* "Meanwhile we have proof that the Communist idea had taken possession, not merely of some individuals, but also of entire corporations, and these the most erudite as well as the most influential. When the Jesuits wished to organize a social order in Paraguay, what were the plans suggested by their previous studies? They were those of Minos, Plato, and Lycurgus. They realized Communism, which, in turn, did not fail to realize its sad consequences. The Indians descended some degrees below the savage state. Yet, such was the inveterate prejudice of Europeans in favor of Communist institutions, always presented as the type of perfection, that the world celebrated the happiness and virtue of these beings without name (for they were no longer *men*) who were vegetating under the yoke of the Jesuits.

"Had Rousseau, Mably, Montesquieu, Raynal, these great preachers up of the missions, verified the facts? Not the least in the world. Could their Greek and Latin books deceive them? Could any one go astray, when taking Plato for guide? The Indians of Paraguay were then happy, or ought to be so, under penalty of being miserable against all the rules! Azara, Bougainville, and other travellers, set out, under the influence of these preconceived ideas, to go and admire such marvels. At first the sad reality could not reach their eyes, for they could not believe it. But they were compelled to yield to evidence, and to state at last, to their great regret, that Communism, seducing as a chimera, is a frightful reality." — *Baccalauréat et Socialism*, par F. BASTIAT.

Jesuit father might enjoy a life of luxury, indolence, and power.

It has been often represented that the early fathers were received and welcomed by the Indians of South America as though they had already been warned from on high of their approach. But this is only one of their own inventions. That the Indians rushed to them as "the hart panteth after the water brook," and cast off the carnal man, and became spiritually new beings, is not only contrary to reason but is denied and repudiated as false by the most reliable writers of the times, and is proved untrue by all contemporaneous history that does not come from the Jesuits themselves. According to Azara, it was not for spiritual, but material, aid that the Indians first came in such large numbers to the reductions. In his own words: —

"The Jesuits say, that, to convert the Indians, their conduct was restricted to persuasion and apostolic preaching. Notwithstanding, two things are to be noticed: one is that their first ten towns were founded within the short space of twenty-five years, and that their zeal and preaching had no other result for one hundred and twelve years, that is, from 1634, the date of the foundation of San Cosmé, till 1746, when they reached the reduction of San Joaquin, and during this long interval they did not establish any other town except that of Jesus, and that less by their preaching than by the aid of the Indians of Itapua; the second observation is that the twenty-five years so fruitful in founding towns are at precisely the time when the Portuguese everywhere furiously persecuted the Indians in order to sell them into slavery, and when the frightened Indians fled for refuge to the region between the Parana and the Uruguay, and to the neighboring forests, where their bloodthirsty enemies could not easily penetrate, and which they did not do. Combining these two observations, there is reason to believe that the famous Jesuit towns owed their formation rather to the fear that the Portuguese inspired among the Indians, than to the persuasive talent of the Jesuits. Indeed, it was natural that those religious persons should subject and direct the Indians very easily, as is always the case with an expatriated and panic-stricken people. The rapid establishment of the first ten colonies, not followed by others, supposing the zeal of the missionaries to have been the same, and that there was no lack of savages, indicate that there must have intervened some other cause in the formation of the towns of the Parana and the Uruguay. That which appears to me most natural is that the terror which the Portuguese had inspired was the same which had induced the Spaniards to establish their towns in Guayara. This idea is, moreover, confirmed in a certain manner by the character of the measures adopted by the Jesuits to subject other towns besides the reductions. They considered useless and entirely discontinued the ways of persuasion, and resorted to temporal means; but they managed these with as much prudence as moderation and skill; wherefore they appear worthy of the higher praise. It is true, that they concealed with great care their conduct in this respect; this was natural, as, being ecclesiastics, they wished to pass as such in all their actions. But I had opportunity to be informed of this conduct, and will relate how it was.

"Knowing that some savage Guaranis existed in Taruma, the Jesuits sent them some small presents, which were carried to them by the Indians that spoke the same language, selected from the older towns. These embassies and presents were repeated, and the recipients were told that they were sent by a Jesuit who loved them tenderly, and who desired to come and live with them, and to furnish them other things much more precious, one of which was a large supply of cattle, so that they could live without labor. The Indians accepted these offers, and the Jesuit set out with what he had promised, besides a considerable number of Indians selected from the missions already established. These Indians remained with the Jesuit, as being necessary to build him a house, and take care of the cattle, that were soon finished off, as the neophytes thought of nothing but eating. The savages then asked for more cattle, which other Indians, selected like the first, went to bring them, and all remained in the place under pretext of constructing a church and other edifices, and of cultivating maize, mandioca, and other things for the use of the Jesuit and all the people. The food, the kindness of the padre, the good conduct of the Christian Indians that had brought the cattle, the feasts, the music, and the avoidance of every appearance of subjection, drew to this village the savages of the whole country around. When the priest saw that his chosen Indians were more numerous than the savages, he one day called them together, and in a few soft words told them it was not right that their brothers should labor for them. Some of them appeared very much disgusted, but seeing the superiority of the forces of the priest, who was wise enough to conciliate some of them, and to punish others with great moderation, and to watch them all for some time, the town of San Joaquin was finally established. The Jesuit did even more than this, for he took away all the savages and distributed them among the missions of the Parana. They escaped, however, and returned to their own country, notwithstanding the great distance."

The colony of San Estanislao was established by similar art, fraud, and cruelty. Swindling was the first step in the plan of conversion. The Indians were cheated into the belief that the padres had come to supply them with cattle, to teach them how, with less labor, they could raise their maize and mandioca; and they could not deny that a religion was highly evangelical which promised them, not only the blessings of a future life, but also in this world beef and indolence. In the first missions, or reductions, of Guayrá, however, the Jesuits had not found it necessary to employ either force or fraud in order to make Christians of the savages. The fear of the Portuguese was enough to cause them to fly to the reductions to seek the protection of the Jesuits. The latter gladly received them, and under their mild rule, supported by the mysterious symbols and gorgeous ceremonies of the church, their pretended miraculous powers, and the promises held out to those who would profess belief and conform to the essentials, the savages were made neophytes as fast as they could be told off.

But the reductions of Guayrá, as we have already seen, were doomed to an early destruction. The story of their fate is one of the darkest in the history of South America. They were exposed to an enemy compared with which all others that had visited them were as mild and gentle protectors. They were marked by their neighbors to the east as victims to that system which honored statesmen, aged bishops, and learned divines within our own times have boastingly characterized as a "divine institution." To the credit of the Spanish government it may be said, that from the first it set itself against the enslavement of the Indians of the Plata. They were subjected to forced servitude to an extent limited by law, but right of property in them and their children was not acknowledged. It is true they were treated with great hardship in many instances, and were, in fact, no better off than slaves, but cruelties practised on them were in violation of the royal orders and to satisfy the cupidity of individuals. The Portuguese in Brazil, however, had no such refined distinctions. They not only forced the natives mercilessly to toil for them, but they bought and sold them like cattle in the market-place, and sent them to labor in districts so distant that no hope could remain to them of ever seeing their native land again. Many thousands were sold in the markets of Rio de Janeiro; some to labor like felons in the streets, others to be sent to the mines, to be used like brutes, till death should relieve them. Catching Indians and selling them for slaves was found to be a profitable business, and any practice that *pays* is sure to have followers and advocates. The province of San Paulo, in Brazil, adjoining Guayrá, seems to have had more than its share of the desperadoes who, after the discovery of the New World, infested both land and sea. The city of San Paulo was a sort of head-quarters for pirates, slave-dealers, and outlaws of every kind; and they scoured the country around to catch the helpless natives and drag them to their slave-marts, thence to be carried into helpless servitude. Bands of these murdering robbers were organized for the purpose of making raids into the Indian country, and bringing in men, women, and children to be sold as merchandise. As the supply gave out in the vicinity of the sea-coast, the Paulistas, or Mamelucos, as they were called, went farther into the interior, and were carrying their work of devastation and death towards the banks of the Parana at the time that the Jesuit fathers began their labors of conversion among the Indians of Guayrá. The reduction of Loreto was the scene of the first Jesuit labors, and that, like those founded afterwards in the vicinity, formed a nucleus around which gathered the Indians who were fleeing from the dreaded Mamelucos. The fathers received them with open arms, and promised them protection in this life and salvation in the next, on condition they would acknowledge themselves converts to the Church, and receive the ordinance of baptism as the visible evidence that they had passed from darkness to light, from spiritual death to spiritual life. As in the nature of things the Indians could understand nothing of the mysteries and symbols in which they were told they must believe, they accepted the terms offered, and became good Christians by name, but changed in little else. They were ignorant savage Indians still, with habits and morals as gross and low as ever.

The rule of the Jesuits at this time, however, was very different from what it afterwards became. The early fathers labored faithfully to benefit the natives, first gaining their respect and confidence and then rebuking their indolence and vices. The success of their efforts in the first instances was such as greatly to exalt their hopes, and other reductions were founded in Guayrá and vicinity. The fathers alleged that conversions made so fast and easily must have been made through the power of God's word as spoken through their sanctified lips. Others say, and especially the Franciscans, that they owed all their success to the fear of the Mamelucos. The coincidence of events would lead to this inference, as the frontier missions were attacked by these freebooters soon after they were founded, and when the neophytes had no means for successful resistance. Many of them were killed, but many were taken prisoners and sent to the human shambles.

Notwithstanding such reverses, however, the Jesuits prospered in their pious work to such an extent that they still proclaimed they were under the special protection of Providence. But about this time an event occurred that would have caused people of weaker faith than theirs to suspect that they were not so miraculously favored as they had supposed. A new Governor for Paraguay was appointed, whose policy and interest were at direct variance with the plans of the Jesuits. His name was Don Luis de Cespedes Jaray. This man was married to a Portuguese woman whose proper position should have been that of queen of the pirates and brigands of San Paulo, rather than governor of the Governor of Paraguay. Her sympathies were with the Portuguese of Brazil, rather than with the Spaniards and Indians of Paraguay. Cespedes was on his way to his post when he first met this Jezebel, whose maiden name was Victoria Correa de Saá. She was connected with a family of wealth and influence in Rio de Janeiro, and Cespedes, during his delay in that city, fell completely into the hands of the Brazilians, and made a bargain with the Paulistas to assist them in kidnapping the people whom he had been sent to govern and protect. Instead of continuing his voyage by sea to Buenos Aires, and thence ascending the river to Asuncion, in obedience to instructions, Cespedes resolved to pass by land across the country. He travelled with an immense escort, more like an Eastern prince returning with his bride from a neighboring court, than as the military and civil ruler of a little-known and half-explored country. The first point he reached within the possessions of the Spaniards was the reduction of Loreto, on the banks of the Ibai, a tributary of the Parana. Cespedes saw the flourishing state of this place, and his eyes fell on the robust forms of the neophyte Indians with such admiring expression as it may be supposed would light up, in former times, the face of a planter or slave-trader from the South at the sight of a school of colored children in New York or Boston.

The Jesuits and their followers awaited the coming of the new Governor with joyful anticipation, as they believed that, coming as he did through the country of the Mamelucos, he must have become fully informed of their atrocities, and would at once use his authority to check them. But Cespedes had made his own interests identical with those of their dreaded enemies. His wife's estates in Brazil needed laborers to cultivate them, and this monster of infamy made a treaty with the murdering, robbing Mamelucos, by which he was to lend them his official influence and power to enable them to sack the reductions and missions and carry off the converted Indians, on condition that he should receive six hundred of the unhappy captives to labor on his lately acquired haciendas. This bargain being struck, a large number of Paulistas accompanied the Governor to the missions, ostensibly as an escort of honor, but really to perfect their plans for future spoliation.

The Jesuit fathers were naturally alarmed at these evidences of a good understanding between the Governor and their enemies, and his conduct towards them was not calculated to dissipate their fears. His manner was haughty, cold, and contemptuous, and he refused even to consider their request that measures might be taken to protect them from the Mamelucos.

Thus left to themselves, the missions of Guayrá fell an easy prey to the slave-captors, and in the following years they were all destroyed. The neophytes were carried off by thousands and sold into slavery. Finding nothing was to be hoped for from the government at Asuncion, and that the only refuge was flight, the scattered fugitives, to the number of some twelve thousand, resolved to abandon that part of the country and seek elsewhere security from the bloodthirsty Mamelucos. They therefore descended the Parana to the Salto de Guayrá, or Great Falls, where they found that they must abandon their boats, and make their way below, through almost impenetrable forests, and over a country so jagged and rough that many perished by exposure and want of food on the way. History furnishes few parallels to the sufferings and patient endurance of these fugitives. The resignation and hopefulness of the fathers, the trusting faith and willing obedience of the natives, should have had an abler chronicler than has yet undertaken to record them. But once, as they thought, at a safe distance from the Paulistas, the fathers again began their work, and founded other reductions, in several instances giving the same names to them as had been given to those they had abandoned. These reductions were located in what has ever since been known as the *Misiones*, and most of them were situate between the Parana and the Uruguay, though some of them were founded on the right bank of the Parana, in what is now Paraguay.

Not only was the Governor, Cespedes, inimical, from self-interest, to the Jesuits, but the Franciscan priests in the capital regarded them with envy, suspicion, and jealousy. These last fomented the animosity of the people against them, so that government, priests, and people regarded with favor, rather than otherwise, the destruction of the missions and the expulsion of their founders.

The disciples of Loyola, however, though coming professedly to convert the Indians, had other objects in view. There was something inherent in the order that seemed to incite its members to universal dominion. They aspired to influence in everything, — things temporal and political as well as spiritual; and while their principal work was the subjugation and conversion of the Indians, they let slip no opportunity for gaining political power in the civil and military affairs at Asuncion. Hence they had provoked opposition, and were generally unpopular. The people and priests of Paraguay were well pleased with the expulsion of the Jesuits of Guayrá. But, like the fox in the fable, the Mamelucos were not satisfied with what Cespedes had offered them. They had no sooner depopulated the Jesuit reductions of Guayrá than they turned their eyes on the Spanish towns in the same province, and thus the towns founded by Melgarejo, — Ontéveros, Villa Rica, and Ciudad Real, — soon shared the fate that, when it fell upon the reductions, had been regarded by the Franciscans with apathy, if not with approbation.

The result of these incursions of the Mamelucos was, that no vestige of a Spanish settlement was left in the province of Guayrá, and that portion of this immense province to the east of the Parana became a part of what is now the Brazilian Empire, — an event that never could have occurred but for the great crime of Cespedes. Had there remained a permanent Spanish colony in Guayrá, we may observe, as we did when commenting on the failure of Chaves to establish a colony on the Upper Paraguay, it would have been impossible for Paraguay to have been so isolated as to have fallen under the absolute rule of that sombre figure that so long hovered over it with remorseless cruelty, and the later tragedy of its depopulation would have been equally impossible.

It is some satisfaction to know that the great crimes of Cespedes at last reached the ears of the Audience of Charcas, which summoned him to its presence, and condemned him to pay a heavy fine, and stripped him of all authority, forbidding him to hold any public office whatever for the space of six years. What became of him afterwards is not known, but Paraguay was never again afflicted nor disgraced by his presence.

CHAPTER VI.

Opposition to the Jesuits by the Government and Priesthood. — They are made Independent of the Government of Paraguay. — Bernardino de Cardenas, Bishop of Paraguay. — Attempts to control the Civil Government by Force of Papal Thunder. — Uses his Influence against the Jesuits. — His Banishment. — Returns to Asuncion. — Elected Governor. — Persecutes the Jesuits. — Demonstration against the Jesuit College. — Cardenas removed from Office. — Francisco Solano, the First American Saint. — Stories concerning him. — Paucity of Words in the Indian Languages. — The Jesuits restored to their Dignities and Privileges. — Their Internal Domestic Policy. — The Spanish Encomenderos. — The System of the Jesuits. — Its Evil Effects upon the Indians. — Prepares the Way for the Rule of Dr. Francia.

THOUGH driven out of Guayrá, the Jesuits did not for that reason abate their zeal and labors. They continued in their new reductions the work of proselyting, and were steadily and constantly working in ways most subtle and insidious to gain influence and power in the capital. The Indians up to this time greatly preferred their rule to that of the military, and gave in their adhesion and services in such numbers that the reductions grew strong and rich; but the government at Asuncion looked upon them with distrust, and the Franciscans, headed by the Bishop of Paraguay, undertook to reap the harvest where the Jesuits had sown the seed and cultivated the soil. The proximity of some of the new reductions to the towns founded by the Spaniards exposed them to great annoyances; so that in these extremities, threatened by the Paulistas on one side and the priests and government of Paraguay on the other, the Jesuit fathers determined to appeal to the crown of Spain and the Pope for aid and protection.

The appeal in both cases was favorably responded to. Their representative to the court of Spain, Father de Montoya, obtained a royal grant that rendered the missions independent of the government of Paraguay. They were also allowed to provide the Indians with firearms to be used in defence of the missions. The response of the Pope would have been equally effective for their protection, had papal thunder and threats been of any force against the godless Paulistas. But men whose business is robbery, whose traffic is in human flesh, and whose whole political creed and system are based on the increase, perpetuation, and extension of human slavery, whose corner-stone of government is a gigantic crime, habitually give little heed to the denunciations of their acts.

Encouraged by the material support of the King and the spiritual approbation of the Pope, the Jesuits undertook their own defence; and when the next raid was made upon them by the Mamelucos, so well were they prepared to receive them, that, though the Paulistas came in large force, numbering not less than one thousand men, very few escaped to tell the tale of their surprise and defeat. After this the reductions were not disturbed by the Mamelucos, and yet troubles ever seemed to follow them. As the capital, Asuncion, was the principal *entrepôt* of all the neighboring regions, the Jesuits necessarily had extensive business relations with that place; and, besides, the fathers, as was ever their habit, were working constantly to increase their influence among the people. Hence it happened that between them and the bishop and clergy of Asuncion, the most of whom were Franciscans, there existed anything but a feeling of brotherly love and Christian charity.

The Bishop of Paraguay at this time figures prominently in the history of the country. His name was Bernardino de Cardenas. He was a man of great ambition and implacable resentments, and he hated the Jesuits with a stronger unction than he ever administered to a dying saint. He assumed the right to dictate in everything, and woe to the person that ventured to thwart him! In that age, the greatest terror that could be held up to frighten the true believer was the threat of excommunication, and Cardenas fulminated his terrible anathemas against all alike who dared stand in his way, from the Governor of the colony to the rival in his gallantries. But the good bishop seemed to forget, that, by using this terrible weapon too often, he weakened the force of it; and the excommunicated, mostly of the better class of citizens, became so numerous and influential that the bishop's fulminations were little feared and less respected. Nevertheless, it was felt by some to be a terrible thing to be under the ban of excommunication, and of those who dreaded this awful curse as the greatest misfortune that could befall a man was the then (1644) Governor of the colony, Gregorio de Hinistrosa. He had ventured to differ from the bishop on some matter, when the latter locked the gates of heaven upon him, and put the keys in his pocket. The people were scandalized at seeing the Governor disgraced, and the bishop trying to control the civil government by force of papal thunder; and there were such signs of an impending tumult, that, to avoid the storm, the bishop left the city and took up his residence at Yaguaron, a town some thirty miles to the southeast of the capital. Hither the unhappy Governor followed him, as an abject penitent, seeking forgiveness. He came before the haughty prelate, and with his face in the dust, kneeling at the bishop's feet, he prayed that the dreadful ban might be removed. The bishop haughtily rebuked and warned him, but granted his prayer as indulgences were granted to the rich, on payment of a heavy fine.

The bishop now, having the Governor prostrate at his feet, had both the civil and spiritual power virtually in his own hands, and his next step was to humble the Jesuits, and destroy their influence. He forbade the fathers to preach within the capital, and closed up their schools. To all these proceedings the imbecile Governor made no resistance. But the high-handed proceedings of the bishop having come to the ears of the Audience of Charcas, both the Council and the Viceroy were indignant at the pitiful part that Hinistrosa had acted. He was severely reprimanded for allowing himself to be overborne and disgraced by an arrogant prelate who had no business to meddle with other than spiritual affairs. Cardenas was denounced as having degraded his cloth, and as being unworthy of his elevated position. As the cry of "Land!" gives more courage to the shipwrecked, famished sailor, so did the action of the Audience give courage and resolution to the faint-hearted Governor. He quietly gathered together a force sufficient for his purpose, and by a quick and silent night-march he appeared with his forces at Yaguaron, before the bishop had received any information of what was coming. The bishop's house was immediately surrounded, and Hinistrosa entered his sleeping-apartment, where he found him but half dressed. The bishop quickly divined that the tables were turned upon him, and retreated from his house to the church. He was followed by the Governor and his party until he reached the steps leading to the altar, when from that elevated position, thinking to strike terror into the hearts of his pursuers, he turned, and, launching forth a string of anathemas as long and strong as rage and hate could express, he demanded of Hinistrosa to know the cause of such violence. The Governor, now no longer prostrate and penitent, replied, in terms equally scornful, that he had come to serve on him a sentence of banishment by order of the Viceroy, for having usurped the power which had been conferred on himself by the King of Spain. Cardenas, finding that his power had departed, and that the people, angrily confronting him, regarded his execrations as so much sound and fury, saw that all his curses were impotent to turn the edge of a single Toledo blade, and then with a bad grace he promised to yield to the sentence of deposition. But though he surrendered to the Governor, his tongue was still free, and he broke forth afresh in a storm of objurgations and abuse against the Governor and his followers, hurling forth anathemas and excommunications against them all, and piling up more curses on their exposed heads than ever Dr. Slop invoked on the offending Obadiah. But the Governor little heeded his curses and objurgations, and took him a quasi-prisoner to Asuncion, where the haughty prelate, finding himself no longer able to pursue his turbulent practices, and utterly without power, declared that such a godless set of excommunicants were unworthy of his sacred presence. With proud scorn, therefore, he turned his back upon the city, — that, notwithstanding, showed great signs of rejoicing by the ringing of bells and various public demonstrations of delight, — and left it to share the fate of Sodom and Gomorrah.

But Cardenas was not a man to abandon his once-conceived projects. He retired to Corrientes, and from there made known his grievances to the Audience of Charcas; and by much importunity he succeeded, after a time, in getting permission to return to Asuncion, for the alleged purpose of arranging his private affairs. He knew that, returning as by authority, he would be able again to wield much influence, if not actually to defy the Governor. But the latter stood in his way only for a little time; for soon after the return of the bishop, and when he had fairly established relations with his old friends and supporters, his old enemy, Hinistrosa, died. In that emergency the choice of a successor was to be made by the people, according to the early edict of Charles V. Cardenas, who less than five years before had left the city before the indignant hootings of the multitude, was now (1648) by the same people chosen Governor, in addition to his spiritual office.

The bishop governor had now full power to carry out his long-cherished purpose, — the expulsion of the Jesuits. He publicly proclaimed that he was determined to drive them from Asuncion; and with this object in view he called together all the people capable of bearing arms, — making use, as usual, of the much-dreaded threat of excommunication in case of refusal to lend their assistance to the work. A large crowd was collected, and the first demonstration was made on the Jesuit college. Its surrender was demanded with threats and menaces, notwithstanding the protests of the rector, who asserted that the order of Jesuits exercised their rights under a royal grant, and would not surrender them. The doors were then forced open by the rabble, and the priests driven out, and all alike, priest and neophyte, sick and well, were dragged to the bank of the river, and placed in boats, and, without sail or oar, cast adrift to the mercy of the current. The college was then sacked, the plate stolen, and the statues of the two great Jesuit saints, St. Loyola and St. Xavier, were changed in form and figure, and converted by a peculiar kind of transubstantiation to represent another sort of saints, after the manner of the showman, who changes his wax figures to be truthful, lifelike statues of the most popular heroes of the time in the town where he is next to exhibit them.

But, in the nature of things, the rule of this worthy bishop could not longer endure. The Audience of Charcas again denounced him, and summoned him for trial to the Grand Council of Peru, and Sebastian de Leon was commanded to put these orders in force. Cardenas, however, was contumacious, and resolved to oppose by force the orders of the Viceroy. But he again found that the thunders of the Church, which he hurled at the malecontents, had no power when not supported by the secular arm of royal authority. He retired, crestfallen, to his native place of Charcas, since called Chuquisaca, and there ended his mischievous and turbulent life.

The disgrace and deposition of Cardenas attached to his party, so that the Jesuits, who were at once recalled, had things for a time pretty much their own way. The Mamelucos, who, owing to the war then existing between Spain and Portugal, and to the persecutions of the Jesuits by Cardenas, had been encouraged to renew their hostilities, were now met and repulsed at every point; and such savage Indians as had taken advantage of the exposed condition of the missions to attack them, as well as some of the Spanish settlements, were quickly put to rout, and perfect quiet and security restored.

The jealousy, however, existing between the Jesuits and the Franciscans was the source of perpetual discord, and the civil government of the Spaniards was generally in sympathy with the latter. The Franciscans had the advantage of having an American saint in their calendar, who had been in Asuncion, which the Jesuits could not yet boast. A saint already canonized, of whose miraculous deeds there were yet living witnesses, was to be reverenced, and his co-workers while he was yet in the flesh were not to be treated lightly.

Of this first American saint, Francisco Solano, little is known, except what he himself reported. On his appearance at Asuncion, in 1589, he told such marvellous stories of miraculous conversions under his teachings, that he was looked upon as divinely inspired. But, besides his own words, there now exists no evidence that he was anything more than a successful impostor. The writers of the time, however, who were nearly all priests, agree in investing him with miraculous powers. He was the popular saint, and both Jesuits and Franciscans strove to magnify his name. To discredit him would have weakened the faith of laymen and neophytes, and, as is always the case with modern miracle-workers, it was thought impious to inquire closely into the truth of his stories.

Francisco Solano, of the Order of San Francisco, reached Asuncion in 1589. He was a native of Spain, and had come to Peru several years before. Thence he crossed the Andes, and, passing through the Gran Chaco, he descended the Bermejo River to its confluence with the Paraguay, and reached Asuncion. It was to this journey that his miraculous works appear to have been limited; and here, according to his own account, he met with a success such as never attended John the Baptist when preaching in the wilderness. He represented that as he came along he learned the languages of the different tribes or nations, and preached to them in their own tongues about the birth, death, and transfiguration of Christ, the mysteries of the Trinity, transubstantiation, and atonement; that he explained to them the symbols of the Church, the papal succession from St. Peter down, and that with his burning words he awakened the Indians by thousands, tens and hundreds of thousands, to a sense of their lost and perishing condition, and that they came in tears and penitence and accepted his words, acknowledged their belief, and, receiving baptism, had been admitted into the fold of the only true Church. It is impossible, at this day, to disprove the statements of Francisco Solano, but their impious absurdity is evident. The languages of the Indians could not by any possible application be made to express the ideas such as he pretended to convey. The poverty of the Indian dialects of the Gran Chaco is scarcely surpassed by that of the dumb brutes. The following quotation from the manuscript notes of Mr. Porter C. Bliss, who in the year 1863 travelled over the same region where Francisco Solano is said to have performed his miracles, will give some idea of the paucity of words among them: * —

"It is well known, that, out of the hundred thousand odd words which are given in Webster's or Worcester's Dictionaries, not more than five thousand are actually used in ordinary conversation, and form the *stock* of an uneducated man. Of these five thousand words, at least half are *synonymes* whose use might be dispensed with. There would remain two thousand five hundred. But of these a large portion are peculiar to the exercise of some profession or industry unknown to savage tribes, another large portion consists of the names of commercial products, animals, plants, and minerals belonging to remote countries; another large portion relates to intellectual and moral emotions of which the savage is incapable. It will be readily seen that these repeated excisions reduce the language of a savage tribe within very moderate limits.

"In fact, the language of a Chaco tribe consists only of some one to two hundred verbs, expressing the simplest actions and emotions; of four or five hundred nouns, which comprise all the animals, trees, plants, and other natural objects known to them; of fifty or sixty adjectives, which (dispensing with synonymes) suffice to express all their ideas of form, size, and character; and of the pronouns, prepositions, conjunctions, etc., which are few in number, and equally necessary in all languages. Thus the verb to *move*, in one of the Chaco languages, when combined with prepositions or adverbs, does duty for the distinct ideas of to *walk*, *run*, *step*, *go*, *come*, etc.

* It may be said that no writer or ethnologist has ever investigated or studied the character and history of the South American Indians so thoroughly as has Mr. Bliss, and probably there is no other man living so thoroughly conversant with the history of the valley of the Plata. Should he ever arrange his vast materials for publication, the work will be an encyclopædia of everything historical, ethnological, or scientific, pertaining to that immense basin.

"An amusing instance of the paucity of words referred to may be given from my voyage of exploration in the river Bermejo, in the Gran Chaco. We had on board a cacique of the *Ocole* tribe, named *Gabriel*, who understood a little Spanish. It was my custom daily to note down a number of words from his mouth, thus gradually forming a vocabulary. One day as we were seated on deck, I pointed out a *crow* on the bank, and inquired its name, which he gave me, — *kidimit*. On another occasion I asked him the word for *pantaloons;* he gave me the same word, *kidimit*. Again, on other occasions, I asked for the separate words *black*, *darkness*, *night*, *sky*, *cloud*, *heaven*, to all of which he responded, *kidimit*. It was only after comparing together my various lists of words that I discovered how many times this word had been repeated. It was then an obvious inference that the fundamental idea was *blackness*, since the crow, the pantaloons, the sky, the cloud, etc. were all black."

How the good priest was to impress his ideas on a people through such a medium as their own language is only to be explained on the theory that he not only had the miraculous gift of tongues, but that the Indians, for the time, were favored with inspired ears. That miracles were wrought by Francisco Solano it is of course impossible to disprove at this time by contemporary evidence, but if they were, they must have been such as to have changed the nature and intellect of the Indians. In their stupid, besotted ignorance, it would have been impossible for them to understand the holy mysteries delivered to them through their own vernacular, unless miraculously gifted with understandings such as they never had before nor since. But if the poverty of the language, the paucity of words, and the utter impossibility of forming any expressions from their meagre vocabulary to convey the ideas of faith, atonement, remission of sins, transubstantiation, the Trinity, and other things essential to be a member of the "Holy Mother Church," are not sufficient to prove Francisco Solano to have been an impostor, there are still other and stronger reasons for questioning the statements of the reverend father.

In these later, degenerate, and sceptical days, the most exacting ritualist or ultramontane believer would hardly pretend that miracles are wrought except for some great, good, and enduring purpose. In this case, however, if miracles were wrought, no such purpose was gained, as it appears that the Indians were not at all improved, for this world at least, by their wonderful conversion. They appear to have soon after relapsed into their original sin, and to-day there is not a vestige of the labors of St. Francisco Solano to confirm his testimony. On the contrary, the Indians themselves, among whom he wrought such wonders, have all disappeared; and when Mr. Bliss travelled over the country where they once dwelt in great numbers, there was scarcely to be found a sign that the country had ever been inhabited. Had a missionary, not of the true faith, done the same as did Francisco Solano, and had similar results followed it, it is to be feared that the "Holy Church" would have declared him an emissary of the Evil One, and that the people had been destroyed as a punishment for going after strange gods.

Francisco Solano remained two years at Asuncion, enjoying high honors, but it does not appear that before so many witnesses his marvellous powers were longer available. The light of intelligent eyes put him out as completely as it does modern spirit-rappers. He was held in great reverence, however, on account of what he pretended to have done elsewhere, and Charlevoix speaks of him as so highly gifted and divinely inspired as clearly to have been assigned by Providence for the special work of evangelizing the Indians. But he remarks, with a simplicity not usual in a Jesuit father, that in the midst of his wonderful achievements he was recalled from the field of his labors by his superiors, as if Providence, in granting him miraculous powers, had forgotten the other necessary steps to make them effective.

The Jesuits, after the banishment of Cardenas (1649), being restored to their dignities and privileges, applied themselves with greater earnestness than ever to increase their power in Asuncion. Their plan was eminently Jesuitical. It was to work insidiously, and, while professing to care only for things spiritual, to really control the civil authorities. By establishing and controlling the schools, the young would be educated to look to their order as the source of knowledge; and, with the educated classes in their favor, they would easily dominate the ignorant multitude. The missions, now grown rich and strong, were already completely under their control, so that they seemed in a fair way of establishing a nation in one of the most fertile regions of the earth, with ample territory to expand till it should become the most powerful in the world.

The growing influence of the Jesuits was naturally regarded with great jealousy and distrust by the Franciscans, and by all others who aspired to authority or influence in the country. The Indians who were not in the reductions preferred the Jesuit rule to that of the civil government, as the former repudiated everything like personal servitude wherever they were not the absolute masters; and in the reductions the service they required of the neophytes was always represented to be very different from slavery, and as being for the common benefit. The system of the Jesuits was very different from that of the Spaniards; and as between the two, for the influence on the character of the Indians, both present and prospective, that of the Jesuits, where their power was absolute, as in the reductions, was infinitely the worst. It had been the plan of Irala to make a homogeneous nation of the mixed Spanish and Indians, and that there should be no privileges on one side or disabilities on the other by reason of difference of race. Prisoners of war were subjected to a limited service to their captors, that worked no disgrace or disability in the blood; and the only servitude known was that which, in opposition to the fundamental law, a cunning people could exercise over a race, simple, credulous, and submissive. From the original union of the races it must inevitably result, that, as very few females had ever come to Paraguay from Europe, the power would soon be in the hands of those of mixed blood, and whatever nationality or civilization might be developed, it would probably contain within itself the men who were to govern it.

But the system of the Jesuits admitted of nothing of this

kind, so far as it affected the natives. They were to be laborers in the common vineyards, having no rights, no power, no liberty, except such as it pleased the fathers to grant; no hope for an improved future for themselves nor for their children; but all was a plain level of communism that must have formed an industrial paradise such as would have delighted Fourier or Owen. No white layman, no one but a Jesuit priest, could ever settle within the precincts of the missions, and hence there was no change ever to be hoped for in the condition of the natives. The power was all in the hands of the fathers, and the Jesuit system never contemplated that the natives should ever be anything but slaves, — slaves to the fathers, but not to be sold to men less holy than themselves, and who might neglect their spiritual interests.

The following extract from Azara gives an idea of the system of the Jesuits. As he writes from knowledge derived from eye-witnesses, and his statements of fact agree with those of the fathers themselves, though his conclusions as to the effects of the system differ widely from theirs, it may be taken as a correct exposition of the internal domestic policy of the missions of the Jesuits.

"The thirty-three Jesuit missions were ruled in the following manner: Two Jesuits resided in each pueblo. The one called the Cura had either been provincial or rector in their colleges, or was at least a grave padre. He did not exercise any of the functions of a Cura, and frequently did not know the language of the Indians. He occupied himself only with the temporal administration of all the property of the pueblo, of which he was the absolute director. The spiritual department was confided to another Jesuit, called *compañero*, or Vice-Cura, subordinate to the first. The Jesuits of all the pueblos were under the superintendence and vigilance of another, named the *Superior* of the missions, who had, moreover, the power to confirm from the Pope. To control these pueblos they had no laws, either civil or criminal; the only rule was the will of the Jesuits. Though in each pueblo there was an Indian called a corregidor, and others called alcaldes and rejidores (mayor and aldermen), that formed a municipal body, like what they have in the Spanish colonies, no one of them exercised the least jurisdiction, and they were only instruments that served to execute the will of the Curas, even in criminal cases. The Curas who inflicted the punishments were never cited before the King, nor before any of the ordinary tribunals. They compelled the Indians of both sexes, and of every age, to labor for the community, without permitting any person to labor at all for himself. All must obey the orders of the Cura, who stored up the produce of the labor, and who had the charge of supplying food and clothing to all. From this it is seen that the Jesuits were absolutely masters of everything; that they completely disposed of the surplus stock of the whole community; and that all the Indians were equal, without any distinction, and unable to possess any private property. There could be no motive of emulation to induce them to exercise their talents or their reason, since the most able, the most virtuous, the most active, was not better fed or clothed than the others, nor would he obtain any enjoyment that was not common to all. The Jesuits have persuaded the world that this kind of government was the only one suitable for the Indians, and had rendered happy those who were like children and incapable of taking care of themselves. They add, that they direct them as a father governs his family, and that they collect and keep in the storehouses the products of the harvests, not for private use, but to make a proper distribution to their children, who, incapable of provision, do not know how to preserve anything for the sustenance of their families. This manner of government has appeared in Europe worthy of such great encomiums, that the lot of these Indians has almost come to be envied. But this is done without reflecting that these same Indians in a savage state did know how to support their families, and that individuals of the same Indians that had been subjugated in Paraguay lived an age before in a state of liberty, without knowing of such community of goods, without the necessity of being directed by any person nor of being excited or forced to labor, and without a public storehouse or distribution of the harvest; and that, too, notwithstanding they had to support the charge of the commanderies that took the sixth part of their annual labor. It seems, then, they were not such children, nor were they so incapable, as the fathers tried to make them appear. But were such incapacity certain, their not having sufficient time in a century and a half to correct such defects, one of the two following causes appears reasonable, — either the administration of the Jesuits was contrary to the civilization of the Indians, or they were such a people as were incapable of emerging from their primitive state of infancy."

The Spaniards, previous to the founding of the Jesuit reductions, had established posts in various parts to serve the double purpose of a local government and of transacting such small business with the Indians in the way of traffic as might be required for the common benefit. These posts were called "encomiendas," and the persons in charge "encomenderos." Under the rule of these encomenderos the Indians were required to give one sixth of their labor for the benefit of the encomienda. Several of these posts, as Loretò, San Ignacio, Miri, Santa Maria de Fé, and other places, were located near the Parana, and in the vicinity of the reductions founded by the Jesuits after their expulsion from Guayrá by the Mamelucos. These encomiendas were regarded with great disfavor by the Jesuits, who at once set to work to break them up. They would have no Europeans near them, except members of their own order. They began by pathetic complaints of the hardships to which the Indians were subjected under the rule of the avaricious, cruel encomenderos; that they had to give one sixth part of their labor to them; that this labor was so severe as to kill them by hundreds and thousands. They complained, also, that the encomenderos were so grossly immoral that their presence greatly interfered with their own mission of conversion, and that altogether they were greatly in the way, and a reproach to their own holy work and pious example. These representations being made to the court of Spain, the encomenderos were compelled to withdraw; and the Jesuits were left in absolute control of the missions and the neighboring country. Then, instead of a sixth part of their labor to be given to the foreigners, the good Jesuits only asked the whole, giving in return what the master usually gives to the slave, — just enough to enable him to support life and strength, so that he may labor the more.

But these charges against the rule of the Spaniards in Paraguay are not sustained by any writers of the times, except the Jesuits themselves. The very system initiated by the great Irala precluded that cruel treatment of the Indians which every other system encouraged. Harshly and unjustly as they were often used after Irala's death, they nevertheless enjoyed rights, privileges, and protection such as no other Indians of the New World ever received at the hands of the Europeans. Indeed, there was little motive among the generality of the Spaniards for treating the natives with extreme severity. Most of them were connected with the natives by domestic ties. The mixed race so preponderated as to have a positive influence not to be disregarded. There were no mines to be worked, no cities to be built from the products of mines, no large establishments of rich conquerors to be adorned and beautified. There was little commerce and less luxury. The only labor to which the encomenderos, of whose oppressions the Jesuits so much complained, could put the Indians, was agriculture ; and all the natives were required to do, or, in the nature of things, could do, for their advantage, was to till so much of the ground as would suffice to supply the actual wants of these few resident Spaniards. Certainly, the hardship of being compelled to provide the maize, mandioca, cigars, sugar, and yerba-mate for one encomendero to each thousand people, when his presence among them not only was intended to be, but actually was, mutually beneficial, was not so grievous as to be insupportable. The labor required for this in a country so productive as Paraguay was very slight. It was, moreover, alleged by the Jesuits, that the Indians were forced to labor in the Yerbales for the benefit of the Spaniards. But at that day very little yerba was consumed, not more than could be gathered and cured by a hundred and fifty Indians. The task of collecting this amount could not have been so very severe on the thousands from whom this small force was taken. The whole history of the Spaniards in Paraguay, before they fell under the baleful influence of the Jesuits, tends to show that instead of seeking to extort fortunes from the natives, — though the pioneers had come with that object, — they soon formed connections with the women of the country, and, giving up all hopes of ever returning to Spain, they only sought to live in ease, indolence and quiet, exacting little from the Indians, since little was required to gratify their simple wants.

But the Jesuits, instead of demanding but a tithe of the products of the Indians' labor, exacted all, and denied to the producer the right of property. The doctrine laid down by Abraham Lincoln, that every man has the right to eat the bread which his hands have earned, did not enter into their political creed. They held rather to the opposite doctrine, that Indians had no rights that Jesuits were bound to respect; that their duty was to labor incessantly, and receive in return such pittance as the fathers thought necessary to keep up their strength, in the same manner as draught animals are fed for the sake of the labor that may be performed by them. In recompense for such services they were at last to be dismissed with extreme unction to another world, where they were to be rewarded without cost to the Jesuits.

In a country like Paraguay, to supply the mere wants, the actual necessities, of life, so far as regards food and clothing, requires very little labor. But the Jesuits must not only be fed, like the encomenderos, but they must have houses and churches of vast proportions and elaborate workmanship, in order to convince the ignorant natives that they were the disciples and followers of "Him who had not where to lay his head." To construct these immense buildings, the Indians were kept remorselessly at work. Besides the ruder kinds of labor, they were taught to work in iron and wood, to spin and weave, and do many things convenient to the Jesuits, but of no benefit to themselves. The fruits of all their toil went to enrich the churches and the Order of Jesus. Whatever they had for exportation, principally hides and tallow, went to buy pictures and gold and silver ornaments for the churches. If the Indians were taught to make and use tools of iron and steel, it was that they might make fine carvings, images, and other trumpery of like usefulness. The doors and window-frames of the churches and colleges, and of all houses that belonged to the holy order, were of the finest workmanship, carved from the hardest, most indestructible woods in the country. Many of these exist to the present day, and, though they have been exposed to wind and weather for two hundred years, they are still well preserved, and show that they were wrought with immense labor and skill.

But even these labors would not have been so great as to have overtasked the Indians, had there not been superadded the task of forging their own fetters, or, more literally, of making the reductions serve as prison-houses to themselves. As the Jesuits would permit the presence of no laymen in their vicinity, so they would not allow the Indians to hold communication with anybody beyond their own precincts. To prevent this, as well as to render desertion impossible, they made a sort of intrenched camp of each reduction, the ditches being dug after the manner of the militia-general in the Mexican War, to guard against the forces within the intrenchments. Guards and sentinels were kept posted at all the avenues of egress from the pueblo. The frontiers of the missions and the dividing lines between them were guarded like a military camp, and the enslaved Indians were not allowed to pass from one to the other. They were as in great prison-pens, with holy fathers for overseers. To render them as helpless as possible, they did not allow the Indians ever to mount a horse, or learn to ride or guide him, except a very few who were required to act as couriers or guard the cattle. But as the same trenches and natural enclosures for the men would serve also to fence in the cattle, few were required as herdsmen.

To render the isolation more complete, the Indians of the missions were not taught any European language. The fathers pretended to educate them in Guarani, and taught them to repeat and chant the formularies of the Church. But they were kept in that condition of ignorance, that, if by any chance a curious traveller or scientific explorer were to meet with one of them, he must first learn the language before he could ascertain anything of the degradation of the people.

The Jesuits paid no tax nor tribute to the King nor to anybody else. Few of them were Spaniards, yet they were allowed an *imperium in imperio* within the dominions of the Spanish crown. Within the missions they were supreme and independent, in virtue of their pious and holy character, and all that was accumulated went to enrich their own order. Being thus absolute in authority, and permitting no other Europeans to come near who might criticise their system or practices, they had the advantage of being their own chroniclers, and they made good use of their own trumpets. They published to the world such glowing accounts of their successes, not only in converting the Indians, but in civilizing them, that it came to be generally believed thoughout Christendom that the fathers of Paraguay ruled with the power of love alone, and that the Indians basked in a state of perpetual ease, peace, and comfort, laboring only so much as health and their own welfare required. No one could contradict them, and therefore their reports went unchallenged. Hence it was that writers of all creeds and denominations, those friendly to the Jesuits and those opposed to them, Catholics and Protestants alike, came to regard the works of the fathers in Paraguay as exceptional and in all respects beneficial. But in effect it was the worst government ever devised by the perverted ingenuity, selfishness, and bigotry of man. The Indians under it were abject slaves, with no possible chance of rising into a condition fit for free men, or men capable of self-government, or self-support. The crucial test of a good and wise administration is that under it the people have advanced in intelligence, and grown self-reliant and capable of self-government, so that, if the existing government or all of its members should be removed, the people would be so accustomed, not only to law and order, but to the responsibilities of power, that they would rapidly improvise another adapted to their necessities, without revolution or serious derangement. But the policy of the Jesuits was precisely the reverse of this. It was to make the Indians as helpless and dependent as it is possible for human beings to be, and preclude every hope or aspiration towards a better condition.

The exercise of absolute power within the missions only did not satisfy the Jesuits. Their influence was to be seen and felt everywhere. It was the same with them in Paraguay as throughout Europe. They aimed at universal dominion. They were not content with attending to merely spiritual affairs, but they must be all the while intriguing to get control of the civil government. Their most subtle idea was to keep the keys of knowledge as far as possible in their own hands, and by giving gratuitous instruction to the youth of wealthy families to make proselytes of them, and through them, or by their aid, to govern the multitude. Their system of government came at length to be regarded as the only one feasible and efficient, both in the missions and throughout Paraguay, and it was but a slight modification of that system applied to a people already prepared to receive it that produced the merciless rule of Dr. Francia. It was the Jesuit system still, when the power was all concentrated in the hands of the cruel Dictator; the difference being that the power was wielded by one man, instead of by a hierarchy. The people were so emasculated of all sense of power or influence in the government, that neither the Dictator nor the fathers ever could conceive of anything so absurd as that any subject could have any rights that did not accord with the interest, caprice, or wishes of the supreme power. This is, and ever has been, since the days of the Jesuits, the conviction, the controlling idea, the consciousness, of those rulers of Paraguay that the country itself has produced. Though the fathers in Paraguay shared the fate of the brotherhood elsewhere, and were long since driven from the country, yet the seed sown by them has produced such fruit that at last the land is left little more than a dreary desert. In the late war the final harvest was gathered in.

CHAPTER VII.

Diego de los Reyes Balmaceda appointed Governor, 1717. — Rebellion of Antiquera. — Defeat of the Rebels by Zavala, Governor of Buenos Aires. — Flight, Capture, and Death of Antiquera, 1731. — Martin Barua appointed Governor. — Return of the Jesuits. — Political Parties. — Second Rebellion. — Battle near Pirayu, December 15, 1733. — Zavala puts down the Second Rebellion. — Jesuitism in Europe. — Sebastian Carvalho, Marques of Pombal. — Expulsion of the Jesuits from Portugal, Spain, and France. — Remonstrance of the Pope. — Charges against the Brotherhood by the Council of Spain. — The Act of Expulsion finally approved and ratified by the Pope, 1773.

FROM the time of the removal of the bishop governor, Cardenas, in 1648, Paraguay remained for a long time undisturbed by any violent internal dissensions, and was left in peace by all its neighbors. There were occasional invasions, at remote points, by unfriendly Indians, and there were petty quarrels between rival aspirants for power; but the general course of events was peaceful, and the colony was all the while growing numerous and rich and strong. The Jesuits made the best of this time of quiet. They had worked successfully to get a controlling interest in the civil government of the colony, and in the missions were absolute. They had had more than a century in which to Christianize and civilize the Indians, and the result was that the missions were as near a state of perfection as could ever be expected under Jesuit rule. The Indians had degenerated into mere helpless, passive machines. And of this condition a late writer, whose narrative* of what he saw does him great credit, but whose historical part seems to be a re-hash of the writings of Charlevoix and other Jesuit writers, says that "the rising generation of Indians, impressed with a profound sense of gratitude for the temporal and spiritual benefits to

* La Plata, the Argentine Confederation, and Paraguay. By Thomas J. Page.

which Jesuit trading had advanced them, contemplated without doubt its permanency." Well they might, for after so long a servitude, with no light or knowledge of the outer world, no memory and scarcely a tradition of anything but the degrading slavery to which they had been born, what hope of change was it possible for them to have? But it is one of the provisions of nature that abuses too gross and too long continued work their own destruction. The bow will not bear too strong a tension without breaking, and human nature cannot be forever outraged without danger of revolt; and the greater has been the tyranny and oppression, the greater the abuses when the chains of despotism are once broken. The excesses of the French Revolution were but the reaction of the human mind long held in galling fetters; and it was only when slavery became the corner-stone, the divine institution, to be defended and preserved though the government and nation and all else should fall, that the American people were roused to declare that the accursed thing should perish forever.

The Jesuits, had they confined themselves to their missions, might long have continued in undisturbed possession, but, as in Europe, the fathers must have a finger in every political pie, and were not contented unless they could control the civil power. At length the time arrived when their influence was to receive a shock from which it was never to recover. Their vaulting ambition had "o'erleaped itself, and fell on the other."

In 1717, Don Diego de los Reyes Balmaceda was named Governor of Paraguay by the Viceroy of Peru. But the nomination was not well received, and, after two years of contention, charges of so serious a nature were preferred against him that they were thought worthy of investigation by the Audience of Charcas. The Audience was occupied for three years in considering the charges and counter-charges. In the mean while Don Jose de Antiquera y Castro had succeeded in obtaining the nomination for Governor to succeed Balmaceda should he be condemned, after which the Audience issued a decree suspending the functions of the latter. Antiquera at once hastened to Paraguay to assume power, although the occasion for which he had been prospectively appointed had not yet arrived. Knowing that he was acting informally and illegally, he thought to cut the Gordian knot of dispute as to which was the rightful governor by making a prisoner of Balmaceda. But the Governor chanced to be absent in the missions at the time of the arrival of Antiquera at Asuncion, and, though the latter made great efforts to catch him, he succeeded in escaping to Corrientes. The violent measures of Antiquera were immediately repudiated by the Viceroy, who declared Balmaceda to be reinstated in authority, and ordered the usurper to give up all pretensions to power. But Antiquera, by the time these orders were received, had organized a considerable military force, and treated them with contempt. He refused to obey the Viceroy, and having gone through the forms of a popular election that he might have some seeming title to the governorship, he then, instead of resigning in favor of Balmaceda, sent a party to Corrientes, who made him their prisoner and carried him to Asuncion. Here, then, was open rebellion against the crown, and the Viceroy sent instructions from Peru to the military commander of the Plata, Don Baltasar Garcia de Ros, who had formerly been Governor of Paraguay, to dispossess Antiquera of his authority, and re-establish Reyes Balmaceda. Garcia Ros hastened at once to Paraguay with such forces as he could readily collect; but, on reaching the river Tebicuari, he found that Antiquera was defiant, and with such forces at command that he must return for reinforcements. This bold attitude of defiance on the part of Antiquera greatly astonished the Governor of Buenos Aires, Bruno Mauricio de Zavala, who had been so confident that Antiquera would not resist the royal authority that he had sent to Garcia Ros requesting him to supply him with troops to assist in the defence of Montevideo against the Portuguese. This letter, intended for Ros, fell into the hands of Antiquera, who, thinking to conciliate Zavala and reconcile him to his remaining in power, sent him six hundred troops armed and equipped. But the news of Antiquera's continued contumacy having reached the ears of the Viceroy of Peru before the arrival of Antiquera's forces, the Governor had received orders to lose no time in putting down the rebellion in Paraguay and re-establishing the legal authority. But Zavala was too busy with the defence of Montevideo to go in person to Paraguay. He sent Ros a second time on the same mission, placing under his command two hundred Spanish troops and all the Indians of the missions. The Jesuits in the quarrel had taken part originally with Balmaceda, and, in imitation of Cardenas, Antiquera had expelled all the members of the order from Asuncion. They therefore lent the services of the Indians with alacrity to put down the usurper. But, arriving again at the Tebicuari, Ros was met by Antiquera with a force of three thousand men, and disastrously defeated and compelled to return to Buenos Aires.

The rebellion had now assumed such proportions that its suppression could not be left to inferior hands. It must either be put down at once, or a part of the Spanish dominions would be wrested from the power of the crown. A new Viceroy having been appointed about this time, he was incensed at his predecessor for not having taken more energetic measures to stop the rebellion. He at once wrote to Governor Zavala, in the most peremptory terms, commanding him to hasten immediately to Paraguay with sufficient force to drive out Antiquera or take him prisoner, and send him to Lima for trial. Zavala set out on this undertaking in December, 1724. Antiquera, now realizing that he had the whole force of the Spanish government in South America against him, endeavored, through the new bishop of Paraguay, Fray José Palos, to persuade Zavala that he would submit, and that therefore he should not push matters to extremities, but return to Buenos Aires. Zavala was not to be deceived, and Antiquera soon learned that orders for his arrest were out should he show himself either in Corrientes or in Santa Fé. Antiquera, now aware of his desperate situation, began to prepare, with renewed activity, to defend himself. But when Zavala had reached the mission of San Ignacio, he was met by the bishop, Palos, who came to assure him, that, if he would proceed without troops to Asuncion, Antiquera would quietly surrender to him. Zavala, however, put no confidence in his promises, and when this was known the followers of Antiquera began rapidly to desert him, and on the 5th of March, 1725, he fled from the country, and took refuge in a convent in Cordova. Thence he went to Bolivia, intending to throw himself on the Audience of Charcas for protection. But he soon learned that he was looked upon as a common enemy. A price had been set on his head, or rather a reward offered for his capture. He was arrested at Chuquisaca in Bolivia, and taken before the Audience, under whose authority he had first aspired to the governorship. The Audience sent him to Lima to be tried, where he was detained as a prisoner till the Viceroy could write to Spain for permission to send his troublesome guest thither to be tried; but the orders came back that he must be tried where he was, and, if found guilty, executed. He was therefore brought before the Audience of Peru, and, after a trial that lasted several years, was found guilty of high treason, and condemned to death. Though so gross an offender, yet his trial had lasted so long that, as in the case of Warren Hastings, the public feeling towards him had been entirely changed from what it was at the time of his arrest. He was a brave, bold, able, and bad man, yet he had the popular sympathies. His offences had not been greater than others', and not so great as those of Cardenas, who was neglected, and left to die in peace, his offences having been pardoned by the Pope before his death; and though he had not the stores of papal thunder to launch on the heads of his enemies, the people could not see why he should be made an example, and treated with exceptional harshness.

The Audience, in passing sentence, prescribed the manner of execution, so as to give as much dramatic effect as possible. The love of sight-seeing, so inherent in the Spanish character that every occasion is taken to gratify it, whether it be a religious procession or ceremonial, a bull-fight, or an *auto-*

de-fe, was not to be disregarded when so eminent a criminal as Antiquera was to suffer. The sentence was, that he should be taken from the prison, clothed in cloak and hood, and mounted upon a horse caparisoned with black ; that he should thence be conducted through the streets, preceded by a herald, who was to proclaim aloud the crimes of the illustrious victim, till they came to the great square, where he was to be executed on a scaffold, in full view of the multitude. The 5th of July, 1731, was the day fixed for the execution. The popular feeling was very strong against the execution of this sentence, and when Antiquera was brought out to be conducted to the scaffold, he found himself surrounded by a frenzied multitude, clamoring for mercy, and denouncing the injustice of his sentence. The crowd gathered round so thick and furious that a body of soldiers was called out to drive them back ; but the citizens paid no regard to this threat, and it was apprehended that a rescue would be attempted, when the Viceroy and his guard appeared upon the scene. His appearance enraged the multitude still more. He found himself surrounded by an angry mob, and himself the object of their imprecations. The Viceroy gave orders to fire on the prisoner. The order was answered by a volley of musketry, and Antiquera and two friars near him fell dead from their horses. This action abashed the mob, and Antiquera's body was placed upon the scaffold and his head severed from his body.

After the flight of Antiquera from Paraguay, Don Martin de Barua was named Governor, and after a little time the Jesuits were allowed to return to Asuncion. They came in great pomp from the missions as returning lords of the manor, and twelve miles from the capital were met by a grand procession, headed by the Governor, bishop, and all the important functionaries, civil and military.

The return of the Jesuits was displeasing to a great many of the people, and especially to the partisans of Antiquera, of whom many were left, and with whom the Governor, Barua, was so much in sympathy, that when a new Governor, Don Ignacio Soroeta, arrived, duly commissioned by the Viceroy, neither government nor people would acknowledge his authority; and so, being without official recognition, and unable to obtain it, he immediately left to return to Peru. In the mean while the country was in a state of political ferment. The people wanted no more governors sent to them from abroad, and they were tired of Jesuit intrigue and interference. The royal rescript of Charles V., by which, in certain emergencies, the people were to choose their own governors, had borne its legitimate fruit. The people had learned to exercise political power, and their best rulers had been those first designated by themselves. The Governor, Barua, secretly favored the plans of the adherents of Antiquera and other malecontents; but not wishing to incur the danger of open opposition to the Viceroy, he resigned, and the state was left without a head. The unsatisfactory condition of affairs in Paraguay, and the belief that the real instigator of the disturbances was the prisoner Antiquera, had caused the Audience of Lima to hasten his trial. But the effect of his execution was the reverse of what was expected. When the news of it reached Asuncion, the indignation of the people was extreme, and they manifested their rage by falling on the Jesuits and expelling them again from the city. There was now a declared party against longer submission to royal authority. The party took the name of *comuneros*, while those who still held out for the King were called *contrabandistas*. The former held the reins of power after Barua's resignation, and they improvised a government composed of a Junta, with a President as the executive head of authority. The first President, Don José Luis de Bareiro, was soon found to be too indulgent towards the contrabandistas, and the feeling against him was so strong that he was glad to escape from the country. His place was promptly filled by a more decided comunero, Don Miguel de Garay.

A hostile collision was now feared between the dominant party in Asuncion and the nearest reductions. The Jesuits had already learned how necessary to despotism is a large standing army, and at this time they had a strong force of their neophytes, or more properly slaves, in the field. As many as seven thousand were stationed as an advanced guard on the Tebicuari. But before a collision occurred a new Governor arrived upon the scene. This was Don Manuel de Ruiloba. Not knowing the reception he might meet with at Asuncion, he first presented himself at the missions, where he found a large military force already organized to his hand. From there he sent forward overtures to the insurgents, such as seemed to satisfy them. At any rate they sent back words of welcome, and promised to recognize and obey his authority. Ruiloba went forward to the capital, and was agreeably surprised at his reception. He entered with all formality on the duties of his office; but, none the wiser for his knowledge of the recent disturbances, and of the tempestuous elements with which he had to deal, he proceeded as though absolute lord and governor of the whole country. One of his first acts was an attempt to disband the comuneros, so that there should be no party or organization to question or dispute his authority. But this was so vehemently resisted that the Governor soon found himself in open opposition to the most numerous party in the state. The rebels openly defied him, and a civil war actually commenced. But in the first action between the Governor and the royalists and the insurgents, which took place near Pirayu, on the 15th of December, 1733, some thirty miles from Asuncion, the unfortunate Governor was killed.

At this crisis of affairs it happened that the bishop of Buenos Aires, Juan de Arregui, who had come to Asuncion to be consecrated, was still there. The rebels resolved to elect him Governor, and the bishop accepted the doubtful and dangerous honor. But he found himself a mere tool in the hands of the Junta, who compelled him to assent to and sign the most sweeping acts of confiscation against the Jesuits, and against such individuals as held out for the King. The Governor soon realized that the commotion which he had at first encouraged was not only beyond his control, but even threatened his own destruction. He therefore embarked for

Buenos Aires to attend to his episcopal functions, content to leave civil affairs to other hands. Before departing, however, he nominated as his successor, Don Cristoval Dominguez de Obelar.

Thus Paraguay was again in a position of defiant rebellion; and this time the people had the same stern, resolute character to deal with as before. Zavala, who was still Governor of Buenos Aires, and who had so successfully extinguished the rebellion of Antiquera, had just been appointed President of the Audience of Charcas when these violent proceedings in Paraguay occurred. With his habitual caution and celerity combined, he blockaded Paraguay at all points. With a small force of veteran troops he then ascended the river to the missions, where he found a force of six thousand Indian troops, that, under Jesuit instruction, had arrived at the perfection of discipline. With these he advanced towards Asuncion till he reached the Tebicuari, that had been the scene of so many combats between the Paraguayans and their invading enemies.

The comuneros had no adequate force to oppose to the well-disciplined troops of Zavala. The skirmishes which occurred all proved disastrous, and showed that it was hopeless for them, unorganized and undisciplined as they were, to resist. They quickly abandoned all idea of opposition. Zavala advanced to Asuncion amid general acclamations. The Jesuits now returned more powerful, more arrogant, and more generally detested than ever. Their presence was hateful to everybody. It was clear that a divided allegiance was impossible wherever they had any power. They aspired to be absolute, and the Spaniards and half-breeds saw that they must become mere passive, blind machines in their hands, like the Indians of the missions, or else the Jesuits must be expelled. Heretofore the latter had had the ear of the King and had been sustained by him in everything. To contend against them, backed up by the Spanish government, was hopeless. The crown must be advised of the real state of affairs, of the tyranny exercised over the enslaved Indians whom they paraded as civilized Christians, of their fraud and duplicity, their design of founding a Jesuit empire, and their military organization. The Spaniards saw the only way to attack the Jesuits successfully was to expose them. Then the truth in regard to their iniquities began to dawn on the civilized world. Then ensued a war of charges and counter-charges, of accusations and denials, of crimes proved and offset by the greater crimes of the accusers. But the result was damaging to the Jesuits. Hitherto they had monopolized the field of letters so far as their own actions were concerned, but the revelations of the Spaniards now showed conclusively that the Jesuit Arcadia was a more absolute despotism than Europe had ever known; that, so far from Christianizing the savages, even their humanity was not recognized, but in all things they were assimilated to and treated like the brute beasts; that the religious forms and ceremonies through which they were made to pass were to them mere forms and drudgery of which they understood nothing.

But the reign of Jesuitism in Europe was drawing near its end. For two hundred years it had tyrannized over kings and courts. Its machinery for governing was so perfect, its contempt for anything like honesty or honor in all things affecting the interests of the order was so palpable, that it was clear to the most stupid king, as well as to the wisest statesman, that unless the Order of Jesus were crushed it must dominate all Christendom. It must perish, or civilization must take the form it had in China and the missions of Paraguay. The dogmas of Loyola admitted of no middle course; no expansion of mind, no elevation, or mental enfranchisement; nothing but a sullen obedience to papal assumption. So powerful had the order become, that kings were afraid to move without its approbation. Its system of espionage was so thorough that there was no longer any such thing as confidence between courts and sovereigns. The most secret and confidential instructions from the monarch to his ambassador were sure to be known to the Jesuit fathers ere they reached their destination. Naturally the sovereigns felt humiliated at their helplessness; but what could they do? The first step towards throwing off the yoke would be at once known, and woe to him who should first venture to break with the holy order. But at last there appeared a man having the nerve and the courage, and, at the same time, such influence with his government that he ventured to grapple with the common enemy. This was Sebastian Carvalho, Marques of Pombal. Though a Portuguese, and representing one of the weakest of the European powers, he boldly took the initiative for the overthrow of the order. He himself had been brought up in their school. The fathers had recognized his great talent and force of character, and had encouraged his promotion by a government absolutely under their control, not doubting that he would be a doughty champion of their cause. And so he was in his early career. Like St. Paul, who verily thought he ought to do many things contrary to the name of Jesus of Nazareth, he persecuted with a zeal that bade fair to secure him canonization. As the agent of his government he was sent to England, where he first saw a people who were not under the control of an infallible Church, and yet were nevertheless none the less virtuous, prosperous, and happy. Afterwards he was employed on other important diplomatic missions, and he found that wherever the influence of the order was weakest there was the greatest general prosperity. His own country, ever since it had fallen under the malign influence of the Jesuits, had been growing weaker and poorer. He saw in them the cause of his country's disgrace. He knew that with men so artful, so unscrupulous, as they were, no half-way measures would avail. For two hundred years they had been supreme in their influence over the Portuguese government, and in that time Portugal had all the while been growing weaker and less respected throughout the world. Pombal, while still a friend to the Jesuits, had acquired a position in the administration such as a strong mind is very sure to attain when it is taken into the councils of inferiors. He became all-powerful, being to the rest of the government something like what, in these later times, Cavour was to Italy and Bismark has been to the government of Prussia.

The occasion of the first open rupture with the Jesuits was the refusal of the fathers in the Paraguayan missions to abide by the terms agreed on by the Spanish and Portuguese governments for the settlement of the questions of boundary of their South American possessions. The Portuguese held the important position of Colonia, on the Plata, nearly opposite Buenos Aires, while there were several missions on the Uruguay in unpleasant proximity to the Portuguese possessions. An arrangement was made by which Nova Colonia was to be given over to Spain, while the Uruguay missions should be delivered over to the Portuguese. When commissioners were sent over to complete the arrangement, the fathers refused to abide by it. Pombal represented this action as defiant and rebellious, and from that time he made unrelenting war upon them till he had the satisfaction of seeing the order broken up and virtually destroyed.

Knowing the craft and the power of the Jesuits, Pombal did not wait to enlist other governments, kings, or ministers to act in concert with Portugal. He knew that if he depended on diplomacy and intrigue the Jesuits would easily outwit him. He knew, however, that they were generally feared and hated in every court of Europe, and took the resolution to act independently. He therefore, in 1759, addressed a letter to the Pope, Clement XIII., informing him that his government had determined to make a donation to him of all the Jesuits in Portugal. Without waiting for an answer, and before the Pope had time to launch out either bulls or excommunications, Pombal had them all seized and shipped to the states of the Church. They were all landed at Civita Vecchia as so much inconvenient rubbish. Having succeeded so well at home, Pombal then endeavored to enlist the other Catholic governments to the same thing. France was the first to follow his example.

The Spanish throne was occupied at this time by Charles III., a sovereign of energy compared with others of the period, which, indeed, is saying but little. But weak kings may have strong ministers. The King of France, Louis XV., was not of sufficient force of character to adopt any violent measure of his own accord. But his chief adviser, Madame de Pompadour, had enough for herself and the King too, and it did not suit her purpose to hold a divided empire over the King. The Jesuits, at that time, could not exist without political power. Therefore they must give way.

In Spain, however, the Jesuits had always had much more influence than in France, bigotry and superstition being national characteristics. The newly crowned King had brought with him from Naples his favorite and adviser, Squillaci. The presence of this favorite was displeasing to the Spaniards, notwithstanding which he was made prime minister. This provoked great enmity towards him; but, having the King's ear, he wished to show the proud and high-spirited Spaniards — a people who had recently been, and still thought themselves, the most powerful nation in the world — that his will was law and they must obey, and that the people, according to a favorite doctrine of the time, had nothing to do with the laws but to obey them. His power over the King was so absolute that even the Jesuits found their occupation gone. Squillaci cared as little for their enmity as he did for that of the hidalgos. He endeavored not only to dominate at court and prescribe general laws, but to interfere with the dress of the citizens. The long cloak and slouched hat of the period was the ordinary dress of the Spanish cavalier. Squillaci undertook to suppress them. A great commotion ensued. If the imported favorite might to-day proscribe one dress, he might put the nation in livery to-morrow. A fierce, angry mob filled the streets of the capital, furious for the blood of the obnoxious minister; but he was not to be found. Then a body of troops, called the Walloon Guards, were called out to disperse the mob by force; but the mob quickly dispersed them, many of the Guards being killed. The King appeared in person, and pathetically begged the people to desist from their violence, promising to dismiss the hated minister, and to do anything else that in reason they might ask. But the words of the weak King fell powerless from his lips, and the mob seemed to be growing more and more furious. At this moment some Jesuit fathers appeared in the midst of the multitude and warned them to desist. The people listened to them, and dispersed without further violence. The King could not understand how he, the anointed of the Lord to rule his people, should be no more respected, while these priests had only to say, "Peace, be still," and they were obeyed. This led him to mistrust that the Jesuits had instigated the mob, knowing that they could control it. Squillaci was dismissed, and the King suspected it was the Jesuits who had forced him to this measure; and for a new minister he selected the Count de Aranda, a man of a very different stamp from the weak but arrogant and haughty Neapolitan.

The King, however, was in mortal fear of the Pope. For a long time the Spanish crown had been, for all ecclesiastical purposes, a mere appanage of the Vatican. The Spanish kings, from the illustrious Charles V., and through the dreary reign of Philip II. and his successors, had regarded it as their first and most sacred duty to war on the infidel; and both Charles and Philip believed that their long and exhausting campaigns were not for empire, but that they were holy wars. Nevertheless, the divine right of the King was not to be questioned; and how could he rule by divine right, when the Jesuits had more power than he? Pombal had acted without consulting the Pope, and Portugal was better off for being rid of the order, its government and King more respected at home and abroad. But to expel the entire brotherhood from Spain, which was their stronghold, and where bigotry and superstition existed in the beauty of perfection, was a far more serious undertaking. The measures taken, therefore, to effect their expulsion, were on a scale corresponding with the magnitude of the work to be done. The royal decree was accordingly issued, banishing the Jesuits from all the Spanish dominions, and forbidding them to return or to hold any intercourse whatever with any subject of Spain or any person residing within its territory. The order was followed by instant measures to put it in execution. The colleges were surrounded, the bells taken possession of by the soldiery, so that no tumult should arise; the fathers were told to secure and take with them such things as their breviaries, linen, money, and a few other trifles, and march forth. They were then escorted, like so many prisoners or criminals, to the sea-coast, and shipped away. They had, and could have, no other destination than Italy, for no other country would receive such a consignment; and even the Holy See already had, thanks to Pombal and Pompadour, an excess of the commodity. The Jesuits were a very convenient engine for his Holiness so long as they were about foreign courts, acting as keepers of royal consciences, betraying state secrets, and making the Pope the arbiter of kings; but a community of Jesuits in his own dominions was, like an army of generals with no soldiers, of little use for active service. The Pope determined not to receive them, and on their arrival at Civita Vecchia they were refused a landing by the Superior or General of their own order, Father Ricci. Though it is probable that this company was not worse than the average of the order, and contained many good, venerable, learned, and pious men, yet so detestable had the Jesuits become in the eyes of laymen generally, that this shipload of holy fathers was as unwelcome at any port in Christendom as was ever a cargo of criminals at Botany Bay. The King insisted that they should be allowed to land; to which the answer was delivered from the guns of the fortress, probably not with the intention to injure the vessels, but as a positive intimation that they must leave those waters. The vessels then put to sea. The doomed Jesuits were now the pariahs and outcasts of the earth. They touched at Leghorn and Genoa, but at each place they were denied a landing. For more than six months were they drifting about, and, like the Flying Dutchman, never reaching a hospitable port. The springs of humanity towards them seemed to be dried up. So many intrigues, plots, treacheries, assassinations, and abominations of various kinds had been laid at their door, that the world generally had come to regard them as an order of conspirators, dangerous to the peace of the world. At last, after much crimination and recrimination, they were permitted to land at Corsica, where they were as unwelcome as they had been to their own General, Father Ricci, on first reaching Civita Vecchia.

A month after the unhappy Jesuits had left the coast of Spain, the King wrote a letter to the Pope in justification of their expulsion. In this remarkable letter he says that as it "is the first duty of a sovereign to watch over the peace and preservation of his state, and provide for the good government and tranquillity of his subjects," he has therefore, "in compliance with this principle, been under the imperious necessity of resolving on the immediate expulsion of all the Jesuits who are established in his kingdom and dominions, and to send them to the states of the Church, under the immediate, wise, and holy direction of your most holy beatitude, and most worthy father and master of all the faithful." To this, which an unbeliever might regard as sarcastic, the King adds the more comforting words, that he has made provision for the payment to each expelled Jesuit of "a sum sufficient to support him for life."

The Pope, however, was greatly afflicted at this step of the King of Spain, and on the 16th of February, 1767, he addressed a brief to him, which, though it commenced with the phrase, "To our dearest son in Jesus Christ, health and apostolic benediction," was nevertheless a bitter remonstrance against the measure, a vindication of the Jesuits, and a severe condemnation of the King. In the face of all that had been said against the Jesuits, the Pope declares that "the body, the instruction, the spirit, of the Company of Jesus is absolutely innocent; and not only innocent, but that it is pious, it is useful, it is holy; and all this considered with reference to its laws, to its maxims, or to its objects."

The Pope's brief was laid before the Extraordinary Council of the King, and was by them treated with scant courtesy; and in reply to the King's request for their opinion, they say the brief is wanting in that spirit of courtesy and moderation due to the King of Spain and the Indies. They intimate, too, that their resolution is taken, and the question will not be reopened, whatever complaints the Pope may make; and that to enter into controversy on the merits of the case would be to incur the most grievous inconvenience of compromising the sovereign prerogative of his Majesty, who is to God alone responsible for his actions. They then proceed to accusations against the Jesuits, notwithstanding the Pope has so solemnly affirmed that their body was "pious, useful, holy." They say that one Jesuit father, "Padre Luis de Molina, altered the theological doctrines; that Padre Juan Aldiuno carried his scepticism so far as to doubt the authenticity of the sacred writings; that in China and Malabar they have rendered compatible at once the worship of God and mammon; that they have lent a deaf ear to pontifical decisions. In Japan they have persecuted the very bishops and other religious orders, in a manner so scandalous that it can never be blotted from the memory of man; while in Europe they have been the focus and *point d'appui* of tumults, rebellions, and regicides. These deeds, notorious to the whole world, have been overlooked in the pontifical brief."

These charges against the brotherhood, thus defiantly thrown out by the Extraordinary Council of Spain, indicate very clearly what was the general opinion of Roman Catholic laymen at the time of the expulsion of the order. There was no question as between believers and heretics, but it had become the almost universal opinion of laymen and priests alike, except those of this one order, and of all who were not Roman Catholics, that the Jesuits were an insufferable evil, not entitled to toleration, and scarcely to existence.

Another of the charges against them was, "that it is proven by the undeniable testimony of their own papers, that in Paraguay they took the field with organized armies to oppose themselves to the crown." This accusation, however, as far as it relates to overt acts, would appear to be unjust; and yet it was evidently their intention to be in a condition to sustain themselves against any forces that might be sent against them, whether they were the King's troops or those in rebellion against him. It is not to be denied, however, that in the different controversies they had given their support to the side of the crown.

The Pope, Clement XIII., still supported the cause of the Jesuits, and died without sanctioning the act of expulsion. But his successor, Clement XIV., having been raised to the Papal See after the Jesuits had lost their influence, and the Church generally being hostile to them, the new Pope was more likely to respect this feeling than was his predecessor, who had found the Jesuits his most useful instruments in gaining and wielding political power. Clement XIV., in 1773, six years after the expulsion from Spain, approved and ratified the act, justified the King, and so strongly pronounced against the Jesuits, recognizing as proved against them the countless charges of almost every crime known to men, that from that time there was no hope the order would ever be re-established or revivified. It had become a defunct body, that no Promethean heat could relume.

CHAPTER VIII.

Expulsion of the Jesuits. — They are sent to Europe. — Great Power and Wealth of the Jesuits previous to their Expulsion. — Their Doctrines and Practices. — Condition of the Indians after their Expulsion. — Hardship and Suffering. — Contest of the Civil and Ecclesiastical Authorities for the Spoils left by the Jesuits. — Conflict of Authority. — Unhappy Condition of the Indians. — Tyranny of Lazaro Ribera Espinosa. — Don Bernardo Velasco. — The Province of Misiones constituted, 1803. — Revolution in Buenos Aires. — Declaration of Independence proclaimed May 25, 1810.

THE expulsion of the Jesuits from Paraguay was included in the plan of the King of Spain. In his letter to the Pope, he said that he was under the imperious necessity of expelling them from all his dominions. This, of course, included Paraguay; and as their expulsion from there was a part of the same general plan, a sketch of the manner of the expulsion from the mother country should necessarily be included in a work of this kind.

So well prepared was the government of Spain to make thorough work of the expulsion, that four days after issuing the royal decree banishing the order from Spain a ship of war was despatched to the Plata bearing peremptory orders from Count de Aranda to the Viceroy at Buenos Aires to take immediate measures for the sudden and simultaneous seizure of all the Jesuits within his jurisdiction, and to ship them without delay to Europe.

The Viceroy at that time was Francisco de Paula Bucareli. He received his orders on the 7th of June, 1767, and entered on his task with a zeal and alacrity that showed his judgment approved the measure. As quickly as possible he despatched sealed instructions to all the governors and local magistrates within his viceroyalty, with orders that they were not to be opened till the 21st of July. On that day in every town where there were Jesuits the seals of these instructions were to be broken, and the magistrates were to find themselves positively commanded, in the name of the King, to seize, on the following day, all Jesuits that could be found, and to send them to Buenos Aires.

The magnitude of the task imposed on the Viceroy may be inferred from his own account, which he gave to the Count de Aranda after it was completed. In this report he says: —

"I had to anticipate all its consequences upon five hundred Jesuits, distributed over a distance of more than seven hundred leagues; possessed of twelve colleges; of one house of residence; of more than fifty estancias, and places where they were building, which are so many more colleges, and settlements made up of a vast number of servants and slaves; of thirty towns of Guarani Indians, with more than a hundred thousand inhabitants; and of twelve thousand Abipones, Macobies, Lulis, and various other nations of Chiquitos; not to speak of many more, of whom, on the Jesuitical principle of keeping the Indians from all intercourse with the Spaniards, we know nothing. . . . . The largest college, that of Cordova, is generally reputed as the head of the powerful empire of the Jesuits. Empire it may truly be called; because, counting Indians, slaves, and other servants, they have in this vast country more vassals than the King."

The news of the expulsion from Spain, however, became public in Buenos Aires on the 3d of July nineteen days before the time fixed upon by Bucareli for the simultaneous arrest of the order. Were he to wait for that day before putting his instructions in execution, the Jesuits, who had a large, well-armed, and well-disciplined army in Paraguay, might be prepared to make an effective resistance. He determined to anticipate the hour and seize the Jesuits, as fast as possible, wherever found, and have them sent directly to Buenos Aires. Commencing in this way, those nearest Buenos Aires were first gathered into the Viceroy's fold. But it was not till August that Cordova was taken possession of by the Spanish soldiery. The Jesuits made no opposition, though the troops came in by daylight, and no attempt was made to surprise them. It had been charged by the Spanish Council that the Jesuits had tampered with the doctrines of the Church. With the troops which entered Cordova, this was a sufficient reason, not only for seizing on whatever property they found belonging to the order, but for destroying their immense and invaluable library, consisting not only of very many rare printed works, but of many manuscripts of great importance, that were thus irretrievably lost.

The captured Jesuits were remitted to Spain from time to time, in groups of forties and fifties, and the King immediately sent them as additional donations to his Holy Father. The fathers of the Paraguayan missions, however, were not disposed to yield without showing a taste of their quality. Their first device was to prepare an address to be signed by those Indians to whom the Jesuits had assigned the duty of enforcing their orders on the community. These were dignified as a municipal government, but they had no other authority than to enforce the commands of the fathers. Twelve of these local functionaries signed this paper, one of whom signed not only for himself, but in behalf of forty-one caciques. This remarkable document is in its language a most humble request from the Indians of the mission of San Luis to their local governor that the Jesuits may continue to live with them. It says: "All this people, men, women, and young persons, and especially the poor, pray for the same with tears in their eyes." As in this memorial the Jesuits are exalted, the friars and priests of other orders who are to replace them are reprobated as having no care or love for the Indians. This paper was not promulgated till after the Jesuits had been taken away from some of the neighboring missions. That it was a trick of the Jesuits with which the Indians who signed it had nothing to do but obey the order to affix their signatures, if so it were they could write their names, was evident on the face of it. Bucareli took it as an indication that the Jesuits would not surrender without an effort to retain their power and vast wealth. He accordingly took such energetic measures as the means at his command would permit to compel them to submit. He sent a body to that pass of the Tebicuari which had been the scene of most of the important battles of the country, besides a similar force at San Miguel, which is some twelve leagues from this pass of the Tebicuari. With another force he ascended the Uruguay, and, to counteract any effect that the letters purporting to come from the Indians might have, Bucareli had another letter prepared, to be signed by the Indian judges and caciques of some thirty towns situated between the Uruguay and Parana, in which they express great thankfulness to the King for having relieved them from the arduous life to which they were before subjected. Their gratitude to Bucareli is expressed in these words: "To him in person, and in the name of your Majesty, it is that we trust for the arrangement of all our differences, and for the rescuing us from that miserable state of bondage in which, like the vilest of slaves, we have been so long held." While these letters prove nothing as to the real wishes and opinions of the Indians, they do prove their utter mental degradation, and that they were ready to do without question whatever they were commanded to do. In the argument, therefore, they make against the Jesuits. But it was now evident that resistance was hopeless. Many of the missions had already fallen into the hands of the Spaniards, and, though they could bring a strong military force of neophytes into the field, they did not venture on this last resort. They were probably actuated by motives similar to those which influenced the Southern slaveholders during the Great Rebellion. These had maintained before the world that their slaves were well fed, not overworked, contented, and happy, and that in case of war they would eagerly take up arms in defence of the lives and property of their beloved masters. So they doubtless would as against a foreign enemy whose purpose it was to retain them in slavery. But when the war came, and with it the prospect of freedom to the slaves, it was not thought advisable to put arms into their hands.

The Jesuits, like the slaveholders, might boast of the happiness of their slaves, their piety, and their love toward themselves. But they had not succeeded, after a hundred and fifty years' seclusion and total darkness, in imbruting them so far that they could be trusted when the question of their own liberation was presented. The author of "La Plata, the Argentine Confederation, and Paraguay," * from whose work most of the popular knowledge of these countries possessed by the American people is derived, is enthusiastic in praise of the Jesuits, "their missionary labors and imperishable glory." His work is of great value, and generally accurate in all matters of which he professes to speak from personal knowledge and observation. But he regards the Jesuits with the eyes of a slaveholder. In the opinion of the authors of the Rebellion, the highest civilization, the best government, is that where the great mass of the people are slaves, and the few live in luxury and idleness on the bread they have never earned. In the history of the Jesuits this system appears in all its perfection. The fathers were so absolute that the Indians had fallen into a condition of imbecility but little removed from beasts of burden; and naturally, when the drivers and overseers were taken away, the helpless neophytes perished rapidly, and the missions that had kept in luxury so many Jesuit fathers, and built such elegant churches, and heaped up such massive stores of gold and silver, had accumulated such fine pictures, statues, and frescos, all paid for by the blood and sweat of Indians who had become passive brutes in the service, soon fell into neglect, and are now but insignificant villages, or, perhaps, mere desert places.

It seems strange, and at first view lamentable, that an order commencing as did the Order of Jesus, with such holy and pious objects, whose founders were men of such devotion and earnestness, who gave up all for the cause of their Divine Master, and were ready to endure anything and sacrifice everything if thereby they might bring the lost to redemption, should thus come to an ignominious end and their memory

* Thomas J. Page.

be ever after almost universally execrated of mankind. But there was a fatal error in their doctrine and practice, and the word "Jesuit" or "Jesuitical" expresses the nature of this error. The early fathers imagined that their purposes were so holy that they might use fraud to attain them, that the end justified the means; and they disregarded the words of the Master they professed to serve, who had forbidden them to do evil that good might come. When men act on this principle, they in effect cut adrift from all moral responsibility. No longer acknowledging accountability to man, they set up their own standard of morals, and then human passions and selfish interests have full sway. The doctrine of non-accountability to man, whether held by kings or by religious orders, is found by experience to lead to both corporal and mental tyranny, and is now pretty well exploded. Charles I. believed in it, and the people cut his head off; and to that tragic act England owes much of its freedom and greatness. The Jesuits believed in it, and they have a name that is a reproach.

All history shows that, the worse a system of government is, the more suffering will a violent and radical change produce among the people. A despotism that forbids all freedom of action, and renders freedom of thought dangerous, will, if long continued, render the subjects of it powerless to help themselves if it be suddenly removed. The natives over whom the Jesuits had ruled till they were as stolid as brutes and as helpless as children must therefore, in the nature of things, suffer incredible hardships if the directing hand of the taskmaster were suddenly withdrawn. But so extensive were the power and influence of the order that their expulsion could only be effected by the most prompt and energetic action. Their policy was so insidious, and they had so many ramifications among all circles of the different courts and governments, that only by a sudden blow could their overthrow be effected. The order for their expulsion coming upon them so unexpectedly, they were doubtless for a time subjected to great hardships, which might have been avoided if the measure would have admitted of deliberation. In Europe, however, the hardships and sufferings were limited to the Jesuits themselves. In the missions of Paraguay it was very different. There they had held such absolute sway over the Indians during their rule of a century and a half, that they had reduced them to be "no longer men, beings without name." * The authority of the fathers being suddenly withdrawn from them, they were as helpless and unprotected as so many sheep. No plan of government, however, suitable for their condition, was substituted by the Spaniards. They were left exposed to such civil and ecclesiastical authorities as remained in Paraguay after their former masters were taken away. Unfortunately, the civil and ecclesiastical authorities were independent of each other, and of course were antagonists and rivals for the power over the Indians and the spoils left by the Jesuits. The condition of the poor natives was now, if possible, worse than it had ever been under their former masters. They had never known the least feeling of independence or personal responsibility, and two sets of taskmasters, rivals in authority, now came in to claim their obedience and services instead of one. The priests appointed two curates for each town to attend to their spiritual wants, while a civil administrator was nominated to manage their temporal affairs. The Indians, who had always before received all their orders from the fathers, could not comprehend how they could be made subject to mere laymen. They therefore frequently appealed to the curates against the administrator, and the former, in order to strengthen their own authority and increase their gains, were constantly fermenting discontent and disregard of the civil ruler. Hence there were perpetual intrigues and rivalries existing between the civil and spiritual functionaries, the result of which was that the poor Indians were ground to powder between the upper and the nether millstones. The evils which they experienced from this conflict of authority are thus described by Don Gonzalo de Doblas, who fourteen years after the expulsion of the Jesuits was appointed Governor of the Province of Corrientes: —

* Bastiat.

"At length the Indians were made to understand that it was only on matters connected with their salvation they were to listen attentively to the curates, but on everything else to their lay administrator only. This put no end, however, to the dissensions between administrator and curates; because, as they both lived in the same house, and, as regards their functions, were, to a certain extent, dependent on each other, they never were agreed as to what was the true balance of power.

"The curates wanted the Indians to attend mass and the counting of their beads every day, and at whatever hour the priests might choose. This was often purposely made a very inconvenient hour. Thereupon the laymen interposed to prevent compliance, sometimes with reason, and sometimes without it. The result was that the curate ordered the Indians that obeyed the administrator to be flogged, and the administrator awarded stripes to those who obeyed the curate. Both chastisements fell upon the miserable Indians, without further delinquency on their part than that of not knowing exactly which party to obey, or of obeying the party they liked best.

"Not even the mayor and aldermen escape this cruel species of torture. They are often bastinadoed by order of both curates and lay administrator, without knowing to which of them it is their duty to adhere.

"From petty jealousies and personal feuds, inflammatory discords are every day kindled into a flame. As the town is obliged to support the curates, and as all provisions are under the control of the administrator, this person, when at war, as he almost invariably is with the curates, takes advantage of this control to avenge himself. He makes them wait; he gives them the worst of everything; doles out to them the most scanty supply; and aggravates the hardship by the infliction of innumerable petty grievances. The curates, it is true, have not always justice on their side; for they often exact rations so superabundant that they not only maintain with them a number of servants, but six or eight adherents.

"As in the towns there are no master tradesmen to work for those who will buy what they make, and as not even a peon can be hired without previous appeal to the administrator, because all are subject to the law of community of goods, as the Indians do not understand what it is to sell the produce of their labor, and there is thus no way of being supplied with many actual necessaries, the practice observed is this: if any functionary wants a pair of shoes, he calls in the shoemaker, gives him the leather, and says to him, 'Make me a pair of shoes.' He makes and brings them. If they give him anything, he takes it, and if not, he goes his way without making any demand. It is the same in everything else. If the curate employs the shoemaker, being on bad terms with the administrator, the moment the latter knows what the shoemaker is about, off he despatches him to work for 'the community,' in order to retard or altogether frustrate the work for the curate. The curate gets to know this, he bristles with ire, and the result of the whole matter is, that the Indian shoemaker has to pay the penalty of stripes from the curate, because forced by the administrator to abandon his last.

"If the Indians view with indifference any property of their own, that which belongs to 'the community' they behold with abhorrence. The time, consequently, during which they are employed in the production of such property, they would as willingly spend in the galleys. The habits to which they have been trained, their great submission and humility, and the constant fear of the whip, are alone sufficient to bend them to their hard task. But even thus it is with the greatest difficulty they can be collected and driven to their work. For every operation it is necessary to name an overseer. There are overseers of the weavers, of the carpenters, of the smiths, of the cooks, of the sextons, of the butchers, and of every branch, in short, of occupation. The same system is necessary in the working of the fields. Now, as all are Indians, it is necessary to place over those first overseers others to watch over them. This second class of overseers is generally taken from among the judges and aldermen; and there is as little confidence placed in them as in those they are appointed to superintend; so that, over all, it is necessary to appoint an overseer-in-chief, the mayor. But even the mayor, as well as all the others, in order that any work may be done, must be watched by the administrator; and when the most is got that under this complicated system of vigilance can be obtained, it is not one fourth of what the men could naturally do."

Previous to their expulsion, as has been said before, the Jesuits had never been content to confine themselves to the missions, but were always interfering with the civil government at Asuncion; and to increase their influence and make it permanent they took it upon themselves to give instruction to such youths of the country as they presumed might in after life exert a political influence. The education thus inculcated was, of course, such as would tend to make them passive subjects in the hands of their teachers, and to instil into their minds the conviction that all matters of government, both civil and ecclesiastic, should be left to the fathers, and that it was presumptuous and sacrilegious for laymen to lay claim to any power in such matters. The influence and the purpose of the Jesuits was, as far as possible, to assimilate the laws and the people of Paraguay to the neophytes of the missions. How well they succeeded will appear as we proceed.

The country, from the time of the rebellion of the comuneros in 1735, for a period of seventy years, may be said to have enjoyed almost uninterrupted peace and quiet. The Indians on the borders were occasionally troublesome, and it was necessary to send troops to chastise them; but none of these forays were of sufficient importance to check the general prosperity. The colony had in these years a variety of governors, but none of any transcendent merit, and some of whom were as bad as their weak abilities would permit. In 1796 one of the worst of them all, Lazaro Ribera Espinosa, was appointed, and he held the office, notwithstanding his arrogance and tyranny, for ten years. His government was in all respects oppressive and odious. The colony was treated by him as a mere dependency of Spain, where the creoles had scarcely any rights as against the avarice and greed of the Spanish officials. All the traffic was monopolized by the Governor and his favorites, so that the native producers realized for their tobacco, their hides and tallow, yerba, and other articles of exportation, but a tithe of what they were worth at the time in Buenos Aires. The principal agent or instrument of Ribera, in his work of spoliation and oppression, was a native Paraguayan by the name of José Espinola. On him was devolved the task of carrying into effect the policy of the Governor; and with such zeal did he apply himself to the work, as to make himself the most obnoxious and thoroughly hated man in Paraguay. The complaints against Ribera's government at length became so grave as to provoke the intervention of the crown, and a man of an entirely opposite character was appointed to succeed him. This was Don Bernardo Velasco, a man whose virtues and unhappy fate will form one of the many sad episodes in the course of this history.

In 1803 the King of Spain issued a decree constituting that broad strip of country between the Parana and the Uruguay which included the site of all the missions between those rivers a separate province, independent both of Paraguay and Buenos Aires. This province was called Misiones, and Bernardo Velasco was appointed Governor by the Viceroy at Buenos Aires. In 1805 he was appointed Governor of Paraguay by the King, in addition to the Deputy-Governorship of Misiones, held under the Viceroy. The licentiate, Benito Velasco, was appointed by the King his counsellor or legal adviser. To him the Governor intrusted the immediate command of Misiones, and as adviser or counsellor, called *teniente letrado,* he appointed Dr. Pedro Somerella.

The revolution in Buenos Aires, by which the independence of that province was achieved, had been, owing to favoring circumstances, accomplished by stratagem and almost without bloodshed. The rule of Spain was odious to all the *Porteños,* as the people of Buenos Aires were called, — for it was always the policy of the mother country to treat her colonies as having no rights that native-born Spaniards were bound to respect. All the higher offices of trust or profit were monopolized by the Spaniards, and all trade or commerce with any nation but Spain was strictly prohibited. Everything, in fact, was managed solely for the advantage of Spain; and the officials, sent over to rule and plunder the colonists, regarded all creoles with contempt, as though they were beings of an inferior order. The successful example of the United States in their revolt against England had not taught the Spaniards either wisdom or moderation, but it had taught the creoles to look to themselves for relief from an odious tyranny. A crisis in the affairs of Spain gave them an opportunity to strike for independence at a time when the mother country was powerless to maintain her authority. The successful arms of Napoleon at this time had so nearly achieved the conquest of Spain, that the weak and unfortunate King, Charles IV., was induced to abdicate in favor of his son, Ferdinand VII.; and, the latter being cajoled into making over his rights to the Emperor of the French, Joseph Bonaparte was made King. The disaffected creoles seized the occasion to manifest their loyalty to their hereditary sovereigns, whom they detested, by refusing to transfer their allegiance. The Viceroy, Cisneros, who held his authority from a king who had abdicated, was a man exactly suited to their purposes, being weak, unpopular, and vacillating. They could dispose of him on the pretence that they were repudiating the Bonaparte king.

The plot for the overthrow of the viceregal government seems to have been confined to a very few persons. On the evening of the 23d of May, 1810, a native by the name of Cornelio Saavedra, colonel of one of the best city regiments, having arranged with certain other subordinate officers to support him, and having his men so disposed as to be ready for any contingency that might arise, quietly waited on the Viceroy, and in terms polite but unmistakable told him that the people had resolved on a new order of things. A similar intimation was made at the same moment to the Audiencia, or Supreme Tribunal, and also to the Cabildo, or Municipal Council; and the latter were compelled to call a *cabildo abierto*, or a sort of mass convention of the people. This assembly decided to depose the Viceroy and establish a governing Junta, to be composed mainly of native-born citizens. Of this Junta, Cisneros was made a member, being thus compelled to appear as one of the body that had degraded him, and to give his viceregal orders for the furtherance of their designs. The spiritless Viceroy, no longer pompous and arrogant, yielded submissively; and thus it went forth to the country that the movement was with his approbation, and that the proceedings taken were not revolutionary, but to defend and maintain the rights of the lawful King, Ferdinand VII. The popular sentiment, however, was averse to having anything more to do with the Viceroy, or with Spain so long as it was a French dependency, and on the 25th of May the final declaration of complete and entire independence of the Bonaparte dynasty was proclaimed. The poor Viceroy having now done all in his power to disgrace himself and injure Spain was immediately put on board a vessel and shipped homewards as a thing no longer wanted in the Argentine country.

The proceedings of the Junta, with the Viceroy acting in concert with it, being made known throughout the provincial towns and among the troops, the measures were generally acquiesced in and approved, so that all foreign authority was strangled for the time without firing a gun. Once fairly rid of the Viceroy, however, the people threw off all pretence of loyalty to King Ferdinand, though, for political reasons, the provisional government assumed to be acting in his name and cause.

CHAPTER IX.

The Revolution in Buenos Aires. — Popularity of Governor Velasco — Efforts of the Junta of Buenos Aires to create a Revolution in Paraguay. — Don Manuel Belgrano's Campaign against Paraguay. — He arrives at the Banks of the Parana, December 4, 1810. — Proclamation to the People of Misiones. — Letter to the Governor of Paraguay. — Barbarous Proclamations. — Crosses the Tebicuari. — Wise Course of Velasco. — Critical Situation of Belgrano. — Battle of Paraguari. — Defeat of Belgrano. He falls back to the Tacuari, to await Reinforcements. — Is there attacked by the Paraguayans under Yegros. — Belgrano saves his Army by Diplomacy. — His Proclamation to the Paraguayan People. — Sows the Seeds of Revolution. — Character of Belgrano.

WHEN the news of the revolution in Buenos Aires reached Paraguay, it created little excitement compared with the manner in which it was received in other places. Paraguay was a thriving colony when the savage Querandis were masters of the country near the mouth of the river. Its government had always been independent of Buenos Aires, and its governors, when not elected temporarily by the people, had always been appointed by the King, or provisionally by the Viceroy of Peru. The people, therefore, did not see how a revolt or tumult there was anything to them. Buenos Aires might rebel, but Paraguay, especially at that time, had no motive to do so. Their Spanish Governor was an exceedingly popular and just man, and the contrast between his rule and that of his predecessor, Ribera, was so great, that people apprehended only evil could result from a change. In due form they were invited to join their fortunes with those who ostensibly had only rebelled against the alien government imposed by Napoleon. But Velasco, who held his commission from the legitimate King of Spain, and who in the perplexed state of affairs at home could hardly tell what superior he was bound to obey, did the wisest thing possible and gave no answer to the self-constituted supporters of an abandoned dynasty. He was invited to repudiate the authority of King Joseph, and, instead, recognize that of King Ferdinand VII. But neither Joseph nor Ferdinand were anything to him, till one or the other could show that he was *de facto* king, and into this imbroglio it was but natural that Paraguay should have no wish to enter. This sensible course was attributed by the revolutionists of Buenos Aires to the influence of the Governor, and they supposed that the popular will had not been allowed an expression, and that, if the fear of the government were removed, the people with one voice would resent being transferred like cattle to a sovereign of whom they only knew that he was a usurper and a stranger in race and language.

With this erroneous idea the Junta of Buenos Aires believed that it would be a well-timed measure to send a military force to Paraguay to liberate their brother patriots, and assist them against the Bonaparte king. A force of nearly a thousand men was accordingly raised, and the command given to Don Manuel Belgrano, a man of unquestioned ability, but at that time without military experience.

Ignorance of the popular sentiment and of the general condition of affairs in Paraguay was, and always has been, not only in Buenos Aires, but everywhere else beyond its limits, most obtuse and profound. Before sending forward this military force, the Junta thought it would be at least courteous first to send an agent to sound the temper of the people, and effect, if possible, an amicable arrangement. For this delicate mission they selected of all men living the one most odious to the Paraguayan people. This was that same José Espinola who had been the principal lieutenant and facile agent of Governor Velasco's predecessor, Rivera, and whose presence could only awaken in the minds of the Paraguayans the memory of that avaricious and cruel despotism from which they had escaped to enjoy the mild and just rule of Velasco. Whatever the merits of the proposition from the Junta of Buenos Aires, the fact that Espinola was their agent was enough to set the people against it. Velasco himself, according to the distinguished and learned author of the *Historia de Belgrano*,* was not hostile to the proposed change in the political relations of the Argentine countries, as he considered that the power of Spain had succumbed, and therefore that the setting up of Ferdinand was but to make him a stalking-horse until they were ready to assert their absolute independence. But the native officers of the Paraguayan army, both from hatred to Espinola and from local or state pride, indignantly refused to entertain the proposition of the Buenos Airean Junta, and they had sufficient influence with the cabildo to outweigh the authority of the Governor and break off all relations with Buenos Aires. They insisted, however, that Velasco, though not fully sharing their opinions or prejudices, should still remain in authority; for all had confidence in his integrity, and he was known to be a brave, able, and experienced soldier, having distinguished himself greatly in the wars between Spain and France, and also in the defence of Buenos Aires against the English.

It was on the 4th of December, 1810, that Belgrano with his army, which had received some small reinforcements on the route, reached the banks of the Parana, opposite the island of Apipé. From this point Belgrano issued a proclamation to the people of Misiones, little consistent with the illustrious character ascribed to him by his distinguished biographer. In this proclamation, which was both bombastic and absurd, he says: "The most excellent government Junta, in the name of his Majesty Ferdinand VII., commands me to restore to you your rights of liberty, property, and security of which you have been deprived for so many generations, serving as slaves to those who have only tried to enrich themselves at the cost of the sweat of your brows, and even of your own blood." Thus avowing that he came in the name of King Ferdinand, the legitimate heir of those sovereigns who had exercised the tyranny complained of, the falsity of his professions was transparent.

* "Historia de Belgrano," by Bartolome Mitre, late President of the Argentine Republic, and Commander-in-Chief of the Allied Army.

Belgrano soon after moved his camp to Candelaria, one of the old Jesuit reductions, on the left bank of the Parana and nearly opposite Itapua, now more generally called Encarnacion. Though a Paraguayan force nearly equal to his own was on the opposite bank of the river, Belgrano effected the passage of his whole army with scarcely any loss, and, that achieved, he felt himself master of the situation; but he was soon undeceived. The country on which he was to enter is thus described by President Mitre: "The Territory of Paraguay, towards the southern part, may be described as a great delta or peninsula formed by the fork of the great rivers, the Parana and the Paraguay. These two rivers are the natural frontiers of the country for more than four fifths of its extent. A large and dense forest stretches out towards the interior, and shuts in on all sides that mysterious region that nature has adorned with all the beauties of the tropics and in which Providence has accumulated her gifts. Long cordons of swamps and marshes produced by the uniform level of the ground, and filled with thousands of poisonous snakes, extend along the coasts of the Parana; and the humidity with which they impregnate the atmosphere, united to the heat of the climate, contributes to relax the fibre of those who are not accustomed to breathe those enervating emanations." The truthfulness of this description President Mitre had opportunity to verify years after, as well as to learn that, after passing the morasses to firmer ground, the country was intersected by several streams of depth and breadth so considerable that they could not be forded unless when low, and only at certain passes even then. In entering such a country, Belgrano, if he did not take such a force as was sure to win, exposed himself to be caught in a trap or "shut up in a bottle." Nevertheless, with a temerity amounting to folly, and having at that time less than a thousand men and without any tidings to encourage his belief that disaffection existed among the Paraguayans, Belgrano, having first proposed an armistice, wrote a letter to Governor Velasco, inviting him, together with the bishop and cabildo, to submit to the Junta of Buenos Aires, and to name a deputy to proceed thither and treat with the General Congress. This letter to Velasco, considering the relative positions of the two, doubtless caused a grim smile to the old veteran; and the mystery is how a man of sense and real ability — and such the subsequent career of Belgrano proved him to be — could ever have dictated anything so pompous and absurd. He said: " I bring you persuasion and force, and I cannot doubt that your Honor will admit the first, avoiding the effusion of blood between brothers, sons of the same soil and vassals of the same King. Do not persuade yourself this is from fear; my troops are superior to yours in enthusiasm, because they defend the cause of the country and the King under principles of sound reason, while those of your Honor only defend your person." The bearer of this letter was sent a prisoner in irons to Asuncion; and had he been the author of it, few would deny that he had been rightly served, unless the plea were allowed that he was *non compos mentis*.

To the commander of the troops immediately in front of him he also, at the same time, wrote a letter in a similar strain, saying: "I bring peace, union, friendship in my hands, for those who receive them as they ought to do; in the same manner I bring war and desolation for those who do not accept these blessings."

While the two commanding generals were waiting, according to the armistice, the reply of Governor Velasco, it appears that a Paraguayan party crossed over the river and committed certain hostile acts on the territory occupied by the invaders. This provoked Belgrano to declare the armistice broken, and he then wrote another letter to the Paraguayan commander that was not only stupid, but stupidly barbarous. He said "that he would have all to understand that he was going to cross the Parana; that any European who should be taken with arms in his hands, or away from his home, would be immediately shot, and it would be the same with the natives of Paraguay, or of any other country, that should fire on the troops of his command." President Mitre says, that, in making this threat, Belgrano but obeyed the instructions of the

Junta. But what a cause must that have appeared to the Paraguayans, when one of its first acts was to give instructions of so atrocious a character; and what general of even ordinary humanity would accept a command with orders to summarily shoot all prisoners taken with arms in defence of their country against an army of invasion!

The duplicity of Belgrano, however, was worse than his barbarous proclamations. His apologists affirm, that, while he was pretending to fight for the rights of Ferdinand VII., he used his name only as a decoy, to be discarded as soon as the Paraguayans had been deceived into acquiescence with the Junta; after this the plan was to repudiate all connection or dependence on any foreign power, and have a king or emperor of their own. Belgrano at that time was not, and did not pretend to be, a Republican. He announced himself as coming to fight for the rights of that reigning family under whose rule Paraguay had been groaning for ages, and those who would not join him he denounced as Spanish royalists, and upholders of King Joseph, who, at least, was not of the race of the oppressors of Paraguay. But the Paraguayans, who knew nothing and cared nothing about King Joseph, and who had a just and wise governor, holding his power from King Charles IV., the father of Ferdinand, and never revoked by the latter, could not understand the subtleties of Belgrano's reasoning, or, perhaps, they understood it too well; and the first answer returned to his haughty summons was that they had done nothing against their much-loved sovereign, but were resolved to defend his rights. Both sides then appeared to be fighting for the same cause, — that of Ferdinand VII. The Paraguayans, under a governor duly commissioned by the King, and whose appointment had never been cancelled, were arming to sustain his lawful successor, while the Porteños, who had rebelled against Spain, made a prisoner of the Viceroy, and banished him from the country, were coming to teach them loyalty.

Flushed with the ease with which he had crossed the river, Belgrano believed that the road to Asuncion was to be but a triumphal march; and so confident was he of sweeping all before him, that he would not wait for the reinforcements, consisting of about four hundred men and two pieces of artillery, that were hastening to join him. He even left behind him a company of cavalry as being unneeded. He had supposed that whatever fighting was to be done would be near the river, and having crossed that, and overcome the strategetic advantage which it afforded the Paraguayans, he considered that the most difficult part of his conquests was already achieved.

But though Velasco did not interpose any serious obstacles to the advance of Belgrano, it was in order that, when he did turn upon him, his ruin might be complete. He ordered his forces to fall back as Belgrano advanced, and that all the inhabitants should precede the troops, leaving nothing behind them that could be of any use to the invaders. The *soi-disant* liberator, therefore, as he advanced, found the country deserted, and instead of the thousands that he supposed would rally to his standard, scarcely a single Paraguayan could be seen. And yet the *liberator* pursued his way, thinking they were all flying in terror before him. In his ignorance of the topography of the country, he had thought to march directly on Asuncion, crossing the river Tebicuari-guazu at the point of its confluence with the Tebicuari-mini.

Before crossing this river, Belgrano committed another of his characteristic mistakes, that should be noticed as showing how completely he was infatuated, — to use no harsher term. In a skirmish between outposts, two soldiers of the Paraguayan army were taken prisoners. One of these, a Spaniard by birth, was shot by the order of Belgrano. His eulogist and biographer, President Mitre, excuses this act, so entirely at variance with his own career as a soldier, by saying that he acted in obedience to the orders of the Junta respecting Spaniards found in arms against him. But this excuse cannot be admitted, as Belgrano, in his letter to the Paraguayan commander, already quoted from, says that Paraguayans taken with arms in their hands would be treated in the same way as foreigners;

all were to be summarily shot. But as in this case it appears that he did not shoot the Paraguayan prisoner, it seems he disobeyed his instructions in one case and observed them in the other, so that it stands clear that he acted on his own authority and according to his own cruel caprice. "This barbarous execution," says Mitre, "as it appears in the official letter of Belgrano, is the only stain on his Paraguayan campaign." And well it might be the only one of the kind, for he was soon to learn that if such savage barbarity were to be the rule of the war, it might be doubtful if he or one of his followers would ever return to tell the tale of their overthrow. He certainly took no more prisoners till the question was not whether he should shoot them, but whether they or their brothers in arms would shoot him.

After this achievement his army crossed the Tebicuari, meeting with little resistance, and Belgrano supposed he had gained another great victory, as a force of four hundred Paraguayans had fled before a scouting-party of fifty. Such easy triumphs convinced Belgrano that he had only to march, slay, and conquer. But these seeming victories were but snares to entangle him. Velasco was well informed of all his movements, and knew that the farther he advanced into the interior the weaker he would be; that he could receive nothing from his base of supplies, while his own forces would be constantly augmenting, and the country through which they retreated furnished everything required for subsistence. But notwithstanding this, Belgrano pushed on, so confident of victory that he gave orders, after the manner of Cortez when he burned his ships, to destroy everything along the route, make a desert of the country, and leave nothing that might afterwards be of service to the doomed Paraguayans, or to his own troops should they ever have to repass the same road. It was not till after he had passed the Tebicuari, and was within twenty leagues of the capital, that it first dawned on the mind of the infatuated commander that he was in an enemy's country. As he proceeded, he saw that, while the Paraguayans were falling back, they were concentrating their forces; and he could also see that, rude and undisciplined as were the troops, their officers did not commit the errors of inexperienced generals by fighting in detachments or allowing themselves to be beaten in detail. Belgrano, however, regarded with supercilious contempt the wise tactics of the veteran Velasco, and, though marching with a force of less than one to seven of the enemy, he divided his small army, the main body proceeding in front at too long a distance from the reserve with the baggage to support it in case of an attack, and liable to be cut off from it altogether. "This imprudent decision," says Mitre, "when the enemy might be supposed near, shows in a new general more temerity than knowledge of the rules of war."

It was on the 15th of January when the invading troops first met the Paraguayan advanced guard, which, as was their policy, fled precipitately before them. Encouraged by this repeated falling back, Belgrano hurried on until he came to an open plain, and saw a small elevation, or hill, at some distance in front. Having gained this point, that commanded the view for a long way, he looked before him to see what had become of the fugitive Paraguayans. From there he saw the Paraguayan army, and that it was several times more numerous than his own; that, in addition to its naturally strong position, it was strongly and skilfully fortified. The Argentine general, however, though up to this time he had evinced little but self-confidence and folly, was not dismayed; and from the moment when he realized his position it must be admitted that he showed great courage and ability. He saw that to retreat was even more dangerous than to advance. Notwithstanding the small number of his troops, being but as hundreds to thousands, he saw that it would give him a great moral advantage to make the first attack. His decision was quickly taken. His troops were better armed and better disciplined than the Paraguayans, and he had a battery of artillery to which the Paraguayans had nothing to correspond; and as many of the enemy were armed only with bows and arrows and rudely made lances, he believed that when he opened upon them they would all scatter in confusion. His little force was posted on the hill before mentioned, where, before making the attack on which he had resolved, he waited for three days to rest his men and gain as much knowledge as possible of the position and strength of the enemy. The Paraguayans remained quiet, but always showed front when the least movement was made by the invaders, and they kept up a lively fire of cannon and musketry, "that," says Mitre, "showed a greater abundance of ammunition than of valor." But what was this waste of ammunition, or lack of valor or of generalship, when compared with the weary years of long-range practice of the allied troops, outnumbering the Paraguayans as three to one, under Mitre's own command, in the next war with Paraguay! Thus situated it would have been fatal for Belgrano to attempt a retreat, and an attack in open daylight would be at least hazardous. Notwithstanding that, Mitre says: "The soldiers they were to attack had never heard the whistling of a bullet, and it was to be expected they would be frightened if they were charged upon with resolution." Alas, what seas of blood it cost to erase from General Mitre's mind this mistake in regard to the Paraguayan character!

The plan of battle was to fall on the Paraguayan camp before daylight, counting on the surprise that such an assault would produce. Having resolved on this mode of attack, Belgrano called a council of war, having first, as his eulogist intimates, made up his mind not to respect its opinion if it differed from his own. In thus acting on his own judgment, Mitre finds much to commend in his hero, comparing him by implication to Charles XII. of Sweden. On another occasion, when he had been outwitted by the Paraguayans, who, feigning to fly in terror and dismay before him, had drawn him into inextricable difficulties and dangers, he compared him to Napoleon in his fatal Russian campaign. On other occasions he excuses his military errors by citing instances of the mistakes of several great conquerors, so that his hero, were he to read his biographer's eulogium, might well exclaim in the words of Pope: —

> "Go on, obliging creatures; make me see
> All that disgraced my betters met in me."

The attack was commenced by a small force of cavalry and infantry with two pieces of artillery, and the surprise of the Paraguayans was complete. They, nevertheless, returned an irregular fire, holding their assailants in check for half an hour. Yet their line was broken and their principal battery taken. As daylight appeared and disclosed to Velasco the turn affairs had taken, he gave up all for lost, if we are to believe President Mitre. But from the context this appears improbable; for in the very next sentence the poet, statesman, soldier, and biographer says, with an innocence bordering on simplicity, that by a casual coincidence, at the same moment the first column fell upon the camp of the enemy, the Paraguayans were just preparing to make a similar attack on the camp of Belgrano. The Porteños, however, being first in point of time, had the advantage of the surprise; and according to Mitre it would have been an utter rout but for another blunder on the part of the general second in command, for which the general-in-chief was justly responsible. Velasco, however, in giving his version of the same affair, while admitting that his raw militia were surprised, and that with such crude material it was scarcely possible to guard against surprise, asserts that but for the fact that the division attacked had not kept together as ordered, but had dispersed or joined themselves with other divisions, they "would have defeated the insurgents." Had the surprise been followed up by throwing the two reserved columns on the broken wings, the result might have proved a great disaster to the Paraguayans; but far from this the cavalry was sent in pursuit of the dispersed Paraguayans, who were already in flight towards the village of Paraguari, situate some seven hundred yards back of the point held by their rear-guard. The *patriots*, as the Porteños called themselves, no sooner entered this town in pursuit of the fugitives, than they began sacking the place, leaving their companions hopelessly exposed, as one to a dozen, against the now confident Paraguayans. Belgrano's troops, however, fought valiantly, and the combat had lasted three hours, and until they burnt their last cartridge; then the signal was given for the scattered forces to gather at one point. But the pillagers of Paraguari, now drunk with the wine and spirits they had found, and considering the battle already gained, gave no heed to it. A worse confusion than this now ensued. On one wing the ammunition was entirely exhausted, and the general in command sent to his chief to ask for a fresh supply. A wagon-load was at once despatched under an escort of cavalry. But so little was there of military order or discipline, that this body of cavalry was taken for enemies by those it was going to relieve, and the cry arose, *Nos cortan,* — "We are cut off," and the general, believing such to be the case, ordered a retreat, thus leaving those who had advanced to Paraguari in the flush of victory to ignominious capture.

The retreat was effected without loss, as the Paraguayans were too undisciplined to take advantage of their success; and when they saw the Porteños falling back, they considered their work done, and neglected to follow up the retreating enemy.

But the victory was clearly with the Paraguayans.

This battle was important as affecting the future of Paraguay; but when we consider the small number of killed and wounded, it appears a very trifling affair, and reflects anything but credit on the invaders. Being better armed and drilled than the Paraguayans, who had little to oppose to them but their unskilled, reckless valor, it was to be supposed that they would have left a large number of their enemies killed or wounded on the field. But they did nothing of the kind. Only thirty Paraguayans were killed, sixteen taken prisoners, and a few wounded. Belgrano, on the other hand, left one hundred and twenty prisoners in the hands of his enemies, and ten killed, though he succeeded in bearing away his wounded. He also succeeded in reaching the Tebicuari and crossing it before any Paraguayans appeared in pursuit. Thence he fell back to the Tacuari, intending there to make a stand and await reinforcements. Though defeated in battle, and though he had not yet seen the first Paraguayan of those he had come to liberate, he had as yet no thought of abandoning the campaign. He still cherished the illusion that he was to free the Paraguayan nation from the yoke of Spanish bondage, though still professing to act in the name of that royal family which had imposed it, and to reinstate a fallen dynasty in power so that it might renew its oppression and tyranny. His experience seemed to have taught him little, or he must have seen that a united and brave people, as the Paraguayans had shown themselves, could never be conquered by any force that Buenos Aires could send against them. Yet he still persisted in a contempt for his adversaries, — the greatest error into which a military man can fall; and after having recrossed the Tacuari he once more divided his forces, sending one fifth of his men to Candelaria, some thirty miles distant, and reserving to himself only four hundred to guard his position on the bank of the river. Such repeated errors, it would seem, ought to be sufficient to render a biographer sceptical of the greatness of his hero. But such is not the case with the author of the *Historia de Belgrano*, for he observes: "To these military errors the Argentine arms are indebted for one of the most beautiful acts of war, and Belgrano the occasion to show the truly heroic temper of his soul."

There, on the left bank of the Tacuari, he proposed to take advantage of the natural strength of the position and wait for reinforcements, and when they should arrive to renew his efforts to bring to allegiance to King Ferdinand VII. the perverse Paraguayans, who had never rebelled against him, and knew no other sovereign.

As soon after the victory of Paraguari as a sufficient force could be organized for the pursuit of the retreating Porteños, Governor Velasco despatched it under command of Colonel Fulgencio Yegros, a man who was to figure prominently in the future history of Paraguay, and, like the Governor himself, destined to become a victim to the future Dictator of Paraguay. The forces under Yegros, though greatly outnumbering the Porteños, did not at first attack them when they came up with them, as it seems to have been the desire of Velasco, that, after the punishment they had received at Paraguari, they should be allowed to leave the country as easily as possible. But when it was found that the invaders did not intend to leave Paraguay, and were waiting till they should be prepared again to take the offensive, Velasco took the necessary measures to compel them to depart. So cautiously did he make his preparations, that Belgrano received no warning of the impending danger, till one morning just before sunrise, and within three minutes after his advanced sentinels had given the announcement that all was quiet, he found himself attacked at three points at once. Thus surprised, the little army of Belgrano made a valiant defence; but, of course, against such odds there could be only one result. The little band appeared to be at the mercy of their foes. All looked to the commander-in-chief, supposing he would surrender. But at that critical moment a flag of truce was seen to approach. The bearer of it came with a summons to Belgrano to surrender at discretion, with the alternative, that, if the demand were not complied with, he and his whole force would have their throats cut. To this proposition, so similar in terms and spirit to the barbarous threat of Belgrano himself on entering the country, the General, now grown wiser, answered that he should never surrender the arms of the King that were in his possession, and to tell the Paraguayan chief to come and take them whenever he pleased.

No sooner had the flag-bearer returned than Belgrano announced to his men that to save themselves they must again take the offensive. His little force, now reduced to less than three hundred, answered him with alacrity, and by a sudden and unexpected attack, aided by the advantageous position which he held, he struck dismay into the minds of his enemies. Such reckless intrepidity caused the Paraguayans to pause, and impressed upon them, as Belgrano intended, the conviction that the little force was resolved to perish to the last man sooner than surrender. Availing himself of this opportune moment, Belgrano then sent in his turn a flag of truce to the enemy, and with it he made such representations as show him to have been more of a diplomatist than a general. He said that he and his army had come to Paraguay, not to conquer its people, but to assist them in throwing off a hated foreign yoke; but their good intentions having been repulsed, they desired to recross the Parana, for which purpose he proposed a cessation of hostilities, that all further effusion of blood between brothers might be stayed. The terms were assented to, on the condition that the whole army should set out on its return the next morning at ten o'clock.

It was now the particular desire of Belgrano not to leave Paraguay without doing something to convince the people that his motives in coming were not those of a conqueror, but rather those of a friend and deliverer. He therefore dropped all hypocritical cant about fighting for King Ferdinand and against the Bonaparte usurper, and in a preamble to the stipulations for the cessation of hostilities he took occasion to recite the grievances under which all the Spanish colonies had long groaned, and to promise the Paraguayan people that, the Spanish dominion once ended, they should have free commerce with the world, and be at liberty to export without hindrance all the products of their country, and especially their tobacco, which had been a monopoly in the hands of government favorites, who bought it at their own prices and exported it to sell at a profit of several hundred per cent. He also said that, as he had come to aid the Paraguayans, and not to conquer them, all the cattle and horses which had been taken for the use of his troops would be paid for in kind. He also presented the sum of seventy gold ounces, to be distributed among the widows of those who had fallen from a mistaken patriotism while fighting against him. This magnanimous conduct on the part of the defeated and disappointed general so won the hearts of the simple Paraguayans, and especially that of the general then in command, Cabañas, that the conviction forced itself on their minds that they had been fighting friends, having a common cause and common interests with themselves, instead of enemies. Belgrano and his officers, after the surrender, sought in every way possible to impress on those Paraguayans with whom they came in contact that it was for their interest, as well as for all other South American colonists, to cut adrift from Spain, and to convince them of the great advantages that would accrue from independence. Cabañas readily appreciated the force of this reasoning, as did Velasco and many others, and before the remnants of Belgrano's army left the country the seeds of revolution were already sown. They were soon to bear fruit.

The campaign of Belgrano against Paraguay thus brought to a close was in a military point of view a most disastrous failure. It appears incredible that a man possessed of the capacity which Belgrano subsequently displayed in his long, successful, and honorable career should have ventured on such an undertaking without more knowledge than he had of the people and of the country that he was to invade. He underrated the fighting qualities of the Paraguayans, as his biographer, President Mitre, the commander-in-chief of the allied army that made the next war on Paraguay, underrated it. The latter might have learned prudence and wisdom from the mistakes of his hero, but he failed to do so; and when in his boasting speech to the people of Buenos Aires in April, 1865, he promised to be in Asuncion within three months, it was with the same vaunting confidence that Belgrano had manifested fifty-five years before.

It is not within the scope of this work to follow the fortunes of Belgrano beyond the limits of Paraguay. The history of his life and times has been written by one of the first scholars and most accomplished gentlemen that South America has produced, but one whose talents, like those displayed by Belgrano in his Paraguayan campaign, are not of a military order. The errors of Belgrano are admitted with a frankness not usual to biographers who write *con amore*. His courage and address are duly applauded, and his general character on the whole fairly estimated ; but yet we suspect that like the poet Archias, who with his poetry had long since been forgotten but for Cicero's defence of him, so Belgrano will be indebted for his name in history less to his own deeds than to the eloquent tribute of Bartolome Mitre.

CHAPTER X.

Revolution in Paraguay. — Don Pedro Somellera. — Success of the Revolutionists. — Incapacity of the People for Self-Government — José Gaspar Rodriguez Francia. — His Origin, Early Education, and Character. — Letters of John P. and William P. Robertson. — Work of Rengger and Longchamp. — Francia pursues the Profession of a *Tinterillo.* — His Tastes, Habits, and Disposition. — His Dislike of the Spanish and the Priesthood. — His Flattery of the Lower Orders. — Anecdote concerning him.

THE army of Belgrano having recrossed the Parana, the Paraguayan troops were recalled to Asuncion, with the exception of some two or three hundred under the command of Yegros, who remained on the right bank of the river till the Porteños should leave that part of the country. There was, however, no longer anything like hostile feeling between the two armies. Familiar intercourse was kept up between the officers on both sides, and Belgrano, who had conceived a great regard for Cabañas, to whom he had finally surrendered, labored successfully to convince him that the object had in view by the government Junta in Buenos Aires was the common liberation of all from the yoke of Spain. The subordinate officers labored in turn with all the Paraguayans they met to impress them with the same ideas, and it took little to persuade them that all had common interests and should be united in a common cause. Velasco was soon advised of the progress made by Belgrano in conquering by reason and argument those who had conquered him in arms. He hastened to the front to stop all communication with the Porteños, but he was too late. The idea had become general that Paraguay should be independent. The seed scattered had taken root, and it was not long before the fruit was ripe for the harvest.

The returning conquerors, who had gone forth to fight in

good faith for their lawful king, and had come back conquered by the tact and statesmanship of Belgrano, and converts to the cause of independence, had no idea of the way to achieve it. Their Governor was popular and much beloved, and they knew of no mode of government except the old Spanish routine. The secretary of the Governor, however, Don Pedro Somellera, was a Porteño, an old friend of Belgrano, and a man of advanced ideas, who fully approved of the revolution in Buenos Aires, and saw that Paraguay could not be longer dependent on Spain if the river below were held by the revolutionists. To him Belgrano addressed a letter, setting forth the real motive of the revolution in Buenos Aires, and the reasons why Paraguay should follow the example thus set by their neighbors. Somellera entered at once into the views of Belgrano. He saw no obstacle in the way of revolution except the old Governor, who, he well knew, would not betray his trust, and had the entire confidence of the people. But Velasco's relations with the cabildo were not entirely harmonious. This body had received early in the month of May, 1811, and after the defeat of Belgrano, an offer from General Sousa, who was commanding a Portuguese army in the Banda Oriental, of a sufficient force to guard and defend the country, should it ever be again attacked by the Porteños. The cabildo, with a stupidity scarcely credible, received this offer as a special interposition of Providence, and decided to accept it. But the Governor strenuously opposed the admission of such a Trojan horse, and had very sharp and prolonged controversies with the cabildo. The latter, however, determined to admit as auxiliaries five hundred men, who were to be supported by Paraguay after once crossing the Parana. A letter was accordingly prepared for General Sousa, accepting his offer on the part of the cabildo, and delivered to his agents, Abreu and Nuñez, who had come to effect the negotiation. To this measure Governor Velasco was strongly opposed as fraught with many dangers to the authority of Spain, while his secretary was opposed to it for the reason that it might interfere with the revolution that he was already planning with some of the military leaders. The letter of the cabildo to General Sousa was therefore taken away from the Portuguese ambassadors, and the project frustrated in that way. "The cabildo," says Somellera, "were astonished, and took unkindly the tenacity of Governor Velasco. They were unanimous in their excitement against this honored chief, and this act was inconsistent with his general moderation. The cabildo attributed the resistance of the Governor to my counsels, and was not entirely deceived."

As it was known to Somellera that Yegros, who had remained near the Parana with two hundred men, had become a convert to the project of independence, it was at first thought prudent to defer any action till his return. But the perverse conduct of the cabildo in deciding to call in Portuguese auxiliaries, and the fear that the plan of a revolution was suspected, determined the leaders to precipitate it before any precautionary measures against it could be taken. The military leader was Don Juan Pedro Cavallero,—a name, like that of all the prominent men of the time, destined to fill a sad page in their country's chronicles. When word was carried to Somellera that their plan was known to the government, he remarked: *Si nos han de ahorcar mañana, muramos hoy; digales V. que esta noche despues de la queda hemos de tomar el cuartel,*—"If they are to hang us to-morrow, let us rather die to-day; tell them that to-night after the last beat of the music we will take the barracks."

This advice was followed by Cavallero, who, with a few followers, at the hour indicated, took possession of the cuartel without opposition of any kind. The Governor's house was not more than a hundred yards from the barracks, but Velasco knew nothing of what was going on till all power was in the hands of the revolutionists. When he learned what was done, he neither made nor counselled resistance. He saw it would be vain and suicidal. The people of Paraguay had become inoculated with the desire to be independent of Spain, and Velasco knew it was for their interest to become so. He therefore resigned his office, and, making no resistance, acquiesced in the new order of things. Thus the independence of Paraguay was achieved without the loss of a life. Says Somellera, there did not occur in it "a single shot, nor wound, nor insult."

A people more unfit to organize a government than were the Paraguayans at that time can scarcely be imagined. It had been the policy of the Jesuits to keep them as ignorant as possible of every duty but that of unquestioning, passive obedience. They indeed had been obliged to share their power with the civil authorities in the capital and elsewhere, outside of their missions, but it was a part of their craft to possess themselves of the springs of knowledge, to have the schools under their direction, and to guard against the admission of any secular learning that might breed doubt or inquiry. And after the expulsion of the Jesuits the government throughout all the Spanish colonies continued to be administered almost exclusively by native Spaniards, holding authority from the King; so that the people, though they knew they wanted independence, and to be relieved from the onerous taxation to which they had long been subjected, nevertheless knew not how to take advantage of their changed circumstances.

In this emergency, the immediate author of the revolution, Dr. Somellera, undertook the work of constructing a government. His plan was to form a Junta composed of three members, of which the two popular military leaders, Cavallero and Yegros, were to be members. But neither of these had any knowledge of the work he was called on to perform. Yegros, though he had won considerable distinction in the war against the Porteños, was a weak, pompous man, and almost as ignorant of letters and of laws as the horse he rode. Nor was Cavellero, whom Somellera had named as president of the Junta, much better. In this emergency it was necessary to find some one, a native of the country, more liberally educated, and who knew something of legal forms and proceedings, to put the Junta in operation. Unfortunately there was but one native Paraguayan in the country qualified for the work. This was the since famous Dr. Francia, who had been educated at the University of Cordova, in the Argentine province of the same name, and whose occupation had been that of a *tinterillo*, or writer to prepare papers, collect and adduce evidence in legal cases, such as was to be submitted to the illiterate judges of such tribunals as then existed. He was at that time about fifty-two years of age, and was selected by Somellera for the third member of the Junta, as being most competent to perform the necessary duties. Of this singular individual, the blight of whose presence has never yet been lifted from Paraguay, it now becomes necessary to speak.

José Gaspar Rodriguez Francia was born, as is generally believed, in Asuncion, about the year 1758. Of his pedigree and early history little is known, and the accounts given by those writers who profess to know most on the subject are conflicting. Francia himself always professed to be of French extraction, and each of the authors of the only works which give a history of his reign has accepted his own account of his origin as the true one. He was, however, of Portuguese descent, as is well known to the older Paraguayans, from some of whom have been gathered many facts in this history which have never before been published. His father, Garcia Rodriguez França was a Brazilian, and a native of Rio de Janeiro. The spelling of the name was changed by the son to encourage the belief that it was of French origin, as his true name, França or Franza, was very common, and is so to this day, among the Portuguese and Brazilians. Some sixty years before the revolution the Spanish government contracted with certain Brazilians to go to Paraguay and establish the manufacture of plug or twist tobacco, and to teach the Paraguayans, especially the Indians, how to cultivate that plant more successfully. Among these Brazilians was Garcia Rodriguez França. These immigrants had all the privileges of Spaniards, and received a salary of two dollars per day. França, though coming into the country as a laborer for daily wages, was evidently a man of more intelligence than most Paraguayans, for not long after he was named as director (*administrador*) of the tobacco culture and manufacture in the town of Yaguaron, or Dogtown, some twelve leagues from the capital. Of the mother of Francia nothing is known, although inquiries have been made of many of the oldest and most intelligent Paraguayans.

So well did the elder França improve his worldly circumstances, that when his son attained a proper age he was able to send him abroad to be educated. At that time the College and University of Cordova enjoyed a great reputation as a seminary of learning. Thither young Gaspar was sent. Somellera, who was at the same University, though long after, says that there was nothing of record or tradition there to distinguish Francia from hundreds of others who went through their course of studies and left, and were never inquired for or heard of afterwards ; and La Guardia, the only other Paraguayan who was ever educated at Cordova, and who had gone there at the recommendation of Francia, and with introductory letters from him, could never learn that his patron had ever displayed talent or scholarship at all above the common level while at the University. His early education he had received at the schools of Asuncion, which had been established by the Jesuits, and which during his early boyhood were probably under their control. But as the order was expelled when he was only some ten or twelve years of age, these schools must have passed into the hands of the Franciscans before he left for Cordova. He entered the University, as he himself said,* as a student for holy orders, as that was the only career open to natives of the country. He continued there until he obtained the degree of Doctor in Theology, and then, as Rengger observes, doubtless using Francia's own words, "the study of the canon law having inspired him with a great inclination to jurisprudence, he decided not to receive orders, and devoted himself to the law." But he never became a lawyer, advocate, or solicitor in any proper sense of the term. He returned to Asuncion with his

* Rengger.

degree of Doctor in Theology, and as such obtained a chair or professorship in the college there. But his arbitrary and quarrelsome character was so intolerable that he was forced to resign, and he then turned his attention to the only kind of law practice known in the country. It was a practice, however, that any one could follow who knew how to read and write, and could draw up papers in the ordinary forms. There were no lawyers in Paraguay at that time, and never have been since, such as they are in other countries. The nearest approach to them were what were called *tinterillos*, — men who prepared the papers and accounts of their clients, to be submitted without verbal argument to the alcalde or judge having jurisdiction. Of this class was Francia. He never could have qualified as a lawyer in Asuncion, for there was neither lawyer nor bar nor teacher of jurisprudence in the country before nor since his time. Rengger, however, assuming that such was his profession, says he must have studied it in the University of Cordova. But that was not one of the branches taught at that ecclesiastical school. Another writer,* generally correct, who had much personal intercourse with Francia during the first years of his reign, also says he was a lawyer, but as he seemed to be aware that he could never have become so in Cordova, he says that, whilst absent from Paraguay, Francia passed over to Chili, and there pursued his legal studies and took his degree. But Francia never was in Chili, and never left Paraguay after his return from the University, and hence never could have been a lawyer. The few persons in Paraguay when Francia came into power who were permitted to leave it, and from whose testimony nearly all that is known of that terrible man has been derived, were men especially favored by him, as is proved by the fact that he permitted them to leave the country. But even these all experienced the cruel force of his iron hand, and, having the awe and dread he inspired among all who approached him, it is not strange that they should regard him as a man of more talent than he actually possessed. But the

* Robertson.

illusion fades as time reveals his acts and shows no glimpse of talent, of learning, or of any redeeming feature whatever. It has been the custom, or more properly the cant, of nearly all who have written on the character of Francia, from Carlyle down to his weakest echoes, to represent Francia as a man invested with very superior mental powers. But he has left no record of having possessed either learning or talent, or even ordinary judgment. A fool with malignity dominating his character might do all that Francia ever did. He had the one quality of stubborn, stupid self-conceit united to such extreme selfishness that reason, or truth, or pity, or natural affection could not affect it.

In the state in which Paraguay was after the revolution, it required neither superior talent nor education to lead the simple people, whose ignorance was their inheritance from the Jesuit fathers. Francia, thanks to the profits of the twist tobacco, had enjoyed for a Paraguayan youth extraordinary advantages of education; and being a recluse in his habits, maintaining an air of great mystery, and assuming to know much of the occult sciences, he passed among his neighbors as a man of marvellous knowledge. With this knowledge he achieved absolute power, and a man once in power becomes an object of interest to others besides the ignorant and superstitious, and whether weak or great, good or bad, people like to know all about him. Flunkyism is a weakness so universal that people generally care more to know of the sayings and doings of a half-idiot king than they do of those of the wisest philosopher or statesman in his dominions. Popular histories are made up, to a great extent, of events of no general importance, as people read with more avidity anecdotes of court scandal and royal duplicity than of the hidden springs of national greatness. What the sovereign head of the government will say in a given contingency is an early question with many, whether he be a great ruler like Cromwell, an idle profligate like Charles II., or a dissolute fop like George IV. Francia, because of his power, which he held so long and with such terrible effect, made himself an historic character. A stronger and wiser, even though no better, man than he, would have seen that his course must have been succeeded by an infamous notoriety; but weak, vain, and conceited, he pursued his dark and dismal way hated by all, and knowing he was hated, and finding his only delight in the misery he could cause to others.

It has seemed necessary to give this outline of the character of Francia at the outset of his history, that the events of his reign, as they will be given in detail, may not grate too harshly on the popular belief as to the capacity for wickedness to which men unrestrained by any other influence than their own ambition and passions may attain. The story of the Dictator's reign will be given in the best chronological order that the data will admit.

The published works concerning Francia's time having any authentic value are very few. Indeed, the latest of those writers who pretended to give any account of him and his government left Paraguay in May, 1825, more than fifteen years before the death of the Dictator, and no one has ever attempted to give the history of those gloomy years. But of the first years of his reign a tolerable idea may be gathered from the rambling letters of the brothers John P. and William P. Robertson, two young Scotchmen, one of whom, John P., first arrived in Asuncion in 1812, and one or both of whom were there till 1816. These letters,* first published in 1838, entitled "Four Years in Paraguay," were followed soon after by others † purporting to be a sequel to the first, under the title of "Francia's Reign of Terror."

Three years after the departure of the Robertsons, two other foreigners entered Paraguay, and were there detained for six years by the Dictator, at the expiration of which time they were allowed to depart. These were Rengger and Longchamp, two doctors of medicine, both natives of Switzerland,

* Four Years in Paraguay; comprising an Account of that Republic under the Government of the Dictator Francia. By J. P. and W. P. Robertson.

† Francia's Reign of Terror; being a Sequel to Letters on Paraguay. By J. P. and W. P. Robertson.

and both naturalists, who in 1818 arrived in Buenos Aires, having come to the Plata with the purpose of pursuing their favorite studies of natural history and botany by a prolonged tour through South America, availing themselves of their medical knowledge as a means to aid them in their scientific pursuits. They found, on reaching Buenos Aires, that, owing to the ravages of Artigas throughout many of the Argentine provinces, there would be great danger in attempting to carry their plans into effect unless they could reach Paraguay, where they heard the most profound peace existed. Though advised of the character of the Dictator's government, they did not suppose that, with objects and intentions so harmless as theirs, they would ever be molested, and therefore they entered the country whence they were to emerge only after six years' detention. They arrived at Asuncion on the 30th of July, 1819, and great was their surprise when they found such a literal reign of terror among the inhabitants that the persons to whom they applied on their arrival for aid or information advised them with bated breath to be careful and circumspect, without daring to explain themselves further. Thus caught in a trap, Rengger and Longchamp made the best of their situation, and so well succeeded in not giving offence to the Dictator, that in May, 1825, they were permitted to leave the country. Once beyond the tyrant's power, Dr. Rengger wrote and published an account of the experience of himself and his companion during their detention, and of what he had seen and knew of Paraguay and its Dictator. These works, both of Robertson and Rengger, are valuable as giving personal experiences and observations. Rengger's book is the evident attempt of a man, knowing he has a strange story to tell, to tell it honestly, without affectation or literary pretensions. The Robertsons' books, though disfigured by tedious attempts at fine writing, are, nevertheless, the work of men evidently intending to tell the truth, but whose vanity and egotism were such that they could not see nor describe anything in which they were not personally concerned and did not prominently figure. But both Rengger and Robertson fell into various errors, most of which were in favor of Francia. Their books when first published were generally condemned as giving exaggerated, if not false, accounts of the government and character of the Dictator. But in the case of that human monstrosity, the adage that the "Devil is not so black as he is painted," should be reversed. The worst acts narrated by either Robertson or Rengger would be regarded by almost any Paraguayan now fifty years of age, if there be any such now living, as events of such ordinary occurrence in his youth as scarcely to excite surprise. During the residence of both Rengger and Robertson in Paraguay, they were more favored by the Dictator than anybody else within his dominions. Both were men of intelligence, who had seen countries that he knew little about, and with them only did he condescend to converse, during the whole thirty years of his dictatorship, with anything like familiarity or ease. His treatment of them was generous and humane compared with his treatment of everybody else, and the crowning act of his clemency was in allowing them to escape from his power. For this they owed him the gratitude that the stork owed to the wolf when he was permitted to withdraw his head from the beast's throat, where he had ventured it to extract a troublesome bone. Perhaps the stork for such favor was bound always to speak of the wolf as a good-natured beast, and perhaps Robertson and Rengger were under like obligations to speak but well of Francia. Against Dr. Rengger's work especially can it be alleged that it shows partiality for the Dictator; it magnifies his abilities, gives him credit for clemency when he does not deserve it, and excuses atrocities whose only apology is the devilish malignity of their perpetrator. Yet Carlyle, in his celebrated essay on Francia, this model hero after the Carlylean standard, complains of the "running shriek," that is heard in all they tell of the Dictator. But the "running shriek," though not agreeable to the ear, is not supposed to endure long. Whoever sits himself to study and learn the history of

Francia and his times must submit to something worse than a "running shriek," for he will find that a chronic, muffled shriek was going up from the bottom of every heart during those dreary thirty years. The subject is as painful a one as history can present, and yet there are those, leaders of public opinion, who would make a hero of this incarnation of every wickedness. In this work, therefore, such use of what has been before published will be made as it has been possible to verify, and a great many facts and incidents will be added, gathered from the witnesses or victims of Francia's cruelty. Nothing in the way of general objurgation or "running shriek" can carry conviction like authentic facts circumstantially related; and therefore, at the risk of being tedious, I shall make such a catalogue of crimes of almost every grade and kind that man ever committed, that even a Carlyle will find scant material for a hero, except of the order of Belial.

From the time of Francia's leaving his chair in the college of Asuncion till the revolution, a period of some twenty-five years, he passed a quiet and obscure life, living part of the time in the capitol, and pursuing his profession of *tinterillo*, and the rest of his time he passed on one of the two small *chacras* that he owned, a few leagues from town. He was a man of very simple, inexpensive habits, and lived like a recluse or misanthrope, without friends, and with only one or two domestics. With such tastes and habits, and surrounded by people for whose good or evil opinion he cared nothing, without a wife or legitimate children, and having no feeling of affection for his brothers, sisters, or natural children, he cared little for the accumulation of wealth. Money had little value in his eyes. He did not need it for his personal uses, for his tastes were too simple; he did not want it that he might use it to make other people happy, for his only pleasure in life was to see other people cringing, abject, and miserable. He did not desire it for his posterity, for he had no natural affection, and his children were all illegitimate. Therefore Francia passed in his transactions as a *tinterillo* for an honest man. He was cynical in his disposition, and generally disliked by his neighbors, and in return he disliked them intensely. Under the Spanish rule nearly all the offices of trust or profit were held by Spaniards, and by Spaniards who had come to the country to acquire wealth. Corruption was therefore a very common practice in all departments. Francia disliked the Spanish, and disliked the rich suitors; and by thwarting them he could not only gratify his spite, but win the favor and support of the lower classes. Hence he was a power in the country, feared, hated, and respected. Being the only Paraguayan (with a single exception) who had been educated outside of the limits of the country, and affecting to be very learned, he might easily pass for an oracle of wisdom among a people over whom the influence of the Jesuits hung for ages like a cloud. To read or speak any other language than Spanish and Guarani was a thing almost unknown among the Paraguayans. And Francia had some knowledge of French, of which he was exceedingly vain, as it not only gave him a reputation for learning, but encouraged the deception that he was of French extraction. He also pretended to a great knowledge of mathematics and astronomy, but of his attainments in those branches no evidence exists, except that it is known that when he tried to apply his knowledge of mathematics practically he made a failure that would have been ridiculous but for its tragical results. There was scarcely any one in the country to criticise his pretensions as a mathematician or to compare notes with him, and he left no proof or record of having any more knowledge of the exact sciences than is possessed by most school-boys of a New England academy. The only books he had on these subjects were of the most elementary kind, yet his slight knowledge of them was sufficient to impose on those who hardly knew the use of the Spanish numerals the idea that his head was the repository of vast learning. The few people who entered his doors saw a small library of books, mostly in a language strange to them. This library, though not so large nor well selected as would be found in the home of most New England mechanics, appeared of Bodleian dimensions to people who did not read at all, or whose reading was limited to the catechism. But what surprised them most was a mysterious instrument through which he used to survey the country far and near by day, while by night it was known he used to look through it at the stars. This, though only a common telescope, or rather theodolite, was a thing whose uses the neighbors of Dr. Francia did not understand; and though they did not trouble themselves to inquire about it so long as he was only a private person, yet when he became absolute in his authority, and had established his system of espionage so thoroughly that the most confidential expressions between man and wife or parent and child, and, as it sometimes seemed, even unspoken thoughts, found their way to him, it is not strange that the ignorant and superstitious Paraguayans should believe that he was conferring with the demons of night through that strange-looking instrument. But that superstition which he fostered when it magnified himself, he utterly abhorred when it made in favor of anybody else. He had a most bitter dislike of the Franciscan priests; for the people of the lower orders, to whom he looked to support him, were the most undoubting believers in all the fathers told them. Their influence over the common people was a great annoyance to Francia, as, however much they might fear him, they could not give up at will their traditional faith. The fathers, unfortunately, as a class, were both ignorant and immoral, and a better man than Francia might have despised them, and despised the people for having any faith in them. Though educated for the Church, he was an infidel in theory, while in practice he seemed to believe in a god of evil that he would placate by his atrocities. His favorite books were the writings of Volney, Voltaire, and Rousseau, a fact that might reconcile Carlyle to more toleration of those free-thinkers if he could suppose that Francia drew the inspiration of his cruelty from their works. But the mental thraldom against which they protested was a mild form of that which he imposed, and his admiration of them was not for their doctrines in regard to human rights, but for their arguments and reasoning against the clergy. The gross ignorance and scandalous lives of the Paraguayan priests made them the object of his contempt and sarcasm, at the same time that their influence over the common people provoked his malice and envy.

The shortcomings of the clergy, however, concerned him very little until he found it necessary, in order that his own power might be absolute, to destroy theirs. He never made pretensions to morality himself, or even decency in his amours. His liaisons were with the lowest, and his natural children were left to follow their mothers in the most menial employment. In his younger days, he had shown a weakness in common with other men. He so far fell in love with a young woman as to ask her hand. The young lady, Doña Petrona Zavala, did not reciprocate, and whether the heart of Francia was wounded or not by the refusal of the young woman it is certain that his pride was, as she was afterwards made to feel. After her rejection of Francia, she married Don Juan José Machain, who received with his bride, as a dowry, the implacable hate of Francia. Yet it was towards this man that Francia behaved, on one occasion, in a manner that would lead one to suppose he was following the Christian precept, "If thine enemy hunger, feed him; if he thirst, give him drink; for in so doing thou shalt heap coals of fire on his head." The anecdote, which has been often told to the credit of Francia, is substantially as follows. Francia was applied to by a man of the name of Domingo Rodriguez to bring a suit against Machain for an amount that, if he could succeed, would prove the ruin of his old rival. Knowing Francia to be a mortal enemy of Machain, Rodriguez took it for granted that he would, for a liberal retainer, undertake his cause. Francia listened to the applicant until he saw that his plan was by fraud and bribery to rob Machain of his estate; that he had no real or just claim, but was relying on corruption and the known enmity of Francia to Machain to effect an impudent fraud. Francia, however, refused to take up his case and advised him to drop it. But when he saw that Rodriguez was resolved to go on with it, he told him that if he did so, instead of assisting him, he would take up the cause of his much-hated enemy. The suit, however, was commenced. Rodriguez was rich, and the judge was known to be accessible. Francia now resolved to interfere. Wrapping himself in his cloak, one dark night, he sallied forth, and went to the house of that enemy whom he had determined to serve. Great was the astonishment of Machain, as he sat at his table with all his title-papers before him contemplating the prospect of his ruin, when in stalked Dr. Francia. Had he come to insult him and to sneer at him in his distress? It was not so. His first words were: "You know I am your enemy. But I know that Rodriguez, who is my friend, is bent on an act of gross injustice towards you, and will certainly succeed unless I interfere. I come to offer you my services." Machain, surprised and thankful, put the case in Francia's hands. The first paper, or "escrito," sent in to the judge confounded that functionary, as he had previously supposed that judgment could be given with impunity in favor of the client that would pay for it most liberally, and the advocates of Rodriguez found that they must lose their case, if any respect were paid to either the law or evidence. The judge, in this unfortunate aspect of affairs, told the leading counsel that he could not give a verdict in favor of his client, unless they would first bribe Dr. Francia to acquiesce. Rodriguez took the kindly hint, and sent his counsel with one hundred gold ounces to propitiate the obstinate Francia. But he had no sooner stated his business and intimated that the judge approved of this way of dispensing justice, than Francia turned upon him and exclaimed: *Salga V. con sus viles pensamientos y vilisimo oro de mi casa!* — "Get out of my house with your vile thoughts and viler gold!" The counsel, abashed and confounded, withdrew, and Francia, without giving the complotters time to consider the changed aspect of affairs, hastened at once to the house of the judge. He first related the circumstances of the interview just held with the opposing counsel, and then told the judge that he was a disgrace to the position which he held; that, knowing his villany, he had him in his power, and that if, the next day, judgment was not given for his client, he would drive him from the bench and make his titles and honors the emblems of his shame and disgrace. The next day came, and with it a decision in favor of Machain.

This affair soon became known to everybody, and Francia's reputation as a just man was greatly extended and magnified. But he was none the less an enemy of Machain than before, as the latter was made to feel years after, which the readers will see when they read the record of the merciless cruelties of the Dictator.

CHAPTER XI.

Inability of the Paraguayan People to form a Government for themselves. — Francia made a Member of the first Junta. — Congress called to determine the Form and Character of the New Government. — Declaration of Independence. — Treatment of Dr. Somellera at the Hands of Francia. — Retirement of Francia from the Junta. — Alleged Conspiracy against the Junta. — The Conspirators arrested and condemned to Death without Form of Process. — Francia interposes, and stays the Effusion of Blood. — Different Accounts of the Affair. — Reasons for supposing it to have been an Infamous Trick contrived by Francia. — Dr. Somellera's Criticisms on the Works of Rengger and Robertson.

THE independence of Paraguay had been achieved too easily. The people were unfit to form a government for themselves, after having thrown off one that greatly oppressed them. The influence of the Jesuits, whose policy it had been to render the people as helpless and dependent as possible, remained for a long time after the order had been expelled. The most intelligent of the native people were mere children in all matters of a political character. They knew little but implicit obedience, and never having had any contact with other people or other nations, they were just in a fit condition to become the willing tools of the strongest man that should arise among themselves. Had they gained their independence after a long struggle with a foreign enemy, the war must have brought out some men of courage and capacity, and have given the common people an idea that there might be a power independent of and apart from the central government at Asuncion. The revolution itself was the work of a foreigner. He knew that the people were tired of paying tribute to Spain, and that, once the government being changed, they would pay the same respect and deference to the new one as to the old. But how to organize a government on a new plan out of the materials at hand was the difficulty that presented itself to Dr. Somellera, after he had succeeded in the overthrow of his chief, Governor Velasco. With no disposition to violence, the people, from the utter lack of all practical knowledge, were on a sea of anarchy. But as the deposed Governor had been exceedingly popular, there was no feeling of resentment towards anybody in the country. Somellera, as a matter of necessity, took the initiatory steps towards establishing some sort of authority, and appears to have followed the course that had been taken in Buenos Aires. This was to establish a Junta. The only real power now left in the capital was in the hands of the military, of which Caballero was military commander. It was with his connivance that Somellera effected the revolution, and he was named for President of the Junta. Somellera himself seems to have had no personal ambition to gratify, and to have been actuated solely by a desire to see the country liberated from the yoke of Spain. He has himself given an account of the part he took at that critical time, in a review that he wrote of the work of Rengger and Longchamp. In this review, which he professes is to correct some errors into which the Swiss doctors had fallen by receiving Dr. Francia's own words as true, he gives from his own knowledge the history of those times which both Rengger and Robertson received at second-hand. He severely criticises many of the statements of Dr. Rengger, and, though giving him credit for a sincere intention to tell the exact truth, he believes that his book is altogether too favorable to Francia, and that it was written rather in his interest than otherwise. From Rengger's book we shall give extracts to show how the Dictator was regarded by an author who was considered as too friendly to him to be impartial by one who knew Francia as well as himself. And we shall afterwards have occasion to show in what terms of vulgar abuse the Dictator spoke of one who had given only a plain narrative of what he had seen, erring only on the side of indulgence and leniency to the tyrant.

Francia had taken no part in the revolution, and, so far as we have any evidence, had taken no part in politics previous to that time. His inordinate vanity had been continually chafed at seeing the Spaniards holding most of the more important and responsible offices, while he, the star-gazer, who could read French and could solve a problem in algebra, and had even gone as far in geometry as the *pons asinorum*, had never risen above a simple alcalde or municipal judge. So far as was known of his political ideas, he had been opposed to the revolution in Buenos Aires. The manner in which he came to be a member of the first Junta is thus given by Dr. Somellera. Having taken the reins of power into their own hands, he says: "We immediately began to consider upon the government that should succeed that of Velasco. I proposed a Junta of three, and that Caballero should be the president until the arrival of Fulgencio Yegros, whose brother Tomas was charged to make public this act, and I proposed that Dr. Francia should be one of this Junta. He was the only Paraguayan that could direct them. . . . . My proposal was generally reprobated; the officers knew that he had been opposed to the revolution in Buenos Aires; but I, who in a meeting called by Velasco the year before, had heard him express the opinion that the Spanish government had fallen, tried to persuade these officials of their mistake; and in support of my opinion I referred to the Padre Fernando Caballero, a pious Franciscan, respected for his age and for the ecclesiastical sway that he held with his order. . . . . He was in Buenos Aires the 25th of May (the day of the revolution there), after that he came to Asuncion, and had advocated the justice of the cause; most of the revolutionary officials knew him, and had conferred with him. His judgment upon the part to which Dr. Francia was inclined, notwithstanding the relationship that existed between him and the Doctor, would suffice to remove their doubts, and I proposed that we should consult the Padre Caballero. They agreed with me, and I arranged that he should come to their quarters. Whilst awaiting the arrival of the Padre Caballero, that part of the work directed to the government Junta at Buenos Aires was attended to, and Don José de Maria was ordered to prepare to start in the morning for Corrientes in a canoe, as soon as the projected Junta should be formed. It was at this moment when Padre Caballero arrived, and he then gave in expressive terms his felicitations to the revolutionists. I impressed upon him what we thought of doing, and spoke of the little security we had in regard to the views of Dr. Francia. His answer was: 'I answer with my blood for the views (*modo de pensar*) of my *sobrino* (nephew) Gaspar.' This tranquillized the officials, and they agreed that the place which I had proposed should be given to Dr. Francia. He was then in his country-house (*chacra*) at Ibirai,* some four leagues distant from the capital, where he had fixed his residence near a year before. I had not seen him since June of the previous year. So I wrote a brief note to Francia, giving him notice of what was done, and I called upon him with urgency that he should take the direction of affairs. I hastened the coming of Francia, because all my desire was to free myself from the compromises I had made, and return with my family to Buenos Aires. At eight in the morning of the 15th (May) Dr. Francia had arrived at the *cuartel*. I informed him quickly of what had transpired, and of the state in which the business was, and of the despatch of a messenger to Buenos Aires."

Thus Francia was named a member of the first Junta, for the reason that he alone of all the Paraguayans in Asuncion had sufficient education and knowledge of forms to organize into working order the improvised government. Somellera was a foreigner, and, besides, he wished to return to his home in Buenos Aires. There was one other man in the country deemed fit for the task, Dr. José M. Baiz, who was not obnoxious to the suspicion of being opposed to the revolution; but he was a son-in-law of Espinola, the detested confidant and agent of Velasco's predecessor in the governorship, and the same who had been so unwisely sent by the Junta at

* The distance of Ibirai from Asuncion is less than two leagues.

Buenos Aires to persuade the Paraguayans to follow their example. But a greater, and indeed an insuperable, objection to making him a member of the Junta, instead of Francia, was the fact that he was not at the moment in the capital. He was in Concepcion, some three hundred miles away, and there was no time to be lost. Francia was accordingly called in, and the Junta was made up. The first act was to call a Congress, which was done on the following day, the 16th of May. This Congress could have little formality and less authority, and was composed of such persons as were invited by the Junta, of which Francia was the scribe and working member, to attend; and it was called only to determine the form and character of the new government. This Congress, or, as it might more properly be called, informal assembly, met on the 17th of June, and adjourned on the 20th, during which time a plan of government that had been prepared by Francia was submitted, and of course approved. According to this plan, the Junta was to consist of five members, including a secretary. Yegros was named President, and the other members were the commander of the troops, Caballero, a priest by the name of Bogardin, Dr. Francia, and Don Fernando Mora. The last was named secretary. The term of their authority was limited to five years.

This Congress issued a declaration of independence, which independence the country has maintained ever since. Buenos Aires, though it had deposed the Viceroy and set up a government of its own, was yet looking for a sovereign to be sent to it from among the royal beggars of Europe, who at that time, owing to the confusion created among them by Napoleon, were both numerous and needy. Paraguay was accordingly the first of the South American states to declare its entire and absolute independence. The declaration was to this effect: —

"1st. That Paraguay should govern itself without intervention from Buenos Aires, proclaiming by that act the Paraguayan independence.

"2d. That, notwithstanding, it would preserve good relations with that Province and send deputies to the general Congress.

"3d. That the custom-house duties should be regularly administered, and that the monopoly of tobacco should be suppressed.

"4th. That in no case should the laws or resolutions of the Congress of Buenos Aires be binding on Paraguay, without being first approved by the Paraguayan general assembly."

This declaration, with such scanty outlines of organic law, having been approved by the Congress, it adjourned. Everything had been done conformably with Francia's suggestions, and thus the government was inaugurated. At this point we will resume Dr. Somellera's narrative:—

"On the evening of the day of the adjournment of the Congress the aspect of affairs was changed. Francia had labored with his colleagues, and already the proposed journey of Don José de Maria to Buenos Aires was reconsidered, and it was determined that Don José Tomas Yegros should go in the character of envoy to represent the Junta as soon as all should be arranged; then I began to observe a certain briskness (*despejo*) in Francia. From my first arrival in Paraguay we had treated each other with frankness and friendship. During the years 1808 and 1809 he had visited me daily. In the former of these years he had been alcalde of the first grade, and in the latter I had labored that he might be named *sindico procurador* (state attorney), and I tried to persuade him to accept the office. We gave each other the title of *compañero*, from having been educated, both of us, in the college of Monserrat in Cordova. This evening I wondered at the ceremony with which he treated me; but I never suspected the extremity to which matters had arrived. On the morning of the 16th, Caballero sent to call me; I found him with Iturbe and other officers; Francia had retired to his house; the call of Caballero was to give me a satisfactory explanation for the detention of the despatch to Buenos Aires as had been agreed upon at daylight the morning before. A little later Francia returned, and he could not dissemble his displeasure at seeing me there with the officers. We went on telling some anecdotes of the night of the 14th that pleased Francia. At my retiring, he spoke to me very particularly. We crossed over the yard to the door of the cuartel, and in this transit he told me it was necessary that each one should serve his country; that I had not failed in Paraguay, and would be of much service in my own country. I answered him that for what

I had done in these times all was with the same idea, and that I thought of going to Buenos Aires with my family as soon as the river should be free. . . . . This innuendo worked, as it was intended, its effects. I did not return to enter the cuartel for a month, when I was carried there. I tried to isolate myself, notwithstanding which some of the officers visited me; they knew not the evil they were doing me."

None but the officers, however, were permitted to see him. He was shut up in a small room by himself, and not allowed to communicate with his family.

This was the treatment that Somellera received at the hands of Francia, so soon as he had the power to inflict it. Being a man of intelligence, the people might, in their extremities, look to him for counsel and advice, and this would interfere with Francia's plans for immediate and absolute power. He was therefore put out of the way. But he was not alone in receiving such flattering attentions from Francia.

"In the same cuartel," he adds, "the members of the cabildo that had been displaced by the revolution were also prisoners. This was one of the things that mortified me most, to see myself a prisoner with those over whom I had just triumphed, and shut up with them in the very place of the triumph. A few days after Governor Velasco entered, a prisoner, and was placed in a cell in front of the one I occupied. There was on guard in the cuartel, Lieutenant Rivarola, who was one of my friends, that I had often met at the house of Don Francisco Recalde. This officer informed me of the imprisonment of Velasco and where he was. He assured me how earnestly Caballero was working for my liberation, and gave me hopes of obtaining it. At nine o'clock in the evening of the following day I was transferred to the public prison, and put in a little room separate from the prisoners. My keeper was only the jailer, independent of the guard of the barracks. I attributed this transfer to the visit of Lieutenant Rivarola. Francia feared nothing so much as my communication with the officers. Here I was better off. I had a window with a view to the river and the Chaco. They allowed me books; my brother Benigno was sent to the same prison, and his company was a great consolation. My jailer was a kind-hearted Biscayan. Notwithstanding, I began to distrust some of his acts of carelessness. Sometimes, at retiring after his evening visit and after bringing us supper, he turned the key, leaving the door open. As I had so many reasons to suspect Francia, I believed that this carelessness was a trick dictated by him to surprise me in flight if I attempted it. When there was such neglect on the part of the jailer, we fastened the door securely within. Everything was to be feared from that tyrant. Francia was not satified with the seclusion to which I was reduced in the prison. . . . .

"About the middle of August I was put aboard of a scow that was anchored at some distance from the bank. As it was a boat without a keel, hard to steer, and loaded with sacks of yerba, it dispelled my fears that they intended to confine me in Fort Borbon. Such a boat could not go up stream. The vessel and cargo belonged to a Spaniard, its captain, or *patron*, was a Brazilian or Portuguese, and to him all the crew were subject. The Portuguese treated me with kindness and respect. My guard was a picket of four soldiers and one corporal, that were on the bank in view of our vessel, and permitted no one to approach it, nor could any one of the guard come on board. The soldiers searched the boy that brought my food. When the weather did not admit of his coming on board, I contented myself with dry biscuit. The Portuguese proposed to me to rescue me from my prison and take me to Buenos Aires, since, making use of a good canoe, he said it would be an easy and a safe thing to do. At the suggestion I remembered the negligence of my jailer in leaving open the door of my cell. I thanked him, and excused my irresolution by saying I could not abandon my family in Paraguay. Some fifteen days after this the Portuguese, on coming aboard, called me to his cabin, and told me in secrecy that a revolution was preparing in the city by the Spaniards against the Junta, with the object of restoring Velasco and the cabildo, and that the scheme was well advanced; that he would advise me of the time of the movement and put me ashore. I asked him who headed this movement; he answered that it was Don Mariano Mallada, and that there were in it all the Spaniards, the prisoners of the cuartel, and many Paraguayans. I knew the incapacity of Mallada, and all the Portuguese had told me appeared to be a fiction. Mallada was a Correntino whom I had known in Buenos Aires since his youth, both of us being then in the school of Matórras; notwithstanding which he was a dunce, a scoundrel, and one of those most in the confidence of Francia. Who knows, said I, that they have not seduced him? I thanked the Portuguese for his information, and begged him to advise me of whatever he might learn of the matter. The neglect of the jailer with the door of my prison, and the invitation to flight of this same Portuguese, came to my mind. But he had given me notice of a revolution of the Spaniards against the government, and for me to keep silence would be a charge that Francia could justly bring against me. On a scrap of paper not clean, and with a piece of lead I had prepared for the purpose, I wrote to Francia all that the Portuguese had told me."

This extract, of such length, from the notes of Somellera, is given to show that it was Francia's system from the first to lay snares for innocent persons, and also to show that his favorite conspiracy, which his apologists always quote to prove that it was the conspirators against his life that transformed him from a just and wise ruler to a cruel despot, was but a trick and device of his own that would give him occasion to murder some and hold all in greater terror. This appears to have been the first of the many conspiracies that were discovered in Paraguay after the revolution; and all that followed for the next sixty years, and till the final overthrow of the younger Lopez, were close imitations of it. All were the work of the ruling despot, and devised as an excuse for destroying suspected enemies and inspiring general terror.

This alleged conspiracy took place in the latter part of September, 1811. Dr. Rengger, who had doubtless received the account of it from Francia's own lips, makes the time when this occurred a year or two later, and when Francia, disgusted with his colleagues, had retired from the Junta. But it was only a day or two after Dr. Somellera, having shunned all the snares laid for him by Francia, had at last been allowed to leave the country. It was, according to Rengger, during the retirement of Francia from the Junta, that this conspiracy against it was formed:—

"It was at this period that Francia distinguished himself by an act of humanity, if not of pure policy, that gained him the good opinion of all just men. The Spaniards and their partisans among the creoles had planned a counter-revolution that was discovered without difficulty. All the accomplices were arrested, and the judges, without other form of process, and in virtue of their simple moral conviction, condemned them to death. Two were instantly shot, and their bodies suspended from a gallows; perhaps they were the least guilty, but they were certainly the poorest. When Francia, who was in his country-house, knew of these executions, he flew to the capital, and stayed the effusion of blood. He knew too well the weakness of the Spanish party to fear any attempts they could make, and he thought that example of rigor was sufficient to restrain them. They only made a part of the conspirators pass under the gallows from which dangled the bodies of the two victims, condemning others to prison for an indefinite period, that was shortened by paying large sums to the state, or to the families of the first functionaries."

This account, written thirteen years after the event, by Dr. Rengger, who never set foot in the country till long after the occurrence, is thus noticed by Somellera:—

"Dr. Rengger does not give the date of this counter-revolution; he does well, for that would have shown all the iniquity of those he tried to applaud; it would have proved that there was no counter-revolution plotted, and that all that tragic farce was a snare set by Dr. Francia, in order to satisfy his desire of shedding blood to frighten the Spaniards. The facts of this affair I will relate as they were told to me at Angostura, three days after their occurrence, by Dr. Ventura Bedoya, a native of Asuncion, who was present; and they were confirmed by many others who were there, and one of whom was an actor in the scenes.

"These are the facts: on the morning of the 29th of September, 1811, a group of soldiers, with some prisoners, all led by an officer, Don Mariano Mallada, rushed out from the cuartel; they brought out two cannon that were under the command of two prisoners, both artillery officers, Juan B. Zavala and Francisco Guerreros. They came forth shouting loudly, beating drums, and crying, *Viva el Rey, viva nuestro Gobernador, y mueran los traidores!*—'Live the King, live our Governor, and perish the traitors!' At the noise, some people, as was common, collected in the plaza where the mob had gathered. Some of those thus coming together were made prisoners by the rioters themselves, and some by soldiers that came out of the cuartel. Among those made prisoners were a Dominican friar, Padre Taboada, a boy who had been a servant of the Governor, a native of Castile, whose name I do not remember, and a Catalonian named Martin, who had a *pulperia* (drinking-shop) in the house of Juan Francisco Decoud. The two last were immediately shot and suspended from a gallows; others were made to pass under it, among whom was the Padre Taboada. I know not why the historian should say that these two unfortunates were certainly the poorest.

"I asked Bedoya if the results had been serious to many, and how the movement had terminated. He said it was a serious affair only to the two who were shot; that after Padre Taboada and others had passed under the gibbet, the cry was raised, 'Viva la Junta!' and then all retired to the cuartel, bearing back the cannon with them. I could but bear in mind the account of the revolution of the Spaniards, which the skipper of the vessel in which I was a prisoner brought to me in the beginning of September, and which I have already mentioned.

"This lamentable event, which Dr. Rengger refers to in order to magnify the humanity of Dr. Francia, is a proof of his iniquitous barbarity. That counter-revolution of the Spaniards, that movement of the 29th of September, was an infamous trap contrived by Dr. Francia. The proofs of it are most convincing.

"In the first place, in the month of September, 1811, there did not exist in Paraguay any Spaniard capable of heading an enterprise against the new order of things. The members of the cabildo and Governor Velasco were all prisoners, and besides, there was no man from whom such a thing was to be feared. . . . . In the second place, that movement of the 29th, headed by Mallada, is the same that in the beginning of September the master of the vessel informed me of, and the same that I denounced to Francia after my arrest. This man, cowardly, distrustful, suspicious, did not heed my information. He did not take any notice of it, nor investigate the origin of the story of the master of the scow. Mallada continued in the same service in the cuartel as he had done before.

"In the third place, the artillery officers, Zavala and Guerreros, who were prisoners, and that appeared in the plaza directing the cannon which they brought among the crowd, were, without doubt, the most culpable in it. It would seem that the rigor should have been exercised towards them; but it was not thus. They, instead of being punished, were rewarded; their salaries that had accrued in the time of the Spanish government were paid to them, and they were set at liberty. Zavala went to Montevideo and entered the Spanish service, and afterwards was often with me in Buenos Aires and told me of this fantastic revolution of Mallada, and of the secret notice that he had given him that it was a trap.

"The reasons given me by Zavala, why he and Guerreros engaged in this plot were the following: first, they knew it was by the connivance of the government; second, if they refused they would have been exposed to be assassinated in their cells, either from the anger that their refusal would cause, or to hide the secret; third, that by appearing to approve they could give notice to the Spaniards so that they would not join in the riot, — as they did not; for, having been forewarned, none of the principal persons of the vicinity went into the plaza. He added that Velasco and the members of the cabildo remained quiet, as they had been warned of this pretended counter-revolution.

"I do not doubt that Dr. Rengger, in relating the event of the 29th of September, has done no more than tell us what Dr. Francia told him. Nobody but himself could invest with colors of humanity an act the most unjust and barbarous. How could this writer attribute humanity to a man of whom he had just said, in the same chapter, he had repressed all tender affections, and knew not friendship? 'Humanity in Dr. Francia! He never appeared to be a man belonging to the human race, and only his death is a proof that he was.'"

Dr. Somellera is equally severe on Robertson, alleging that every act instanced either by him or Rengger as indicating humanity or justice in Francia was prompted by utter selfishness and malignity on the part of the Dictator, and that he acted solely with the conviction that it proved him to be a being of superior order when all trembled in his presence, and only held their lives subject to his pleasure or caprice.

CHAPTER XII.

The Indecision of the Junta. — Francia withdraws, and La Cerda is named Asesor. — His Popularity and Manner of doing Business. — Francia in Retirement. — His Intrigues for Restoration. — Condition of Paraguay at this Time. — A Day's Festivities. — Dona Juana Ysquibel. — Arrival of Don Nicholas Herrera as Special Envoy from Buenos Aires — Francia recalled to the Junta. — He assumes Absolute Power. — Banishment of La Cerda. — A Congress convoked. — Character of the Congress, and Description of the Members. — The Junta abolished, and Francia and Yegros appointed Consuls. — Abuses corrected. — Espionage. — Quotation from Robertson.

THE violent and unjust measures that characterized Francia's first elevation to power are not to be laid to his charge alone. To the weakness, timidity, and ignorance of the Junta may justly be ascribed the crime of permitting a mind so sombre and wicked as his was known to be to obtain absolute power. When he entered their counsels he was not absolute, as is evident from the fact that after some six months he retired from it, disgusted because he could not have everything his own way. It was impossible that men like Caballero and Yegros, ignorant as they were, yet having some sense of dignity, and too proud to engage in any act of baseness, would engage in such low tricks as suited the dark, sinister purposes of Francia. He was not yet strong enough to venture on their arrest and execution, and then to set himself up as absolute ruler, nor were they sufficiently self-confident to defy him, and rid themselves and the country of his ominous presence, by those strong measures that they knew to be necessary. Francia, however, knew their weakness and his own power. He knew that if he left the Junta he would leave all the other members in a state of confusion ; that they would hardly know how to make a law, or, if made, to put it in force. Somellera had left the country, and there was no other one of whom he need feel jealous. He therefore at the end of a few months left the Junta to get on without him, and retired to his country-house at Ibirai.

Francia having withdrawn, the Junta was reconstituted, and in his stead, Don Gregorio de la Cerda was called in to make up the full number of the body as organized by Somellera. La Cerda was taken for two reasons; one was his popularity, and the other was that he had sufficient education to draw up official papers. Necessarily he was made the secretary, or, as they called it, the "asesor," of the Junta. This Don Gregorio was an important character in many ways. He was one of those good-natured, ever-serviceable men, that, affecting much knowledge, hold it at the service of everybody. He had a pleasant word for every beggar, and a compliment for every pretty face, and bore so little malice in his nature, that, while he was on good terms with all the fathers of the more respectable families, the mothers almost universally looked to him to be godfather (*compadre*) to their children. Hence it was that he was a sort of general godfather, or *padrino;* and as the godmothers, or *madrinas*, were many, he came to have a kind of relationship with nearly all the best families in the capital. Of course his influence was great among the people, and correspondingly great was the anger of Francia when he saw him called to fill the place he had himself vacated.

To give an idea of the simple, unsophisticated way in which the government was administered by Don Gregorio, as well as to show the general condition of the people and the way their business was managed, we shall give the following extracts from Robertson. It should be here premised that Robertson was largely engaged in merchandising; that, at the time, Buenos Aires was at war with Spain, and the ports of Paraguay were closed to all foreigners. Robertson, however, by use of his credits in Buenos Aires, and with the proceeds of a cargo of merchandise that had come consigned to him from that port, had purchased from the merchants of Asuncion, and others who were desirous of making remittances below, a large quantity of Paraguayan produce, consisting mainly of hides, tobacco, and yerba. Naturally he was anxious to get permission to ship it below, and as Don Gregorio de la Cerda was virtually the government, he made it his business to get into his confidence and good graces. Of course there was nothing easier than that with a person so exuberant with good-nature. Having first propitiated the general compadre, he had an interview with him which he thus relates:—

"'*Señor Don Juan*,' he said to me one day, '*es preciso que de algun modo V. me permita servirle*,'—'Mr. Robertson, I insist upon it that in some way you permit me to serve you.'

"There was no one in Paraguay who could so well serve me as Don Gregorio. He was lord paramount there, and directed all the operations of the government.

"'Well, Senor Don Gregorio,' I replied, 'you know the port of Paraguay is now closed against the egress of both persons and property. You know, too, that I have a great deal of the latter locked up in unprofitable stagnation here. Besides, I desire very much to return for a season to Buenos Aires. Now, if you will obtain permission for me to take away both my person and property in one of the many ships lying empty and inactive in the river, you will do me a very essential favor.' The best of compadres and friends instantly replied, '*Por hecho*,'—'Consider the matter settled.' 'There are,' he continued, 'some difficulties in the way. There will be great jealousy on the part of all the merchants on account of your being authorized to break the embargo. The Spanish marines, you know, are in the river, and making prizes of all vessels which sail from neutral ports; and Vattel lays it down as a principle of national law, that no neutral can be allowed to carry his property from one belligerent port to another, unless the ship in which it is be under the flag of his own nation and be manned by at least one third subjects belonging to it. But never mind, we will find a way of smoothing these difficulties, provided you have really made up your mind to run the risk, which you know is imminent, of capture.'

"'That,' I replied, 'is entirely my affair; and my mind is quite made up on the subject.'

"Don Gregorio was one of those active and fidgety spirits that, having once undertaken a business, give themselves no rest, day or night, till it is accomplished. He immediately sat down and dictated to an amanuensis the petition to government, embracing all the points of my request, and of the fate of which petition he knew himself to be sole arbiter. He explained and mollified, in the present instance, the objections of Vattel; he made out a very ingenious case of hardship for me; and he called on the government, as it valued the friendship of Great Britain, to grant the reasonable request of the only British subject then in Paraguay. There were a number of technical formalities to be gone through in the way of taking the opinions and informes (dicta) of the various lawyers and men in office. The cabildo, or court of aldermen, were to give their informes, the judge of commerce and the director of customs were to give theirs. The juez de alzada, or judge of appeal, was to give his opinion, and the fiscal his. Every one of these honorable and learned gentlemen were compadres of Don Gregorio (he was godfather to the children of each), and the idea of one compadre's opinion being against another's, especially as Don Gregorio was the government 'asesor,' was not to be entertained. Every one of them therefore set down exactly what the compadre dictated. Within eight days from the time of presenting my petition all was granted."

Thus were affairs managed by the great La Cerda after Francia had left the Junta, and while the latter was brooding over the slight put upon him by attempting to carry on the government without him.

He was not idle, however, in his retirement. He had tasted the sweets of power, and like the tame tiger, that is harmless as long as he is fed only on milk and vegetable food, having once tasted blood has ever after an unappeasable thirst for it, so Francia, now some years past fifty, thought only of regaining power and slaking his thirst for revenge with human blood. His first step was to make people realize that they were badly governed. They were almost invariably contented with the existing order of things, and, save a few Spaniards who had held official positions, there was scarcely a person in the country who did not rejoice that they were no longer subject to the grinding oppression of Spain. That the river was closed, or nearly so, to commerce, was no fault of the Junta; and it was therefore idle for Francia to talk to the farmers and landholders in the interior of their material sufferings and grievances. He nevertheless sought interviews with them, and as they came to and went from the capital they were induced to visit his house, where he would receive them with courtesy, show them his books and mysterious theodolite, and then seek to make them discontented with the government by telling them that they were the wise men, they were the Solons who ought to be in authority, instead of such vulgar, ignorant fellows as Caballero, Yegros, La Cerda, and the others. The revolution he represented to them to have been a failure, for though it had been successful in so far as it had overthrown the Spanish authority, yet it had been succeeded by a government much worse, as it was composed of ignorant pretenders, whereas it should have been in the hands of such wise, experienced, and able men as were his auditors. Of the Junta, Yegros and Caballero were particularly his aversion, as they were both generals, both had acquired distinction in the war against Buenos Aires, both had favored the revolution, and both were held in much awe and respect by the people. As military men they were entitled to wear gold lace, and wherever they went the common people gave way and looked upon them as great conquerors and national deliverers. To a man of Francia's inordinate, self-devouring vanity, one who could read French and make an equation in algebra, the sight of these men with their trappings and escorts was a thousand times worse than was to Haman the sight of Mordecai, the Jew, sitting at the king's gate. To the more wealthy and influential landholders, or *estancieros*, therefore, who lived scattered about in different parts of the state, he managed to make known the grievances they had not before realized. Aroused to a sense of their wrongs and importance, these now dissatisfied persons would secretly visit Francia at his country-house, where he would dilate on their sufferings, boast of the reforms he had introduced or projected while a member of the Junta, and promise them all a surfeit of honors and wealth should he ever return to power. To the lower classes of the capital Francia was at the same time particularly condescending, and in every way tried to make it appear that he was their champion against the more wealthy, whom he treated with ostentatious contempt.

Gradually the public mind became impressed with the idea that Francia, though in retirement, was a power, was the coming man. The *estancieros*, who came in from the country, with wonderful unanimity spoke of him as the man for the times. His acts of extreme severity when he was in the Junta had been confined to foreigners, of whom those who still remained in the country had little influence. The Junta was inherently impotent to do anything to stem the current that was setting in against it and in favor of Francia. Some of the old and more intelligent Spaniards saw to what things were tending, and with gloomy forebodings awaited the result which they had no power to avert. They had already so far divined the character of Francia, that had he propounded the question of Hazael, "Is thy servant a dog, that he should do this thing?" they could have answered in the affirmative.

But what was the actual condition of the country at the time? Was Paraguay in so miserable a condition as Francia represented, and was Asuncion so like Sodom or Gomorrah as Carlyle would have us believe when his hero angel stepped forward to rescue it, and avert from it the flames of consuming heaven? An extract from Robertson, though only a chance and rambling description of a day's festivities, will convey a very clear idea of the condition of the people and the liberty then enjoyed.

At the time of Robertson's residence in Paraguay, there lived at a distance of some two leagues from the capital an old woman having a large estate, who took a great fancy to the young Scotchman and offered him her country-house, putting at his service her horses, her cooks, grooms, and everything that he could possibly require in the way of eating and drinking that could be obtained in Paraguay. This strange character was very rich for a Paraguayan dame, and had some designs on the heart and hand of our ungallant author, who thus describes her: "The old lady was eighty-four years of age; rich, hale, healthy, vigorous, and active; and she was in the habit of riding to Asuncion from her country-house and back again three times a week. Though a wrinkled skeleton and brown as an Egyptian mummy, she was erect; she did not totter at all; and her utterance, even in Spanish, was clear, unbroken, and distinct. Her name was Doña Juana Ysquibel."

This gay and amorous damsel having made some advances towards the Scotch youth of twenty-one, even at that age beginning to take lessons on the guitar on his account, was very properly told not to make a fool of herself. At this rejection of "her hand and fortune," the enraged woman broke out in furious ejaculations and reproaches, and Robertson concluded that on the following morning he would change his domicile. But the morning brought to the mind of the disappointed Doña Juana the reflection that her guest, Don Juan, was in the right, and had given very good advice, and she sought an interview with him to prevent, what she had foreseen might happen, his departure from her house. Don Juan promised to stay on condition that he was to supply his own wants and should hear no more of her love and music. To make the reconciliation complete, however, Doña Juana insisted on celebrating the day of their common saint, St. John, by giving a grand entertainment at her house in Campo Grande to all the aristocracy of Asuncion. To this Don Juan assented, on the condition that it was to be at his own expense, and the two set off for the capital in order to give out the invitations. The youth of twenty-one and the dame of eighty-four, each well mounted and each accompanied by a servant riding in the rear, proceeded towards the town, calling, in their circuit, at the houses of the better class of the people, bidding them come to the feast. The social distinctions there were not clearly marked, and before they had gone the rounds of the town a large number of people had been invited to the festivities. It was intended to be, however, a very fashionable and aristocratic affair. All the members of the government were invited, and all the officials of any rank or note in the vicinity. The priests were invited as a matter of course; the officers of the barracks, the old ex-Governor, General Velasco, and farmers, merchants, and shop-keepers, all were bid to come and help celebrate the festival given in honor of the saint of Don Juan and Doña Juana. The next thing was to make the necessary preparations for so grand a celebration; and the assistance of several of the neighbors was called in, and ample provision was made that none who came should depart dissatisfied with their entertainment. To quote the words of Robertson: —

"The natal day of Saint John dawned auspicious on Ytapúa. The most sumptuous and abundant arrangements were made by Doña Juana, as well in honor of her saint as for the good cheer of her guests. These amounted to about two hundred, and embraced all grades, from the members of the government down to the shop-keepers of Asuncion. Doña Juana's first care was to decorate with uncommon splendor a large image of Saint John the Evangelist, which, in a costly crystal box, she preserved as the chief ornament of her principal *sala*, or drawing-room. He was painted anew and regilt; he had a black velvet robe purchased for him and trimmed with deep gold lace. Hovering over him was a cherub; and with more historical propriety than I should have expected from a Roman Catholic artist in Paraguay, there were thrown up behind the saint some artificial rocks, moss, and trees, meant to represent the Isle of Patmos, in which he wrote the Apocalypse. Every friend of Doña Juana had lent some part of her jewelry for the decoration of the holy man. Rings sparkled on his fingers, collars hung around his neck, a tiara graced his venerable brow, the lacings of his sandals were set with pearls, a precious girdle bound his slender waist; and six large wax candles were lighted up at the shrine. There, imbosomed in fragrant evergreens, — the orange, the lime, the acacia, — stood the favorite saint, destined to receive the first homage of every guest that should arrive. The orange-groves on either side of the house were festooned with variegated lamps ready to be lighted. The tables were laid out by the best confectioners in Asuncion; the old Governor's cooks were hired for the occasion, and every one was requested to bring as many of his own domestics as he could."

All being arranged, Doña Juana awaited the arrival of her guests; and as it was about sundown there was a general setting forth of the invited guests, some on horses, some on mules or donkeys, and some in carts and carriages. The straggling procession had at their head a company of Franciscan friars, preceded by the band of music from their own monastery. The friars, though clothed according to the rules of their order to show their humility, rode on fine, well-groomed horses, richly caparisoned, and in this way they indulged the pride which was in their hearts, though conforming to the rules of their order. They were followed by the Dominicans and Recoletanos, and all approached, uncovered, and knelt before the image of the saint, and then reverently retired.

"The priests were followed by the wives of the members of the Junta, who came in the state carriage, a lumbering old wagon nearly a hundred years old. They were escorted by their husbands, mounted on horseback and dressed in ball-room costume. Their heavy sabres dangled by their sides; yet they were clothed in short knee-breeches and silk stockings, while their horses, trained for such special occasions to dance, moved on by the side of the carriage that dragged its ponderous weight through ruts of sand often eight and ten inches deep. This party was succeeded by Don Gregorio de la Cerda and twelve or fourteen of his comadres. The latter were in caravans, with awnings over them, and mattresses under the ladies to break the shock of the constant jolting of the clumsy wagon. They were drawn each by four oxen, and moved at the rate of two miles an hour. Then six out of the twelve comadres had infants with them. Don Gregorio (their guardian angel) was mounted on a superb white horse, caparisoned after the highest style of Spanish luxury and antiquity, and he had one favorite godson before and another behind him. No man was ever so rich in godchildren as Don Gregorio, and therefore no man was so potent. If a man wishes to become, in that country, a first-rate character, let him lay himself out to become a general godfather. After Don Gregorio came groups of officers in full dress, escorting each on horseback his favorite dulcinea. In many cases the lady rode on a pillion behind her dragoon, and not a few palfreys were mounted by two Paraguayan sylphs, escorted by their favorite *paysitos*, or young country beaux.

In poured the *tenderos*, or shopkeepers, in all their finery of upstart wealth and vulgarity; in came Dr. Burgos, powdered and pomatumed and frizzled from top to toe; in came the merchants, full of 'wise saws and modern instances'; and finally in came the late gentlemanlike, modest, and dignified Spanish Governor, General Velasco. He was attended simply by his butler and *valet-de-chambre* (for the faithful man served him in both capacities) and a groom.

"All his power was gone; his honors were laid in the dust; there were his rivals revelling in those attributes and distinctions which but a few months ago were exclusively his own; and yet not a frown not a symptom of jealousy or mortified pride clouded his brow. Good man, how little he deserved the awful fate which at a subsequent period overtook him during Francia's indiscriminating and unrelenting reign of terror!

"By the time the whole party was assembled, the shades of evening were beginning to throw their sombre hues over the scene of the lawn. The sun set in great splendor, and the moon rose in equal brightness. What added greatly to the romantic simplicity of the scene was, that, ever and anon, little groups of Paraguayan peasantry, uninvited, except by the report they had heard of the rejoicings that were to take place at Doña Juana's, came through the valley in different directions. They were escorted by one or two *guitarreros* (players on the guitar), who accompanied themselves on that instrument to some plaintive *triste*, or national ballad. As they emerged from behind the copses, or came out from the surrounding dark woods, in their white dresses, they looked in the distance like inhabitants of another world; and as their simple and harmonious music came undulating from different quarters upon the breeze, one might have fancied it a choral contribution of the shepherds of Arcadia.

"Very different were the revels within and immediately around the dwelling of Doña Juana. Some were dancing on the lawn, some in the saloons; some were cracking jokes amid peals of laughter loud and long; here was a party of friars busy at *malilla* (or whist), and there another rejoicing in the pleasures of the tempting wines and viands which were spread out for all. A few of the more bold of the holy fathers were winding through the mazes of the dance. They were distinguishable chiefly by their bulk from their fair partners, both being clad in petticoats.

"Here was a personage named Bedoya, nearly seven feet high, and with latitudinal amplitude much more than proportioned to his longitudinal dimensions. Still he was dancing with no small glee, and perspiring with no little profusion. The members of the government threw off all restraint, and danced, drank, and smoked cigars just like the rest of their subjects. Up got Doña Juana, in her eighty-fourth year, and danced a *sarandîg*, or heel-dance; swains with their nymphs crowded the orange-grove, and each there wooed 'his ain kind dearie.' The servants collected in groups round the fires lit in the groves for their cooking purposes; every little singing company, as it came up, was accommodated with room, and entertained with good cheer; defiance seemed to be bidden to the ills of life; and, uncouth as was the music of the church choirs, and vociferous as was the din of the guests, yet the whole scene had an air thrown over it of abundance, simplicity, and cordial hilarity, which I shall not soon forget.

"Both the light and the music of the revels must have reached Dr. Francia's cottage; and at this very time he was planning those schemes which have since been carried into execution, and have at once hushed hilarity and extinguished the light of liberty.

"The old Spanish Governor, Velasco, observed to me with remarkable and foreboding emphasis: 'Ah, Mr. Robertson, I am afraid this is the last scene of festivity we shall ever see in Paraguay!'

"At length the envious day broke in upon our revelries. The ladies began to look very wan, and the candles and lamps to grow very dim. The lungs of the musicians were exhausted; some of the friars had lost their money at cards, and many of the guests their wits over their wine. Mothers looked after their daughters, servants after their carriages and carts. Many husbands were, by their wives, caught napping, but all were obliged to obey orders. They ran into the paddock to catch their horses, and afterwards busied themselves in saddling them. Warm coffee and chocolate were handed round; servants bustled and equipages started; troops of hallooing horsemen took the road; off went the friars, and off with them the musicians. By nine o'clock in the morning there was nothing left to behold but the vestiges of the gayety of the night past."

Certainly this is not an unpleasant picture of domestic life. It does not indeed present a very high order of refinement or morality, but in all that for which the government was responsible it appears to have been unobjectionable. The people were happy and contented; they had freedom of thought and expression, and from the highest to the lowest were permitted without question the inalienable rights of "life, liberty, and the pursuit of happiness." If the morals were easy and the habits careless and unthrifty, it was not for the temporal power to correct them. The province of government is to give security of life and property, not to enforce sumptuary laws nor interfere with personal liberty so long as it does not offend public decency or the rights of others. If the standard of morality was low, it was the spiritual guides and teachers against whom this charge should be brought, not against the civil government whose functions are, or should be, limited to matters of material polity, leaving all questions of faith and ethics to private judgment. But not "to consider too curiously" the question of morality, it must be admitted that the Paraguayans were a happy people. There existed that freedom from constraint and that simplicity calculated to entice the romantic adventurers of all countries to emigrate thither; and the future of Paraguay, when the Spanish dominion was once thrown off, was full of promise. Yet this was the time when, according to Carlyle, "there occurred fatuities, mismanagements innumerable; then discontents, open grumblings, and, as a running accompaniment, intriguings, caballings, outings, innings; till the Government House, fouler than when the Jesuits had it, became a bottomless, pestilent inanity, insupportable articulate-speaking soul." Indeed, so corrupt was everything, according to our reviewer, that the one just man in Paraguay, the only hater of shams, the only man "who would do himself an injury to do a just or true thing under the sun," had left the government Junta with his moral sense shocked and disgusted. It was during this retirement that the *fête champêtre* of Doña Juana took place.

The signal for the return of Francia to become a second time a member of the Junta was the nomination, by the government of Buenos Aires, of Don Nicholas Herrera as diplomatic agent to proceed to Paraguay for the purpose of making a treaty of commerce and comity between the two nations. When the news of this nomination reached Asuncion, there was great consternation in the Junta and little less among the revolutionists generally. Francia busied himself by magnifying the importance of the impending negotiation, and labored to create a suspicion that the Porteños, having failed to subject Paraguay to her dominion by force of arms, was now seeking by diplomacy to accomplish the same thing. The public anxiety was naturally excited, and even of those who hated Francia, most admitted that he was more competent to treat with the coming envoy than any member of the Junta, or than any other Paraguayan. The old Governor Velasco was fully competent, and had the entire confidence of the people; but he was a Spaniard, and had been opposed to the revolution, and so it was with all the other Spaniards of wealth, education, or influence. The other members of the Junta, Yegros, Caballero, Bogarin, and Mora, felt their own incompetency, and they knew that their asesor, La Cerda, great as he was at managing neighborhood difficulties, competent as he was to demolish Vattel, and popular as he might be as godfather to all their children, the making of a treaty with a foreign power was not within the range of his peculiar talents. Francia was accordingly recalled to the Junta with the general acquiescence. In the mean while and during his retirement, he had managed to gain over to his support the officers in immediate command of the troops, and with them at his beck the real power was almost absolutely in his own hands. On his return, therefore, he did not come in as a member, but as director or ruler of the Junta. La Cerda was dismissed contemptuously, and Francia took the post of asesor. Mora was also dismissed, and, more fortunate than La Cerda, he was allowed to live for a while in the country. This, it should be borne in mind, was as early as 1813, and before there had ever been any hostile attempt against Francia either personally or politically. The date is important as showing that the excuses which have been made for Francia's cruelties were based on erroneous statements of facts. It has often been alleged that he had been driven to these severities by the repeated attempts on his life. As has been shown, the only outbreak since the revolution was a trick of his own to ensnare the unwary and find an excuse for murdering them; yet almost his first act after coming again into power was to order the arrest of La Cerda, and decree his banishment from the country within eight days. Of him says Robertson: "The universal compadre, the zealous friend, the powerful patron of almost all the principal people in Asuncion, they one and all deserted him, not, certainly, because in his misfortune they esteemed him less, but because they esteemed their own safety more. Such were the fears which they had already begun to entertain of the ruthless and jealous temper of the restored member of the Junta, Francia." When Robertson, who at that time was treated with familiarity and confidence by Francia, ventured with more fidelity and courage than discretion to speak to the asesor in behalf of his friend, who to do him a favor had demolished Vattel, he was answered thus: "I think it proper to send him out of the way, because he had the impudence, on my leaving the government, to take the assessorship of it, knowing I both hated and despised him." This in 1813, and Francia lived till 1840, and each year, as resistance became more hopeless, his tyranny became more severe, his acts more cruel.

The colleagues of Francia in the Junta did not venture to oppose him, as they well knew that the military were debauched, and that the officers in authority were ready to execute any order of the asesor. In fact, Francia was already absolute, though as yet feeling insecure in his position, and fearing lest too arbitrary measures should produce a reaction against him. The chains for the people were already forged. His next measure was to compel them to fix them irremovably on their own limbs. The means adopted to effect this was to convoke a Congress, and by intrigue and threats pass such measures as would be suicidal to individual liberty. Instructions were accordingly issued, soon after Francia's return to power, for the inhabitants of the different districts to send deputies to the Congress that was to decide on the important measure of a treaty of commerce and amity with Buenos Aires. Francia had long been preparing for the time when a Congress should be called, and now he took good care that the members sent from the different districts should be entirely at his control. As for the town members, he cared little whether they were friends or enemies, as he was sure to have a majority sufficient to overcome all opposition. In some cases his declared enemies were named members of this Congress for the very purpose of impaling them by their own acts. Let them vote against Francia or any of his proposed measures, they knew the awful fate that awaited them ; let them vote for him, and they would be committed to his policy.

The envoy from Buenos Aires, Don Nicholas Herrera, in due time arrived. His reception was similar to what a hawk might receive on alighting in a farm-yard full of poultry. People had already learned to be in mortal fear of Francia, and it was well known that he disapproved the idea of a treaty, and that whoever should show courtesy or hospitality to Señor Herrera would do so at his peril. The Minister is soon aware that he is an unwelcome guest. He is given inferior accommodations, and finds himself watched and followed at every step. He hears rumors of personal danger, and it is more than a week before he can get an interview with any member of the Junta.

In the mean while the time arrived that had been named for the meeting of the Congress. The deputies came in from all parts. Francia now became the prince of hosts, the most polite gentleman, the most attentive friend. He told them all that affairs were to be administered in a different way from formerly. The shop-keeper was to have greater ease and freedom in obtaining his wares from abroad, and in exporting the produce of the country; the more wealthy *estanciëro* was told that he was a man of great importance, and thenceforth should have a voice in the government ; the Indian alcalde was promised whatever he might chance most to want. In this way Francia conciliated the country deputies so that they were prepared to do the only work he had for them, and that was to rivet the fetters he had prepared for their own limbs, at the same time that they might be flattered into the belief that they were in reality the governing power.

The manner of convoking congresses in Paraguay from that time to the present has been somewhat different from what it is in the United States. The local officials in the different districts, or *partidos*, hold their authority direct from the supreme government at Asuncion, and they are bidden to send such and such men to the capital to attend the Congress. In these later years they pretended to go through a kind of election, but the names announced by the local judge, *juez*, and the chief of police, or *géfe*, are always unanimously returned. In Francia's time, however, the persons whose presence was desired at the Congress were called directly, and they dared not disobey the summons. This first Congress called by Francia consisted of about two hundred members. The large majority was from the country, and, from the appearance they made on their arrival in the capital it is believed that they had not been selected because of any superior ability as debaters or statesmen. In fact, they knew no more of the duties of a congressman than they did of the differential calculus. They were a motley set of Indian caciques, half-breeds, boatmen, country farmers, and village shop-keepers. The Indian thus honored would be the head man of an Indian village, who, holding a sort of commission from the central government, and acting in concert with a couple of friars, had authority over the natives. He would have all the Indian's love of finery and gaudy display, united to the formality and gravity of a Spanish hidalgo. Draped with ribbons and tinsel, borrowed probably from the priests for the solemn occasion, he would ride through the town, attended by two servants, in a dress like that worn before the first sin of Adam. Before leaving home they had all been made to understand that the great potentate before whom they were to appear was the Carai (*Lord*) Francia. On reaching the capital, therefore, each one would approach the Government House, before which there was, and is, a fine lawn, and pay his respects to the lean, scowling figure standing in the veranda to receive his homage by making his horse perform sundry tricks, after which he would solemnly file off and withdraw to make room for another deputy, who, though a landed proprietor, or shop-keeper, or *vaqueano* (herdsman) would go through a form of salutation as grotesque and absurd. In these exercises, which were repeated every day for weeks, the deputies thought they were fulfilling their duties as statesmen, overweighted by their responsibilities. But as the day for the opening of the Congress was postponed for two months after the arrival of the deputies, they got tired of the labors and honors of public life, and wanted to close up their official duties and return, the Indian to his village of mud-huts, the farmer to look to his crops, the vaqueano to his herds, and the shop-keeper to his store. They received no pay for their services, and the delay in opening the Congress was prolonged purposely by Francia, in order that the money they had brought with them should get exhausted, and the country members should become so tired of the city, and so eager to get home, that, when it should finally meet, they would ask no questions, but vote through everything submitted without hesitation or question.

During this time that the members were waiting in the capital till it should please Francia to open the Congress, they had been duly indoctrinated with a wholesome dread of any connection with Buenos Aires ; and when at last the day arrived, and they were summoned to attend the august assemblage, the question of the treaty was the first submitted to their consideration, and of course the measure was rejected. To consider that subject had been the ostensible motive in calling the Congress together, but Francia, finding it so plastic in his hands, proposed a measure of reform in the government that completely changed its character. This was to abolish the old Junta of five, and substitute for it two consuls, himself and Yegros, with joint and equal power, who were to be the government for the following year. This measure was sprung upon the Congress, and passed almost before any one but its contriver was aware of its meaning and purport. Francia was named the First Consul, and Yegros the Second. The selection of Yegros had been made for two reasons: first, he was popular with the people, and especially with the soldiers; and, second, he was ignorant and vain, and Francia was well aware that, by proposing him as his colleague, he would at the same time conciliate the people, while in no respect would his own power be divided.

These two measures having been acted on, the Congress was instantly dissolved, and the members, having seen "how absolute the knave was," were glad to escape from the city and return to their homes, fully satisfied with congressional honors.

Having attained all but absolute power, Francia set himself to improving the machinery of government, and doubtless effected some much-needed reforms. Routine, circumlocution, and delays had long been felt to be grievous evils in all matters of official administration, and it was well understood that justice was of that kind which could be had for a consideration. These abuses of subordinate officials who corruptly assumed power and responsibility were entirely inconsistent with Francia's plan of being absolute in everything. The abuses were stopped. The corrupt officials were degraded, and laziness and procrastination were no longer tolerated. Francia required prompt returns to him of everything that had been done by every petty official. Only by having everything quickly brought to his attention could he know and direct all.

The system of espionage that he had been gradually extending for years and while he was in retirement was now brought to a degree of perfection never known before. It was so thorough that people soon began to find that their most insignificant acts were known, and that opinions expressed the most confidentially, or, as they thought, not expressed at all, had reached the ears of the First Consul.

People might well think the theodolite had marvellous powers.

He now began that mode of life that he never varied till his death, twenty-seven years later. He personally attended to everything, without trusting to any one more than the dry, mechanical details, and all these were carefully inspected by an eye that gleamed with joy whenever it found an error, as it promised a feast of torture. Though no beadle of a parish workhouse was ever more inquisitive after the fragments, or more jealous of his power and the dignity due to his position, yet he was anxious to be regarded as the head of a government having its different departments and bureaus, each having its proper and independent duties. He would speak of "my government," "my people," "my army," "my marine," with all the pompous dignity of a speech from the throne of England. The following extract from Robertson, however, will show how well this dignity was kept up, and that while nature made Francia so ill that he was the worst possible ruler of a nation, he would have been stupendous as the governor of a poorhouse or as warden of a prison. Says Robertson: —

"Meantime my intercourse with the Consul not only continued, but increased. I had frequent citations to attend him at the Government House, or, as it was officially styled, Palace. Our interviews were always in the evening, and were sometimes protracted till eleven o'clock. Francia's greatest pleasure consisted in talking about the 'War Department'; and he would go into the most absurd minutiæ with a positively childish delight. On one occasion the gunsmith came in with three or four old muskets repaired. Francia held them up one by one to his shoulder, and pointing them, as in the act of firing, drew the trigger. When the flint struck good fire, the Consul was charmed, and said to me, 'What do you think, Mr. Robertson, will my muskets carry a ball to the heart of my enemies?' Next, the master tailor presented himself with a tight fit for a grenadier recruit. The man for whom the coat was made being ordered in, and stripped to try it on, got at length, after some very awkward attempts, his arms into it. The fit was not a very soldier-like one in my eyes; for I thought the high waist and the short, the very short, tails of Francia's grenadier coat rather uncouth. Still it was a fit according to the Consul's fancy, and he praised the tailor, and told the soldier to mind how he ever got a stain or *mancha* upon it. Last of all came in two sturdy mulattoes, one with a grenadier's bearskin cap, and another with brown belts and cartouch-box. They were all fitted on the martyr of a soldier, into whose hands finally Francia put one of the muskets. He then said, 'There, Mr. Robertson, this is the style in which every one of my grenadiers shall be equipped.' Such exhibitions as these were of frequent occurrence, and they always elicited glee and good-humor from Francia. His grenadier company was his great hobby; and I never saw a little girl dress out her doll with more self-importance and delight than did Francia, with his own hands, dress and fit out each individual grenadier of his guard."

What a hero for the great hero-worshipper! "Thou lonely Francia!"

CHAPTER XIII.

The Joint Consulship. — Francia's Views and Aspirations in Regard to an Alliance with Great Britain. — His Ignorance of European Affairs. — Perfects his System of Espionage. — Arbitrary Measures. — Decree concerning Marriages. — Its Influence upon the Morals of the Country. — Francia becomes the Head of the Church. — A Vicar-General appointed to administer the Spiritual Affairs of the Country. — Another Congress called. — The Consulship abolished. — Francia made Dictator. — Personal Habits of the Dictator, Mode of Life, Treatment of his Subordinates, Personal Appearance, Grotesque Costume, Vanity, and Egotism. — Military Displays.

THE joint consulship lasted but a year, when it expired by limitation. While it lasted, Francia directed and controlled everything as much as though he had been sole consul. But as Yegros desired to have some appearance of authority, it was arranged that orders should come nominally from him for the first three months, then from Francia for three months, then again for another quarter from Yegros, and the last three months from Francia. To give an idea of the united wisdom possessed by the two consuls, the following anecdotes from Robertson will suffice: —

"We had received letters from Buenos Aires, and were giving the consuls the latest news from Europe. We mentioned, among other things, that the Emperor Alexander had joined the general alliance against Napoleon, and that several vessels loaded with arms and munitions of war had been despatched from England to Russia. '*Malhaya!*' said Yegros, after considering awhile, — '*Malhaya soplara un viento sur largo y recio que trajese todos estos buques aguas arriba!*' — 'O that a long and strong south-wind would blow, and force all these vessels up the river.' Yegros fancied that if the south-wind blew long enough it would force every vessel bound for the Baltic up the Paraguay and into the port of Asuncion. 'Just consider,' said Francia, after his compañero, as he called him, was gone, 'if such an animal, such a fool as that, be capable of governing a republic!'"

Certainly this does not show Yegros to have been a geographer like Humboldt or Malte Brun. But his ignorance was shared by almost the entire people, and to this day nine tenths of the people of Paraguay imagine that all the countries of Europe and North America are situate *aquas abajo,* down river, and there are few who can tell whether London is in England or England in London, whether Europe is in North America or North America in Europe. They have heard the names of these countries, but have no other idea of where they are than that all who come from them come up the river. Francia, having been educated at a university, could hardly be so ignorant as that, but the following anecdote will show that his general knowledge was but little superior to that of his colleague.

The business of Robertson required his presence in Buenos Aires, and he also desired to return for a brief period to England. The port of Asuncion, however, was closed against all egress, and only by special favor of Francia could he get permission to leave the country. This he succeeded in obtaining, as the Consul had reasons of his own for wishing him to go to England. When he was about ready to start, Francia one day summoned him to his presence, and what happened afterwards I give as related by him: —

"On arrival at the Palace I was received with more than ordinary kindness and affability by the Consul. His countenance was lit up into an expression that almost approached to that of glee; his scarlet cloak depended in graceful folds from his shoulder; he seemed to smoke his cigars with unusual relish; and quite in opposition to his usual rule of burning only one light in his small and humble audience chamber, there blazed in it on that evening two of the best mould candles. Shaking hands with me very cordially, 'Sit down, Don Juan,' said he. He then drew his chair close to mine, and desired I would listen very attentively to what he had to say. He addressed me thus: —

"'You know what my policy has been with respect to Paraguay;

that I have kept it on a system of non-intercourse with the other provinces of South America, and from contamination by that foul and restless spirit of anarchy and revolution which has more or less desolated and disgraced them all. Paraguay is in a more flourishing state now than any of the countries around it; and while here all is order, subordination, and tranquillity, the moment you pass its boundary the sound of the cannon and the din of civil discord salute your ears. As may naturally be anticipated, these internal broils paralyze industry, and chase prosperity from the land. Now, whence arises all this? Why, from the fact that there is not a man in South America but myself who understands the character of the people, or is able to govern them. The outcry is for free institutions; but personal aggrandizement and public spoliation are the objects alone sought. The natives of Buenos Aires are the most fickle, vain, volatile, and profligate of the whole of Spain's late dominions in this hemisphere; and therefore I am resolved to have nothing to do with the Porteños. My wish is to promote an intercourse with England direct; so that whatever feuds may distract the other states, and whatever impediments they may choose to throw in the way of commerce and navigation, those states shall themselves be the sole sufferers. The ships of Great Britain, triumphantly sweeping the Atlantic, will penetrate to Paraguay, and, in union with our flotillas, will bid defiance to all interruption of commerce from the mouth of the Plate to the Lake Jarayes. Your government will have its minister here, and I shall have mine at the Court of St. James. Your countrymen shall traffic in manufactures and munitions of war, and shall receive in exchange the noble products of this country.'

"At this point of his oration the Consul rose with great emotion, but evident delight, from his chair, and calling to the sentinel at the door, desired him to order in the sergeant of the guard. On appearance of this person the Doctor gave him a significant and peremptory look, and told him emphatically to bring 'that.' The sergeant withdrew, and in less than three minutes returned with four grenadiers at his back, bearing, to my astonishment, among them, a large hide package of tobacco of two hundred weight, a bale of Paraguay tea of similar dimensions and exterior, a demijohn of Paraguay spirits, a long loaf of sugar, and several bundles of cigars, tied and ornamented with variegated fillets. Last of all came an old negress with some beautiful specimens of embroidered cloth made from Paraguay cotton, and used there by the luxurious as hand-towels and shaving-cloths.

"I thought this very kind and considerate; for though I could not but wonder at the somewhat barbarian ostentation in the mode of making the present, yet I never doubted that the accumulated native productions, now arranged in order before me, were intended as a parting manifestation of the Consul's regard. Judge, then, of my surprise (you will see it cannot bear the name of disappointment) when, after ordering his soldiers and the negress out of the room with a *vayanse* (begone), he broke forth in the following strain: —

"'Señor Don Juan, these are but a few specimens of the rich productions of this soil, and of the industry and ingenuity of its inhabitants. I have taken some pains to furnish you with the best samples which the country affords of the different articles in their respective kinds, and for these reasons: You are now going to England; you know what a country this is, and what a man I am. You know to what an unlimited extent these productions can be reared in this paradise, I may call it, of the world. Now, without entering upon the discussion as to whether this continent is ripe for popular institutions (you know I think it is not), it cannot be denied that, in an old and civilized country like Britain, where these institutions have gradually and practically (not theoretically) superseded forms of government originally feudal till they have forced themselves upon legislative notice in a ratio proportioned to the growing education of the majority, they are those best adapted to secure the greatness and stability of a nation. And that England is a great nation, and that its people are knit together as one man upon all questions of momentous national concern, is undeniable.

"'Now, I desire that, as soon as you get to London, you will present yourself to the House of Commons, take with you these samples of the productions of Paraguay, request an audience at the bar; inform the assembly that you are deputed by Don Gaspar Rodriguez de Francia, Consul of the Republic of Paraguay, to lay before it these specimens of the rich productions of that country. Tell them I have authorized you to say that I invite England to a political and commercial intercourse with me; and that I am ready and anxious to receive in my capital, and with all the deference due to diplomatic intercourse between civilized states, a minister from the Court of St. James; I also will appoint to that Court an envoy of my own.

"'Such a treaty of commerce and political alliance may then be framed as shall comport at once with the dignity and interests of the great empire of England, and with those of the rising state which I now rule. Paraguay will be the first republic of South America, as Great Britain is already the first of European nations. The alliance seems, therefore, natural; and how beneficial for the European state, you, Señor Don Juan, can fully elucidate and explain.'

"Such were the terms, and almost the words, in which Francia delivered himself of his views and aspirations in reference to an alliance with Great Britain. I stood, as you may imagine, aghast, at the idea of being appointed a minister plenipotentiary, not to the Court of St. James, but to the House of Commons. I was charged especially not to take a private interview with the head of the executive. 'For,' said Francia, 'I know well how apt great men in England are, unless under the fear of responsibility to the House of Commons, to treat questions even so important as this with levity or disregard.

"'Present yourself,' continued he, 'at the bar of the House, and there deliver my message, as of old the ambassadors of independent states delivered theirs to the senate of Rome. According to the reception which they shall give to you, one of their countrymen, and above the suspicion, therefore, of being a witness in my favor, shall be the reception (*acogimiento*) which I will extend to their ambassador to this republic.'

"Never in my life was I more puzzled how to act or what to say. To refuse the Quixotic mission, and thus incur at once the Consul's displeasure and draw down upon my own devoted head the ruinous consequences of it, was an alternative too horrible to be thought of. The only other was to acquiesce; and to this I came, in spite of the strong sense of the ludicrous which pressed itself upon me, as I drew a picture of myself forcing my way to the bar of the House of Commons; overpowering, with half a dozen porters, the Usher of the Black Rod, and delivering, in spite of remonstrance and resistance, at once my hide-bound bales of Paraguay merchandise, and the oration, verbatim, of the First Consul. But Assumption was a great distance from St. Stephen's. I therefore bowed assent to Dr. Francia's proposition, and trusted to the chapter of accidents for providing me, when the time should come, with a suitable apology for having been unable to get into the predicament which he had so graciously prepared for me.

"Having taken leave, the sergeant and grenadiers, heavily laden, followed me home, where I not a little astonished the new-comer, my brother, with the account of the diplomatic interview to which I had been called. I bade defiance to his scepticism on the subject, by making the soldiers unload at his feet the ponderous physical evidence by which I sustained the truth of my tale.

"At a subsequent interview, Francia made out a long list of commissions for me to execute. I was to bring him gold lace, a cocked hat, a dress sword, a pair of double-barrelled pistols, sashes, sabres, soldiers' caps, musical and mathematical instruments, with a very protracted detail of et ceteras. About the procuring of these, however, I had by no means so many misgivings as in regard to my power of persuading Mr. Speaker and the House of Commons to accede to the political and commercial league of which the Consul was so full.

"Thus did matters stand. I was to sail in a fortnight, with an exclusive license for the exportation of my property and person, and upon an understanding that, if I proceeded home, I should do there my endeavors to bring about an intercourse between England and Paraguay, which I was about as likely to effect as a junction between any two of the planets the most remote from each other in our system.

"A circumstance occurred, during our interview, curiously illustrative of the growing despotism, the abrupt manner, and rude disregard of propriety which Francia was taking daily less pains to conceal, whenever his capricious humor was at variance with anything said or done by those around him. The question with him was not how unconsciously offence might be given : it was enough that it was taken. He stopped not to inquire whether it was the result of ignorance, or even of well-meant deference and assiduity. His irritable and jaundiced temper sought, at the moment, something on which to vent its spleen ; and the innocent and guilty were alike immolated at the shrine of his caprice. In the instance referred to, while Francia was dilating to me upon his prospective alliance with Great Britain, the sentry announced as being in the lobby the Minister of Finance. This office was then united with that of Director of Customs, though the double functionary was no better than a subordinate clerk of the Consul. It was the duty and the daily practice of the financial minister to be in attendance, at a certain hour, in the lobby of the haughty Doctor, at once to give an account of the transactions of the day and to take instructions for to-morrow. The hour of this accustomed interview was now occupied by Francia in the opening up to me of day-dream projects, much more fraught with importance to him than the routine account of a day's receipt and expenditure of the treasury, albeit, on ordinary occasions, this was exacted, to the last maravedi, with scrupulous and inquisitorial severity.

"'*El Señor Tesorero aguarda,*'—'Mr. Treasurer waits,' said the sentinel. '*Que aguarde,*'—'Let him wait,' replied the Consul. Two hours did the Consul's harangue to me and subsequent explanations occupy; and when, at the close of it, he saw me off, escorted by the grenadiers with the tobacco and yerba bales on their shoulders, the treasurer was still pacing up and down the corridor of the Palace, and waiting, as he had been ordered to do, his master's further commands. Upon seeing Francia come out, the Minister of Finance went up to him, and, most respectfully taking off his hat, asked him if he were that night to give in his accounts. 'Take him to the guard-house,' said the supercilious despot. 'Did I not tell the fellow (*el bribóor*) to wait? and now he must needs ask questions.'

"Off was the Chancellor of the Exchequer marched to the guard-house, and there, on a bullock's raw hide, in company with the soldiers, was he constrained to ruminate all night on the danger of breaking in upon the Consul's associations, even for the purpose of rendering an account of his stewardship."

The cannie Scotchman prized his life and liberty too highly to tell the Consul to his face how ridiculous was the mission on which he proposed to send him. That he did not tell him so at the time and march off to prison immediately afterwards, to be shot at the tyrant's convenience, instead of seeming to acquiesce and thus save his life to write and publish his recollections of Francia's atrocities, seems greatly to have surprised the hero-worshipper. "A man who said he would do, and then did not do, was at no time a man admirable to Francia." *

* Carlyle's Essay on Francia, Foreign Quarterly Review.

During the year of the consulship, Francia worked incessantly to perfect his system of espionage. He was insidiously working through the lowest and vilest agents to find out family secrets, to learn from the servants if they had ever overheard anything to his disparagement. He was then preparing for his great work of vengeance. But as if to provoke inimical expressions he resorted to a measure the most revolting and humiliating to the old Spanish families that could possibly be devised. This was the publication of a decree prohibiting all Spaniards from contracting marriage except with negresses or mulattoes. This bitter insult proclaimed through the town by a crier, accompanied by a drum and fife, was felt not only to be shamefully degrading, but it blighted the hopes of many who were looking forward to a life of virtue. It was the more galling from the superiority that the Spaniards had always assumed over the creoles. The native Spaniards, not only in Paraguay, but throughout all South America, even though they were but tinkers, cobblers, or rag-pickers at home, considered that they were doing honor to any part of South America in which they should condescend to reside, and that the richest and oldest families must needs be flattered by their attentions. This conceit Francia took as a direct insult to himself, for was he not a native of the country?

The effect of this cruel insult was such as might have been expected and was doubtless intended. It not only humbled the Spaniards, so that those who had been accustomed to boast their *sangré azul* might well envy the native-born Paraguayans, even those having a shade of the Indian tint, but it prevented marriage and encouraged licentiousness. Persons previously engaged, finding they could never marry, adopted the practice of illicit cohabitation, and as the proudest and most intelligent were among the first to set the example, it soon ceased to be a scandal, or illegitimacy a reproach. Even before Francia's time the morals of the people were extremely slack. The influence of the Jesuits in this respect had been entirely and wholly bad, as their system encouraged profligacy in their neophytes in the same way as was lately the custom on the slave plantations of the South. Men and women were made to live together in one case as it pleased the padres, and in the other as it suited the planters, with no respect to family ties or the loves and likings of the persons most interested. After the expulsion of the Jesuits, the influence and example of the priests were equally bad, as they were generally scandalously dissolute, and the coif or cowl was considered but as a covering for a licensed seducer. Their nasal sanctity, under cloak of which they imposed on those who feared their displeasure, gave not only the cynical Francia, but every intelligent person, reason to despise them. But it was not because of their lazy and dissolute lives that he hated them. The morals of the people gave him no concern. But the priests, in spite of their gross sensuality, had great influence, especially among the lower classes, among whom Francia was resolved to be all powerful. A church government like that existing in Paraguay, which exercised authority independent of the civil power, being, as it was, of a secret and inquisitorial character, was inconsistent with his absolute rule, and he destroyed it as ruthlessly as he had destroyed all the other barriers to his despotic sway. He did not object to people confessing to the padres, but the padres must then confess to him all they had heard in the confidence of the confessional. These requirements greatly scandalized the bishop and some of the priests, when Francia made short work of their scruples by taking all the church property into his own hands, degrading and persecuting the bishop till he became insane, and appointing a creature of his own, whom he called the vicar-general, to administer the spiritual affairs of the country. The principal convent, that of San Francisco, was taken for soldiers' barracks, the street processions were suppressed, the assembling in the churches at night was forbidden, and Francia was head of the church within his own dominions.

The joint consulship expired in October, 1814, but before its expiration Francia took good care to have another Congress called, and such a one as he could easily control. This time the order was given that the Congress should consist of a thousand members, and the different partidos were assessed for the number they must send, in much the same manner as they were required to contribute cattle for the use of the state. The local magistrates holding their authority from Francia, whose word was law with them, made the selections, and when all was ready set out for the capital, driving along their conscripted members of Congress as though they had been recruits for the army or cattle for the shambles. Of the thousand deputies thus favored with office and honors, seven eighths at least were from the country districts; and as they could expect no pay for their services, and money was a very scarce commodity with them, they brought with them such country produce as they had to defray their expenses while serving the state. As on the former occasion, the members were anxious to get through their business as soon as possible and get away. Francia arranged the order of proceedings to his satisfaction at two preliminary meetings, at which his confidential friends had the whole direction. His first object was to get Yegros out of the way, as both he and Caballero were, in spite of all his efforts, still dangerously popular with the rank and file of the troops. The first measure proposed, therefore, was that, instead of two consuls, there should be one chief magistrate, to be called a Dictator.*

The subsequent proceedings are thus described by Robertson: —

"The proceedings were opened by Mr. Speaker about nine o'clock in the morning, and notwithstanding all the precautions which Fran-

* Among the deputies was Francisco La Guardia, who, like Francia, had been educated at the University of Cordova. He had gone thither at the recommendation of Francia, and taken letters from him certifying to his attainments and character. He was absent twelve years, and on his return Francia was the secretary, or asesor, of the first Junta. He was living when I was in Paraguay, and from him I learned many things of Francia and his times. He proposed in the Congress, that the choice of a Dictator, the question of a dictatorship having been already settled, should be decided by lot. Though this proposition was rejected, Francia was greatly displeased with his quondam *protégé*. Yet, strange to say, he survived the Dictator.

cia had taken, some awkward inquiries began to be made about the propriety of a dictatorship. The services and abilities of Francia were spoken of in the highest terms, indeed he was loaded with the most extravagant praises; but it was doubted whether a dictatorship would conduce so much to his glory as a more limited power, assisted by a national Congress. Hereupon debates commenced and heats ensued. I went up myself to the church about twelve o'clock. The doors were shut, but great confusion seemed to prevail within. At last one of the dimity-jacketed members came out wiping his forehead, and seeming to have suffered much either from the heat of the church or of the debate. 'How go things within, my friend?' said I to the Representative. 'Why,' replied the honest member, 'to tell you the truth, these are matters that I do not pretend at all to understand; but I judge from the noise that all goes well.'

"About two o'clock, as the members of Congress were still in warm debate, Francia got impatient, and very politely sent a numerous guard of honor to wait on the members. The troop was well armed, and quite surrounded the church. This hint was sufficient even for the clod-pated deputies in dimity jackets; besides, the dinner-hour was past, and hunger as well as the mustaches of the Quarteleros hastened a decision. At this juncture, one of the most energetic of Francia's partisans rose, and in a stentorian voice called silence. 'Gentlemen,' said he, 'why should we waste our time here? The Carai (Lord) Francia wishes to be absolute, he ought to be absolute, and I say' (here he struck the table at which he stood with his whole force) 'he shall be absolute!' The question was then put to the vote, and without one dissentient voice Francia was invested with the dictatorship for three years. The Congress dissolved itself instanter; the Quarteleros marched to the Government House with flying colors; and Francia heard, with the malignant sneer of a devil on his face, that Paraguay was all his own.

"The insensate populace celebrated with mirth and music and festive meetings that night the decision of the Congress. Alas, the low sobs and moanings of those who were destined soon to be bereaved widows and wretched orphans, the heavy sighs of the prisoners, and the groans of those whose blood was erelong to irrigate the streets of Asuncion, ought alone to have announced that Francia was Dictator of Paraguay!"

Nearly fifty years later, the people of Paraguay were called upon to rejoice at the happy result of another election. A worse than Francia had succeeded to power, — one whose career was to be marked by acts of violence and cruelties compared with which those of Francia were mild and gentle, and they were to cease only when the extermination of the race should leave no more victims to his vengeance. At that time there were no insensate cheers; though the cannon belched forth their salvos, and bands of music played martial and joyful airs, and wine and spirits were freely circulated, there was no popular enthusiasm, no joy on any face. The people seemed to have a premonition of their impending fate, and that the peals of the cannon were but heralding the doom of their extinction as a people!

Though Francia had won over to himself most of the subordinate officers, yet the rank and file of the troops were very much dissatisfied when they found that the new Congress had left their old and favorite general out of the government. So great was the disaffection that an outbreak was feared. But the commandant of the cuartel, Caballero, who had been in the first Junta, had fought with credit against Belgrano, and been one of the most influential promoters of the revolution, though known to be an enemy to Francia, sacrificed his personal feelings and went to the cuartel, and by his personal influence among the troops prevailed upon them to return to duty and accept the new arrangement. This magnanimous act on the part of Caballero was afterwards requited by Francia as he and his imitator Lopez requited everybody that ever did him or the state a service. To deserve well of the state was enough to make a mortal enemy of Francia, and as we go on following his career we shall find the road strewn with the heads of the men who deserved the gratitude of their countrymen.

The motion submitted to the Congress to make Francia Dictator included the two provisions that he should be styled His Excellency and receive the annual salary of nine thousand dollars; but with ostentatious self-denial he refused to receive but a third part of that sum, saying that the state had more need of the balance than he had. He might as well have refused to accept anything, for the whole revenue of the country was paid directly into his hands, and he confiscated at pleasure the fortunes of everybody, and gave no account to any one of the way in which the money was expended. The income of the country was neither more nor less than Francia's salary; and from that day till the end of the Lopez rule, if any person had ventured to inquire how the public revenue was spent, he would soon have found himself where his complaints would not reach beyond four walls.

And here it seems opportune to speak of the personal habits of the Dictator. His mode of life was always very simple and regular. He cared nothing for good eating or drinking. He seldom took wine, and his meals never consisted of more than two or three very plain dishes. Like all Paraguayans he smoked a great deal. Before he aspired to rule, he was addicted to gambling, and was a gross libertine, whose mind had been so corrupted by indulgence that his tastes led him to seek such intrigues that a half-breed slave would scorn to be his rival. After he attained the supreme power, he gave up gambling and intrigues that might draw attention, never allowing any woman to approach him except his negro domestics. His temperance and frugality in regard to the pleasures of the table have been much commended, as though these were great and extraordinary virtues. His indifference to all his kindred has also been often adduced as evidence of his honesty and disinterestedness. But what if his table expenses, instead of being half a dollar a day, had been fifty times that sum, it would have been as a grain of sand on the sea-shore compared with the hundreds of thousands he was constantly extorting from his miserable people. His own fortune was amply sufficient for all his wants, and that he did not squander the money of the state for what he had no taste or desire for is made a merit by his excusers. It was his only one, and well may they make the most of that. That he never favored any of his blood relations at the expense of the state is in itself to his credit, but Francia was so intensely selfish, so egotistical, and so indifferent to everything but his own power and person, that he knew no such thing as ties of kindred or natural affection. His nearest relatives he imprisoned or put to death without remorse or compunction, and no one could assign any other reason for it than that he wanted to impress on every one how terribly, unmovably, absolute he was. What merit not to enrich at the expense of the state those whom at the slightest whim he was ready to murder!

Francia, like all tyrants who give way to their cruel propensities, was a great coward, and in constant fear of assassination. From the time that he first became Dictator till the final expulsion of the younger Lopez, conspiracy and assassination were the perpetual dread of the despot in power. They all seemed to realize that they had committed such cruel injustice towards individuals and families, there must necessarily be many who, if the opportunity were offered them, would improve it by ridding themselves of the perpetrator. To guard against any attempt upon his life, the Dictator, in the early days of his power, ordered that every person who happened to be in the street as he passed through it should stand motionless and uncovered, with his arms by his sides and head bowed, until he had gone by. This, however, did not seem to be a sufficient precaution, so that his guards were instructed frequently to cut down with their sabres such people as chanced to be in those streets through which he was to pass. After that, as soon as it was known that he was out, people fled to their houses, shut their doors, and the town, so far as he could see, had the appearance of being entirely deserted. He had several houses in which he was accustomed to sleep, but no one knew until the afternoon before which one he would select for the coming night. His more usual residence was in the old Government House, which is yet standing, though he passed a great deal of his time at the hospital, which was a little out of town, upon an acclivity on which no other buildings were standing. His object in changing so often was supposed to be to defeat any plan of conspiracy that might possibly have been concocted without his knowledge. The life that a man must lead in this constant fear, with no other reason than that he knows he has given many people good cause for assassinating him at sight, one would suppose to be as wretched as it is possible to endure in this world. Francia, however, passed a life of this kind for nearly thirty years, which could hardly have been possible had he not been conscious, during the last years of his reign, that all hope of escape from his tyranny, and even the natural feelings of resentment, had ceased to exist in the minds of the people, and had he not become aware that whatever he might do would be as passively submitted to as a decree of fate. After the departure of the Swiss doctors, there is no record or tradition that he ever spoke to a human being, though he lived sixteen years longer, except as to a dog or to an abject slave. He never conversed with anybody further than when some unhappy subject would apply to him for some slight favor, on which occasion, if the person were permitted to enter his dark and narrow room, he would rise up from his table, having two loaded pistols lying upon it before him, and when the humble suppliant had entered the door, he was compelled, not only to keep his hands down, but to keep them rigid and fixed at an angle of some fifteen or twenty degrees from his body, to show that he had no weapon in either of them, and if he had any about his person, this position would enable Francia to make use of his own pistols before the petitioner could do him any harm. The unhappy man, half frightened to death, would stop as soon as he was within the room, some fifteen or twenty feet from Francia, when the haughty Dictator would ask what he wanted. The petitioner would make his petition, when, according to the whim which took the Dictator, he would either grant the request and send him away, or perhaps pour out a torrent of abuse, order his arrest, and send him to the prison or the *banquillo*. This was the extent of his social intercourse for sixteen years. Even to his domestic servants he maintained his gloomy taciturnity. Of these he had three, all females, one of whom was supposed to hold another relation to him. None of them, however, ever dared to speak to him to tell him that anything was wanted in the house, even to supply his own necessities. He allowed them a few reals a day to obtain the food necessary for the house. The cost of what he consumed himself did not probably exceed a single shilling a day. A little soup, or *puchero,* a bit of bread (or *chipa,* a substitute made from the flour of the mandioca), a taste of *dulce,* of the preserved fruit of the country, together with, occasionally, a glass of milk, and the frequently taken *maté,* or Paraguay tea, sufficed for all his wants in the way of eating and drinking. In the evening, when the sentinels were set and the spies at work, he would sit for hours with his chair leaning against a tree in the yard, his chin upon his breast, apparently absorbed in thought. No one could approach him, no one of his servants would venture to address him, unless to convey to him a message from the outside. So great was the dread of his servants, that they dared not speak to him of any domestic matter. They moved about as silently as if in the presence of death, and yet they were sometimes afraid lest they might offend him by not advising him of what was required for the next day's necessities. On such occasions, two of them would contrive to be near him and whisper to each other, intending to be overheard, that there was this thing wanted for the Carai's (Lord's) dinner the next day; that there was no milk, no more yerba, no money to go to market with. Thus advised of what was required, Francia would provide whatever was needed, and give such orders as would relieve the servants of their difficulties. He had no pet or favorite animal, and in fact he lived, as it were, conscious of being universally feared and hated. In this way his life was passed, not a friend to console, not an eye to greet him except in distrust and fear. "Thou lonely Francia!"

Of the all-absorbing vanity that on his attainment of power caused him to disregard every sentiment of honor and every feeling of pity, which are supposed to affect all the human race, but which certainly never affected him, there is very little recorded, and in the nature of the case little more of it can ever be known than what has been recorded by Robertson and Rengger. These were the only persons that in a period of more than a quarter of a century he ever allowed to approach him with anything like familiarity. The former left the country in 1815, and the latter in 1826. The dark days of his reign are considered as having hardly begun before Robertson quitted the scene. He had up to that time put no one to death, except those that were killed in his pretended counter-revolution. But even then, and while he was Consul, his countrymen approached him with such fear that their words would almost stick in their throats.

"Sometimes," says Robertson, "while conversing with me, his guard would announce visitors; they were often sent away, sometimes admitted. In this latter case Francia assumed a cold and stern inflexibility of feature. He stood erect. The crouching applicant came to the door. 'What do you want?' Francia would abruptly and harshly say. The want was expressed with tremor or with profound reverence. '*Bien-retirese,*' — 'Very well, retire.' The self-constituted intruder would retire accordingly, too happy to escape from the presence of the haughty Consul; and then the latter would turn to me and resume his discourse. . . . . His conversation was chiefly of a political nature, and he himself was the centre of perfection to which all his observations pointed. If he touched on scientific or literary subjects, it was still to boast of some acquirement of his own. His vanity, under a thin skin of pretended indifference to fame or applause, oozed out at every word he pronounced. His own government, his own political sagacity, his wisdom, his acquirements, he constantly contrasted with those of others, and as constantly to his own advantage. Paraguay was a Utopia realized, and Francia was the Solon of modern days.

"He spoke contemptuously of all Europe with the exception of England. Paraguay and England, England and Paraguay, — these were the enlightened countries which he wished to see united, like the Siamese twins, firmly and irrevocably in one.

"He could not bear to hear of the celebrity, glory, or renown of any South-American but himself. General San Martin, the great and honest champion of South American independence, and General Alvear, at that time the successful and energetic leader of the fortunes of Buenos Aires, he hated with a deadly hate. It was when speaking of them alone that I used to see all the malignity of Francia's character. He always began his discourses about his celebrated contemporaries with affected and bitter contempt; but he invariably ended with violent and passionate declamation."

Though Francia, with the exception of England, despised all Europe, including France, he yet condescended to think and speak highly of Napoleon, whom he complimented as being very like himself. How this must have soothed the great captive at St. Helena could he have known it, and also known of the military exploits of his South American champion! In some way Francia had become possessed of one of those unsightly caricatures of Napoleon, such as were very common in many parts of Europe at the time that his great military successes were astonishing the world, and he was painted as a monster or an ogre whose daily rations were "three sheep a day and all the children he could catch." This caricature represented the great captain as dressed in a most grotesque manner. But Francia had taken it for a real likeness, and adopted the style of dress, doubtless thinking that two men so much alike should dress in the same manner. We have no copy of that picture, but from the style of dress that he adopted on his military parades we may judge how like it was to the well-known gray overcoat, cocked hat, and generally plain attire, that is always suggested by the name of Napoleon. Though Francia affected such contempt for everybody, yet, as we have seen, it was gall and wormwood for him to witness public admiration and respect for any one but himself. Yegros and Caballero, who had distinguished themselves in the war and in the revolution, and who, being military men, moved about in gold lace, would by general accord have places of honor assigned to them, and wherever they might go people would give way to them or respectfully salute them as they passed. Such deference to them, while Francia passed unobserved and unnoticed, was to a man of his insensate, intense vanity nothing less than criminal. But he had his revenge. The time came when he too could dress in uniform, not indeed like a poor general of gauchos, but like the other famous warrior, the great Napoleon. But it is hardly probable that even the caricature showed a uniform so grotesque as Francia thought necessary to adopt in order to display his multiform greatness. He must have a dress symbolical of his many great qualities. Unfortunately, nature had not given him the physique of a hero.* He was about five feet ten inches in height, lean and cadaverous almost as a mummy, with bony, shrunken hands, and legs so attenuated and fleshless that the genius of Famine would have disowned them. A "whiskered pander" he could not be, for though he tried very hard he could never coax whiskers to his face. On his upper lip he succeeded in beating up some straggling furze that would pass for mustaches, but on his cheeks and chin he could never raise enough to more than show the barrenness of the soil. His long, dank, coarse hair, drawn back, hung about his neck and shoulders, while his sharp features, sallow face, and devilish black eyes made him appear as hopeless a figure to pad or stuff into anything officer-like in appearance as ever perplexed a court tailor. It had long been his habit, before he was

* I have never seen or heard of but two pictures that pretended to be likenesses of Francia. An engraving from one of these is given in Robertson's Letters on Paraguay. In this he is represented as a tall, well-formed man, answering to the following description as given in the book: "I beheld a gentleman of about fifty years of age, dressed in a suit of black, with a large scarlet *capote*, or cloak, thrown over his shoulders. . . . . The stranger's countenance was dark, and his black eyes were very penetrating, while his jet hair combed back from a bold forehead, and hanging in natural ringlets over his shoulders, gave him a dignified and striking air. He wore on his shoes large gold buckles, and at the knees of his breeches the same." The picture is evidently a sketch from memory, and in no sense a portrait or likeness, as it is certain that Robertson, leaving Paraguay as he did, could not have brought away a portrait of the Dictator, and he had no communication with him afterwards.

The engraving given as a frontispiece to this volume is from a painting of which there were several photographic copies in Paraguay a few years ago. I could never learn when it was painted or the name of the artist. The old people there who remembered the face, figure, and garb of the Dictator, said it was an excellent likeness, and that the style of dress in which he is represented is that in which he always, for more than twenty-five years, appeared in public. The attitude and surroundings of the portrait are such as a pedant and charletan would naturally select.

Dictator, to dress in knee-breeches, silk stockings, and light, thin shoes, and he boasted that he had never worn boots since he was a student. Whether or not the caricature of Napoleon represented him with his lower extremities thus clad is not now known; but if it did not, Francia would not for that reason give up his tights and pumps. He probably thought these gave him more the appearance of a civic ruler. His entire costume, when he went forth, was as follows: First his knee-breeches and stockings, both of silk, fastened at the knees with gold buckles; his low, light shoes, also with gold buckles, and his military spurs fastened over his stockings; then a Spanish military coat, with much gold lace and many bright buttons; and upon his head a high cocked hat, with a large, erect, red feather, and a cockade brilliant and gaudy. On his left breast he wore a star of dimensions so grand, and so elaborately wrought with different colors, as to resemble a lamp-mat inlaid with blue, red, and white beads. This star or badge, says Robertson, was copied from the Nuremberg caricature. Around his waist he wore a blue satin sash, with a large tassel at each end. At his side he carried a long cavalry sword with steel scabbard. Thus gorgeously arrayed, he was prepared to mount his charger. The steed destined to the honor of bearing this mighty conqueror was caparisoned with bridle and saddle heavily mounted with silver, and a pair of holsters, in each of which was a loaded double-barrelled pistol. These arms were probably worn to show his valor, as we have known many who, before "the age of *Southern* chivalry was gone," always, in times of the most perfect quiet and order, went about loaded down with revolvers and bowie-knives to show that they were men of courage. But his outfit is not complete without his emblem of civic authority, which consists of a cane, or staff, with a gold head and black tassel, that has a socket fitted to hold it affixed in front of him to the saddle. With all these insignia of military and civil power he mounts his horse to marshal his legions. With his sabre drawn, he leads forth his two or three companies of cavalry. These men, who are a sort of "old guard," have every one been equipped under his own eye, and they follow him to the field where glory waits them. "At slow time!" exclaims the Dictator. "At quick time!" he next cries out, as soon as they come into an open space. "Charge at full gallop!" when they dash forward against the enemy, who would doubtless turn and fly, or fall by thousands, if they were only there. But as none except imaginary foes were to be found, after half an hour's slaughter of them the order would come to halt, when, instead of distributing prizes or conferring the order of the Legion of Honor, he would send his aids to beat over the head and shoulders any one who had been unable, from having an inferior or fractious horse, to keep in the ranks. These were all the military achievements that Francia ever took part in. During the long term of his reign, there were many occasions when the Indians of the Chaco and to the North became troublesome, and parties were sent to chastise them, but Francia never ventured where he imagined there was any danger. His cowardice was consistent with his whole character. Hating everybody and delighting in cruelty, he had a consciousness that everybody hated him, and would, if they could or dared, do him an injury. In every act of his life he acted on that hypothesis; and devoured by the conceit that he was of more importance than all else in the world, he would put to death the best men in the country with no more compunction than most persons would feel at killing a troublesome mosquito.

CHAPTER XIV.

Condition of the Country under the Rule of the Dictator. — Government Spies: their Modes of Operation. — Universal Distrust. — Officers and Soldiers licensed Libertines. — The Dictator in Public. — Humiliating Observances. — Another Congress called, 1817. — Francia made Perpetual Dictator.

A GOVERNMENT like that of Francia could only be supported by force. The fears of the people might cause them to endure a tyrant whom they detested. Of this Francia was well aware, and he gradually gathered into his own hands all the reins of authority by surrounding himself with persons of low character, who were entirely dependent upon him. Suspicious of every one, he resorted to every device to learn the sentiments of all who had either wealth or influence. The whole military force of the country was subject to his orders, and his first thought was so to organize it as to make it a grand engine of *espionage*. In imitation of Dionysius, who had a room so built that every whisper uttered in it would reach his own ear in a distant apartment, Francia sought to make Paraguay a great whispering gallery, where every word expressed or thought entertained should come to his knowledge. It was the duty of every policeman and every soldier in the country to be a spy, and report all he saw. Woe to him if he knew aught that could be construed to any one's prejudice, and failed to do it! To effect this, those officers and soldiers who had been for some time in the service, and who had friends or families in the capital, were gradually weeded out, and replaced by others from the lowest ranks, and mostly from the interior. These were taught to look to Francia for every benefit and for everything necessary to existence. They soon found that the most direct road to favor was by insolence and rapacity towards the better class of people, and especially the old Spanish families and those creoles having most Spanish blood in their veins. Their discipline was of the severest kind in all things relating to their duties as police, soldiers, or spies, and they were shown no mercy if caught delinquent in the least point of their assigned routine. But off duty they were permitted to indulge in almost every license. They were privileged ravishers, against whom it was dangerous to protest. For more than a quarter of a century the dread of these favored libertines was such that no woman who wished to be regarded as respectable dared venture into the streets, unless so accompanied by her family or friends that their very number might protect her from insult or worse. The houses of such were all this time like prisons. There were no social gatherings; there was neither laughter nor social converse, except in subdued tones and on the most commonplace subjects. Every man feared his neighbor as being a spy on his actions; and yet, notwithstanding the greatest caution, every little while some person's absence from his home and haunts would be noticed by his neighbors, and some servant or member of his family would be seen taking his food through the streets towards the prison. Nobody would know what had been his offence, nor would any one dare to inquire. A question regarding any act of the Dictator was enough to insure the inquirer years of imprisonment.

So searching and thorough was the system of espionage that distrust was universal, and no one dared to trust a secret to any other person. The object of the Dictator seemed to be to make everybody afraid of everybody else, so that, whatever animosity his tyranny might create in the breast of any individual, he would fear to confide in any friend or companion. In this way, he would be sure that there could be no combination against him. To create this impression, he resorted to every kind of eavesdropping; he would have his secret police in league with the servants of the better class of families, to gather from them any chance remark, any expression of discontent, that might be made from husband to wife, or wife to daughter, or daughter to lover. Somehow, and in a way that people could not imagine, all their secret thoughts seemed to reach the Dictator, till it came to this, that no man dared speak to a living soul of anything that might reflect on the beneficent rule of the Dictator. But it was not enough to say nothing. It was expected that every man should constitute himself a spy on everybody else, and if his own wife were to let fall an expression of discontent, that he should hurry to the Dictator to denounce her. If he failed to do that, and it came to the Dictator's ears by any other channel, away they would both be sent to prison, whence, in all probability, they would never come out alive.

His two favorite and most trusted spies, in the earlier part of his tyranny, were his barber, and an inspector of yerba named Orrego. The barber, who was a black, dirty, fat, and lazy fellow, was the last person one would suspect of being a spy. He was so good-natured as to appear almost silly, and always ready to condole with those who were afflicted, and to express sorrow for those who had incurred the Dictator's displeasure. But woe to them if, in his hearing, a question, or even a sigh, escaped them! His innocent, stolid face would show nothing but compassion or pity, but in his next attendance on the Dictator the whole story of his discoveries would be revealed. But the blow would not fall immediately; time would be allowed to elapse, so that the barber might not be suspected as the informant.

The inspector Orrego, who, besides being a government official, kept a *pulperia*, or drinking-house, is thus described by Robertson: —

"He was a joyous and good-natured-looking little man, not much more than five feet high, with a portly body, a round and laughter-loving face, and a look of easy indifference and simplicity which would have made you believe him altogether incapable of guile or deceit. He used to wear a gaudy-colored handkerchief about his head, with a small coarse hat stuck on the top of it. His *calador*, or long steel probe, sharp at the end and hollow in the centre, with which he pierced and drew out samples of yerba from the *sernos*, was always in his hand; and he went gossiping about in the prosecution of his business, received by all and suspected by none. This little man I found was one of Francia's principal and most confidential spies. Seeing the open favor shown to me by Francia, and knowing that I would not betray him, he could not help boasting to me of the secret intimacy which he was permitted with the Consul. He was *reconocedor del Gobierno*, or government inspector of yerba, and this lulled any suspicion which might arise from his being frequently seen with Francia. Little Orrego, when his public-house was filled with the lower orders, would hold forth in eloquent strains of Guarani in praise of 'Caria Francia,' and when going about the stores or warehouses and shops of the better citizens, he caught up all that was said of the Consul without appearing to listen to a single word. While a conversation was going on, I have seen the little fellow astride of a bale of yerba, striking the hard substance under him with his calador, half whistling or humming a tune, in apparent abstraction of all that was going forward, and yet drinking in every word that was uttered around him. 'But, Orrego,' said I one day, 'I hope you do not betray your friends.' He fidgeted, and looked uneasy. 'Ah,' said he, 'Carai Francia is a hard man to deal with. I do my best to let things go on as quietly as possible, but I *dare* not deceive the Consul. He has many others besides myself, and *I do not know who they are;* if through any of them I was detected in a falsehood, or in anything like equivocation, you know what would be the result to me.' I knew, indeed, but too truly, that the result would be imprisonment and irons for life. Orrego was a cunning though good-hearted little man; and you will perceive what an admirable sort of tool he was with which to work out dark ends like those of the First Consul. Most of the spies, I believe, were chosen with the same keen observation of character."

During the time of the joint consulship, Francia was accustomed to ride out every day, attended by a guard of only three or four. At his appearance everybody in the streets was expected to stand still, the men and boys with hat in hand and heads bowed, to wait for his Excellency to pass by. These humiliating observances were more strictly enforced after he became sole Dictator. His body-guard was increased to a numerous escort, and his title of Excellency was then changed to that of *El Supremo*, The Supreme. In his all-devouring vanity he could think of no inferior title that would express his transcendent greatness, and as no language has a term to express a power or being superior to that of the Almighty, poor Francia was obliged to rest content at that of equality. From that time till his death, no one was allowed to allude to him in any way but as El Supremo. After his election as Dictator, any hesitation in stopping instantly when he appeared in sight and waiting with uncovered head was sure to call down on the delinquent several sabre-blows, and, in some instances, from the edge of the weapon. To this requirement is ascribed a practice that prevailed until the commencement of the late war. This was the custom of giving hats to all male children from the time they are large enough to run about the streets, and when they have not another article or shred of clothing about them. They must have hats to hold humbly before them, and thus show their respect for El Supremo ; but they could go till they were full grown with no other garment, unless from shame they were induced to cover themselves. The practice thus begun was continued under Francia's successor as a habit rather than a police regulation; and up to the time that the war begun, and so long as hats were procurable, it was the custom for the children of the lower classes, from the age of four to ten, to go about with no article of dress or protection from sun, wind, or rain, but a straw or palm hat to salute any person they might see in uniform.

But after the expiration of the first dictatorship and Francia had been made "perpetual Dictator," it was found that the most humble demeanor frequently would not save a man who was unfortunate enough to meet El Supremo as he was out on his daily *paseos ;* and people hid in their houses, or fled from the streets through which he was to pass, as though a whole caravan of wild animals had been let loose in the public plaza.

As he would ride through the streets, surrounded by his escort, he would seem to notice nothing. His head always fell forward, and his chin rested on his chest; and the centaur-like garb, half military, half civic, that covered his fleshless limbs, rendered him an uncouth figure to look upon. But though he seemed to see or direct nothing, some of his escort evidently knew what would prove agreeable to their master, and what persons they could outrage with his approbation. An illustration of this was related to the author by his old friend, La Guardia, before mentioned as having been sent to the University of Cordova as a *protégé* of Francia, and who, on his return, kept up intimate relations with him until his elevation to power. But after he became Dictator he tolerated no familiarity or intimacy with any of his countrymen, and he was esteemed the happiest man who attracted least notice from El Supremo. La Guardia, one afternoon as he was walking through the town, found, as he turned the corner of the street, that the guard which always rode a hundred yards more or less in advance of the Dictator was directly abreast of him. Following at the usual distance was Francia with a single soldier at his side, having a drawn sword in his hand; in the rear followed, at a respectful distance, the other members of his escort. At the sight La Guardia considered himself a lost man. It was too late to turn and fly. The craven fear that people always exhibited in presence of the Dictator would enrage him, though he did all he could to create it, and an air of confidence was sure to bring death or imprisonment to any one that assumed it. La Guardia therefore stood still, his hat in hand and his head bowed, thinking that perhaps his time had come. But to his great relief the cloud passed by, and the lightning did not fall. Fifty years after this the old man related the circumstance as a remarkable escape.*

* "The owner of the house in which we lived, Don Pascual Echagüe, was a native of Santa Fé, but married to a Paraguayan lady of good family and settled in Asuncion. A pasquin on the Dictator was found one morning, stuck on the wall of the house in which our landlord resided with his family. To suppose that Echagüe himself had stuck it there was monstrous and absurd; yet that day he was thrown into prison and into chains. His unhappy wife, after her husband had languished in solitary confinement for some months, contrived to get an interview with the Dictator. She threw herself at his feet. Her tears and

The first dictatorship expired, according to the law creating it, in three years; and though long previous to its termination an order of the Dictator announced by the town crier was unquestioned, and passed as the unassailable law of the country, as much so as if a part of the organic act establishing the government, Francia decided to call another Congress to re-elect himself, instead of proclaiming by a decree that his term was perpetual. Accordingly, in 1817, he called another Congress. But by this time no one thought of questioning anything that he might propose. The persons named by himself as members of this body came as ordered, voted as they knew would please El Supremo, and, as soon as he permitted, adjourned and went to their homes. To save himself the trouble of convoking other congresses, he had himself made perpetual Dictator; and this done he sent away the deputies, and never after pretended to do anything except as might please his own sweet will. From 1817 to 1840 there was no sign or pretence of authority except the will of Francia.

her sobs choked her utterance. 'Woman,' said the tyrant, 'what do you want here?' 'O my husband, my husband!' was all the unhappy lady could articulate. Francia then turned to his guard and said: 'Order another *barra de grillos* (iron fetters) to be placed on Echagüe, and an additional one every time this mad woman dares approach me.' The wretched husband, like many other victims, died in his prison and in his chains." — ROBERTSON, *Letters on Paraguay.*

"Some time after the ineffectual application in favor of Echagüe by his wife, another but more distant relation of his, having been employed in some matters by Francia, ventured once more to intercede for the imprisoned, enchained, and dying man.

"'Sir,' said the Dictator, 'I have permitted you to approach my person, not because you deserve it, but because I chose it. You now pretend to *dictate* to me, and, by interceding for your friend, impugn the judgment by which he has been consigned to perpetual imprisonment and chains. Go where he is, and there, like a dog as you are, rot and die in the contiguous dungeon.'

"The friend of Echagüe thus rotted and died." — ROBERTSON, *Reign of Terror.*

CHAPTER XV.

José de Artigas. — Gauchos and Estancieros. — Antecedents of Artigas. — Commences his Career as Captain of Banditti, 1808. — Ineffectual Attempts to put him down. — Receives a Commission from the Crown of Spain. — Deserts, and joins the Revolutionists in Buenos Aires, 1813. — Again deserts and fights "on his own Hook." — His Relations with Dr. Francia. — Duties assessed upon Paraguayan Vessels. — Destruction of the Missions of Entre Rios. — Overthrow of Artigas. — He escapes to Paraguay. — His Treatment at the Hands of Francia.

WE may here diverge for a time from the dismal story of Francia's career, and rest from the "running shriek." So long as one writes of him, he can have nothing to tell but a catalogue of crimes committed by a man possessed of no redeeming quality. Throughout the whole of the perpetual dictatorship, the history of the country is but a prolonged wail of misery. Paraguay for all that time is a land where mirth and laughter are unknown, where confidence and friendship do not exist, where home is indeed "no home," for home confidences are feared lest El Supremo should know of them.

Events are now transpiring on the borders of Paraguay and in the provinces below that have an important bearing on the subsequent history of all the countries of the Plata, and we have to consider a state of things in some respects worse than existed in Paraguay. The provinces next below Paraguay, on the left bank of the Parana, were at this time the home of the worst gang of banditti ever known in America. The condition of the inhabitants on the whole, however, was better than that of the Paraguayans, in the same way that the condition of people in those sections of Italy infested by brigands is better than that of the condemned wretches whose prison is near the "Bridge of Sighs." It is possible to get out of one, but not possible to get out of the other. So, if life or property were too insecure in Corrientes and Entre Rios, the inhabitants could sometimes go away and stay away; but it was not possible to leave Paraguay.

It was before the election of Francia as perpetual Dictator in 1817 that he found himself menaced by his neighbors to the South. Indeed, as long before as 1814, he had been greatly annoyed by the armed freebooters that ravaged, and we may say governed, the provinces of Corrientes and Entre Rios. The leader of this band of cut-throats, whose name for some six years was a terror to all decent people, was José de Artigas. This man was a famous character in his day, and his influence for evil was greater, perhaps, than that of any man in South America during the time of his lawless career. He was born in or near Montevideo, about the year 1768. His family belonged to that class of cattle-raisers who, having early begun in that business, which afterwards became very profitable, acquired considerable wealth, though leading a life but few removes from the barbarous. This scion of the family was therefore brought up, or allowed to grow up, as a gaucho, receiving no education but that of riding and breaking wild horses, throwing the lasso, and catching, marking, and slaughtering cattle. In these accomplishments he greatly excelled, and became at once the terror and the admiration of other gauchos. He had the qualities for a leader of desperadoes, and the state of society at that time in the Banda Oriental * was such that there was always a great number of that class of restless vagabonds, whose whole character, as it was then and is now, is expressed by the one word *gaucho,* — men with no interest in the country, and no desire for any; who know no more of the comforts of civilized life than the Indians of the Gran Chaco, and who differ from them mainly

* The Banda Oriental, as it is almost universally called in the countries of the Plata, is usually designated on the maps as the Republic of Uruguay. Being situate to the eastward of Buenos Aires, the Porteños gave it this name, signifying the eastern side or section. In official documents it is styled *La Republica Oriental del Uruguay,* — "The Oriental Republic of the Uruguay."

in the fact that they are not so lazy, are more athletic and sanguinary, and have more animal spirits. A horse and his trappings, and their own peculiar garb, a knife and a lasso, are all the gaucho requires. Let him acquire by plunder or otherwise thousands of dollars, and he will not rest till the last dollar is squandered in gaming and dissipation. The gaucho is *sui generis*. No other part of the world but the pampas of South America has ever produced any similar race of beings. To the peculiar geographical features of the country must be ascribed this anomalous development of character. Those vast plains extending almost from the ocean to the foot of the Andes, and from Paraguay to Patagonia, having an area sufficient for four kingdoms as large as France, or some eight hundred thousand square miles, is even yet to a great extent an uninhabited, unreclaimed waste. In the time of Artigas it was much less advanced than now from the state in which it was when, near three hundred years before, Sebastian Cabot first cast his eyes over this wide domain. There were many towns of more or less importance scattered about and generally situate on the banks of the navigable rivers. But the interior was only settled by estancieros and their dependants. The capitalist who succeeded in getting a title to a large tract of land, generally many thousand acres, would erect on it such buildings as were indispensable, and commence the raising of cattle and horses. These were only valued for their hides and tallow. Here, far removed from everything like society or civilization, the estanciero would settle down with his wife, and raise up a family of children. To take care of the herds many men would be required, and these would have their mud hovels near the large estancia, where they would live and breed like savages. The children of the proprietor would grow up untaught in everything except the labors of the estancia; but being privileged to lord it over the sons of the dependants, they early develop into juvenile tyrants, and soon pass beyond all constraint except their own bad passions. When grown to be men, and when they come to inherit the estates of their fathers, they have no taste for any of those refinements or comforts that partially modified the manners and customs of the first settlers, whose early life, perhaps, had been spent in towns or cities. After this first remove from civilized society, the estanciero became to all intents and purposes a gaucho ; as much so as any man who labored for him for no other reward than the beef he might require to eat. With the thousands and hundreds of thousands of horned cattle, horses, and sheep that in time came to roam over his vast possessions, the estanciero must have great numbers of peons, or laborers, to take care of them. Over these the illiterate estanciero would reign supreme, with no one to dispute or even question his authority. Literally, he "was monarch of all he surveyed." Having scarcely any intercourse with the outer world, being unable to read, and only going to the nearest market town when it might be necessary to sell his hides and tallow, he saw his flocks increase, and lived undisturbed, unless an occasional foray of the Indians might interrupt his ease and indolence. A French writer, M. Chevalier St. Robert,* has given a description so correct and so graphic of the race of gauchos, that no apology will be needed for introducing so long an extract as the following : —

"His children and his domestics, gauchos like himself, pass the same sort of life, that is to say, without ambition, without desires, and without any species of agricultural labor. All they have to do is to mark and to kill, at certain periods, the herds of oxen and flocks of sheep which constitute the fortune of the estanciero, and that satisfy the wants of all. Purely carnivorous, the gaucho's only food consists of flesh and water ; bread and spirituous liquors are as much unknown to him as the simplest elements of social life. In a country in which the only wealth of the inhabitants arises from the incessant destruction of innumerable flocks, it can be easily understood how their sanguinary occupation must tend to obliterate every sentiment of pity, and induce an indifference to the perpetration of acts of cruelty. The readiness to shed blood — a ferocity which is at the same time obdurate and brutal — constitutes the

* Le General Rosas et la Question de la Plata. Par M. Chevalier St. Robert. Translated by M. B. McCabe.

prominent feature in the character of the pure gaucho. The first instrument that the infantile hand of the gaucho grasps is the knife; the first things that attract his attention as a child are the pouring out of blood and the palpitating flesh of expiring animals. From his earliest years, as soon as he is able to walk, he is taught how he may with the greatest skill approach the living beast, hough it, and, if he has the strength, kill it. Such are the sports of his childhood; he pursues them ardently, and amid the approving smiles of his family. As soon as he acquires sufficient strength, he takes part in the labors of the estancia; they are the sole arts he has to study, and he concentrates all his intellectual powers in mastering them. From that time forth he arms himself with a large knife, and for a single moment of his life he never parts with it. It is to his hand an additional limb; he makes use of it always, in all cases, in every circumstance, and constantly with wonderful skill and address. The same knife that in the morning had been used to slaughter a bullock or to kill a tiger aids him, in the daytime, to cut his dinner, and at night to carve out a skin tent, or else to repair his saddle or to mend his mandoline. With the gaucho the knife is often used as an argument in support of his opinions. In the midst of a conversation apparently carried on in amity, the formidable knife glitters on a sudden in the hands of one of the speakers, the ponchos are rolled around the left arm, and a conflict commences. Soon deep gashes are seen on the face, the blood gushes forth, and not unfrequently one of the combatants falls lifeless to the earth; but no one thinks of interfering with the combat, and when it is over the conversation is resumed as if nothing extraordinary had occurred. No person is disturbed by it, not even the women, who remain as cold, unmoved spectators of the affray. It may easily be surmised what sort of persons they must be of which such a scene is but a specimen of their domestic manners. Thus the savage education of the estancia produces in the gaucho a complete indifference as to human life, by familiarizing him from his most tender years to the contemplation of a violent death, whether it is that he inflicts it on another or receives it himself. He lifts his knife against a man with the same indifference that he strikes down a bullock; the idea which everywhere else attaches to the crime of homicide does not exist in his mind; for in slaying another he yields not less to habit than to the impulse of his wild and barbarous nature. If perchance a murder of this kind is committed so close to town that there is reason to apprehend the pursuit of justice, every one is eager to favor the flight of the guilty person. The fleetest horse is at his service, and he departs, certain to find, wherever he goes, the favor and sympathy of all. Then, with that marvellous instinct which is common to all the savage races, he feels no hesitation in venturing into the numerous plains of the pampas. Alone, in the midst of a boundless desert, and in which the eye strains itself in vain to discover a boundary, he advances without the slightest feeling of uneasiness; he does so watching the course of the stars, listening to the winds, watching, interrogating, discovering the cause of the slightest noise that reaches his ears, and he at length arrives at the place he sought, without ever straying, even for a moment. The lasso which is rolled around his horse's neck, the bolas suspended to his saddle, and the inseparable knife, suffice to assure him food and to secure him against every danger, even against the tiger. When he is hungry he selects one out of the herd of beeves that cover the plain, pursues it, lassos it, kills it, cuts out of it a piece of flesh, which he eats raw or cooks, and thus refreshes himself for the journey of the following day. If murder be a common incident in the life of a gaucho, it often also becomes the means to him of emerging from obscurity and obtaining renown amongst his associates. When a gaucho has rendered himself remarkable by his audacity and address in single combats, companions gather around him, and he soon finds himself at the head of a considerable party. He commences a campaign, sets himself in open defiance to the laws, and in a short time acquires a celebrity which rallies a crowd about him."

Of this class was José Artigas. He was a gaucho by instinct and inclination. Though born near Montevideo and passing much of his boyhood there, he took to the wild life of the pampas as readily as a young duck takes to the water. It is even said that in his youth he never learned either to read or to write, and only when he became an important chieftain did he constrain himself to this disagreeable task. His whole ambition was to be a leader of others much like himself, and the terror of all who would not pay tribute to him. He was as ignorant as the horse he rode of all the world beyond the plains which he aspired to rule. Possessed of great physical strength and endurance, he early became a leader of the criminals from all the neighboring country, and of such other gauchos as found the quiet life of the estancia too tame or unremunerative. He was soon strong enough in numbers to despise the law and put its officers at defiance. He and his band roamed where they listed and took all that they required. Such as gave up willingly what was wanted, and made no complaint, were not further molested, but whoever protested or appealed to the government for protection received no mercy. His flocks and herds would be driven away, and he and his family would be no more heard of. Hence many people compounded with him, paying such tribute as he might exact. His control over his men was complete, and whoever could show a band of his marauders the tax receipt of their chieftain had his property respected.

This bandit commenced his career in a small way as early as 1808, some seven years before Montevideo achieved its independence. But as the street sewer gathers in what is foul and useless, increasing in volume as it passes through the populous city, so Artigas, as he went on in his career of crime, gathered around him all the vile scum of society, — outlaws, thieves, murderers, and such gauchos as were too dangerous or too lazy to be tolerated near the estancias; all flocked to his standard, for he could protect them and save them from the penalties due to their crimes. The whole force lived by robbery, either in the way of blackmail levied on those who would pay him to be protected from his troops, or by the direct plunder of others who could not or would not make terms with him. At first his operations were comparatively on a small scale, and he neither aspired nor pretended to be anything but a cattle and horse thief, selling his surplus plunder sometimes in the Banda Oriental and sometimes in Buenos Aires, where he always found a ready sale for all the cattle and horses he could bring to market. As his forces became more numerous, he grew more daring, and swept over not only the Banda Oriental, but even sent his bands of marauders into the Brazilian province of Rio Grande to gather up the herds of cattle and horses, and whatever else could be easily carried away, and then retreat so rapidly as to render futile every attempt at pursuit.

The Governor of Montevideo several times sent such forces as he could collect to put down this modern Cacus. But the royal troops were invariably defeated, as in a country like the Banda Oriental a force like that of Artigas could not be overcome by ten times their number of organized troops. Like a later gaucho chieftain whose history we have yet to relate, it was not the policy of Artigas to fight, except with everything in his favor. Were he known to be in one place with a large force, and a body of royal troops was sent to capture him, before they could reach his camping-ground he would be a hundred miles or a hundred leagues distant with his whole band. His followers required no commissariat. If their horses gave out, they selected fresh ones that were to be found in great numbers on the intervening estancias; and for food they only had to kill and eat the cattle and sheep they were sure to find grazing on the estancias by which they passed. The lasso, the rude saddle called *recado*, the sheath-knife, were all that the gaucho soldier required to secure him against every want. His clothing was such as in his maraudings might fall into his hands, though the true gaucho dress was his favorite costume. This consists, when complete, of a shirt and a square piece of cloth brought around the hips so as to form two loose bags for the legs, and fastened about the waist with a broad leather belt, ornamented with all the silver coins, having eyes, soldered to them like buttons, that he is the owner of. Over his shoulders he wears a *poncho*, which is a thick woollen cloth about five feet long and three and a half wide. Through a slit made lengthwise in the middle of this the wearer thrusts his head, and the garment, falling from his shoulders and about his sides and hips, effectually protects him from cold, wind, and rain. A brigandish hat and huge spurs, with or without boots, complete the uniform of the gaucho.

For warlike purposes, however, Artigas found it necessary to have other arms for his men than the sheath-knife; and it was to obtain these that the cattle stolen from the estancieros of his own country were sent to the market of Buenos Aires. Arms, ammunition, and the cloth requisite for their rude dress, were about all that they could not secure in their favorite pastime of robbery.

The Governor of Montevideo, being unable to subdue Artigas, whose forces were constantly increasing, and whose range of devastation was as constantly extending, proposed to treat with the gaucho chieftain. He proposed to make Artigas his ally in support of law and order, to give him a commission in the service of the King of Spain as captain of mounted militia, or, as they were called, *Blandengues*. Artigas accepted the terms, and entered Montevideo with his murdering band. But desperate and lawless as they were, they were all implicitly subject to him. There was no trifling with his authority among his followers. His word was law. His men were now regularly paid, and their wants were provided for; and their leader told them to stop robbing and murdering and serve as a general police for the country to maintain law and order. For a time the novelty of an honest life satisfied Artigas, and for a time the people of the country around Montevideo, and indeed the whole Banda Oriental, enjoyed a security and prosperity which they had not known for a long time before.

At this time the revolution in Buenos Aires took place, and war in Spain ensued. Artigas, tired of inaction, and the novelty of an honest life having worn off, would fain take part in the war; and as he was already in the King's service, and in honor bound to fight his battles, he, of course, deserted, and went over to the other side. He passed over with many of his followers to Buenos Aires, and in 1813, when Montevideo, that still held out as a Spanish colony, was besieged by the Porteños under General Alvear, Artigas, then having the rank of colonel, served with that zeal and malignity that are at all times peculiar to deserters and traitors. But the service under a Porteño general was not congenial to the tastes of Artigas.

He was a red-handed, ignorant gaucho, and his presence was an offence to the revolutionary leaders of Buenos Aires, who were men of education, and who believed in conducting war with some regard to humanity and the rights of private persons. So with characteristic treachery, while the siege was yet going on, Artigas again deserted, taking with him his whole command, consisting of eight hundred men, all of whom were his own countrymen and most of them gauchos like himself.

The double traitor now adopted the course of warfare suited to his tastes. Nominally fighting against Alvear and the Porteños, he was in no way subordinate to the Governor of Montevideo. He was literally "fighting on his own hook." He assumed the title of "Lord Protector," and, marching to the northward toward Entre Rios, the gauchos in great numbers flocked to his standard. Two different expeditions were sent against him, one under General Quintana being detached from the besieging force, and the other under command of Baron Holderberg, a German adventurer in the service of Buenos Aires, who, with a force of less than one fifth of that of Artigas, crossed over the river at Santa Fé, nearly opposite to what was then called the Bajada, and where now is the city of Parana, the capital of the Confederation from 1852 to 1861. Of course the Baron was defeated, and he and all his force taken prisoners.

The Most Excellent Lord Protector now had full sway. Buenos Aires, having the war with Spain on her hands, must devote her whole resources to the maintaining of her independence, and must leave the wild gaucho to ravage the upper provinces till a more convenient season should arrive for making war upon them. Of the country lying between Buenos Aires and Paraguay, and of the larger part of the Banda Oriental, he became for the time the absolute sovereign. Though he never crossed the Parana, yet in Santa Fé his authority was so far acknowledged, during the later part of his career, that such tribute as he demanded was paid as the price of exemption. So that whole vast country was converted into one great region where no law prevailed but the will of the Most Excellent Protector, a man who knew neither mercy, truth, nor justice. And yet, withal, he was none of your sceptics or humanitarians, for whom Francia's eulogist has so much contempt, albeit he does not praise his hero's piety. He had a priest always at his ear, acting as counsellor, secretary, friend, and confessor. He was surrounded by cut-throats, for none others were congenial companions. But of them all, says Rengger, the most infamous was this friar, whose name was Monterroso, and, like another bishop of whom we shall speak by and by, he always advised the most sanguinary measures.

The proceedings of Artigas, so far as they were damaging to Buenos Aires, were entirely such as were agreeable to the Dictator of Paraguay. Francia greatly dreaded a collision with the Porteños, for though the army of Belgrano had been conquered by the Paraguayans under Velasco, he knew that he and his government were so detested that if Paraguay were again invaded by an army from Buenos Aires, every man that could desert to it would do so. Buenos Aires was his great terror and aversion. From no other power had he reason to fear any interference with his absolute despotism. From Artigas's banditti he had little to dread, for he had sufficient troops stationed at the passes of the river to repel any force that the Protector could spare on such an expedition. And while Artigas kept up his marauding warfare, it was certain Buenos Aires could never send any force against him. He served as a buffer between Francia and his most dreaded enemy.

Francia, however, needed arms from abroad as well as Artigas, and the latter had the power, if not to stop all river navigation, at least to render it very difficult and dangerous. The vessels that attempted the long and perilous voyage from Buenos Aires to Paraguay always sailed under the flag of some neutral nation, generally the English. But this did not give immunity to contraband of war; and as it was not in accordance with the interest or policy of Artigas that Francia should receive munitions of war, he kept a sharp lookout for all vessels that might be making their way *aguas arriba* (up river). This interference with the Dictator greatly irritated him. The "Most Excellent Lord Protector" and the "Supremo" were jealous of each other. The presence of an army like that of Paraguay, so near the territory that he claimed as his own, was a constant menace to Artigas; and, on the other hand, his own habit of taking whatever arms he could find in vessels bound to Paraguay, and of detaining those bound *aguas abajo*, or down river, loaded with the produce of Paraguay, till they should pay such toll as he might demand, greatly exasperated Francia. That they might not thus annoy each other, but make common cause against Buenos Aires, Artigas several times proposed terms to Francia whereby they should both engage not to molest each other. But Francia treated the advances of Artigas with scorn and insult. At this Artigas was greatly enraged, and by means of his gaucho troops, among whom were Indians and half-breeds, he induced the Indians of the half-ruined missions of Entre Rios to revolt. These missions still belonged to Paraguay, and were kept in subjection by the troops of the Dictator, who was well aware that they could not hold their position against the forces of Artigas. He therefore gave orders that at the first outbreak his troops should retire, burning as they went every sign of a habitation, and destroying everything that could be of use either to the Indians or their gaucho allies. The order was obeyed, and thus fifteen of the old mission towns, and those the most flourishing yet remaining, were entirely destroyed.

After this, Francia closed up more closely than ever all communication between Paraguay and the outer world. He would not risk his troops across the river to make war on Artigas, but he would nevertheless prevent him from assessing duties on vessels going below with Paraguayan produce. He therefore shut up the ports completely, and allowed neither vessel nor person to leave Paraguay. It is true this was ruinous to his own subjects; but the interests of his people never troubled Francia. His own dignity and greatness were so vast that his mind could contain nothing else.

Artigas, like Francia, had a mortal hatred for the native Spaniards; and whenever such fell into his power, it was his delight to torture them by means of unheard-of cruelty. One of his happy conceits was to have them sewed up in the green hides of bullocks just flayed, and then leave them in the burning sun till death should set them free. In justice to Francia it should be said he never tortured for the mere sake of torture. The people whom he put to death were in his eyes too insignificant to merit so much attention. He would, indeed, cast persons into prison, and load them with fetters, knowing they must expire under the protracted agony, and he would look with fiendish complacency at his victims as they were shot and bayoneted before his eyes. But this was all in the way of business. He never would prolong their misery before his eyes, that he might delight in their shrieks and groans. In this respect he differed from Artigas, and from the tyrant of Buenos Aires, Rosas, who subsequently distinguished himself as the most ingenious torturer from the time of the Inquisition to that of the second Lopez.

The disputes and hostile demonstrations between Francia and Artigas began early in the career of the former as supreme Dictator. Indeed, they commenced in the time of the joint consulate, and the knowledge of the atrocities of Artigas in the adjoining provinces served to some extent to reconcile the Paraguayans to the tyranny of Francia; while Corrientes, on the opposite bank of the Parana, was overrun by bands of murdering gauchos, Paraguay enjoyed the peace and quiet of the tomb.

To give an idea of the state of affairs as they existed in the two countries, I must ask indulgence for again citing the testimony of the already often-quoted Robertson. In fact, as far as the reign of Francia is concerned, there are only two authors to quote, — Rengger and Robertson. They only — with the exception of Molas and of Somellera, who left Paraguay before the "reign of terror" had fairly commenced — have ever published anything from personal experience and observation, and until now I am not aware that any one has ever given to the world anything additional respecting the horrors of Francia's time.*

Robertson, as it appears, had, after that memorable interview with Francia, when he was commissioned to go before the House of Commons with bales of tobacco and yerba, and demijohns of rum and molasses, to prove by ocular demonstration the great wealth and resources of Paraguay, ventured to return to Asuncion without fulfilling his high diplomatic mission. Apprehending that the Dictator would be greatly disappointed should he return without bringing word that the English government was anxious to form an alliance offensive and defensive against all the world besides with such a powerful and wise potentate as himself, Robertson thought to placate his resentment by taking to him a small quantity of arms and such other things as he thought would be most acceptable. At the time there was no declared war existing between the different provinces of the Plata. Artigas was regarded by the government of Buenos Aires as neither more nor less than a bandit and an outlaw, and Francia claimed to be neutral and independent of them both. Under these circumstances Robertson, having first consulted the commander of the English squadron then lying in the Plata, and having obtained a sailing license from him, loaded a small brigantine with such wares as he knew to be most in demand in Paraguay. Before departing, however, he was solicited by General Alvear, who was then director of affairs in Buenos Aires, to endeavor to open a negotiation with Francia by which arms and ammunition were to be supplied to Paraguay on condition that the Dictator would furnish a certain number of troops to Buenos Aires. It should be borne in mind that at this time

* The notes of Don Mariano Molas, which have recently been published in book form in Buenos Aires, contain a list of Francia's decrees during the first half of his reign, and they also give an account of his principal acts of tyranny during the same period. Molas was a prisoner for many years, and it was not till long after his death that his manuscripts saw the light. I have never been able to get a copy of the published volume.

the population of Paraguay exceeded that of all the other Argentine provinces together, excepting only Buenos Aires; and Alvear believed that, by acting in concert with the Dictator, the gaucho rule might be easily put down. Robertson, however, very properly, as a neutral and a merchant, refused to have anything to do with the transaction. But as his vessel was to take a letter-bag to Paraguay, the government might avail itself of the opportunity to send its proposals direct to Francia by means of a sealed letter. Such a letter was accordingly sent, and the vessel left for Asuncion.

The voyage was about half accomplished, and the little vessel was one evening, owing to head winds, fastened to the bank of the river, and the proprietor had gone on shore to shoot partridges, when it was suddenly pounced upon by a band of *Artigueños* (soldiers of Artigas). These ragged, fierce-looking ruffians took possession of the vessel, seizing poor Robertson just as he was coming on board, unsuspicious of danger, and not without many kicks and sabre-blows he was pinioned and fastened to a ring-bolt on the deck of the vessel. The scenes that followed are thus described by him: "The deck was in possession of between thirty and forty of the very worst class of the marauding soldiers of Artigas; the hatches of the vessel were open, and the cases and bales of merchandise, every one of them more or less violated, lay strewed about; my scattered wardrobe was partitioned off among the robbers; wine was spilt and glass broken in every direction; one man was lying on my bed in a state of intoxication, and by his side sat three more, wrangling over a pack of cards; and as if gambling were not of itself a sufficient excitement, they were quaffing large libations of raw spirits. Every one of the demon-like gang was more or less in a state of intoxication; and while, with frequent reference to me, significant gestures were passing from one to the other, commingled with open threats of instantly taking my life unless I discovered to them all the valuable property, and especially the money, they supposed to be in the vessel, I was left in profound ignorance of the cause and origin of so barbarous a violation of law. Night came on; sentinels were placed over the crew on shore; I was more tightly bound; and, after witnessing for hours a scene of license and debauch too frightful to be conceived of and too gross to be portrayed, I was thrust into the hold of the vessel, and had the hatches closed over my head."

In the morning a soldier, by birth an Indian, was sent below to conduct the prisoner on deck, and "when he reached there," continues our author, "every sort of menace was resorted to in order to extort from me a secret which I had not to reveal. 'Where is your money?' and 'Where are the rest of your arms?' were the oft-reiterated demands. They had got all I had of both, but my protestations to this effect seemed of no avail. Twice was I taken out of the vessel to the shore, and twice were the men drawn up to shoot me."

But the man was not shot, as he lived to record the tale. Among these ruffians there was a sort of tacit understanding, almost an established rule, that any soldier who had distinguished himself by any peculiar excesses should be entitled to ask a favor of his chief, which the latter was bound to grant or to refuse with the prospect that the party refused would take it as a personal affront, and cut his throat at the first convenient opportunity. Robertson was already tied to a tree, and the soldiers were ready for the word, when the same Indian who had conducted him from the cabin stepped forward from the ranks and asked that he might not be shot. The request was granted, and as the *protégé* of the Indian who had saved his life the cords were removed from his limbs. The robbers, however, took all his clothes that were on board the vessel and distributed among themselves; but as he had not sufficient to clothe the whole party of forty, they were obliged to put up with something less than full dress for all. One would take a pair of pantaloons, another a shirt, and a third a swallow-tailed coat, dispensing with the two former articles; one took a pair of boots, another an opera-hat; one took his watch-chain, seal, and keys, and another his watch. So rigged out in a style more motley than even one of Francia's congressmen, they left the lawful proprietor with nothing but a tattered great-coat and an old greasy poncho.

After a series of trials, being shut up in the mean while in a sort of prison-pen among those who had distinguished themselves for their crimes to such an extent that it was deemed unsafe for them to be at large, he was fortunate enough to get sight of an old acquaintance, a servant formerly in his employ. To him in hurried words he communicated his situation, and bade him fly to Buenos Aires and inform Captain Percy, the commander of the British squadron there, of what he had seen. Fortunately this officer was not like some admirals, and at once despatched a war vessel to the brigand head-quarters, with a letter to the gaucho chief demanding the instant release of Robertson and the restoration of his property. This prompt action on the part of the English naval commander had the intended effect. The prisoner was at once released, and his property, so far as possible, restored to him. The arms had been too much needed and too soon distributed to be returned to their owner.

The vessel, with the remaining part of the cargo, was again despatched for Paraguay, but this time without the owner, who resolved to visit Artigas in his camp and recover damages for the losses he had sustained.

Making his way to the head-quarters of the Most Excellent Protector, he found him seated on a bullock's skull at a fire kindled on the mud floor of his hut, eating beef from a spit, and drinking gin out of a cow's horn. He was surrounded by a dozen officials in weather-beaten attire, all similarly engaged. The Protector was dictating to two secretaries, as, unfortunately, his early education was so limited that he could little more than write his name. They all had a squalid, brigandish look, and the party had the appearance of ferocious banditti, who had no more sense of decency or regard for cleanliness than so many swine. Still, there was something ludicrous in the scene, for strewn about the room and trampled on the mud floor were a great number of envelopes from all the different provinces in the confederation addressed to "His Excellency the Protector." Outside, however, there was an appearance of business, as couriers were arriving frequently on panting, overridden horses, with despatches, while fresh horses stood at his door ready for them to mount and carry his orders to his lieutenants in different parts. The Most Excellent Protector sat upon his bullock's skull as upon a throne, smoking and eating and drinking and swearing, while he despatched the business brought to his notice and sent his couriers to execute his orders. They were coming and going all the time, and each one, while waiting to be again despatched, would cut a slice from the slaughtered bullock that was near at hand, and, half roasting it in the fire, would appease his hunger, and soon be ready for another gallop across the plains. When he found that Robertson had brought a letter from the commander of the English gunboat, he at once became very civil to him; for while he felt that he could hold his own against the government of Buenos Aires or Montevideo, distracted as they were by intestine feuds, and straining every nerve to maintain themselves against the power of Spain, he yet did not wish to give offence to England, or to force her to become an ally of Buenos Aires in effecting his overthrow. As it was, his situation was desperate enough; for, knowing himself to be the common enemy of mankind, he was almost constantly expecting an attack, and therefore he always had around his hut a large number of horses ready saddled and bridled, sufficient for himself and his staff to escape in case of a sudden attack; and it was the same with his followers, who were bivouacked near by. As horses were plenty, and as their only cost was the stealing of them, they, as a rule, had two or three to each man, so that all the time every one of his soldiers had a horse ready to mount at a moment's notice, and in five minutes after the word was given his whole army could be put in motion. The celerity with which they would move was most astonishing; and as they had no object in sparing their horses, they would ride them in full gallop at the top of their speed until they were about to give out, when they would catch others, and, transferring the trappings, would in three minutes' time be again sweeping at full speed over the country. I give the remainder of this description in Robertson's own words: "He had about fifteen hundred tattered followers in his camp, who acted in the double capacity of horse and foot soldiers. They were chiefly Indians, taken from the decayed establishments of the Jesuits, admirable horsemen, and inured to every species of privation and fatigue. The sloping hills and the fertile plains of the Banda Oriental and Entre Rios furnished abundant pasture for their horses, as well as numerous herds of cattle for slaughter. They wanted little more. A scanty jacket, and one poncho tied around the waist in the form of a Highlander's kilt, while another hung over their shoulders, completed, with the foraging-cap and a pair of *potro* boots, large spurs, a sabre and blunderbuss, and a knife, the Artigueno's attire. Their camp was made of rows of hide huts and mud hovels, and these, together with about a dozen cottages of a somewhat better description, constituted what was called the 'Villa de la Purificacion.'"

Such was Artigas in his prosperity. It is hard to conceive of a character worse than his. He was an enemy of his kind, and his whole delight was in desolation and rapine. It is no wonder that the mild and peaceable Paraguayans, on hearing of his atrocities, should cower and shrink under that even worse rule which was reducing them to a state of slavery, in which even their thoughts were punished as capital crimes. This dread of Artigas was artfully used by the Dictator, in the early part of his despotic career, to make his own person more absolute. But at length Artigas found insubordination in his camp, and one of his lieutenants, Ramirez by name, revolted against his chief, and so thoroughly routed his remaining forces that the Most Excellent Protector, in stress of intrigue, fled to Paraguay. He threw himself on the clemency of a ruler who never before had known clemency or mercy. This man had given Francia more cause for enmity than any other living. He had waged war upon him, embargoed the navigation of the river, taken his property, and thrown defiance in the face of the Supremo. But Francia's treatment of him was an exception — and, I believe, the only exception — to his general conduct. Instead of having him immediately shot or immured in a prison till he died, he was sent to the district of Curuguati, a distance of some sixty leagues from the capital, and allowed a pension of thirty dollars a month until the death of Francia.*

What passport Artigas had to the good graces of Francia is unknown, and it is probable that the credentials which secured him the clemency of the Dictator were his reputation of having cut more throats than any man then living. He had one characteristic, however, in common with Francia, and this may have won the regard of the Dictator. He too, like the Supremo, was utterly destitute of natural affection. This is evident from his mode of life after entering Paraguay. He retired to the residence allotted to him, and never more learned or inquired anything about his fellow-robbers, his family, or his friends, if, indeed, he had left any.

* "The bandit" (Artigas) "cultivated fields, did charitable deeds, and passed a life of penitence, for his few remaining years." — CARLYLE.

As a specimen of Carlyle's accuracy, this will do pretty well. Artigas entered Paraguay in 1817, and lived there till he died in 1851, thirty-four years,— surviving Francia by nearly eleven years

"But in that year, 1819" (in fact it was 1817), "the firebrand Artigas was finally quenched ; obliged to beg a lodging even of Francia, his enemy, and got it hospitably, though *contemptuously*. . . . . Francia's treatment of Artigas, his old enemy, the bandit and firebrand, reduced now to beg shelter of him, is good, humane, even *dignified*." — IDEM.

CHAPTER XVI.

Last Years of Artigas's Life. — His Apotheosis. — Banda Oriental. — Republicanism in Spanish America. — M. Aimé Bonpland. — Arrives in Buenos Aires, 1817. — Explorations and Observations in the Interior. — A Missionary of Civilization. — Establishes a Colony in Corrientes. — Experiments with Paraguay Tea. — Destruction of the Colony, and Seizure and Detention of Bonpland by Dr. Francia. — Ineffectual Attempts to obtain his Release. — Other Foreigners allowed to leave the Country. — Bonpland's Labors in Paraguay.

IN his later years, after the death of the Dictator, the quondam Most Excellent Protector left his "cultivated fields" and the scenes of his "charitable deeds," — never heard of in Paraguay, — and moved to Ibirai, where he passed his remaining days. Though he now lived near the capital, and was occasionally visited by strangers from Buenos Aires and Montevideo, he took no interest in anything or anybody beyond his own household. He had never had any ties of affection, and never inquired about any of his old acquaintances. In his younger days his life had been that of a wild beast that robbed and murdered for the pleasure it afforded him. In his later years he was the same beast, with his teeth drawn and his claws clipped.

And yet the worst thing in connection with Artigas is still to be told. It is the story of his apotheosis. While he lived it was impossible to make anything of him better than a savage, a beast. But after his death, and when his ferocity or brutishness could no longer rebuke the gaucho spirit that would magnify him into a hero, his remains were honored with ceremonies and a mausoleum such as no other South-American ever received; and there have been South-Americans of as lofty patriotism as the world has known, — men who have realized the gaucho disposition of their countrymen, and who have sacrificed everything to change it. The best have fallen by the wayside, and ere the achievement of any high reputation. But the names of San Martin, Balcarca, Sarmiento, and many others, must always appear on the page of history as meteor lights to prove that there is no redemption for the race which they aspired to lead to a higher civilization. Not from want of leaders, but from inherent gauchoism, have these nations and peoples remained in a state of semi-barbarism, and from which of themselves they can never emerge.

In dearth of material for heroes, people sometimes magnify into such doubtful or positively vicious characters. The little state of the Banda Oriental, or Republic of Uruguay, never as yet has had but one man whose reputation has extended beyond South America. That one is the great robber, Artigas. The name of no other Oriental that I could mention would be remembered as ever having been heard of before by any American or European; and I hazard nothing in saying that no reader of this book, unless he has actually been in the countries of which I am writing, can recall the name of a single Montevidean or Oriental excepting Artigas. But notwithstanding this dearth of superior men, and perhaps by very reason of it, it has always been one of the most pugnacious, belligerent, quarrelsome states in South America. It has, in fact, no right to a separate national existence. Its territory does not exceed seventy-five thousand square miles in extent, and its population is but about three hundred and fifty thousand. But with the exception of Paraguay, it is the most fertile and productive district of South America. Its climate is one of the finest in the world, and the face of the country is that of a vast rolling prairie, diversified with undulating hills capped with abundant timber. In all parts it is watered by living streams that preclude, to a great extent, the dangers of the drouth, or *seca*, that frequently proves fatal to thousands of sheep and cattle on the level pampas of Buenos Aires. It is the favorite region where European emigrants prefer to settle; and with a stable and honest government it would in a few years become one of the richest and most prosperous countries in the world. On the east it fronts directly on the Atlantic, and to the south on the broad Rio de la Plata. The site of its principal town, Montevideo, is of very great importance in a military point of view to both of the neighboring powers, Brazil and the Argentine Republic, and each is jealous of the other lest it gain a preponderating influence in the national councils.

It is most unfortunate, that, after the expulsion of the Spaniards, this fine province was not permanently annexed to the Argentine Confederation, or even to Brazil. In either case, there is no reasonable doubt that the wealth and population of the country would have been double what it is. In the latter event, however, it would in all probability have united with the large and powerful province of Rio Grande, far the most powerful of the Brazilian provinces, and have formed a separate republic of respectable proportions and of sufficient resources to maintain its independence against either of its neighbors. But this union would have had many disadvantages, chiefly arising from the difference of race. The antipathy existing between the Spaniards and Portuguese has existed for ages, till it is a part of the nature of each to hate the other. It is, perhaps, more intense and bitter between their American descendants than it ever was among their ancestors. The subjection of the Spaniards of the Banda Oriental, therefore, to the rule of the Brazilians, could only have been effected by force so long applied as virtually to destroy the Spanish race and influence. But none of these objections to a union with Buenos Aires existed. Of the same race, language, and religion, nothing but local prejudices and party feuds could prevent such union. Both gravitated from mutual interest towards such a result.

It was at this time that Artigas with his hordes of robbers appears as a great marplot. First turning traitor to his own country, he passes over to Buenos Aires; then he deserts his new friends and sets up as general freebooter, and by devastating the interior provinces the union that in all probability would have followed a speedy fall of the Spanish authority in

Montevideo was postponed and delayed till circumstances so changed it never was effected. For his instrumentality in this bad work, and for the results that followed from his devastations, — results that he neither foresaw nor desired, and in which, when effected, he took no interest, — he was regarded after his death by the Montevideans as the preserver of their independence. The occasion was therefore taken in 1857, six years after his death, when, owing to certain angry disputes with Buenos Aires, the feeling in favor of a separate national independence ran high among all parties, to testify to the world their appreciation of the services of Artigas. A deputation of the most influential and respectable citizens of Montevideo was appointed to proceed to Paraguay and disinter the great throat-cutter, and remove his remains to Montevideo. They performed their work as if engaged in honoring the remains of a canonized saint; and on their arrival at Montevideo the funeral ceremonies were so gorgeous, the masses and processions so numerous, the candles and incense so profusely burned, a heretic might have well thought the crimes of the defunct must be enormous, and that prayers and penances enough to save a city like Sodom were necessary to save Artigas from an endless woe. A magnificent tomb was erected over his remains, and the visitor to the cemetery of Montevideo, when he views the marble pile, may well ask what hope there is of a nation or race that thus deifies a monster of human depravity.

Nominally the Banda Oriental has preserved its independence and nationality, and its people boast of it as though they had thereby saved themselves from a hated foreign yoke. But the limited territory and the geographical position of the country forbid that it should ever be anything but an insignificant state, unable to defend its rights at home or protect its citizens abroad. Only people who have travelled considerably in foreign countries can realize fully the advantage of being the subject of a great and powerful government. Such governments assume to defend the rights of their citizens wherever they are, and any contemptible despotism that delights to show its power by persecution of foreigners is very sure to discriminate in favor of those nations that have the largest squadrons. On the other hand, the subject of the petty dukedoms and principalities of Europe are absolutely at the mercy of the governments into whose territory they happen to stray. Of the truth of these propositions, we shall have numerous illustrations in the latter part of this Paraguayan history. And yet the Orientales are as boastful and proud of their independence as though it had brought blessings instead of calamities, peace and prosperity instead of anarchy and ever-recurring civil war. They yet honor Artigas as their national hero, as the representative gaucho. In my own time I have known one of the best of them, a courteous, well-educated gentleman, a young man respected by his government, and holding the office of Secretary of Legation in Paraguay, of distinguished talent, amiable character, and great urbanity of deportment, to go on a pilgrimage to the former residence of this pest of society, and carry away as a sacred relic a brick or a tile of the house in which he had lived. When such are honored, who would not desire the refuge of obscurity!

As family quarrels are hardest to reconcile, and neighborhood disputes are more angry than those that are participated in by large communities, so are party feeling and political feuds more intense and bitter in proportion as the country is small and insignificant. In a great nation there is a multiplicity of interests and numberless questions affecting the politics, the religion, the commerce, and the morals of the entire population, and the people in the different communities generally agree with each other on some points, and differ on others. But in a nation too small to have such varied interests, people are prone to range themselves into parties on questions of local importance. Hence family feuds grow into national questions, traditional animosities divide people into hostile parties, and the politics of the country have reference mainly to the past. In the United States, and indeed in most popular governments, men aspire to power and influence by proclaiming their principles, and by trying to convince the people that the policy they will carry out, if elected, is the best for the general interest. But there is nothing of this kind in the Spanish American countries. No candidate comes forward with a programme of principles, and tries to prove that with such a policy the country must prosper. Like the wit who wrote for antiquity, they legislate for the past, and people are called upon to vote for men, not for their merits, nor for what they propose to do if elected, but because their fathers or grandfathers were killed in some former civil war, the animosities of which remain in all their intensity.

The first idea of a republican government is a thing utterly unknown throughout all Spanish America. At a popular election the party having for the time being the reins of power almost invariably returns its candidates. Hence the changes are almost always effected by revolutions or civil wars. But the defeated parties do not hold themselves under any obligation to abide the result. If they ever enter the contest hoping to win, like the gambler who quietly pockets his winnings as long as the cards run in his favor, but, on losing, grabs the pool, or like our "Southern brethren" after the first election of Mr. Lincoln, they do not, if out-voted, consider themselves as morally bound to respect the result. If they can get up a revolution with a reasonable chance of winning, they are sure to do it.

And how is all this to end? Many people will say, let them change their form of government and establish monarchies, and call to each one of these distracted countries a scion of royalty, and then let all the people rally around his throne. But the people will not have a monarchy, and if foreign sovereigns were to attempt to impose one of their throneless adventurers on them as a ruler, the lesson of Mexico proves how all would unite to expel the invader. Besides, the form of government has little to do with changing the character of a people. Were the popular leader of either of the parties in any South American republic a prince of any royal family of Europe, the people would still be as prone as ever to revolution and civil war. There is that fatal want of respect for law or for constituted authority which, in one word, may be described as gauchoism, and which seems to be a quality inherent in the race, and would be the same under one form of government as another.

The evil, however, is effecting its own cure. While the natives of the Spanish or mixed blood are wasting their possessions and destroying each other, there is a tide of emigration setting in from Europe that erelong must completely swamp the gaucho influence. These emigrants are mostly from England, Ireland, Germany, and Italy. They care nothing about the traditional family and party feuds rife among the natives of Spanish descent. They only want security and protection for life and property, and of course are opposed to everything like revolution or civil war. The returns which they have received for the investment of capital have in times past, and whenever the country has been quiet for a few years, been enormous. They are fast acquiring possession of landed property, and the available active capital is mostly in the hands of foreigners. Hitherto they have generally abstained from any part in politics ; but this cannot always last. They have too large interests at stake to allow the political power to remain much longer in gaucho hands. Every war and every revolution, however, increases their relative strength. They pursue their peaceful avocations while the gauchos are engaged in their favorite pastime of exterminating each other. The war with Paraguay may, for this reason, prove of advantage to the Valley of the Plata as far as it has been destructive to a race that can never be improved, and left the regions of their excesses to become the homes of a law-abiding, industrious, and thriving population. From iniquitous beginnings good results may flow. The gaucho race as a disturbing element has been very much weakened by the war. Brazil has been forced, in the exigencies that have arisen during its progress, to provide for the speedy abolition of slavery, and the despotism of Paraguay, whose existence was a source of danger and embarrassment to the adjoining countries, and a reproach to the age, has been forever destroyed.

The connection of Artigas with the history of Paraguay has led me into an inevitable digression upon the condition of the other countries of the Plata, and especially of the Oriental Republic of the Uruguay. The relevancy of this will appear long before the conclusion of this history. It will be found that in the political condition of the Banda Oriental the first hostilities of the war that resulted so disastrously to Paraguay had their origin.

A few years after the overthrow of Artigas and his band, and the escape of the gaucho chief to Paraguay, another individual equally noted, but enjoying another kind of celebrity, and in a different sphere of society, fell into the power of Francia. This was the celebrated naturalist, M. Aimé Bonpland. The companion and fellow-traveller of the still more celebrated Humboldt had fixed his attention on the interior of South America as offering a rich and unexplored field for his favorite investigations and pursuits, in which all the civilized world was interested. He arrived in Buenos Aires in 1817, accompanied by his wife and daughter, and remained there and in the vicinity for about two years, engaged in his favorite occupation, and in 1819 set out on an exploring expedition through the provinces of the interior. He had observed that throughout a large part of South America the use of the Paraguayan tea, or yerba maté (*Ilex Paraguayensis*), was almost universal. He observed that people who were accustomed to it had a great fondness for it, preferring it to the tea of China, to coffee, cocoa, or any other beverage whatever. An analysis showed to him that it had all the essential qualities of China tea, and he believed that by cultivating and curing it with more care it could be made to supersede the use of the China tea in other countries than South America. He therefore determined to make a thorough experiment, and wait the results. He established himself at Candelaria, on the left bank of the Parana, in the province of Corrientes, nearly opposite Itapua, or, as it is now generally called, Encarnacion. Here he gathered around him a colony of Indians, whom he employed and instructed in cultivating the soil. He never employed force, for he had none at his command, but by his example and his kindness towards them he so won their confidence and affection that his word was law and his precepts were their religion. He taught them to depend on the labor of their hands for their support, and showed them how easy, by a little care and forethought, it was to have abundance of food for the whole time, instead of depending on their former precarious means of support, — like hunting and fishing, — that sometimes exposed them to great destitution. He was a man exactly calculated to be a missionary of civilization to the savages. He had great skill as a physician, and his knowledge of plants and herbs enabled him to effect such wonders in the healing art as to appear miraculous to the simple natives.

The colony prospered exceedingly. The enterprise was one that, it would seem, could provoke neither jealousy nor enmity. The great work of Bonpland was to investigate the secrets of nature, and learn how far the fruits of this prolific country could be made useful to mankind. Even the gauchos respected him. True he had neither flocks nor herds to tempt them, and they had not the wantonness to destroy his colony from the mere love of destruction.

He had been about two years thus engaged; he had transplanted his slips of the yerba maté, that promised well; he had proved to the Indians that a better life was possible to them than they had ever known; and he was laboriously seeking to ascertain the mercantile and medicinal value of the woods, trees, and plants of that part of the world. His mission was one of philanthropy and self-abnegation. He had gone into the wilderness to spend his days as a benefactor of mankind.

While thus engaged, and knowing that he meditated harm to no one in the world, and laboring only to be of use to his fellow-men of all nations and countries, his work is suddenly brought to a close by the Dictator of Paraguay. The jealous Francia has observed his proceedings, and stealthily, while Bonpland has been pursuing his peaceful avocations, he has collected a force on the opposite side of the river. The first that the naturalist and his people know is that an armed force has entered the colony and begun cutting and slaying alike men, women, and children. It is a body of Francia's troops, consisting of four hundred men, sent to break up the establishment. The Indians are killed without mercy, and Bonpland himself receives a dangerous sabre-cut in the head. The defenceless Indians who are not slain escape to the woods and jungles ; and Bonpland, heavily loaded with fetters, is taken across the river.

The establishment being thus broken up, and Bonpland secure within the territory of the Dictator, his shackles were taken from his ankles, and he was permitted to reside as a prisoner at large, at Santa Maria, some sixty leagues to the southeast of Asuncion. But as he had cut no throats, nor baked anybody in the sun, as had Artigas, he had not the necessary title to the gratitude of Francia, and did not, like the great gaucho, receive any pension from the Dictator. On the contrary, he lived in extreme indigence, at first in absolute want. But his passion for his favorite studies did not desert him. If he could still pursue them, he would be comparatively happy. He asked permission to visit Asuncion, but his request was not granted. He then asked to be allowed to explore other parts of the country, simply as a naturalist, that he might discover what wealth yet unknown might be found in the plants, herbs, gums, and woods of the interior, to discover sources of wealth of which Francia would be the sole beneficiary. But this petition was as ungraciously refused as the other.

Francia, in recounting to Rengger the circumstances of Bonpland's capture, alleged, in justification of it, that his cultivation of the yerba maté would diminish the revenues of Paraguay, which at that time had a monopoly of the article. He alleged, as another reason, that the territory where the colony was established belonged to Paraguay. But as he never before or since exercised jurisdiction there, and it was known and acknowledged to be within the province of Corrientes, the assertion was absurd and impudent, as was the other accusation against Boupland, that his object was not to cultivate the yerba, but to co-operate with Ramirez, the gaucho chief who had rebelled against Artigas, and was afterwards Most Excellent Protector. "But at this very time," says Rengger, "and for long before, the head of Ramirez was exposed in an iron cage to the eyes of the public in the city of Santa Fé."

At last, after long waiting and hoping that the Dictator would relent toward him, Bonpland settled down at Cerrito, a place near Santa Maria, where he endeavored, on a miniature scale, to gather around him a colony of natives, and be to them as a father and messenger of civilization, as he had been to his larger colony at Candelaria. His skill as a surgeon and physician was again in requisition, and he soon won the love and confidence of all around him. He had no society except the ignorant semi-savage natives, no books, and therefore could not pursue his favorite studies except at great disadvantage; but he never complained, never meddled with anything but his fields and gardens.

But Bonpland, though he knew it not, was not forgotten in his misfortunes. His seizure and detention were made the subject of much comment among all civilized nations, but Francia had him hard and fast, and the more foreign governments and people complained of the act, so long as they sent no vessels of war to enforce their demands, the more self-complacent was he, as, by defying them, all the more important a character did he think himself to be. First the court of Rio de Janeiro attempted to so far placate the tyrant as to induce him to release Bonpland. But the effort was ineffectual. Afterwards the Institute of France took up the matter, and sent a special agent, who went as far as the banks of the Parana, for the same object. The agent, M. Grandsire, himself a naturalist, wisely kept out of Francia's reach and communicated with him only by letter. Even in him Francia could see only a political envoy and spy, and, instead of complying with the request, he only restricted and watched Bonpland more closely than before.

In the mean while several other foreigners who had been detained for years were allowed to leave Paraguay, and among them were the two Swiss doctors, Rengger and Longchamp. The English Chargé d'Affaires in Buenos Aires, Sir Woodbine Parish, had so far imposed on the vanity of Francia as to make him believe that something like what the Dictator had proposed to Robertson some seven years before could be effected if he would relax his rule a little towards Englishmen, so that they would not be afraid of detention in case they entered Paraguay on commercial business. The bait was eagerly swallowed by Francia, and the English, a few Porteños, and some of other nationalities, were allowed to leave a country that had for nearly a dozen years been their prison. Having thus acceded to the request of Sir Woodbine Parish, Francia in imagination saw an end of all his troubles. Indeed, he had but one; that was the lack of arms and ammunition, of which the governments below would not permit the transmission up the river. But now Francia had allied himself with England; Paraguay and England, England and Paraguay, were to form a union that should be the envy and the wonder of all other nations. Francia imagined that, if necessary, England would send her whole fleet to the Plata, in order that he might get a few muskets, and then he could hurl defiance at Buenos Aires and all his enemies. He communicated to Sir Woodbine, that, having shown so friendly a disposition towards England, he should expect the British government to keep the river open for him to import munitions of war. But that was more than the minister could promise. He wrote a courteous letter of thanks, however, to the Dictator for permitting his countrymen to leave Paraguay, but informed him that his government could not guarantee to him the free navigation of the river. He at the same time took occasion to renew his request for the liberation of M. Bonpland, stipulating that, if he should be permitted to leave the country, he would respect any conditions that might be imposed upon him.

The anger of Francia was unbounded when he found that England would not protect him in the importation of arms. He had been outwitted by Sir Woodbine, and he had no remedy. The English subjects were safe and beyond his reach, and he could not glut his rage by his favorite diversions of shooting and imprisoning. The letter from his Majesty's Chargé d'Affaires was returned to him with no other comment than what might be inferred from the superscription on the envelope containing it, which was thus: "To —— Parish, English Consul, Buenos Aires." Of course poor Bonpland was left to linger in his misery. He was not permitted to know of the interest taken in him beyond the limits of Paraguay, or of the efforts made for his release. His wife was incessant in her labors to interest influential parties in his behalf. But there was only one influence that could affect Francia, and that was the influence of fear. A threat of sending a squadron of war vessels to Asuncion to knock his capital about his ears would have doubtless made him eager to concede all that was asked. But none of the European powers would do that, so the Dictator knew, and the neighboring powers were too much occupied with their own intestine feuds, and were too jealous of each other, to attempt anything of the kind.

But M. Bonpland had within himself the means of his release. His life was a rebuke to Francia. With nothing but his own hands and kindly heart, he had, in the course of years, made himself a comfortable home, surrounded by willing subjects, who looked to him as their guide and father. He taught the natives how easy it was to live in comfort and plenty. He instructed them in the use of tools, and encouraged them to cultivate the soil to a greater extent than had been their wont, to have better houses, to clothe themselves decently, and give up their semi-savage habits. Under his watchful eye the flocks and herds increased, and the natives, whom he had found little better than wandering savages, under his direction had become a thriving colony. The French captive governed them as he pleased, for they obeyed him as their best friend. All this was observed by Francia, and his never-failing vanity was touched. That any of his subjects should look to any one but El Supremo for anything was an insult to his government. It was easy enough for him to shoot Bonpland or to imprison him ; but he seemed to feel that that would cause too great a scandal, and call down upon him more obloquy than he cared to face. To be rid of him he therefore took another way.

One evening Bonpland was visited by one of Francia's officers, and informed that he must leave Paraguay the same night. He was permitted to take a few clothes and a few dollars in money, and then hurried to the bank of the river, whence he was taken in a canoe to the other side and left to his fate. Nine years had he been in Paraguay. During this long and cruel detention he had, by his industry and kind treatment of the natives, and in spite of all disadvantages, accumulated considerable property, that he held in trust for those around him. But as before Francia had forced him to abandon all and enter penniless within his gloomy dominions, so now, when he had ties of interest and affection for the simple people by whom he was surrounded, he was cast out destitute by the envious despot.

The seizure and detention for so many years of M. Bonpland is not properly entitled to so large a space in the history of Paraguay as I have given it, as it had no political importance, and neither during his captivity nor afterwards did it have any influence for good or evil on the general policy of the Dictator or his relations with other nations. It is given at such length as an instance of the acts of Francia, not so bad as hundreds of others, and only of more interest than they by reason of the distinguished character of the sufferer.

CHAPTER XVII.

General Isolation. — The Closing of the Ports. — Effect upon the Commercial Condition of the Country. — Improvement in Agriculture and Manufactures. — These Forced Improvements but Incidents of Acts of the Grossest Tyranny. — Francia as a Cattle-Doctor.

AFTER the defeat of Artigas by his lieutenant, Ramirez, the latter with his bands of gauchos hung upon the southern frontiers of Paraguay, making occasional forays and keeping the Dictator in a state of constant fear. Vessels leaving for Buenos Aires were liable to capture by any band of gauchos that might get sight of them. Francia therefore, soon after he came into power, forbade the departure of any vessels, except at very rare intervals, when he had some purpose of his own to subserve. But from the time that Robertson was permitted to leave, in 1815, till 1825, when Rengger, Longchamp, and several English were allowed to do the same, all egress from the country was absolutely prohibited, and to the time of the Dictator's death, in 1840, no other person, except Bonpland, left the country. The merchants, therefore, who had at the time of the revolution accumulated large quantities of the produce of the country, consisting principally of hides, tobacco, and yerba maté, found themselves suddenly ruined. The risks from Ramirez and his men at that time, it is true, were great, but if overtaken by them they could generally, on payment of a sum of money, get permission to go on with that part of the cargo that was of no use to the gauchos. Besides, these very dangers gave a pretext and occasion for charging high prices. Excessive profits among business men imply extreme risks; and when large fortunes are speedily made, they are usually acquired by those bold speculators who take all the chances. The profits of the

Paraguay trade were then enormous,* and so far from being detrimental to the interests of those engaged in it, the gaucho robbers were an actual benefit to them, as they prevented competition, and left the whole business to be monopolized by a few. But Francia refused permission for any vessel to leave the port, and after that the general commerce was virtually at an end. The goods rotted in the storehouses, and the vessels rotted in the river. The prices of everything from abroad naturally increased enormously, for nothing was allowed to be imported.

This state of things did not fully accord with the interests of the Dictator, as some articles from abroad were needed for the purposes of the state. But the general isolation, that allowed him full power, with no one to criticise his acts whose voice he could not instantly silence, was exactly to his mind. Beyond the confines of Paraguay it was indeed reported that he ruled his people with an iron hand, but of the individual acts of his tyranny nothing was known. He therefore sought to open communication so far as to allow the admission of such goods as he wanted, without permitting any personal communication between his prisoners and the outer world. The port of Ñeembucu, now called the Villa del Pilar, was accordingly made a sort of *entrepôt*, to which a few vessels were permitted to ascend. This was the lowest town of any importance on the river, though some fifty miles above the confluence of the Parana and Paraguay. The country below there, forming the delta, is a succession of marshes and lagoons, alternating with level plains, on many of which the trees and underbrush form an almost impenetrable jungle. In the one, tigers and pumas held undisturbed possession; and in the other, alligators and snakes abounded. This broad waste served the purposes of Francia most effectually, as in later times, from its strategetic position, it served another purpose. It served Francia as a barrier to prevent egress

* Robertson gives an instance where a quantity of salt taken in as ballast, that cost two hundred dollars in Buenos Aires, was sold in Paraguay at a profit over and above all expenses of sixty thousand dollars.

and ingress, and it afterwards served to facilitate the extermination of the nation.

To this point vessels, having first obtained permission from the Dictator, were allowed to ascend. But before going even thus far, the captain or supercargo of each vessel was obliged to forward a manifest of his cargo, which was sent on to Asuncion, when the Dictator made a selection of the goods to be admitted, and named the price he would pay for them in the produce of the country, generally in yerba maté. The vessel was then allowed to go up to Ñeembucu and make the exchange, but the strictest caution was taken that no word of intelligence from the outer world should penetrate to the interior. The goods were taken thence to the capital, and deposited in the government storehouses, and such as were not used for the army were sold out to the inhabitants at prices unknown elsewhere within the last two centuries. A common silk handkerchief, such as would cost in England from two to three shillings, would sell in Paraguay for as many sovereigns. A yard of broadcloth, worth five dollars in Buenos Aires, would cost ten times the amount in Asuncion. A black fur or silk hat would sell for sixty dollars, and a yard of black silk for an ounce. And these were the prices when the products of the country were nearly valueless; when the cattle had increased to vast herds throughout the country; when the tobacco could not be exported, and was only raised for home consumption; when the hides were not worth preserving, as they could not be shipped away, and the bales of yerba maté were rotting in the storehouses of their owners. A good horse could be bought for a silver dollar, and a fat ox for two or three shillings, so that a hat would cost the price of sixty horses or eighty horned cattle.

Thus shut in and forbidden all communication with the rest of the world, the people of Paraguay, finding that any exhibition of thrift, or restiveness, or talent was sure to expose them to the merciless jealousy of the Dictator, fell into a state of apathy and stolidity. But the people were not savages. They must have some of the comforts and necessaries of civilization, and to obtain them they must make them for themselves. The protectionist doctrine was strictly applied by Francia. The natural result followed; people learned to manufacture for themselves. They made themselves chairs and tables, rough boxes to hold their clothes, and bedsteads with strips of green hide for bed-cords. They learned, too, to spin and weave. But in their mode of doing these things there had been no improvement since the days of Penelope. Even to this day the spindle is the principal thing used besides the fingers for spinning the cotton. This, in order to be worked, must be prepared, whipped, and combed with great care; and then with a spindle about six inches long, to which the thread is attached, they draw out the fibres with a twirl, which when sufficiently twisted they wind up on the spindle in a way that no skill or dexterity can make otherwise than tediously slow; then another yard is spun in the same way and wound up, and then another, till the spindle will hold no more. How many yards a woman can spin in a day one person may imagine as well as another, but it is apparent that the labor requisite for a yard of cloth is a matter of weeks. Occasionally a coarsely made, old-fashioned spinning-wheel, imported in the colonial time, may be seen in the houses of some of the better class. But these are used only for fabrics of coarse texture, and are so imperfectly made that spinning with them is still a slow process. The weaving is done on looms made in the country; and as there are people who make that their speciality, the process, though so slow that it would exhaust the patience of any one not a Paraguayan, is comparatively a short operation. But with the weaving given out by the piece, it is yet a good year's labor for a woman to make a fine cotton shirt. Some of them, it is true, are uselessly fine, and have an amount of embroidery hardly comporting with the bare feet and half-wild aspect of the wearer. Many of the women attain great skill in the working of this embroidery, and the men were compelled to learn something of the use of tools that they would not have needed to learn had the ports been open. But further than that there was no improvement in anything. The labor required for decent clothing was so great that people soon learned to go half naked and think nothing of it. A single bullock's hide would buy more cloth, and of a better quality, in Buenos Aires, than a woman in Paraguay could make in a year. But the hides where they lay were not worth a penny, for it was the Dictator's policy that there should be no commerce.

The improvement in manufactures, however, such as it was, has been adduced by the apologists of Francia as a proof of the wisdom of his policy. In the same way it could be proved that the wisest policy for any nation is to shut up the men in prisons, and put them to work at mechanical trades, as it is found that criminals so placed do learn to be tolerable artisans. In fact, the best mechanics in Paraguay at that time were the state prisoners; men who for dreary years were kept in prison, generally for having so much intelligence as to be objects of suspicion. Some of these unhappy men were allowed to beguile their time by making small fancy articles, such as required few tools; and some even made boots, shoes, saddles, bridles, and other horse-trappings. These men, thus shut up for many years, would naturally learn to do well what they chose to do, as they were allowed to enjoy the fruits of their labor in so far as to assist in their own support, and thus lighten the burden of their families.

The closing of the ports also compelled many of the more wealthy citizens to depend on the home production for many of those luxuries of the table which they had been accustomed to import. Hence more attention than formerly was given to the cultivation of cotton, — which it had before been found more profitable to import already manufactured, — and of those fruits of which sweetmeats were made, to the culture of the sugar-cane, and to the manufacture of the rum, or *caña*, of the country. The grape, however, was neglected, and has been to this time; and though the soil and climate are well adapted to it, yet it has never been cultivated, except to be eaten as fresh fruit. No wine of any consequence has ever been made in the country.

The character of the Paraguayan people was naturally so docile, that only by general and intense personal suffering could they be provoked to turn on their oppressor. Francia understood their peaceable disposition, and he was aware that so long as the masses of the people did not lack for food they would not be dangerous, unless they were incited to resistance by men of military prestige and superior capacity. All such it was his early care to put out of the way, and he took especial pains that the lower classes should never be driven to those excesses to which hunger and want will excite the most quiet and docile. The soil was naturally so fertile that scarcely any labor was required to make it produce all the sugar-cane, tobacco, mandioca, and Indian corn that the inhabitants required for their own consumption ; and as nothing was allowed to bc exported, there was no inducement for them to cultivate anything more than sufficed for their own necessities. The cattle, that ever since the time of Cabeza de Vaca had been multiplying at an astonishing ratio of increase, were so numerous as to be of scarcely any value after the closing of the ports put an end to the export of hides and tallow. Hence the people in the country lived in lazy abundance, and grew indolent, vicious, and immoral, as any people would under such circumstances. In the towns the lower classes, the lazy, thriftless, and dissolute, were encouraged in their gross and idle habits by the Dictator's policy compelling the rich estancieros to send their cattle to the public slaughter-houses to be butchered, and then distributed gratuitously to the vicious and abandoned. This class naturally soon learned to regard Francia as a benefactor ; and the fact that the meat they consumed had been robbed from the better class of citizens caused them to regard all such persons as their natural enemies, to be accused to the Dictator in case they resisted their insolence and extortion. This was more particularly the case with the soldiers, who, if they were scrupulous and exact when on duty, knew that there was scarcely any excess in which they might not indulge with impunity at all other times.

The compulsory gift of cattle to feed the poor, however, was but a trifling hardship in itself, as the herds had become so numerous that the increase was greater than the consumption. Besides, a large portion of what was required, both for the food of the soldiers and for gratuitous distribution, was taken from the estates that, as a part of the machinery of the conspiracy, had been confiscated when the owners were executed. But it was a more serious matter when the Dictator ordered all the cattle in several of the populous districts of the state to be indiscriminately slaughtered. At one time a kind of tick, called there the garrapata, had become so numerous, and so infested the cattle, as to cause very great loss and annoyance. The indolent owners took little or no pains to destroy them in the embryo state, or to separate cattle that were covered with them from ranging with the herds. Francia's remedy was like that of the physician who cut off the patient's head to prevent him from dying of a fever. He ordered the herds of cattle among which the garrapata had appeared to be all killed off without exception, and the owners were compelled to see these orders executed. Sometimes these herds contained as many as two or three thousand head, and the work of slaughter was a labor of weeks. But the Dictator had commanded, and the unhappy estanciero knew that anything like hesitation in obeying would be followed by imprisonment and death.

But the garrapatas were not exterminated, notwithstanding the sweeping measure of Francia. They have continued from that day to this to infest the cattle and other animals, but the people find no difficulty in so far destroying them that they are regarded as of trifling consequence.

These forced improvements in agriculture and in mechanic arts are all that the reign of Francia has to show of domestic benefit derived from his rule; and these were purchased at a price far beyond their value, and only followed incidentally from acts of the grossest tyranny. But anything to vary the current or relieve the "running shriek," anything in the history of those dark times that is not a story of blood or torture, is a relief. Henceforth, until the event of death destroys the illusion that had come to possess the people of Paraguay that Francia was the fiend incarnate, gifted with supernatural powers, this history can be little more than the chronicles and details of his atrocities.

Not only were the people compelled for their own convenience and comfort to learn to some extent the use of tools, and to manufacture certain articles which they had before been accustomed to import, but they were obliged by the Dictator to make the clothes with which his soldiers were clad, and also to make the saddles, bridles, and other trappings for the horses of his cavalry. For a man in the government employ to botch his work, though he had never been taught any trade, was a crime, in the eyes of Francia, against the government; and in one instance a shoemaker who had been ordered to make some belts, which, either from ignorance or clumsiness, he had made badly, or at least not according to the fancy of Francia, was subjected to a reprimand which, in that instance, seems to have served to make him, if not more skilful, at least more careful, for the future. Being called to the door of the Government House by the sentinel, the Dictator ordered the delinquent to be taken to the gallows across the way, where he was to walk beneath it three times, and the admonition given him that if his next belts were not better made he should be hung thereon. He was accordingly passed and repassed under the gibbet, and the next belts that he made so well suited the Dictator that he was approved by him for his greater skill, and made belt-maker-general for the army. Whether this implied that his labor or his remuneration was increased is not mentioned either by Rengger or Robertson, both of whom mention the circumstance. This act is commented upon with much satisfaction by Carlyle, as showing great wisdom on the part of his hero, and as a most excellent way of quickening the intellects and improving the handicraft of unskilful laborers. Even Rengger, whose work appears to all who have had any personal knowledge of the reign of terror as altogether too favorable to Francia, and to be written in an apologetic spirit rather than otherwise, in mitigation of the judgment against his cruelties, commends this act as having had a good effect in stimulating artisans and all other laborers, inciting them to greater care and skill. Indeed, whatever the Dictator did, having in any respect a good result, notwithstanding the suffering and the expense of life or property it may have cost, is largely credited by this author to the tyrant, while the reviewer rings many changes upon it as evidence of his wisdom and his beneficent rule. According to this reasoning, it would be a most blessed thing if some Francia might obtain absolute control of the government of Australia, New Zealand, or other British province, and rigidly prohibit all communication with the outer world. No doubt certain kinds of native industry would be stimulated, but no doubt, also, the mind and spirit of the people would be dwarfed and stunted, until they might passively submit to become mere machines, without ambition or hope ever to emerge from their misery and degradation.

CHAPTER XVIII.

Scarcity of Data for a History of Francia's Times. — Capricious Character of his Government. — His Jealousy of all Persons of Intelligence. — He gives a Levee. — Unnatural Conduct towards his Father. — Treatment of his Natural Children. — Religious Belief. — Banishment of Mendez. — The Prisons. — The Chamber of Truth. — Tevego a Place of Exile. — Executions. — Persecution of the Spaniards. — Forced Contributions. — Marriage discountenanced; forbidden except with Negroes. — Francia makes himself the Head of the Church. — Question of his Insanity. — His Motives in closing the Ports and excluding Foreigners.

FROM this time till the death of the Dictator, there is little to be said that can properly be called history; no living, moving diorama in which individual men occupy the foreground, each acting the part to which his talents, his education, or his ambition, lead him. It is only a dark level, a gloomy stationary scene; and the only figures that appear on it, save only the sombre Dictator, whose presence clouds it all, are the victims whose clanking chains we shall see and whose death-groans we shall hear. The country was reduced so entirely to the will of one man, that, having no foreign policy, no connections abroad, no change within, and no other incidents of interest than the arrest and execution of suspected or obnoxious persons, the country had no history except the cruelties of Francia. For all the rest it was the same one day, one week, month, or year as another. There was neither social intercourse nor domestic confidence. Nor did it seem that a change would ever come. The tyrant lived much beyond the allotted age of man, and to the last evinced the same inflexible love of persecution and the same pleasure in causing fear and despair. None knew who were safe or who in danger. They only knew that about the same number of victims would be taken each year, some to be shot, but the greater part to lie in prison till the death of the Dictator or of themselves should set them free. This work from this time to the close of the dictatorship might properly be called "The Diversions of Francia," but the reader is here warned it will be but heavy diversion to him, a story of continuous horrors, and for all purposes of the historic progress of the country may as well be omitted.

Indeed, it is scarcely possible to give anything like a connected or chronological account of the cruelties of the Dictator during the last fourteen years of his life. No records of anything, so far as I have been able to ascertain, were kept; there was no printing-press in the country, and the ports were so closely shut and guarded, lest the darkness and ignorance of the outer world should break in to obscure the light which glowed around El Supremo, and blind the people to the blessings they enjoyed, that scarcely anything in regard to those gloomy years was ever published in any other part of the world. During Francia's lifetime no person could have ventured, even if so disposed, to keep such a thing as a journal of passing events without the greatest danger to himself; and after his death the succeeding government discountenanced all unfavorable allusions to him, and therefore no one, when the circumstances of the times were fresh in people's memories, ever made a connected relation of the events of Francia's reign. Hence nothing is now to be learned but from the recollections of people living at the time; and as full forty years have passed since many of the tragic incidents occurred which I have to relate, it is impossible to obtain anything like accuracy of dates. At the commencement of the late war, there were many people still living who had a vivid recollection of the circumstances of the arrest and imprisonment or execution of their friends; but such things were so common, and were kept up through so many years during which there was nothing to distinguish one year from another, that those who remembered well the events had often very vague ideas of the dates of their occurrence.

Nearly all that is or can be known of them, with the exception of the brief reminiscences of Rengger and Robertson, is derived orally from persons who were living at the time. These people are now nearly all dead, though less than thirty years have passed since the decease of Francia. From the oldest and most intelligent of them I endeavored to collect such reminiscences of their youth as they could give me, and from notes taken thus I shall endeavor to make out such an account of the events as they were able to give; but as the acts of Francia could generally be traced to no motive, and there was seldom any antecedent event to give warning of his most severe measures, my informants could only tell me of the occurrences, not pretending to give the dates within two or or three years. After the Dictator had fairly got the machinery of his authority in order, people took little note of time or of the year; and probably, at his death, not one quarter part of the inhabitants knew how long he had been in power, or in what year of the century they were living. To show intelligence above the ordinary level was dangerous; and to evince any disposition to inquire into the acts of Francia, or any curiosity to learn what events were then transpiring, either in or out of Paraguay, was fatal; and had there been in all Paraguay a person disposed to make a record of what was going on around him, he could not without great danger, in the general distrust that prevailed, have committed the first item to paper. Husbands were afraid of their wives, wives of their husbands, brother was afraid of brother, and all were afraid of the prying eyes of their servants and slaves. As Carlyle says, "One desiderates some biography of Francia by a native." But how was a native to gather the materials of a biography? Francia destroyed, not only his own principal records, but took good care that no one else should make or preserve any. And therefore, if I give an account of the treatment of some of the prominent people of Paraguay, especially those who had attained some position, influence, or reputation previous to his accession to power, the narrative will be as connected as anything that can be formed from the materials that now exist.

When Francia was first elected Dictator, partly from vanity and partly with the desire to show himself to the people with the trappings of authority, and to remind them that he was the central figure of the country, to whom the obsequious attentions that had formerly been paid to the governors of the Spanish *régime* were all to be directed, he so far unbent from his habitual reserve and cynicism as to hold a public levee, which all the principal persons of the capital were permitted to attend. On this occasion, dressed out in a fantastic manner, he showed the delight and self-conceit of a boy at sight of the bright buttons on his first suit of jacket and trousers. Anything of this kind, however, was repugnant to his character; and ever afterwards, as throughout his previous life, unless during a short period when he was laying his plans for gaining power, he evinced too great contempt for everybody to put himself to the inconvenience of another reception. Ever since his return from the University of Cordova, he affected to despise everybody in Paraguay. After being dismissed from the College of Asuncion he lived for a time with his father at Yaguaron, of which the old man was the *géfe*, or chief of police. There the future Dictator lived the life of a recluse, shut up in a room by himself, and holding scarcely any intercourse with his own family or any one else. He made no visits, but passed the whole time at his own house in a kind of twilight, with the door slightly ajar, but sufficiently open to admit the light for him to read. He took no interest in the amusements of the place, had no social intercourse, and did not go abroad, except occasionally he would go out partridge shooting. The people of the village took it for granted that a man who lived thus shut up, with no companions but his books, must be a prodigy of learning and wisdom. His father, however, thought that this was done more from affectation than any love of knowledge, and used to say that "his son Gaspar was either a great philosopher or a great fool."

The son, however, could not long live at peace with the father, and Gaspar left the family abode at Yaguaron and took up his residence at Ibirai, a league and a half from the capital, and from that time his family were to him as other people. The ties of consanguinity, if they had ever existed, were entirely severed; and though his father afterwards made some overtures of reconciliation, they were treated with contempt by Francia. He was as indifferent to the welfare and happiness of his brothers, sisters, and parents as to that of his natural children, whom he permitted to follow the fortunes of their low and abandoned mothers, and make a precarious living in menial occupations, dependent on charity or on the offal and refuse of the market which was thrown to the dogs and the beggars. On his death-bed, the elder Francia, or França, made a last effort at reconciliation with his son, for he feared to enter the unseen world bearing with him the unrevoked curse of his unnatural child. He therefore sent to beg that he would visit him in his last moments. Francia declined doing so, and another message was sent to him more urgent and piteous, stating that his father feared he might not enter the gates of paradise unless the two should be reconciled. To this dying request Francia replied, that, if his father could not enter heaven without his forgiveness, he might enter the abode of the damned, for he would not go near him. The accuracy of this anecdote of Francia's implacable resentment has been questioned by those who would make a hero of him. The tradition of it, however, was familiar to many during my residence in Paraguay, and there, among those who knew his character and his acts, no one had any more doubt of its authenticity than of the murder of Yegros, Velasco, or Cabañas. It may be said, perhaps, in extenuation of this unnatural act of Francia, that he did not attach the same importance to death-bed confessions, or regard the efficacy of extreme unction, as did most Paraguayans. He was an avowed infidel, a disciple of Voltaire and Volney, and his scanty library was composed mainly of infidel works.

He was not, however, possessed of one arm of power which has since been used with terrible effect. The priests he treated with contumely and harshness, making no distinction between them and others, except that, as they had more influence, he persecuted them with greater severity. But he did not resort to the plan practised by his successors of extorting from them the secrets of the confessional, or compel them to disclose to him what they had extorted in the hour of death. This expedient for a more perfect system of espionage was not unimproved, however, by his successors. The elder Lopez treated the priests with more respect, and sustained them as an arm of the civil power, and encouraged the people to confess to them, and directed the fathers to impress it upon all, that only through full confession could they ever escape the doom of eternal misery. The younger Lopez, as we shall see in the proper place, reaped the fruit of the seed thus sown by the father. He particularly imposed it as a duty upon all the priests to question the dying in regard to their feelings towards him and his government, and if they knew or had ever heard of any other person's giving expression to any feelings unfriendly to him, or reflecting upon his actions. In this way, as we shall see, the innermost thoughts of the whole people were made apparent to Lopez; so that his country became literally a Dionysian Gallery, and not only the expressions, but the thoughts, of all were sure to reach him.

Not long after the occurrence of his only levee, however, Francia took a more effectual mode to impress upon the people, and especially the native Spaniards, a sense of their helplessness and of his own power. At this time Francia kept a secretary by the name of Martinez, who was dignified with the title of Prime Minister, or Secretary of State,—a pompous, ignorant fellow, combining these two qualities, so often united in similar persons, servility to superiors and insolence to dependants and inferiors. By Francia's order he summoned all the old Spaniards to appear in front of his house, but for what purpose they were not at the time informed. In obedience to the summons, they all appeared at the hour designated, which was in the hottest part of the day. When all were assembled, the Secretary of State appeared on the veranda in front of them, arrayed in a fantastic dress, and surveyed the unfortunate men before him, who stood hat in hand, exposed to the scorching rays of the sun, anxiously awaiting what he might have to say. After smoking his cigar, sipping his maté, and surveying with evident satisfaction the faces of those before him, he began to address them, calling them a lot of brutes and beasts who deserved to be hanged, to be shot, to be treated like dogs. He told them that they were the natural enemies of the Paraguayan natives, and that they were conspirators, rebels, enemies of his Excellency the Dictator, and that they had been engaged in intrigues and treason, and were greatly beholden to the Dictator that they had not all been destroyed. This harangue, which was intended to be as insulting and humiliating as words could make it to the native Spaniards, served to convince them, if the august presence of his Excellency at the levee had not already done so, that they had a master over them with whom it would be dangerous to trifle; that they were all marked victims of his tyranny.

To add to the other terrors of the rule of Francia was its complete mystery. Every one was in constant fear, for the reason that no one could tell what offence had been committed by those who were arrested, imprisoned, or executed. People the most cautious and the most inoffensive were liable at any time to be taken without any notice or suspicion of the reason therefor. They would be sent into exile or taken to prison; and in the latter case, if they were not executed, their families would only know that they still lived by the fact that they were permitted to send them their meals. An instance mentioned by Robertson will serve to illustrate this practice.

A man by the name of Mendez, from Montevideo, lived in Paraguay with his family, consisting of a wife and three children, for some years before the revolution. He was a shopkeeper, and by close attention to his business was so successful that his wife, a very handsome, sprightly woman, was able to appear in the society of Asuncion in a style to which the simple natives were not accustomed, and the house came to be regarded as a favorite resort for foreigners and persons accustomed to those social observances with which the Paraguayans were unfamiliar. Mendez was a man who took no part in politics, and could have done nothing to provoke the enmity of Francia. He would, however, furnish a striking example, and accordingly one evening, when he was holding a little levee, or *tertulia,* in his house, a messenger from the Dictator appeared at his door and called him out to tell him that he and his family were banished a distance of some two or three hundred miles into the forests of the interior. The sufferings which he and his family underwent before they arrived there were, as described by Robertson, of the most terrible character. But these things were so common in Paraguay during the time of the Dictator, that there is no particular reason for describing this case in preference to those of others ; though this was at the commencement of the dictatorship, and when Francia had scarcely begun to show his true character. So much was he dreaded, that, so soon as any one was found to have incurred his displeasure, all his neighbors and friends were compelled from fear of their lives to forsake him, to leave him to his fate. Says Robertson : "From the moment that Mendez' banishment became known, his house, his family, and himself were all deserted as if a mortal and contagious disease were in the dwelling. Not a soul in all Paraguay but was terrified to go near the banished man, dreading a participation in his doom. His business had been pretty extensive ; none now dared to act as his agent, recover his debts, or take charge of his property ; no one would pay him ; no one would purchase, at any price, anything he had. He could not, on any terms, get a single person to charter him a vessel that might carry himself and family to the port nearest to his place of banishment. The mark of Cain seemed suddenly to be branded on his forehead. All men fled from him as from the plague ; in the midst of a populous city he was at once abandoned to the solitude of the desert." *

* "There was an old Spaniard who lived next door to me, and whom I had

The prisons of Paraguay are, and always have been, of the most noisome description, suited to the character of the government. In Francia's time, says Rengger, there were two clases of them : —

"The first were rather regarded as houses of detention, or to keep prisoners in safety before they had been condemned, or while they were waiting for their cases to be considered. This prison was one hundred feet long, with an L of the house projecting. It had only one story, divided into eight rooms, that enclosed a large yard, or *patio*. In each room were thirty or forty prisoners, who not all being able to sleep on the ground, some of them suspended their hammocks above the others. What must forty persons suffer, shut up twelve hours in the twenty-four in a little room without a window or any other breathing-place, in a country where three quarters of the year the heat rises to from 23° to 28° Reaumer, and under a roof that the sun heats all the day up to above 50°. Thus it is that the sweat of the prisoner runs from one hammock to another until it falls upon the ground. In the yard of the prison were little cabins, which served to shelter those individuals detained on suspi-

known from my first arrival in Paraguay. He went by the sobriquet of 'El Pelado,' 'the bald man.' His real name was Milleres. He was an inveterate enemy of the creoles, and a great bigot. . . . . He was a man of a fiery, irritable temper ; but still he was a man under the check of practical prudence, and being a mere shop-keeper, from whom most people kept aloof because of his forbidding manners, he was, perhaps, of all men in Asuncion, the least formidable to the Dictator. . . . When Francia proceeded to annihilate and debase the monastic orders, he converted into barracks some of their monasteries. This so exasperated the poor Pelado, especially as his hopes at the time were raised to a great pitch of excitement by a false report of a Russian squadron being on its way to Paraguay, that he gave loose to the following remark : 'The Franciscans have gone to-day ; but who can tell that Francia's turn may not come to-morrow ?' By some busy and malicious tongue this short but fatal speech was conveyed to the ears of the Dictator. He summoned the Pelado to his presence, and addressed him in these terribly emphatic words : 'As to when it may be my turn to go I am not aware ; but this I know, *that you shall go before me*.' Next morning the Pelado was brought to the *banquillo* placed not far from Francia's window ; and the Dictator delivered with his own hands, to three soldiers, the three ball cartridges with which the unfortunate man was to be shot. The aim was not effectual, and the executioners were ordered to despatch him with their bayonets. On the whole of this scene of barbarity and blood Francia looked from his window, being not distant more than thirty yards from the place of slaughter." — ROBERTSON, *Reign of Terror*.

cion and those condemned for slight crimes. Some of the prisoners in the yards were sent out during the daytime to labor on the public works, and could thus have some exercise. In these cases they were chained together, two and two, or they had only the fetters, that consists of a heavy ring of iron upon the foot, whilst the greater part of the other prisoners carried another kind of fetters, whose weight was often more than twenty-five pounds, notwithstanding which it permitted them to travel. The state gave a little food and some clothes to those prisoners who were occupied on the public works; the others were maintained at their own cost, or by charity that two or three of them daily went out to seek through the city, accompanied by a soldier, or that some people sent to the prison, either for charity or in fulfilment of some promise. In these prisons were seen the Paraguayan, the Indian, the mulatto, the white, and the negro, the master and the slave; all classes and ages confined together; the innocent and the guilty, the condemned and the simply accused, the footpad of the roads, the assassin, and the betrayer, and many times were they tied together by a chain. But what fills the complement of this picture was the demoralization always increasing of the greater part of the prisoners, and the fierce joy, the ferocious delight, that they manifested at the arrival of a new victim. The female prisoners, fortunately very few, dwelt in a room and in a part of the yard fenced off from the larger one, where they could communicate more or less with the men. The women who from some cause had fallen into disgrace with the Dictator were there mixed with prostitutes and criminals, and exposed to every insult from the prisoners. These women dragged their fetters the same as the men, and not even pregnancy was sufficient to ameliorate their condition."

The jailer of this prison was a man named Gomez, of whose efforts to alleviate the sufferings of the prisoners Rengger speaks in the highest terms. He says of him, that, before being assigned to this duty, he himself had suffered many years in the same prison, where he had been shut up many years as a prisoner of state; that, after he had been given his liberty by the Dictator, he was assigned to the post of jailer, which he was obliged to accept.

"The prisons of state consist of small cells, without windows, and in damp holes, where it is impossible to set the foot except in the mud. These prisons appear to be designed for objects of the vengeance of the Dictator, some suffering there a solitary seclusion, while others are shut up two, and even four, in each cell; all wear fetters, and are not permitted to communicate with each other, a sentinel being always in sight. By day the door is open, but at sunset it is closely shut, and it is not permitted them to have light, nor to occupy themselves in anything, so that an unfortunate prisoner, an acquaintance of mine, having succeeded in taming some mice in his prison, the sentinel hunted and killed them. The beard, hair, and nails grow long, but they have no permission or means to cut them. Their families are not permitted to send them anything to eat more than twice a day, and this must consist of the food that is considered the most cheap and common, such as beef and mandioca root. The soldiers to whom the food is delivered at the door of the prison turn it over with their bayonets to see if it has any papers or instruments. Many times they keep it for themselves, or throw it upon the ground. When any of the prisoners are sick, no kind of assistance is given to them except in their last moments, and even then it can only be done by day; by night the door is shut, leaving the unhappy victim abandoned to his sufferings. Not even to the last agony is he relieved of his chains. The total number of prisoners at our departure from Paraguay was at least five hundred, a tenth part of whom, at least, were of that class."

In addition to the prisons before described, Francia had another which he denominated "The Chamber of Truth," and it was here that his victims who were suspected of having knowledge of anything which he was not already possessed of were tortured. Into this dark chamber the accused were taken and questioned in regard to whatever had been suspected by Francia; and if, as was generally the case, they knew nothing in regard to the matter, they were then beaten until their memories should be quickened to such admission as Francia desired to obtain, or until they expired under the repeated application of the torture. He had not learned the refinement of the art as some fifty years later, in a more enlightened age, it was practised by Lopez. But Francia differed from his successor in this, that he only flogged and starved his victims for a purpose, and not for the simple pleasure of inflicting misery for the delight which it afforded him. If he conceived the idea that a person was concealing anything which he wished to know, he resorted to torture as the readiest means to make him divulge it. But the suffering and agony were to him a matter of perfect indifference. For an accused person to confess, however, was only to secure him a more speedy termination of his sufferings. When Francia had obtained from him by this means all that he desired, his next step was to order him to be shot or hung.

To the other punishments which Francia visited upon the unhappy Paraguayans, that of exile was added. His system was in no respect confined to the capital. It was as rigorously enforced in the remotest parts of the state as in Asuncion and vicinity. Hence a mere decree or order from the Dictator for a person or family to retire into any remote part was easily enforced. And if, for any reason, Francia wished to remove persons from the city, and did not care either to execute them or hold them as prisoners, he had only to decree their banishment and assign them the place to which they must retire. He had, however, a place selected, especially for criminals of a low class; and he therefore established a sort of criminal colony at a place called Tevego, one hundred leagues northward from Asuncion. It is now called San Salvador. The spot is low and unhealthy, and was then exposed to attacks of the Indians, and the soil was of that sandy character capable of producing but little, so that the colonists were constantly exposed to inundations and starvation. A guard of soldiers was kept there to prevent them from escaping; and there, exposed to the malaria of the marshes, without the comforts of civilization, the poor wretches soon succumbed, and it was only by recruits sent from other parts that the colony was kept up. The abandoned character of the people, however, rendered it in some respects a place which it was desirable for Francia to have at hand, as whenever a person of respectability was sent there to end his days, it was a stigma and a disgrace which execution by torture or by shooting could never attach. The number of people who, during Francia's reign of nearly thirty years, were sent into this exile is not known, and never will be, but it is certain that there were a great many. The colony was kept up for more than twenty-five years; and as the exiles were supposed to perish within two or three years after their entrance into this abode of misery, their number from first to last may be reckoned by thousands.

His executions were attended by circumstances of peculiar horror. He always superintended them himself, and if he did not experience the same delight in witnessing the miseries of his victims and hearing his torturers' accounts of their contortions, shrieks, and agonies as did his successor, Lopez, he had equal delight in contemplating the ghastly fear that he inspired among their relatives and friends. The Government House, where he spent most of his time, meditating upon the deeds of terror either done or to be done, was situate in the Plaza, fronting a fine lawn or plot of ground extending towards the bank of the river. His window commanded a view of this plaza, on the other side of which stood an orange-tree. Beneath this tree — "the tree is living yet" — was placed a stool or bench called the banquillo, on which the doomed man was seated for execution. Francia himself acted as chief executioner. He was so parsimonious of his ammunition (or perhaps it was from sheer cruelty) that he would allow but three cartridges for the despatch of one victim. These he would give with his own hand to as many soldiers, who, having taken their posts at a convenient distance from the banquillo, at the word discharge their pieces, Francia viewing the scene either from the corridor or window of his house. But as he was too economical of his ammunition to waste it for the purpose of saving from prolonged misery the objects of his vengeance, and his soldiers, knowing little of the use of fire-arms, sometimes but slightly wounded the man they were to kill, they would afterwards despatch their victim with their bayonets, while the Dictator would look on, indifferent to everything except to satisfy himself that the man was finally dead. It was not sufficient, however, for him to see the victims butchered; they were always left for the whole day to lie before his window, that he might feast his eyes on the sight, sharing his joys with the vultures that were gathering about, anticipating a less brutal repast than the Dictator had gorged himself upon. There they must lie through the heat of the day, to be seen by all who were compelled to pass in that vicinity, — few others would pass, — and when night fell the friends of the family might take them away and hide them from the further vengeance or desecration of either the Dictator or the vultures.

To obtain the arms and ammunition which Francia required, it was more convenient for him to send away money to purchase them than the productions of the country, inasmuch as it was easier to get gold and silver out of the country than the yerba and tobacco, which, being more bulky, were in consequence more liable to fall into the hands of the freebooters on the banks of the river below. It was, therefore, very unfortunate for a man to be thought rich, or to have money about him, for in Francia's eyes it was as grave an offence to be rich as to be a Spaniard. When, therefore, he had determined to make a forced contribution from any person whom he supposed either had money or could obtain it, he would send a soldier to notify him that El Supremo commanded his presence at the Government House. Such a command was invariably followed by instant obedience, and the person thus called, with fear and trembling, would accompany the soldier to the dingy room of the Dictator, where, being admitted, he would stand humbly to receive his sentence, probably not having the least suspicion of what offence he was to be accused. Standing in front of the haughty Dictator, with his arms extended towards the ground, he would meekly await his sentence. The Dictator, if he had determined to extort money from him, would begin after this manner, "You villain! you are an enemy to my government." To which the man, not daring to raise his eyes, would probably reply, "I have never said a word against your government." "But you have heard others speak against it, and you did not denounce them." "Your Excellency, I do not remember to have ever heard any one speak against you or your government." "You don't, villain! I will make you remember. Bring me five thousand dollars within three days, or you go to the banquillo." "Your Excellency, I have not five thousand dollars, and know not how to obtain it." "Away to prison." The poor, trembling wretch would then be marched off to the public prison, where he could communicate with his family and friends and inform them that unless within three days he could raise the money for his ransom his life would be the forfeit. Sometimes they would be able to raise the money; and then the offender would generally be let out, though frequently it happened that, notwithstanding the money was paid by his friends, he was left to rot and die, or perhaps was finally executed by the order of the Supremo.

On one occasion, before the ports were entirely closed to commerce, Francia being desirous of raising a considerable sum of money, brought three of the most wealthy and respectable merchants in town, Aramburu, Garmendia, and Recalde, before him, and accused them of having sent, or attempted to send, money out of the country. Each protested in turn that he had done nothing of the kind. Francia, however, would not listen to their denials, but told them that they were his enemies, and enemies of the government, and ordered them, under penalty of death, to bring him from sixteen to thirty thousand dollars each within a stipulated time. They were all sent to prison, to remain until the money should be forthcoming. Aramburu was to give thirty thousand dollars; and being a man of very large property for that country, and having been engaged in merchandising, he had so large a portion of this sum at his command, that, with the aid of his friends, before the fatal day arrived, the whole thirty thousand dollars was deposited with the Dictator. Recalde was also able, with the assistance of friends, to raise the amount required. Garmendia, however, could not collect or raise the sixteen thousand dollars which he had been condemned to pay. His wife, upon hearing of his imprisonment and the amount necessary to save him, had exerted herself, with many of her friends and relatives, to obtain the money, and succeeded in getting together the larger half of it, which she took to the Government House and left there, begging for more time to raise the balance. Francia took the money and kept it, but the deficit was never made up, for, when the allotted time expired, Garmendia was taken from the prison to the banquillo and there shot, and left lying beneath the fatal orange-tree for the buzzards and the Dictator to look upon until the night should come, and his friends and family might take away his remains for burial.

In most cases, however, Francia did not condescend to allege any offence against his victims. They were fined, imprisoned, banished, or shot, nobody knew why or dared to ask his neighbor. There was gloom over all the country, so dense that never was heard the shout of laughter, never were meetings of young or old for amusement or conversation. The shadow of Francia's presence was over all like a pall, and though men lived, labored, and raised their children, all were in a state of chronic terror such as perhaps never existed elsewhere than in Paraguay before or since.

Hypocrisy is said to be the homage which vice pays to virtue. Such homage, however, was never rendered by Francia. He made no pretensions to virtue. Like the Arab, he scorned to be the slave of his word, and people who endeavored to observe the forms and appearances of a correct and moral life were, for that very cause, the more obnoxious to him. The affected superiority of the Spaniards over the creoles had doubtless often excited his gorge and contempt long before he became the head of the government; and it was certainly calculated to inspire anything but admiration for the native Spaniards, when a poor adventurer from Spain, who might have been a cobbler or a tinker in his own country, considered that he was doing honor to any part of America in which he might take up his residence. But this did not excite the jealousy of Francia so much as the sight of well-to-do people, who, from the very fact that they were moral and respectable, commanded influence and respect. He had a double motive, therefore, for forbidding all marriages of Spaniards with any other than negroes or mulattoes.

For the priests he had an aversion even stronger than for the Spaniards or the intelligent, respectable, and wealthy creoles. Their pretended sanctity, under cloak of which they imposed on the superstitious young daughters of mothers and fathers who feared their dipleasure, gave the cynical Dictator reason to despise them. But it was not because of their lazy, dissolute lives that he hated them. In spite of their gross licentiousness they had great influence, and especially among the lower classes, where Francia was resolved to be all powerful. A church government like that existing in Paraguay, that exercised authority independent of the civil power, being, as it was, of a secret and inquisitorial character, was inconsistent with his absolute rule, and he made short work of bishop, priests, and church property. He would tolerate nobody who acknowledged any authority independent of himself, and, after the example of Henry VIII., he made himself the head of the Church within his own dominions. The Convent of San Francisco was taken for barracks, and the bishop was badgered by the Dictator until he became insane, when he was superseded, and a vicar-general appointed to administer the spiritual affairs under Francia's direction. Religious processions in the street were suppressed, and the assembling in the churches at night was forbidden, lest people might take such opportunity to engage in dangerous conspiracies. Thus, in the early part of his career, did he labor to destroy every influence that might in any way militate against his absolute will. He had indeed destroyed all opposition, at least so far that no one dared to speak a word against his most arbitrary acts before his three years' time as Dictator expired. Having thus become absolute, it was very easy for him, through the Congress which he called, to have himself declared perpetual Dictator.

It appears that so long as the Robertsons or Rengger and

Longchamp were in the country, the Dictator occasionally invited them to visit him. They could tell him something of events transpiring in the outer world, of which he was lamentably ignorant; and up to the time that the Robertsons left they occasionally received letters and newspapers from abroad, the contents of which Francia was naturally desirous of knowing. He was particularly anxious to know what the rest of the world was saying about him and his government. He in this respect resembled that African prince who was seated beneath a palm-tree, clad in a red, ragged, cast-off monkey-jacket, without pantaloons, with an old glazed cap on, and the hilt of a broken sword beside him, and two of his subjects, almost nude, standing by to serve him, when, as some French officers from a war vessel in the offing passed by, he inquired of them if there was much talk about him in France. So Francia was curious to know if the world was mainly concerned in discussing his transcendent merits. Of all the eminent men, he seemed to think that Napoleon was most like himself, and accordingly regarded him as most worthy of his admiration. Perhaps the author of "Heroes and Hero Worship," who seems to have about the same admiration for one as for the other, may see the same resemblance between these two heroes.

It has often been alleged, in extenuation of Francia's conduct, that he was more or less insane, but never yet lived a man whose acts were all more consistent with his general character. There was too much method in his madness, the same line of conduct was too long sustained, to leave a doubt in regard to his sanity. There were no aberrations in his general course, no spasmodic acts of clemency or consideration, nothing, in fact, to show that every word and deed of his life was not the result of a deliberate purpose. That the purpose was bad, selfish, cruel, argues nothing against his sanity; and his extreme consistency with himself, through all the long years of his power, proves conclusively that his mind was always obedient to his will. His vanity was the controlling principle of his character. He delighted to see and feel himself absolute, and to have all around him crouch and tremble as before a superior being. To offend this vanity would incite him to torture the offender; but in other instances, and as the general rule of his actions, he shot, imprisoned, or banished his people for the deliberate purpose of causing himself to be feared. It has been sometimes alleged in evidence of his mental aberration, that at some periods, especially when the wind was from the north, he was much more morose and vindictive than at other times. As it is the experience of all, not only in Paraguay but throughout the regions of the Plata, that the warm humid, winds from the regions of the equator always produce a feeling of lassitude and depression of spirits that undergo an instant change when the wind veers and the cool breezes from the south set in, it is probable that Francia's evil passions were more demonstrative during the time that the weathercock pointed to the north. Other people were also less amiable, but they were not charged with insanity on that account, and it would be as silly to do it as to question the soundness of a person's mind who happened to be under the very common mental depression arising from indigestion. No, Francia was not the man to become insane. His mind was too narrow for any tumult or confusion of ideas, his thoughts too selfish to deviate from one channel.

His object in closing the ports and destroying the whole commerce of the country was in keeping with the other dark aspects of his character. If the river were left open and free to navigation, and foreigners could come and go, the world would learn of his horrid practices, and his people would also learn that there was sunshine in the sky, though the dark clouds of his power had involved their own land in darkness. He therefore, immediately after getting the reins of government into his own hands, began by putting such restrictions on trade and such difficulties in the way of commerce that no more vessels ventured into Paraguayan waters, and most of those already there were not permitted to leave the country. Nearly all of them remained in the river during his long and dreary dictatorship, rotted, and fell to pieces. Previously the trade of Paraguay with Buenos Aires had, for the number of people in the country, become very large. The wood of Paraguay was of immense value for very many purposes, as it has a finer grain and harder texture, and is more durable, than any other wood so easily attainable in any other part of the world. Francia forbade its exportation for the same reason that he had prevented the export of the other productions of the country, that its sale for export would necessitate communication with the other provinces. Tobacco, hides, and the yerba maté, were at first, however, allowed to be exported in a few instances, and in return for them foreign merchandise was admitted under the same restrictions which had existed before the revolution. But the coming and going of the small vessels that for many years had carried on this business were incompatible with the rule of the Dictator. If foreign vessels entered Paraguay, and the subjects of foreign countries commanded and navigated them, their governments would demand for them security and protection; and as most of these vessels carried the English or French flag, Francia could not venture to provoke hostilities by dealing with them as with his own subjects. If he permitted foreigners to enter the country for the purposes of trade, he must treat them as human beings, or their governments might declare him a common enemy of mankind; and as he had no fleet or navy, they might easily send a force against him that would soon put an end to his authority. He therefore determined to keep foreigners entirely out of the country. This was not done, however, according to any fixed plan, nor was there ever any general law promulgated of which the foreign owners of vessels detained in Paraguay could complain. The mercantile class in Asuncion, and the owners of vessels in the river, were mostly Spaniards, though their vessels were obliged to sail under the flags of other nations. Whatever outrage, therefore, Francia might commit against them or their vessels, the Spanish government was powerless to give them any assistance or protection, for at that time Buenos Aires was at war with Spain, and though directly interested in having free trade with Paraguay, Buenos Aires became the defender and auxiliary of Francia in his work of destroying the commerce of the river. It was impossible for any of these merchants or ship-owners who had accumulated property to leave Paraguay after the reign of Francia had fairly commenced. The Dictator not only wanted to destroy the commerce, but he wished to ruin those who had been engaged in it. This he accomplished by fines for alleged offences, for payment of which there was no other alternative than death. But he had another way to ruin them, which was more in accordance with his dark and sinuous policy. For months he would allow no vessel to load or leave the country, and the accumulated hides, tobacco, and yerba would remain at large expense in the hands of the merchants, until deteriorated in quality, or perhaps ruined; and then an order might be issued permitting them to load the vessel and depart. But when the cargo had been taken on board, and the vessels were ready to start, out would come another order for them to discharge everything; until finally there was no business, no trade. The vessels lay moored in the river until they rotted and fell to pieces, and Paraguay was shut out from the world as effectually as if it had been surrounded by a wall of fire. For his own purposes he nevertheless found it necessary to keep up a connection with the outer world. He wanted instruments to enforce his tyranny; arms and ammunition, iron for fetters, and a few tools, were indispensable. To obtain these he occasionally made an exception, and particularly in the case of the Robertson brothers, who were allowed to carry on a small river trade at an immense profit until they were driven from the country in 1815.

CHAPTER XIX.

The Yegros Conspiracy. — Its Counterpart. — The Chamber of Torture. — Execution of the Alleged Conspirators. — Espionage. — Francia turns Land Surveyor. — The City laid Prostrate. — Needless Destruction of Property. — Reconstruction. — Francia's Treatment of Old Spaniards. — General Velasco. — Francia's Letter in Reply to Rengger.

THE most interesting work that could be written on Paraguay, could all the facts be ascertained, would be a complete account of the several conspiracies that have been invented by the different dictators. From all that is known of them, or from all the existing evidence, it is the belief of the most intelligent Paraguayans yet alive, or that were living a year or two ago, that none of them ever had any existence except in the mind of the supreme head of the government. With the exception of that first revolution, instigated by Francia and instantly suppressed in accordance with his previous plan, there never was any pretence of more than one conspiracy during the Dictator's reign. The story of this is to the effect, that about the year 1818 a person by the name of Valta Vargas was sent by the government of Buenos Aires into Paraguay, in order to stir up a revolution; that he was arrested soon after entering the country and made a prisoner, though Francia was unable to connect him with any suspicious circumstance. Other parties, however, were observed by the spies and the police to behave in a very mysterious manner, and it was ascertained that they were in the habit of meeting at the house of a certain individual who was suspected of being unfriendly to the Dictator. This conspiracy, like all the other Paraguayan conspiracies, seems to have been going on for a long time, as much as a year having passed, after the arrival of Valta Vargas, before anything definite or positive was known in regard to it. The conspirators embraced all the principal men left in the country, including Francia's colleague during the consulship, General Yegros. The plans of the conspiracy, after so long a time in maturing, had advanced so far that a concert of action had been agreed upon by which the Dictator was to be attacked in the streets and summarily despatched. One of the conspirators, however, previous to taking part in the affair, which might involve himself in personal danger, confessed to a priest, and the priest in turn informed Francia of the plan.

"That night," says Robertson, "the groans of the state dungeons were augmented by the wailings of more than fifty of the best inhabitants of Asuncion. Every member of the former Junta was arrested, and every friend and relation he had. Their property was confiscated, and the house in which the conspirators had held their meetings was razed. The blacksmiths could not forge chains fast enough; the rigor and privations of a system of imprisonment already sufficiently callous were augmented; all that demoniacal ingenuity could devise, or fear, hatred, and jealousy wrought to a pitch of frenzy could invent, was had recourse to; the cup of bitterness held up to the prisoners was drained to the dregs; terror and consternation were spread among those who escaped the dungeon. The Dictator felt his arm strengthened by the detection of the plot, while, at the same time, it offered to him a plausible pretext for the multiplication of every precaution which jealousy could suggest and every cruelty which revenge could devise. One motive, and only one, prevented his doing instant execution upon the conspirators. *He was still afraid.* Connected as they were with every family of distinction in Paraguay, he feared to draw down upon him the odium or to raise the rebellion that might, and probably would, be consequent on the wholesale slaughter of his enemies. He left them, therefore, to languish in the state dungeons, unshaved, unshorn, unwashed, badly fed, wretchedly clothed, without communication with a human being, with their nails unpared and their bodies fetid from filth, till death, as he paid his frequent visits, was received, even by the greatest lover of life, as a welcome guest."

This extract from Robertson might be applied with equal

propriety to another conspiracy, of a similar character but more formidable dimensions, that was alleged to have been formed fifty years later. The latter conspiracy resembled the former in almost every particular. In the opinion of the older Paraguayans with whom the author became acquainted, there never was, in the first instance, any conspiracy whatever. It was a device of Francia's to furnish a pretext or excuse for putting the more influential and respectable men of the country out of the way. There is not a word of proof to the contrary. All the evidence that exists in regard to the matter at this time is that Francia arrested, imprisoned, and executed these people, and that through his spies and informers he announced that they had been detected in a conspiracy. Francia's word, therefore, is all the evidence that now exists to sustain the accusation that he then made; and the only proof that exists of the later conspiracy is the word of one more mendacious and cruel than Francia. It is said that Francia became more cruel, distrustful, and suspicious after the detection of this conspiracy than before; but this can be accounted for from the fact, that, knowing it to be a false accusation, and that the idea of the conspiracy originated in his own perverted mind, he had created a degree of enmity and hatred in the minds of the people which was before unknown to them, and which might lead to more desperate measures than they would otherwise venture to attempt. Having invented a conspiracy and then throttled it, he may have afterwards suspected that something like what he had pretended to discover might exist in reality. As he passed through the streets, he feared an assassin at every corner; and therefore, to guard against the danger of suddenly coming into close proximity with a band of assassins, he caused every hedge and bush, and even the houses behind which men meditating evil might conceal themselves when he passed by, to be levelled with the ground. The existence of so many persons of note, though prisoners and in fetters, was a source of anxiety to the Dictator, for the reason that he did not care to put them to death lest it should provoke an uprising of the people; for supreme as he was, he feared his shadow and dared not trust to his own power, and, so long as they were living, they would be a source of more or less danger. The overthrow of Artigas, however, and his flight to Paraguay, where he threw himself at the feet of the Dictator, served to remove one of the principal dangers with which Francia had been threatened for a long time. The successor and vanquisher of Artigas, however, Ramirez, attempted to hold some correspondence with the conspirators that Francia already had loaded down with fetters in his dungeon; and a letter from this gaucho chief addressed to General Yegros, the president of the first Junta, is said to have fallen into the hands of Francia. That any such letter was ever sent by Ramirez, or, if it were, that Yegros had ever done anything to invite it or to encourage Ramirez in his designs against Francia, no evidence exists, and it is believed that Francia's pretext that he had discovered such a letter was but a part of his original plan; that, having marked his victims for destruction, he desired to have some pretext, after they had been in prison for a long time, for putting them to death; and they were all successively taken to the Chamber of Truth and tortured until some of them expired, and some not only confessed to their participation in the conspiracy, but implicated others, so that after this mode of eliciting truth got fairly under way, each day brought in new accessions to the band of conspirators. How closely this proceeding of Francia was imitated years after will appear in its proper place. The closing scene is thus described by Robertson: —

"Three demons alone were accessory to the inquisitorial investigations of the Chamber of Torture, — Francia himself, a legal functionary, and a registrar. No one but these ever knew the results of the examinations. The result was only revealed to the public by the corpses of the prisoners as day after day they perished on the banquillo, glutted the eyes of the despot, tempted to voracity the birds of prey, and, after exposure to them for a whole day, were conducted in the evening, often mangled, by their despairing relations, to a dark and silent grave. Poor Don Fulgencio Yegros was first shot and then bayoneted; Don Fernando de la Mora followed in the same way; Galvan, Yturbide, and fifty others, all went in succession. Then came the turn of Don Pedro Juan Cavallero, the second member of the original Junta, and the most beloved by the troops of all the officers in Paraguay. The sentinels came into his cell in the morning to drag him forth to the banquillo, but he had eluded their clutches and given defiance to further tyranny. He had managed to strangle himself during the night, and on the morning destined for his execution was found a ghostly corpse under an epitaph which, in these words, he had written in charcoal upon the wall of the dungeon: '*I know that suicide is contrary to the laws of God and of man, but the tyrant of Paraguay shall never exult in having spilled my blood.*'"

According to the ideas of most men, it would be no crime to conspire against such a government as that of Francia's. On the contrary, it would be considered meritorious, and that people who would submit to the rule of such a despot without attempting to throw it off deserved all that they received. But in Paraguay, from the time of Francia's election as Dictator until the downfall of the younger Lopez, a conspiracy of five persons was a thing impossible. People who have not lived in Paraguay can have no idea how thorough was the system of espionage, or in what dread every man lived of all who were around him. It was dangerous for one man to introduce the subject of politics to his nearest relation or most intimate friend. Whoever might listen to it would be instantly suspected of being a spy of the Dictator, and he would dare to hear nothing of the kind; the man might be his most intimate friend, and on all other matters save the government the two might be on the most confidential terms. But it was known to be the special will of Francia that every person who heard the question of his government criticised or discussed should immediately report it, and that, if he failed to do so, he would be himself considered a criminal and a traitor. Therefore, whenever a man might hear anything of that kind, — and the same is true not only of Francia's time but throughout the reign of the two Lopezes, — he would consider himself already an accused person, and that he was in the power of the man who had been talking to him about the government. He had listened to criticisms of the Dictator's policy, and by not having reported the fact he had made himself obnoxious to his vengeance should it ever be discovered. Therefore it was that it came to this, — there were no two persons in Paraguay sufficiently intimate to discuss the character of the acts of the chief magistrate. If they were to do so, it would be a race between the two to see which should denounce the other first. Hence it was that from first to last a conspiracy of Paraguayans was a thing entirely beyond the limits of possibility, and so does every man say who ever resided in that country for as long a period as one short year. The older inhabitants of Paraguay who were living three years ago did not believe in what was called the Yegros conspiracy. They had no evidence, of course, either way; but from their knowledge of the country they knew a conspiracy was impossible, and there was no evidence that it ever existed, except the word of Francia. And of the subsequent conspiracies that have been alleged the same may be said; there is no evidence that they had any existence, except the word of the Dictator or President who accused obnoxious persons as an excuse for their execution.

The Dictator, besides fancying himself to resemble Napoleon as a warrior, considered that he ought also to resemble him in his public improvements; and his labors in that line are so extraordinary, that they serve to illustrate, not only his character, but his capacity.

The city of Asuncion, as originally built, had no regularity of plan. The site had primarily been selected for a military post, from the fact that the hill to the south had a bluff from which both the neighboring country and the river up and down could be overlooked; and the paths and trails used first by the Indians, and afterwards by the soldiers, came in time to be the streets of the town. Hence they were crooked and irregular, though adapted to the natural configuration of the ground, which, being uneven and broken, could not be laid out into a city with streets crossing each other at right angles without destroying the natural beauty and many of the natural advantages of the place. On these streets were a considerable number of good houses, some of which are yet standing. They were built usually of adobes, or of adobes faced with bricks on both sides, and the walls were sometimes as much as three feet in thickness. The architecture was somewhat after the old Moorish style, being one story in height, with large yards, or *patios*, in the centre, and having wide corridors, or piazzas, upon the street, with heavy pillars to support them, and with other and similar corridors within, surrounding the patios. There was very little uniformity, however, either in the streets or buildings, and Francia conceived the idea of rearranging the plan of the whole town. He, therefore, without any regard to the natural topography of the country or the convenience of the inhabitants, determined to lay out the town in regular squares. Without consulting any one, or making any preliminary surveys, he set forth with a force of chain-bearers, masons, and clerks, to correct the plan of his capital. He carried with him his terrible theodolite, which was calculated to impress the people, who might otherwise doubt his infallibility or his wisdom in what he was to do, that he had been inspired by superior power to the course he was pursuing. Taking his position at what he supposed to be the most convenient starting-point or landmark, he planted his theodolite, took a direct line to the northwest, and ordered everything to be cleared away, whether houses, trees, fences or hills, to make way for a street forty feet wide. The manner and result of these strange proceedings is thus described by Robertson: —

"His plan was to lay out the city in capacious streets, intersecting each other at right angles, and in straight lines, in a direction of due northwest and southeast. Three new squares were to be built on sites now covered with houses, and one square was to be altered and enlarged. Salient angles were to be lopped off, narrow streets were to be made wide, lanes were to be abolished, orange-trees were to be hewn down, fences were to be exterminated, for huts there was to be no commiseration; while babbling springs were to be choked, and gurgling rills to be dammed. Against brooks and stagnant waters a war of extermination was declared, and the sandy surface of Asuncion was to be overlaid by granite brought from many leagues' distance. Down went the theodolite, and down for its management came the Supremo from his horse. The very first line marked out in the direction of northwest swept off a dozen houses all standing obtrusively in the way. The next line in the transverse direction called for the annihilation of a dozen buildings more. These two first measurements a little staggered the land surveyor; but his one invariable appeal to himself was, 'Am I not El Supremo?' Soon were his scrupulous objections to his own original plans silenced. 'The houses *must* come down,' said he to himself; and he proceeded on his way without misgiving and without remorse. His first afternoon's work devoted eighty tenements to destruction; and another week's use of the theodolite and chain marked out a hundred more habitations for immediate demolition.

"So far was the land surveyor's conscience from being moved by a contemplation of the misery which such a step must entail upon the inhabitants of the devoted dwellings, that he looked upon every one of them as enemies to the amelioration of the city, and as obstructing and thwarting his plans for its improvement. With his usual impetuosity and haste, he issued orders to every one of the owners of the obnoxious houses 'to quit,' and not only so, but to be themselves the demolishers of their own dwellings, free of all expense to the state. One poor man applied to know 'what remuneration he was to have'; and the Dictator's answer was, 'A lodgement, gratis, in the public prison.' Another asked where he was to go, and the Supremo's answer was, 'To a state dungeon.' Both culprits were forthwith lodged in their respective new residences; and their houses were levelled to the ground.

"The surveying department, or rather the surveyor-general, after devoting upwards of five hundred houses to demolition, sent the inmates to substitute for them huts in the woods, and left every inhabitant of Asuncion unequivocally to infer that if his house interfered with the lines of northwest and southeast, especially if any objections were made to the proposed plans, that he (the objecting tenant or owner) must be prepared at once for ejectment and for banishment. Consequently no further remonstrance was made; and the levelling theodolite, under the scientific hands and unscrupulous conscience of the Supremo, proceeded on its angular and rectilineal process of destruction.

"The mathematical science of the Dictator was so scanty, that, before he could fix the *true* lines in which the new houses of the projected city were to run, he was obliged to demolish a great many buildings which the result of his final admeasurement showed him might as well have been left standing, inasmuch as they would not have interfered with the contemplated symmetry of the embryo capital of Paraguay. The result was that the first demolitions of brick and mortar were adopted as mere preliminary steps to pave the way for a more accurate mensuration and a more complete destruction.

"The streets of Asuncion were not only streets of sand, but were often formed into ravines by heavy rains, and in all cases rendered by these, and by numerous springs and brooks, of a very unequal surface. In order to remedy this obvious defect in the thoroughfares, our engineering, architectural land surveyor caused all the rubbish and *débris* of the demolished houses to be cast into the gaps and chasms and ravines of the *old* streets, so as to approximate them to the level on which he had determined that the houses of the new city should be built. Little hillocks which stood in the way of this levelling process were cut down, and little valleys which offered an obstruction to it were choked with rubbish. At length the site of the intended city was made as level as the engineer deemed it possible to make it; and to work went all hands to raise the superstructures which were to embellish it. Four hundred wretched prisoners in chains were set to work as bricklayers, masons, and carpenters; the carts, horses, asses, and mules of every laboring man were pressed into the service; no pay was ever awarded to them; the Dictator observed that they ought to be proud of serving the state gratuitously, since he condescended personally to superintend for them the erection of a city destined to be the most beautiful and important in the New World.

"Onward pressed the Dictator in his great undertaking, scattering the population of Asuncion, pulling down their houses about their ears, sending them to seek for shelter where they might best find it, obliging many of the more substantial inhabitants to build houses in substitution of those which he had made them demolish, and on spots selected according to his fancy. Slowly, however, even with all the Dictator's potency, did the work of reconstruction proceed; for though he was master of many Paraguayan slaves, even the Congress had not been able to confer upon him the power of contending with the elements, of changing the course of nature, or of evoking at his nod the waters from the dry land. Besides, in his anxiety to rear a superb superstructure, he overlooked the essential point of laying a solid foundation. A tropical storm of one night often swept away the works on which five hundred men had been engaged for a month. As the streets were not paved, the torrents of rain swamped and undermined all the rubbish that had been lavished upon them. The old cataracts, chasms, and ravines were reopened; the springs which the mighty engineer had choked in one place burst forth in another; the houses were no longer level with the streets; the windows of some of them were choked with mud and sand forced up against the walls by the impetuosity of the roaring torrents; and the foundations of others were laid bare by the sweeping storms by which they were inundated and undermined.

"Many of the smothered streams found vent in the very heart of the rising edifices, and, seeking a level, spouted forth with irresistible impetus, till reaching the elevation of the mortar-built walls, back fell the water to its mother earth. The *jets d'eau* were beautiful, not finer than some of those at Versailles; but water having a tendency, where there is nothing but newly laid bricks and mortar to resist it, to make awkward inroads, the mortar was attenuated, the bricks were loosened, and the next day exhibited to the Dictator, as he rode along with his plumb-line, theodolite, and squares, so many chinks and apertures as to convince him that the half-constructed edifice must come down. In some cases he set his men to the work of demolition; in others, nature saved him this trouble; so that, between the development of the destructive organ of the Dictator, in the elements, and above all in the contumacious springs, the city of Asuncion was no sooner half built than it was laid wholly prostrate. Nodding and tottering to its fall stood every edifice; the backs of many of the old houses were turned upon the new streets, as if in contempt of the Dictator's operations; crumbling to the ground came one day half a dozen structures; crash the next came half a dozen more; and all-persevering as was the besotted architect, yet, after five years' labor, not one fourth of his edifices had attained the security afforded by a roof; whole streets were laid off with stakes of dry reeds, not marking where a house *had been*, but where houses *were to be*; the town presented the appearance of having sustained a lengthened bombardment; and though by degrees, after his five years of frustrated plans and disappointed hopes, Francia succeeded in having some tolerably good houses erected, yet of the mass and his whole undertaking it may be safely asserted that there never was, nor is ever likely to be, so remarkable, and especially so literal, a fulfilment of the latter part of a striking parable: 'He shall be likened unto a foolish man, who built his house upon the sand; and the rain descended, and the winds blew, and beat upon that house, and it fell: and great was the fall thereof.'"

Of the old Spanish residents in Paraguay at the time of the revolution none escaped persecution, and few, if any, survived the Dictator. Many of them were arrested, tortured, and executed, as being members of the first conspiracy. Those who were not included in this general accusation were for other reasons, unknown to themselves, subjected to the same or similar treatment. In 1821, a year after the tragedy of the pretended conspiracy had ended, all the Spaniards in Asuncion were commanded to present themselves in front of the Dictator's house; here a series of grave accusations against them was read. They were charged, not only with being unfriendly to the government of Francia, but with being engaged in designs against his government. To these accusations they had nothing to say, for they were permitted to make no reply. They stood, however, some three hundred in number, from early in the morning until about sunset, afraid to move, not knowing what might be the next order of El Supremo. In the evening they were all taken to prison, and there they remained for weeks and months, and no further reason was ever given for their imprisonment, nor had they any intimation of what was to be their fate. Of course, those of them who had been engaged in business were financially ruined, and their families, in many instances, reduced to absolute poverty, and yet no one dared venture to bespeak pity or pardon of the Dictator.

It is unnecessary perhaps to cite other instances of the

practices of Francia. No one of them is exceptional; his policy and his conduct were uniform, — to arrest, imprison, torture, and destroy all of his people who had intelligence enough to command respect or influence. It is the same dreary level. His career is irradiated by no acts of clemency, of kindness, or of wisdom. He neither evinced ability in improving the condition of the country or of the people, nor in any way showed any capacity except that of a remorseless destroyer. From his efforts to improve the city we are able to judge of his scientific attainments and his practical sense, but we have little by which we may judge of his literary merits. No state papers of any importance were left by him. The records of his own times and deeds he was careful to destroy, and we are only to judge of his capacity and talents from his acts. On one occasion, however, he was provoked to put forth a letter in defence of himself and in reply to the accusations made against him in Rengger's book. This was the weakest act in his whole government, as it revealed completely the capacity of the man. Had he never allowed such letter to appear, it might have been imagined that a man who could control an entire people so absolutely as did Francia the Paraguayan nation must have been possessed of remarkable talents. This letter, however, must dispel any such illusion as that, for there are few criminals of the lower class arraigned before the criminal courts of our large cities who, if given time and opportunity, could not make a better defence than this which Francia makes of himself. As it is the only paper which we are able to produce from him, it is here given nearly entire.* Rengger's

* *Notes made in Paraguay by the Dictator Francia on the Volume of John Rengger.*

"The Swiss John Rengger came to Paraguay with his companion and countryman, Marcelino Longchamp, to establish himself as a physician. It was not long before Rengger leagued himself closely and seditiously with the old Spaniards, and with the Frenchman Saguier, a notorious spy of the royalists, and who established himself here as a so-called botanist. It was shrewdly suspected that they had both been banished from Europe. Here Rengger occupied himself with the poisoning of such American patients as he could lay hold of;

book, it should be borne in mind, was severely criticised by Robertson, and by Somellera, and, in fact, by nearly everybody else who from personal experience knew the facts in regard to Francia and his reign of terror. Rengger himself, and his companion Longchamp, were treated better by Francia than any other foreigners who were in Paraguay at the same time with themselves. They complained of nothing personal,

and, among others, no sooner had the treasurer Decoud swallowed the deleterious beverage than he fell into mortal agony, while the wretch of a physician from that moment abandoned his patient, nor would return to see him, in spite of repeated solicitation to this effect.

"During the three months in which Rengger attended the barracks of the regiment of men of color, he despatched more than twenty of them, and was on this account sent about his business, when at once the mortality ceased. No wonder that the fellow (el Bribon) avoids in his volume all allusions to this barbarous massacre. He knew well he should not find his account in making that public.

"Himself bitterly inimical to the cause of America, Rengger did all in his power to seduce others into his views. He persuaded the Saxon, Gustavus Leman, an ally and correspondent of the patriots, to desert them, and take part with the old Spaniards, on the allegation that he would receive better treatment at their hands than at those of the Americans.

"The Dictator, at length, in order to avoid the necessity of sending this wretch to the scaffold, — this assassin, this poisoner, this seducer and intriguer with factious enemies, — refused to grant the request which he made, that the government would allow him to remain in Paraguay in the exercise of his medical vocation. His principal object, however, in desiring to remain, was not this, but that he might marry the daughter of the rich old Spaniard Antonio Recalde. Of that lady the poor doctor was desperately enamored; but see if in his book he says anything of the rejection of his addresses, and consequent discomfiture of his marriage plans. The object of such omission is clear; it was to lull suspicion as to his mendacity in the fresh piece of iniquity of which he has been guilty in attempting to pass off as history a tissue of abominable falsehoods: and in doing this, and stamping himself as an unblushing liar, he has done exactly what was wanted to complete his character. So odious in Paraguay had this barbarous atheist made himself, so well had he established his character for perverseness, that the Paraguayans, in mockery and derision, gave him no other name than that of 'John Rengo.'* Some people who were walking on the banks of the river, and saw him embark, called aloud also, 'Adieu, pill-doctor! Adieu, purger! Adieu, poisoner!'

"Chafed and enraged not less from being unable to effect his marriage, on account of the government's prohibition, than from being banished the country and mocked by the patriots, the malicious Rengger left Paraguay like a dog with an old kettle tied to its tail. This is the man, who, coming into the country and

* A bad pun upon Mons. Rengger's name, and signifying "John the Limper," or "Lame Man."

and Rengger, in his narrative, gives Francia credit for ability and good motives, in many instances, when the others alleged that he was not entitled to it. He believed in the Yegros conspiracy. He also gave Francia credit for the improvements in the manufacturing arts which his system of non-intercourse compelled the Paraguayan people to adopt. He also gives Francia the credit of having stimulated or com-

cloaking over his secret mission, has published a pretended historical essay, of which the object evidently is to undermine the reputation of the Dictator; but the raving contemptible volume ought rather to have been styled an Essay of *Lies*. It may, without exaggeration, be affirmed that, as regards Paraguay and its government, it contains not a word of truth.

"Even in those parts in which there is some foundation of reality, everything is changed, disfigured, distorted. All is dressed up with fictions, and evidently meant to lower the character of the Dictator. Things the best known and the best authenticated are, with malice the most perceptible, and disingenuousness the most culpable, slurred over or kept out of view, simply because they do not dovetail into Rengger's plan. There is ample evidence on the face of the book that it is made up of disfigured accounts, slanderous tales, impostures, and stories, not only accommodated to the tastes of Europeans, but invented by them in revenge for the frustration of their repeated conspiracies, machinations, and plots. Take, for example, the mad-brained, or, rather, ridiculous fiction of the Marquis of Guarani, Envoy to Spain; and the hidden schemes by which they thought to lay prostrate the Dictator, with whom they are at rancorous variance, because he is a firm and decided patriot and viewed by them as an insuperable stumbling-block in the way of their particular theories and plans. Rengger, as being accredited with them for every species of iniquity, has lent a helping hand to increase the catalogue of such stories; and that by means of his fresh lies, fictions, and misrepresentations, and of the pure inventions of his own fantastic imagination.

"He has given himself up, without a blush, to the infamy of acting the mendacious and calumnious impostor; and this because of his engagements with the Europeans, of his declared aversion to the patriots, of his desire to revenge himself for the denial of his application to the government, and of the contempt and mockery which he suffered in consequence of the frustration of his connubial plans.

"These were likewise the causes which impelled his impudence to the pitch of inventing sayings and of forging conversations of the Dictator, which never took place. We are in no ignorance, nowadays, of the objects and implacable malice of such men. The single object of these rascals, devoid of soul, is to disburden themselves of vile passions; and for this purpose they avail themselves of sinister machinations and intrigues. It is a vain, and even a risible, effort in this ungrateful vagabond and low calumniator to speak about that of which he understands nothing.

"Rengger, foreseeing the charge of falsehood which would be brought against pelled the Paraguayan people to improved modes of agriculture. These things, however, are repudiated and derided by all who knew the real motives that actuated him. Notwithstanding, however, that Rengger was generally blamed for representing the character of Francia as less dark and cruel than it really was, the Dictator thus repays his forbearance and moderation.

him, hastens in the Preface of his Essay of Lies to adduce as a witness of the truth of his impostures the person of the name of Longchamp, already mentioned. But this man is nothing more nor less than the countryman of the other, and took up his miserable abode with him in a hut, as his gaucho companion, and as an accomplice in all his iniquities.

"The malignity of this calumniator has not been confined to Paraguay; it has extended to the patriots of other states. After his departure from hence, two letters of his were intercepted which he wrote from Buenos Aires on the 22d of September, 1825, — one to the wife of the Recalde already mentioned, and the other to her daughter Angelica. There are some curious things revealed in them. To the mother he writes in these studied terms: 'In Buenos Aires I do not feel at home. The Porteños have adopted the bad qualities of all the European nations, without one of their virtues. The city is like a house in ruins, which they have painted outside like whited sepulchres, while within all is hollowness and decay.'

"Who knows but that in Buenos Aires he flattered and gratified many by abusing the Paraguayans at the very moment when he was writing to Paraguay in vituperation of the Porteños and of their city?

"These short notes shall suffice to give an idea of the character and depravity of this infamous impostor and villanous man, who, emerging from the mountains and crags of Switzerland, actuated by an innate perversity of disposition, and desirous of making a figure, and of giving to himself an adventitious importance, dares, with insolent brutality, to interfere with the government of Paraguay!

"If it were necessary, it would be easy to show in detail the impostures and falsehoods which pervade his whole volume, for the enlargement of which he has after all been obliged to have recourse to impertinences and despicable frivolities, all the progeny of his own perverted brain. But the best answer to malevolence, to its abandoned authors, to scoundrels, and to traitors, is that of contempt."

CHAPTER XX.

The Urdapilleta Family. — Father and Son condemned to Death. — Saved by the Death of the Dictator. — The Schoolmaster Escalada's Testimony. — His Contempt for Francia's Scientific and Literary Attainments. — Francia's Treatment of his Brothers, Sisters, and Natural Children. — The Different Versions of the Yegros Conspiracy. — Devised by Francia as a Pretext for Killing off all the Leading Men. — The Example imitated by the First Lopez and improved upon by the Second. — The People not permitted to know Anything, except that Certain Persons have been arrested and executed, and their Property confiscated. — The Observance of Legal Forms. — The Confiscation of Cabañas's Estate. — Iturbe. — The Arrest and Suicide of General Caballero. — Francia's System perfected by Lopez.

THE singular and, as it would seem, providential escape of the Urdapilletas from the death to which Francia had condemned them is probably the only instance in the history of the Dictator's reign in which his orders were not executed. Captain Pascual Urdapilleta was a Spanish officer of artillery at the time of the revolution in Buenos Aires, and had taken part in the defence of that place and Montevideo against the English, after which he went to Paraguay, where he married and had a family. At the commencement of the late war, his two sons, Andres and José Vicente, were still living. They both belonged to the upper class of society, and were, at the time, from fifty to sixty years of age; both were men of fine appearance, and, for Paraguayans, men of much intelligence. Though their father was a Spaniard, and therefore very obnoxious to Francia, he had been permitted to live, and had not been seriously molested until the year 1828, twelve years before the death of the Dictator. About this time the father and his son Vicente had the misfortune to get hold of an old musket, which they were examining or handling, when it was accidentally discharged and wounded a mulatto slave belonging to the father. The matter, however, was hushed up by the connivance of a Dr. Vidal and the juez of the district until the mulatto died, and then the facts of the case coming to the knowledge of the Dictator, the father and son, together with the physician and the judge, were arrested and detained in the public prison until the death of the Dictator. They were not confined as prisoners of state, but were in the open prison allotted for lesser criminals, or for those who were simply held for trial. The family was allowed to supply them with food, with some books, and with clothing sufficient to cover them. In the daytime they were permitted to occupy themselves in some industry on their own account. This privilege they improved by spinning cotton supplied by their families into thread, and weaving it into the ponchos and hammocks of the country, in making straw hats and stockings, horn spoons, and bridles and fancy trappings for horses. In fact, the prison was a vast workshop, somewhat similar to the public prisons of many of the States in which the convicts are compelled to labor. There was this difference, however, that they were not in solitary confinement, as in each cell there were many persons, and conversation was permitted among them. Moreover, the labor they performed was all voluntary, and on their own account. In this place the persons held for trial were kept until it should suit the good pleasure of the Dictator to pronounce judgment upon them. Few who once entered the walls, however, ever went forth again, except to execution, to the state prisons, or to the Chamber of Truth; but they were nearly all detained many years before Francia troubled himself about them any further.

Notwithstanding he had destroyed, in the early part of his dictatorship, all whom he considered in any wise dangerous, he seemed to think that he must keep up his pastime of making arrests and executions, lest people should become oblivious of his presence and power. It was to guard against this that he kept up the practice of arresting and executing at such irregular periods as his caprice might dictate. The Urdapilletas had already been twelve years in prison when Francia gave the order for them to be taken out and executed. This order was given one day just as a heavy tempest was commencing, and before it could be executed the storm came on with a fury and violence unknown in our higher latitudes. The thunder and lightning were of the most terrific character, and the rain came down in such quantities that the streets were filled with torrents of water, so that it was with extreme difficulty a foot-passenger could get across the streets, and utterly impossible for a cart to pass through them. This storm was exceptional even for that country, and it seemed as though the elements had at last conspired to put an end to the Dictator and save his remaining victims from his fury. The water ran down through the streets with such force that it broke through in many places into the houses, and even came rushing into the government hospital, where Francia was at that time, inundating the floor, so that the mighty Dictator himself had his feet wet, and, in consequence, took a severe cold. The storm continued in the afternoon and evening, so that the order for the execution of the Urdapilletas could not be carried out. The officer to whom the charge had been intrusted, not having obeyed his orders, did not on the following morning attempt, without further instructions, to execute them. They were to be shot, and when prisoners were thus put out of the way they were taken to the banquillo, where Francia could witness their execution from his window. But Francia was prostrate, and no additional command was issued; and the officer who had received the order to superintend the execution waited with anxiety, doubtless expecting that when the next command should be given it would be to some other official, and that he himself would be included with the Urdapilletas in the next sacrifice. Francia, however, never rallied sufficiently to put in force any more of his unfulfilled plans. And thus, as it were by the interposition of Heaven, the Urdapilletas were saved.

It may be said, however, that the younger Urdapilleta, José Vicente, was reserved for a worse fate than that for which he had been intended by Francia. During the time of his long imprisonment, having been permitted to receive books from his family, he had become much addicted to reading, and the habit was continued until he was again arrested, twenty-five years after. This man's name will be found to figure in another alleged conspiracy, more extensive and more sweeping in its character than any devised by Francia. Something of his career during the twenty-five years between his first and second imprisonment may here be given. His house, during the latter part of my residence in Paraguay, was but a short distance from mine. He was a shopkeeper and had an interesting family, consisting of a wife and three or four very pretty daughters. He was understood to be, for a Paraguayan, in easy circumstances; and as I frequently passed his door, I almost invariably found him with a book in his hand. His reading was confined almost entirely to the literature of former times, as very few modern books, and scarcely any periodical of recent date, were to be had in Paraguay. His large reading enabled him to converse on some topics with a great deal of intelligence and judgment.

Unfortunately for him, he became acquainted with the ill-fated Dr. Carreras at the time of his first visit to Paraguay. In the absence of men of learning in the country, those who had education and general knowledge sufficient to write tolerable Spanish were, at different periods, forced into some government position. In some such position was Urdapilleta at the commencement of the late war, and when called upon to make out some official document or statement he applied to his friend Carreras to assist him. Carreras readily prepared the paper, evincing a perfect knowledge of the subject, and expressed it in terse and forcible language. When this was offered to Lopez, he imagined, or affected to imagine, that it was the production of Urdapilleta himself; and thereupon he was made Chief-Justice of Paraguay, having, and pretending to have, no more knowledge of law, or even the forms of law, than any other shopkeeper in the town. The fate of his successor, Don Bernardo Ortellado, was in some respects more tragic than that of Señor Urdapilleta. For him was reserved the task of being the judicial instrument for the execution of his predecessor and of his colleagues in the government, and afterwards to suffer the same tortures and horrible death that at the dictum of his master, he had pronounced against some of the best and some of the worst men in Paraguay. Urdapilleta lived very quietly, attended all the festivals given in honor of his Excellency the Marshal President, always made speeches in his favor, and was liberal in his contributions for the costly presents which the people were constantly making to Lopez, and which they were obliged to declare in the public assemblages were spontaneous, though they knew that refusal or reluctance to make such voluntary offerings would be at the peril of their lives. He knew well the character of Lopez and the situation of the country, and therefore, like all Paraguayans, he never spoke of anything of a political nature unless it was in a public way, when he would indulge in patriotic outbursts against the Brazilians and in favor of the great Lopez. As I was not intimate with him, he never ventured to speak with me except on the most commonplace topics, such as the weather, his health, or that of his family; but invariably, if I asked him if there was any news, the reply was, "None." Had he known anything, he would not have dared to mention it, unless it had previously been published in the *Semanario*, in which case he knew I should have been informed of it as soon as he. But for all this, at the time when Lopez had made all his preparations for the subsequent conspiracy, and had determined to sacrifice all the best men in the country, Urdapilleta was included among them. He, as well as his brother Andres, was taken in irons to headquarters, and there subjected to all the horrible tortures which Lopez had imitated or invented for his victims. He was flogged, starved, and put in the *cepo uruguayana*, until, when about to die, he was taken out and mercifully shot, and this ended the last but one of the chief-justices of Paraguay.

As neither the Robertsons nor Rengger and Longchamp could give any account of the occurrences in Paraguay, subsequent to the departure of the latter in 1824, except from rumors which they were never able to verify, it was an object with me to make the acquaintance of such of the older men in the country as, having the most intelligence, could give the most information of the later years of the dictatorship. Among these was Juan Pedro Escalada, a native of Buenos Aires, who came to Paraguay when a child, and at the time of the revolution was about twenty years of age. His employment from that time to the commencement of the late war was that of a teacher, and he was allowed to pursue his calling and receive pupils during the whole time of Francia's reign, notwithstanding that in his youth he had been a sort of favorite of Governor Velasco, and enjoyed his friendship until his arrest. In fact, he was so much a favorite of the Ex-Governor that he used to apply to him for assistance in solving algebraic and geometrical problems while he was yet a student. He had a most excellent opinion of the abilities and kindness of Velasco, and regarded him, not only as a wise and excellent governor, but as a man of superior scientific attainments; while he regarded Francia as a charlatan, a pedant, and a pretender. He ridiculed his practice of looking at the stars through his famous theodolite, for he said Francia knew nothing of astronomy, and his star-gazing was only practised to impress the people with superstitious awe and a belief in his supernatural power. His account of the family of Francia differed somewhat from that of Robertson and Rengger, though it agreed with them in saying that he had no natural affection either for his brothers or sisters, of whom there were two of each. His elder brother, Pedro, was given the position of administrator of the large Indian village of Ita, some thirty miles to the south of Asuncion. Like his brother the Dictator, Don Pedro was eccentric in his habits, though in all other respects entirely unlike him. He was a corpulent, good-natured man, regarded as of very little capacity, and utterly without ambition. To be the chief man among the Indians, to live a life of indolence, and at the festivals to appear among them with the trappings of authority, satisfied his highest desires. As he never cared to leave his post of administrator, or in any way took any interest in affairs beyond the precincts of his own limited authority, it is hard to conceive how he provoked the wrath of his implacable brother. Such, however, was the case, and he was arrested and thrown into prison, and there left to expire. Robertson speaks of him as having been subject to fits of insanity of a harmless character. This, however, Escalada denies, and thinks it far more probable that, having married the daughter of the chief of Yaguaron who had succeeded to the position of the elder França, and who for some reason had incurred the enmity of the Dictator, his brother had been made to atone vicariously for the sins of his father-in-law. Of the other brother of Francia, Don Juan José, nothing was known by Escalada, except that he lived near Ibitimi, some twenty-five leagues from Asuncion, and, strange to say, died there without the assistance of his brother the Dictator. The sisters of Francia were treated with as little consideration by him as were his brothers. The elder married a man by the name of Marecos, in Villa Rica, and had several children. One of these children was executed by Francia. Another married José del Rosario Miranda, the adopted son of Cabaños, who had figured so conspicuously in the revolution. Miranda was long imprisoned by Francia, but was not executed. The other sister of Francia, Petrona, was married to a tinterillo by the name of Galvan, who was imprisoned by the Dictator. This sister was permitted by the Dictator to live in the family mansion, and to teach school. She survived her brother some ten years, and was well known to many people of my acquaintance. She resembled her brother to some extent, as she was extremely severe to her scholars, and very capricious and arbitrary in her treatment of them. To her Francia intrusted the making of his cigars, as he had not sufficient confidence in anybody else to smoke one made by other hands than hers; and yet so constant was his fear of being poisoned, he never ventured to light a cigar, even though made by her, that he had not first unrolled to see that it contained nothing but the harmless tobacco. Dr. Francia, according to Escalada, had several illegitimate children, the most of whom he declined to recognize in any way, though it was well known that they were his. One of his children, for some reason, inherited his property near the Trinidad. This property, however, was taken by the Lopez family. The woman married a man by the name of Cañete, and the two were servants of General Barrios, who married the eldest daughter of Carlos Antonio Lopez. Although the man held the position of *capataz* on the fine estancia of General Barrios, yet they were, in reality, no better than slaves.

Escalada also had the honor of being the first teacher of Francisco Solano Lopez, and under him the future President studied arithmetic, grammar, and a little Latin. When questioned as to the aptitude and abilities of this pupil, Escalada declined to speak except in terms that left it to be inferred that, if he was not a dunce, he was not a desirable pupil to have in his school. The teacher evidently took no credit to himself for having aided in developing a character like that of Lopez.

The "Yegros conspiracy," as it was called, was alleged to have been discovered in 1818, or forty-seven years before the commencement of the late war; and after such a lapse of time little was known about it by persons still living, except what had been given out by Francia at the time, or promulgated among the people by his authority. The dread and fear of the Dictator was so general that no one would dare question his neighbor in regard to the facts, or express a doubt about the guilt of the persons accused of participation in it. Yet, from the facts that were patent to all, it was clearly evident that the version of Francia was false in many respects, if not entirely fictitious. While so many arrests of the principal men in the country were being made, as in the later conspiracy of the second Lopez, people supposed that something of a dangerous character had been discovered; but in both instances they had no means of ascertaining the truth, and could only draw their inferences from the acts of the government. Hence, in the absence of any other evidence than the words and deeds of Francia, the people who, forty years later, ventured in confidence to speak about it, had different versions of the affair to give. One of the most intelligent men in Paraguay during the writer's residence there was an old Frenchman by the name of Charles Dupin. His version of the "conspiracy" is somewhat different from Robertson's, and particularly in regard to its discovery. As, after it was once suspected, all the parties implicated were immediately thrown into prison, and could never communicate with any one outside previous to their execution, nothing is known of what they confessed or admitted, and no one of those accused was permitted to escape and give any explanation of the affair. If there were a conspiracy, Francia was careful to destroy all the proofs of it, unless it were the confessions made under the torture, and of these, as far as is known, no records were ever kept. The account of M. Dupin, as received verbally from him, and which he said he received some two or three years afterwards, was that a certain Spaniard had noticed a suspicious gathering of persons at the house of a man named Rivarola, which stood on the corner of Calles Comercio and Encarnacion.* He did not concern himself particularly about these meetings, however, till one night he was summoned into the house, where he found the conspirators assembled. They then informed him of the plan, and told him he must keep it a secret on pain of death if he divulged it. Alarmed at the possession of such a dreadful secret, the poor man resolved to reveal it to Francia; and that he might not be detected going near him by the conspirators he blacked his face, and, thus disguised, went by night to the Dictator and told him of the whole plot. Francia told him to continue his attend-

* This house has now another tragic interest, as it subsequently came into the possession of Saturnino Bedoya, who was tortured to death by his brother-in-law, the second Lopez, on the charge of being engaged in another conspiracy.

ance at the house and report all he saw. When Francia had thus learned all their plans, he suddenly arrested every person engaged in the plot, for form's sake including the Spaniard who divulged it, though he was soon after released. Strangely enough, the conspiracy embraced every man in the country having a leading influence, including all those who had distinguished themselves in the war against Belgrano, among whom were Velasco, Yegros, Gamarra, Caballero, and many others, all of whom, with the exception of those who died in prison or committed suicide, were afterwards shot together. The less important persons were executed at subsequent periods, in groups of from two or three to eight persons.

Such was the account of this conspiracy, so far as Dupin could remember the vague rumors that he had heard of it during the forty years succeeding. Yet he could make nothing of them, as he knew that during the whole year or more that the conspiracy was maturing it was impossible, as during all those forty years afterwards, for as many as four persons to hold two secret meetings in Asuncion without its being known to the government. That under such a government people engaged in a conspiracy should court detection by frequent meetings continued through a twelvemonth is too absurd for belief; yet in Paraguay, as in other countries, history repeats itself, and nearly fifty years afterwards another conspiracy of a like character to this, but much more extensive, was discovered by a worse than Francia, but of which no one but himself knew, and which the parties engaged in it were for a still longer period engaged in concocting.

Two other versions of the same plot were given by Don José Vicente Urdapilleta, the unfortunate victim of both Francia and Lopez, having been kept a prisoner for twelve years by the former and tortured and executed by the latter. His story was that the originators of the plot were two brothers named Montiel. One of these, José Joaquin, was a sergeant of Francia's guard in the hospital; and their plan was betrayed by a relative named Caballero. This sergeant was understood to be a great favorite of the Dictator, and to enjoy very much of his confidence; and his plan was to take advantage of this circumstance, and, as if acting under orders, remove all who might interfere with his enterprise to distant parts, and then with his fellow-conspirators fall upon the Dictator and kill him. This plot would seem to be entirely distinct from the other, yet it was doubtless a part of the same, as the two Montiels were executed with Yegros and his companions.

Still another version entirely different from all the others was extant, and this is the one mentioned by Robertson. According to this account the betrayer of the plot was a Paraguayan named Lisardo Bogarin, who, just as it was to be carried into effect, revealed it all to the confessor, Padre Atanacio, who sent him with his story to the Dictator. The head-quarters of the conspirators, according to this version, were in another house from that mentioned by Dupin; but the fact that this house was ordered to be destroyed by Francia, while the other was left standing, would indicate that the latter version was the one approved by the Dictator. Probably there was as much truth in one as in the other, and the discrepancies in the accounts given by the Paraguayans so many years after arose from the fact that at the time of the occurrence it was all shrouded in mystery, and so fearful was the reign of terror which prevailed that no one dared to ask a question or express an opinion in regard to the affair during the lifetime of the Dictator, and hence these different versions were but the surmises of different people, that long years after took the forms here given. The only facts the survivors were certain of were that all the leading men in the country were arrested and put to death on the pretext that they had been detected in a conspiracy against the Dictator; and this is believed to be all the evidence in the matter that now exists.

Subsequent to the Dictator's death it was never permitted to question the justice or propriety of his acts. Probably his successor might have thrown some light on the conspiracy, and shown the whole thing to have been but a device of Francia for ridding himself of all persons obnoxious to him from their influence or respectability. But he was as tenacious of absolute power as was the Dictator, and would not permit any statements or opinions to circulate among the people implying that the government could err. Besides, it was an exercise of statecraft that he found it convenient to imitate, and in his time he originated similar conspiracies on a smaller scale, under cover of which he put out of the way obnoxious people whom he could not prove anything against; and it was not convenient that the people should question the justice or wisdom of his conduct, any more than they had that of Francia.

During the first years of Francia's power he pretended to observe the forms of justice, and not to ruin people at his arbitrary will, but according to the laws of the country. This practice was continued by his successors, and the forms of a secret trial were always observed, and confessions of guilt were always obtained, unless the accused expired under the means employed to compel them to speak as the government desired. What the object was in obtaining such confessions it is hard to surmise, for in most cases they were known to be false, and it was only the false confessions that were wanted; and it is hard to divine any motive in extorting them, unless it was to have them preserved in the government archives for the use of future historians, that they might show to the world that only the confessedly guilty had been condemned.

The legal proceedings instituted by Francia in order to possess himself of the estate of Don Manuel Atanacio Cabañas will serve to illustrate the regard that Francia had during the early part of his reign for legal forms. Cabañas was an officer of high rank in the war against Belgrano, and greatly distinguished himself. He was chief in command at the important battle of Tacuari, and afterwards took a prominent part in the revolution; and after the independence was secured he retired to his estancia, situate in the Cordilleras, some thirty leagues from Asuncion. Fortunately for himself, he died before Francia had invented his conspiracy, as being a man of large means and great influence he was eminently eligible for a conspirator, and if condemned and executed as one his estate would be confiscated. Having died too soon for that, Francia, according to M. Dupin, adopted the following process of legal confiscation of his estate.

The commandante of the troops at Asuncion at the time Somellera carried into effect his plan of revolution was Vicente Iturbe. His co-operation had been essential to the success of the plot; and when Francia became the controlling spirit of the Junta, he received his orders from him and seconded him in his arbitrary acts. To reward him Francia sent him as his commandante to the villa of San Pedro, some thirty leagues above Asuncion. Afterwards, having for some reason determined to ruin him, and to make him useful in his fall, he sent a copy of a letter to Artigas to him, with orders for him to sign it. The bearer of this letter from Francia to Iturbe was a man by the name of Aldecoa, who, having obeyed his orders, was soon after arrested and taken with his mulatto slave, who had accompanied him on his visit to Iturbe, to the Chamber of Truth. Here he was met by Francia's secretary, Patiño, and the question was asked him, who had given him that letter? Aldecoa promptly replied that it was his Excellency the supreme Dictator. "That cannot be," said Patiño; "think again. Was it not Don Manuel Cabañas?" "No, señor," said Aldecoa. A hundred lashes were then administered to both him and his servant to quicken their memories; and so well were they laid on that the mulatto died under the infliction, and Aldecoa, on being again interrogated, replied that the letter had been given him by Cabañas. On this he was instantly released, and a decree was issued denouncing Cabañas as a traitor and his estate consequently confiscated. Iturbe, to whom the letter was sent by Francia, was also arrested and thrown into prison, where he lingered for twenty years, and was finally shot in 1838.

Among the others accused of being parties to this conspiracy was the former Governor, General Velasco. This man, as we have before seen, had won the regard of the entire Paraguayan people, natives and foreigners. His administration, succeeding one of the worst under the colonial rule, had been marked by justice and liberality. He was a man of excellent presence, of fine appearance, and of courtly, affable, engaging manners. It was the general complaint that the Spanish officials who were sent to Paraguay abused their power to enrich themselves, but this was never said of Velasco. His habits being inexpensive, he had just sufficient means to keep up the appearance of gentility in the most limited and economical way. He was a man, besides, of such classical and scientific attainments as in the eyes of the better educated people to be a reproach to the charlatanism and pretensions of Francia. When the small remnants of his property which he had about him at the time of his retirement from public life were consumed, the native Spaniards, from respect for and regard to his character and services, continued to make such contributions for his support as would not wound his self-respect nor create any feeling of dependence. His only servant, that he had brought with him from Spain, regarded his old master with such veneration and love that he insisted on serving him long after the General had told him he had no means of remunerating him for his services. The faithful domestic, however, refused to leave him, and with his own little earnings, if necessary, he eked out the supplies for his master's table without his knowing whence they came. Velasco had acquiesced in the revolution as a wise and necessary measure, and after that, when he was no longer Governor, he abjured politics entirely, and lived isolated and retired. But neither the respect entertained for him by the people of Paraguay, his past services, his venerable hairs, his quiet life, nor his amiable character, could save him from the vengeance of Francia. Both he and his servant were arrested and thrown into prison, and the unfortunate Governor was left to linger there, neglected, sick, and half starved, until at last death relieved him from his sufferings.* His faithful servant sur-

* Robertson says that Velasco died in prison. Escalada, the schoolmaster, however, informed me that he was released before he died, but that his sufferings had been so great, while a prisoner, that he perished immediately afterwards.

vived him but one day. Thus perished one after another, in the same miserable way, all, or nearly all, the better class of both Spaniards and Paraguayans.

These traditions that have been preserved of the accusations against all the leading men living in Paraguay at the time of Francia's accession to power are necessarily of doubtful authenticity, from the fact that everything was done in secret, and people dared not make inquiries to ascertain the truth; but as the persons most obnoxious to Francia were generally men of wealth and respectability and of family influence, it was but natural that when they were killed, and their property confiscated, their ruined families would treasure up all the incidents that could be gathered from the soldiers, police, and others who were compelled to execute his orders, and that, in spite of all the Dictator could do, many incidents should become known that he would have preferred should never be divulged; but in the first years of his power it was far more difficult to keep every unpleasant fact hidden than it afterwards became. The people had not learned the necessity of absolute silence on all they saw, as they did afterwards. In time, however, after it had been for a generation or more the practice of incarcerating every one who gave currency to an unwelcome truth, the people learned that their safety lay in discussing or alluding only to such subjects of a political nature as had been treated of in the official organ. In the time of the younger Lopez, had words like those inscribed on the walls of his prison by Caballero been discovered by a policeman, he would have instantly reported the circumstance to the government and been warned that if it ever became known it would be through him. The obnoxious words would then be obliterated, and the unfortunate depositary of the secret for some other alleged offence would be put out of the way. No disclosure of anything of this kind was ever made in the time of the second Lopez. The system of Francia had by this time become too well perfected for any such leaks.

CHAPTER XXI.

Last Years of the Dictator. — His Death and Funeral Ceremonies. — Superstition of the People. — His Tomb broken open and his Remains carried off. — A God of Evil. — Terror inspired by his Name. — His Character.

UNTIL that terrible tempest, which saved the doomed Urdapilletas while it hastened the death of Francia, there was no mitigation of his terrible rule. Though all the leading men in the country whom he had reason to fear from their talents, wealth, or influence had been destroyed, he did not remit the practice of the early years of his dictatorship of arresting, imprisoning, and killing. It had become a habit with him, and the Paraguayans with whom I became acquainted all spoke of his latter days as those when his power was most remorselessly exercised. The prisons at his death were all full, as they had been for twenty-five years. The annual percentage of deaths among the prisoners was very large, but what it was can never be known. The treatment to which they were subjected could not have been otherwise than fatal to a large proportion of those who were subjected to it. As there were nearly seven hundred confined in them at the time of his death (and that was about the average during the long period of his power), the number who died at his hands, either in prison, from torture, or at the banquillo, must have been several thousand. As many more, though generally of an inferior class, were sent to their long account through the purgatory of exile at Tevego, or other places of a like character. People had come long before his death to look upon their condition as their normal state, to feel that they were under a spell, and that there was no escape for them so long as the Dictator might live. Many had come to regard him almost as a god;

as his life was prolonged so much beyond the ordinary period allotted to man, even the hope that death would remove him had nearly ceased to exist. When it was first announced that the Dictator was dead, they could hardly believe it; they feared it was a device of his to entice them into some expressions of relief or joy, for which they would yet be compelled to answer before El Supremo. Of the manner of his death little is known, or ever can be, beyond the fact that after the tempest that flooded his room his orders were not executed. The native physician who was summoned to attend him was living till within a year or two. His name was Estagarribia. He was an eccentric, reserved man, and though I made several attempts, through other persons, to learn something from him of the last days of Francia, he would communicate nothing. This man doubtless perished with the hundreds of thousands of others sacrificed to the ambition and cruelty of Francia's imitator, the younger Lopez. What, therefore, were the last thoughts or words of a man so strange and remarkable for his evil deeds as was the first Dictator of Paraguay will never be known. But it is certain that his last public acts were in character with the man and his whole career. The machinery of his government was kept in motion, however, by his chief secretary, Patiño, through whom his orders, when not given verbally by himself, were transmitted to his subordinates. The directions for the funeral services were given by this man, and the remains of the Dictator were deposited with awful solemnity in the tomb in the church of the Encarnacion; and, strange as it may appear, a priest was found to preach his funeral sermon. This priest, Manuel Antonio Perez, it would appear, shared the fears of the common people lest the mighty Dictator should appear in the flesh again to assert his authority. He did not and could not allude to the pious and Christian character of Francia, as it was known that Francia was not only a scoffer at religion, but had done everything in his power to bring the Church and the priests into contempt; and had he ventured on any such bold eulogium, he might have dreaded lest the Dictator should start from his tomb and order him to the banquillo. But he confined himself to speaking of the Dictator as a great ruler, one who had preserved the country from anarchy at home and had repelled invasion from abroad, who had straightened the streets of the city, and saved his people from numberless evils. It may be alleged in excuse for this profane, if not blasphemous, eulogium of the Dictator, that it was delivered to a people, many of whom had come to regard the subject of it as a god, and that, if he had ventured to speak of him as he was, a cry of horror would have gone up from the crowd. But if the priest Perez did not extol the piety and religious character of Francia, or assign him a place in the abodes of the blessed, it certainly is to be placed to his credit.

But though dead and buried, many people yet feared his speedy resurrection, — that he would appear among them to punish them for any failure in showing respect for his remains or his memory, and the poorer and more ignorant people would gather at the church and worship at his tomb. This was not continued, however, very long; for some months after his death, on opening the church, it was found that the monument over the remains of Francia had been overturned, the tomb opened, and the dust and bones of the Dictator had disappeared. Still, this did not dispel the illusion that he was a god, but it caused those who had before thought him so to consider him rather as a god of evil, and the people no longer assembled to offer their prayers to him. The terror which his name inspired, however, was so general, that for many years it could not be mentioned in the presence of a Paraguayan without causing fear and alarm. In fact, among the natives his name was seldom or never mentioned, and if they found it necessary to speak of some event or circumstance connected with him, they called him "El Difunto," or made use of some indirect way of alluding to him. The word "Francia" had an unwelcome sound to everybody. So complete and long continued had been the dread and awe of the dreadful Dictator, that the people who had lived during his reign always evinced such fear and consternation when speaking of him or the events of his time that their children born after he was dead grew up with the impression that he was an ogre or a demon ; and twenty-five years after his death, if a stranger ventured to mention his name or to make any inquiries in regard to his time or his acts, the whole household would be instantly hushed, all would look about to see lest some suspicious person might overhear, the doors would be closed, and the people would intimate by their acts and their appealing looks their wish that the subject should be dropped.

Francia's character is to be judged only by his acts. He had no confidences, and left no records or memoranda of his plans or theories for the government of his people. So far as is known, he was under no illusion that his government either promoted the general happiness at the time, or would have that effect in the future. The happiness of the people did not seem to be a motive with him. His ambition was rather to create that universal fear and abject perpetual dread which rendered the life of all around him dark, hopeless, miserable. The rejoicing of others enraged him, and innocent amusements showed forgetfulness of his power, and he would not tolerate them. He had not the ordinary motives that influence other men, and in this was so different that many who suffered from his tyranny doubted whether he belonged to the human family. The ordinary motives of other men give us no clew to his character, as he was not influenced by them. Hence by his acts alone is he to be judged.

The plea of insanity that has been so often advanced as an explanation of his unnatural conduct cannot be admitted, for the reason that all the parts of his life were consistent with each other and with the same general character. There were never in his whole career any outbreaks of tenderness, any displays of affection, any sympathy with the human race. His cruelties, his cynicism, the apparent want of motive for many of his most pitiless and wanton deeds, all indicate a mind always under control and consistent with itself, and differing from other minds only in that it had no sympathy with human nature. His acts show that he was inhuman, not insane.

Of his early career scarcely anything is known; and as a student at the University of Cordova, all that we can learn is that he in no way distinguished himself. On returning to his own country, his morose and overbearing temper soon arrayed everybody with whom he came in contact in opposition to him, so that he lived ever after as a misanthrope and recluse. He had no desire for the love of any human being, nor yet of any pet animal. His love and admiration were all centred on himself, and so completely was he lost in the consciousness of his own greatness that he could not contemplate a superior being. His vanity and egotism made him an infidel, and when he commanded his unhappy subjects to call him the Supremo, their obedience and helplessness sustained him in the assumption. With the desires and appetites of other men he had as little in common as with their affections and sympathies. His beardless face was the index of a character never stirred by love or passion towards any of the other sex, and his indifference to the grosser pleasures of eating and drinking closed up the last avenue through which all other tyrants known in history have realized one feeling in common with their subjects. To his nearest relatives he was as merciless as to the worst criminal, sending his curse to his dying father, and subjecting his harmless, inoffensive brother to torture and execution. His natural children were to him of as utter indifference as were the dogs that contended with them for the offal of the butchers' shambles.

Such was his character as a private citizen, and his after life, when he had become the absolute ruler of an ignorant, amiable, unambitious people, was in keeping with it. His narrow mind was never intoxicated by his elevation to power, for he evinced the same feelings and the same indifference to the happiness and the misery of others afterwards as before. Constitutionally timid and distrustful, he first, on attaining authority, turned his eyes towards those who would be most likely to profit by his overthrow; and these he regarded as his natural enemies, and as a pretext for their taking off he invented the conspiracy system that has been so often used by his successors. The consciousness that he had put to death so many thousands of innocent people was accompanied by the conviction that he was universally feared and hated. He therefore inferred that nearly every person in the country desired his death, and he saw in every one an enemy who would gladly take his life if he could get an opportunity. Hence his orders were to his guards to strike down any person to be seen in the streets when he was passing through them, for his first thought was that he might be an assassin laying in wait to murder him. In time this frame of mind became habitual to him, and he lived in perpetual dread, his only pleasure being found in the fear and misery he could inflict on others. To secure the fidelity of the very few that approached his person, he granted them almost unlimited license, as the more obnoxious they were to the people the more interest they had in preserving his life and his power. But even these were so distrusted that he was always on his guard whenever one of them came near him, and ready to shoot or strike him dead at the first suspicious motion. His dread of assassination was such that it haunted him perpetually for many years, and half his time seemed to be spent in devising plans to defeat the imaginary conspirators. His several places of residence were kept up, that he might change from one to the other, seldom sleeping for two nights in succession under the same roof, and never returning to one of them by the same road he had gone, thus thinking to defeat any band of conspirators who might be lying in wait for him. To circumvent them he was constantly studying to be in places where his coming could not have been foreseen, and no body of assassins be waiting to waylay or entrap him.

But the most remarkable thing in the character of the man is that he could endure a life such as he led so long. That a human being could exist through so many long years, shut up in its own self-inflicted prison, through which no ray of human sympathy could penetrate to the congealed heart within, and on looking out from its hiding-place could only behold wretches whom it had made miserable, and all of whom regarded it with hate enhanced by fear, is a psychological phenomenon such as the world has perhaps never seen before nor since; nor is it at all strange that the simple, superstitious and kind-hearted Paraguayans should regard a person so differently constituted from themselves as a being of a different order, and that "his death alone should prove to them that he was a human being."

"The evil that men do lives after them." The terrible system of Francia continued when he was no more. The people had for a whole generation been held in such abject terror that at his death they were spell-bound and helpless, so completely divested of all sense or feeling of self-reliance as to become the passive, resistless victims of a weaker and a worse than Francia. It was his to destroy all who had given proof of intelligence, patriotism, or ability; to sow the seeds of entire submission and unquestioning obedience; but to reap the fruit, to sacrifice, as it were, the entire people, irrespective of sex or age or rank, to reduce the country to a desert waste, and to raise a tomb for himself on the whitening bones of the entire Paraguayan nation, was left to his disciple and imitator, FRANCISCO SOLANO LOPEZ.

CHAPTER XXII.

Condition of the Country after the Death of Francia. — Policarpo Patiño. — The Junta. — Imprisonment and Death of Patiño. — The Triumvirate. — Carlos Antonio Lopez. — Congress convoked. — Lopez and Alonso made Consuls. — Antecedents of Lopez. — Reforms in the Government. — Francisco Solano Lopez. — Education. — Crude Laws. — Gradual Extinction of Slavery. — Removal of Commercial Restrictions. — The Consulship abolished and Lopez elected President, 1844, for three Years. — Independence of Paraguay. — Foreign Emigration encouraged. — Alliance with Corrientes. — Edward A. Hopkins. — United States and Paraguay Navigation Company.

THUS closed the gloomy career of the Dictator, a man remarkable indeed, but remarkable only for the absence of every human feeling or affection. Without talent, without learning, and without a friend, for twenty-nine years he held absolute sway over a people naturally brave and generous, till the lights of intellect and hope became dim and obscure in their minds. From a joyous, careless, confiding, and happy people, much addicted to amusement and hospitality, they became sullen, distrustful, and treacherous. Says the author of Six Years' Residence in Paraguay: "The imagination of a Paraguayan saw an informer in every person that approached, and the first thing he thought of was to keep closely mute, in order to preserve his sad and uncertain existence. The greater part of the youth, without occupation, without harmless diversion, without means of instructing themselves, wishing to employ their leisure and find excitement, gave themselves up to games of chance and licentious pleasures, wasting thus their health and scanty fortunes." The people of Paraguay had morally and intellectually deteriorated during the rule of Francia. They had grown poorer and more ignorant, less frank and hospitable, and less fit for self-government whenever death should relieve them of the presence of the Dictator. If it be a true test by which to judge of the merits of an administration, that under it the people have learned self-government, then was Francia's the worst, unless that of the Jesuits be excepted, of which history makes mention. He had made it his pleasure and business to put out the lights of intelligence as much as possible, by killing off all the men possessing more than ordinary capacity or education. He made no provision for the administration of the government in case of his death, and it would seem as though he contemplated with grim delight the helpless anarchy in which those people would be left whom it had suited his purpose not to destroy.

When it was known that the Dictator was dead, the people could with difficulty realize it. At first they feared to speak of it to one another. Was it not a trick of his to give out that he was dead, and if any one dared to say a word against him to send him to the prison or to the banquillo? And even if he were dead, they feared he still had power to do them harm. Had not men been flogged, imprisoned, and shot for opinions that they had never dared express; and if he had power to read the stars, and divine men's thoughts while in the flesh, could he not still reach them with his malign influence? Their condition might be compared to a cargo of prisoners of different nations and languages, who could not understand each other, confined in a ship's hold with the light of heaven shut out, all dreading shipwreck, but all cast at length on a beautiful fertile island. What confusion and anarchy might be anticipated before anything like order or confidence could be created! That results did not follow as had been predicted, and that there was no outbreak nor violence, proves only that the spirit of the people had been so completely crushed they dared not harbor even resentment. Natural feelings and anticipations had been found too dear a luxury to be cherished, for they had cost the lives of hundreds and thousands. Besides, the people had for nearly thirty years been so powerless, there had been such complete silence imposed upon them, that there could be no union, no harmony of action, even among a few. They must learn gradually that they had the power before they could try to exercise it.

The secretary of Francia, Policarpo Patiño, had been so long the servile tool through whom his orders had been transmitted, that he imagined he might carry on the government himself in the manner of his master. To prove himself an apt scholar, he caused several persons to be arrested immediately after the Dictator's death, among whom were the old Frenchmen Dupin and Saguier. To wield the power that Francia had wielded, however, it was indispensable that he should have the support and co-operation of the military chiefs in charge of the government barracks. As Patiño was to them, as to everybody else, nothing but a hated instrument used by Francia, and as in the lifetime of the latter there could have been no correspondence between them, it could not but happen that there should soon be disagreement. Patiño, however, to conciliate them, having as yet the machinery of the government in his hands, called together the four officers in command of the four respective bodies of troops stationed in the capital, together with an alcalde, Manuel Antonio Ortiz, in order that they might go through the form of establishing a government; Patiño being resolved all the while to keep the real power in his own hands, and to use the commandantes only as agents to install himself in the seat left vacant by his master. He therefore formed a Junta composed of these five officers and himself, reserving to himself the post of secretary. His plan, however, sadly miscarried. The Junta selected by himself put him in prison within a few days after Francia's death, where, conscious of the odium he had excited and that the mighty Dictator could no longer protect him, he hanged himself in his cell.

The others of the military chiefs, not satisfied that the authority should be left entirely in the hands of the five, determined that a Congress should be called. Not knowing what else to do, the Junta named one of themselves, Ortiz, as general military commander, to preserve the public order until a Congress could be convoked. But with no one in the country who knew how to take the preliminary steps towards forming a government, the Junta was perplexed, and, not knowing what to do, only busied themselves in listening to the petitions of those whose friends were in prison. The dungeons were still full of Francia's victims, and no one assumed the authority to set them free. About three months after the Dictator's death, on the 23d of January, 1841, the people having become tired of this inaction of the Junta, it was displaced by a movement of the troops in the San Francisco barracks, headed by two sergeants, Ramon Duré and one Campos. But the people seemed to have an idea that only a general Congress could give them a government that would be respected; and when the first Junta was dissolved, a triumvirate was announced in place of it, whose business it was at once to call a Congress. This triumvirate consisted of three citizens, who, not knowing what to do, did nothing. In the mean while there was one man busily at work laying his plans for the succession,—a man as ignorant of laws and forms of government as the rest, but possessed of cunning, shrewdness, avarice, and ambition. This was Carlos Antonio Lopez. He was at that time about forty-seven years of age, and though destined to play an important part in the subsequent history of Paraguay he was then little known. Indeed, during the long reign of terror, no one in the country was permitted to have any prominence except the Dictator. To be prominent by reason of wealth was dangerous, to be so by reason of talents was fatal. But when the Dictator was no more, then was the time for those to show their talents who before, like Junius Brutus, had feigned not to possess them. Lopez had been cunning enough not to provoke the Dictator's jealousy by anything more than very slight exhibitions of capacity. It is true that two years before his death he had been banished to Rosario for having shown too much astuteness in a legal paper he had drawn up which fell under the eye of Francia. But he accepted the exile without a murmur, and kept strictly quiet till the Dictator's death, when he returned to his home near the city. From there he witnessed the attempts of the people of the capital to form a government, and saw that the sceptre of Francia could be easily seized and wielded by the first strong hand that would resolutely grasp it. But he had no prestige as a civilian, and was not a military man. He therefore arranged his plans with the commandante-general of the national arms, Mariano Roque Alonso; and then by exciting discontent among the people at the inaction of the triumvirate it was superseded, and the authority and force to improve it remained in the hands of Alonso, with Lopez as his secretary. A general Congress of three hundred members was at once called, and on the 12th of March, thirty-three days after the overthrow of the triumvirate, it assembled in the capital. Of course, scarcely a member of it had any definite idea of what was to be done. They could only vote for or against the projects submitted by the military commander. The crude plan of a fundamental law drawn up by Lopez was submitted and adopted on the first day of the session; and the second day after, two consuls were elected for the term of three years, who were to exercise jointly the executive authority. The consuls, of course, were those who had called the Congress together, Carlos Antonio Lopez and Mariano Roque Alonso.

Alonso appears to have been a well-intentioned, harmless man, who had been selected by Lopez as the prime mover in establishing a government, for the reason that from his position as military chief under Francia he had control of the national arms and forces. Of Lopez and his antecedents it is now necessary to speak more at length.

He was born near the Recoleta, at a distance of a little more than a league from Asuncion, about the year 1787. The family was one of the lowest in the country, and was considered to be, not only of base blood, but, before the hand of Francia had destroyed all respect for the forms of morality, of disreputable origin. Under the old Spanish *régime* there lived in Asuncion a man by the name of Juan Bautista Goyez. He was a man of some education, but of profligate character. When past middle age, and after Francia became Dictator, he was employed by him as a clerk or accountant of his treasury, a position which he held for many years. He was never married, but lived with a mulatto woman, by whom he had one child that he acknowledged and treated as his own. When grown to womanhood this child married a poor journeyman tailor of mixed Spanish and Guarani blood, by the name of Cirilo Lopez. Her worldly prospects were so much better than his as to overcome the repugnance which is cherished to this day by the Paraguayans to amalgamation with the negroes. They were accordingly married, and by the aid of his wife's fortune he was enabled to purchase a piece of land near the Recoleta and build a house on it, large and commodious for that country. He continued, however, to follow his occupation of tailor, either as journeyman or master, being mainly dependent upon the work of his hands for the support of his family. This family in due course of time consisted of six sons and two daughters, of which Carlos Antonio was destined to be the President of the future Republic. The schools of the capital at that time, though better than they ever have been since, were very defective, the object of the clerical teachers being to inculcate the dogmas and superstitions of the Church, and also that all matters of authority, both secular and ecclesiastic, should be left in the hands of the priests. Young Carlos, having mastered the rudiments of the Spanish language, was sent to the College of Asuncion, where he received such education as the monks and priests could give him. He improved his opportunities so well, that, after the conclusion of the course, he was named as Professor of Theology in the same college, and also filled the chair of Philosophy. But, like Francia, Lopez was more inclined to the law than to theology, and like him he gave up the instruction of youth in sacred things and took up the practice of the law; but as he never was outside of Paraguay, he had no other knowledge of it than he could pick up in a country where a regularly educated law graduate had never existed. He gained, however, sufficient knowledge of the forms and principles of law to be as competent as any in the capital; and being possessed of great natural cunning he obtained considerable practice, and enjoyed the reputation of being zealous and faithful in the interests of his clients. He was still a young man when Francia came into power, and soon saw the dangers attending the practice of law, and also that there could be little practice in a country where one mind was absolute and judged everything by sheer caprice. Lopez saw his danger in time to avert it. Before he had done anything to provoke the Dictator's resentment or awaken his suspicions, he quietly withdrew to the family residence at the Recoleta, and lived as retired as possible, knowing and seeing as few of his neighbors as possible.

There was living at this time, in one of the districts to the northeast of Asuncion, a rich estanciero by the name of Lazaro Rojas. He had numerous estancias in different sections, and on each of them were large herds of cattle and horses. Like many others of the older families, he had lived in a kind of rude splendor, his house containing silver plate enough to set off a royal palace. A part of this property he had received with his wife, who at the time of his marriage was a widow by the name of Carillo. At the time of this marriage the widow had but one child, a daughter named Juana. It appears that Don Lazaro had an eye for the person of the daughter as well as for the estate of the mother. The result was that he found, after a time, that it would be convenient to have the young woman married off; and in casting about for a suitable match for his step-daughter, he selected Carlos Antonio Lopez as the most eligible person, inasmuch as he was a man of intelligence above the average, and, having some negro blood to boast of, the union would not be a violation of that law which Francia had promulgated, forbidding all marriages of those claiming Spanish blood except with negroes. The marriage was therefore permitted, and, the first fruit, not of, but after, the union, was Francisco Salano Lopez. The putative father always recognized the child as his own, and it was only known to a few Paraguayans that he was not sc. Some of the older inhabitants of the vicinity, however, knew all the circumstances, and after a long residence among them I obtained so much of their confidence that they dared to reveal the facts to me. But among themselves they would no more have whispered such a thing than have plotted a conspiracy. My informants are all dead ere this, most of them killed by the illegitimate son of Lozaro Rajas and Juana Carillo. With his wife, Carlos Antonio received a considerable portion in lands; and on the death of Rojas, many years after, his whole fortune was bequeathed to Francisco Solano, the unnatural child, whose career was to be marked with cruelties and crimes that spared neither age nor sex nor ties of kindred nor friendship, who at last, after imbruing his hands in the blood of all his near relatives, including brothers and sisters, spared not the mother who bore him.

After his marriage, Lopez passed a great part of his time in superintending the estancia he had received with his wife, seldom visiting the capital, and whenever he did so despatching his business and leaving as soon as possible. Necessarily he read little during these years of enforced silence and seclusion, for he had few books, and it was not possible to get more. To the inhabitants of Paraguay their country was the whole world, and for twenty-five years they knew absolutely nothing of what was transpiring beyond the confines of the Dictator's dominions. Under the old Spanish rule the doctrine of the divine right of kings was recognized and inculcated, and, before the modern ideas of republicanism, of the inherent right in the people to choose their own form of government, had reached Paraguay, it was shut out from all communication with the world; and when the Dictator died, no one in the country had any knowledge of any other government than his and the routine and forms introduced by the Spanish governors. They had therefore to rely almost entirely on intuition and common sense to extricate themselves from their anomalous position, and there is no doubt that Lopez well understood the character of the people, and under the circumstances managed affairs with moderation and wisdom. Francia being dead, all authority was paralyzed. There was no one to command, and none to obey. The task was to make a government that would be respected before anarchy or license should render it impossible.

It was six months after the death of the Dictator before the election of the two consuls. In that time nothing had been done to ameliorate the condition of the people, except that they were no longer in fear of his terrible power, and the arrests and executions for unknown causes had ceased. But the prisoners were still in prison and in fetters to the number of more than seven hundred, some of whom had been there for more than twenty years. One of the first acts of the consular government was to set all who were not proven criminals at liberty. This act was an indication that a new order of things had been commenced, and never, probably, was more complete and universal joy felt by an entire community than that which pervaded Asuncion when this decree was made. From five to six per cent of the entire population, and these nearly all taken from the best families, were in prison; and when the doors were opened and the fetters knocked off, it was a sight such as was perhaps never before witnessed, to see the families and friends of the long-immured prisoners flying to the embrace of friends and kindred whom they had not hoped ever more to greet in this world. Some of them, during their long imprisonment, had fallen into hopeless idiocy, and knew not their kindred who had come to welcome them. The man of middle age, who had been long before consigned to a cell, came forth decrepit and old, perhaps to find all his relatives dead, and all his property taken and disposed of by the Dictator.

To carry out his destructive measures, Francia had been obliged to have many subordinates to execute his orders. Those who were forced to this ungrateful task were not friends of his, and generally it was fear for their own safety that induced them to show neither mercy nor favor. Nevertheless there was a deep feeling of resentment against those who had only executed their master's instructions, and people who had seen their houses razed, their cattle killed by thousands, their relatives imprisoned and executed, were disposed to seek redress and vengeance at the expense of the Dictator's agents. It was therefore a difficult work to smooth down asperities between those who had had their property destroyed and those who had been forced to destroy it. The consuls, however, appear to have acted wisely, justly, and cautiously; confiscated lands and houses were restored to the families of those who had been executed, and such small returns as the state could pay were made to those who had been ruined by fines and imprisonment. It was the policy of the consuls to have the transition gradual, that the people should feel their improved condition before they had begun to cherish any hope of a great or radical change. In Francia's time the towns were filled with his soldiers and spies, who reported everything to him, and any criminal caught in the act would be condemned to death, imprisonment, or nothing, just as the whim of the moment took him. The consuls, however, soon arranged a police system which, though crude and imperfect, was a great improvement on the caprice of the Dictator. A judicial system was also established, and judges appointed of different grades, and their respective powers were defined. As there had been no courts, laws, or lawyers in the country, it may be supposed these first tribunals had an original way of proceeding; but as the judges were selected from the more substantial and respected citizens that Francia had suffered to survive, they could award justice in the simple cases brought before them, even if they had to improvise a law for the occasion. During the twenty-nine years of Francia's reign, education had been neglected, and at his death the most profound ignorance prevailed. Some few females in the capital, like the Dictator's sister, had taught children the elementary branches; but as there was no college or seminary for teaching anything beyond these, the Spanish language was all the while giving place to the Guarani, so that children whose fathers had been liberally educated in Spain grew up hardly able to speak, much less to read or write, in any dialect.

The people, ignorant as they were, had sense enough to be aware of their ignorance; and the very first act of the Congress, even before choosing the consuls, was to pass a law for the founding of a state College. The consuls also took early measures to establish primary schools, not only in the capital, but throughout the country. It was necessarily slow work. The darkness of nearly thirty years had left few capable of teaching even the elementary branches. Nevertheless the work began, and in time the clouds began to lift, not so much at first by reason of any education that could be acquired as from the opening of the ports and the admission of foreigners, whose presence and conversation proved to them — what they were before scarcely conscious of — that there was a world outside of the limits of Paraguay.

It is amusing to read of the first acts of this makeshift government. In their ignorance of all forms, and their desire to do what other nations did, they committed many ludicrous acts. In time these errors and absurdities were discovered, — often from the ridicule they excited among their neighbors. This caused greater caution afterwards, and doubtless had a great effect in causing Lopez, in his subsequent career, to be very punctilious on all matters of ceremony, as fast as he learned what was expected and exacted by other potentates.

The condition of the soldiery in the more remote parts of the country during the time of Francia was most miserable. Young men were taken from their homes and sent to remote and unhealthy points, and there kept under the most severe treatment for years, being allowed nothing for their service but a single ration of beef per day. The length of service was unlimited, and a soldier once taken and despatched to the frontier could never hope to return until the earth was rid of the Dictator. How it was that he was able to retain them on the southern frontier, where it was possible to escape, is almost inconceivable. But such was the dread of his terrible power, and so fearful were the tortures inflicted, and so possessed were they of the belief that everything was known, even to their thoughts, by the star-gazer, that they remained faithful at their posts till relieved by death. This condition of things was very soon changed by the consuls. It was no longer the object or policy of the government to keep foreigners out of the country, or make a close prison of it for everybody within its limits, and most of the soldiers were recalled and discharged, and, where necessary, others were sent to replace them.

In the capital the soldiers under Francia were allowed every license, if they only closely followed his orders while on duty. On parade they must be clean and sober, and go through all their evolutions with precision, as sentinels they must be vigilant and inquisitive; but off duty they might get as drunk as they pleased, might insult any private citizen with impunity, might outrage any woman that they fancied, and there was no redress, — for seldom, if ever, was a soldier punished by Francia for any outrage on private persons. But the government of the consuls at once put a stop to all this. The miserable instruments that had been employed by Francia to degrade and insult the most respectable of the inhabitants seemed to disappear with the Dictator. They instinctively recognized the fact that their "occupation was gone," and were soon lost to sight. In this way the acts of vengeance and retaliation that must have taken place had they remained among the people familiar with their atrocities failed to occur.

The difficulties under which the new government labored will appear more striking by reading some of its crude laws than from any other evidence that can now be produced. One of its first acts was to provide for the instruction of youth in several branches not taught in the primary schools. So a law was decreed by the two consuls for what was fancifully called a Literary Academy. A professor of Latin and another of philosophy were decreed, and an old priest, who knew little of Latin and nothing at all of philosophy, was intrusted with the duty of organizing the institution. Soon after, however, the arrival of two Jesuit priests from Buenos Aires, whose lives had been dedicated to the education of youth, enabled the government to give more form and comeliness to their Literary Academy.' These priests appear to have entered on their work with zeal and judgment. But they did not stay long, and whether it was because the consuls feared that this would be but an entering wedge for the re-establishment of Jesuit influence, or whether the ideas of the government were so absurd in regard to what a Literary Academy ought to be, does not appear. Perhaps the two causes combined to secure their departure. The latter will appear sufficient, however, if we observe the very original and curious features of the organic law. In this the government appears to be head schoolmaster. It declares there shall be a professorship of Latin and another of the Spanish language and *belles-lettres;* another of "rational philosophy in the didactic method; that is, logic, metaphysics, ethics, general and particular, physics, general and particular." There was also to be a professorship of dogmatic theology "in the didactic method"; another of moral theology in the same method. Besides this, it defines minutely the duties of the professors, who were also assigned the hours of instruction to be given in each branch. A translation of the duties of the first professorship will serve to show the general character of the whole five.

"Latin shall be taught from seven o'clock in the morning until nine; afterwards, half an hour of recreation. At two and a half in winter and at two and three quarters in summer, in the afternoon, shall begin the teaching of Latin for two continuous hours. On Saturday mornings, lessons will be given on the elements of the Christian religion for one hour after the ordinary task, instead of recreation." The other four professorships have each their duties assigned them in similar detail, all teaching about the same branches; and the whole would appear to be copied from the rules of some ancient Spanish schoolmaster, and repeatedly divided and subdivided to make it appear that the Literary Academy had as many learned professors as had colleges of learning in other countries.*

* When the Jesuits went away, there was but one man in the whole country capable of teaching anything beyond such elementary branches as reading, spell-

Not only are the duties of the professors thus definitely prescribed by the organic law of the Academy in statute form, but rules for the conduct and deportment of the students are given at such length as would confound the monitors of a normal school. Even the parents are commanded to attend to it that their children come well washed and combed and dressed,—the latter of which was easily complied with, as a boy of twelve or fourteen was considered in full dress with nothing more than a loose shirt, and girls of ten or twelve generally dispensed with that, being perfectly content with nothing but their rosaries. Then there is incorporated into the law rules of study and deportment to be committed to memory, and, in fact, all the details of conduct for both teachers and pupils from the rising to the setting of the sun.

This law for the establishment of a literary institution was doubtless intended to be drawn with a skill and literary perfection corresponding with the exalted nature of the subject. The law, however, declaratory of the regulations to be observed in regard to the public cemetery and the burial of the dead, if less dignified in phraseology, is none the less curious and minute in its details. The following extracts taken from this law will show how, in this state of pupilage, the new government made some very singular enactments:—

"The undertakers and grave-diggers shall be paid each five dollars per month, the hearse-driver five dollars, and the peon that takes care of the mules twenty reals. No person shall ride in the dead-carts except the corpse that is carried, and, therefore, nobody shall get up and ride behind.

"The graves shall always be of the same depth, that is, six hands deep and seven feet long; and the bodies that have coffins shall be lowered with two cords, one at each end."

Among the thirty-nine similar provisions of this law there

ing, writing, and arithmetic. And this one most competent of all, Don Juan Pedro Escalada, who, if not executed by the second Lopez, is probably living yet, and from whom I have received much information in regard to those times, was only a private teacher, and never had the honor of a chair in the Literary Academy.

is this moral reflection interjected as one of the articles: "It is against Christian piety to bury people with irreverent actions, or drag them in hides, or throw them into the grave without consideration, or in a position contrary to the practice of the Church."

But crude and undigested as were these laws, — for as yet there was no constitution, and there was no more formality in a decree upon the most important questions of state policy than in one fixing the salary of a peon, — there was one act promulgated very early in the time of the consular government, so wise and just as to redeem the faults and defects of all the others, — a law that stands forth as a rebuke to the leading statesmen of the United States at the time, many of whom were laboring to strengthen and perpetuate that "sum of all villanies" which this government, composed of two ignorant, unlettered consuls, from a mere instinctive sense of sound policy and natural justice, were seeking to abate and finally destroy. This law provided for the gradual extinction of slavery; though in its provisions it is cumbered with ludicrous details, yet had this law been passed in the United States at the same time, it would, before leading to civil war, have rendered slavery extinct, and saved the nation from the Great Rebellion.

This law was first promulgated November 24, 1842, and was to take effect on the 1st of June following. It provided that all children of slaves born after that time should be free, the males at twenty-five and the females at twenty-four years of age. The result proposed was to make all the children of slaves born after the law was published absolutely free at the end of the year 1867. These were not styled slaves, but *libertos*, or freedmen. The slaves in the mean while were constantly diminishing in number, as no more were born after that date to perpetual bondage, and the last vestige of slavery must cease with the lives of those slaves who had been born previous to the year 1843. This law may seem too slow in its operations to suit the ideas of the present age. We have seen the institution of slavery, which was so firmly rooted that it seemed impossible to destroy it, entirely cut up and its four millions of bondmen set at liberty within the space of four short years. Yet, slow as it was, the influence of such a law practically abolished the system long before all had been made free through its direct operation. The law respecting the treatment of the *libertos*, or freedmen, which was but a counterpart of the one providing for the gradual abolition of slavery, was so liberal that there was little difference between a slave and a peon or other laboring person. A slave who was not well treated, or who disliked his master, might go to a justice of the peace and make a complaint, and the latter was bound to find him a new master, and the former must be satisfied to receive only such price for his services as the hirer was willing to pay. A slave was no more subject to corporal punishment than any other person of low condition. In fact, during all my residence in Paraguay, I never heard of the castigation of a slave unless it was administered by a government employee. The operations of this law, however, were brought to a sudden termination during the late war, as Lopez, to recruit his army, made no distinction between slaves and their masters. All were alike taken for soldiers; all alike were sent to the field of battle, and, with very few exceptions, all perished, either on the battle-field, in prison, or from disease, hardship, or exposure in the camp.

During the time of the consulate there was an effort made to obtain the recognition by Buenos Aires of Paraguay as an independent republic; but Rosas, the Dictator and tyrant of that country, then in the zenith of his power, refused such recognition, and it was not till 1856 that it was granted.

A protracted and angry correspondence took place between Rosas and the consular government, and the former, not being able to make a warlike attack on Paraguay by reason of being at war with Corrientes, shut up his ports to all Paraguayan commerce, so that the country still continued practically closed to the rest of the world until that sanguinary and cowardly tyrant was driven from power and from the country he had long afflicted.

The consular government having been chosen for but three years, a new Congress was called on the 12th of March, 1844. To this Congress the government presented a report of its proceedings, all of which were approved. And ever since, though professing to have a constitution and published laws, it has been the invariable custom for the government to make such decrees and do such acts as may please it, and when a Congress is convoked to submit a report of what has been done, which the Congress duly ratifies and approves without a word of debate.

During the time of the consular government, Lopez, in imitation of Francia nearly thirty years before, managed to hold the entire power in his own hands. His colleague Alonso, though a well-meaning man and of fair intelligence for that country, had neither the cunning nor the ambition that distinguished Lopez. The latter, like Francia, while Secretary of the Junta, had no sooner tasted the luxury of power than he commenced to lay his plans to make himself absolute, and the measures that had resulted so favorably to the Dictator he resolved to imitate. The older people could remember that Francia had appeared to derive his authority from a Congress, and the impression yet remained that only a Congress could invest with due authority the head of the government.

Lopez, therefore, before the expiration of the consulship, had ordered a Congress to be called, taking good care that it should be composed entirely of members who were favorable to him and his plans. This it was not hard to do, as up to that time all his acts had been marked with moderation and humanity ; and, besides, all ambition had been so effectually extinguished among the people that no one else cared to question or dispute his claims.

On the assembling of this Congress, Lopez submitted his plan for a change in the form of government. A dictatorship, by that name, was too odious to be repeated, and a law was therefore proposed to establish a government republican in form, and with a President as chief magistrate. This law was passed without debate or dissent, and thus Carlos Antonio

Lopez, then about fifty-one years of age, was unanimously declared President of Paraguay for ten years. It may be here remarked, that this Congress, like all others which were called during the reign of the Lopezes, was unanimous in everything. A dissenting voice was never heard in one of them. A minority vote was never reported in one of those august assemblages. The work for which the Congress was convened having been done, it was dismissed, to be called together again, or rather a new Congress to be called, when it might suit the President's purposes, or when the ten years should expire and he should desire a re-election. In the organic law there is no provision for the assembling of a Congress except when the President shall call it; so that, the Congress that had elected Lopez being dissolved, the new President was as absolute as ever had been the old Dictator.

But his policy and conduct at first were very different from those of his predecessor. Instead of shutting up the ports, he was anxious to cultivate friendly relations with other nations, and to have free commerce with the rest of the world. Though unable to obtain from Rosas the recognition of Paraguay as a sovereign independent state, he succeeded in getting the commercial restrictions removed as early as the 27th of March of the year of his election, and in June following the independence of Paraguay was acknowledged by Bolivia. In 1852 it was acknowledged by the Argentine Confederation, to which the Province of Buenos Aires did not then belong. In 1853 it was recognized as an independent power by England, France, Sardinia, and the United States, though with the latter, for reasons to be hereafter explained, the treaty was not ratified till six years later.

The first newspaper, the *Paraguayo Independiente*, was issued in April, 1845. It was a government organ, and was intended not so much as a newspaper as to make known the official decrees, and to give the President, who seemed to have an exalted opinion of his own abilities as a writer, an opportunity to display his talents, abuse his enemies, and commend himself. Two other laws first promulgated about this time gave unmistakable evidence of the President's desire to cultivate friendly relations with other nations, and to induce foreign immigration. One of these provided that whoever should introduce any new invention should have the exclusive use of it for five years, and the same exclusive privilege was granted to whomsoever should introduce any new industry into the country. The other was that in all things foreigners resident in the country should enjoy all the rights, privileges, and immunities of natives. They should not be subject to military duty, should not be molested for their religious opinions, and their property of all kinds was to be respected and inviolable, both in times of peace and in times of war; but should war occur with any other nation, the citizens of such nation resident in the country could continue unmolested in their business so long as they respected the laws. This law was liberal in its terms, but how from the first it was a dead letter, and how it was always violated whenever it suited the caprice or interest of the President to violate it, will appear frequently hereafter. In the enforcement of any law of Paraguay there was never any such thing as reciprocity between the subject and the sovereign. The former was expected to obey the laws, but the latter always did just as he pleased, and set aside laws under which foreigners had acquired vested rights at his own good pleasure.

The war between Rosas and the Correntinos continued, and as it was the avowed purpose of Rosas, after he should bring Corrientes into subjection, to attempt the same with Paraguay, President Lopez entered into an alliance offensive and defensive against the Dictator. Active measures were now taken to increase and organize the army, and in the month of December war was publicly proclaimed against Rosas.

Lopez, more wise than Francia, and yet as eager for absolute power, instead of arraying whatever was left of a religious element in the country against him by persecution of the priests, sought to make the church a support to himself. He was intensely avaricious, and already was using his influence and position as President to enrich himself and his family.

His brother, Basilio Lopez, was made, at the request of the President, Bishop of Paraguay, as thus the influence, patronage, and perquisites of the office would all be secured to the family; beside which the position of bishop was, in the popular estimation, so important, that its possession by any other person might imply a division of power, and it was the determination of Lopez to be, like his predecessor, absolute in both temporal and spiritual things. The extent to which he afterwards carried this practice of nepotism, especially towards his children, was perhaps never equalled. In this he showed that he had human affections, in which respect he differed from Francia and from the younger Lopez, who tortured and executed all alike with entire impartiality.

But the event most important in its consequences on the future of Paraguay that occurred during the year 1845 was the arrival of a young American in Asuncion as a sort of special agent of the United States government. His name was Edward A. Hopkins. He had been a midshipman in the navy, but having, for reasons of his own, resigned and left the service, the government of the United States, in accordance with its general policy of giving early recognition to all South American republics that had thrown off the Spanish allegiance, had selected Mr. Hopkins as its special agent to proceed to Paraguay and express its felicitations that a republican form of government had succeeded the colonial period and the dictatorship, and to inquire into the general condition of the country, with the object, on the part of the American government, of recognizing Paraguay as an independent power whenever the proper time should arrive. The person selected was very young for a task of this kind. He was a man of extraordinary energy and fair intelligence, but without that moderation and judgment that might have been expected in an older person. He was not only enthusiastic in whatever he undertook, but had the faculty of inspiring others with faith in his schemes and enterprises; unhappily, however, he was of so arrogant and overbearing a disposition that no one could long act with him in any enterprise, so that, though successful in this and in his subsequent career as the initiator and promoter of important and useful works, his withdrawal from them was essential to their ultimate success. But he had not that great fault of most of his countrymen of being embarrassed and hampered by excessive modesty. To this may be added that he was a man of fine appearance, of herculean strength and iron endurance. He was also a fine musician, and could sing a song or play the guitar in a way that astonished the simple Paraguayans. He could tire out the strongest gaucho in a gallop over the pampas, and was possessed of considerable miscellaneous information, with an imagination at all times ready to help out where facts were wanting, and a volubility that could deluge with assertions whoever opposed him in controversy. Such a man was the first government agent ever sent into Paraguay by the United States; and had the whole country been searched, not another could have been found better calculated to impress on the isolated Paraguayans the fact that the outside barbarians were not so much, physically and mentally, their inferiors as they had supposed.

That the modesty of Hopkins was not so excessive as to embarrass him will appear from his first official communication with the government of Paraguay. In this, although authorized by the government only to investigate and report with a view to recognition, he tells President Lopez that the next Congress of the United States will acknowledge the independence of Paraguay, and he also informs him that he is authorized to offer the mediation of the United States in the war pending between Paraguay and Buenos Aires.

The appearance of a messenger from the great republic, bringing such promises of recognition and sympathy, appeared to Lopez like a special providence for his especial benefit. What cared he then for the ephemeral governments of his neighbors, that were always fighting among themselves, always exposed to, if not engaged in, revolutions? Had not the great Colossus of Republicanism learned of his wisdom and the greatness of his country? and would he not strike hands with his "great and good friend" the President of the United States, as Francia had proposed to do with England, when there should be but two nations of the first class in all the world, Paraguay and North America? — for that the United States and North America are not one and the same no Paraguayan could ever yet understand. What cared he, then, for his neighbors? Hopkins assured him that by concessions to American citizens he could induce men of capital and enterprise to come to Paraguay, who would introduce steamers and factories of various kinds, and the wealth of the country would vastly and rapidly increase with the development of its resources, and Carlos Antonio, instead of being at the head of a petty republic scarcely known to nineteen twentieths of the civilized world, would be the chief magistrate of a great and flourishing empire that would make his name resound throughout the world and would add millions to his private fortune. Lopez listened, well pleased, to all of Hopkins's flatteries, and thought him a marvellously proper man. He gave him his confidence and asked his advice, and bade him go forward with all his plans, and rely on him for assistance and protection.

Hopkins, finding himself in such favor, at once set to work to take advantage of the offers of his friend, Carlos Antonio. He told him that he had wealthy connections in his own country who would introduce many and important improvements into Paraguay; that a company could be formed with a capital of three hundred thousand dollars, and the aggregate wealth of its members would be not less than ten million dollars. If it so pleased his Excellency he would return to the United States, and have the company take immediate steps to realize their great project. The President, cunning and Jesuitical as he was, was completely dazzled with the representations of Hopkins. He saw in the future himself as a great sovereign, famed the world over for his wisdom, and, which was more, he saw the prospect of increased wealth to himself, and this was the impelling motive of his life. Hopkins told him of the great advantages to result from the introduction of improved agricultural implements, like cast-iron ploughs, cultivators, harrows, corn-shellers, cotton-gins; so that Paraguay, instead of being dotted all over with mud houses, each with its little patch of indian corn, cotton, tobacco, mandioca, and sugar-cane, would have great plantations finely improved, and steamers and sailing vessels would in a few years be coming daily to Asuncion to bring the needed manufactures from other countries, and bear away millions of the wealth that the improved culture of the land would produce.

President Lopez having, as we have seen, passed the best part of his life shut out from the world, experienced great difficulty in getting his government into anything like working order. Though he desired to be absolute, he yet wished to have the forms and departments of an organized government to be administered in its details and branches by subordinate officials. But we have already seen how jumbled together were the provisions of his laws, as in the organic law of the Literary Academy it is decreed what clothes the pupils shall wear, what hours shall be devoted to this or that branch, and when they shall have religious exercises instead of recreation; we have also seen that in the law for the establishment of a public cemetery it is provided that, in going to that cemetery, no one shall ride in the dead-cart but the corpse, nor shall any one be allowed to get up and ride behind. From such absurdities and incongruities Hopkins could warn his friend, and could assist him in the work of general organization. Lopez, finding him very useful, treated him with great kindness and attention, and an affection grew up between them as great as that between David and Jonathan or Damon and Pythias. Lopez promised Hopkins everything, and Hopkins, in his turn, wrote glowing accounts of Paraguay to be published in the newspapers of the United States, setting forth the wonderful fertility of the soil, the salubrity of the climate, the vast wealth in the gums, woods, dye-stuffs, medicinal plants, tobacco, cotton, and sugar-cane of the country, and also of the great wisdom, liberality, and good disposition towards foreigners, especially Americans, of its most excellent President, Carlos Antonio Lopez. The government of the United States, however, did not approve all that Hopkins had done in promising recognition of Paraguayan independence and offering mediation between Paraguay and Buenos Aires, and revoked his commission. Though Lopez could not understand the cause of the delay of the former, he was not aware that the promise of Hopkins was made without authority, and it is not probable that the agent ever told him of his reprimand and recall. To carry into effect the great plans that the two had projected, it was concluded that Hopkins should return to the United States and at once set to work to complete the organization of his company, and return with the implements and skilled workmen that were to effect an industrial revolution in Paraguay. To give him more authority, Lopez thought it would be well for him to take a sort of consular commission from him. But he knew nothing of official forms, and Hopkins was obliged even to write out his own passport.

Thus armed with promises Hopkins returned to the United States. But before he left he had been in correspondence with an eminent American citizen, since Governor of his State and United States Senator, in relation to an enterprise of profit and speculation in South America. This gentleman in his youth had travelled much in South America, and had seen the marked contrast between the natural resources and the development of the countries of the Plata ; and it occurred to him that there was a fine field for a profitable business that would yield large fortunes to the promoters, and be of incalculable service to the people of the country. The whole valley of the Plata was in a state of incredible backwardness in all matters of modern improvement and discovery. That noble river, navigable for steamers for a distance of twenty-five hundred miles above tide-water, having towns and cities of considerable size at that distance from the sea, was as yet innocent of steam navigation. The people were almost as primitive in their habits as they had been two hundred years before. The soil was so productive that very little labor sufficed to supply the wants of nature, and people knew little of luxury or of artificial wants. Whatever they had in the way of furniture or clothing was of the rudest and crudest sort, and yet, from lack of tools and skill, was made with infinite labor. The cotton was first separated by hand from the seeds, then it was picked apart and made soft and workable by the same method, then it was spun with no other utensil than a wooden spindle twirled in the fingers, and then it was woven in looms of a construction that even Lucretia would have regarded as old-fashioned. The only plough used was of wood, of a model as old as the Pyramids; and for household utensils they had little more than home-made clay pottery, with one knife for a family and a horn spoon for each individual. Yet these same people had the lingering traditions of gorgeous luxury inherited from their cavalier ancestors, and all that was required to redeem them from their state of semi-barbarism was to establish a free and easy communication with the rest of the world. They had mines of wealth in their woods alone, in their medicinal plants and gums, in their yerba maté, their dyestuffs, their hides and tallow; yet, remote as they were from all civilized countries, all these availed them but little, and they passed lives of helpless ignorance and indolence. The plan of Hopkins, though like all schemes of private enterprise founded on a love of gain, was, nevertheless, a plan for redemption from semi-barbarism to civilization. President Lopez was sagacious enough to see the great advantages that would result to his country and people from the introduction of such new industries as Hopkins proposed to establish; but at first he did not consider that their successful working would be incompatible with a government like his, that the presence of a colony of intelligent and enterprising Americans would soon dispel the illusion of his people as regarded himself, and that his absolute authority would not be tolerated. He desired to let in light so far as to enable his people to make improvements in agriculture and the mechanic arts, but he never considered that if they went thus far they would soon take an inconvenient interest in the state politics.

On returning to the United States, Hopkins was enabled

to show that the schemes of his distinguished friend were exactly in accordance with the views and aims of the very person who could do most towards their realization. Lopez had promised everything, — a monopoly of steam navigation for many years, full protection in executing his plans, and exclusive privileges for all new industries he might introduce. Over and above this, he represented that Don Carlos Antonio was a marvel of intelligence and liberality. A company was then easily formed, and a charter granted by the Legislature of Rhode Island under the title of the United States and Paraguay Navigation Company, composed of men of substantial wealth and character; in fact, made up of the most respectable and influential men of the State of Rhode Island, and the president of which was the individual before referred to who had originated the scheme. A steamer was purchased, her name changed to the El Paraguay, and one or two other vessels chartered, and all were freighted with such things as might be most useful. The cargo was well selected, and consisted of steam-engines, horse-powers, cotton-gins, millstones, saw-mills, ploughs, hoes, shovels, scythes, ox-yokes, sugar-boilers, blacksmith's tools, and many other articles, such as are most needed in a new country. In addition to the machinery and tools, engineers and experienced workmen in all the new arts and industries that they proposed to introduce accompanied the expedition. The most profitable crop for exportation in Paraguay is tobacco; but owing to a lack of care and skill in curing it, it commanded but a low price in the market, and in its manufactured state it was quite unsalable. This company therefore took with them several persons who had been engaged in Cuba in curing tobacco, and were familiar with all the processes of improving its flavor, and also in making the best quality of cigars. Thus freighted with the implements for a great enterprise, the El Paraguay sailed from New York the 21st of March, 1853. But she was destined never to reach Paraguay. She experienced a succession of gales, so that by the time she arrived off the coast of Brazil she was obliged to put into

Maranham, where she was condemned and she and her cargo sold. This was a loss to the company estimated at many times the intrinsic value of the vessel and cargo. It not only entailed heavy expense in addition to the direct loss, but it embarrassed and delayed the enterprise, so that it did not get into fair working condition for a long time, and not till Lopez had had time to realize that such a company as this might prove a very Trojan horse within his dominions. The shipments sent by other vessels were of little value except as supplemental to what was sent in the El Paraguay. Nevertheless the agent of the company, with the men employed, went forward and began operations as best they could, sending back to have duplicated those articles of the most pressing necessity. The company regarded the direct loss of the property as insignificant compared with the franchises promised by Lopez. With the privileges that would enure under them, and the law giving monopolies for the term of five years to whoever should introduce new industries, they saw that if good faith were observed by all parties the undertaking must be immensely profitable and give fortunes to the stockholders.

CARLOS ANTONIO LOPEZ.

CHAPTER XXIII.

The United States and Paraguay Steam Navigation Company. — Difficulties with Lopez. — Expedition of Lieutenant Thomas J. Page to the Plata. — Opposition of Lopez to the American Company. — Insults and Annoyances. — The Enterprise broken up. — Lieutenant Page succeeds in extricating the Company from the Power of Lopez. — Treaty between the United States and Paraguay. — The Water Witch sent to explore the Waters of the Parana. — Fort Itapiru. — The Water Witch fired upon. — Eagerness of Page to avenge the Insult to the Flag. — Commodore Salter refuses to take any Action in the Matter. — Duties of Naval Officers.

LOPEZ had been so greatly elated at the magnificent projects of Hopkins, that he not only promised him most extraordinary privileges and monopolies, but even lent him money to the amount of ten thousand dollars to assist him in returning to the United States and organizing his plans. He had expected that the company would commence operations on an extensive scale, and was evidently disappointed when, owing to the loss of the steamer El Paraguay and the delays incident to this misfortune, the company was able to commence only in a very small way. Notwithstanding this, however, when the company began its operations, he manifested an interest in its success, and showed a disposition to conform to the promises which he had made previous to the return of Hopkins to the United States. The point selected for the head-quarters of the company was a place called San Antonio, about eight miles below Asuncion. A tract of land was here purchased from the owner with the approval and consent of Lopez; and in spite of the disasters which the company had incurred on the voyage everything seemed to open prosperously, and the company were for a time in high hopes of a successful career. They had erected and set in operation a saw-mill, and commenced the manufacture of cigars of a superior quality to what had ever been known before in Paraguay. The company had taken with them several experienced cigar-makers from Cuba, and as the tobacco of the country was of a superior quality, though the rude manner in which it had previously been cured had given it a very low price in the market, they anticipated a very large revenue from this source. Lopez had engaged to permit the employment of as many natives as they needed, and the skilled Cubans immediately set to work to teach their employees how to convert their hitherto nearly valueless raw material into cigars that would bring a good price in any part of the world. Lopez saw, however, that the company were working rather in their own interest than in his, and soon became uneasy at the presence of such a company; and Hopkins, who had returned from the United States with a commission as consul for Paraguay, did not try to conciliate him, either by deferring to his wishes in small things or by making him a partner in the prospective profits of the company. It was soon evident to all that Lopez had changed his mind in regard to the whole project, and that the company were regarded by him with fear and aversion. This was at first apparent from the changed manner of the native people. Under his system of government he could easily convey to all of his subjects the fact that any persons had fallen into disfavor, and that it was safe to treat them with disrespect and discourtesy and to have nothing to do with them. It required no official decree or public announcement for him to make known his desires. If an official who was understood to be high in his confidence was known to be rude to any foreigner, all were aware that he acted by authority, and that it would be prudent for them to imitate his example. Nevertheless, nothing of a serious nature occurred, until one day, as the brother of Mr. Hopkins happened to be riding out in company with the wife of the French consul, he met, at a short distance from the capital, a native Paraguayan driving before him a small herd of cattle. The cattle at the sight of the lady and her attendant turned back, or ran into the bushes and woods near the road. The

Paraguayan in charge of them, who was, of course, well aware that the Americans were no longer in favor, showed great anger, and, riding up to young Hopkins, drew his sword and beat him with it over the head and shoulders. When Consul Hopkins learned of this outrage he was very indignant; and hurried into the presence of Lopez, and, without observing those forms and ceremonies in which the Spanish-Americans are always very punctilious, recounted in an angry and energetic manner the insult and indignity to which his brother had been subjected, and demanded the punishment of the soldier. During all the time that Lopez had been at the head of the government he had never before been addressed except in the most obsequious and respectful terms; and when he saw the stalwart American before him, in top-boots and spurs, with his hat on and whip in hand, violently gesticulating and demanding satisfaction, he was both alarmed and angry. He, however, complied with the request, and said the man should be punished, and that he would order the infliction upon him of three hundred blows. This did not satisfy Hopkins, who demanded not only that the man should be punished, but that the official newspaper should publicly announce it, that others might learn from his fate what they were to expect if any further indignities or offences were given to members of the company. The old man refused to accede to this demand, and as soon as he could recover from his fright he commenced a series of annoyances and outrages that rendered the property of the company valueless, and left the members of it exposed and helpless. His people were privately forbidden to labor for the company or traffic with them, and in some instances the company's property was taken by him and in others it was destroyed. The land which had been bought by the company, to the purchase of which no objection had been made at the time of the bargain, was declared to have been illegally sold, and that there were claims upon it by others than the former owner, so that the deed of purchase was null and void. This pretence of illegality was clearly trumped up for no other object than as an excuse for ejecting the company from their rightful possessions. But the company had no means of redress. Lopez had determined to drive them from the country and break up the enterprise, and as he was responsible to no power in the world but his own arbitrary will, it was hopeless, at this stage, for the company to contend with him. His action towards them, however, was somewhat embarrassed by the fact that an American man-of-war was in the river; and though this vessel had not been built for warlike purposes, and as a war vessel was of very little account, it was nevertheless capable, with its small armament, of destroying his capital.

Some time before this, as early as 1852, Lieutenant Thomas J. Page, an officer of the American navy, who was possessed of a commendable spirit of enterprise and adventure, and a man of considerable scientific knowledge, had so far interested the United States in the affairs of the Plata as to induce the government to send out an expedition to explore that river and its tributaries, and report upon their navigability and of the field which they offered for commerce with the United States. It was a scientific expedition in which all commercial countries were more or less interested, as previous to that time the character of the upper waters of the Plata was almost entirely unknown. Lieutenant Page was commissioned also to negotiate a treaty of commerce and navigation, either by himself or in conjunction with our ministers to Brazil and the Argentine Confederation. The vessel detailed by the government for this expedition was the steamer Water Witch. She left the United States in the early part of the year 1853, and proceeding first to Brazil, Lieutenant Page there made known to the Brazilian government the object of the expedition, which was to explore the tributaries of the Plata, especially the waters of the Upper Paraguay, that had their rise in the Brazilian province of Matto Grosso. At first permission was granted to him to ascend only to a point called Albuquerque, which is but a short distance from the Paraguayan frontier; but after a great deal of diplomacy, prevarication, and delay, characteristic of the Brazilian government, permission was finally given to explore any of the tributaries of the Paraguay River. After leaving Rio, the Water Witch proceeded to Montevideo and Buenos Aires, and thence on its voyage of exploration and discovery up the river to Asuncion, where it arrived in October, 1853. Lieutenant Page, on making known to President Lopez the object of the Water Witch in ascending the Paraguay, was received by him with unusual courtesy and attention, for at that time the Rhode Island company had not commenced operations in the country and Lopez was particularly well affected towards Americans. Having made all the preparations necessary for the continuation of his voyage, and having built a small steamer to explore the smaller tributaries of the river and obtained the promise of assistance from Lopez in securing a supply of fuel and any assistance that might be required from the people farther up the river, he continued his voyage up beyond the limits of Paraguay to the town of Coimbra, in the Brazilian province of Matto Grosso. Not having at that time received permission from the Brazilian government to go higher, he was obliged to turn back at this point, and found, greatly to his mortification, that the habitual delay of the Brazilians in granting him permission to go higher up had defeated to a great extent the object of his expedition, though he found, when too late for it to be available, that the desired permission had been given. Returning down the river to Asuncion, he ascertained that the disposition of President Lopez towards himself, his expedition, and all Americans, had undergone an important change. Some members of the Rhode Island company, with their agent, Mr. Hopkins, had arrived since the time of his first arrival there and his return from the Upper Paraguay, and had commenced operations, though the difficulties between the company and Lopez had not yet commenced. The President affected great displeasure because the Water Witch had ascended beyond the frontiers of Paraguay, alleging that having permitted an American steamer to do so, he would next be called upon by Brazil to permit the same privilege to her vessels, which might lead to difficulties and complications with that government. The wrath of Lopez, however, was so far appeased, that he permitted Lieutenant Page to complete the little steamer for the exploration of the Pilcomayo and the Bermejo, both of which streams have their head-waters far to the west of the Andes, and find their way through the Gran Chaco until they unite with the Paraguay, the former near Asuncion and the latter near its confluence with the Parana. Lieutenant Page improved his time and opportunities most efficiently. He made charts of the different rivers and obtained a great variety of information, all of which he held at the service, not only of his own government, but of Paraguay and the whole civilized world. Having an adequate force of assistants, well instructed in botany, mineralogy, and zoölogy, he collected specimens of many rare plants and birds, and of the animals peculiar to the country; and up to the time when Lopez saw fit to interrupt his explorations his expedition had been one of the most successful and creditable to the United States that had ever been despatched from their shores. While engaged in his explorations, being absent in the interior of the country, he learned of the difficulties which had occurred between Consul Hopkins and President Lopez. He returned immediately, and learned that the hostility of Lopez to the company, which had long been repressed, had finally reached its climax with the assault of the Paraguayan soldier upon the brother of the consul. Hopkins had complained of this outrage, and demanded that the soldier should be summarily punished and the reason for it be publicly announced in the official organ. What followed is thus described by Lieutenant Page: —

"President Lopez took exception to the language in which the complaint was made. A paper war ensued; crimination followed recrimination. The consular *exequatur* was revoked, and the wrath of the chief magistrate extended to the members of the American company of which Hopkins was the agent. They had been permitted to occupy the cuartel of San Antonio; had improved the grounds, purchased some adjoining lands, erected a saw-mill, and established a cigar-factory. They were now forced to give up the cuartel; the controversy waxed hotter and hotter; decrees, or *bandos*, intended to embarrass their operations, were issued, and at last the cigar-factory was closed, thereby virtually closing the business of the company in Paraguay. I give a few of the *bandos*, which, though applied to all foreigners, were at this time intended for the special embarrassment of the Americans: —

"'1. No servant shall engage in the service of a foreigner without a written agreement or notification given and approved by the government as to the amount of wages.

"'2. All meetings of foreigners, except for the ostensible purpose of visiting and innocent diversion, are forbidden, by day and by night.

"'3. All foreigners must take out a license to engage in any commercial or industrial pursuit.'

"The last article was reasonable; but the company, though going on for a year, had not before been required to take out a license; and when Mr. Hopkins made an application for it, in the character of 'general agent,' having paid sixteen dollars for the stamped paper, it was refused on the ground of his being 'general agent.' This title was objectionable to the government, and would not be recognized. He must apply as 'agent,' without the 'general.'

"I am to this day mystified by this phase of the difficulty. There was but one general in Paraguay, the son and heir of the President; but by what process of reasoning the title of the 'general agent' reflected upon the head of the military arm I am unable to say; neither do I see why it should not have been relinquished. There are other petty annoyances, seemingly of a general bearing, but in fact aimed at the American company.

"Affairs had reached this crisis when I arrived at Asuncion, and found Mr. Hopkins determined, by reason of the course of the government, to leave the country, with the members of the company and such of their effects as could conveniently be removed."

Lieutenant Page called on President Lopez with the object of arranging the difficulties which had arisen, and in reply Lopez complained of the indignity which Hopkins had offered to him in the interview which took place after the outrage committed by the soldier on his brother, and said that for that reason he had withdrawn his *exequatur*. He said Hopkins was personally obnoxious to him, but that the other members of the company would enjoy full protection in conducting the business, and that they should be protected from all further insult or injury. It was evident, nevertheless, to Hopkins, who had lived long in the country and knew how absolute Lopez was in everything, that he had determined to break up the company. In fact it was already broken up, as Lopez had violated all the contracts or arrangements which he had previously made with it. He therefore determined to abandon the enterprise and to look to his own government to exact such redress and restitution as the laws of nations might demand. Without the aid of the Water Witch, however, neither he nor his companions could leave the country, for none of the small sailing vessels in the river would dare to take them away without the permission of Lopez, as the owners knew that to attempt to do so would call upon them the displeasure of the government, which was then directed to Hopkins and his company. Lieutenant Page continues: —

"I replied, 'I will see the President, and if no arrangement can be made for your leaving the country by a trading vessel, I will receive the members of the company and their effects on board the Water Witch, and convey them to Corrientes,' — this being the point at which he wished to establish them.

"I called again at the Government House, stated again the apprehensions of Mr. Hopkins, and suggested that he should allow the captain of the port to procure a vessel which would at once set at rest the fears of any shipmaster as to the consequences of receiving the Americans. He said, 'This shall be done.' 'Now, sir,' I asked, 'what forms must be complied with to enable the company to leave Paraguay with their property?' He replied, 'They will simply be required to procure passports, and a "permit" from the custom-house for the shipment of their effects and merchandise, all of which they are at liberty to take with them, paying the export duty on such articles as are the product of the country.' They had about eight hundred arrobas of superior tobacco.

"A vessel was engaged, passports obtained, and I concluded that all was satisfactorily arranged for the departure of the company, when one of its members came on board the Water Witch and complained of fresh insults by the chief of police.

" Again I called on the President. It was my last interview with his Excellency. I reminded him of the assurances he had given me as to the personal treatment of the members of the company, and stated the new complaint, informing him at the same time, in decided but courteous language, *that my duty obliged me to watch over the rights of American citizens wherever I should meet them abroad*."

The chief of police being examined, the President informed him of the charges made against him, which, as he doubtless had been previously advised to do, he positively denied. And it appeared that the last difficulty had arisen from a cause such as perhaps never before in the history of the world engaged the attention of the head of a great nation. The company, in gathering together such of their effects as they wished to take away, had left a small tin sign on the building which they had occupied, and Lopez demanded that they should take it away with them and give a receipt for it, lest the claim should be made that their property had been withheld. Lieutenant Page quickly solved this difficulty by saying that he would send one of his boat's crew to carry away the obnoxious sign, and thus this important state difficulty was arranged. He continues: —

" I had scarcely got on board the Water Witch, congratulating myself that the difficulties were over, when another note was received from Mr. Hopkins. On applying for a 'permit' to ship the goods, it had been refused until he should surrender the papers, deeds, etc., which secured to the company certain lands purchased and paid for.

" Before taking any further steps I sent my clerk to ascertain from the collector if I must understand that he refused a 'permit' for the despatch of the company's merchandise on the grounds mentioned. He returned with a reply in the affirmative.

" I had been long enough in the country to know that the collector would not dare to take such a step without instructions from the President. It was in direct violation of every promise his Excellency had given me, and I saw clearly that the moment had arrived when my action in this difficulty should be a matter of record. I addressed a note to the Minister of Foreign Relations, stating the facts of the case, repeating the assurances of the President, and telling him what would be my course for the relief of the members of this company if they were not allowed to depart by the usual mode of conveyance."

In endeavoring to extricate Hopkins and his company from their difficult and dangerous position, Page soon found himself as obnoxious to Lopez as they were. He was requested to send a translation of the notes which he addressed to the government, to which he properly replied that he would do nothing of the kind, and he adds: —

"Failing to coerce me into this measure, — the sole object of which was to exhibit to the people of Paraguay his authority over a foreign officer, — my notes were returned the following day, with one from the Minister of Foreign Relations, Mr. José Falcon, informing me that the President did not read English, and desiring that I would translate them into Spanish, when they would receive proper attention.

"I replied to Mr. Falcon, stating that the contemptuous treatment of my official communications, addressed in courteous language, was a thing unprecedented in this age of civilization; that it deprived me of the means of arriving at the intentions of the government relative to the departure of the Americans, and forced upon me the inference that my request had been refused, thus making it an imperative duty to remove them in the Water Witch. At the same time I informed the captain of the port that I should receive them and their effects on board, and leave Asuncion at a certain hour."

Lopez, to save the appearance of having been bullied, instantly had the permits issued, though he pretended that he had not understood the contents of the notes which demanded them. The Americans, however, were already on board, or going on board, the steamer, before the permission for their departure had been made known to them.

The following, describing the appearance of Asuncion at this time, will show, not only how absolute was the authority of Lopez, but how silently he could make known and enforce his orders throughout the town: —

"Before getting under way, having occasion to pass through a good portion of the town, I observed that it presented an unusual appearance; not a soul was abroad. Asuncion was not at *siesta*, for it was not the hour; moreover, heads were peering through half-opened doors, showing that curiosity was stronger than fear or sleep. Something was wrong, and the people were anxious to know what difficulties were brewing with the 'supreme government.'

"The plaza, usually the gayest and noisiest place imaginable, was deserted. I missed the picturesque groups of market women, with their white cotton mantas, seated upon the ground, encircled by fruits, vegetables, and an eager crowd of buyers. Not a man, cart, or horse was to be seen, except a few conveying the effects of the American company to the beach. What was feared? The following explanation was made:—

"Last night at midnight the President called a consultation of his advisers, at which your letter was considered. The wise-heads thought they saw in it another 'Graytown affair.' His Excellency thought, as heavy bodies move slowly, it would be well to be prepared; so he sent for a machinist to examine his carriage, and see that all was in good *running* condition. Orders were issued that no one should appear in the plaza or streets after eleven o'clock this morning, and not a horse or cart, except those engaged in transporting the goods of the American company, was to be seen.

"The submission of the people to the present grinding system is only simulated. They are not insensible to their thraldom, and the President really feared that if you fired at the Government House the people might avail themselves of the opportunity to rise and change the order of things, and he was prepared to run."

In this way the Rhode Island company, with their obnoxious agent, were enabled to escape from the power of Lopez, their enterprise having been broken up, and their property seized and rendered valueless or virtually confiscated. The Water Witch was prevented from continuing her explorations, and the object in sending out the expedition was to a great extent defeated.

In the treaty which had been previously made between the United States and Paraguay, by an inadvertency the United States of America was called the United States of North

America. The error was detected in Washington, and before the treaty could be passed upon by the Senate and ratifications exchanged, it was returned, that the mistake might be rectified; and when Page, after leaving Paraguay, had arrived at Corrientes, he met a messenger from the United States with the treaty duly corrected in order to exchange ratifications. The bearer of this treaty, Mr. R. C. Buckley, also brought letters from the Secretary of State, William L. Marcy, to Lieutenant Page, instructing him to propose the exchange. The treaties between Paraguay and France, England and Sardinia, which had been negotiated at the same time with that of the United States, had been ratified long before, and doubtless that of the United States would have been but for this error of description. As soon as the Water Witch left Paraguay, Lopez issued a decree prohibiting the entrance of all vessels of war into the Paraguayan waters. This decree, though general in its terms, was specially intended to prevent Lieutenant Page from returning to continue his explorations of the upper waters, either of the Parana or the Paraguay, or any of those streams that have their source in Bolivia. As the Water Witch was technically a war vessel, Lieutenant Page could not return to Asuncion on board of her for the purpose of exchanging the ratifications of the treaty; and he therefore despatched two of his officers with a note to Lopez, or his Minister of Foreign Relations, advising him that he had been commissioned to exchange ratifications, and desiring to know when and where he should meet the person duly authorized to act on the part of Paraguay. This note was returned with an insolent and insulting reply, complaining that it was not accompanied by a translation. Subsequently the United States sent a special commissioner, Colonel Fitzpatrick, to Paraguay, to effect an exchange of ratifications, but Lopez would have nothing more to do with the Americans, and the commission of Colonel Fitzpatrick failed to reconcile him.

The Water Witch, having extricated the unfortunate company from the hands of Lopez, proceeded to Buenos Aires in order to obtain supplies for the purpose of exploring the waters of the Parana, over which Lopez had no legal control. The commander of the expedition now decided to divide his forces, and proceed himself, with a part of his crew, to the exploration of the river Salado. On returning, the Water Witch was despatched by Lieutenant Page, under command of Lieutenant Jeffers, to ascend again to the confluence of the Paraguay and Parana, thence to ascend the latter river as far as the island of Apipé, a distance of over a hundred miles from the confluence of the two rivers. The object in sending the Water Witch to this point was, besides a general survey of the river and its banks, to ascertain how far it was navigable. As that part of the Parana which Lieutenant Jeffers intended to explore flowed between Paraguay and the province of Corrientes, Lopez made no pretension of controlling it, and it was not anticipated that he would interfere in any way with the voyage of the Water Witch. In fact, it was the opinion of Lieutenant Page that he had left Lopez and his country behind him, and would be no more troubled by them. The Water Witch accordingly again commenced her ascent of the river, and, having reached the confluence of the Parana and Paraguay, continued her course towards Apipé. About two leagues from the extreme southern point of Paraguay stood the small fort of Itapiru. This fort stood upon a rock or point of land that jutted into the stream, so as to give it a commanding position ; just above it was a small island, and the main or deeper channel of the river was towards the right bank, and between the island and the Paraguayan shore. As the pilot of the steamer was ignorant of where the main channel was, he undertook to pass to the south of the island, and next to the Corrientes side. The vessel, however, struck a sand-bar and could not go on, when she was backed off, and the attempt was made for her to pass through the other or principal channel. Says Page :—

"When the Water Witch was within close shot, two or three blank cartridges were fired from the fort, followed by a *shot.* At what part of the vessel it was aimed I can only judge from President Lopez's despatch to our State Department, where he magnanimously says it was directed so as to 'pass ahead.' If so, it struck wide of the mark, and was unfortunately effective; for it passed through the after port, cut away the wheel, and killed the helmsman. Lieutenant Jeffers had disregarded the blank cartridges, and up to this time had withheld his fire. Indeed, his means of defence, with three howitzers, — one twenty-four-pounder and two twelve-pounders, — were small against a brick or stone fort. But when this shot came he returned it as rapidly as the reduced number of officers and crew and the disabled condition of the helm would admit. The accuracy of the fire was seen in cutting away the flagstaff, and in the shrapnel grazing the low wall, — for the guns were mounted *en barbette*. We learned afterwards that several Paraguayans were killed; some reports said eleven, others fifteen. The Water Witch was struck ten times, but the first was the only shot that did any execution, though we learned that the firing from the fort was directed by a person formerly of the French navy, who had entered the service of Paraguay."

Page was already on his way down the river towards the mouth of the Salado, when, to his great surprise, he saw the Water Witch coming after him, and great was his astonishment when he learned that the vessel had been fired into while it was in waters over which Lopez had neither jurisdiction nor rightful control. It seemed as though Lopez, in his arrogance and isolation, had intended to commit so gross an insult against the flag of the United States as to provoke war against him. Commander Page was indignant. The flag of his country — alas that it should be said! the flag he himself afterwards betrayed, and endeavored to disgrace and humble — had been insulted, and he was eager to avenge it so promptly that it should ever after be respected in those waters. The United States had an idle squadron on the South Atlantic Coast, and he hastened to communicate with the commander of it, Commodore W. D. Salter, and inform him of the insult the flag had received from President Lopez, and to request him to send one of his large vessels immediately to Paraguay, and demand such redress, apology, and satisfaction as so gross an insult merited. The two large war vessels of the squadron, the Germantown and the Savannah, were at Rio de Janeiro at this time; and Lieutenant Page despatched an officer to that place to represent the condition of affairs to Commodore Salter, and by personal appeal support his application for a large vessel to proceed immediately to Paraguay. Commodore Salter, however, did not see that any occasion had arisen for such action. He seemed to have adopted the ideas which have long been prevalent in the American navy, that in time of peace our ships of war are sent to foreign stations for the convenience and pleasure of the chief officers of the squadrons; that they were to respect no representations from any source except the Navy Department, and, whatever insult may be offered to the flag, they are not to resent it without specific and direct orders from the Secretary of the Navy; that the flag officer of the squadron is to take no responsibility upon himself, but to make his flag-ship a pleasure yacht, and do no service further than to exhibit the vessel to the eyes of foreign nations, and the uniforms of the officers in the streets, courts, and saloons of the cities which they visit. This attack upon the Water Witch was as gross an insult, and as direct a violation of the flag of the United States and the laws of nations, as can well be imagined; yet the commander of our squadron could see nothing serious in it, or nothing that required him to vary or interrupt the course of his voyage of pleasure. Lieutenant Page demonstrated the fact that there would be no difficulty in taking the Germantown up the river at that time, and of so frightening Lopez that he would have consented to any terms, both in regard to the outrage on the Water Witch and the wrongs of the Rhode Island company, if by so doing he could have persuaded her to depart from the country, and leave him in peace to tyrannize over and rob his own people. It was all in vain, however. The spirit and feeling which at a later period have been manifested in a more lamentable manner by high officers of the navy, that the Navy Department is established and supported by the government, but owes no corresponding duties to it; that it is an *imperium in imperio*, so independent as to have nothing more to do than maintain its discipline and secure promotion for its officers, and is under no obligations to render assistance to the other branches of the government at times when the national character and the honor of the flag are at stake, — so thoroughly possessed the commander of this squadron at the time, that he did not seem to realize how such an outrage as that committed by President Lopez on the Water Witch was a matter of sufficient importance to require any action from him.

CHAPTER XXIV.

The United States Government takes up the Cause of the Rhode Island Company. — An Expedition with a Special Commissioner sent to Paraguay to demand Indemnity. — Urquiza obtains a Copy of the Secret Instructions and visits Lopez. — Arrival of Commissioner Bowlin in Paraguay. — Negotiations. — A Convention formed. — The Expedition returns to the United States. — The Commissioners meet in Washington — Result of the Arbitration. — Chagrin of President Buchanan at the Decision. — His Message to Congress.

THE Rhode Island company having been driven out of Paraguay in defiance of all right or semblance of law, they appealed to the United States to compel Lopez to make compensation for the injury that they had suffered at his hands; and the Secretary of State, William L. Marcy, on investigation of the circumstances of the case, officially declared in favor of their right to indemnity. Of this our government never had any doubt, and the only question with it was as to the amount of damages to which the company was entitled. But before any demonstrations of force were made, a special commissioner was sent out, with instructions to present to the Paraguayan government a claim for indemnification for the losses which had been sustained. The commissioner, Mr. Fitzpatrick, was also instructed to exchange ratifications of the treaty which had been made some two years before, but which had not been ratified by reason of the verbal error to which allusion has already been made. But the commissioner was repelled with rudeness by Lopez, who refused to exchange the ratifications, and also refused to admit his liability to the company or make any compensation in damages. Mr. Marcy assumed as a fact not to be questioned or discussed, that injustice had been done to the company, for which that government was accountable; and when Congress met in December, 1857, the President, in his message, declared that a demand should be made for redress, and recommended that if it were not granted the Executive should have authority to employ force. Congress, by decided majorities, adopted the recommendation of the President, and passed an act authorizing him to use force if necessary to obtain justice from Lopez. An expedition, consisting of twenty-three vessels, was accordingly fitted out and sent to the Plata, with instructions to obtain redress, — forcibly, if necessary. It was badly arranged in its details, and was made needlessly expensive. It has been charged that the controlling members of the administration had other objects in view in fitting out this expedition besides vindicating the flag and obtaining redress for the company. Certain it is that the same high officials who approved of the expedition were soon after found fighting against the flag which had been so outraged by Lopez that the national honor required satisfaction. And it is equally certain that the sailing of this expedition was made a pretext for withdrawing from the forts and arsenals of the North all the munitions of war, thus leaving them unprovided with arms whenever the plans for the Great Rebellion should be matured. The Secretary of State, General Cass, however, had no such ulterior views. He had sufficient respect for the national credit to encumber the expedition with instructions that, if followed out, would vindicate the flag and teach other nations that the American government was prepared to defend the rights of its citizens in whatever part of the world they might be. He maintained, that, by sending an expedition to demand reparation for damages, the government assumed there was no question in regard to the wrong inflicted and the just liability of the wrong-doer, and that Paraguay must either pay the damage or feel the strong hand of a strong power in actual war. But it was not the policy of Davis, Floyd, and Toucey to begin a war even with so weak a power as Paraguay. The country was so remote that perhaps this great expedition would be unable to conquer it; and, once engaged in it, there would be no way but to go on, and perhaps a larger force might be required, so that before the business was concluded the government might find itself with a large naval force and a greatly increased regular army. This would render the expedition worse than nothing. The President, without entering into their views, was only wax in their hands. But it was not so with the Secretary of State. If the expedition were to sail, it must go under such circumstances that it could not prove a ridiculous failure and bring disgrace on the President, Secretary of State, and the whole country. As the success of an expedition of this kind would depend very much on the tact and ability of the diplomatic agent who was to accompany it, common sense would have dictated that a shrewd, experienced diplomatist should be selected for the position. The commissioner, however, appointed by President Buchanan, was the Hon. James B. Bowlin of Missouri, — a gentleman who had served several terms in Congress, but whose experience as a stump orator in the West was not of the kind to render him a formidable antagonist to one brought up in the schools of the Jesuits. The secretary to the mission was Mr. Samuel Ward of New York, whose appointment was approved by the company, as he was a relative of some of the leading members of it and friendly to them all. They did not then think that he would ever betray them.

The instructions of General Cass to Commissioner Bowlin were strong, clear, and explicit. These instructions, necessarily secret, were to the effect that the expedition would proceed to the Plata, and the commissioner and his secretary, leaving the fleet at some convenient point, were to proceed with only one or two vessels to Asuncion, and there represent to President Lopez the demands of the United States government, and endeavor to make a pacific arrangement of the matter in question. The company claimed that they had suffered injury to the amount of $ 1,000,000 from the unlawful acts of President Lopez. The Secretary of State, however, considered that they had overestimated their prospective profits, and, in his instructions to Commissioner Bowlin, told him he was to insist on

$ 500,000 as the minimum he could accept as compensation. "And if, therefore," says the Secretary, "the government of Paraguay should consent to the payment of the sum of $ 500,000, in full discharge of the entire claim of the company, you will not refuse to make the adjustment for that account." This was the first condition imposed by the instructions of General Cass. If President Lopez would pay half a million in hard money, then Commissioner Bowlin was authorized to accept it; but if Lopez would not listen to the conditions, then the fleet was to be employed to bring him to terms. And if they must fight before he would make compensation, then they were to exact, not only the half-million for the company, but another half-million towards paying the expenses of the expedition. The question of liability was treated as a foregone conclusion by General Cass, as he was a statesman of too much experience to countenance an expedition that was to cost the country millions of dollars, unless the question of the justice and rightfulness of the claims were already established, and the consequent liability of the other party. To send such an expedition eight thousand miles to ascertain that it had no business to go at all, as there were no wrongs to redress, was too gross an absurdity, and therefore General Cass made it an indispensable preliminary that the liability of Paraguay to make compensation should be acknowledged. But if the sum of $ 500,000 was deemed excessive by Lopez, and he would submit to an impartial investigation of the damages sustained by the company, and abide the result of an arbitration, and pay whatever a joint commission might declare to have been the losses sustained by the company through his acts, then Commissioner Bowlin was instructed to assent to such mode of adjustment. This he could do only on condition that Lopez acknowledged the liability of his government to the company. If Lopez would not acknowledge the liability, waiving all questions of right, and would not pay the $ 500,000, then the commissioner was to call on Commodore Shubrick to obtain double that amount by force. Thus fortified with instructions, it was the purpose of the government, or at least of the Secretary of State, that the fleet should proceed to the Plata ; that the commissioner, with Commodore Shubrick and Secretary Ward, should ascend to Asuncion with only one or two vessels, and then endeavor to effect an adjustment without resorting to force.

The news of the extensive preparations made by the United States had reached Lopez long before the arrival of the expedition. The country was at that time almost defenceless. The only fortifications on the river were at Humaita and Asuncion, and at that time they were not sufficient to endanger a single steamer of the squadron, had they all tried to pass at full speed. Lopez was in a great fright, while the hopes of the people of Paraguay were greatly elated by the prospect of a war which they hoped would result in a change of government. Some even went so far as to intimate that Lopez was not autocrat of all the world, and that he was about to receive a lesson. Words then spoken were afterwards remembered, as we shall see by and by.

The most influential man at that time in these regions was the President of the Argentine Confederation, General J. J. Urquiza. This man, who from poverty and obscurity, by a life of fraud, rapacity, and robbery, had obtained possession of the better, if not the larger, part of the province of Entre Rios, so that he always had a large army under his control, had been at one time the ally and supporter of Rosas in his infamous and blood-thirsty career. Believing himself, after a time, to be sufficiently strong to dethrone his chief, he made war upon him, the result of which was that Rosas was driven from power and into exile, and Urquiza became the head of the government. The province of Buenos Aires did not long submit to his rule, and he in time was driven out and obliged to retire to his own province, where he raised another army, and this time made war on Buenos Aires, not to liberate it from one tyrant, but to subject it to another, — himself. In this, however, he had not been successful, and afterwards was obliged to content himself with being virtually, if not nominally, the head of the Confederation, with Buenos Aires no longer a member of it. Urquiza looked with distrust on the approaching armada, for if real war were to be begun by the Yankees, the result would most likely be disastrous to his ill-gotten and ill-used power. He at once opened communication with Lopez to avert the impending catastrophe, and as soon as the fleet arrived at Montevideo, he set the necessary means in operation to ascertain what were the secret instructions of Commissioner Bowlin. It is enough to say that a copy of the instructions was given to young Don Eduardo Guido* to translate for the use of Urquiza. No sooner was the latter possessed of these instructions than he saw that if Lopez were assured of their tenor and purport there would be no danger of a collision. He therefore immediately took a special steamer, and, hurrying to Paraguay, advised Lopez to haggle for the least amount possible; not to deny liability, but finally, if he could not induce the expedition to depart without too large a payment, to await the offer of arbitration which he knew that Bowlin must make before proceeding to extremities; to avoid a collision at every sacrifice, and if an arbitration only could avert it, to trust to duplicity and corruption to secure a favorable result.

Lopez took the advice of his friend, and when the commissioner arrived treated him with respectful courtesy, but denied that anything was rightfully due the Rhode Island company. He indulged in gross abuse and vituperation of Hopkins, and claimed to have done everything in accordance with the laws of the country. Bowlin, however, told him that he had not come to discuss the merits of the case. His instructions were to demand \$500,000 as the minimum that he could accept. Lopez refused to give it, but said that though nothing was justly due the company, he would, in order to get rid of the expedition, give them \$260,000. He thought it would be better and safer to pay this amount than to run the risk of an arbitration. Had he not been previously advised of Bowlin's instructions, he doubtless would have paid the full

* These facts were given to me by Guido himself.

sum demanded, or even double that amount, sooner than go to war. But owing to treachery he had the cards already in his hands, and knew that in refusing to pay it he was in no danger of being attacked. Consequently, he refused the payment of the half-million demanded, and when the arbitration was offered he accepted it. Commissioner Bowlin, in offering to submit the case to arbitration, considered that the only point to be passed upon was that of the amount of loss incurred by the company; and that question he engaged to refer to a mixed commission of two persons, — one of whom should be appointed by President Lopez, and the other by the President of the United States. In case of the disagreement of the two commissioners, they were to select a third, who should act as umpire. A convention was therefore ratified in form, by which it was agreed by the two parties that the two commissioners should meet in Washington, and after a full presentation of the case in all its bearings they should decide and adjudge the amount of the losses sustained by the company. The words of the convention were as follows : —

"ARTICLE I. The government of the Republic of Paraguay binds itself for the responsibility in favor of the United States and Paraguay Navigation Company which may result from the decree of commissioners, who, it is agreed, shall be appointed as follows : —

"The two high contracting parties, appreciating the difficulty of agreeing upon the amount of reclamations to which the said company may be entitled, and being convinced that a commission is the only equitable and honorable method by which the two countries can arrive at a perfect understanding thereof, hereby covenant to adjust them accordingly by a loyal commission. To determine the amount of said reclamations, it is therefore agreed to constitute such a commission, whose decision shall be binding," etc.

Two commissioners were to be appointed under the terms of this convention, one by President Lopez and the other by the President of the United States; and according to the terms of the convention they were to meet in the city of Washington to investigate, adjust, and determine the amount of the claims of the above-mentioned company. The convention having been duly signed by Commissioner Bowlin on the part of the United States, and by Nicholas Vasquez on the part of Paraguay, Commissioner Bowlin and his secretary bade adieu to President Lopez and returned to Montevideo.

It was now clear that no warlike demonstrations were to be made in the river, and General Urquiza was so pleased with his success in obtaining the secret instructions, and by means of them having circumvented the United States government, that he received the commissioner with profuse demonstrations of respect and hospitality, and in testimony of his gratitude or obligations he presented him with a diamond snuff-box of the value of $ 5,000. With this trophy the fleet, the commissioner, and his secretary returned to the United States; and the commissioner reported to the government that the expedition had been eminently successful, and that an arbitration had been obtained according to the conditions of his instructions.

The commissioner on the part of President Lopez was Don José Berges, a man of much acuteness, and, for a Paraguayan, of superior attainments. Berges, though appointed as commissioner and sworn to act with impartiality, was, nevertheless, the agent or advocate of Lopez. If inclined to be otherwise, and disposed to consider all the questions at issue with the impartiality of a judge, he knew very well that if he let slip any opportunity for advancing the interests of the cause of his chief he could never venture to return to Paraguay without incurring the penalty of imprisonment and probable death. He knew also that all his property, of which he had considerable, would be instantly confiscated by Lopez, and therefore he must act rather as the attorney of Paraguay than as an impartial arbiter between that country and the Rhode Island company. Under these circumstances it would have been legitimate and proper for President Buchanan to have appointed some one known to be favorable to the interests of the company, as, according to the terms of the convention, if the two commissioners could not agree, they were to choose a third person to act as umpire between them. In this way, and in this way only, could a fair and just decision be expected. President Buchanan, however, with an obtuseness or perversity which characterized his whole administration, selected a man — the Hon. Cave Johnson of Kentucky — whose prejudices were strongly against everything that originated in New England; and it might have been foreseen, that, though he intended to act justly and honorably, his feelings would be adverse to the company. The commission accordingly met in Washington, and though it had been expressly stipulated in the convention that they were only to decide upon the amount of claims for which Lopez was liable to the company, the attorney for Paraguay, in opening the case, took the ground that the whole question of liability was before them, and that he had a right to go into the origin of the alleged wrongs committed against the company, and to show that Lopez had done nothing from the beginning but what, according to the laws of his own country, he had a right to do; and that therefore, if the Rhode Island company had suffered through the operation of those laws, it was their misfortune, for which the government of Paraguay was in no wise liable.

The counsel for the company protested against this, but instead of refusing to appear before the commission, or to prosecute their case unless that which had been stipulated in the convention was admitted by the commissioners, they contented themselves with objecting to this assumption of the opposite party, and entered into a discussion of the entire merits of the case. The American commissioner, not understanding the Spanish language, was dependent for all the information he had in regard to the laws of Paraguay, the customs of the country, and the operations of Lopez's government, on the secretary of the board, who was the same Mr. Samuel Ward that had gone out as secretary and interpreter to Commissioner Bowlin, and of whom the company complained then, as they have ever since, that for some reason unknown to them he was too well affected towards Lopez to be impartial. The result of the arbitration was as might have been foreseen. The commissioners decided on the 13th of August, 1860, that having examined the whole case, and conferred and deliberated upon it, and listened to the arguments on both sides, the company had neither proved nor established any right against the government of Paraguay by reason of the losses they had incurred, and that the said government was not responsible for any pecuniary loss or indemnity in the premises.

Lopez had now apparently succeeded, not only in destroying and seizing the property of the American company and in driving the members of it from his territory, but this commission had decided that he did nothing more than he was legally and justly entitled to do. In this matter he had clearly circumvented and outwitted all his enemies. Commissioner Berges had succeeded so well in serving the cause of his chief that he ventured to return to Paraguay; but notwithstanding the decision had been so entirely in conformity with the interests and desires of Lopez, when he reached Montevideo he for a time hesitated whether it would be safe for him to return. He knew the inexorable, tyrannical character of the master whom he served, and for some time hesitated whether it would be safe for him to risk himself again in the power of Lopez. His very success might endanger his liberty or his life, as he knew full well Lopez arrogated to himself the credit of everything favorable either to him or the country. As by this time the Paraguayan people were well aware that an important question had been in negotiation of which he had had the management abroad, Lopez would feel it incumbent upon himself to do something which should humble and disgrace him on his return, so as to remind the people that he, and he alone, was the source and fountain of all power, to whom all credit and all honor were to be given.

When the decision of this commission was made known to President Buchanan, he was greatly astonished and mortified. The commissioner appointed by him had decided a case that had never been referred to him; and more than this, he had said that the President had put the country to an expense of nearly three million dollars without first knowing whether he had any just cause of action. The United States, according to this decision, had precipitately incurred an immense expense on insufficient and incorrect information, and the President had been the instrument through whom this great folly had been committed. Mr. Buchanan accordingly sent a message to Congress, setting forth that the commissioners who had been selected to arbitrate on the Paraguay difficulty had not decided the question that had been referred to them, they had only decided a matter which the United States could not consistently with its dignity submit to arbitration ; they had decided, in effect, that the United States never had any case against Paraguay, and the question of the amount of damages sustained by the American company had been left untouched. The President therefore expressed the opinion that the whole matter was left open as it was before the expedition had been despatched. Millions had been lost to the Treasury, and the only satisfaction which the company or the United States had, was that the commissioner had received a diamond-mounted snuff-box, and the case stood just as it was before the government had expended a dollar in the prosecution of it.

CHAPTER XXV.

The Family of Carlos Antonio Lopez. — Paraguay and Corrientes make Common Cause against Buenos Aires. — The Paraguayan Army. — The Alliance abandoned. — Lopez's Appearance in Public. — Dissolute Character of his Sons. — Pancha Garmendia. — Lopez invents a Conspiracy. — James Canstatt, an Englishman, included among the Conspirators. — Interference of Consul Henderson. — Energetic Action of the English Government — Lopez as a Mediator between the Province of Buenos Aires and President Urquiza. — F. S. Lopez as an Ambassador of Peace — Attempt of the English Gunboats to make a Prisoner of Lopez. — A Hostage for Canstatt. — The Tacuari blockaded till Canstatt is liberated. — Lopez forced to make Restitution to Canstatt.— Re-establishes Friendly Relations with England. — Execution of the Brothers Decoud. — Libertinism and Vengeance.

THE worldly circumstances of Carlos Antonio Lopez were entirely changed and greatly improved by his marriage with the step-daughter of Don Lazaro Rojas. The family, however, continued to reside at the Lopez homestead after the marriage, and in the course of the next dozen years Doña Juana bore to her husband four children, besides Francisco Solano, the son of Rojas. They consisted of two sons and two daughters, and were born in the following order: Inocencia, Venancio, Rafaela, and Benigno. In their childhood they were sent to the school of Don Juan Pedro Escalada, and by him were taught the rudiments of the Spanish language. During Francia's time they were on an equality with their neighbors, as any assumption of superiority or wealth would have brought down upon the whole of them the attention and persecution of the Dictator. In the year 1837, however, Lopez had drawn up some legal paper for a neighbor who had a case pending before one of Francia's tribunals. This paper, falling under the eyes of Francia, excited in his mind the apprehension that the author of it knew too much to be a safe subject so near the capital, and he therefore banished him to an estancia belonging to his wife, near the town of Rosario. Here he remained until the death of the Dictator, when he returned to his former residence, and his sons were again sent to the school of Señor Escalada, where Francisco Solano commenced the study of Latin. According to Escalada, however, he showed little aptitude or inclination for study, and in no respect distinguished himself from the generality of his pupils. Soon after Lopez became the head of the government his two elder sons were devoted to the army; and when at the age of seventeen, Francisco Solano was made brigadier-general, and his brother Venancio, then about thirteen, was promoted to the rank of major.

Lopez, during the first years of his authority, experienced great difficulty in keeping open communication between Paraguay and the outer world. Rosas, the avowed enemy of Lopez, refused to acknowledge the independence of Paraguay, and treated it rather as a dependency than as a distinct, separate nation. In a decree issued by him on the 1st of August, 1844, he declared that the navigation of the river was only open to Argentine vessels, so that whatever commerce Paraguay might have with other nations was at all times subject to be interrupted or destroyed by Rosas. At this time the province of Corrientes was in open opposition to the authority of the Dictator of Buenos Aires, and Lopez, who believed that it was the purpose of Rosas sooner or later to destroy Paraguayan independence and annex the country to the Argentine Confederation, made common cause with Corrientes, and on the 4th of December, 1845, declared war against Buenos Aires. His army was meanwhile under the command of the young Don Francisco Solano, though the entire military discipline was under men of more experience, those who during the time of Francia had learned something of the routine and order necessary for a camp life. The army was but poorly armed and badly organized, and yet in August, 1846, it was sent across the river to Corrientes, to assist the Governor of that province in his struggle against Rosas; but it engaged in no action, as it was impossible for the Paraguayan army to act in concert with any other. The Governor of Corrientes, Madariaga, could not move in harmony with an ally who arrogated to himself the same power over the troops of another nation that he exercised over his own implicit, unquestioned, enslaved troops. The alliance was therefore abandoned, and young Lopez retired with his troops to Paraguay without having heard the sound of a cannon or the whistling of a bullet. He had learned, however, during his brief military career, to be charmed with the routine of military life, the deference paid to the commander-in-chief, and the exercise of absolute power; besides, he had learned that it involved no personal danger. The liberty and license allowed to the young General and his brothers after this time by their parents appears incomprehensible. The deference which was exacted from all the people towards the Lopez family exceeded anything known in the despotic countries of Europe; the three sons, when they appeared abroad, being always treated like princes of the blood, to whom any appearance of disrespect would be construed as an insult to the government. In many things Lopez sought to imitate Francia. He did not, indeed, forbid the people to appear in the streets whenever he might be passing through them, nor did he forbid their assembling for purposes of festivity or amusement; but whenever he or any of his family were passing through the streets, all were required to stop and remain in a reverent position, hat in hand and head bowed, until he had passed; and on all occasions of public assemblages it was taken as an indication of disloyalty and hostility to the government unless the occasion was improved by one or more of the assembly to indulge in the most fulsome praises of Lopez and his government, and of expressions of gratitude for the great liberty and prosperity which they enjoyed.

In his style of dress, on all public occasions, he made himself as ridiculous as did his predecessor. Though he had no military rank or title, and regarded himself in no respect as a military man, when he went out in his carriage (as for a long time before his death, owing to his immense obesity, he never went on horseback) he was dressed in a uniform as fantastic

Copied from Du Graty. *From a Photograph.*

CARLOS ANTONIO LOPEZ REVIEWING HIS TROOPS.

as that of Francia when he led his legions over the hills around Asuncion. The appearance of the old man as he rode through the streets in his low carriage, with his cocked hat and blue coat with enormous epaulets, holding his sword by the hilt, would have led one to suppose that some harmless, demented buffoon was playing king for the diversion of the rabble in the streets. He was always attended by a numerous guard, all well mounted, and generally composed of large, fine-looking men, so that his squat, uncourtly figure appeared more ridiculous from the contrast.

His sons, however, were left almost entirely to their own sweet will. All were afraid of them, and had they been neither better nor worse than most young men from fifteen to twenty-five years of age, it was but natural that their lives would be most scandalous and dissolute. Such, indeed, was the case. Francisco Solano was a licensed ravisher, and his brother Venancio was in this respect no better than he. The eldest, having even at that time visions of power and authority, was more guarded in appearances; but Venancio, who was of a coarser and more stolid character, was the terror of those families that, not belonging to the upper class, had yet some regard for decency and the reputation of their daughters. Whatever either of them might do, there was no remedy for the wronged and injured. No one ever dared to appeal to Lopez against one of his sons, or complain of any outrage that had been committed by either of them. Very early in his career as the head of the government, Lopez gave great pecuniary privileges to each of his sons and daughters. The land which had never been sold to individuals, and which belonged to the state, was parcelled out to them at nominal prices; and they were allowed, all of them, to call upon the people of their respective neighborhoods to furnish any amount of labor that might be required for the cultivation of their estancias or for the erection of buildings. They were also allowed to participate in the government monopolies, to collect the yerba maté in the interior and to send it abroad without paying the duties to which others were liable.

They also could possess themselves of any property which they coveted belonging to individuals, as the fear of them was so great that it was seldom a private individual dared to refuse an offer from one of the royal family.

In consequence of these privileges all of the children became enormously wealthy. All of them had numerous estancias, from two to ten or fifteen leagues square. Each of the sons had a fine house in town in which he lived in open concubinage, besides having the same arrangements at his different estancias whenever he chose to visit them. In fact, the lives which the young Lopezes were permitted to lead without any restraint by the government were such as in any other country would have caused their assassination a thousand times. In Paraguay, however, they were secure; and each pursued his own inclinations, regardless alike of broken hearts and ruined families. The only instance known where resistance was made to the lewd and lawless designs of either of the Lopez sons had so melancholy a result that no one ever ventured to repeat it. Among the victims of Francia the name of the merchant Garmendia has been mentioned. This man had been ordered by the Dictator to pay into the public treasury the sum of $ 12,000, and was thrown into prison until that sum should be raised. His wife made every exertion to collect the amount from her relatives and friends, but with all she could do she could only raise $ 8,000. This she took to Francia, and begged that he would remit the balance of the penalty or give her further time to collect the amount that was lacking. Francia took the $ 8,000, but Garmendia was sent to the banquillo and there executed. This unfortunate man at the time of his death left a young child, a little girl, who was about the age of the eldest of the Lopez boys. Her name was Francisca, or, as she was generally called, Pancha. She was a most beautiful child, of fair complexion, elegant figure, and possessed of great vivacity and intelligence. Her father's property having been all taken by Francia, she and her mother were left dependent, and lived with one of the sisters of the Barrios family. Early in his career of profligacy, young Francisco had fixed his eyes upon her and marked her for his victim. She, however, from the first, conceived an aversion to him, and would never listen to any of his proposals. He therefore resorted to the persecution of her two brothers, and they were subjected to every indignity that he could invent, and compelled to leave the capital and live as exiles in the interior. This was permitted by the old man, who seemed to care nothing for what his sons might do, provided they accumulated property and did not interfere with his authority. On one occasion the sister, hearing that one of her brothers had been sentenced to some severe punishment, took a companion with her and ventured into the presence of her admirer. On seeing her enter, he appeared at first to be greatly pleased, and saluted her with great courtesy; but when she made known the object of her visit he answered very roughly, and told her to be gone. She retired in tears, but had not reached her house before she was overtaken by one of his staff and told to go back, but to return alone. She did not obey the order, and young Garmendia was left to his fate. Subsequently, this modern Tarquin made an arrangement with the brother of the lady with whom she was living to be permitted to enter her room at night when she was alone, and no one else was in the house to whom she could appeal for protection. But, greatly to his surprise, Lopez did not find in Pancha another Lucretia. She turned upon him like an enraged tigress, and drove him with indignation and blows from the room. From that time she was no longer pursued by him, except as a victim of his malignity. After that she had several eligible offers of marriage, one of which she was very desirous of accepting; but her lovers were all put out of the way, and she was always exposed to such petty annoyances and insults by the acknowledged mistresses of Lopez, that she seldom ventured out of doors, but lived a life of seclusion and retirement. She was always spoken of with the greatest respect and esteem by all Paraguayans, and was invariably mentioned as the most beautiful woman in Paraguay; and yet, during my long residence in the country, though I attended many balls, festivals, and assemblages, I never got a view of her except from the window of her house, which was to her literally a prison. Her sufferings and tragic death at the hands of her relentless persecutor will be related hereafter.

The American squadron had no sooner left the river, and the danger that had threatened the authority of Lopez from that quarter been averted, than he sought to reinstate himself as the absolute despot he had been before his power was menaced from abroad. When it was known that the great Republic was bearing down upon him with a large squadron, the people within his dominions, and especially the foreigners, began to conceive a hope that better times were coming, and that the system of government which they had so long endured in shame and silence was near its end. They hoped that the day was near when a man might talk with his neighbor of the common events of life, without having everything reported to head-quarters and exposing him to be imprisoned, sent off as a common soldier, or executed. It is probable that some of these hopes found expression in words, though of that no other evidence exists except the fact, that, as soon as the danger from the Americans had passed, a large number of persons were arrested and thrown into prison. They were nearly all Paraguayans belonging to the best families; but there was one of them who was the son of an Englishman, though born in Montevideo. His name was James Canstatt. What offence had been committed by any of them was never known, as nothing was ever proved against one of them. Lopez, however, desired to show to the people that he was as absolute as ever; and as the persons arrested had probably rendered themselves obnoxious by some trifling acts or expressions that could not be tortured into crimes, they were all accused of conspiracy. They were kept in solitary confinement and in fetters for a long time, and subjected to inquisitorial examinations. Fortunately for Canstatt, the English government then had a consul at Asuncion, who interfered in his behalf. This consul, Mr. C. A. Henderson, claimed Canstatt as a British subject, and insisted that he should be tried according to the laws and usages of civilized nations; he should have the benefit of counsel and be confronted with his accusers. But Lopez would not listen to such a proposition. An innovation of this kind would be fatal to Paraguayan republicanism. The system of Francia would not admit of open trial, or that accused parties should be permitted to defend themselves or disprove the charges against them. It was enough for the government to allege that a party was guilty, and it was taken as an insult if any one doubted the truth of the allegation. Mr. Henderson, however, would not accept the accusation of Lopez as proof of guilt, and reported the facts to the British government. He was sustained in the position he had taken, and instructed to insist on such a trial for Canstatt as it was the right of all accused persons to demand among civilized nations. Lopez would not yield, however; for were he to give a fair and open trial to Canstatt his case must break down, and his charge of a conspiracy would be proved to be a miserable invention of his own. Henderson therefore broke up his consulate and withdrew from Paraguay.

In the mean while Lopez proceeded with the trial of Canstatt according to his own fashion. He was subjected to very harsh treatment and examined at great length. He was questioned in regard to a thousand insignificant acts, and the answers he made were taken down, not as he made them, but as his inquisitors desired them to stand. Then, after each examination, he was forced to sign his name to the statements that had been made for him. But instead of affixing his name immediately below the last answer, he was compelled to have a large blank space between that and his signature, so that if anything were added afterwards, in the same handwriting and without his knowledge, it would all alike appear to be his own confession. Having predoomed Canstatt before his arrest, the trial had no other object than the manufacturing of testimony; and the result, of course, was that he was condemned and sentenced to be shot. Twelve others were condemned, as his fellow-conspirators, to suffer the same penalty.

Lopez was greatly embarrassed by the white elephant he had caught when he laid his hands on Canstatt. Had he supposed that the English government would have claimed him, he would never have included him among his conspirators. But having done so, he could not let him go without incurring the obloquy and odium that would follow his release, when he well knew he would expose the manner in which his confessions had been extorted from him, and would deny that there had been any conspiracy whatever. He could not torture, for he might afterwards be forced to give him up, and then he would subsequently be brought to account by England for his barbarity. He would therefore hold him prisoner till he could see whether or not the English government would follow up the case, and, if it did not, he might conveniently die in prison. But Consul Henderson, who had lived several years in Paraguay, had learned the character of Lopez so well that he knew if any lukewarmness were shown in the matter Canstatt's life would be the forfeit. In fact, Lopez had become by this time furious against Canstatt, against Henderson, and against the English government. The *Semanario* had indulged for many months in abuse of them all, had denounced Canstatt as a conspirator who had been detected in a plot to assassinate Lopez and overthrow his blessed government, and had declared, in defiant language, that the laws of the Republic should be enforced and the rights of Paraguay defended at every hazard.

But while Canstatt was still lingering in prison, other events were transpiring in the Plata which were availed of by the British government to effect his release. For a long time the attitude of the province of Buenos Aires towards the Argentine Confederation had been unsatisfactory, and ever threatening war. The existing relations were such as could not long continue without open war; and it was the interest of all that the old questions of dispute between Urquiza on the one hand and the government of Buenos Aires on the other should be buried, and that the single province containing the great city of the valley, and more important than all the others, should be reunited to the Confederation. In this crisis (1859) of affairs, it occurred to Lopez that he would offer his mediation. He therefore sketched a plan for the arrangement of the questions at issue, and despatched Francisco Solano, the general-in-chief of his armies, as mediating ambassador. The offer was timely and was well received by all parties, and a convention was formed according to which Buenos Aires was again incorporated with the Confederation, for which happy result due credit was given to the two Lopezes.

Young Lopez was then quite a hero in Buenos Aires, and like a conqueror covered with laurels he proposed to start on his return to Paraguay. All this while, however, poor Canstatt was in prison, and the elder Lopez had given no intimation that he would ever leave it except for execution. Situate as was Paraguay in the middle of a continent, her autocrat was confident that England would never go to the expense of millions, as the United States had done, to force him to terms. He refused to abide by the laws of nations, and defied England and the whole world, assuming that he had a right to seize the citizen of any nation, imprison and execute him, on his own allegation that he had committed a crime, and without producing any proof of the fact. It was useless, then, to treat with Lopez, with any view of saving Canstatt, as with the head of a civilized nation, notwithstanding that England had some six years before acknowledged Paraguay as one of the family of nations. The English government was then represented at Montevideo by Hon. Edward Thornton, as Chargé d'Affaires, and Admiral Lushington was in command of her Majesty's South Atlantic squadron. The conduct of this admiral was in striking contrast to that of an American admiral in the same waters some years later. He knew that a man claiming to be a British subject was held a prisoner by a cruel despot who was bent on taking his life in defiance of all law or justice, and that only by extreme measures of doubtful legality could he be rescued from the tyrant's power. He therefore determined, if possible, to seize young Lopez and hold him as a hostage for the safe delivery of Canstatt.

Accordingly, when the elated young diplomat took passage on his own war steamer, the Tacuari, to return home, he found two English gunboats, the Buzzard and the Grappler, with steam up, at a little distance in the harbor, evidently waiting to intercept him. The Tacuari, however, moved out a short distance; but as, from the blundering movements of the gunboats and from a blank shot fired by one of them, it was clear that it was their intention to capture the Tacuari, she put back into the harbor and dropped anchor again. One of the gunboats took up her position alongside of her, and constituted herself a guard over her.

This act of war in the very harbor of Buenos Aires was indisputably in defiance of the law of nations, not only towards Paraguay, but also towards the Argentine Confederation. Lopez, greatly crestfallen, went on shore, expecting that Buenos Aires would resent this act of war in contempt of its sovereignty. But the people and government were well pleased at the course of the English admiral, only regretting that his subordinates had so badly managed their business that they had not waited until the Tacuari had got beyond the Argentine jurisdiction, and then captured her and made a prisoner of Lopez. Though the mediation of Paraguay had been accepted, yet the existence of such a government as that of Lopez in such dangerous proximity had long been regarded as an obstacle in the way of opening up and developing the upper sections of the Valley of the Plata. The large standing army that Lopez always maintained also rendered him a dangerous neighbor, as at any moment he might precipitate a force into the Argentine territory and commit extensive ravages before an army adequate to resist him could be collected. Hence, though the detention of the Tacuari was illegal, and insulting to Buenos Aires, yet the people acquiesced in it, hoping that the task of humiliating and disarming the isolated barbarian would devolve on Great Britain.

Lopez, finding that the English gunboats were permitted,

undisturbed by the Argentine authorities, to hold the Tacuari blockaded in the harbor of Buenos Aires, chagrined and mortified, started to return by land to Paraguay. The Tacuari was held as security for the life of Canstatt. The Paraguayan despot had been overreached at his own game. In his isolation and fancied security he imagined he could defy the laws of nations and treat the citizens of all other nations as he was accustomed to treat his own people. But the English government said by its acts, "If the laws of nations are not to be respected, let each avail itself of its natural rights and obtain satisfaction how and when it can."

When President Lopez learned of the means resorted to by England in behalf of Canstatt he was greatly enraged, and doubtless deeply regretted that he had ever started his device of a conspiracy. He must make up his mind to release Canstatt or else to lose the Tacuari, which with her armament had cost him at least $150,000. The loss of the Tacuari would not mend the matter, however. The English government by this time had taken up Canstatt's case in earnest, and if he were not released would undoubtedly follow up the detention of the Tacuari by sending an expedition into Paraguay, the result of which would probably be his own overthrow, and the expulsion of his family from Paraguay. He therefore, after having poured forth in his *Semanario* column after column of abuse of England and Englishmen, and protesting that the Republic would never yield to the insolent *gringo*, opened negotiations, and released Canstatt on the understanding that the Tacuari should be permitted to return to Paraguay.

The English government, however, was not satisfied with the bare release of Canstatt. He had been arrested when quietly pursuing his business as a merchant, and the government of Paraguay had failed to prove anything against him. The charge that he had been engaged in a conspiracy, with nothing but Lopez's assertion to sustain it, was not entertained for a moment. Canstatt, when at liberty, denied all knowledge of any such plot, and gave the full particulars of the manner of his examination, and how he had been forced to sign statements he had never made, and to leave blank spaces over his name to be filled in with other confessions of which he knew nothing. These papers, however, that he had signed, were never produced against him by the Paraguayan government; and the object in making them is to be explained only on the supposition that the examinations were made with the intention of killing him, and then to produce them, if necessary, in proof of his guilt, if ever called on by the English government to justify the act. But as Lopez could prove nothing in justification of his arrest of Canstatt, the destruction of his business, and the confiscation of his goods, the English government insisted that he must be indemnified for the losses he had sustained. Lopez, however, demurred to this, and sought by every means to re-establish friendly relations with Great Britain, leaving that question in abeyance. He sent a diplomatic agent duly accredited to the Court of St. James to renew diplomatic relations. But Lord Russell refused to receive him or have any relations with him until restitution had been made, not in England, but in Paraguay, to Canstatt. The agent of Lopez submitted his case to eminent English authorities on international law, among others to the distinguished writer, Dr. Robert Phillimore. The question submitted, however, was not one that touched the merits of the case at all. Stripped of its verbiage and special pleading, it was simply this : If the government of Paraguay discovers a plot to overthrow it and to assassinate its chief magistrate, and arrests the conspirators, among whom is an Englishman, and after a trial according to the laws and usages of the country they are condemned to death, can the English government rightfully claim different treatment for the Englishman than is adjudged to the Paraguayans? and if the President should in his clemency remit the punishment of death, and set him at liberty, can his government rightfully claim indemnification for him?

To the question put in this form the answer must obviously be in the negative, and such was the response of Dr. Phillimore. But Lord Russell was uncivil enough to discredit the whole story of the conspiracy, and to virtually say that the pretence that there had been any was an impudent fraud on the part of Lopez. Finding, therefore, that England would not recede from her position, and that he must always remain under a menace of war from that dreaded power, he finally invited negotiations for an adjustment, and the English Minister in Buenos Aires, Mr. Thornton, again went to Paraguay, and a settlement of all the pending difficulties was effected. Lopez agreed to pay the amount demanded as indemnification for Canstatt, but begged so piteously that no allusion should be made to that matter in the treaty that Mr. Thornton consented to omit it. To his own people, therefore, Lopez appeared to have come out triumphant from the Canstatt difficulty, and in the *Semanario* he boasted that the English government had conceded all that Paraguay had ever claimed.

This settlement of the long-pending difficulty was not definite or binding until ratified by the English government, and the terms granted by Mr. Thornton were not wholly satisfactory to Lord Russell, who insisted on their modification. Mr. William Doria, who, during the absence of Minister Thornton, held the position of her Britannic Majesty's Chargé d'Affaires in Buenos Aires, was accordingly sent to Asuncion to effect such modifications as Lord Russell regarded as indispensable. Before his arrival, however, the elder Lopez had died, and the younger was not at that time disposed to reopen a question which he had hoped had been already settled. He therefore, after long wrangling and prevarication, accepted the changes as proposed by Mr. Doria, the points in dispute were all arranged or waived, and the money was finally paid over to Canstatt.

Twelve persons besides Canstatt had been condemned to death by the same secret tribunal that had condemned him. These others were all Paraguayans, and Lopez could do as he pleased with them, being responsible to nobody. Some twenty others who had been arrested at the same time with them had been released as not guilty. The discussion of the

Canstatt case by the newspapers of Buenos Aires and Montevideo had served to convince Lopez that his pretence of a conspiracy was thoroughly understood, and that the execution of the alleged conspirators would be regarded as the cold-blooded murder of innocent men ; and had he been left to his own impulses he would probably, after having kept them in prison till all excitement had passed away, have set them all at liberty. Ten of the twelve were thus released, but the other two were not so fortunate, as they were held accountable vicariously for the sins of a brother who had swindled Lopez out of a large sum of money and gone to Europe, where he could not be reached.

These two unfortunate men were brothers of the name of Decoud. They belonged to one of the most respectable families in Paraguay, and were men of good character and enterprising, industrious habits. An older brother of theirs had been selected by Lopez as his business agent in Buenos Aires, where he made sales of the yerba maté, the tobacco, hides, and other products of Paraguay, that the government or the Lopez family had to sell, besides making purchases of such commodities in the markets of Buenos Aires as were required in exchange. As Lopez kept his accounts very loosely, and seldom inquired into the acts of his agent, the latter betrayed his trust and made false returns of the moneys received. So ignorant was Lopez of his own affairs, that, before he suspected anything, Decoud had embezzled nearly a million of dollars. The President, when he learned of the breach of trust, gave no intimation to his agent that his frauds were discovered, but politely expressed great satisfaction at the manner he had managed the finances of the Republic, and invited him to revisit Paraguay, as he wished to intrust more important negotiations to his charge. Decoud, however, suspected the snare, and did not go, and soon afterwards, when a Paraguayan steamer was in the harbor, he was invited on board to dine with the captain. This invitation he also declined ; and Lopez, having seen that he was too wary to be caught, sent another agent, Don Felix Ejusquiza, to supersede him.

But if the fraudulent agent could not be punished in person, yet Lopez could be revenged on him by persecuting his family and relatives who were in his power. Vicarious punishment was a favorite means of vengeance with him throughout his whole career, and it was carried by his successor, the younger Lopez, to a refinement of cruelty such as was never known before. Three of the brothers of the defaulting agent were accordingly arrested, and, after the prolonged mock trial, were condemned to death as conspirators. The hour was named for their execution, and one evening they were advised that they were to be shot early on the following morning. When the morning came, however, one of them was pardoned and set at liberty. The other two had offended in another way than in being brothers of the dishonest agent. One of them had in some way interfered with a business speculation of the younger Lopez, the returned diplomatist, general-in-chief of the army, and heir presumptive to the Presidency. The other had offended the heir apparent in a more sensitive point: he had crossed him in one of his brutal passions.

The license permitted to the young Lopezes by their parents, and the system of government which made everything tributary to the family, naturally encouraged them in their excesses, so that they thought they were doing honor to any other family by an illicit alliance with any member of it, even of a temporary character. Francisco Solano, as the prospective heir, was more guarded in his amours than his brothers, and prided himself on having his mistresses belong to the best families in the country. If a young woman of good family and fair person had the misfortune to attract his attention and please his fancy, he considered that he had a right to her for so long a time as might suit his pleasure. Unfortunately, soon after his return from Buenos Aires, his attention was caught by a beautiful young girl who was contracted to be married shortly after to Carlos Decoud, one of the brothers of the defaulting Paraguayan agent. She belonged to one of the best families in the country, and so much superior to that of Lopez, that very likely the father of the President had felt himself highly honored by being permitted to make the coats and pantaloons of her grandfather. Nevertheless, young Francisco marked her as his victim, and made infamous proposals to her. But she turned from him with scorn and loathing, as had previously the beautiful Pancha Garmendia, though not in so demonstrative a manner. Lopez saw in Carlos Decoud a rival, one who stood between him and his right, and he resolved on his revenge. Decoud was included among the conspirators, and with Canstatt, his two brothers, and one other, was condemned to death. After the rescue of Canstatt, and the whole plot of the conspiracy had been discovered to be but a clumsy trick of Lopez, it was believed that the President would not execute any of the condemned, for, with all his faults, Carlos Antonio Lopez was not, for a Spanish-American, naturally sanguinary. Two of the Decouds, however, had given personal offence to Francisco Solano, and were both shot, and it was the belief of all who dared even to speak on the matter, that it was only at the instigation of the young man that the old President had ordered the execution. The young woman who had thus become the unconscious instrument of her lover's death, it is needless to say, did not become the mistress of his murderer.

CHAPTER XXVI.

Francisco Solano Lopez sent Ambassador to Europe. — Mrs. Lynch. — Colony of French Agriculturists introduced into Paraguay. — Hardships and Sufferings. — Attempt to desert. — Isolation of Paraguay. — The Gran Chaco. — Barbarous Treatment of the French Colonists. — Efforts of the French Consul in their Behalf. — Action taken by the French Government. — They are finally allowed to leave the Country. — The French Claims. — Lopez increases his Army. — Relations with Brazil. — The Brazilian Squadron. — Negotiations. — Treaty concluded. — Line of Steamers established between Rio and Cuyuba. — Measures taken by Lopez to increase his Revenue. — Yerba Maté. — Customs. — Internal Revenue. — Incomes of the Lopez Family. — Government Lands. — Influence of Lopez's Government upon the Industry of the People.

THE independence of Paraguay having been acknowledged, and treaties of friendship, commerce, and navigation having been formed with France, England, Sardinia, and the United States, President Lopez thought the time had come when he should send an ambassador to Europe to represent him at the different courts. For this duty he selected the young general, Francisco Solano, then about twenty-four years of age. The young diplomatist was accordingly despatched on his mission with an outfit and an escort such as in modern times has seldom, if ever, accompanied a simple ambassador to any court. His suite consisted of some forty persons. His secretary was Juan Andres Gelly, who, though a native Paraguayan, had been abroad on different occasions as a sort of special agent of the government, and in this way had had considerable experience in diplomatic affairs, and was, in fact, the minister, as young Lopez, though nominally the head of the embassy, had yet to learn everything that regarded diplomatic usages and duties. The other members of the escort consisted of military and naval officers of different grades, his brother Benigno, and a large following of servants. Paraguay had at that time no navy of any importance and no steamers, and the ambassador was obliged, therefore, to cross the Atlantic as ambassadors of England, France, the United States, and other countries usually do, in the humble capacity of passenger on board a merchant steamer. But besides the large retinue which the young minister took with him to give importance to his mission, he had ample means provided to support the style and equipage becoming a general, ambassador, and prince of the blood. The old man put to his credit in England and France a sum of money sufficient to maintain him and his suite in a style such as no other ambassador at Paris or London could pretend to rival.

On arriving at Paris, young Lopez left the details of all business to his secretary, gave loose rein to his naturally licentious propensities, and plunged into the vices of that gay capital. With an unlimited bank account and with the free use which he made of it, it was but natural that he should secure a certain following of those sharp and needy adventurers who are ever ready to attach themselves to any persons who will entertain them liberally, in return for which they magnify their importance and minister to their vanity and vices. Coming in such state and making such a display of wealth, it was not difficult to create the impression that he must represent a country of immense resources; and, as little was known of Paraguay, it was thought, by some persons of influence and official position, that immense commercial advantages were to result from the cultivation of intimate relations with the newly opened country. Young Lopez was accordingly presented to the Emperor, and was also, in accordance with general usage, honored with a private audience. In England, however, where he spent his money with equal profusion as in France, and made the same semi-barbarous display, he was not so successful in impressing upon the government either the importance of himself or his mission. In fact, he was greatly enraged at the little consideration he received there, and an incident which occurred soon after he had presented his credentials greatly aggravated his wrath.

He had expected to be formally presented to the Queen, and Lord Palmerston had fixed the day when he would make the introduction. Some other matters, however, of more importance in the eyes of the Premier having intervened so as to make it inconvenient to present him at the time agreed upon, the presentation was deferred to another occasion. Lopez was greatly indignant at this seeming disrespect and want of courtesy, and therefore her Majesty was compelled to forego the honor of an introduction to the Paraguayan ambassador. The slight was never forgotten by Lopez, and though he afterwards had many Englishmen in his employment, always had a great antipathy to them and their country. He had been sent by his father, however, to accomplish certain purposes, and among other things he was to obtain two steamers for the Paraguayan service, and make arrangements for the manufacture and shipment of arms and munitions of war, and for the manufacture of the machinery necessary for the establishment of an arsenal in Paraguay. He accordingly purchased the steamer called the Rio Blanco, which was sent out to Paraguay under command of an English captain by the name of Morris ; and arranged for the purchase of another steamer of a superior quality, which was to be ready to cross the Atlantic whenever he should himself wish to return home. In the mean while Lopez spent most of his time in Paris, where he became familiar with the worst phases of Parisian society. Among the members of his suite was a young man by the name of Brizuela, who, mingling in the questionable society that his chief most frequented, had made the acquaintance of a woman of abandoned character, belonging to what is there called the *demi-monde*. This woman, whose maiden name was Lynch, was born in Cork, Ireland ; and her family, while she was yet a child, had moved to France, where she married a surgeon in the French army by the name of Quatrefaghts. Her character was such, however, that she soon separated from her husband, and at the time of the advent of Lopez in Paris she belonged to that class of public women so numerous in Paris, always on the watch for strangers with long purses and vicious habits. This woman having made the acquaintance of Brizuela, and learned from him of the circumstances under which he had come to France, and the magnificence and princely munificence of his chief, contrived to make his acquaintance. Brizuela boasting to his patron of the conquest he had achieved, Lopez, who had not forgotten his Paraguayan habit of supervising and inquiring into the conduct of those who were about him, was anxious to meet with the lady whose charms were so vaunted by his subordinate, and on meeting her he was greatly infatuated with her appearance; so much so, that he made an arrangement with Brizuela in some respects similar to that which his father, Lazaro Rojas, had made with the elder Lopez. In both cases the woman was to be transferred for valuable money considerations. Madam Lynch was thenceforward the favorite mistress, counsellor, and friend of Lopez. She accompanied him in his travels to different parts of Europe, and went with him to the Crimea, visiting the camps of the allies then engaged in war against the Czar. When Lopez was about to return to Paraguay, Madam Lynch was desirous of accompanying him; but being doubtful how the old man would receive him if accompanied by such an encumbrance, it was decided between them that she should remain behind and allow him to precede her, and first learn whether he had fallen from grace during his absence or still retained the confidence of the old man, so that he might venture to introduce such an improvement into the country.

Young Lopez, before leaving Europe, also conceived the project of introducing a colony of French agriculturists into Paraguay; and for that purpose, while in Bordeaux, made a contract with a merchant there to send some five hundred emigrants to Paraguay, stipulating that the government of Paraguay should give to each family, on its arrival, a house, and as much land in a healthy part of the country as it could well cultivate, besides the provisions necessary to support it for eight months; and that the colony should pay nothing for ten years, and should be free from all military service, only being liable to serve in the national guard when the security of the colony might demand it. The colonists in return bound themselves to cultivate this land as their own property until they had reimbursed the government of Paraguay from the productions of their harvests for the expense it had incurred. It was a condition of the contract that these colonists should be Roman Catholics, and born in the province of Gascony, whose idiom closely resembles the Spanish. The contractor, whose only object was to secure the commission for each colonist, paid little regard to the character of the individuals whom he selected, and picked up any persons who offered that were in destitute circumstances, without regard to their fitness for the life to which they would be subjected in Paraguay. They were neither farmers nor mechanics, but were generally servants, petty tradesmen, barbers, valets, *chevaliers d'industrie*, and, in fact, composed of that needy class which in a city like Bordeaux, having no fixed or reliable employment, would be the first to offer themselves for any expedition that promised subsistence. They were not advised of the character of the country to which they were going, nor of the kind of government to which they would be subjected ; they were only told that it was a fine, fertile section, where the climate was warm, and nature so prolific that but little labor would suffice to supply all their wants, and that the terms under which they were to enter Paraguay were such that they all, within a few years, would be independent owners of houses and lands, and surrounded by every comfort and luxury. The colony thus selected contained some very estimable people, besides many who could not be regarded as a valuable acquisition to any community. Their passage to Paraguay was paid by Lopez, but they were provided with the worst accommodations while at sea, and experienced great sufferings before they reached their destination.

On arriving at Asuncion, instead of finding their troubles at an end they learned that they had just begun. They had anticipated that on their arrival each family would be assigned to its house, with its bit of land and provisions for their subsistence until they could raise more for their own use. They were all taken to a place some four leagues above Asuncion and thrust ashore on the right bank of the river, on territory to which both Bolivia and the Argentine Republic laid claim as well as Lopez. The provisions provided for them were totally insufficient and of very bad quality, and they were subjected to a military discipline under the republican government such as they had never witnessed or heard of in the empire of France. They were also exposed to the incursions of the Indians of the Chaco. They, however, set themselves to work to build houses and cultivate the lands; but they found that the land, though sufficiently productive, was of that hard, clayey character which rendered it very difficult to cultivate, and which the first year yielded scarcely anything in return for their labors. The colonists were treated precisely as so many slaves, having no rights whatever which the government regarded. Special regulations were drawn up according to which they were to be governed, and a person was appointed to rule over them under the title of justice of the peace and purveyor to the colony. The emigrants were greatly exasperated at finding they had been imposed upon, and that the treatment they received was utterly at variance with the terms of the agent at Bordeaux. So disappointed were they when they found themselves thus situated, and that to all their complaints the justice-purveyor only returned contemptuous answers, accompanied with threats of what worse they might expect if they did not cease from their complaints, five of the emigrants attempted to desert. The military guard, which was kept constantly on watch over their actions, soon missed the fugitives and pursued them; but they were not overtaken and were never heard of more, whence the presumption is that they all perished from starvation in the wilderness or at the hands of the savages.

And here it seems necessary to explain something of the isolation to which the government of Paraguay has been able to subject its inhabitants for so many years without the possibility of their escaping from its all-searching despotism. It should be borne in mind that on the west and right bank of the river, for nearly the whole distance from Asuncion to many leagues below the confluence of the Parana and the Paraguay, is a dense, unbroken forest; that this vast extent of territory, which is called the Gran Chaco, is composed of immense marshes filled with the rankest vegetation, that forms an almost impervious jungle, and through which it is impossible to pass except in large bodies, that carry with them the necessary implements for cutting away the vines and bushes, and for making the rafts necessary to pass over the numerous streams and lagoons that they are sure to meet on their way. During Francia's long reign, attempts were made by several parties to leave the country through this vast forest, but no one, so far as is known, ever succeeded; no one who made the desperate attempt, unless caught by Francia's soldiers, was ever heard of again.

It was not known, at the colony, whether the deserters from the French colony had escaped or not; but as they were not caught and brought back it was thought possible that they had succeeded in getting through to Corrientes, and on the 28th of August, 1855, twenty others also attempted to desert. They were pursued so actively by the guard, however, that they were overtaken, captured, brought back and put in irons, and were afterwards condemned by a Presidential decree to several months' imprisonment; to be turned out of the colony and deprived of the concession of land which was to become their property after cultivation; and after this term of imprisonment should expire, they were to be located separately in different parts of the interior. By the same decree it was declared that any future attempts to abscond, or the mere fact of being on the line of outposts, would be punishable by death, as would also the crime of advising any of the emigrants to desert. The French consul then at Asuncion, Count de Brayer, protested against this barbarous Draconian decree, but without effect. In the mean while Lopez made no attempt to improve the condition of the colonists, who were now in a state of extreme suffering, but thought to cause them to cease from complaints by increased vigor, and by subjecting them to more aggravating and intolerable hardships. In fact, their condition became so insupportable that, notwithstanding the fate of the last deserters, on the 24th of October following seven others also attempted to desert, two of whom were living with another Frenchman by the name of Dorignac and a woman called Anna Prat. These two persons were arrested, put in irons, and threatened with death by Colonel Barrios, the son-in-law of the President, if they did not reveal the way the fugitives had taken. They both answered that they knew nothing about it, and for their contemptuous conduct they were both most brutally beaten. Dorignac was flogged until nearly dead to make him disclose, but as deserters and fugitives seldom tell even their friends what road they are to take, poor Dorignac could have given no information had he been disposed to; and Barrios, — whose character from the time he first attracted public notice by being taken into the Lopez family until he was made to expire under the same treatment, received at the hands of young Lopez, that he had inflicted with so much alacrity on many others, rendered him a fit person for such services, — finding that flogging would not make him reveal, ordered his head to be plunged into a bucket of water and held there until he was nearly drowned. This was repeated several times until the man was nearly dead. But Dorignac did not reveal anything, for the very good reason, if he had no better one, that he had nothing to reveal. The French consul, whom Lopez could not prevent from visiting the colonists, learning from them of the atrocities to which they had been subjected, complained officially to the government of the treatment to which his countrymen were subjected. Lopez, however, audaciously denied all the charges, though they were as notoriously true, and known to be so by everybody else, as that he was President of Paraguay. The last fugitives, however, had not succeeded in their attempt to escape. Five of the seven were captured, and according to the report of the soldiers sent in pursuit of them, the two others, who had hidden in trees, and refused to come down when summoned, had been shot. This was the report which was promulgated by the guard immediately on their return ; but Lopez, fearing that such a report would be construed to his prejudice if it were not denied, caused it to be announced that the two deserters who were not returned had escaped, and the soldiers who had first described the manner of their death in one way dutifully modified their first statements, and declared that they were false, and that the missing Frenchmen had got away.

From that moment vexations of every sort were accumulated on the unfortunate emigrants to such an extent that the colony was brought to a state of desperation bordering on insurrection. On the 26th of December the President went to visit the colony. He assembled the colonists and expressed his satisfaction at the amount of labor they had performed, and ascribed the scanty harvests to the unfavorable season. He expressed his regret that any of the colonists should be, as he had heard some were, dissatisfied, and said that the government of Paraguay never wished to detain people against their will, and that if they were desirous of leaving they had only to give their names to the justice of the peace. The next day three hundred and thirty-nine individuals had given their names, and very shortly after all the rest, with the exception of one family of four persons, who had been in the country at the time of the foundation of the colony, and one female servant. No proof could be more conclusive of the bad faith of the Paraguayan government, and the hardships to which the colonists were subjected, than the unanimity with which they desired to leave the country. Though they had come to one of the finest regions on which the sun shines, and brought with them their household gods, intending there to spend their days, so infamous and barbarous had been the treatment they had received, they all were not only willing, but eager, to leave the country, destitute and helpless, provided they could set foot beyond the limits of Paraguay and where the power of Lopez did not extend. Finding the colonists so unanimous, the President on the 29th of December issued a decree by which all the applicants were ordered to leave the country within a week, which order was so far modified as to grant them fifty days to reimburse the government for their passage-money and the advances made to them, according to the contract, in provisions, tools, seeds, and other articles which they had received. In the first days of January they were all driven from the colony, and the poor wretches, about four hundred in number, were landed at Asuncion, where, without provisions, and having no means of earning anything, they must inevitably have starved but for the assistance rendered them by the French consul, Count de Brayer. On the expiration of the fifty days given the colonists to reimburse the government, none of them were able to do so; and on the 23d of February, 1856, another decree appeared, condemning the debtors to forced labor in the mines, brick-yards, and other public works of the state, until full payment should be made. But Count de Brayer protested so earnestly and energetically against thus reducing French subjects to slavery that the decree was never put in force. The French government, on learning of the treatment which the first colonists received, prohibited the departure of any other emigrants to Paraguay, and in a despatch to Count de Brayer, to be communicated to the government of Paraguay, expressed its painful surprise that such harsh measures had been committed against French subjects, and its decided opinion that the colonists were under no pecuniary obligations to the government of Paraguay. In consequence of this action by the French government, President Lopez, by a decree of the 13th of June, 1856, renounced all claims against the French colonists and ordered them to leave the country. The emigrants were therefore provided by the consul with passes to Buenos Aires, and, as opportunity occurred, all, with the exception of some half-dozen, departed.

The experience of these colonists was enough to convince the French government that the less it had to do with Paraguay, so long as it remained under the Lopez rule, the better it would be; and Count de Brayer leaving Asuncion about this time on account of ill health, the consulate was allowed to remain vacant for about two years. Lopez, however, was very anxious that his government should be recognized by the great powers of Europe, and that they should not only acknowledge the independence of Paraguay, but should send diplomatic and consular agents to his country, as they did to all other countries having any pretensions to civilization, or any importance, political or commercial; and having expressed a desire to satisfy the claims of the French government respecting the affairs of the colony, another consul, Count de Brossard, was sent in place of M. de Brayer. His first official act was to make a claim against Lopez for repayment of all expenses to which the French government had been put to rescue its subjects from his power, and to this Lopez was obliged to add the humiliating concession of ten thousand francs to the martyr Dorignac, who had become entirely idiotic from the prolonged tortures to which he had been exposed. In this case, however, as in the Canstatt affair, when Lopez was obliged to make compensation to the injured party for the wrongs he had done him, no mention was made of the circumstance in the convention or agreement that was to be made public. In both cases Lopez consented to pay the money on condition that neither government should ever publish the terms to which he had yielded. He was thus enabled, without exposing his mendacity to his people, to assert that in all things he had carried his point, and that the governments both of France and England had been forced to acknowledge the justice of Paraguay, and to apologize to him for ever having doubted it.

Lopez having had this experience, both with the Americans and with the French, became very suspicious of all foreigners; and the few who went there to do business generally found themselves so much embarrassed by his official regulations and by hindrances put in their way that few cared to remain. He was obliged, however, to tolerate the presence of foreigners as artisans, engineers, and physicians, as he found the latter were indispensable to the life and health of his troops, and without the former he could not establish his shops for the manufacture of many articles which, with his enforced labor, it was much cheaper for him to manufacture than to purchase and import.

Having driven out the American company and the French colony, Lopez was left to pursue his peculiar administration of affairs with no one to question his justice or criticise his policy. He was as absolute at that time as ever Francia had been, and during the time that the obnoxious strangers were in the country he had not only revived to its full extent the system of espionage of Francia, but even improved upon it. He had quarrelled with the American, French, and English consuls, and all of them had left the country, firmly convinced that Paraguay was a country to be shunned by their fellow-countrymen. The Portuguese and Brazilian consuls, however, remained there; but as they had been a long time in the country, and fully understood the character of the people and of their ruler, and besides had few duties to perform, they were careful in no way to interfere with the government or complain when their fellow-countrymen were maltreated.

During the later years Lopez had been largely increasing his army, and had introduced a large quantity of arms, besides a vast amount of gunpowder, which were stored in the capital. His position towards Brazil had always been one of disagreement, as there had been from long before his time a question of boundaries between the two countries. During the whole of Francia's reign, and up to the year 1855, Paraguay, having had control of the river from Tres Bocas to its northern frontiers, had permitted no vessel of any nationality to ascend the river to the Brazilian province of Matto Grosso. This province, which is half as large as Europe, was almost inaccessible except by the river. To reach it by land from any point on the coast, it was necessary to pass through such dense forests and cross so many streams as to render it a labor of several months; yet as there had been, from long before

Francia's time, a number of settlements there, and as the country was believed to be rich in mines, and capable of supporting a large population that would add much to the strength and wealth of the empire, Brazil was not disposed to submit to the pretensions of Lopez in prohibiting all communication by way of the river with the province. Lopez, however, was inexorable, and would concede nothing either to threats or diplomacy, until in 1855 the Emperor sent a squadron, consisting of eleven war vessels and eight transports, to exact what was clearly and indisputably a right. The conduct of the Brazilians on this occasion was in keeping with that displayed by them a dozen years later in the great war. There were no fortifications then on the banks of the river below Asuncion, and the entire squadron might have proceeded at once to Asuncion and dictated any terms to Lopez that the Brazilian envoy might have desired. Lopez had not yet the nucleus of a navy, yet when he found the Brazilians were coming he had nothing to oppose them but the guard, consisting of twenty-eight men, at Cerrito, a post on the right bank of the river, some ten leagues below the since celebrated fortress of Humaita; but the officer in command, though utterly without means to enforce his orders, forbade the higher ascent of the river by more than one of the Brazilian steamers. The minister acceded to this demand, and, leaving the rest of the squadron at Tres Bocas, ascended in the admiral's ship to Asuncion. Lopez soon learned that, of the things which the Brazilians had come for, fighting was not one of them, and was careful to treat both minister and admiral in such a way that neither of them would change his mind. He temporized with them, and induced them to defer a settlement of the questions to another time, so that the expedition returned to Brazil having effected nothing. Lopez now saw that it would not do to expose himself longer to an invasion by the river without having some means to prevent it, and he therefore commenced fortifying at Humaita, a point admirably adapted, from the winding course of the river and the topographical configuration of the country, to impede the ascent of a hostile fleet.

When it was known in Rio how completely Lopez had deceived and hoodwinked their minister, the feeling of indignation against both was intense; and another and a stronger expedition, with a different minister, and an admiral not averse to fighting, was about to be fitted out to enforce what the former expedition had been sent to do. But Lopez, who had his paid spies in Rio, was soon advised of the danger which was threatening, and, without waiting for official notification from the Brazilian government that it would no longer submit to his impositions, he despatched a minister to Rio with instructions to renew negotiations. The minister despatched on this embassy was Don José Berges, and a treaty was there made in which the privilege was conceded to Brazil of access by the river to her northwestern province, while the questions of boundaries were left in abeyance. The Brazilians now believed that they had obtained by diplomacy what they had failed to get by threats and a display of force. It was almost a barren triumph, however, for although vessels could go and come from the upper waters of the Paraguay to Buenos Aires or Rio, they were subjected, while passing through the Paraguayan waters, to such annoyances, delays, and vexations as to make the treaty appear to be only a delusion. The Brazilian government, however, was not disposed to have the spirit of the treaty defeated by treachery, or to be cut off from its distant province by a series of petty annoyances, none of which were of sufficient importance to justify a declaration of war. It therefore despatched its ablest diplomat and most unscrupulous statesman, Counsellor Paranhos, to make a new treaty, and one which should clearly specify the rights of each party. Paranhos was far too astute to be overreached by Lopez, and by impressing upon the old man the conviction that he must concede to the Brazilians the privilege of communicating with their own province without interference from him, or else be prepared for a war with the Empire, he succeeded in forming a treaty so clear and precise in its terms that it could not be misconstrued. This treaty having been ratified, the government of Brazil, in order to encourage emigration into Matto Grosso, granted a subsidy to a steam-navigation company, which was to make eight round trips a year from Rio to Cuyuba, a distance of nearly four thousand miles. This service was performed in three different steamers; one from Rio to Montevideo, there to connect with a river steamer to Curumbà, and then with another steamer of lighter draught to Cuyuba. This line being established, continued in operation without molestation some five years; and the first act of the war which was to be so expensive to Brazil and so fatal to Paraguay was the seizure of a steam-packet of this line, the Marquis d'Olinda, in October, 1865.

The importation of so much machinery, and so many arms and munitions of war, with the employment of many foreign artisans, greatly increased the expenses of the government above what they had been in the time of Francia, or in the early days of Lopez's rule. To increase his revenue, therefore, he resorted to numerous measures, which, judicious in themselves, were, as conducted by him, acts of unmitigated tyranny. The revenue previously had been derived mostly from the sale of yerba maté and the export of tobacco and hides. The yerba business was entirely a government monopoly; but as it was an article used only by a limited number of people in the adjoining countries of South America, the amount to be realized from it could not be increased above a million and a half or two millions of dollars a year. The demand for this article had greatly diminished during the time of the dispute with Brazil, as large quantities of it had previous to this been consumed in the Brazilian provinces. Lopez, in order to spite the Brazilians, and as if to bring them to his terms by such a petty device, forbade the export of yerba maté from the country; and the result was that thousands of people who, since the death of Francia, had begun to regard it as a necessity, and to consume it in large quantities, not being able to obtain it longer, learned to live without it, and to make use of tea, coffee, and cocoa in its stead; and afterwards, when the difficulties with Brazil were arranged, and the yerba maté was again allowed to be exported, the number of people who used it was greatly reduced. To a great extent they had lost their taste for it, and the demand for the article was never again so large as it had been.

To increase the amount of general exports of tobacco and hides, Lopez engaged in the protective system so thoroughly as to order the people regarding the number of roods or acres which they should cultivate. He paid little regard to those productions which would all be consumed in the country, but for those that could be exported he issued orders as to the number of rows that should be planted by each individual. He also increased the export duty on everything that was sent out of the country, and the taxes which in one way and another he extorted from the people amounted to more than one third of their entire productions. In the first place, the diezmo, or one tenth of all that was raised by everybody in the country, was taken as the property of the government, another tax of twenty per cent of the value was exacted at the time of export, and the taxes for inspection, for wharfage, and for the stamped paper, amounted in the aggregate to so much that before an article left Paraguay it had paid thirty-six per cent of its value to the government. In addition to this a tax of twenty-five per cent was required on all importations, and after this the amount collected for stamped paper, and for fees of various kinds, was such that all people doing business were compelled to pay to the government officials from ten to fifteen per cent in addition to the direct tax on their goods.

The revenue, therefore, which the government derived was, considering the population of the country and the general poverty of the people, enormous; though the sum realized was greatly reduced by reason of the reductions made in behalf of the different members of the Lopez family. All of these had special privileges, and were exempt from internal taxes and export and import duties. The old man and his wife were constantly adding to their landed estates and making improvements upon them, while the three sons and two daughters were each imitating their thrifty example, so that at least twenty-five per cent of all collected from the Paraguayan people during the latter years of the Presidency of the elder Lopez went, directly and indirectly, to enrich the Lopez family. Besides the revenues thus taken from the people, the government had what was derived from the lands of the state, as notwithstanding so many of the finest estancias in the country had, through favor of the President, become the property of his children, there were many very fine tracts of land that were still said to belong to the state, and over them was always placed some agent of the government, generally an officer of the army, either a lieutenant or an ensign, who had the care of them. The peons, or laborers, of all the neighboring estancias were subject to the orders of this official; and he could demand of their masters at any time to send them all to work on the government estates, and they had no alternative but to obey. They must send, if so required, their men, their oxen, and their horses to labor without any compensation; and the government official, or *capitaz*, was held to the strictest accountability for the government property, and compelled to furnish from the lands under his charge whatever the government might require. The people, therefore, who lived near these government estancias, found it for their interest always to pretend to the greatest poverty, as thus they would escape contributions to the state. The better and more wealthy class of the people were compelled to furnish most of the laborers and most of the oxen, and whenever the government required cattle or horses to put upon the government estancias, it compelled the neighboring people to provide them. Thus the people were afraid to show any signs of prosperity or abundance; they were afraid to make good houses, or to show any signs of wealth or prosperity, for any such display was sure to bring upon them greater exactions from the government. In fact, every man felt that he had nothing he could really call his own; he had nothing but what the government might take from him at any time, whether it was oxen for the government estancias or sons for the army. The people under this government saw that thrift and industry added little or nothing to their own comfort, as it all went to the state or to enrich the Lopez family; they saw that their true interest was to raise just what was required for their families, so that they should not suffer for the absolute necessities of life, but beyond that they had no aspirations, or, if they had, they dared not show them.

CHAPTER XXVII.

The Question between the United States and Paraguay at the Inauguration of President Lincoln. — A Resident Commissioner appointed to Paraguay. — He is accompanied by an Agent of the Rhode Island Company. — Lieutenant William H. Macomb. — Arrival in Asuncion, November 14, 1861. — Lopez refuses to reopen the Question of the Rhode Island Company. — His Grudging Civility towards the Commissioner. — Physical Aspects of Paraguay. — The Parana and Paraguay Rivers. — Early Settlements. — The Tres Bocas. — Gran Chaco. — Cerrito. — Humaita. — The Vermejo. — Villa del Pilar. — The Tebicuari. — Villa Franca. — Villeta. — San Antonio. — Lambare. — Asuncion. — Arsenal. — Custom-House. — San Pedro. — Concepcion. — San Salvador. — Description of a Paraguayan Town. — The General Configuration of the Country. — The Forests. — Dwellings. — Productions. — Characteristics of the People. — The Future Paraguayan Race. — The Natural Wealth of the Country. — The Fruits. — The Climate. — Diseases brought in the Train of War. — Sufferings of the People.

IN the convention made between Paraguay and the United States, by the terms of which the amount of the claims of the Rhode Island company was to be submitted to arbitration, it was also stipulated that the decision to which the commissioners might come should be announced by the two governments in presidential proclamations. President Buchanan, however, being of the opinion that the commissioners had decided another question than the one referred to them, did not issue any such proclamation, but sent a message to Congress setting forth these facts; and thus the matter stood at the time President Lincoln was inaugurated. The new administration, taking the same view as the preceding one, determined to send a resident commissioner to Paraguay, with instructions to notify President Lopez that the decision of the commissioners had been irregular and did not conclude anything, and that as it was on a question not submitted to them it was not binding upon the United States, and therefore the whole question was left open for further negotiation. The writer of these volumes was appointed to this office, and accordingly left the United States on the 27th of July, 1861, and proceeded to the mouth of the Plata, where he took passage up the river on the United States gunboat Pulaski. This vessel was under the command of Lieutenant William H. Macomb, one of the most promising and energetic officers in the American service. He realized that it was the duty of a naval commander, not only to implicitly obey the orders of the Secretary of the Navy, but, even without waiting for instructions from him, to render any assistance in his power to the agents and representatives of the United States in other branches of the government to facilitate them in the discharge of their duties in a manner comporting with the character of the government and the dignity of their offices. On the 14th of November, 1861, the Pulaski reached Asuncion; and the new commissioner having presented his credentials and been formally received, the vessel returned to the mouth of the river. The Rhode Island company, having been advised of the nature of the instructions which the government had given to the commissioner, took it for granted that Lopez would not force the American government to the extremity of sending another expedition, but would rather make such compensation to the company as would induce them not to further prosecute their claims. They therefore supposing that the United States government was committed to secure them justice, sent an agent with authority on their behalf to conclude an arrangement of the question. Lopez, however, being well aware of the difficulties in which Mr. Lincoln's administration was placed, saw that it was in no condition, and would not be for a considerable time, to send another expedition against Paraguay. The civil war having commenced, the result of which he believed would be the destruction of the Union, he assumed a defiant attitude, and refused to reopen the question or entertain any proposition to discuss it. It was a rule with him, not only never to fight, but never to yield till the last moment, and he then saw that the last moment had not come ; that he could put off the day of settlement, and believed that if at last he must yield, he could do so on as favorable terms afterwards as at that time. The agent therefore returned empty-handed to the United States, and the commissioner, having advised his government of Lopez's refusal to reopen the question of the Rhode Island company, remained to await further instructions. Lopez seemed to regard his remaining there as a constant threat, and though he was careful to commit no act of which the commissioner might complain, he was as churlish and uncivil as he could be without danger of aggravating his already delicate relations with the United States. He carried this so far that at one time the commissioner intimated to him that unless he changed his course he would be compelled to leave the country, go to Buenos Aires, and there wait until his government could be informed of his incivility and rudeness. Anything of this kind, however, Lopez was very anxious to avoid, and hastily made amends, asserting that it was through a mistake or misunderstanding of his Minister of Foreign Affairs. After this he was coolly civil in all things, though the people, being aware that he looked with disfavor on the commissioner, considered it the safest course for them to keep as much aloof from him as possible without committing any acts of rudeness or incivility.

The rivers Parana and Paraguay both have their rise in the mountains of Brazil that form the divide between the valleys of the Amazon and the Plata. The sources of the Parana are among the Cordilleras of Goyaz, about 18° south latitude, where the many tributaries uniting, the river is called Parana. Its course is at first southerly, and then, bearing to the west for a while, it again assumes its former direction until it reaches nearly to the southern extremity of Paraguay, when, taking a southwesterly course, it keeps on until its confluence with the Paraguay at 27° 18′ south latitude. The Paraguay, rising more to the west, in the province of Matto Grosso, has its source in the same range of mountains. The general direction of the Paraguay is very nearly due south, and its course from the northern frontier of Paraguay until near its confluence with the Parana is nearly parallel with that river, and the country known as Paraguay is situated between these two streams. The Parana being much more difficult and dangerous for navigation, and being off the general line of direction by which the early adventurers into these regions hoped to establish a line of communication with Peru, the first settlements of the country were made upon the banks of the Paraguay. The seat of government also being on this river, numerous towns and villages were founded in its vicinity; and hence the western part of the territory soon contained a numerous population subject to the government at Asuncion, while the eastern section, or that nearer to the Parana, was neglected, and the greater part of it has remained until this day an unbroken wilderness, uninhabited except by a few roving and miserable Indians. To obtain a general idea of the physical aspects of the western or more cultivated and populous part of the state, that part which before the late war was inhabited by a numerous population in a state of semi-civilization, the traveller in ascending the river first approaches the Tres Bocas (*Three Mouths*), so called from the fact that two islands are so situated in the river that it unites with the Parana through three channels. Below this point he has found the Parana very wide, and so full of islands, that, in some places, he must have been at a loss to tell where the channel of the river was, and must have been impressed with the feeling that it really could be no river, but an immense sea or lake, dotted with little islands just high enough above the level of the stream to permit the growth of verdure so rich and luxuriant as to form apparently an impenetrable jungle; and approaching the Tres Bocas he would observe that while the river which comes in from the eastward, the Parana, preserved many of the characteristics which it had below that point, the Paraguay was confined within narrow limits, and very soon after commencing its ascent above the confluence he would observe it to be restricted to well-defined banks. On the opposite side of the river is the dense Gran Chaco, stretching hundreds of miles to the west; and at this point the land is so nearly on a level with the river, that when the water is high it seems to be but one great swamp, in which the rank vines and creeping parasites are so intertwisted among the larger trees that only by immense labor can they be penetrated. The extreme southern point of Paraguay, below which the three rivers mingle their waters, is a spit of hard land, opposite which to the west is the Chaco, and to the south the province of Corrientes. Just above this southern extremity of Paraguay, and a little distance inland, there are immense swamps as well as impassable jungles, and this is the general character of the country for a distance of some forty miles. There are, here and there, small tracts of hard ground sufficiently elevated to be above high water even when the rivers are highest; and they are generally surrounded, on three sides at least, by swamps and lagoons, which are so broad and deep and difficult to pass that an army which should attempt it in the face of an enemy must be exposed for hours to a merciless cannonade. Ascending the Paraguay from the Tres Bocas, at a distance of about two leagues the land on the Chaco side becomes slightly more elevated and firmer, and here for many years previous to the war was established the guard-house of the Paraguayan government called Cerrito. Here was always maintained a force of some twenty or thirty men in the time of the elder Lopez, to prevent any vessels ascending above there without his permission, and also to prevent the flight of any unfortunate persons who might seek to escape from their prison by way of the river. Continuing the voyage above Cerrito, the Gran Chaco will be found very much as it was below there, and the Paraguayan bank appears to be but a continuous marsh or swamp, producing only the weeds, swamp-grass, and bamboos which are peculiar to low places in those latitudes. Ascending higher, however, it will be seen that the river makes a sudden bend, and as we turn the lower point of it, it will be observed that the left bank of the river is elevated several feet above the level of the river, and the land is hard and dry, denuded of trees or brushwood. Here was the fortress of Humaita, of which a description will hereafter be given. Passing above this point about four leagues, we come to the mouth of another river, the Vermejo, which unites with the Paraguay. Taking its rise at the foot of the Andes, it flows for an immense distance through the Gran Chaco, and finally here joins the Paraguay. This river takes its name, Vermejo,— the word signifying red,— from the color of the water, as, like the Red River of Arkansas and Louisiana, it is greatly discolored by earthy particles which it gathers from the soil over and through which it flows. The next point of any importance is Villa del Pilar, formerly called Ñeembucú. This, for a long time, was the only port in Paraguay to which vessels from below were allowed to come. During the long period of isolation in which Francia held Paraguay, occasionally a vessel would be permitted to come to this port with a cargo of goods, a manifest of which would be sent forward to the Dictator at Asuncion, when he would select such articles as he wished to purchase and name the prices which he would pay in the produce of the country. Towards the latter part of his reign, however, this trifling traffic ceased, after which the people of Paraguay were entirely dependent on what was produced within the country for every article of necessity or comfort.

About ten leagues above Pilar the river Tebicuari, that, rising in the central or northern section of the state, flows southwesterly through the most fertile and populous part of the country, here falls into the Paraguay. This river is free from rapids or falls for a considerable distance, and is navigable for small steamers for more than a hundred miles. The next town, situate at a distance of about seven leagues above the mouth of the Tebicuari, is Villa Franca; and four leagues above this is Villa Oliva, after which there is no town of any importance before reaching Asuncion, except the village of Villeta, situated at a distance of about twenty-five leagues above Villa Oliva. Between this and the capital, however, is the district, or partido, of San Antonio, situated some three leagues from Asuncion. This is the place where the American company undertook to establish their works, and from which they were driven with violence by the President of Paraguay. About half-way between San Antonio and Asuncion is the hill called Lambaré. This hill is of basaltic origin and of conical form, and though of an elevation of only three hundred and twelve feet, yet, standing as it does in the midst of a country nearly level, it may be seen at a long distance, and gives the impression of a mountain many times larger and higher. Above Lambaré the river makes a bend to the east as we ascend, but following the channel in approaching Asuncion we pass under a high bluff, immediately after which we find ourselves in a deep basin of still water almost directly in front of the town, and the first objects liable to arrest attention are the large arsenal on the right hand and the custom-house on the left, — the latter of which, having been erected according to the new ideas of architecture of the elder Lopez, stands on a slant so steep that one would suppose he had intended, when completed, to launch it like a ship into the river, and move it to some other part of his dominions. Directly opposite Asuncion are a few buildings and a brickyard belonging to some of the members of the Lopez family; and beyond that and the huts necessary for the occupation of the laborers employed in making brick and in taking care of the cattle of the state, a few hundred of whom are thus occupied, on that side of the river the whole country appears uninhabited until arriving at Villa Occidental, or New Bordeaux, the place in which the unfortunate French colony were confined until they obtained their deliverance and were permitted to leave the country. Farther on are other towns near the bank of the river, of more or less importance, the principal of which are San Pedro, which stands some distance back on the Jejuy; Concepcion, a larger town, some forty leagues higher up; and beyond that the town now called San Salvador, which in Francia's time was called Tevego, and was the place to which so many unfortunate Paraguayans were exiled during the time of the Dictator. The different towns passed in the ascent of the river are, with the exception of the capital, very like in appearance, and those throughout the country were very like them. The site of a Paraguayan town was generally on an open plain, and the founders had usually exercised good taste in selecting the spot. The central point of the village was the church. This was generally a rudely built structure of adobes, having a tower and a bell. Around the church, at a distance of about sixty yards in all directions, was a smooth-cropped and open lawn, and beyond this on each side was a row of houses. These houses in many of the towns were built of mud or adobes, and had thatched roofs; though in others near the capital, and especially along the bank of the river, many of them were built of brick, with tile roofs to them. These houses about the capillas were owned mostly by the better class of farmers living in the vicinity, who did not reside in them, but were compelled by the government to have a house in the town and keep it in order, and in which frequently some poor dependants would reside. In nearly all the capillas the best houses belonged to the government, and were reserved for the chief of police, or gefé, and the judge, or juez, who, though not often living in them, were obliged to be in attendance at their offices a given number of hours daily, and were held responsible for the good conduct and decorum of the people, and for their fidelity to the government.

Ascending the river from Tres Bocas, as the lakes and lagoons are left behind the country becomes more and more interesting; and approaching Villa Oliva, Villetta, and San Antonio the general appearance is most charming and attractive. The rude adobe houses, with their thick walls, thatched roofs, and deep corridors, have an air of refreshing coolness, and the dense orange-groves that stand near, with awnings of grape-vines, and the luxurious vegetation, the abounding fruit, with the general appearance of indolence and unthriftiness among the people, give one the idea that this must be a suburb to the Castle of Indolence, and that the whole life of the people is but one dream of lazy idleness and harmless delights. The general configuration of the most densely populated parts of Paraguay has been compared by some one to a chess-board, on which every dark spot was a gentle hill, and every white spot a plain or valley ; the hills cropped with the various woods of Paraguay, — which for mechanical uses are the best in the world, — with medicinal herbs of numerous kinds, balsam, juniper, gum-elastic, indigo, and almost every plant or herb of value produced in the tropics ; while the plains, through which course unfailing streams of water, have an abundance of grass of a finer, richer, and more nutritious quality than is known elsewhere in the world. The comparison to a chess-board would be a good one if we suppose that after the hills and valleys were placed in their regular order, some convulsion of nature occurred that had so far deranged this order that they had partially run into each other, and the courses of the waters had at the same time been opened, so that the streams had found their way from one plain to another, until they were finally discharged into the great rivers of the country. The wooded hills stand in their primeval grandeur ; for, owing to the policy which the government has pursued ever since colonial times, practically forbidding the export of timber, the forests are now the same to all appearance as when Sebastian Cabot first cast his eye upon them. Just in the selvage or on the borders of the woods, next to the plains, the inhabitants have their dwelling-houses, and a description of one will in its main features serve for a description of four fifths of them all. The house is usually made of adobes and thatched, and having two or three rooms, the largest of which is perhaps fifteen by twenty feet. This is the dining and sitting room, while the others serve for sleeping-rooms. Besides this main house there will probably be several smaller hovels for the occupation of the slaves, or peons, besides the cook-house. Invariably there is an abundance of orange-trees surrounding the house, and generally there is near by a rude mill for grinding the sugar-cane ; also a sugar-house, or shed, under which one or two boilers are set for the purpose of boiling the juice of the cane down to sirup at the time of the harvest. The gathered maize is suspended or stacked in the husk near the house, elevated from the ground, so that it cannot be destroyed by the mice or other vermin. As there were no mills in the country for grinding the corn, it was reduced to meal by pounding in wooden mortars. These mortars were made from a log of the lepacho-tree, generally about eighteen inches in diameter and three feet high. One end being hollowed out, the corn was thrown in, and then the peons or slave women would gather round with their pestles, and, striking in, would beat a kind of dull music till the corn was sufficiently pulverized. As every house of the better sort had a large retinue of slaves and peons of both sexes, there were always a large number of children of all ages running about, and usually in a state of nudity. These peons were generally of mixed Spanish, Indian, and negro blood, the Indian largely predominating over the other two.

SLAVES AND PEONS.

A stable is a thing unknown, as it is seldom needed. In front or in the rear of the house is a cultivated field, seldom of more than two or three acres in extent, and yet in this field will be raised all that the family has to consume for the year. There will be a patch of Indian corn, another of sugar-cane, another of cotton, another of mandioca, and another of tobacco ; but the whole aggregate would seldom exceed two acres in extent, and on the produce thus raised the family would mainly subsist for a year. The cattle which belonged to the different occupants grazed in common on the plains in front, and each family would have a sufficient number of cows to supply it with all the milk required. They would have likewise a number of chickens ; and as the cattle were very cheap, beef was always to be had at the market of the capilla at a very low price.

About the only article that was counted a luxury by the Paraguayans was the yerba maté, and it was for the purchase of this, more than any other, that they parted with anything that they had raised on their little patches. The tobacco which they grew was always in demand, and would command money in Asuncion ; and it was from the money realized from this crop principally that the inhabitants purchased the much-coveted maté. Something also was required for the purchase of imported muslins, handkerchiefs, and shawls by the women, and for some articles of clothing worn by the men ; but the amount of clothing worn was so very little that the cost of it was very light. The tastes of the people were so simple, so primitive, that they were almost totally ignorant of what other people would call luxury. The women had a great love of jewelry ; and poor as a woman might be, it was seldom but that in the course of years she would manage to acquire a quantity of beads and ear-rings, finger-rings, and gold-mounted combs, to the value of several ounces, sometimes to the amount of several hundred dollars. As this jewelry was invariably in fine gold, the government having carefully watched the goldsmiths, and prevented them, under heavy penalties, from manufacturing their wares of gold that was inferior to the average ounce in circulation, the amount of gold in the country before the war, for a population of such general poverty, must have been enormous. The food was always of the simplest kind, and seldom or never did the natives have any article upon the table except what had been produced upon the place. A *puchero*, or stew, of beef or chicken, with rice, sufficed for the principal dish; a bit of the boiled mandioca was laid beside each plate, and also a bit of corn bread, or *chipa*, and after this came a *dulce*, or sweetmeat, as a dessert. When the meal was concluded, a gourd of water would be passed round to each person at the table, and with a large draught the meal would be concluded. This, with slight changes, would be about the average meal of a family from one year's end to another, for dinner and supper. Tea and coffee were scarcely known to them, and wine was only used at public festivals, — never in their own houses. Their wants were so few and so easily supplied that there was little inducement to hard labor, and it seldom happened that such a thing as absolute want was known. For three fourths of the year, at least, the oranges were so plentiful and cheap that in the country they could be had for the asking; and they formed an important article of food, the oranges of Paraguay being so rich and sweet that while they are abundant no one ever suffers from hunger. With oranges, a little yerba maté, a bit of *asado*, or broiled beef, or of boiled mandioca root, a Paraguayan would be perfectly contented; and if permitted to lie for three quarters of the time in his hammock and thrum his guitar, he would regard himself at the height of earthly bliss.

The Paraguayan people having been so nearly exterminated by the war, it may be presumed that the next generation will be of a very different character from the last. It is not likely, however, that it will be at all improved. Of those left when the war terminated, nine tenths were females; and it will probably be found, that, after the troops of the allies left the country, many thousand deserters and low camp-followers, nearly all of them of negro or of mixed Indian and negro blood, will remain there to prey on the unhappy remnants of the Paraguayan people and become the progenitors of the next generation.

It may be presumed that, as the country is naturally so healthy and prolific, it will receive a considerable emigration from Europe. This may counteract to some extent the evil influence of the worthless dregs left from the allied armies. The emigrants will find thousands of abandoned ranches to which there are no claimants, and can secure to themselves large tracts of excellent land for almost nothing. But laborers will be scarce and difficult to obtain, and the country, if it is ever to arise from its prostration, must depend for its prosperity on the more substantial and staple articles, like the native tea, tobacco, cotton, corn, sugar, hides, and timber, rather than on any of those trifling productions that, though existing there, can never be exported in sufficient quantities to be of any considerable importance to the general prosperity. Travellers who visit such out-of-the-way places as Paraguay, and learn that fruits, resins, and herbs of medicinal value grow there spontaneously, are prone to magnify the resources of the country, and to represent that only science and industry are required to convert them into a source of perennial wealth. But a little observation would show that the same labor employed in raising tobacco or sugar-cane as would be given to collecting the sarsaparilla or balsam, or in manufacturing the dulces, would in the first case give more than double returns. To make the collection of rare gums and plants such as are used in medicine at all profitable, the business must be done in a small way, and even then the labor employed is that of the natives, who expect scarcely any recompense. But all that Paraguay can ever yield of such products can never be sufficient to reward the emigrant or business adventurer for diverging from the ordinary pursuits of agriculture or the regular channels of commerce.

As in the old colonial period the exports from the country were limited almost entirely to the yerba maté, timber, tobacco, and hides, so it will be in the future. The wealth in the forests of timber, however, must in time be immense. Owing to the non-intercourse policy of Francia and the jealousy of Lopez, the forests of noble trees yet remain in their primitive splendor. The woods are generally of a peculiar quality, and resemble nothing known in North America. The quebracho, lapacho, and urundey all grow to a size as large as the hemlock or yellow birch of New England, being straight and free from limbs some fifty, sixty, or seventy feet from the ground. They are of very fine texture, and so heavy as to sink in water like iron. They are exceedingly hard to cut and work, and take a beautiful polish. But the greatest value of the wood consists in its durability. No kind of exposure seems to affect it. Sills of houses that have been exposed on one side to the sun and rain, on another to the ground, and on the other two to varying dampness and darkness, still appear to be as sound as when first put in their places, three hundred years ago. For railroad ties they must be superior to anything else known, as while larger and holding to the earth more firmly than iron, they are certainly durable enough, and hereafter will be far less costly.

The fruits of Paraguay are, with the exception of the orange, of little account. The oranges, however, grow in great abundance, and are equal, if not superior, to those produced in any other part of the world. Though not so large as those of Bahia, they are equally sweet, and of a finer, richer flavor. The wild or bitter orange grows in great profusion in many of the forests, and in time it may be found profitable to collect and convert them into marmalade and other sweetmeats, or dulces, but as yet they have never had any value. The guava and the pomegranate are also produced in great abundance. The latter is regarded as of small value, and the former is seldom eaten except when preserved with sirup or sugar. In this form it is one of the favorite dulces of the country. There are numerous other wild fruits of the country that the Paraguayans manufacture into most palatable sweets. The raw fruit generally has a peculiar flavor that is not agreeable to foreigners.

Pineapples and bananas are also grown occasionally. The former are much smaller than those of Brazil, and the latter are in no respect superior.

Paraguay, although it lies in a low latitude, with nearly half of its territory within the tropics, is probably as healthy a country as any in the world. In the summer time it is extremely warm, and to a stranger accustomed to higher latitudes the heat is frequently oppressive. The changes of temperature are, within the limit of some twenty degrees, very sudden, though they are seldom such as to endanger the health. During summer the mercury will frequently stand for several days at 92° to 98° Fahrenheit, but I have never known it to go above 100°. The nights are almost as warm as the days, and when the weather continues for a week or two without change, a person not acclimated feels it to be very oppressive and debilitating, and has a great disinclination to labor or exercise. During these periods the winds are from the north, and have a depressing effect, not only on the physical system, but on the spirits. So long as the wind holds in the same direction it grows hotter daily, until it culminates in a tempest or thunder-storm. The wind then veers to the south, and after a violent shower, sometimes lengthening into a storm, it clears off, and the air is cool and invigorating. But each day afterwards is warmer than the preceding until the same point is reached again, when another shower follows, succeeded by a cooler atmosphere.

In the winter time the nights are always cool, though it is very rare that from twelve to two of a fair day the rays of the sun are not so strong as to cause people to seek the shade. The evenings and nights are frequently so cool that a fire is desirable; but such a thing as a fireplace is not known in the country, and among the poorer classes, who have but little clothing, there is always a great deal of suffering during the winter months. This was particularly the case with the soldiers in the army, who, besides being poorly fed and scarcely clothed at all, had no shelter from the storms, and were obliged to sleep on the damp ground.

The war brought with it pestilence and famine. Before that there had never been any epidemic in the country, or any diseases incident to the climate or soil. Fever and ague was indeed known there, but it was very rare. Cholera and yellow fever had never penetrated so far into the interior, and of the other diseases to which mankind is exposed there was no one which was not equally common in all the neighboring countries. Among the lower classes the morals were so low that they had become very generally contaminated with diseases caused by vicious indulgences, but it was the opinion of medical men that this was less fatal among the Paraguayans than among Europeans. A person whose whole system was corrupted would still appear to enjoy perfect health. When such persons, however, were wounded in battle, they scarcely ever recovered.

The first disease that made any serious inroads on the army was the measles. It had been so long since this troublesome, but seldom dangerous, disorder had visited the country, that nearly the whole army was liable to take it; and when it got into the camp at Itapiru, so many were prostrated at once, and so inadequate were the means for taking care of the convalescents, that for very want of care and proper shelter and attention many thousands died, and the whole army was in such a condition, that, had the enemy moved upon the camp, scarcely a show of resistance could have been made.

Afterwards the cholera invaded, not only the camp, but the principal towns throughout the state. In Asuncion there were few houses that it did not visit; and as there were scarcely any medicines in the country, and no doctors to administer them if there had been, nearly every case proved fatal.

But the most troublesome complaint both in and out of the army was the chills and fever, or *chuchu*. This disease, that had previously been of so rare occurrence, was in almost every family. The usual remedies for it were not to be had at any price; and as many of the people affected by it had neither the proper food to sustain their strength nor the clothing necessary to keep up the heat of the body, it caused immense misery, and in thousands of cases proved fatal.

The war had brought all those evils in its train. They were but incidents, however, to the final catastrophe. Those who perished then escaped the worse fate of tens upon tens of thousands who afterwards died of starvation in the wilderness.

CHAPTER XXVIII.

Personal Experiences and Adventures. — Society in Asuncion. — Hospitality of the Paraguayans. — The Club Balls and Banquets. — New Fashions. — The Casal Family. — Wealth and Extravagance without Comfort. — José Mauricio Casal. — His Sons and Daughters. — News from Home. — Domestic Arrangements. — Food of the Country People. — Amusements. — Dancing. — Harvest of the Sugar-Cane. — Ballads and Music.

THAT the reader may have a more definite idea of the character and domestic habits of the Paraguayan people, I will give a brief sketch of personal experience and intercourse with them during the first three years of my residence in the country. I arrived there in November, 1861; and as the old question of the Rhode Island company was still hanging in suspense over the head of the President, Carlos Antonio Lopez, I was not received, either by government or people, with much cordiality. However, this mattered little to me, as I then talked little Spanish and no Guarani, and at that time there was a considerable number of intelligent foreigners in Asuncion, who were disposed to welcome the arrival of a foreign minister, or indeed of any stranger having fair intelligence, as an important acquisition to their little society. Lopez had been fortunate in securing the services of not only capable, but very superior, men for directors of his public works. The chief engineer and superintendent of his arsenal, Mr. Whytehead, was thoroughly competent in all the branches of his department, and of extensive general information; and the chief engineer of the railroad, George Paddison, was a man of very extensive reading and of very liberal, cosmopolitan views. There were also several English physicians, all well educated and skilled in their professions; besides which there were several civil engineers, a naval constructor, a few merchants, and others, that formed a circle sufficiently numerous to render it of little importance to me whether the Paraguayans were ordered to cultivate or to avoid my society. There were also several consuls there, some of whom had families, and all of whom were courteous and intelligent gentlemen. The American consul, however, who had no salary, and was dependent on the fees of the office for compensation, left within a few months after my arrival, as the fees were so small that the office was an expense, rather than a benefit, to him. The French consul, M. Izarie, also left soon after the American. His wife was the accomplished daughter of an American long resident at Buenos Aires, and, having lived for a considerable time in the United States, regarded herself more as an American than a Porteña, and was a gallant champion of the Union against the English, who at that time had a strange liking for slavery and the Rebels.

The native people of Paraguay, though inclined to hospitality, have a peculiar way of manifesting it. In Asuncion they appear to be aware that their ways are different from those of people from other countries, and will expose them to criticism, and perhaps ridicule, if they attempt to entertain strangers as guests or invite them to their tables. Therefore they never do so. During my long residence there I never knew a foreigner to be invited to dine or sup with a native family in Asuncion. Neither the President nor any of his ministers ever entertained in any manner; and of the foreigners in the country, so few were in a condition to do so, that it is no exaggeration to say, that though the American legation was maintained in a style that in most countries would be considered as none too liberal for a private gentleman, yet it offered more hospitality to strangers visiting the country than all the rest of Paraguay.

The "National Club" at Asuncion was made to do duty in various ways. The building belonged to the government, and had a large hall, well fitted up, in which most of the public banquets and balls were held. It was supported by a tax on the members, who were mostly business men in the town, both natives and foreigners. The better class of natives had no option but to belong to it and pay their assessments, and a reluctance to do so on the part of a foreign merchant would be set down to his prejudice by the government. The banquets were always on a liberal scale, and the tables showed that the caterers who furnished them had learned their art in other countries than Paraguay. The balls were also given in a style to surprise one who had only seen the people in their own homes. The young ladies seemed to have an instinctive good taste, and their cheap lawns and laces were always so well matched and tastefully worn, that, at a little distance, the wearers appeared to be not only elegantly, but richly dressed.

Though the dresses of the young ladies were but cheap imitations of richer stuffs, the balls were a hard tax on many families. On the national anniversary days — such, for instance, as that of Paraguayan independence or the birthday of the President — it was an offence to the government for people invited to the balls not to attend. The printed invitations that were sent around specified what grand event was to be celebrated; and if it were anything personal to the reigning family, then it was a patriotic duty for all to be present. During the week of the President's birthday a ball would be given nearly every night; and after the younger Lopez became President, the joy and happiness of the people must have been doubled or trebled if the festivities celebrated were an indication of their joy. In 1864, the balls of various kinds began on the 24th of July, the birthday of the President, and it was not before September that all classes of people had ceased to celebrate the natal day of a man who was to be their almost universal destroyer. The introduction, by the future President, of his Parisian courtesan, was followed by a marked change in the style of the official balls. Before that, the young ladies would attend, dressed in their best, but they were not compelled to obtain purposely for such occasions ornaments or dresses beyond their means. If they went barefoot, as many of them belonging to respectable families did, no one took affront at it, for it had not been many years since the daughters of his Excellency had discarded the *tupoi*, and taken to wearing stays and moroccos. But the new queen of fashion set an example of extravagance that the more wealthy tried to imitate; and they, in turn, dragged their poorer neighbors along the same road of folly. It was no longer proper to appear in the same dress at two balls. Poor as many of the families were, the young ladies must not only go, but they must observe the new order of things, that required the observance of a custom which, being the rule at the courts of Europe, the court of Paraguay could not ignore. Very likely the expense to which this rule subjected them obliged them to scrimp themselves in many other things, and they may have had little to eat for days before but oranges and mandioca; yet the state balls must be worthy of a court, and any shortcomings would, sooner or later, be followed by severe penalties.

The young ladies always went to the balls and other festivals attended by their mothers or by some elderly relatives to act as duennas; but the latter never entered the dancing-hall. They sat in the adjoining anteroom gossiping, taking maté, and smoking. When the supper-hour arrived, however, the old ladies took precedence at the table, and all the younger people of both sexes showed them great deference and respect. The watchful eye of the mother was never withdrawn till after the supper and dance were concluded, and she had seen her daughters safely at home and the doors locked against their partners of the evening. It was assumed and taken for granted there, as in most Spanish countries, that young women, if left to themselves, will go astray. No confidence whatever was ever placed in them by their parents; and owing to this, rather than from any natural perverseness or disposition to wanton, stray lambs were very plentiful in the country. The parents thought they did all in their power to prevent them from wandering by keeping watch over them; but as they took little pains to make moral impressions upon them or cultivate in them a sense of their own responsibility, they were too apt to show by their conduct that they needed watching. If there were several daughters, it was regarded as a great misfortune for one of them to go astray, and yet she was never disowned or cast out upon the world.

Soon after my arrival in Paraguay I took a new and commodious house, situate but a short distance from the Church de la Encarnacion. Adjoining my premises stood a poor adobe ranche, inhabited by a family of the poorer sort. They, nevertheless, had visitors from the country apparently of a better class than themselves. I soon made their acquaintance, and was invited to visit them in the country. They lived about six leagues from the capital, and about a mile from the village, or capilla, of Limpio. My first visit to their home gave me a better impression of the character of the Paraguayan people than I had before held, but subsequent acquaintance convinced me that this family was in many respects exceptional and superior to any other with which I became acquainted while in Paraguay. The father's name was José Mauricio Casal. He was at that time above seventy years of age, a widower, with two sons and five daughters, — one of the latter being married, and living with her husband and children on one of the old man's estancias near Caapucu, a town some thirty leagues to the south of Limpio. The father of Don Mauricio had been one of the richest estancieros in the country under the old Spanish *régime*, being possessed of as many as eight very large estancias. These estancias varied in size, being from three to eight leagues square, each of them numbering their cattle by thousands. He was the nephew of General Gamarra, one of the most distinguished officers in the war against Belgrano. Like many of the rich old Spanish families in South America, that of Don Mauricio had indulged in the most profuse extravagance in articles of luxury, while, following the universal custom of the Paraguayan people, they lived in a very primitive style, not even knowing the want of many things regarded as indispensable in more civilized countries. The silver plate which the house contained was to be estimated by hundreds of pounds, if not by the ton. The richest silks, brocades, and damasks wrought with gold and silver threads were bought and stored away, while the necessary furniture and fixtures of the house would, perhaps, not all be of the value of one hundred dollars.

It was in the early days of Francia's reign that Don Mauricio became heir to this large estate. Judging by the number of dependants upon him in his old age, whose claims to kinship he allowed, he was not distinguished for propriety in his younger days. One of these was the old woman, my next-door neighbor in Asuncion. During the long period of Francia's power, Don Mauricio managed so as to avoid the fate of nearly all of his class in the country, and survived the Dictator. He never provoked the enmity or suspicion of Francia, but, on the contrary, so ingratiated himself with him by his liberal donations of cattle and horses to the state, that about fifteen years before his death he got permission to marry. His wife, like himself, was of pure Spanish blood, and both of them were of sufficient intelligence to know that Paraguay was but a prison, and to realize that it was relapsing, under the rule of Francia, to its primitive barbarism. As their children grew up, their mother cherished the hope of seeing them, after the rule of the Dictator had passed away, fit to appear in civilized society, and not only utterly forbade the use of the Indian dialect in her family, but taught her older children to read and write.

But when the reign of Lopez commenced, the affairs of Señor Casal seemed no longer to prosper. He became involved in litigation with his brother-in-law, Argaña; and one estancia after another was sacrificed to the tribunals of Lopez, and the best of them soon after worked into the hands of that family. His silver plate went next by instalments, and it all went in the same direction. The last relics of it, consisting of eight arrobas, or nearly two hundred pounds, was sold but a short time before my arrival in Paraguay to Don Venancio, the second son of the President.

The old homestead estancia had been sadly shorn in its dimensions at the time I first saw it. It had once extended for two or three leagues to the south and west, taking in a large plain, or rather opening, — beyond which was a rolling

RESIDENCE OF DON MAURICIO CASAL, LIMPIO.

plain, overlooking the surrounding country to the east, but descending on the other side to the broad river Paraguay, and beyond this, as far as the eye could reach, nothing could be seen but the dense dark forest of the Gran Chaco. All had once been the property of Don Mauricio, but as it was the finest spot for miles around for a country residence, it had been coveted by the Lopez family, and had been given as a dowry to the ill-fated Doña Inocencia, the daughter of the President and wife of Colonel Vicente Barrios. The other estancias of the old man had also, all but two, passed from his possession. Of these the largest was near Caapucu, in charge of his son-in-law; and the other, near Oliva, was left neglected, for he had not the capital to stock and take care of it, and, besides, he had found that the state took all that a man could raise, save only a bare subsistence. That he could easily make on what remained of the homestead. His two sons were the only Paraguayans that did not seem to be enervated by the climate and disposed to loiter in idleness, passing the day in smoking cigars, playing the guitar, in love-making and dancing in the evening, that I ever met. They, on the contrary, seemed to think it a duty to redeem by industry the fortunes of the family. On reaching manhood, they had therefore set to work to build a brickery near the homestead, and had just got it in good working order when the war commenced, and both were taken for soldiers. Though they boasted the pure blood of Spain, they worked among their peons like day laborers, and were just beginning to realize large returns for their enterprise when everything was paralyzed by the preparations for war.

The old man was proud of his sons and daughters. He had been a gay Lothario in his youth, and shared the Spanish American idea that the only safety for young girls was in constant watchfulness. Their mother being dead, he had taken this task on himself, and never had they been as prone to go astray as he gave them credit for, could they have avoided his watchful care. I was always received with the greatest kindness and hospitality, and would sometimes take my gun and dog along with me to hunt for partridges in the plains, or ducks and pigeons in the lagoons and fields, and would stay for one, two, or three days at a time. The semi-monthly steamer for Buenos Aires left regularly about two days before the incoming one was due ; and, having despatched my mail, I was naturally in a great state of impatience and anxiety for the next news from town. As an almost invariable rule, a Reuter telegram would come by way of Lisbon to the Plata, giving as the latest news a report of a reverse or disaster to the national arms ; and during the time that the friends of the Rebels at the North were boldly asserting their purpose of arming to prevent loyal troops from marching against the Southerners, who only wanted to be left alone, and were raising mobs to oppose the conscription, and threatening to transfer the scenes of war from the South to the North, they were indeed anxious days for the American in foreign lands, who knew not if, when the war should be over, he would have a country to return to or not. The two or three days, therefore, between the departure of one steamer and the arrival of the next, were days of intense anxiety ; and usually, as soon as the first was started, I would jump on my horse and gallop out to Don Mauricio's, and spend a day or two roving about with my gun, or sipping maté, smoking cigars, eating oranges, and talking bad Spanish with him and his pretty daughters. The experience of one day there may serve to illustrate the life of the better class of Paraguayans in the interior before the war.

As early in the morning as the first streaks of light were to be seen the old man would be out, and ere sunrise his example would be followed by the whole household. The fire would be lighted in the kitchen, and if the weather were cool the slaves and peons would huddle about it until they got their morning cup of maté, after which the women servants would milk the cows and the women of the family would put the house in order. The peons would some of them drive up and yoke the oxen to plough the field, or, as the season might be, to plant the seeds of the tobacco, cotton, sugar-cane, and maize, or to harvest the crop. The sons, with their peons, would go to the brickery and commence the day's labor. Breakfast was a thing unknown; but as soon as the water could be made to boil in the kitchen the maté was served to all, and if there were guests in the house who were laggard in rising they were served in bed. Then followed the inevitable and almost perpetual cigar. Smoking is a universal habit, and is as common with the women as the men. Children learn to smoke, among the lower class, as soon as they can walk, and before they quit the breast. During the forenoon I would saunter about the premises, or go out to shoot birds, and a little before noon the dinner would be ready. The dishes were always about the same at every meal, and though prepared in a different way from what I had ever seen before, they were always relishing and palatable. The *asado*, or roast beef, was the most invariable course. It was prepared by cutting the meat in strips, through which wooden spits were run, and then stuck into the ground near the fire until they were thoroughly cooked. The *puchero*, or stew, was also a favorite dish, and was prepared by cutting up the beef or the chicken, and stewing it with rice and some leaves of a kind of cabbage that gave it an excellent flavor. Eggs and beefsteak were a frequent course.

Potatoes are not raised in the country. The mandioca, however, is a very good substitute. This is a root something like the sweet potato, but more nutritious. It grows usually to the length of from six to ten inches, and is from an inch and a half to two inches thick, and covered with a thick rind, or skin, that readily peels off. It is eaten boiled or roasted. When boiled it has very little taste, and unless cooked soon after it is ripe it does not become soft or boil to pieces, but remains heavy and sodden. A fine flour is made from this root, which is prepared in the same manner that starch is made from the potato. It is from a variety of the mandioca that the tapioca of Brazil, with which all are familiar, is manufactured. The flour, as prepared by the Paraguayans, is used for making the *chipa*, or bread of the country;

though no cereal enters into its composition, and it is not, properly speaking, bread, it is an excellent substitute for it. It is made by mixing the flour with pulverized cheese and lard or suet, and then baked. When well made and fresh it is delicious, though, probably owing to the cheese it contains, somewhat indigestible. It soon hardens, however, and becomes stale and unpalatable. A cheaper and coarser kind of *chipa* is made by using pounded corn meal instead of the mandioca flour; and these are the nearest like bread of anything known to the Paraguayan people. Wheat is not raised in the country, and the flour that was imported before the war was nearly all consumed by foreigners.

After the midday meal, and sitting long enough for digestion to commence and to smoke a cigar, the house would be closed, the sun and light shut out, and every person about the premises, from Don Mauricio to the naked little *chiquitos* of the peons, would take a siesta for a couple of hours. After siesta the maté was again served, and the labors of the peons would be resumed and continued till nightfall. Strolling musicians were common, who wandered about from house to house, being always welcome, as they asked for nothing but their food in return for their music. A harpist, a guitarist, and a fiddler would often appear at Don Mauricio's when I was there, and on such occasions a dance in the evening was the invariable custom. The Paraguayan young ladies dance with exceeding grace. They are accustomed to it from early childhood; and those of the better class never indulge in any of those rude and boisterous dances in which strength and endurance are the qualities most in requisition. On the contrary, there is among them a natural grace and ease of motion, which all strangers who have been among them have remarked and admired. Politeness and grace of manners is natural to them, and to any attention or courtesy they respond with charming frankness and propriety.

The time of harvest of the sugar-cane was always a gay season in Paraguay as long as there was cane to harvest or people to gather it in. At nearly every house was a rude mill, built very much after the style of an old-fashioned cider-mill, for grinding the cane. Close by stood the sugar-house for boiling down the juice. The boilers were set at one side of the room, so as to leave a large open space for dancing. The fires once lighted, they were kept up continuously; and during the long night, while some were engaged in watching the boilers and cooling the bubbling sirup, the others would be dancing till the morning broke. The troubadours would vary the monotony of their instruments by singing some of the old Spanish ballads, in which the young ladies would sometimes join. The younger daughters of Don Mauricio had most sweet voices, though of small compass; and the simple music they essayed always had a most sad and plaintive sound. This seems to be the case with all Spanish ballad singing; but in Paraguay the sweet and plaintive voices seemed to be attuned to a most melancholy refrain, and the low, soft strains seemed to be the sighs of sadness and despair, and I fancied I could hear in it the story of the national enslavement. How is it that the songs and airs of Scotland have such a bold, inspiring tone, while those of Ireland are so sad and plaintive? Is it because the Scotch have always maintained their independence and self-respect, and breathed out in their ballads liberty and defiance? And are those of the neighboring isle so different, because the Irish have so long been an oppressed and enslaved people, and their misery and despair has found expression in the wail of music? However this may be, it struck me that those airs, songs, and ballads of Spain that were most sad and plaintive were those that among the Paraguayans had struck the key-note of the popular heart, and thus unconsciously, as it were, to themselves, did they give expression to thoughts and feelings that for generations they dared not express in any other way.

CHAPTER XXIX.

The Yerba Maté. — A French Savant. — Visit to the Yerbales. — Capiatá. — The Hospitable Cura. — Itaguá: Nicholas Troya and Alexandro Cavallero. — Pirayu. — Paraguari. — The Grotto of St. Thomas. — The Fernandez Family. — Ibitimi. — The Tebicuari. — Villa Rica. — Caaguazu. — The Gefé and the Club. — The Yerbales. — Collecting and curing the Yerba. — Life at the Yerbales. — Subsequent Fate of all who showed Attention and Hospitality.

OF the productions peculiar to the soil of Paraguay, the tea (*ilex paraguayensis*), or yerba maté, as it is usually called, is the most important. So far as is known, it grows nowhere in the world but in the northern or northeastern part of that country. An article of an inferior quality grows in some parts of Brazil and in the Argentine district of Misiones; but though it passes under the same generic name as that of Paraguay, and has some of its peculiar qualities, it has little of the flavor or aroma of the Paraguayan article, and is never used when the other can be had. As the grapes from which some of the most delicate and expensive wines are made will only grow to perfection in certain small districts, or as only some parts of Cuba will produce the tobacco from which the finest Havana cigars are manufactured, so is the yerba maté of the best quality only to be found in that part of Paraguay to the north of Asuncion and at the distance of from twenty-five to fifty leagues inland from the river. Here, however, it grows in great abundance; but as all the country producing it belongs to the state, it was during all the time of the Lopezes a government monopoly, and only so much of it was allowed to be gathered each year as would meet the demand at a high price. It yielded an enormous profit to the government, which allowed less than one fourth of its market value in Buenos Aires to the favored individual who was permitted to gather and cure it.

AN ORANGE-GROVE.—RESTING BY THE WAYSIDE.

In the month of March, 1863, a Frenchman professing to be a *savant*, or scientific explorer, arrived in Asuncion. He called himself a doctor, Dr. S——, and expressed a great desire to travel through the country for purely scientific objects. It was believed, however, after his departure, that he was a political emissary of the Emperor Napoleon, and that his real object was to learn and report the political and social condition of the country. About that time the Emperor, being under the delusion that monarchy could be re-established in several Spanish American countries, was engaged in making his unfortunate experiment to that end in Mexico. The presence of his emissaries was suspected in the mushroom republics of Central America, and such evidence of their machinations was furnished to certain members of our Congress that a call was made on the Secretary of State for any information he might have in regard to the matter. The Secretary, Mr. Seward, replied, that the Department was fully advised by our ministers of what they knew and what they suspected, but that the information given was of a confidential nature which ought not to be made public. There were many indications that the countries of the Plata were receiving the special attention of the Emperor, all of which was duly reported to the State Department.

This *savant* proposed to visit the yerbales; and as I had long contemplated such an excursion, and had often talked with my friend Don Domingo Parodi, an Italian apothecary of high scientific attainments and a gentleman in the best sense of the term, we concluded to accompany Dr. S——. We accordingly started from Asuncion at about seven o'clock in the morning of the 28th of March. The Frenchman evidently thought he was going on a long and hazardous expedition, for he took with him seven mules and three peons. Parodi and myself had but one peon each, and no other animals than the horses we rode. The incidents of the journey to the yerbales I will quote from my journal.

"At eleven o'clock we reached the capilla of Capiatá and stopped at the house of the cura, with whom Parodi was acquainted. Distance, five leagues. We commenced a repast on the bread, sardines, and canned oysters we had brought with us, but the priest had bestirred himself so actively that we had hardly commenced when he invited us to join him at his table, which was copiously supplied with asado, chipa, mandioca, and milk, on which we feasted with keen relish. Then the padre conducted us to a room in which were stretched three nice clean hammocks, and we took a two hours' siesta. A woman in the house is sick, and the two doctors have prescribed for her. The good padre looks hearty, and as if he lacked for nothing. In form and color he looks as though he took a great deal of aguadiente, and on some occasion had swallowed a keg that had got crosswise inside of him; so that at a front view he looks tall and spare, but sideways appears bulged out like a demijohn. But he treated us well, and he has my best wishes for his present and future welfare."

I never saw the man afterwards to speak to him, and my good wishes as thus expressed were not realized, as he was some five years afterwards arrested, tortured, and shot as a traitor. As I go on quoting from my journal, it will be found that nearly every one I met on this excursion had a similar fate to this good priest.

"At 4 P. M. we set forth again, and, moving at a slow amble, we reached Itagua in about two hours, where we put up with an Italian by the name of Nicolas Troya, who entertained us with great hospitality. Don Nicolas is married to a Paraguayan, and has two pretty children, one of which, a little girl five years old, is partially paralyzed in one side of her body, but is still playful and happy. We called on the judge, or juez, Don Alexandro Cavallero, who is a relative of my friends, the Casals, in Limpio. He is a man of large wealth for this country, and is supposed to be high in the confidence of the government, as he has held his present office for fifteen years."

Don Alexandro was removed from his office about a year after this; and in the general conscription of the next February, he and all his slaves and peons were taken as common soldiers, and sent to Cerro Leon. Two or three months afterwards, seeing one of his old servants suffering from the cold, he gave him money to buy a poncho. Unfortunately, the poncho thus bought had been stolen, and Don Alexandro was arrested and *flogged to death*. This took place before the war had begun. The fate of our host, Don Nicolas, may be learned from the following extract from the official register of General Resquin, captured at Lopez's head-quarters some five years later: —

"The following accused traitors were executed on the same day," [August 22]: "Francisco Rodriguez Larreta, James Manlove, William Stark, Nicolas Troya, José Vicente Urdapilleta," [thirty-two names in this list are here omitted,] "except Nicolas Troya, who died before execution."

"*March 29th.* — We started about sunrise, after taking a Paraguayan breakfast, — that is, a sip of maté. Our road lay through a beautiful country, now over wooded hills and now through the open valleys. We reached Pirayu about ten o'clock, and put up with my old friend Concha, a fat, jolly old Paraguayan, who seems to be so delighted whenever foreigners call upon him, he cannot do enough to show his gratitude for the honor they do him. As he had not anticipated our coming, he had no time to prepare such a feast as he desired to set before us; but with the keen appetite we had acquired from the ride, and from having taken nothing but the morning maté since the night before, we found the beefsteak and eggs, with fresh *chipa*, amply sufficient. After siesta and a cup of maté, we again started, and pursued our way through the beautiful valley towards Paraguari."

Our host, Señor Concha, was also taken for a soldier within a year from this time, but, more fortunate than Don Nicolas of the night before, he died soon afterwards.

"We reached Paraguari at dusk, and put up with a couple of Frenchmen, who kept a shop there, and were engaged in the manufacture of caña. Their names are Clugny, and they are brothers of the school-teacher at the capital. They entertained us the best they could, and yet the Paraguayan hospitality always seems to me to be more gracious and cordial than that of any foreigners."

These Clugnys are now all dead. Two died natural deaths, and the third was arrested as a conspirator and shared the fate of all the Frenchmen who were in Paraguay at that time.

"This town of Paraguari is situate about forty miles from Asuncion, and is said to be the coolest place for a summer residence in Paraguay. The range of hills to the east of the valley by which we approached it here terminates abruptly with the cerro of San Tomas, a bold precipitous mountain, that, rising gradually at first, afterwards shoots up vertically on the side next us for some three hundred feet to the summit. In this mountain is the celebrated grotto where St. Thomas left his cross when he visited America some hundreds of years before Columbus was born. To this day this cave is occasionally visited by the good saint for whom the mountain is named. At least our servants tell us so, and also that his cross is transferred miraculously to other parts of the country, where it is shown to work miracles and confound doubters, and then returns, without the aid of human hands, to the sacred grotto.

"*March 30th.* — It was all still and calm when we left Paraguari half an hour after sunrise; but when the first breath of air moves up or down the valley, it will all be compressed in the narrow pass where the town stands, and ere nine o'clock a strong breeze will be sweeping through.

"At a league from the capilla we passed the estancia of the Fernandez family, one of the richest and proudest in the country. It was at this place that Captain Page, of the Water Witch, received such a cold welcome as to lead him to make a note of it, and complain of the lack of hospitality. But it has no such character here. We should have pushed on to it last night, except for the fact that we were all strangers; and, knowing they would accept no recompense for their trouble, we thought it would be an imposition on generosity and good-nature for so large a cavalcade to quarter itself upon them without warning. Before noon we met a friend and countryman of Parodi on his way to the capital from his residence in Ibitimi, at which place we were intending to stop for the night. He insisted on returning to entertain us at his house. We reached there before sunset, and fared sumptuously, as usual.

"*March 31st.* — We started about the usual hour. This part of the country is very charming to the eye. At about 9 A. M. we passed the estancia of the Herreros family. It is one of the finest in the country. One of the sons is a lieutenant in the navy, and was educated in Europe, and is a great favorite with the President. At eleven o'clock we reached the banks of the Tebicuari, which we crossed in canoes, swimming our horses. The river here is about five feet deep and forty yards wide. On the left bank we found a small straggling village of miserable huts, at the best of which we obtained some maize for our horses, and took our siesta under the shade of the orange-trees. The patron gave us a *puchero* of stewed chicken and some milk. At two o'clock we started again and reached Villa Rica before sunset, and were made most welcome by Don Manuel Madruga, the brother of the Portuguese consul in Asuncion. A new house, which is but just finished, he has provided with beds, chairs, and tables for our use, and is almost oppressive with his excess of hospitality.

"*April 1st.* — This is one of the largest and best built towns in Paraguay, and we propose to stay here a day or two to give the *savant* a chance to pursue his scientific investigations. He seems a queer man for such service, as he knows nothing of botany or geology, and is dependent on Parodi, who is well versed in both, to tell him how to describe and classify any plant or tree that strikes him as peculiar, or to give the geological formation of the country. Don Manuel is married to a Paraguayan, and has but one child, a son about sixteen, — a very handsome and intelligent youth that he wants to send abroad to be educated.

"*April 2d.* — We learn that the yerbales are about twenty-one leagues to the northwest of us. Those nearest this place are of limited extent, and an Italian by the name of Queirolo, who lives in this place, has the privilege of working them. They are situate about seven leagues beyond the capilla of Caaguaza, where Señor Queirolo is now making preparations to commence work in a few days. This being Passion Week, the religious Paraguayans will not labor. A Porteño merchant here by the name of Quintanilla invited us in the afternoon to go and see some native people about two leagues out and near the monté. As at almost every house we have stopped we have found one or more sick persons, the doctors are always welcome. Here the *patron* was an old man, who said there were lots of monkeys in the woods near by. We rode down to look for them, and soon saw several. Dr. S—— shot a large one, called here a mono, which was brought home to be skinned; the skin to be stuffed and the carcass to be cooked. Some of the party said they saw a large boa constrictor moving along on the ground. I was not near, and saw nothing of it. The doctor *fit* it by running away.

"*April 3d, Thursday.* — We have spent the day wandering about the town, conversing with many people. We were intending to start for the yerbales this afternoon, but the capataz was so late with the animals, we have concluded to start early to-morrow morning. The native people here, some of whom seem to be very respectable and well-to-do, are rather reserved towards us all. They are civil, but show a distrust, as if they either thought we were spies, or that attention and hospitality towards us might bring them into trouble. Señor Quintanilla and the son of Quierolo, a youth of eighteen, propose to join us in the trip to the yerbales.

"*April 4th.* — We got an early start this morning, and by daylight were at least three leagues from Villa Rica. It then began to rain, and we sought shelter under the roof of an old native who lived near the road. He had just got his fire started, and treated us to maté, which was very grateful to us, as the morning was cold, and the rain had overtaken us some time before we reached his hospitable, though humble abode. The rain held up about nine o'clock, and we again set forth. Before starting, however, the old man gave us some milk, which we ate with some bread of our own, the doctor eating a piëce of roast monkey. He said it was good, and I took his word for it. After starting again we pursued our journey till near 12 M., when we entered a wooded country, and our road lay over high hills and through deep ravines. Yet even here there is nothing grand or picturesque about the country. The trees that line the road are many of them very large and would be of great value in other countries. We reached Caaguazu about 6 P. M., having rode fifteen leagues during the day. Señor Quierolo has a house and shop here, and has received us with great cordiality. He tells us his men will not begin work in the yerbales till next week, so we must manage to while away a couple of days here.

"*April 5th.* — The gefé of the partido, waiving the ceremony of the first call, came early this morning in full uniform to pay his respects to the guests of Señor Quierolo. He is a large man, enormously fat, and was profuse in his offers of attention and service. The capilla is situate in the midst of a beautiful lawn, and that is all there is beautiful in sight. It is a poor miserable place of about eight hundred people, and not a family in it pretending to respectability. We have been looking for game in the adjoining woods, but have seen nothing but two monkeys, that at sight of us fled into the forest, jumping from tree to tree much faster than we could follow through the tangled underbrush below. In the evening the gefé got up a ball in our honor, in what is called the "Club." Judging from the building, the aristocracy of Caaguazu are not so extravagant in their habits as the denizens of Pall Mall and Fifth Avenue. The dancing-hall of this Club is nothing but an open shanty with a thatched roof and clay floor. The dancers were all barefoot, and not a comely face among them. The room being open on one side, the tallow-dips flared so as to give but a dim, uncertain light, yet the gefé seemed to take great pride in thus showing off the refinement of his people. The music consisted of two or three rude guitars, or banjos, a cracked fiddle, a tambourine, and a triangle. The refreshments consisted of a bottle of *caña*, or native rum, that was passed from mouth to mouth, and which, though it had a villanous smell, must have been good, judging from the frequency with which the old gefé applied it to his lips and passed it round. The musicians had an eye to profit as well as pleasure, for not long after we had taken our seats beside the magistrate to view the gorgeous mazes of the dance I heard them improvising a song in my honor. The import of it was that *el senor ministro norte americano* had come to honor the ball of the Caaguazu Club, and that they were proud and grateful to him for his condescension. No sooner was the song finished than the tambourine was passed towards me. I asked Parodi for advice, and he told me to give them two dollars. Having obtained it, they improvised another song in honor of the French doctor, for which his two dollars was immediately forthcoming. Parodi's turn came next, and though he protested to us he had not merited the honor they had done him, as he was an old resident of the country, he paid his two dollars, after which we left the gay circle, leaving the old gefé too far gone to observe our departure.

"*April 6th.*— The day has been as unprofitable as yesterday, but the religious scruples of these people will not permit them to labor during Passion Week. Another ball was given at the Club in our honor, but, the novelty having worn off, we did not go.

"*April 7th.*— As the men will begin work to-morrow, we set off this morning for the scenes of the yerba harvest. Señor Quierolo and the gefé both accompanied us. The latter is so fat and unwieldy that no horse he had could carry him faster than a walk. We had but seven leagues to go, half of which was through a heavy rolling country, and the rest through a dense forest. At about 3 P. M. we reached the camp of the yerbal. It was a damp, cold day, and the place had a dismal look. An opening had been made in the forest on a hard, level spot, and a low thatched house erected for the use of the *patron*. It contained the stores required for the use of the peons, and had a large bin, about six feet by twelve, and four feet deep, nearly full of yerba that had been cured previously. Around this principal house were several miserable huts that served as dwellings for the laborers, and near by was the place where the process of curing the yerba leaves was performed.

"*April 8th.* — This morning the work of collecting the yerba commenced, the process of curing which is as follows: A dry, level place is selected, and a circular spot some twenty-five feet in diameter made perfectly smooth and hard, and a layer of damp clay spread over it and stamped down till it becomes a hard and smooth floor. Within this space a large number of small trees are set into the ground in a circle of about eighteen feet in diameter. The tops of these trees are then bent over and interwoven into each other so that an oval roof is formed. Then commencing some three feet from the ground, long withs are woven in longitudinally, with the upright poles forming a sort of open basket-work to the top. The peons next go in search of the yerba, which they collect and bring to the camp. They take with them a sort of basket made of thongs of raw hide, that they adjust on their shoulders and neck in such a manner that they carry enormous loads.

"Provided with this and a hatchet, the swarthy native plunges into the wood to look for the yerba. That most coveted is the bush from six to ten feet high, which he cuts down, and then, chipping off all the branches and leaves, whips them into his basket. It is the medium-sized shrub that is most sought. Sometimes the bush grows to a tree of twenty-five feet or more, but these are left unmolested when the smaller shrub can be found. So soon as the peon collects as much as he can carry, he returns to the camp, and the branches, having the leaves still on them, are passed quickly through the blaze of a hot fire, and then the leaves are stripped off and thrown upon the ground. When a sufficient quantity has been gathered in this way, the leaves are all taken up and worked into the wicker-work of the oval structure before described. They are worked in with great care and so as to be of uniform thickness over the whole surface. When this is finished the floor beneath is swept out, and a pile of wood, that has been long before cut and seasoned, is placed underneath and a fire kindled. The heat soon becomes very great, and much care is taken that it reaches all parts overhead alike, so that

CURING THE YERBA.

none of the yerba is scorched and none that is not completely dried. To cure it thoroughly, every particle of moisture must be driven away; and as there are always more or less stems of the wood of considerable thickness, it is not considered safe to withdraw the fire till it has been in full flame for some thirty-six hours. When the roasting process is finished, the fire and ashes are drawn out, the floor carefully swept, and the now cured yerba is shaken to the ground. It is then gathered up and placed under cover, ready for packing.

"The packing process is not the least singular of the yerba-curing operations. First the green hide of a large ox is taken, and a strip about five feet by two and a half taken and sewed up with thongs from the same hide in the form of a square pillow-case. It is then attached to strong stakes driven into the ground, and a quantity of the yerba is put into it when a couple of stout peons proceed to press it down with heavy sticks of wood in the form of hand-spikes. It is a very slow process, as the yerba is beaten and hammered in till the mauls, though pointed at the end, can hardly make an indentation. When as much has been forced in by this operation as possibly can be, the open side is brought together and laced up with the thongs of green hide, and then it is left to harden in the sun. What with the close packing and the contraction of the hide by exposure to the sun, it becomes almost as hard as a rock. The bales, called here *tercios*, usually weigh from 150 to 200 pounds each.

"The yerba, in the process of curing and packing, is reduced to a fine powder. It is called the yerba maté from the way it is invariably used. The maté is a small gourd, holding, usually, less than a gill. When the gourd is growing it can, by great care and attention, be made to have a long and curiously twisted stem. A hole an inch in diameter is then made in one side of it, and it is used thus, or is mounted with silver or gold according to the caprice or means of the owner. The maté is always taken with the *bombilla*, which is a silver or tin tube, having a bulb at one end punctured with small holes. This bulb serves as a strainer to prevent the fine particles of the yerba from passing into the mouth.

"To prepare a maté, the cup or gourd is taken with the bombilla already inserted, and is filled about two thirds full of the yerba. Boiling-hot water is then poured in, and the bombilla is taken between the lips, and is made to do the duty of a straw in a sherry-cobbler or at the bunghole of a barrel of cider. The hot water may be renewed to the same yerba for three or four times before all its strength is extracted. Taken in this fashion, it is very strong, and is not agreeable to persons unaccustomed to use it. But to Paraguayans it is the one indispensable luxury. Wine, spirits, and even tobacco, they can live without, and they are simple and temperate in their eating; but the yerba they will have if they can get it. With the old people it is indeed "the cup that cheers, but not inebriates," and the means resorted to to obtain it are often as ingenious as were ever employed by a veteran tippler to obtain his morning dram.

"Having witnessed with our own eyes the curing process of the yerba, we were glad to get away from the comfortless camp. Our accommodations had been none of the best, and the fare was not inviting. Our party consisted of seven persons besides our servants, and our host could give his guests but one course, and that was served in primitive style. It was always the same, and consisted of *choclo*, or beef and maize stewed together in a large pot, that was placed in the middle of the group, who were seated on dried hides around it. Two or three of the most honored guests were provided with plates and horn spoons, but the others all helped themselves direct from the steaming vessel in the centre. The old gefé was the impersonation of good-nature, and as he sat by the caldron of steaming choclo at supper, his face illumed by the light of the blazing fire, holding the bottle of caña to his mouth, he looked the very picture of animal enjoyment.

"On our return we tarried but one night at Caaguazu, and the next day found our way back to Villa Rica. Here my companions, Dr. S—— and Señor Parodi left me and came back to Asuncion. I wished to see more of the country around Villa Rica and to return by a different road from that we went. A few days, however, satisfied my curiosity, and, bidding my good friends the Madrugas *adios*, I turned my face towards the capital, which I was more pleased to reach than I had been to leave."

I will here anticipate the chronological order of events by relating in this place the subsequent fate of all the persons whose names I have mentioned in this narrative. Queroli was so fortunate as to die a natural death early in the war. His son was taken for a soldier, and perished either in the camp or on the battle-field. Of his wife and younger children I have no information, but have little doubt that they are all dead,— that they perished from want and exposure. Young Madruga was shot through the heart while on picket duty in 1867, and the fate of his father is thus noted in Resquin's register of prisoners under his charge: "July 15th. Died, the accused traitor Manuel Madruga, a Portuguese." Several others are mentioned as having died on the same day. Generally those whose names are thus entered on the list expired under the torture, though many died from starvation and exposure, or the diseases resulting from their cruel treatment.

Quintanilla, who accompanied us to the yerbales, was arrested early in the war for the crime of being a Porteño, and kept a close prisoner for many months at Humaita. He was afterwards set at liberty for a while, but subsequently arrested again, and kept a prisoner till, by a catastrophe unforeseen by Lopez, he was taken prisoner, and thus escaped.

The Italian who entertained us so hospitably at Ibitimi was made prisoner in the general harvest of foreigners, and was honored with a place among the conspirators, and consequently his property was taken by Lopez, and he was tortured and executed.

Of the brothers Clugny, with whom we put up at Paraguari, one died before the war began, and the other was declared a conspirator when the great swoop on all persons in the country supposed to have money was made. He had accumulated considerable property during the three first years of the war, and as he had converted it to a large extent into coin, he was accused of being, not only a conspirator, but of having robbed the public treasury. His money, as a matter of course, was seized, and he was executed. Concha, our good-natured host at Pirayu, died. Troya and Cavallero of Itagua were killed, one for being a conspirator, and the other for buying a poncho that had been stolen ; and the priest at Capiata had the fate of thousands of others, all of whom were just as innocent and just as guilty as he.

CHAPTER XXX.

The Elder Lopez not naturally of a Sanguinary Disposition. — Treatment of Foreign Diplomats. — His Peculiar Etiquette. — Disputes with the Pope. — He retains the Church Property. — Bishops of Paraguay. — The Constitution. — Ignorance and Indifference of the People in Political Affairs. — All Power with the Executive. — The Subserviency of Congress. — How chosen. — Lopez, in Imitation of Rosas, declines a Re-election. — An Awkward Failure.

THE current of internal affairs during the long reign of Carlos Antonio Lopez had little to disturb it. When he had once obtained absolute power, he governed with a firm hand, closely watching for any signs of disaffection and promptly suppressing them. He was averse to taking life, and it is doubtful if a man ever reigned before with such absolute authority and for so long a period without condemning more persons to death than he did during his twenty-one years of power. The execution of the brothers Decoud is the worst, if not the only, instance in which he took life on the pretext that the sufferers were political offenders. But those conversant with the facts ascribed his severity in this case to the influence of the young general, who, at an early period of his life, evinced a tiger's thirst for blood. One instance of a summary execution was remembered against the old man, that was rather an evidence of his bad temper, which was known to be violent and ungovernable, rather than of a disposition deliberately cruel. A merchant in Asuncion, having some goods in the custom-house which he wished to withdraw, went to the stamped-paper office and took out a permit, paying therefor, as he supposed, the amount of the duty. On reaching the custom-house he was told that the sum paid was not sufficient for the tax on his goods, and therefore his stamped paper was worthless. Enraged at the loss, he tore up the paper and went away to his own house. This insult to the government in tearing up a piece of paper bearing its stamp upon it and trampling it under his feet was immediately, as a matter of course, reported to Lopez, and the man was instantly arrested, and executed by shooting the same afternoon.*

To the common people of the country the disputes with other governments were of very little importance. When they heard that the American expedition was coming, many hoped a better day was at hand, and that the system which had then endured for more than forty years, and which made them, not only slaves, but dumb slaves, was to be broken up. It is possible that some persons were so unguarded as to let a sigh to that effect escape them, and that this caused Lopez to invent the conspiracy which might have proved "as good a plot as ever was laid," and as successful as the "Yegros conspiracy," got up by Francia forty years before, had he not unfortunately included the Englishman, Canstatt, among its members. Of the wrangles and quarrels, however, which the President was having almost continually with foreign ministers who came to treat with him, unsupported by any military or naval force, the people knew nothing except what was told them in the *Semanario*. In this hebdomadal the old President gave free vent to his spite against all who had offended him. Though nothing appeared in it which was not either written or approved by him, it purported to be edited by some one else, so that his modesty was not offended by the fulsome praises of himself, and he was not responsible for the gross abuse of other governments and their representatives.

His treatment of the different diplomatic agents who came to treat with him was peculiar to himself. He seemed to think that diplomacy consisted in rudeness, discourtesy, and fraud. He was exceedingly jealous lest he should not be treated with the same respect and deference as were exacted

* The facts in this case are substantially as I have related them, and as they were told to me by several persons cognizant of them. But as I made no note, at the time, of the details of the affair, it is probable they are somewhat different from the version as given here.

at royal courts in approaching the sovereign, and his punctiliousness on this point, led to some incidents of a ludicrous character. Until a few years before his death he persisted in wearing his hat whenever he gave a reception to any foreign minister. This boorishness was resented by a certain English Minister, and he said that it was disrespectful to the Queen of England thus to treat her representative. But Lopez said it mattered not whether he wore a crown or a hat; he was the head of a government whose sovereignty and independence were acknowledged by the family of nations, and that as at official receptions the Queen of England wore her crown, he had a right on similar occasions to wear his hat. The Minister, however, ingeniously rebuked the cacique President. Having arranged for an interview in which he was to present his secretary and some officers of the gunboat that had taken him to Asuncion, they all went in company, and, as usual, found the old President seated at his table with his big bell-crowned hat on his head. Entering the room uncovered, and bowing as they advanced, the Minister introduced the others, one after another, when, seeing that the old man still kept his hât on, he turned to his companions and said: "The President is right; the air is a little fresh here, 't is better to keep your hats on"; and suiting the action to the word he put on his own hat, and the rest followed his example and remained so till the interview was concluded. Finding that persistency in his own ideas of etiquette might lead to serious embarrassment, and that he could not dictate rules of courtesy to foreign ambassadors, he gave up the point on the hat question, and afterwards received official agents of other countries in a more civilized manner.

As we have already seen, Francia, soon after he had succeeded in making himself absolute, took possession of all the church property and turned the priests adrift. In closing the ports to the ingress of foreigners, he made no exception in favor of papal nuncios or agents, but confiscated to his own use everything that belonged to the church. He appointed a creature of his own, with the title of Apostolic Vicar, to be the head of the church in Paraguay, and to whom all the priests were to be subject and make their reports. The latter were so persecuted, however, that they scarcely ventured to exercise any of their functions, except to receive death-bed confessions and administer extreme unction. Lopez, however, found that he could put the priests to a better use, and that he could make them auxiliaries to his power. He re-established them in the different partidos, and in many cases gave them civil authority in addition to their spiritual functions. But in everything they were required to report to him, and the secrets of the confessional all came to his knowledge as fully as the returns of the custom-house or the diezmo.

He also wished to renew relations with the Pope, that had been entirely suspended during Francia's time. While he was yet consul he made overtures of reconciliation, and asked for the appointment of a bishop, recommending his own brother, Basilio Lopez, for that office. The request was granted, so that he had both the civil and spiritual authority at command.

Basilio Lopez, the bishop, was an eccentric, good-natured priest, without ambition and without avarice, the two qualities that were the guiding principles of Carlos Antonio. He lived in extreme poverty, and gave away nearly all his income in charity. He ridiculed the pretensions of his brother to royal honors and dignities. As bishop he had no authority or power beyond what was conceded by the President, with whose arbitrary rule he never pretended to interfere. He died in 1859, when the Pope was requested to appoint another Bishop of Paraguay. But the Holy See required that an account of the property belonging to the church, that had been withheld for nearly fifty years, should be rendered to him, and restitution made to the church. He also claimed the right of sending a bishop not a Paraguayan, who was to be responsible to him, rather than to the President of Paraguay. Lopez would not listen for a moment to either of these propositions. He would not restore the property, nor would he have a bishop thrust upon him who was not first recommended by himself. He was resolved to be the head of the Church within his own dominions. The Pope threatened to cut off not only Lopez, but all his people, from the body of the true Church, and leave them all to share the fate of the heretic and unconverted. Such threats had no terrors for Lopez, and in a long letter which he addressed to the Pontiff he reviewed the peculiar situation of affairs both temporal and spiritual in Paraguay, and set forth that a divided authority was not compatible with the maintenance of peace and order, and that therefore he should not yield to the demands of his Holiness. If therefore, he added, the Holy Father should shut the gates of Heaven against him and his people, and forevermore refuse to unlock them, he hoped and believed that the good Father and Creator of all would find some other way by which they, his loving and dutiful children, might enter into the abodes of the blessed.

The Pope, finding he could do nothing with such a refractory disciple, finally appointed the person recommended by Lopez for bishop. This was an old priest by the name of Juan Gregorio Urbieta, who was very aged and very infirm. The papal bull authorizing his ordination was received in the latter part of the year 1860.

In giving the history of a republic, it would naturally be supposed that near the close of each constitutional term of office a period of political discussion and excitement would occur. But nothing of that kind was ever known in Paraguay. The people were not allowed to interfere in, or even to talk of, such matters. The Constitution imposed no limits on the power of the President, except that at the first election his term should be for ten years. His own will was his only law. This instrument, prepared by Lopez himself in 1844, and duly ratified by the same Congress that elected him, had some of the provisions of a republican constitution. It provided that the Congress should have the power of making and interpreting the laws, while the execution of them should reside with the President. But practically it left the nomination of the members entirely to the President. All the military and naval forces of the country were declared to be absolutely at his disposal. "He could appoint and remove civil, military, and political employees"; "he could nominate business agents and diplomatic envoys"; "he could exercise the patronage of the churches, the livings, and ecclesiastical persons according to the laws; he could name the bishops and the members of the ecclesiastical senate"; "he could celebrate concordats with the Holy Apostolic See; concede or refuse his approval to the decrees of the council or any ecclesiastical constitution; give or deny the exequatur to the pontifical bulls or briefs, without which requisite nobody should enforce them"; he was to be final judge in appealed causes; "he could augment or diminish the salaries of the public employees." "He could appoint such ministers and secretaries as he pleased, and they were to have the salary he chose to allow them. No minister could give any order without the approbation of the President."

This remarkable Constitution showed a great deal of the Jesuitical cunning characteristic of the first President, as under it, and without violating any of its provisions, he could rule as absolutely as Francia had ever done. It was free from some of the crudities of the first decrees that he promulgated as the organic law of the country, but it gave the whole power to himself. Though it provided that the deputies to Congress should be elected, all the judges and police chiefs who had charge of the elections in the different partidos were appointed by himself, and they sent only such as they knew would be acceptable to him. An instance to the contrary was never known.

The people knew they had no voice in the choice of these deputies, and therefore took no interest in the elections. They only knew that each five years certain men were ordered to the capital, and there something called a Congress was held. Their duties were very simple, and were quickly discharged. As soon as they had organized, Lopez would send in a report of his transactions during the intervening time since the last Congress. Some member known to be in his confidence would move that all his acts be ratified and approved, and the motion was always carried unanimously, without question or debate. Having gone through with this form, the Congress would be declared closed, and the members would return to their homes.

The first term of the Presidency expired in 1854, and a Congress was convoked in the usual manner to ratify his acts and elect him again. But this time, for some reason of his own, he chose to be elected for three years instead of the constitutional term of ten. At the end of that time another Congress was called, when he declined to be a candidate. He had probably taken the hint of declining, and then being forced to accept by the tears and entreaties of the people, from his old enemy Rosas.

For several years before his fall, the tyrant of Buenos Aires, as his term of office was about to expire, would announce that he was tired of public life and sighed for rest and retirement. The people knew but too well what this announcement meant. They took it as a notice that they must all go and beg him not to abandon them to anarchy and ruin, but still extend over them his protecting and paternal care. Therefore every native of sufficient importance to have his absence noted would, on a given day, proceed to his country residence, a league and a half from town, and implore him with tears and protestations of love to remain with them and save them from their own wicked passions for another year. Such an appeal would be too much for the tender heart of Rosas. He would consent to serve one year more, and the people would return to their homes, each man feeling sure that, had he failed to take part in that humiliating scene, he would have had Rosas's mazorcas at his throat within forty-eight hours. The pitiful spectacle, however, served the purpose of Rosas. He had his hirelings in Europe, whose business it was to manipulate the press and deceive the world as to his true character. People in distant parts could not understand how it was, that, if Rosas was the monster that some represented him to be, the whole population should join in such a procession. But when Rosas fell the veil was suddenly lifted. The spell was broken the instant it was known that the hated tyrant had been driven from the country. A universal scream and shout of joy went up from every heart, and the very men who a few months before begged him not to desert them, now, as soon as the spell was broken, wildly sought to destroy everything that reminded them of their former degradation.

People who have never lived in South America cannot understand how, among reasoning, intelligent beings, such things can be. It is hard to give an explanation or account for them. Yet the facts are so; and it will be found that a more terrible spell held the entire people of Paraguay for two generations, and that as a flock of sheep driven by a storm will, heedless of what is before them, rush into a stream where they will all drown, so the Paraguayan nation all yielded, unresisting, to the remorseless tyrant, seemingly having no power to break the charm that inthralled them.

The difficulties that Lopez had had with the English, French, and American governments had caused it to be generally known that he was a tyrant and his government an unmitigated despotism, and it was probably with a view of counteracting this impression that he resorted to the stale trick of Rosas. But he managed the affair in so bungling a manner, his scheme was a laughable failure. When he sent the message to Congress, saying that he declined a re-election, he neglected to take the precaution of telling any confidential friend that he did not mean it, and the members, taken by surprise, believed him to be in earnest. Taking it for granted that the old man intended Francisco Solano for his successor, one member proposed him as a candidate, and he had actually been unanimously elected when the old man learned that his stupid Congress had taken him at his word. He instantly despatched a messenger to announce that he had reconsidered his resolution to decline, and would consent to serve another term of seven years. The election that had just taken place was therefore passed over as informal and void, and Carlos Antonio was again proclaimed elected President of the Republic.

CHAPTER XXXI.

F. S. Lopez in Europe. — Armies moving to the Crimea. — His Visions of Military Glory. — He inaugurates a New Policy for Paraguay. — Warlike Preparations. — Steam Vessels. — Military Arsenal. — Railroad. — Great Increase of the Army. — Death of Carlos Antonio Lopez. — Francisco Solano assumes the Control of the Government. — Character of Carlos Antonio Lopez. — Condition of Paraguay under his Rule. — Government Exactions. — Internal Improvements. — Public Morals. — Education. — Foreign Relations. — Condition of Paraguay as compared with Argentine Provinces.

THE visit of the younger Lopez to Europe had the natural effect of convincing him that Paraguay was not all the world, nor even an important part of it. Educated and indulged as he had been in his youth, and accustomed all his life to have his will over all with whom he came in contact, and to hear his country spoken of as the pivot of civilization and greatness, he learned, when he went abroad, that in the opinion of the people whom he met, his country, instead of being the principal subject of intrigue and interest among foreign governments, was scarcely known beyond the regions of the Plata. It was to him a most humiliating thought, that, great as he was in Paraguay, he was nobody in Europe, and he could not conceal his chagrin that he was not received and treated as the heir apparent of an important empire; and for years after, when speaking of his European tour, he would allude in bitterness of soul to the fact, that, go where he would, the people whom he met did not know where Paraguay was.

Unfortunately, his visit was made during the time of the Crimean War; and having made the campaign of Corrientes, and, according to the *Semanario* established his fame as one of the greatest warriors of modern times, he wondered why he was not consulted by the allied generals. But as they had never heard of the campaign of Corrientes, and only knew of Paraguay as they knew of Patagonia or Sitka, he could only look on at the reviews as a spectator. The sight of great armies in their gay uniforms appealed to the half-Indian nature of the travelling diplomat; and as he found that the heaviest battalions command the greatest attention and respect from the multitude, he returned home with the fixed purpose of making a figure as a military character, and causing it to be known to the world that there was such a country as Paraguay. He had seen that the commanders-in-chief were not expected to take the posts of danger. Their spurs, it was true, had been won by courage and daring, but he was at the head of the Paraguayan army, though he had never seen an enemy or heard the whistling of a bullet. He had entered the ship's cabin through the window, and never seen the forecastle. It was for him to be a great hero without seeing danger, exposure, or fatigue. He returned home after disporting himself for two years in Europe, swelling with these ideas. He had been mortified that he who was so important a character in Paraguay, and in Europe scattered his money with unheard-of profusion, could never cross his stumpy legs beneath an English gentleman's table; but he would return and make a name that should command respect and admiration. The one strong quality of fixity of purpose he possessed to a degree that trespassed on stupidity, and on his return his whole thoughts were turned on making Paraguay a military power.

During the time of Francia the military had never consisted of more than five thousand men, but under the system of the Dictator these were sufficient to overawe the whole country. The number had been much increased by the elder Lopez, and after the return of Francisco Solano the whole policy of the government seemed to be directed to increasing the war power of the nation. The difficulty with Brazil and the American question had arisen at a time when Paraguay was well-nigh powerless for resistance. By duplicity and fraud the impending dangers from these sources had been averted for the time. The policy of the elder Lopez was peace, and he was prepared to make any concession rather than provoke any strong nation to war. But the threats of Brazil and the United States inclined the elder to listen to the counsels of the younger that Paraguay should be put in a state of defence. As we have seen, the fortifications at Humaita had been hurriedly constructed at a time when the Brazilian squadron had been waiting for further instructions, and it would seem that afterwards Francisco Solano had it pretty much his own way in regard to the military disposition of the country. One of the first requisites for effecting his purposes was to obtain a fleet of steam vessels. During his tour in Europe young Lopez had purchased the Tacuari, a fast steamer of light draught, and the Rio Blanco was purchased and sent out while he was yet there. But it would evidently be too expensive to place the country on a war footing, if all the materials for land and naval armament were to come from abroad. Accordingly, before leaving England, young Lopez made arrangements for commencing a military arsenal in Asuncion. He engaged with the established house of J. and A. Blyth, Limehouse, London, machinists and builders, to furnish whatever might be required in their line and to act as general agents, and engaged as director of the establishment and chief engineer for the government Mr. William K. Whytehead, a man of great professional capacity, but who, like most who entered the service of Paraguay, found it a veritable wolf's den whence there were no returning footsteps. Engineers for subordinate branches were brought out from England, and also a master shipbuilder. A couple of light-draught steamers were built to run between Buenos Aires and Asuncion, and all arrangements were perfected by which any amount of arms and ammunition could be introduced into Paraguay, and no one of the neighboring governments be any the wiser for it. At a later period — in 1859 — a railroad was commenced, which was projected to run from the capital to Villa Rica, a distance of about one hundred miles to the eastward, and through the most productive and thickly populated part of the country. It was already completed and in running order for about half the distance — as far as the town of Paraguari — at the commencement of the war. Whether the construction of this road was a part of the war programme of young Lopez or not, it is nevertheless certain that it was of incalculable service in bringing supplies from the interior ; and if the road was begun as a war measure, the fact does credit to the sagacity of the projector. The influence of the younger man with the elder was all directed to increasing the military strength of the country. The standing army was gradually augmented, and at the time of the old man's death was more than double that of the United States before the great Rebellion, or about twenty-five thousand men. Indeed, there had not been a time for the ten years preceding the death of the elder Lopez but that a stranger would imagine, from the number of troops to be seen in the streets of the capital, that he was in some fortress, or at least in a town that for the time was the seat of a military encampment. In effect, martial law prevailed as absolutely as ever it did in a camp. The forms of law were but a device to impose on foreigners, but with the natives it was never necessary to pretend to any forms of legality. The old President, unwieldy and fat, in cocked hat and gorgeous in gold lace, went forth to drive in his carriage, accompanied by a large escort in uniform, and all his orders were obeyed with military promptness and precision. The young expectant went out to ride on horseback with a still larger escort ; and at the doors of each of their houses stood orderlies and lieutenants, cap in hand, ready to mount their waiting horses and dash off as though an enemy were approaching the town.

But it was not all show and parade. The soldiers were all the while being severely drilled, and the people becoming more and more accustomed to a rule entirely military. The war material in the country was being quietly increased at a rate that the neighboring powers would have forcibly objected to had they known anything about it. But all was permitted to go on without interference until the death of Carlos Antonio.

On the accession of the younger Lopez to power, his first measures were of a political character; as we have seen, his first acts were marked with a cruelty that would have appalled his father. His object appears to have been to crush out all hope of anything like a constitutional government, in which some people had been indulging during the latter part of the reign of Don Carlos. He wished to inspire such dread and awe of his person, that all the resources of the country should be absolutely at his disposal, and that his will should be supreme and absolute over the life and property of every individual.

While thus engaged in drawing tighter the ligaments of despotism, he was busily occupied, not only in importing war material from abroad, but in manufacturing it at home. By this time the arsenal was in excellent order for turning out various kinds of work, including steam-engines, cannon of various calibres, and shot and shell to fit them. An iron-mine some thirty leagues to the southeast of the capital, which had been previously opened and worked on a small scale, was put in active operation with a largely increased force. At the same time munitions of war of various kinds were being largely imported. What was the amount of gunpowder introduced into the country during the three or four years before the commencement of the war there is no means of accurately estimating, but it must have been enormous, for it sufficed, with that captured at Coimbra, for a war of more than five years' duration, in which the country lost nearly all its population.

The preparations for war on so grand a scale were commenced when there was no immediate question pending between Paraguay and any other country, nor was there then any more probability of an attack being made upon her than there had been at any time for twenty years. They had all evidently been made with the deliberate purpose of provoking a war, that Francisco Solano Lopez might make a figure as a military character.

The extensive warlike preparations that were being made

during the last few years of the life of Carlos Antonio Lopez were universally attributed to the influence exercised over him by Francisco Solano. The old man, though during all his reign having a large standing army, always professed a great disinclination for war. Though he bore himself insolently in dealing with other nations, he always yielded rather than incur the dangers that might follow in the train of hostilities once commenced. But he had allowed the young man to have his way in increasing the army and accumulating arms that could have been intended only for an offensive war. He was, moreover, in failing health, and during the last years of his life was a great sufferer from a complication of diseases. His complaints were of a chronic character, from which no person at his age ever recovers. He was aware of his approaching dissolution, and had prepared an instrument providing for the succession. What the purport of this paper was will probably never be known, as no one now survives who ever saw it, and from the moment of the old man's death his successor had the custody of all his papers. An impression, however, gained currency among those who had been most intimate with the old President and his wife, that a different instrument, one providing for a temporary triumvirate, had been left by the deceased, and for which the document that was published, naming Francisco Solano as Vice-President, was substituted. His last sickness was very painful, though to the last he held the power absolutely in his own hands, and only relinquished it with his dying breath. As the hour of dissolution approached he was surrounded by his entire family and two English physicians, Drs. Stewart and Barton. The sorrow manifested by his wife and all his own children was undoubtedly sincere and profound ; for, however tyrannical he had been as a ruler over the people, he had certainly never neglected the interests of his family. On the contrary, his worst acts had been committed that he might enrich his wife and children at the expense of his other subjects. They also had more reason than any others to regret his death, for they knew better than anybody else the character of the man who was next to rule, and had greater reason to fear the change. The dying man, like his predecessor Francia, had always been a scoffer at religion, though observing its outward forms, and held the Pope as his natural enemy. His family, however, were anxious to have him reconciled to the Church, and just before he expired he received extreme unction, which the priest, Padre Maiz, was hardly able to complete before he had drawn his last breath. He expired on the evening of September 10, 1862, his son Benigno supporting him in his arms, while Francisco Solano stood at a little distance watching for the last breath; and when Dr. Stewart, seeing that the spirit had fled, turned from the bedside, he said to him, "Is he dead?" The doctor replying in the affirmative, Francisco instantly hastened to the closet where the old man had kept his private and most important papers, took possession of them, and assumed control of the household and of the government. Orders were issued the next morning for the funeral and burial of the deceased President; and on the following day he was taken to the Church of the Trinidad, which he had himself erected years before, and in which a vault had been constructed, by his directions, to receive his remains. Orders were given for the whole population of Asuncion to attend his funeral, and they were implicitly obeyed. To judge from the concourse of people who went from the capital to the Trinidad, a distance of about a league and a half, the loss of the old President was greatly deplored. They were soon to have reason to feel real grief instead of that which on this occasion they manifested under orders.

The period during which Carlos Antonio Lopez was at the head of the government of Paraguay was the most prosperous that the people of that country have known since they achieved their independence. He was a man of a great deal of astuteness and cunning, an indefatigable worker, and of good administrative talent. He came into power as the successor of a despotism such as the world had never known before, and his ideas of government were those which he had learned from the Jesuits and from Francia. Isolated as he had been during the days of his younger manhood, cut off from all intercourse with men of liberal and advanced ideas, and without books, he had no knowledge of any other mode of government than that of an absolute despotism. He had found, early in his public career, that to govern absolutely he must know of all that was going on, and to do this he must keep up a system of espionage similar to that employed by his predecessor. He was not naturally either blood-thirsty or cruel, but he was intensely selfish and greedy for wealth. It was for money that he contracted a matrimonial alliance that would in most countries have made him the derision of all people pretending to respectability ; and like Micipsa, he preferred Jugurtha to his own legitimate children. He trusted and honored the son of Rojas above his own children, because of the estates that, by adopting him, he had brought into the family.

During the time of his reign, the country in some respects made considerable advancement. Yet the common people of the interior were not so well off as they had been in the time of Francia. The governmental exactions during his time had increased fourfold above what they were under the dictatorship, and the people found that it was unsafe to show any signs of prosperity, and that to avoid contributions to the state they should have nothing accumulated above what was indispensable for a bare subsistence. He, however, opened the ports of the country to commerce and navigation, though under such restrictions as were very annoying to all engaged in business. He had built an arsenal, and had brought into the country a large number of skilled artisans ; he established a ship-yard, built a number of sailing vessels and several steamers, and commenced the construction of a railroad from the capital to the central part of the state. The morals of the country, however, rather deteriorated than improved during his time. His three sons, who were regarded politically and socially as at the head of society, all lived in open profligacy ; hence it could hardly be disreputable in others to follow their example. The old man seemed to disapprove of marriage, as he not only permitted but encouraged his sons in their dissolute careers, and he would not listen to the marriage of either of his daughters until the elder had gone astray. He had made some efforts towards the education of the people, but they were so badly directed that at the time of his death not one fourth of the number were able to read and write that there were in the time of Governor Velasco. The language of the country people still continued to be the Guarani; and though parents were required to send their children to school, the teachers were generally so ignorant that the pupils learned little or nothing. If a teacher could read and write Spanish, though but indifferently, he was considered competent for an instructor, and the children would be taught their letters without knowing a word of anything but Guarani; they were also taught to read and spell without knowing the meaning of a single word. The result of all this was, that, at the time of the death of the elder Lopez, few of the people were able to speak, much less to read or write, any written language, and the most of those who could were aged persons who had been taught in the schools that existed before the time of Francia. Since then nearly fifty years had passed, and in that time the mass of the people had relapsed into greater ignorance and barbarism.

In his dealings with other nations Lopez had shown a great deal of ability, and an utter disregard for truth and common honesty. The great defect of his character was an utter disregard of truth, and a want of respect for it in others. He would make the most audacious misstatements, knowing not only that they were false, but that the parties to whom he made them likewise knew them to be false. He had no shame in lying, but he had a policy in it, and this was to magnify himself in the eyes of his own people. He cared little what people beyond the limits of Paraguay might say of his mendacity, of his treachery, or of his bad faith; but he did care that his official papers should set forth such statements of fact as he desired, and that his people should believe them. During his own time the system pursued by him had been successful. If in his intercourse with other nations he had not always outwitted or swindled them, he at least had brought upon himself no armed hostilities and no public humiliation. That this policy would not have served him much longer in this age of progress, when commerce is pushing its wares into all the more remote corners of the earth, is apparent; but it availed so long as he lived, and he seemed to care little for what might come after him. He had contrived, during his long term of power, to get the ill-will of every government with which he had had anything to do, and had never manifested any desire to conciliate them, or to make the friendship of some in case he should be assailed by others. In fact, he was a sort of common enemy; and holding the position he did, where he could not be attacked except at enormous expense by any government that he might offend, he magnified himself in the eyes of his own people by the insults which he offered to his neighbors. The aggregate wealth of the country during his time had not only diminished, but property was so differently distributed that the generality of the people were made sensible of a poverty they had never felt before. Under the reign of the Dictator the cattle were so plenty that the poorest need not suffer for beef, and very little labor was necessary to produce all the corn, mandioca, tobacco, cotton, and sugar-cane required to supply their simple wants. But Lopez, in partially opening the country to commerce, had first consulted the interests of himself and family, and regarded all improvements in the condition of the people as of secondary importance. He sought by every means possible to monopolize every branch of profitable trade and every new industry for his own benefit; and the best agricultural tracts of the whole state were either held by him, under the fiction that they belonged to the government, or became the property of his children. The common people had discovered that there were luxuries in the world they had never thought of in Francia's time; and now they had learned of their existence, they found them beyond their reach.

Though the wants of the people had increased, their means of purchase had not; and yet, for all the tyranny to which they were subjected, and all the evils which in many ways they experienced from the government of the elder Lopez, it may be questioned whether he was not a benefactor to the country. It is true, that, for the small population of the country, he had kept up an immense army, which the people had been obliged to support, he had taxed them without justice and without mercy, and had extorted immense wealth from other people to enrich his own family; yet the country had been all the while at peace, he had kept out the gaucho banditti of the Argentine Confederation, and had introduced some of the arts of peace to which his neighbors had no pretensions. If we institute a comparison between Paraguay and the neighboring province of Corrientes, or any of the states of the Argentine Confederation during the time of Carlos Antonio Lopez, we shall find that the condition of the former was in many respects far preferable to the latter. In Paraguay there was always security for life and property against anything and everything except the government; in Corrientes there was no security, either against the government or the gauchos, who were ever ready to indulge in a rebellion, or to follow any leader that would promise revolution, plunder, and immunity for crime. Notwithstanding this, there was to the peaceable citizen, to the man disposed to attend to his own business, a freedom and a feeling of independence that were utterly unknown in Paraguay. In Corrientes a man could speak of the affairs of the government, could approve or condemn, could transact business without being under the surveillance of spies or informers, could hold social intercourse with his neighbors, and no one would question his right to do so; he could leave whenever he wished, and return when he pleased; he could send his children abroad to be educated, or have them taught in the schools of the town. But in Paraguay he could enjoy none of these privileges. Everything that he did was sure to be made known to the government. He could not discuss the political condition of affairs, or even allude to them; he could not leave the country without the permission of Lopez; and at any time it was in the power of the government to ruin him financially, of which he could never complain without danger of greater evils. Hence it was, that, notwithstanding the gauchos and the revolutions, the instability and insecurity in Corrientes and the other Argentine provinces, people from abroad would go there and engage in business, preferring all the dangers and evils to which they might there be exposed to the enforced silence and slavery of Paraguay.

CHAPTER XXXII.

The Constitution of Paraguay. — Francisco Solano Lopez secures his own Election. — His Treatment of the Friends of the Deceased President. — The Meeting of the Congress. — The Mode of Business and the Debates. — Discussion between Varela and Vasquez. — Fate of Varela. — Padre Maiz and other Priests. — Arrest, Torture, and Death of Chief-Justice Lescano. — Another Conspiracy alleged to have been discovered. — Treatment of the Accused.

THAT somewhat mythical instrument called the Constitution of Paraguay, which few people have ever seen, and a copy or sight of which could not be obtained for many years by any person in the country except Lopez, confers on the President the power of appointing a Vice-President whenever he may choose so to do ; and it provides, moreover, that in case of the death, resignation, or disability of the President, the Vice-President shall act in that capacity until a Congress can be convened and a new president chosen.

Francisco Solano having, on the death of his reputed father, seized all his papers, nothing is known of the provision the deceased President had made for the future, beyond what may be inferred from the acts of his successor. Immediately after the old man's death, Francisco Solano caused it to be announced that he had himself been named Vice-President, and soon after he issued a proclamation for the assembling of a Congress. His next public acts were to cause the arrest of those persons who had enjoyed most of the confidence of, and had most influence with, the late President. Among these were the Chief-Justice of Paraguay, Lescano, and Padre Maiz, both of whom had been the counsellors of the deceased President, and the latter had been the trusted confessor of Francisco Solano's mother and the rest of the family. A number of priests besides Padre Maiz were arrested about the same time, and there was a large increase of the military force stationed in and near the capital. The guards around Lopez's house and the patrols of the streets were doubled, trebled, or quadrupled in number ; and though nothing was known by the general public of the reason for these precautionary measures, there was an impression among the foreigners that something of an important character had been discovered by young Lopez on his getting the entire power into his own hands. The judges, police chiefs, and curas in various districts outside the capital, who had enjoyed more of the respect and confidence of the late President than was pleasing to his successor, were displaced, and men on whom he could entirely rely were substituted for them. The curas, however, who were then removed, were mostly thrown into prison, while those sent to replace them had, in addition to their spiritual duties, the task assigned to them of serving as spies to ascertain if there was any disposition on the part of the chiefs or the judges, or indeed of any others, to elect anybody as president other than Francisco Solano Lopez. The most extreme care was taken to make sure that no one should be selected for the Congress who was not favorable to his election, and well aware of the danger of expressing any doubt or hesitation in the matter. The people of the different districts were not to be consulted at all ; in fact, they never had been from the first Congress called by Francia. The judge, the chief, and the cura were to meet together on a certain day at the office of one of their number, and then and there name the member of Congress for that district, and usually one of their number was selected, and the one that Lopez had privately intimated to them was his choice. The members named from the capital were generally those citizens who were most intelligent, and would give respectability and character to the general body. Some of those, however, who were first selected, had their names struck from the list afterwards by Lopez, with orders to substitute others, they having ventured to discuss with their neighbors the propriety of certain changes in the organic law of the country. One man, in particular, by the name of Manuel Rojas, a man of large wealth and of more general information than was often possessed by a Paraguayan, had ventured to express an opinion that, as there was to be a new Congress, and a new president elected, it would be a favorable time for the adoption of a constitution such as would define the powers of the Executive, and could not be superseded or disregarded at his pleasure or caprice. This man's name was immediately struck from the list of Congressmen, and he fell into disgrace; and though not arrested for some time after, he could never regain the lost favor of Lopez, and finally perished, as a common soldier, in the trenches.

The members of Congress thus selected assembled in Asuncion; and on the 16th of October, 1862, the Congress was formally opened in the Government House, or *cabildo*. The Vice-President presided over their deliberations. A large military force was kept in readiness for any emergency, and the public parades, which were made in front of the Government House, served the double purpose of displaying the perfection of the drill and discipline, and of warning the members against any act that might cause their arms to be turned against themselves. The Congress being opened and the message of the President read to them, and the object of their being called together having been announced, Don Nicolas Vasquez, who had been at one time the Minister for Foreign Affairs, and was perhaps the best-informed man on political matters in Paraguay, in a highly flattering and eulogistic speech proposed the name of Francisco Solano Lopez as the choice of the people of Paraguay for the Presidency. But in spite of the care that Lopez had taken to have no one in the Congress who would make any embarrassing suggestions or ask any impertinent questions, one man ventured to suggest the propriety of having a constitution adopted for Paraguay. Lopez, who in all his preliminary arrangements had manifested great fear lest questions might be started that would lead to discussion, and knew if the members were permitted to state their grievances the result of the Congress might be very different from what he desired, instantly arose and said to the convention that he would allow no such insult to the memory of his father as was contained in that suggestion; and the member, in his ignorance and simplicity, sunk back into his seat. Notwithstanding his discomfiture, a member by the name of Varela, a man of large wealth for Paraguay, — indeed, by far the richest man in the country except the different members of the Lopez family, — rose to his feet, and after expressing the greatest admiration for the talents and patriotism of the Vice-President, and alluding to the debt of gratitude which all Paraguayans owed to him, said he was still in doubt whether he was eligible to the Presidency. Though disposed to support him for that office as the most fit and proper man for the position, he was embarrassed by the fact that the constitution of the country provided that the Presidency should never become the property or heritage of any family, and that as Francisco Solano Lopez was the son of the late President, he did not see how he could, with due regard to that instrument, approve of his election. He would, however, be greatly pleased to hear the views of other persons, and if this objection were removed he should support the person whose name had been presented with the greatest pleasure. Vasquez replied to him, stating that although the Constitution did have that provision, nevertheless it was not the meaning of it that the people or the Congress should be thereby fettered or restricted in their choice, the true meaning of the clause being, that no President should ever transmit his power to any member of his family by will or official decree, but that the Congress might elect whomsoever it pleased; the article in the Constitution was not intended to restrict or limit the people in their choice, it was only to prohibit the head of the government from transmitting his power in defiance of the will of the people. Varela, in reply, said that the speech of Vasquez had removed all doubt in his mind in regard to the constitutional provision, and that therefore, without any hesitation, he should vote for the election of Lopez. No further discussion was had, and Lopez was declared to be elected President of the Republic of Paraguay for a period of ten years, and the booming of cannon soon announced the glad tidings to the people of Asuncion. The Congress was then dissolved, and the members, with the exception of Varela, returned to their homes. Though no account of the proceedings was ever published, and the meeting had been secret, yet it was soon after known by several persons who were not members of the Congress that Varela had hinted an objection in regard to the eligibility of Lopez, and at first it was supposed that the discussion was but a farce which had been previously arranged, by order of Lopez, between Varela and Vasquez ; that the former was to start the discussion and the latter to refute his objections so clearly and forcibly that all the others, if they entertained any doubt, might be convinced, and it would hence appear that the members had had the subject before them and voted understandingly upon it. This idea, however, was soon after dispelled, when it was known that, on the adjournment of Congress, Varela was immediately arrested, his property confiscated, and himself thrown into prison, from which he never went forth alive. How long he lived, or when he died, or under what circumstances, was never made public.

Lopez, being now duly installed as President, proceeded to the trial of those persons whom he had caused to be arrested immediately after taking the reins of power. Padre Maiz and Chief-Justice Lescano were subjected to a military trial. Maiz had usually been regarded by the people of Paraguay as a man of great purity of life, and was by far the best educated of all the priests in Paraguay. He was at the head of the theological college at which candidates for orders received their education, and the offence charged against him at the time of his removal from that position and his arrest was that he had taught his pupils some heretical doctrines. He was placed in solitary confinement and treated with great brutality, and for three years subjected to a series of the most cruel tortures and indignities. Being about the age of Lopez, in their youth they had been schoolmates together, and Maiz being in appearance and natural abilities the superior of the two, he had even at that early period provoked the jealousy and enmity of him who now had it in his power to obtain satisfaction. The chief of the tribunal that investigated the charges against him was Colonel Wenceslao Robles, the military officer next in rank to Lopez himself, and though the proceedings of the trial were secret, it was given out as by authority that the prisoner had confessed to a multiplicity of crimes; that, while it had been supposed that his conduct had been extremely pure, and that he had always observed that sanctity and chastity which the rules of his order enjoined upon all its members, his life had really been one of the deepest hypocrisy and lewdness. These reports, though put in circulation as it were semi-officially, were nevertheless discredited by the better class of the people in Asuncion. They could have believed such stories of any other priest in the country, but of Padre Maiz they had never heard anything inconsistent with the life of a saint.

Chief-Justice Lescano was subjected to similar treatment to that inflicted on Padre Maiz, but from his age he did not long survive his fall and disgrace. He was a man of about sixty years of age, of large frame and full habit, of very dark complexion, showing that he was more Guarani than Spanish. He had been selected for the position of chief-justice for nothing but the personal regard of the elder Lopez, for he was an ignorant man, having no knowledge of law and very little of anything else. He had lived all his life in the interior, until summoned to the capital to take this office, and had no ambition whatever, except to pass his days on his estancia with his family, living in rude plenty as the most important and influential man of his own *partido*. What offence he had committed against the new President will probably never be known. He was thrown into prison immediately after his accession to power, loaded with heavy fetters, supplied with the coarsest kind of food, with a sentinel over him all the time, and probably ignorant of the cause of his disgrace. After being confined for several weeks in a dark and damp room, he was taken, with his fetters still on him, through the streets and across the plaza to another prison, near the President's house. He, however, was spared the mortification of being seen by many people in this humiliating plight, as he was removed from one prison to the other at siesta time, when few people were abroad to witness his disgrace. He was accompanied by a guard of soldiers with drawn swords, and forced to make his way on foot with his heavy fetters, consisting of iron rings on his ankles, with a bar between them so heavy that it was with extreme difficulty that the old man could make any progress. After reaching his new quarters he was subjected to such cruel treatment that he rapidly sunk under it; and as it was evident he could not long survive, he was sent to the hospital, and, a few days after, expired. Among the lowest class of the people a report got into circulation that he had been poisoned, which coming to the ears of the President he caused a post-mortem examination to be made by two English physicians, who certified in an official report that he had died from natural causes. As soon as his death was made known to the chief of police, he sent for the wife of the deceased and told her she was then at liberty to go and visit her husband; that he was then free, and she might go to the hospital and take care of him. Delighted with the unexpected news she hurried thither only to find that her husband was laid out for the post-mortem examination. The man so honored by the late President was sent to his last resting-place in a rough cart, accompanied only by a single slave. None of his near relatives were permitted to give him a decent burial, and none of his other friends in the capital could venture to show any respect to his memory without exposing themselves to a like fate.

It was also announced that a conspiracy had been discovered. In fact, Lopez told several individuals (foreigners) that such was the case, and that Padre Maiz and his brother Benigno were the principal instigators of it. He said each had long been scheming to have himself elected to the Presidency whenever the office should become vacant, that each had a considerable number of delegates in the Congress, who were secretly in their favor, and that only a day or two before the Congress met did he learn of the dangers that surrounded him. He said he had early suspected Padre Maiz, and had taken measures to circumvent his plans; but it was only a few hours before the session opened that he became aware of the treachery of his brother Benigno. He said that the heart of one of the persons in his brother's interest had failed him about thirty-six hours before the Congress met, and he had come to him and confessed the whole plot of his younger brother, and he then ascertained that the number of those who were pledged to the support of Benigno would have been sufficient, with those whom he knew to be in the interest of Maiz, to have defeated his own election. He professed to have been greatly surprised, grieved, and mortified when he first learned of the perfidy of his brother, for whom he pretended such affection that he could not proceed against him as he did against Maiz and some others. He was, however, banished into the interior, and ordered to remain upon one of his estancias, and was not permitted to leave it for several months, and then only at the solicitation of his mother. Maiz, however, was kept about three years in prison. After the war began he was taken to head-quarters, where after a while he succeeded in making his peace with Lopez, and subsequently became his chief inquisitor, and had the satisfaction of repaying Lopez for his treatment of him by being made the instrument of destruction of nearly every one of the friends who surrounded him at the time of his own incarceration.

It may also be stated here, that Benigno and Robles were both afterwards executed by order of Lopez; the former was first tortured by his unnatural brother until death would soon have relieved him from his power had he not been executed.

CHAPTER XXXIII.

Revolution in the Banda Oriental. — Venancio Flores. — Juan F. Giro elected President. — Treachery and Violence. – Machinations of Paranhos. — Flores made Minister of War. — Flight of Giro. — The Triumvirate. — Flores as President. — His Overthrow. — Don Luis Lamas. — War between Buenos Aires and the Argentine Confederation. — Bartolome Mitre. — Battles of Cepeda and Pavon. — Rebellion of Cesar Diaz. — Antonio de las Carreras. — Bernardo P. Berro elected President. — The Flores Invasion. — Florencio Varela. — "La Tribuna" of Buenos Aires. — Progress of the Revolution. — Flores sustained by Outlaws and Brazilians.

BEFORE proceeding further with the course of events in Paraguay, it is necessary to turn aside and consider the political situation of affairs in the three countries that afterwards became parties to the Triple Alliance. The immediate occasion taken by Lopez to interfere in the political questions of the lower countries of the Plata having been the revolution in the Oriental Republic, a brief sketch of the origin and progress of that revolution will here be given.

The leader of the small band of gauchos that in 1863 invaded the Banda Oriental with the avowed object of overthrowing the established government was one Venancio Flores. He had been long known as a leader of gauchos, or *caudillo.* He was of mixed blood, the Indian predominating over the Spanish. Inferior in natural parts to Artigas, he was nevertheless distinguished for all the bad qualities of that famous freebooter. Of iron frame and tireless activity, the wild life of the gaucho was, in his opinion, the perfection of human happiness. Crafty, cruel, and ignorant, all his tastes and instincts found free indulgence as a leader of banditti. The luxuries and comforts of civilized life were things which he could not appreciate.

In the course of his career as a gaucho leader, whose vocation was revolution and whose subsistence was the plunder of the estancieros, now making a foray into one section, now skulking for his life in another, he naturally acquired an intimate knowledge of the topography of the country, and knew every path, trail, and crossing throughout its whole extent. In his youth he distinguished himself as a leader of the gauchos, and during the nine years' siege of Montevideo, which was maintained by Rosas and Oribe, Flores attained the rank of colonel. He belonged to the inside or colorado party, as it was called, but achieved no marked distinction. Of regular warfare he was entirely ignorant, and as he had no education and no marked abilities of any kind save as a guerilla leader, he held a subordinate position until Rosas had fallen and the long siege was raised. The party to which he belonged previous to the siege had come into power by a revolution, and the partisans of the ejected government had, under General Oribe, made the great error of calling in the aid of Rosas, in order to regain their power. They formed then, as they have ever since, much the most numerous and respectable part of the population, and but for allying themselves with a cause so odious as that of Rosas, would doubtless soon have regained their ascendency. But the despotism of that unnatural tyrant was so sanguinary and so obnoxious to foreign nations, that the English and French governments were both induced to give countenance and support to the revolutionary colorados, and in this way, and by the assistance thus rendered, they were able to defend themselves for the long period of nine years. With the fall of Rosas all foreign intervention ceased, matters soon resumed their normal state, and the blancos again came into power. The colorado party contained more of the gaucho element than the other, or blanco, party ; and yet, after the nine years' siege, though it had been finally successful, it was now in a hopeless minority.

The first election that took place after the fall of Rosas and Oribe resulted in the choice of Juan Francisco Giro as President. He was elected with little opposition, for though known as a blanco, he was regarded as a man of good character and of liberal principles. The election of Giro as President in a manner which clearly showed him to be the choice of a majority promised to put an end to the miseries of the Orientales. But the gaucho element among the colorados preferred anything rather than peace and the enforcement of the laws. There was no complaint of the administration that it was of a partisan character, or that the colorados were persecuted under it. On the contrary, its policy had been to harmonize the discordant elements by forming a cabinet of a mixed character,—even going so far as to make General Cesar Diaz, the future revolutionist, the Minister of War,—and by ignoring as far as possible old party feuds. The election and inauguration took place on the 1st of March, 1852. All seemed to promise well, and the country appeared to be entering on a course of peace and consequent prosperity. But this condition of affairs did not accord at all with the gaucho ideas of some of the colorado chieftains, and the 18th of July, 1853, was the occasion of a formidable outbreak. This day is the anniversary of Oriental independence, and is always observed as a holiday and national jubilee. The various military companies, as usual, took part in the festival, and on the morning of that day a stranger would have imagined, on seeing the different bodies of troops, some composed chiefly of blancos, others entirely of colorados, uniting to celebrate in perfect harmony the common independence, that the era of good feeling had indeed arrived.

Though the day opened thus auspiciously, some of the colorado leaders took advantage of it to effect a revolution which in all its aspects was eminently characteristic of the Spanish-Indian character. The troops of the line that had formerly been colorados, and who were mostly negroes, or of mixed negro and Indian blood, were in the morning secretly served with ball-cartridges, for what purpose they were not then advised. They were marching through one street at the same time that a body of the National Guards, composed mainly of young men of the best families in Montevideo, was passing through another. The colorado leaders arranged to have their troops drawn up in a line on the main plaza of the town at a time when the National Guards should pass by with their music playing and banners flying. When directly in front of them, the troops of the line, who by this time had learned that something desperate was expected of them, received the signal to fire. A ruthless massacre followed. The National Guards, taken by surprise, with their arms not loaded, and having no ball-cartridges, could make little resistance, and what they did make was at great disadvantage. The only resource left to those who had not been killed or wounded was to fly. As many as thirty-eight of the young blancos, who had turned out in the morning for a holiday, lay dead on the plaza or in the streets.

As was to be expected from his character and antecedents, Flores was one of the instigators of this treacherous plot. The city was for the time at the mercy of him and his fellow-conspirators, and they followed up the advantage gained by other acts of violence and terror intended to strike dismay into the blancos and prevent them from rallying to the support of the government. President Giro at the first outbreak undertook to quell the disturbance, but he soon discovered that the slaughter of the men was not the work of an excited, purposeless mob, but that it had been instigated by leading colorados for political objects. Giro was an amiable man, and enjoyed the respect of all people and parties to a rare degree, but it was that respect which is awarded to honesty and good intentions, and not that which firmness and energy command. Instead of treating the authors of this outbreak as ruffians and traitors, and calling upon the people to sustain him, he began to temporize with them and treat with them for terms. The whole people, not only in Montevideo, but throughout the entire Republic, were shocked and disgusted at the conduct of the gaucho leaders. Even the colorados, the few respectable people among them, were tired of war and wanted peace. At this time an envoy of Brazil, like a night-bird of ill-omen, was hovering nigh, watching the occasion again to embroil the beautiful Banda Oriental in war. This envoy, whose hand may be seen in almost every bad thing that has been attempted by Brazil for the last twenty years, — and the number is very large, — was then in Montevideo as minister. He was a man of great talent and address, one who combined in himself the tact of Talleyrand and the principles of Machiavelli. With Judas-like affection for Giro, he counselled him to treat with the colorados. The President weakly yielded to his advice, and made conditions with the authors of the massacre, that, instead of being executed as traitors and murderers, they should be admitted into his counsels and have the most important and influential positions under his administration. Afterwards it was found that the whole plot for the massacre and revolution had been the work of the Brazilian envoy, though at the time Giro suspected nothing. Indeed, the bland face and amiable manners of José Maria de Silva Paranhos were enough to disarm men far more astute than Giro of suspicion or distrust. Irresolute and distracted by insidious counsels, he began to parley with the chiefs of the revolution. He asked what were their demands; and they, having nothing to allege against his government, made some jumbling pretence about the necessity of constitutional guaranties, — which guaranties were that the chief offices of trust and power should be conferred on themselves.

Giro yielded to their terms, and Flores was named Minister of War, after which he showed his regard for constitutional guaranties and established authority by conduct so arbitrary and violent, that the President, in fear of his life, fled on board of one of the neutral war vessels in the harbor. Giro feared another riot, in which event he was well aware that his War Minister would take good care to make him the recipient of a vagrant bullet. The threats of Flores having thus accomplished their object, the Minister of War declared the Giro government to have terminated with the flight of the President. He then assumed to himself provisional powers as the executive head, and organized a government to suit himself. This was a triumvirate composed of himself and two old partisan generals, Lavalleja and Ribera, both of them so advanced in years as to be nothing but lay-figures in his plan of administration. In fact, they both died soon after having this doubtful honor conferred upon them, and Flores was then left free from any encumbrances so long as his military forces sufficed to repress the dissatisfied blancos. But he saw that he could not hold his position without some pretence of right. He therefore convoked a body of his partisans, and, calling it a Congress, bade them choose him President, and they duteously obeyed. He then took the title of President of the Oriental Republic of the Uruguay.

But it was not in the nature of things that an illiterate gaucho should long be tolerated as the President of a people so advanced and so well informed in the principles of constitutional government as were the Orientales at that time. Montevideo, which is to the country as Paris to France, is eminently a commercial and cosmopolitan city, and its interests were too important to be intrusted to such a semi-savage as Flores. Many members of his own party soon became disgusted at the spectacle which their chief presented, and in 1855, the year after his pretended election to the Presidency, they made a demonstration against him and overthrew his government, and, in place of Flores, declared Don Luis Lamas provisional President.

Flores, after his overthrow, fled to Entre Rios, and threw himself on the hospitality of General Urquiza. The latter gave him shelter and protection, but Flores soon passed over to Buenos Aires, then a province by itself, independent of the Argentine Confederation. It had been so since the fall of Rosas in 1852. To all intents and purposes it was an independent state, though not formally recognized as such by foreign nations. The Governor was in fact the sovereign executive head of the nation, and his office was more important than the Presidency of the Confederation.

Flores, soon after crossing over to Buenos Aires, was employed by the government there to chastise the pampas Indians on the frontier, who at the time were very troublesome, making frequent raids into the more advanced settlements, and driving off in large numbers the cattle and horses of the inhabitants. He was exactly fitted for this service, and successfully accomplished the work he was sent to perform.

Afterwards, in 1859, when war broke out between Buenos Aires and the Confederation, Flores offered his services to the former, though his old friend and benefactor, Urquiza, was President of the latter, and commander-in-chief of its armies. The Buenos Airean forces were under the command of a young general distinguished at the time as a soldier, but distinguished rather as a scholar, historian, and orator than for any military successes. This was Bartolome Mitre, author of the History of Belgrano. This brief campaign resulted disastrously to the Buenos Airean troops, who suffered an irretrievable defeat at the battle of Cepeda, a place within the limits of their own province, and near the line of the frontier that separated it from the province of Santa Fé. By the fortune of war, Buenos Aires now, instead of dictating the terms of union with the Confederation, as was its purpose in taking up arms, was a supplicant for peace and union on the best conditions that could be obtained. The conditions conceded by the victors were just and liberal, but Buenos Aires, which in disputes with the provinces had always arrogated to itself the lion's share, was not long satisfied with them. The terms made by the sick lion would not content him when he had recovered his strength, and it was not long before an occasion was found for breaking the compact agreed upon after the unfortunate affair of Cepeda. A revolution in one of the interior provinces, San Juan, was made the occasion for a demonstration against the central government. By this time General Mitre had risen to be Governor of Buenos Aires. The people of that city and province were restive and discontented under the peace of Cepeda. The capital had been established at Parana, and the provincial towns above Buenos Aires had the right to import directly from foreign countries, under a system of differential duties, in such vessels as did not touch at Buenos Aires. Thus the principal *entrepôt* of the river was liable to lose its long-abused privilege of taking toll on all foreign merchandise introduced into the interior. A rupture, therefore, was inevitable. The then President of the Confederation, Dr. Santiago Derqui, had been put forward as the candidate of Urquiza, of whom he had been the principal minister; but having obtained the power, he was not the pliant instrument in the hands of his chief that the latter had expected to find him. Urquiza, therefore, encouraged a conflict with Buenos Aires, not doubting that he should be at the head of the military of the provinces, and that, having successfully dispersed the Porteños, he could easily dispose of President Derqui, and again put himself at the head of the entire country as President of all the provinces, including Buenos Aires. But fortune, which had hitherto greatly favored the famous gaucho of Entre Rios, now jilted him. The two armies came face to face on the opposite banks of a small river called the Pavon. The Porteños were commanded by General Mitre. The immediate command of the cavalry, however, was given to General Flores. The forces of Urquiza were about equal in number to those of Mitre, and his cavalry were under the command of a famous desperado and cut-throat named Saá. The two cavalry commanders were well pitted against each other, both men of personal courage, and both of that peculiar ferocity only found in the mixed Spanish and Indian races which delights in the amusement of cutting throats.

This battle of Pavon could hardly be called a battle at all. Neither party seemed to have any stomach for the fight, and, as far as the cavalry were concerned, there seemed to be a rivalry as to which should first run away. The main body of each fled simultaneously before crossing lances, though Flores kept in hand a sufficient number to render important service at the critical moment, and convert defeat into victory. The infantry of Urquiza, however, behaved better, and apparently the day was won, when he, at the moment the Porteños were giving ground, took fright and ran away, and was soon followed by the whole army, except the cavalry that had got the start of him in the flight. Both armies considered themselves at that moment defeated, and Mitre was on the point of ordering a retreat when he learned that Urquiza and all his army had fled. He therefore ordered an immediate march on Rosario, which place he entered as a conqueror. It was thus that the victory of Pavon, by the aid of Flores, was won by General Mitre; and the battle was not only the turning-point in his own fortunes, but in the history of South America.

The defeat of Pavon and the flight and disgrace of Urquiza, the only man having influence and prestige enough to make resistance to the pretensions of Buenos Aires with any hope of success, left the Porteños complete masters of the situation. A convention was soon after called, at which all the provinces were represented. President Derqui having fled, his office was vacant, and it was proposed to make Mitre acting President till a general election could be held. The question of the capital was the only one on which the convention was divided. All acknowledged Mitre as having both capacity and prestige equal to the occasion, but many of the provincial delegates objected to Buenos Aires as the seat of the federal government. Mitre, however, quickly cut this knot of dispute by peremptorily refusing to accept the provisional Presidency unless Buenos Aires were made the capital. He was then Governor of the latter, and said he preferred to remain so to accepting the Presidency of the whole Confederation, if by so doing he must follow the government to some provincial town. The delegates had no alternative but to give him his own terms, and the convention passed a resolution establishing Buenos Aires as the capital for five years. The next year, 1862, in the month of October, a presidential election was held. Mitre was the only candidate, and he was accordingly unanimously elected for the constitutional term of six years.

In the mean while, Flores, after the battle of Pavon, was living a fugitive from his own country, and debarred his favorite pastime of stealing horses or ravaging the country. To support himself he entered the service of a rich estanciero, who had large tracts of land on the frontier, and whose flocks were exposed to the raids of the neighboring Indians.

But the life of a cattle-tender could not long content a person so restless and ambitious as Flores. His own country, the Banda Oriental, had, since his absence, enjoyed a degree of prosperity never known before. The people had so far forgot their partisan animosities, that the blancos and colorados, in May, 1856, united to elect Don Gabriel Antonio Pereira as President, notwithstanding he was of colorado antecedents and during the long siege of Montevideo had belonged to the inside party. But he was considered a moderate and just man, and his counsellors and ministers were nearly all taken from the blanco party. Thus there seemed at last a prospect that old party antipathies might pass into oblivion, and that the powers of the government might be directed to developing the resources of the country, rather than to avenging past transgressions. The President had been elected in such a manner that no one questioned that he was the choice of the majority, and the country soon assumed a condition of peace and quiet entirely unprecedented. Emigrants began to pour in in large numbers, and capital, as it could be invested to great advantage, flowed in freely. The material wealth of the country began to increase at a rate almost without parallel. With the Spanish-American the itch for revolution is a chronic disease, and at this time, notwithstanding the great prosperity that the country was enjoying as the result of peace and good government, a wild and foolish attempt was made to effect another revolution. It had, perhaps, less justification and excuse than any revolution ever attempted before or since. The head-quarters of the revolutionists was in Buenos Aires, where public meetings were held to raise money and enlist men for the invasion of the Banda Oriental, though the government professed to be at peace with its neighbor and to frown on all attempts at invasion of a friendly country. But the Governor, Don Valentin Alsina, was notoriously in sympathy with the filibusters, and winked at their open violations of law while he encouraged their more secret proceedings. At length, when all was supposed to be ripe for the revolution, Flores set out with a small force of gauchos to wait the course of events and make a diversion in the northern part of the country ; and soon after a vessel belonging to or chartered by the Buenos Airean government, with arms and ammunition taken from the public arsenal at Buenos Aires, with such a force of men as by fraud and force could be pressed aboard, was despatched to Montevideo to effect a landing and set up a standard of rebellion.

The person in command of this party was the ex-Minister of War, General Cesar Diaz. He was a turbulent demagogue, of military experience sufficient to render him a dangerous subject, and therefore, to keep him quiet, he had been sent to Buenos Aires in the capacity of consul-general for the Banda Oriental. Here he fell in with outlaws and other traitors, and began his machinations to subvert the government he was sworn to support. His treason becoming known, he was removed from his post as consul, when he threw off all pretensions of loyalty, and began openly to denounce as a hideous tyranny the government to which his country was subjected. With the connivance of the government of Buenos Aires, backed up by arms and ammunition publicly loaned to him from the national arsenal, he set forth on his ill-starred expedition. He reached Montevideo and effected a landing without opposition on the side of the river opposite the town. The government was in a fright and quandary. The ministers resigned, and everything bade fair for the capture of the town by the invaders. At this time President Pereira called into his councils another class of men, one of whom was a young lawyer named Antonio de las Carreras, then but twenty-eight years of age. He was a violent partisan, a man of great energy, and, for his years, of great influence, and was perhaps the only man in the country equal to the emergency. He was asked to take the direction of the departments of government and of foreign affairs. He refused to accept the position except on condition that he should be unfettered by any superior authority. The President yielded to his terms, and the fate of the rebellion was sealed. With marvellous energy he caused to be organized a force far outnumbering the invaders, and all who, since their landing, had joined their standard. These troops, under command of General Medina, were sent after Diaz, with orders to despatch him and his followers as nothing more nor less than outlaws and robbers. Diaz, surprised at the energy of the government, fell back, and retreated to the Rio Negro. Here his little force, now dwindled down to some four hundred men, was surrounded at a place called Quinteros, and compelled to surrender at discretion. Medina promised no terms, and indeed, had he done so, he would have exceeded his authority, for his orders were to pursue them as outlaws, robbers, and traitors. Nevertheless, after the surrender he hesitated to execute his instructions without direct orders from the government. These orders were promptly sent to him. He was commanded to summarily execute all the leaders and such notorious criminals as had taken refuge in his ranks. Diaz and eight others of the political traitors were accordingly shot, besides fourteen of the well-known gaucho murderers.* This energetic action on the part of Carreras had its intended effect. The revolutionary spirit was quelled. For the first time in the history of the Plata the promoters of

* The execution of these prisoners taken at Quinteros has been the subject of a great deal of controversy in the Plata, and many versions of the affair have been published by those who justified and those who condemned it. By the latter it has been called a cruel, unnecessary massacre, and the number of persons executed has been often stated to have been some two or three hundred. My own account of the affair was derived from Dr. Carreras himself, with whom I afterwards became intimately acquainted, and whom I found to be a most reliable and courteous gentleman. He was a very violent partisan, but he always justified his action in the Quinteros affair, as it has generally been justified by his own party. It is certain that the spirit of revolution which had been so rife in these countries as to render anything like permanent prosperity impossible received a severe check from this act. But whether it was wise and just or not, it rendered Carreras the most odious and unpopular man among the colorados, gauchos, and revolutionists in the state; and when afterwards he was again called into the government to put down a greater rebellion, he was denounced as an assassin, and every opprobrious epithet was applied to him by the colorado party in Montevideo and their sympathizers in Buenos Aires. His terrible death, however, years later, at the hands of Lopez, seemed to disarm even his worst enemies, for not one of them could have desired for him so cruel a fate as he finally suffered.

a revolution thoroughly unjustifiable, and set on foot solely to serve the ambitious and selfish purposes of treacherous neighbors and gaucho chieftains, had been summarily dealt with. Instead of being bought off, as on previous occasions, and promised honors and offices if they would lay down their arms, the leaders were shot, as they deserved to be. The revolution-makers saw their occupation was gone. Men of peace saw a new prospect opening, and that they were not so liable to be robbed and murdered every time a poverty-stricken gaucho thought to better his fortunes by attempting a revolution. The spirit of the chronic revolutionists was broken, the caudillos had received such a check that for years none of them ventured to get up another rebellion, and the country enjoyed peace and prosperity until 1863, when the same Flores, who unfortunately did not share the fate of his fellow-traitor Diaz, began a revolution that was to involve the whole valley of the Plata in a general war.

After the suppression of the Diaz-Flores invasion, the country continued in a state of quiet and prosperity until the end of President Pereira's constitutional term of office. The state being at peace, the blanco party, as a matter of course, elected their candidate, Don Bernardo P. Berro, as the successor of Pereira. Though a blanco, the new President was very little of a partisan, and probably as little obnoxious to the colorados as any man in the country not of their own party. There was little or no opposition to his election, and no one pretended to question that he was the constitutional President for the prescribed term of four years. The administration of President Berro was extremely fortunate for the material interests of the country. The Diaz revolution having proved so disastrous to its leaders, the spirit of gauchoism seemed in a great measure subdued. Emigrants in great numbers came in with capital and bought land, and the sheep, cattle, and horses multiplied prodigiously. The interest realized on investments was enormous, and, extravagant as it may seem, it is not too much to say that the aggregate capital of the country more than doubled within the period of six years from 1858 to 1863 inclusive.

But to this general aspect of affairs in the Republic of Uruguay an exception is to be made in regard to that part of the country bordering on Brazil. For a long time affairs on this frontier had been in a most unsettled and turbulent state. An insignificant stream called the Cuaraim separates the two countries for a part of the distance, and during the time of the long siege of Montevideo many Brazilians crossed over into Uruguayan territory, where they bought lands and established and stocked estancias. The country along this frontier is the finest grazing section in all South America, and would be a source of great wealth to Uruguay if it could be controlled by the Montevidean government. But the Brazilians there were so numerous and wealthy, consisting of at least fifty thousand persons, or one sixth of the entire population of the country, that they defied the laws, and being beyond the jurisdiction of their own government they were almost independent of any restraint. Between them and the natives of the country there existed not only the intense antipathy which prevails between the two races, but the feuds and collisions between parties had been so frequent that they had come to regard each other as natural enemies. The Brazilian intruders, whenever they were molested in their attempts to run off their cattle without the payment of the export duty, or were interfered with in any of their unlawful proceedings, appealed to their own government for redress ; and it was both the policy and practice of Brazil to encourage them in their encroachments by listening to their appeals and promising to exact indemnity from Uruguay. Both Brazil and Buenos Aires had long coveted the Banda Oriental, and the policy of each had long been to make it an integral part of its own territory. Thus this little tract of country, the finest in South America, became an apple of discord, jealously watched by its two powerful neighbors.

Though under the strongest treaty stipulations to respect its independence, they seemed to be ever watching for an occasion to violate it, and each of them was bent on annexing it to its own possessions. The party in sympathy with the colorados of Montevideo was the more numerous and powerful in Buenos Aires. The administration of President Mitre notoriously sympathized with the outlaws and traitors, whose crimes rendered their residence in their own country incompatible with the public safety. Flores, restless and uneasy, was tired of his life of cattle-tender, or *capataz;* and, leaving the care of his flocks and herds, he came to Buenos Aires to try his fortune again as traitor and invader of his native land. He had great personal claims on President Mitre. He had rendered important services at the battle of Pavon, which was the turning-point of Mitre's fortunes and had made him President of the Argentine Republic. The more influential newspapers in Buenos Aires openly encouraged him to proceed, and called on the people of Buenos Aires to come forward and aid in raising both men and money for the army of the "liberator," who was to redeem the suffering people of the Banda Oriental from the grinding tyranny of Berro. The leading newspaper, *La Tribuna,* frantically called on the rich to give their money and the poor to give their services in the great cause of Oriental liberty. The conductors of this paper were natives of Montevideo and intensely partisan. They were the sons of Don Florencio Varela, a man of great talent and influence in his time, who had fled from Buenos Aires to escape the knives of Rosas's organized assassins, and, during the siege of Montevideo rendered great service to the inside party. Being sent on a diplomatic mission to Europe, it was through his influence that France and England were induced to take sides with the besieged. Rosas's favorite mode of getting rid of persons obnoxious to him was to send out his *mazorcas* to quietly assassinate them. That was the end of the affair; for as everybody knew by whose orders these things were done, nobody dared, except in very rare cases, to make comment or inquiry. But Varela was beyond the reach of the mazorcas. Rosas therefore ordered his general, Oribe, to find some other means to put him out of the way. Oribe obeyed, and sent a wretch by the name of Cabrera to do his bloody work. This hired murderer succeeded in getting within the lines of the besieged and executed his terrible commission. Naturally the sons of this man were intense in their hatred of Rosas, and of Oribe, and of the blancos who called in the aid of such allies, and, forgetful of all questions of right or justice or international law, they advocated, in their paper, doctrines in justification of this Flores invasion that would disgrace the King of Dahomey or the Emperor of Abyssinia. Their journal did not advocate open and manly war against the Banda Oriental, for it was impossible to devise a pretext for that; but it took the ground that the minority of any country, when they could not get what they wanted under the established forms of law, were justified in making a rebellion and overturning the government by force of arms. If outnumbered and outvoted, they were under no obligations to submit. This was the very spirit of gauchoism, and as an evidence how strong this element still is, even in Buenos Aires, no stronger proof is necessary than that such anarchical, detestable doctrines were so popular that the government had no power to resist it. Meetings were publicly called and openly held, for the purpose of obtaining material aid for Flores. In a free country and under a constitutional government the right to assemble thus is admitted. The Fenians exercised it in their foolish appeals in behalf of the Irish republic, and the English exercised it when they assembled to furnish aid and comfort to another republic whose corner-stone was to be human slavery. But until some overt act on the high seas or within the territory of the menaced country was committed, no violation of international law could be alleged. The government of Montevideo, however, complained of these demonstrations as showing an unfriendly spirit, and alleged that they were not only tolerated, but encouraged, by the government of Buenos Aires.

There was very little response, however, by the people of the Banda Oriental to these "liberators" who were coming to free them from a government under which they were enjoying a degree of prosperity before unknown; and among those who approved of the invasion there were scarcely any who cared to venture their own safety on an expedition so hazardous, if not hopeless. The government of Montevideo was distracted in its counsels, and taking no effective steps to throttle the invasion should it be attempted. Of this Flores was well aware. He knew, if he could effect a landing with a small force, he could easily escape should he see any such energetic proceedings on the part of the government as were taken at the time of Diaz's invasion. But if indecision and apathy prevailed, he could gradually gather to his standard the loose, floating, gaucho population that takes to marauding as naturally as the young partridge takes to the woods. With such recruits, if not too numerous, he could easily keep himself out of the way of any regular troops sent in pursuit of him. The country was then in a very different condition from that which obtained when Diaz made his invasion. The estancias, with their herds of horses, cattle, and sheep, were much more numerous; and, if pursued, his followers could, after every day's flight, supply themselves with fresh horses and the needed provisions at the expense of the estancieros, whereas any regular troops must move with such means as they could legally obtain.

With this prospect before him, Flores, on the 16th of April, 1863, embarked in a whale-boat at Buenos Aires, with only three attendants, for the Banda Oriental. He landed without opposition at a point on the Uruguay called Rincon de las Gallinas, and raised his standard. The government heard of his invasion and knew of the small force that attended him, but it took no measures adequate to the circumstances. Carreras was not in the Cabinet, and his calls on the government for more active measures had not only been disregarded, but his censures of its apathy had caused his counsels to be treated with contempt. Berro, whose administration had been marked by such wonderful general prosperity, was averse to such measures as had proved so successful against Diaz. His term of office had nearly expired, and he was anxious to tide over the constitutional limit of his Presidency without engaging in anything like active war. He also had his choice for the succession, though he was himself ineligible for a second term. The crisis required that some man of military experience and energetic character should be placed at the head of military affairs; but the only two men answering to these conditions would, it was well known, so soon crush out the rebellion that whichever of them was called to the position would most likely be afterwards elected to the Presidency. These two were General Lucas Moreno and Colonel Leandro Gomez. Berro hesitated and did nothing. Old General Medina, then an octogenarian, was called upon to organize the army; but while he was considering how to do it, Flores was actively ranging the country, stealing horses and recruiting gauchos. He found none of the respectable people, however, not even the colorados, to welcome him. He accordingly made his way across the country to the Brazilian frontier, where he knew that many of the traditional enemies of his country would, for reasons of their own, and which will appear hereafter, espouse his cause. As he passed through the country he scattered his proclamations, calling on the people to rise and throw off the tyranny under which they groaned. But no person of any influence responded to the call, until he reached the Brazilian frontier, where he found a mixed crowd of Brazilians and Oriental outlaws ready to join him. They had already been collected together by a noted Brazilian chieftain, who had previously been in communication with Flores, and had assembled his forces to be prepared to join him at the opportune moment. This ally of Flores, General David Canavarro, had long been known as one of the most dangerous and influential enemies to the independence of the Oriental Republic within the Brazilian Empire. But this mattered little to Flores and his colorado sympathizers, who all professed to be the peculiar champions of the national independence.

CHAPTER XXXIV.

Policy of Brazil and Buenos Aires respecting Paraguay and Uruguay. — Correspondence between Lopez and Mitre. — Lopez's Preparations for War. — The Province of Rio Grande. — Smuggling Expeditions. — Invasion of Flores. — His Mode of Warfare. — Weakness and Vacillation of President Berro. — Don Antanacio C. Aguierre Acting President. — Don Felipe Netto's Efforts to involve Brazil in a War with the Oriental Republic. — José Antonio Saraiva. — Brazil sends Commissioners to Montevideo. — Imperial Designs of President Lopez. — He is disappointed in his Matrimonial Designs. — He assumes to be the Champion of Republicanism.

THE favor shown to Flores by both the government and the people of Buenos Aires had been regarded from the first with jealous interest by Paraguay, or rather by President Lopez, who, so far as any expression of opinion was allowed, was both government and people. Paraguay and Uruguay were two little republics between the Argentine Republic and the Brazilian Empire, the latter having twenty-five and the former six times the extent of territory of them both put together. It was the traditional policy of Buenos Aires to make itself the capital and emporium of all the territory of the Plata and its confluents that had been originally settled by the Spaniards. It was with this idea that the war of Belgrano had been commenced in 1810; and although through the long gloom and isolation of Francia's reign, and during the twenty years of the despotism of the elder Lopez, there was no organized effort to conquer or annex it, yet the feeling was still general, that, from its geographical position and its kindred population, it ought to be one of the provinces of the Argentine Republic. For the possession of Uruguay there had been long and bitter struggles. It was coveted by both Brazil and Buenos Aires. Brazil had intrigued and made war in alliance with the renegade Flores to get possession of it; and Buenos

Aires had years before sent one of its war vessels with Diaz and his recruits to make the revolution that came to so disastrous an end at Quinteros. Both countries were watching the opportunity to seize on the little Republic, and each was watching the other. The only mode in which annexation could be effected must be with the ostensible assent of the people of the country, for other nations could not be expected to look on passively and see it subjected by force to a foreign yoke. The only feasible plan was to employ some renegade or traitor to get up a revolution, and, while professing neutrality, to give such material support as to make it successful, and that he should afterwards, when he had had time to go through the forms of an election that should give a color of legitimacy to his authority, make over the country to his employers, while yet he held the knife at the throats of the people. This appeared to be the plan of Diaz and Alsina, and the antecedents of Flores were such as to leave no doubt that he would be as willing to sell his country to Buenos Aires as he had formerly been to sell it and himself to Brazil.

In making his previous revolution, Flores had been able to make terms and to be received as a member of the government which he had sought to overthrow. On this later occasion, finding that he had not met with the reception he expected, and that with his bands of outlaws he could never hope to conquer the country, an effort was made to bring about an arrangement between him and the government through the mediation of the English, Brazilian, and Argentine ministers. This attempt was abortive, and could hardly have been made in good faith on the part of Brazil and the Argentine Republic, as they both had designs of their own on the Banda Oriental, and both were seeking to make use of Flores as their instrument. The former had declared that it would remain neutral, and the Oriental government, trusting to these professions, did not doubt that it could put down the Flores rebellion. For this reason, and because it did not wish to recognize in Flores anything more or less than an outlaw, robber, and murderer, the proposed mediation was scarcely entertained.

Not without reason the Paraguayan government looked with great interest on the issue of the Flores invasion; for if successful, or if in any way the independence of the Oriental Republic were overthrown, Paraguayan despotism would have but a precarious existence. The government of Montevideo, at the first mutterings of the impending storm, had foreseen that the interests of Lopez were involved with its own. It had sent as its minister resident at Asuncion Dr. Octavio Lapido, one of its most trusted and promising young men, with instructions to represent to the government of Paraguay the common danger, and propose, in confidence, that a secret alliance should be made between the two countries against the Argentine Republic, as at that time the most imminent danger to them both was apprehended from that quarter. Lopez, however, demurred to the alliance, and put Lapido off with promises of assistance whenever the Oriental independence should appear to be in danger. But in the month of September, 1863, and during the residence of Lapido at Asuncion, Lopez sent a note to President Mitre, demanding explanations concerning the violations of neutrality notoriously committed, not only with the sanction, but with the approval and assistance, of his government. Mitre denied any responsibility for acts committed by irresponsible parties against the Oriental Republic, alleging that his government had observed the strictest neutrality in all things. This answer was far from satisfactory, as it neither acknowledged past faults nor promised greater circumspection in the future. The reply of Lopez to this was the last of the personal and ostensibly friendly correspondence that had been carried on for some time between the two Presidents. This correspondence is a curious specimen of diplomatic writing, in which, under the forms of official etiquette, both parties try to conceal their real feelings towards each other. Lopez looked upon Mitre as the prominent figure of the countries of the Plata, as the shadow or curtain that prevented the light of his own greatness from shining forth and illuminating the world; while Mitre regarded his brother President as a semi-savage, whose tyranny was a disgrace, not only to South America, but to the human race. Yet in their personal correspondence they billed and cooed as gently as sucking doves. This, however, could not continue with the warlike attitude that both parties were assuming. In the last letter of Lopez, he intimated that thenceforth considerations of friendship would no longer avail, but that Paraguay would be governed in the future solely by its own judgment and sense of interest.

This menace was followed by the general conscription of February, 1864, throughout Paraguay. There was already a standing army in the country of some twenty thousand men, and this recruitment increased the number to nearly sixty thousand. A camp was formed at a place called Cerro Leon, ten leagues from the capital, and situate at the base of a range of hills and near the line of the railroad. The recruits were immediately subjected to severe training, and there was every indication that real war was intended. The materials for a telegraphic line and a competent staff of engineers and operators were ordered from Europe; several additional physicians for the army were also engaged by the Paraguayan agent in London, all of whom reached Asuncion about the middle of the year (1864).

But a new danger was now threatening the Oriental independence. Hitherto Brazil had taken no part either for or against Flores, and all the military preparations and demonstrations of Paraguay had been with a view of confronting the ambitious designs of the Argentine government. Now, however, as the Berro government was gradually getting its military forces together, and it was becoming evident, that, without more aid from abroad than could be derived through the connivance and secret assistance of Buenos Aires, the revolution could have no hope of success, there were heard the first threatening sounds from the north.

We have already seen how the Brazilians of the province of Rio Grande had been for years encroaching on the territory of the Banda Oriental. Many estancieros from this province had entered this fine grazing region belonging to the latter, and by purchase or occupation gained possession of large tracts, on which they had vast herds of cattle, sheep, and horses. Being beyond the jurisdiction of their own country, they, of course, paid no taxes to it; and the export duty on their stock they contrived to evade by attempting revolutions or minor disturbances, under which they would run off their cattle scot free. These intruders had some of them acquired immense wealth, and desired a continuation of their immunities, which they could not expect to enjoy long if the rebellion were put down and the peace that had prevailed under Pereira and Berro were re-established. Among those Brazilians having the largest possessions in this fertile region were General Netto, General Marquess (afterwards Baron Porte Alegre), General Osorio (afterwards Baron Herval), and Colonels Saldanha and Illa. These men had all been conspicuous in the attempted revolution in 1837 of the province of Rio Grande, the most southern province of Brazil, and one of the most valuable and important of the Empire in its resources. They had joined in this movement in the belief that their province was strong enough to establish its independence and found a nation to be called the Republic of Piratiny. The Empire was then in a weak and inefficient condition, and was scarcely able to make an effort to put down the rebellion; and a state of affairs which they called war dragged on for ten years, when the government was able to make such terms with the leading revolutionists that they returned to their allegiance. The favorite Brazilian weapon, gold, was successfully employed. The leaders of the rebellion were left in peace to pursue their depredations in the Banda Oriental.

This border section being so fine a district for grazing, the Montevidean government sought to derive a revenue from it by an export duty on cattle.

Against this the Brazilian government would not complain, but the people who were affected by it found a way, in most cases, to avoid its payment. Whenever it was desirable to send over a large number, it was an easy matter to get up a feigned rebellion or insurrection, that would engage the attention of all the Oriental officials, and in the smoke run off all the cattle that they wished to export. The parties engaged in these smuggling expeditions were often attacked by the revenue officers, who were sometimes supported by a considerable military force. This systematic evasion of taxes was a dangerous business, and in the course of years a good many of the smugglers were, at different times, killed or made prisoners. The Brazilians, however, had the impudence to demand reparation for the injuries received by their countrymen; and the claims of this sort that had accumulated during some fifteen years were finally alleged as a justification for uniting with Flores and making war on the Banda Oriental. Even kidnappers, who had attempted to steal and carry off free negroes and sell them into slavery in Brazil, if caught and punished had their cause espoused by the government, and reclamations made for the injustice they had sustained. Doubtless there was much violence and wrong-doing on both sides, but there is little doubt that the Brazilians were the principal offenders; and if the accounts for wrongs and injuries had been justly investigated, a large balance would have been found due to Uruguay.

This state of open defiance and contempt of the laws of the Montevidean government had endured many years; for during the long siege, and for years after, Brazilian interlopers were little molested by any pretended authority of the Uruguayans. But with the peace and prosperity that succeeded the expulsion of Flores after his first revolution the nation and government waxed strong, and the lands bordering on the frontiers, and next to those occupied or owned by the Brazilians, became valuable, and the great smugglers saw that they were liable to lose their long-enjoyed immunities. Hence anything that threatened war to the Banda Oriental was hailed by these Brazilians as likely to give them a longer lease of their abuses. A civil war would be to them the most welcome, as while that lasted they would be unmolested by either party, and, while the substance of the native people was being wasted, the Brazilian influence would be constantly growing stronger.

The chief reliance of Flores, therefore, in making his invasion, was on the hereditary enemies of his country. Besides the forces that had been collected by Canavarro, he was also able to count on other reinforcements which a gaucho chieftain, General Nicanor Caceres, had raised on the opposite side of the river Uruguay, in the Argentine province of Corrientes. With such patriots as these, not one seventh of whom were natives of the country they were to liberate, Flores, or, as he was called by his followers and the newspapers that supported his cause, the "Liberator," set out on a second march, or rather gallop, through the country. His forces now began to increase quite rapidly, as little knots of gauchos from more remote parts had by this time heard of his adventure and come to join him. The first encounters with any government troops took place in the month of June, 1863, and resulted favorably to the invaders. Their success gave them prestige, and many of those Brazilians dwelling within the territory who had at first kept aloof, fearing lest it might prove another Quinteros affair, came forward in large numbers to join the standard of the "Liberator."

Thus was the little Republic, that during a few years of peace had attained to such prosperity, launched on the sea of civil war. As yet both Brazil and the Argentine Republic, though giving both moral and material support to Flores, professed the strictest neutrality. This wicked connivance and breach of national faith was to cost them hundreds of thousands of lives and hundreds of millions of dollars, and to Brazil was to prove her financial ruin, if not her national dismemberment.

It is beyond the scope of this work to follow the fortunes of Flores after his first successes against the government troops. His mode of warfare was the one best adapted to harass and ruin the country, and at the same time to advance his own interests. The estancieros and other peaceable citizens, who were satisfied with the government as it was and had been for years, and who deeply deplored the invasion, were afraid to take sides against him, as they knew full well that a suspicion of that would expose them to be robbed and murdered by any of his marauding gangs. This was the experience of such as had ever been prominent as blancos. The army of Flores, consisting of the worst materials the earth could produce, scoured the country, stealing horses, cattle, and sheep as they were needed, wantonly slaughtering the herds of those they considered as unfriendly, but robbing friend or foe with great impartiality whenever their necessities required. In fact, it could not strictly be called war that he prosecuted ; it was in robbery and assassination on a large scale, purposely carried on to ruin and exhaust the country, and not as the leader of an army making war against another army, that he employed his troops. Finding fresh relays of horses at every estancia, his men were always well mounted ; and they scoured the country from one end to the other, falling like a tempest alike on the large estancias and the unpretending hamlets, and on any small bodies of national troops that had been detached from the main army to learn the whereabouts of the "Liberator." A great many skirmishes of more or less importance took place between the opposing forces ; but Flores always avoided anything like a pitched battle, nor did he venture to attack any town of importance. The whole native population was so unanimously against him, that the people of any large town would have defended it until government troops could come to its relief. His warfare was against the rural districts. Five times he approached near Montevideo, never venturing to attack the town ; and fleeing away before the government, that showed all the while a criminal sluggishness, could collect sufficient force to give him battle, he would be off, with all his forces, on another devastating raid through the country. The little skirmishes were magnified by the newspapers of Buenos Aires and Montevideo into as many great battles, and, of course, great victories ; but the newspapers, according to their partisan bias, in every case disagreed as to which party had gained the victory.

The public sentiment of Buenos Aires, from the first favorable to Flores, grew enthusiastic as the revolution proceeded and promised ruin to the neighboring Republic. Two or three newspapers openly justified the invasion, and the *Tribuna* frantically appealed to the people to come forward with material aid for the "Liberator." Recruiting for his army was openly carried on; and public meetings were held, in which the people were called upon to make war on a country against which the government had not declared it. The government, to the shame of President Mitre, connived at and approved all these proceedings. It secretly instigated a kind of warfare against a weak neighbor, towards whom it professed peace and friendship in a way that no other word will characterize so well as "sneaking." Men and arms were embarked at Buenos Aires without any attempt on the part of the authorities to interfere. On the contrary, the arms which these recruits bore were, many of them, taken from the national arsenal; and on one occasion an open boat, filled with these liberators ready armed for service, was taken in tow by an Argentine national steamer.

Such neutrality as this called forth strong protests from the Oriental government; but unfortunately the only strong thing it did was to protest. Its internal administration was weak and vacillating. Berro, who had guided the ship of state very well while the waters were calm, became not only confused and imbecile, but stubborn and perverse, when the sea became rough. He would not call into the civil service men of energy like Carreras, nor men of military prestige and capacity like Lucas Moreno or Leandro Gomez. He feared lest they should gain military prestige, and neither of them was his choice for the succession to the Presidency. He would not believe the rebellion was so formidable that it could not be put down without any serious interruption of the political programme which he and his friends had formed for the future. Old General Medina, then past eighty-five years of age, was continued as the commanding-general of the army; and the result was that nothing effectual was done to recruit a force such as at that time could crush out the rebellion. As yet the army of Flores was weak in comparison with the forces that the government might have put into the field. But the rebellion was allowed, nevertheless, to drag along until the end of Berro's term, in March, 1864. Medina had indeed been changed for General Servando Gomez, who, if not quite as old, was even more inefficient.

Berro's term having expired, the duties of the Presidency devolved on the President of the Senate, Don Atanacio C. Aguierre. No election of a successor had taken place, as according to the Constitution of the state no presidential election can take place during the time of civil war. Aguierre had not the capacity of Berro, nor did he possess in any high degree the public confidence. But he was free from the prejudices of his predecessor, and was not in the interest of the same parties, who, for their own selfish ends, had counselled a course of action that exposed the country to destruction. His situation was one of great difficulty, and one requiring a high order of executive ability, for a danger more pressing than the abused and treacherous neutrality of Buenos Aires now loomed upon the horizon of the devoted little Republic. Brazil, that at the commencement of the rebellion had declared it would remain neutral, now threatened to interfere. The border men on both sides of the dividing line between Uruguay and the province of Rio Grande, who had carried on for years their traffic in the territory of the former in defiance of all law, now demanded that the imperial government should declare war against the little state whose power they had so long defied. Without waiting to be accused, they turned accusers, and in the Chambers of the Brazilian Parliament they proclaimed the wrongs they had suffered. The person of most wealth and influence in Rio Grande, and the one having most pecuniary interest in the overthrow of the Oriental independence, was General Felipe Netto, who had once led a rebellion with the object of detaching the province of Rio Grande from the Empire and setting up an independent republic. A large part of his fortune, which consisted of millions, had been gained in supplying the army of General Oribe with cattle during his nine years' siege of Montevideo. But though Oribe was the king stork that Rosas had sent as his deputy to the Banda Oriental, ostensibly to rehabilitate the blancos in the government, yet when this party had succeeded to power, after the fall of both Rosas and Oribe, the aggrieved Netto had his budget of wrongs done to him by the blancos to complain of. In the Lower Chamber of the Brazilian Parliament, his representative, Felipe Nery, a native of Montevideo, but of Portuguese ancestry, came forward with a series of grave charges and accusations against La Republica Oriental del Uruguay. The wrongs endured by his countrymen who had crossed over into the Banda Oriental to kidnap free negroes or smuggle cattle were depicted as national outrages, and he called on the Brazilian government to demand instant redress of grievances. At the same time, Netto was ready with arguments stronger than those used by his representative. He took apartments in Rio de Janeiro, and lived in a style entirely eclipsing royalty or anything ever before seen in the Empire, and entertained the members of the Chambers in a style of more profusion than elegance, but gorgeously extravagant. His banquets were the marvel of the newspapers, and his liberality in all things toward the congressional deputies was beyond praise, — far beyond. Gold, as I have said before, and as I shall have occasion to prove repeatedly hereafter, is the great motive-power on which Brazil always counts for success. Netto knew his country and his countrymen, and what between Nery's eloquence and his own money a majority of the Lower House was converted to his views, and a committee was named to proceed to Montevideo and demand immediate satisfaction for the wrongs endured by Brazilians at the hands of the Oriental people and government.

It should be noted that these claims for damages were few of them of recent origin. The most of them had been held in abeyance for many years, and the country under the Pereira and Berro administrations was fast arriving at a condition in which it could easily liquidate all just claims against it. The only hope that they would ever be paid consisted in the probability that the peace would continue. But Netto and the other complainants neither hoped for nor expected peace. He was the veritable wolf who had been worried by the lamb. He wanted a cause for a quarrel, and the unpaid claims were made the pretext for it, even though aware that by promoting a war the holders of just claims would have far less chance of ever obtaining their dues.

Netto had been preparing for war before he succeeded in forcing his measures through the Congress. His troops were already organized to the number of one thousand or more, and they were hovering over the frontier and ready to pounce on the Banda Oriental as soon as he should give the word. That he was resolved to do, sooner or later, and the Congress and the Emperor knew it. He was too powerful a subject to be controlled; and if he could not make war by and with the consent of the imperial government, it was well known he would do it on his own account, and that he would be supported in it by nearly the whole province of Rio Grande. Netto, it was also known, had never relinquished his ideas of twenty years before, of forming the province into an independent republic, and nearly all the men of wealth and influence in the province were equally weak in their loyalty to the throne. Once in arms and without authority of law, it was not likely that the leaders would be satisfied with a simple invasion of the Banda Oriental. They would doubtless soon after raise the standard of rebellion and again set up their republic. War, therefore, of some kind, was at the door; but whether the imperial arms should be directed against such Brazilian subjects as might choose to rebel, or against the inoffending and already afflicted Banda Oriental, was the question to be decided. The Emperor deprecated war of any kind, and especially deprecated such a war as the Congress, instigated by Netto, was trying to force upon him. But he at length reluctantly and weakly yielded, and this fatal step precipitated the Empire into a war which cost it at least six times the number of able-bodied men that existed in the whole province of Rio Grande, and five hundred millions of dollars.

The committee appointed for this work were two of the most eminent statesmen in the Empire. The senior member was the Counsellor José Antonio Saraiva, a man of great experience, having often held the positions of most importance and responsibility under the government. The junior commissioner, Dr. Taveres Bastos, was yet a young man, but one whose antecedents and services should have excused him from a task so calculated to bring reproach to the nation. His various measures for internal improvements, his projects of extending the national commerce, all of which evinced careful study and enlarged statesmanship, had called attention to him as the rising man of the country. But the measure which reflects most honor on his career was one which called down upon him the enmity and opposition of the rich and aristocratic classes. Before the great Rebellion in the United States he had proposed a plan for the gradual extinction of African slavery, and had urged the measure with great earnestness and persistence, taking the high moral ground that slavery was a crime against God, man, and nature, and must in the end bring ruin and desolation on the country. This man, however, who was then but twenty-five years of age, and whom all looked upon with respect as the man of most promise among the younger statesmen, was nominated on this committee to perform a work that brigands might well shrink from.

The instructions given to this committee were not made public, and the two commissioners proceeded to Montevideo ostensibly only as a committee of inquiry. The people there supposed that they were coming to investigate the question of claims and counter-claims ; and as they believed that the balance, on an honest examination, would be largely in their favor, their arrival was hailed with great satisfaction. The newspapers were filled with long articles written in the belief that the time to obtain redress of grievances from Brazil had at last arrived.

Great, therefore, was the surprise and indignation of the

people of Montevideo when they learned that the commissioners, instead of coming to examine, arrange, and adjust all the pending questions, had made a demand for the immediate recognition of claims amounting in the total to fourteen millions of dollars! The whole population of the country, after deducting the Brazilians on the frontier, who did not pay taxes to the Montevidean government, did not at that time exceed three hundred and fifty thousand souls. To meet this demand of Brazil, therefore, would require a tax of more than forty-three dollars on every man, woman, and child in the entire Republic.

It was in this discreditable manner that Brazil became involved in the civil war of the Banda Oriental. The government at Rio de Janeiro allowed itself to be controlled by the turbulent feudal lords of Rio Grande, and to become the ally of a rebel against a weak neighbor with whom it had no just cause of war, and at a time when to take advantage of her weakness and internal dissensions was both cowardly and dishonorable. By this act it gave a pretext for the interference of Paraguay in the affairs of the Banda Oriental, and put itself morally in the wrong in the eyes of all the other nations of the world. By her own wrongful acts Brazil had first become involved in the cause of Flores; and when Lopez, in utter contempt of the laws and usages of civilized nations, commenced war against her after the manner of the barbarian and savage, few people made the distinction between the two issues, and the generality believed that in her wrongful and treacherous course towards Uruguay she had begun the war against Paraguay.

It is not unlikely, however, that Brazil would soon have been forced into a war with Paraguay had she not interfered in this discreditable manner with the affairs of the Banda Oriental. Other events were transpiring which greatly incensed President Lopez against the Emperor. It had been the dream of Lopez from his youth to change the form of the Paraguayan government, on his accession to power, from that of a republic to an empire; and on his voyage to Europe he had stopped at

Rio, where he had been treated with great consideration by Don Pedro II., and after his return to his own country he made advances to his Imperial Majesty to ascertain if he could count on his support and assistance in taking such a step. It will probably never be known how far he was encouraged in this ambitious idea by the Emperor, as it is unlikely that the latter will admit that he has ever had any secret negotiations with a man capable of such atrocities as Lopez was guilty of in his subsequent career. The fact, however, that Lopez, immediately on his accession to power, began, in minor things, to imitate the forms and customs of royalty, and in some of the more remote districts of Paraguay to have his name hailed as Francisco Primero, instead of Excellentissimo Presidente, leads to the inference that his imperial designs were not disapproved by the Emperor. In fact, Lopez, on one occasion, distinctly stated to the writer of this work that the Emperor of Brazil had urged him to make the change. He said, moreover, that so far as his own people were concerned, he could do it without any difficulty, but that such was not his purpose or plan. And on another occasion he stated that "the Emperor of Brazil would find that he had made a great mistake when he ventured to come in contact with or thwart the plans of Francisco Solano Lopez." It was his ambition, not only to found an empire, but to establish a dynasty; and to do this he saw that he must not only have the support and approval of the Emperor of Brazil and the heads of other monarchical governments, but they must so cordially support him as to encourage a matrimonial alliance with some princess of royal blood. In fact, his whole scheme depended on the good-will and approval of the Emperor; for unless he would agree to recognize him as Emperor of Paraguay, he could not expect any of the European powers to do so. The elder Lopez had always regarded the Brazilians, their government, and the Emperor, with the greatest aversion and contempt. In speaking of them to third parties, his almost invariable rule was to call them *macacos* (monkeys); and he carried his enmity so far, that, at the time of his death, there was not in all Paraguay a single Brazilian except the consul. The young President, however, on his advent to power, did not seem to share in this aversion to his neighbors, but, on the contrary, always spoke of them with respect; and while indulging through his official organ in the most unstinted abuse of his Argentine neighbors, he allowed nothing to appear in it inimical or disrespectful towards Brazil. As imperialism has but a precarious hold in America, he naturally thought that the only empire would be strengthened in its position by having another established to make common cause with it against republicanism; and thinking Pedro II. would so regard it, he hoped for his cordial and earnest support in all his plans. The Emperor had two daughters then approaching marriageable age, and if he was disposed to aid him in his imperial designs, the most effectual way for him to do so was to offer him the hand of his second daughter, the Princess Isabella, to be his empress and share his throne. But the Emperor, who, if he had encouraged Lopez in his imperial aspirations, had probably done so with the hope that such a step would prove to be his ultimate destruction, had long regarded the existence of a government like that which obtained in Paraguay as an evil, and as an obstacle and perpetual hindrance to the development and progress of South America, and would never understand the allusions made by Lopez as to the manner in which he could best serve him. Had there been no other objection to the alliance, it was enough that he knew the character of Lopez. He knew him to be licentious, dissolute, and cruel; for as in his youth it had been probable that he would succeed to a position in which it was important for the governments of the neighboring countries to know his disposition and character, he had taken pains to inform himself of them, and had learned that, while he had cultivated the forms and usages of society so as to have the manners of a gentleman, he was at heart a jealous tyrant, with the savage instincts of the gaucho. The Emperor was also well aware that Lopez had for years lived with a favorite who had great influence over him, and who was as ambitious, as false, and as cruel as himself; that by her he had had many children, and that for them alone had he ever shown any affection; and that any person whom for state or ambitious purposes he might take to share his throne would hold but the second place in his regard, and be in reality but the servant and captive of his mistress.

While Lopez was recruiting his army and making such extensive preparations for war, as was generally supposed, against the Argentine Republic, in which he had believed he would have the sympathy, if not the active support, of the Emperor, who, he hoped, was to be his father-in-law, all his hopes were suddenly dashed by learning, through the newspapers, that his Majesty, who had never officially responded to his advances, but had rather encouraged his warlike preparations against the Argentines, had contracted alliances for both his daughters with European princes. This information reached him about the time that General Netto was urging the imperial government to the invasion of the Banda Oriental, and great were his wrath and anger at finding that the Emperor had been encouraging him with vague intimations of support in his ambitious designs, rather as an Indian cacique than as the head of an independent nation. It was not until this time, to judge from his acts and from the tone of his paper, that he had ever contemplated hostilities with Brazil; and the attitude of the Emperor towards the Republic of Uruguay had not disturbed him, as he supposed he might contract an alliance with the imperial family that would unite in a common cause the interests of the two empires. But as soon as he found the Emperor had designs entirely independent of him, from that moment he assumed to be the champion of republicanism against the ambitious projects of empire entertained by Brazil; and his newspaper, the *Semanario*, from that moment began to assail the policy and conduct of the Brazilian government, and ceased to a great extent its attacks on President Mitre and the Argentine Confederation.

CHAPTER XXXV.

Intervention of Brazil in the Affairs of Uruguay. — Correspondence between Saraiva and the Oriental Minister for Foreign Affairs. — Don Cesar Sauvan Vianna de Lima. — Hon. Edward Thornton. — Don José Vasquez Sagastume. — Lopez declines to form an Alliance with Uruguay. — Violation of Confidence. — Official Receptions. — Lopez assumes the Character of Arbiter. — The English in Paraguay. — Case of William Atherton. — Advice of the English Minister. — Carlos and Fernando Saguier.

THE Emperor of Brazil had little anticipated the effect which his rejection of the overtures of Lopez towards a more intimate alliance would have upon him ; and when he yielded to the demands of his Rio Grande subjects that he should espouse the cause of Flores and make war on the Banda Oriental, he supposed that, by acceding to their wishes, nothing more would follow than that the lawful government of that Republic would be overturned and another substituted, the head of which would not be inimical to himself. Flores was known to be already in the interest and confidence of President Mitre, and if, through the aid of Buenos Aires alone, he were to overturn the existing government and set up another, with himself as President, the country might become a province of the Argentine Republic. It may have been that it was to avert this result that he acceded to the demands of Netto and his followers, as the alleged grievances of which his government complained had little or no foundation either in justice or fact.

The correspondence that took place between his minister, Saraiva, and the Oriental Minister for Foreign Affairs, Don Juan J. Herrera, is perhaps without parallel in diplomatic history. The insolent assurance on one side was so coolly and effectively met by facts incontrovertible and notorious on the other, fixing the burden of the wrongs on the Brazilians, that the question of right was made palpable to all who read it; and had the Montevidean government had the sagacity to despatch a competent representative to Europe and the United States to press on the attention of different governments the merits of the controversy, the pretensions of Brazil must have been condemned and rebuked. It was but a repetition of the old story of the wolf and the lamb, except that the wolf did not attack the lamb at a time when it was being harried by dogs.

The Brazilian government, at the dictation of Netto, had determined to avail itself of the distresses of its neighbor to make war upon Uruguay at the very moment when the Flores invasion had assumed such formidable proportions as to threaten the existence of the legal government. It was the bully's time to strike. Herrera answered the arrogant note of Saraiva with dignity, against his claims alleging counter-claims of greater magnitude and as well sustained by proofs. He at the same time declared that his government had the best disposition to satisfy all just demands, while it would expect the same justice from the government of his Imperial Majesty. It was known that the pretensions of Brazil had been put forward at this time only as a pretext of intervention in behalf of Flores, as the military preparations for his assistance had already been made by raising troops to send to his aid,—a fact which Saraiva, with an effrontery almost sublime, admits in his first note to Herrera. He says that, "in order to hinder the passage of reinforcements through the southern frontier of the province of Rio Grande to General Flores, and to make them respect the territory of the Empire, the imperial government has resolved to increase its force stationed on that frontier." No one doubted that this force was intended to be launched into the Banda Oriental to aid Flores as soon as the terms proposed by Saraiva should be rejected, and which it was known and intended by the instigators of the war would be rejected.

The government of Uruguay, from the commencement of the Flores rebellion, had nourished a hope of assistance from Lopez; and notwithstanding he had rejected the alliance proposed by Dr. Lapido, it sent some months afterwards, in May, 1864, another minister, Don José Vasquez Sagastume, to reside at Asuncion, and bring about some sort of an arrangement under which Uruguay and Paraguay might be united in the common cause. The Minister was accompanied by Francisco Rodriguez Larreta as secretary, — a young man of fine attainments belonging to an excellent family in Montevideo, and whose melancholy fate will be narrated at length in a subsequent chapter. The Oriental government had previously rejected all overtures of reconciliation with Flores, — both those made by Lopez the preceding year, and those offered by the ministers of England, Brazil, and Buenos Aires. Previous to the menace of Brazil to interfere in behalf of Flores, the Oriental government had felt no apprehension that the Emperor could be provoked to take the part of such a notorious outlaw.

The demands of Saraiva, however, opened their eyes to the dangers that beset them, and then they hastened to make terms with Paraguay, and, if possible, form an alliance offensive and defensive against Brazil. This, however, Lopez refused to do. In an arrogant note addressed by his Minister for Foreign Affairs, José Berges, to the Oriental minister resident in Asuncion, he reviewed the situation at great length, complaining of the course hitherto pursued by the Oriental government. In this note, though the two governments were professedly aiming to adopt some means of common defence, Lopez did not scruple to make use of the confidential communications of the former Oriental minister, Dr. Lapido, and immediately afterward publish them in the *Semanario*.* Whether this was done to prove his own superior astuteness, or to show that he was not to be bound by the ordinary principles that are supposed to obtain between governments in matters confidential, does not appear from the note itself. At the time of the publication of this note in the *Semanario*, the government

* . . . . "El Dr. Lapido presento confidencialmente á este Ministerio una carta particular que le dirigia el Señor Berro Presidente de esa Republica y aventuró despues la idea de la oportunidad y necesidad de que la Escuadra paraguaya en combinacion con la Oriental se apoderasen de la Isla de Martin Garcia." — *Note of Minister José Berges*, August 30, 1864.

of Paraguay was figuring prominently in the politics of South America. Lopez had avowed that his object in interfering in the affairs of the neighboring countries was to maintain the balance of power, and prevent the larger states from absorbing the smaller ones. His assumption of the character of arbiter, whose dictum other nations must respect, caused great mirth and ridicule, at the time, in both Rio de Janeiro and Buenos Aires. But Paraguay, small as it was, and insignificant as it was commercially, had a standing army, well drilled and well armed, larger than all the neighboring states, and it could become a formidable enemy or a powerful ally. No one of the neighboring countries wished to quarrel with it; for besides having a large army, it had such advantages of position that it could inflict much injury on its enemies at little risk or damage to itself. For a civilized and strong power to make war on Paraguay would be like the attempts of the man to shear the wolf,— the wolf might, indeed, be shorn, and be damaged in the operation, but the fleece was sure not to pay the shearer.

The Brazilian government at this juncture took measures to conciliate Paraguay by sending Don Cesar Sauvan Vianna de Lima, as minister duly accredited, to reside at Asuncion. Brazil had latterly been represented at Paraguay only by *Chargés d'Affaires*. Lopez, it was well known, was ambitious to have his government recognized as of such importance by other nations as to merit, and require, diplomatic agents of a high rank. It little comported with his swelling greatness that Paraguay should be treated by the leading powers like Congo or Madagascar. A minister resident was therefore sent, at this crisis of affairs, to both flatter and placate the man who had set himself up as the preserver of the equilibrium of nations.

The appointment for this important office—the most important, as events proved, that the imperial government ever had it in its power to bestow — was not fortunate. Señor Vianna de Lima was an accomplished gentleman and an experienced diplomatist; but nearly all his diplomatic career had been passed in Europe. His last residence there had been in

Turin as the Brazilian *Chargé*, and his promotion from *Chargé* at Turin to Minister at Asuncion must have caused him feelings of mingled disgust and satisfaction. He accepted the situation, however, in the line of his career; and to give the more appearance of a friendly disposition and of intention to remain, he was accompanied by his entire family and with all the outfit that it might be supposed would be required for a long residence. But he regarded the time to be passed as so many months or years of exile. Brazil was a great empire, and its agents were highly respected at the different courts of Europe. But Paraguay was an insignificant little state, scarcely known beyond South America. Its existence, even, as a separate state, was regarded by his government as an evil that should be abated on the first opportunity. It had been long tolerated, because it had not hitherto been quite convenient to extinguish it. With opinions of this kind, which, though entertained by his government, it was not diplomatic to manifest, Señor Vianna de Lima entered Paraguay.

He was not received graciously by Lopez. On the contrary, an incident occurred on the day of his formal reception that tended to excite both anger and contempt. Petty despotisms are always very punctilious on those matters of form and etiquette that in great states scarcely excite a thought. They fear that any non-observance of a mere formality is intended as a slight that would not be practised towards a great power; and they stand on their rights and dignity in trivial matters with a pertinacity of form often inconvenient to themselves and always offensive to others. Another minister had arrived at the same time with Vianna de Lima. This was the Hon. Edward Thornton, her Britannic Majesty's minister plenipotentiary. He had been several times before in Paraguay on the business of her Majesty's government, but now he came to present his credentials as minister. He had resided for some time in that capacity in Buenos Aires, and had spent nearly twenty years of his diplomatic life in Spanish American countries. Neither he nor Vianna de Lima were likely, therefore, to omit any form or point of etiquette; and if they were not well informed on those matters, they did not go to Paraguay to be instructed. After their arrival they both formally announced the fact to the Minister for Foreign Affairs, and requested an audience with the President to present their credentials. The day and hour for the reception of each was named, the English Minister taking precedence as being of the higher grade. They were advised, that, at the appointed hour, the state carriage would be sent to convey them to the Palace. Mr. Thornton and his secretary of legation were accordingly in readiness, dressed in full uniform, when the coach arrived; but great was their surprise, when they attempted to enter it, on being told that the carriage was only for the minister, and that the secretary could not go in it. This was an unexpected predicament. Mr. Thornton had seen many diplomatic receptions before, and it had always been an object to have as many of the countrymen of the minister holding any official rank — such as consuls, naval officers, and even prominent citizens — in the train as possible; and generally several carriages were provided to convey them all, both to give *éclat* to the affair and to indicate the good disposition of the government. But here he was refused the company of his secretary of legation, and so, "lone and lorn," he entered the coach and was driven to the Palace, where he formally presented his credentials with the ordinary platitudes of congratulations, in which he said that he was deputed to express the deep interest felt by the Queen in the welfare and prosperity of Paraguay. To this President Lopez replied, saying that he was pleased to know that her Majesty was so deeply interested in *his* welfare. Perhaps he was thinking of recognition into royal circles of the Lopez dynasty, and of the time when he should call the Queen *my sister*. The Brazilian Minister, being advised that the state coach was not to be contaminated by bearing in it any person of lesser rank than a minister, did not expose himself to be taught the same lesson that had been so unceremoniously administered to Mr. Thornton, but went alone, without offering to take his secretary of legation.

This act, insignificant in itself, was not so in its results. It confirmed Vianna de Lima in his impressions that he had fallen among semi-barbarians, and could only be excused by Mr. Thornton on the ground of ignorance. This, however, the Paraguayan government never confessed. To the personal demand made afterwards to the President for an explanation of the affront, the usual excuse was given, — that the officer in charge had mistaken his orders. During my long residence in Paraguay, the government, from jealousy and excessive punctiliousness, made many similar errors, that, being seen afterwards, made it appear ridiculous, but it was always the fault of some official who had not understood his duty ; and this though everybody knew that there was no official, civil or military, in the country who dared do the most trifling act without express authority.

But Mr. Thornton had more serious questions than those of form or etiquette to settle with President Lopez on this occasion, and the latter was not disposed in the least to conciliate him. On his previous visits to Paraguay he had had to deal with the elder Lopez, who had treated him with respect, and with whom he had arranged the long-standing difficulty of the Canstatt affair. At that time his feelings towards Paraguay were most friendly and cordial, and his position was such as to give his representations in regard to the condition of Paraguay great weight with the English government. The successor, however, was so conscious of his own great powers, that he felt he might defy everybody ; and his treatment of certain English subjects, at this time, was such that the Minister could not disregard it. A case had arisen, just before Mr. Thornton's arrival, in which the rights of an Englishman had been most grossly infringed, and the newly accredited minister must either obtain redress or advise his government that his countrymen had no rights there that were respected, and that it was utter folly to maintain diplomatic relations with a power that had no regard for the laws of nations. The person whose affairs had thus complicated the situation was a merchant by the name of William Atherton. He had brought considerable property into the country about a year before, which he had embarked in business as a general dealer. This man had entered into a negotiation with a couple of Paraguayan subjects, who had been wise enough, on seeing the tyrannical and destructive policy that the new President had adopted, to get out of the country before their purpose of keeping away from it was suspected. The persons referred to were the brothers Carlos and Fernando Saguier. The elder of these, Carlos, was a man of education and fine business talents, and in the time of the elder Lopez had been much consulted in business matters, and had received many favors from him in the way of privileges for collecting and exporting the yerba maté, and for any other business that he chose to embark in. The old man had generally monopolized every branch of trade or commerce that promised large profits to his own family. But Saguier was courtier and man of the world enough to get exceptions made in his favor; and as he had travelled abroad a good deal, his opinions in business matters were often consulted. He had been in his youth the most intimate companion of the young Francisco Solano, who, notwithstanding his arrogance and sense of superiority to all around him, felt that he must have some one to treat with as a companion. In appearance, education, and natural gifts, however, the courtier was far superior to the prince; and when the latter succeeded to power, the former knew enough of the character of the young sovereign to be aware that any offence would be pardoned sooner than superior ability. The strange conduct of the new President in seizing and throwing into prison so many of the richest, most respectable, and influential men in the country immediately after his accession naturally caused Saguier to fear lest his own turn might come next; but he kept as secluded as possible, and quietly attended to his business, not even going near the much-dreaded tyrant. Some time had passed after the inauguration, when he received an invitation to visit his Excellency the President. Of course he lost no time in reporting himself in the anteroom.

In the interview which followed, the President reproached

his old companion and schoolmate for keeping so much aloof, telling him that though he was now the head of the government, he desired that their old relations of intimacy and confidence should continue, as then, more than ever, he needed his counsel and advice. Saguier replied that he desired those relations should still exist, and that if his opinions were asked he should tell them frankly, approve when he could, and condemn when he must. "Certainly," replied Lopez; "speak freely your opinions, and tell me what you think of the present state of affairs, and of my government thus far." "There are some things I do not understand the reasons for, and, not understanding, I cannot approve." "How is that?" said Lopez; "what is it you do not approve?" "I do not understand why so many of the best men in the country have been thrown into prison; and it appears to me that the policy begun by your Excellency, if followed up, will not only prove disastrous to the country, but unfortunate for your own fame and reputation." "How, sir!" said Lopez, turning fiercely upon him; "do you not know that I can put you in the calaboose in three minutes, where you will no more insult me by your insolence?" "I am aware of your power," replied Saguier, "but as you asked my opinion, it was my duty to you as an old friend to tell you my honest convictions." "Very well, I need none of your advice." The interview closed, and Saguier was allowed to return to his own house "a sadder and a wiser man." He now realized to the full his own situation and that of the country, and at once made his plans for escape.

But to get away from Paraguay without the consent of the government was, and had been for fifty years, next to an impossibility. He must play the courtier and sycophant till he had reinstated himself in the good graces of his Excellency. This it was not easy to do, as he had previously offended the favorite mistress, who was supposed to be the only person having any influence over Lopez. The manner in which he had incurred the anger of this Jezebel is worthy of record, as showing the state of morals that obtained at the time.

CHAPTER XXXVI.

The Funeral of Carlos A. Lopez. — Rivalry of his Sons' Mistresses. — A Fancy-Dress Ball. — The Saguiers escape from Paraguay. — Treatment of Atherton. — The People forced to appear happy and devoted to Lopez. — Frauds on English Employees. — Paraguay repudiated by the English Government. — The French Consul, Laurent Cochelet.

AT the death of the late President, his remains were taken to be interred in the church of La Trinidad, some four miles from the capital. There was a great funeral procession, as a matter of course, and the railroad train was put in requisition to convey people to the station, situate some quarter of a mile from the church. The immediate family went in carriages; but as carriages were scarce in Asuncion, those not in requisition for the family were employed to convey the near relatives to and from the station. After the ceremonies, and while people were leaving the church, Carlos Saguier, as master of ceremonies, escorted the Lady President and her daughters to their carriage, and was making himself useful in every way. As it happened, a vacant carriage stood near, — in fact, the carriage of the favorite. She was not at hand, and as fate would have it the mistress of her paramour's brother Venancio stood there ready to go. Saguier, without reflection, told her to get into the coach, and ordered the postilion to drive to the station and return. But scarcely had the carriage started when the favorite appeared, with her children by her side, her face covered "to hide the tears she did not shed." No sooner did she catch a glimpse of the carriage moving away with her despised sister-in-law — or, more properly, sister-out-of-law — than she forgot her grief, and turned furiously on Saguier to know why she had been thus insulted. Saguier protested the best intentions, and said he had supposed the carriage would return before she would require it, and did not know that it was purposely for her. Scornfully telling him he lied, she moved off indignantly on foot for the station, and for the first time that day she then wept real tears, and would not be comforted.

But in time he managed to placate the wrath of the offended mistress, and was called by her to consult on matters of display and ceremony. A fancy-dress ball being given a few months after, he was obsequious in his attentions and assiduous in his services. This ball, like most balls in Asuncion, was strictly an official affair. People were invited to attend, but the invitation among the natives was equivalent to a command. The imported favorite was the leader of fashion, and had the almost unlimited direction of all such matters; and the custom of having a new dress for each ball, which when a grisette of Paris she had observed, she enforced in Asuncion among people who would have danced much more at their ease barefoot and in the Paraguayan *tupoi*. At this fancy ball she prescribed the dress for all, — assigning the garb of a Swiss shepherdess for one, an Italian fruit-seller for another, and prescribing for each some peculiar style of costume, but arraying herself in the gorgeous style of Queen Elizabeth. Carlos Saguier, as the Doge of Venice, paid court to the Queen; and the affair passed off so well that he seemed to regain the favor which he had lost, both with the favorite and the President. He and his brother Fernando continued their business affairs ostensibly as before, though gradually contracting their operations, collecting their dues, and sending their proceeds to Buenos Aires. They had a contract with the Brazilian Navigation Company to supply the coal in the Paraguayan ports for the line of steamers running from Montevideo to Matto Grosso. This profitable contract they had held for years, of course with the consent and approval of the government, as no subject was ever allowed to transact any business that the government did not approve. As yet, up to the latter part of the year 1863, there were no indications of a rupture with Brazil, the coal contract was in full force, and the business of the Saguiers seemed to be going on as prosperously as ever. But they knew the character of the man that was over them, and they saw the ruin that was impending as clearly as Elisha foresaw the cruelties and tyranny that would be inflicted on his people by Hazael. Fernando, alleging that his business affairs required his presence in Buenos Aires, asked for a passport, — no one was allowed to leave the country without a passport, and stowaways and fugitives were unknown, — and it was granted. Before his return Carlos did the same thing, having first, in a familiar conversation, mentioned his desire to make his usual visit at carnival time to the Porteños. He, too, obtained his passport; but he had hardly escaped beyond the reach of Lopez when it appeared that the English merchant, Atherton, had purchased nearly all their personal property, including their contract with the Brazilian Navigation Company, and all the coal then on hand. The wrath of his Excellency, when he found that these men had outwitted and escaped him, was Achillean. For a person to escape from his grasp was an insult to his clemency and justice. To resign his power over an individual was like giving up his heart's blood. Throughout his whole career, if a person was once in his power he held to him with an iron grasp, as we shall cite numerous instances to prove; and even those who had incurred danger and toil to enter his country to serve him found that country was to them a very cave of Cacus, and that for them there was no egress during the lifetime of the friend they had come to serve. The appropriate motto to have placed over the entrance to Paraguay was that which Dante saw at the entrance of the Inferno, "Let him who enters here leave hope behind."

But if the Saguiers had escaped him, yet Atherton was still in Paraguay. His purchase had been in accordance with the forms of law, the papers had been duly signed and witnessed, and there was no just reason why, on showing them, he should not take possession. But he was suddenly interrupted in his negotiation. One morning a large police force entered his premises and arrested him, searched every nook and corner of his house, and seized all his account-books with every letter, bill, paper, or scrap that had a word written on it, and carried them away. These were examined minutely to find if Atherton had not in some way evaded or violated the law. He himself was afterwards examined at great length, in the expectation of finding something illegal in his conduct. An examination by Paraguayan officials, whenever they wished to make out a case against a man, was nothing more nor less than a protracted torture. In the case of Atherton, he was taken early in the morning to the office of an *escribano*, or clerk, who began by asking all sorts of irrelevant questions. Then, if an answer was not satisfactory, he was threatened with dire punishment for his contumacy, and finally the answer would be written down as the government desired it should be. The examination conducted in this manner was continued all day, the man not knowing whether he was to be sent to prison at night, taken out and shot the next morning, or again set at liberty. He was allowed nothing to eat all day, and even a glass of water was refused him by the churlish escribano. He was permitted to return to his house to sleep at night, but the examination was continued till his answers as written out by the escribano inculpated him in serious offences. The property bought from Saguier, consisting of a coal-hulk and coal, and two or three tanneries, was seized by the government; and when all was arranged to its satisfaction, and Atherton was made to appear to have committed many and gross offences, he was compelled to sign the testimony, not given by him, but as written down by the escribano, and certified to by him as being a true and correct report of his evidence.

It was when the affair had arrived at this stage that Mr. Thornton arrived to present his credentials as minister plenipotentiary to Paraguay. Naturally he was very indignant at such treatment of an English subject by the direct action of the government, which, if perpetrated by a great power, would be followed by a peremptory demand for reparation. His energetic protests were followed by a return of Mr. Atherton's books and papers, and he was allowed to resume his former business. The Saguier property, however, was not restored to him. The government, though it could prove nothing against Atherton or the regularity of the purchase, had another way to effect its plan of sequestration. The Saguiers had a younger brother, Adolfo, who never having been connected with them in business, and, being an employee of the government, they had supposed he would not be implicated with them. This brother was now brought forward and forced to assert a partnership interest with the brothers, and a suit was commenced ostensibly in his behalf. The judgment was, of course, in his favor. Atherton, nevertheless, appealed to a higher court; but the government having the property tied up and secure against both him and the Saguiers delayed any further action till the death of Atherton, which took place a year or so later, after which there was no foreigner to move further in the matter.

This action of Lopez, in the case of Atherton, convinced Mr. Thornton that Paraguay was no place for his countrymen or for any foreigners. Though he had been in Paraguay several times before, he saw that in the short time the new President had been in power he had established a reign of fear and terror such as he had never seen before. The popular festivities of balls, bull-fights, races, and games were kept up during all the time he remained; and every evening there were bonfires in the plazas, around which the people gathered in large numbers, and danced till late at night to testify their joy and their love for the great Lopez, in whose honor these demonstrations were made. Yet even by a stranger it was easy to be seen that it was all forced, and that there was no real joy or hilarity among the people. Processions were sent every evening, under direction of the police, with bands of music, through the streets; and they would always stop in front of the residence of the different foreign ministers and consuls and perform some dance of the country. The object of these forced demonstrations was to show the representatives of foreign governments how happy the people were, and how devoted to Lopez. It had the contrary effect; for not even the ominous hints of the better class of people, the prisons full of the best men in the country, or anything else, so completely proved the abject fear and slavery of the masses as these forced attempts to appear happy.

While Mr. Thornton was there, I remember that one day, at about 3 P. M., I went to call on him. He had rooms in the Club on the same street with, and very near to, Lopez's private residence. It was an oppressively warm day, slight showers and sunshine alternating with each other, and not a breath of air stirring. Yet at this hour a band of music was playing in front of the President's house, and about fifty of the lower class of men and women were trying to make it appear that they were dancing, laughing, and shouting from excess of joy. The disgust of her Majesty's Minister at such a shallow device to impose upon him was intense, and the language he used in expressing his opinion was certainly free from diplomatic generalities.

Exhibitions of this kind, and the other evidences that a reign of terror had set in which he saw, served to convince the Minister that the best advice he could give his countrymen was to leave Paraguay as soon as possible.

But, with few exceptions, they were all of them under contract with the government. They had been engaged in London by the agents of Paraguay, and all of them were dissatisfied with their treatment. The conduct of these agents, J. and A. Blyth, machinists and founders, Limehouse, was scandalous and dishonest. They would receive orders to engage a certain number of machinists, draughtsmen, engineers, physicians, or any class of men skilled in their profession whose services were needed, under contract generally for three years, at a stipulated rate of wages. By advertising in the newspapers, or in some other way, they would make known that such men were needed, and candidates for the situations would apply to them for the terms and the services required. The answer would always be that they were wanted in that modern paradise, Paraguay. But as probably not one out of ten had ever heard of such a place, and those who had could not tell whether it was approached from the Pacific or Atlantic, they naturally desired more definite information as to the character of the country, the sort of government they would be under, and the expenses of living to which they would be subjected. The Blyths could not speak from personal knowledge, they had never been in Paraguay; but they had a witness at hand, — a convenient and swift witness, and one paid by Paraguay for the very purpose of lying and deceiving young men into a service which few would ever leave alive. This man is since dead, and as no good purpose can be subserved by fixing the stigma on his name which his offences richly merit, I withhold it. He had been employed to take out to the Plata the steamer Rio Blanco, which had been purchased in England in the year 1854. He remained in Paraguay some two or three years, and after his return was pensioned off as capper, or witness, for Paraguay. To him the unsuspecting victims would be referred, and the bluff, honest old seaman would invite them to dine with him. Over the dinner he would descant on the glories of Paraguay, its beautiful and healthful climate, its luscious fruits, its amiable men and lovely women, and, above all, its free and liberal government; a republic, too, where the poor young stranger found every avenue for wealth and distinction open to him, with no effete aristocracy to monopolize all the places of honor and profit. And then the expenses there were as nothing. The country was so fertile and prolific that twenty pounds a year was sufficient to support a family; and the government was liberal with strangers, especially the English, giving them houses rent free, and loading them with favors at all times. Well might he call it liberal! It was probably paying for the dinner they were eating, but it was the bait for gudgeons. In justice to this man it should be said that his treatment by the Paraguayan government was doubtless much better than that of his countrymen whom he induced to go there. But the abuse was continued so long, and so many complaints went back to him and to the Blyths from their unfortunate dupes, that he must have known he was grossly deceiving all whom he afterwards encouraged to go there.

The contracts made with these men were for a stipulated number of pounds sterling. Nothing more was ever said to them on that score. But as soon as they reached Paraguay they found that a pound sterling was just what the government chose to consider it. A pound sterling in the other countries of the Plata is equivalent to $ 4.90 silver, and a gold ounce is reckoned at sixteen Spanish dollars. In one of these three, it was immaterial which, they had expected to be paid. But on arriving at Paraguay, they, for the first time, learned that only one half of their wages was to be paid in coin, — and this in ounces at $ 17.25 each, instead of the current mercantile rate of $ 16. If paid in *patacones*, or silver dollars, they were reckoned at ten reals each, or one fifth more than their value, so that on the half paid in coin they were forced to submit to a reduction of from six to twenty per cent. The balance, or other half, of their wages they were obliged to receive in the Paraguayan currency, on which from the first they suffered a still greater loss. Previous to the war the price of ounces varied from twenty-one to twenty-five dollars, currency, so that the average loss on this half of their stipulated salary was about thirty per cent. After the war commenced, the paper money rapidly depreciated ; and by the middle of the year 1867, ounces sold as high as eighty to eighty-five paper dollars. None of the foreign employees, however, received any part of their pay in ounces after the war was fairly commenced ; and towards the latter part of it they were obliged to submit to a loss of twenty per cent on the half paid in silver, and of eighty per cent on the half paid in paper. But even this was not the worst. Those whose contracts expired seldom cared to make new ones, and they were forced by intimidation to work for the government on its own terms and take their pay all in paper.

The principal engineers of the railroad, Mr. Percy Burrell and Mr. Henry Valpy, were both treated in this way ; and, strange as it may seem to those familiar with the events of those terrible times, they both had the good fortune to be taken prisoners by the allies before Lopez had either shot them or tortured them to death, after the manner he had served nearly all the other foreigners in the country. Mr. Burrell was not only a man of much ability in his profession, but so much of an architect as to make the plans for the President's new palace, one of the finest buildings in South America. He had made a contract with the Blyths in London by which he was to receive eight hundred pounds sterling a year. At the commencement of the war he desired to quit the service and leave the country, but was not permitted to do so, and was afterwards ordered to the camp to perform service as military engineer. He complied, and made the plans of the encampment at Cerro Leon ; but when requested to render similar service in front of the enemy at Itapiru he declined, and was glad to save his life and liberty by consenting to continue his services as railroad engineer for half his stipulated salary, paid all in paper. Both he and Valpy were ultimately forced to perform duty in the camp under such threats that they considered the only alternative to military service in the field would be imprisonment and fetters. There were other cases of similar hardship, but this will serve as an illustration of the way Englishmen who had made contracts in London were treated after they had reached Paraguay.

On the arrival of Mr. Thornton they complained to him of the fraud that had been practised upon them. But he could only tell them, that, having made contracts to serve a foreign government, they had forfeited all protection of their own, that they could only look for justice and protection to the country whose service they had entered ; and that, if the government chose to maltreat and rob them, they had no remedy so long as their contracts lasted. But he advised them as fast as their engagements expired to leave the country, and told them if they chose to remain after that time, knowing the character of the government, it would be at their own risk. The British interests in Paraguay were not of sufficient importance to justify the English government in sending an expedition to chastise Paraguay for maltreatment of its citizens. The United States government had done that at an expense of three millions of dollars, and the expedition that went for wool came back shorn. England was not disposed to incur any such expense, nor was she disposed to have any number of her subjects exposed to the tyranny of a government that respected no law human or divine, but was subject only to the caprice of one man. Therefore her Minister advised his countrymen to leave Paraguay, and warned them that if they remained they would be at the mercy of a cruel tyrant. He said that the English government would not send a consul to Paraguay, as that would encourage more Englishmen to go there; and it was not its policy to encourage its subjects to enter foreign countries where it could not protect them without incurring millions of expense, and could not leave them to be persecuted without incurring general censure.

Having thus advised his countrymen to save themselves while there was yet time, the English Minister left Paraguay. He had received a personal affront, and had seen that Lopez was a savage and paid no regard to the rights of foreigners. His representations to his own government must have been in accordance with these impressions. Paraguay was represented to be like Abyssinia, and Lopez like King Theodore. A despotism so situated was an obstacle in the path of civilization. Insignificant in itself, it could impede the development and progress of all its neighbors. Its existence was a nuisance, and its extinction as a distinct nationality, or the overthrow of the reigning family, would be a benefit to its own people and to all the world besides.

At this time, however, President Lopez felt so strong in himself and his position that he thought he might defy the world. He was about to enter on a war for which he had been years preparing, while his enemies, whoever they might be, — for as yet he did not know against whom the war was to be made, — would be undisciplined and unprepared. A short campaign would establish his fame as a great warrior and the arbiter of South America, and then he would neither ask nor need the favor or sympathy of foreign nations.

But the projects of Lopez sadly miscarried; and when, a year after, he found he had greatly miscalculated the endurance of his adversaries, and was calling for aid from abroad, he thought it very strange that England and all Christendom did not rush to his rescue. Mr. Thornton, in the mean while, had been promoted to be her Majesty's envoy extraordinary and minister plenipotentiary to Brazil, where, instead of being snubbed at presenting his credentials, and forbidden to take his secretary with him, he had been received with unprecedented honors, and all the fine carriages that could be obtained were sent in procession to convey him and his whole suite, besides naval officers, consuls, and private citizens who chose to honor the occasion of the renewal of diplomatic relations between the two countries.

In entering upon a war that may be long and exhausting, a ruler of ordinary sense will so forelay his plans as to be on as good terms as possible with the great powers of the world. Lopez, however, pursued a course the opposite of this in regard to both England and France. He took every possible opportunity to annoy the French consul, M. Cochelet, and render his residence in Paraguay disagreeable. He would not commit any act of so gross a nature that the French government could make it a *casus belli*, but he caused it to be so well understood that the Frenchman was not in favor that scarcely anybody would visit him. The English, with one or two exceptions, dared not go near him. On one occasion Lopez called Burrell and Valpy before him, and broke forth in a furious tirade against them for their intimacy with M. Cochelet. His rage on that occasion, as described by them, was more like that of a wild beast than anything human. He raved and frothed at the mouth, accusing them of hostility to himself and friendship for his enemies. They protested that they were unconscious of any act of which he could complain. At this he launched forth still more furiously, and they supposed their hour had come. Under these circumstances they were glad to promise to serve him for mere nominal wages, and retire from his presence and never go near the obnoxious Frenchman again.

For the consul of a great nation, perhaps no man ever had so disagreeable a position as was that of M. Cochelet. For eleven months he was without a word or line from his government or from anybody beyond the limits of Paraguay. Scarcely a soul, native or foreigner, dared come near his house; and he and his family, in a city of some fifteen thousand people, were almost as isolated from the world as though they had been cast on a desert island. Not being prepared at that time to do violence to the consul himself, Lopez seemed to take a fiendish delight in arresting, imprisoning, and maltreating other French subjects purposely to annoy the consul. Of course, when the latter got an opportunity to send away his despatches he represented Lopez as he had found him; so that during the whole war the French Foreign Office could not but regard him as the common enemy of civilized nations, and give all the sympathy and moral support that a neutral nation might do to the powers allied against him.

Mr. Thornton's despatches to his government were of a similar character. He advised Earl Russell that to the despotism of Carlos A. Lopez had succeeded one that was indescribably worse; that the new President had already developed into a tyrant so vain, arrogant, and cruel that there was no misery, suffering, or humiliation to which all within his power were not exposed. Thus Lopez before the war began, and as if to show his contempt for the great powers, went out of his way to insult their representatives. He afterwards wondered why, when he was reduced to desperate straits, they did not come to his rescue; but it was no wonder to Minister Thornton or to Consul Cochelet.

CHAPTER XXXVII.

Banda Oriental. — The Demands of Brazil. — Gauchoism in the Ascendant. — Leandro Gomez. — Carreras sent to Paraguay. — Lopez declines an Alliance with the Banda Oriental, but protests against the Occupation of Oriental Territory by the Brazilian Forces. — Carreras constituted the Government. — Operations of the Brazilian Squadron. — Bombastic Circular of the Admiral. — Seizure of the Marques de Olinda, and Treatment of those on Board. — The Brazilian Minister. — Efforts in his Behalf. — Interview with the President. — Discussion of the Military Situation. — Privileges of Foreign Ministers. — Official Correspondence.

WHILE the events related in the last chapter were transpiring in Paraguay, the correspondence between the governments of Rio de Janeiro and Montevideo was approaching a conclusion. To the answer of the Oriental Minister for Foreign Relations, Don Juan J. Herrera, in which he had set up counter-claims to those made by the Brazilian commissioners, and proposed an amicable adjustment of all, the reply of the Brazilians was tantamount to this: We want our claims paid now, but yours can stand over, and unless you accede to our terms we will blockade your ports and take possession of your territory. This was the substance, expressed in diplomatic phraseology, that, unless the long-pending demands were immediately satisfied, the government of his Imperial Majesty would proceed at once to make reprisals. This note, to the credit of the little Republic, was returned unanswered, as insulting and disrespectful. The senior member of the commission, Señor Saraiva, thereupon withdrew from Montevideo and went to Buenos Aires, and presented his credentials as envoy extraordinary. So notorious and well understood was it that the Buenos Airean government was in collusion with Flores, that the announcement of this fact was universally received as a proclamation that Herod and Pilate had shaken hands and made an alliance with the unrepentant thief. From thenceforth the legitimate or blanco government, that before the Flores invasion had no opposition, and represented nearly all the wealth and respectability and four fifths of the population, was doomed. Gauchoism was again in the ascendant.

The threat of reprisals made by Saraiva previous to his departure for Buenos Aires to concert measures of aggression with that *neutral* power was carried into effect in September, 1864, by the attempt of a Brazilian gunboat to capture the Oriental steamer Villa del Salto. The effort was not successful, for by this time the Montevidean government so far realized its desperate situation as to forget the petty jealousies existing between rival factions, and call into the service its ablest men. Leandro Gomez, a man in whom all had recognized a reserved or latent power that had so clearly marked him as a natural leader as to cause him to be looked upon by all the aspirants for the Presidency — and their name was legion — as the only obstacle in their way, had at last been called upon to take command of the national forces. He was a man without military education or experience, but with a natural valor and capacity that supplied all defects, — a man whose career was too short to fill a prominent place in history, but "the deep damnation of his taking off" makes a blot on the ink-dyed page of Brazilian colorado treachery. He was then stationed at Paysandu, with a force of some eight hundred men. The Brazilian squadron had already besieged Montevideo, and its gunboats were plying up and down the river, with orders to seize any Oriental vessel that might be encountered. The steamer Villa del Salto was lying in the port of the town of the same name. Gomez sent an order for it to proceed to Paysandu. It started out into the stream, and the commander, who is accused of having been corrupted by the Brazilians, purposely kept his course on the right or Argentine bank of the river, so that the vessel was within the Argentine jurisdiction at the time. But whether or not this was done by previous agreement, it is certain that the first act of hostility on the part of Brazil took place in Argentine territory, that was at the time professing the strictest neutrality. This violation of its territory, however, was never complained of by the Argentine government. Its acquiescence in the act, on the contrary, was taken as evidence of complicity with Brazil, and Paranhos paraded the fact in the Brazilian Chambers as a justification of his own conduct. The steamer returned to the port of Villa del Salto, where, by order of Gomez, she was destroyed, to prevent her from falling into the hands of the Brazilians.

But a more important step had been taken by the Oriental government than the calling of Leandro Gomez into the military service. In July, 1864, it had despatched Antonio de las Carreras to Paraguay on a special mission. This fact being known, it was evident there was to be no more child's play or petty jealousies to distract the attention of the government or waste its resources. Carreras was extremely unpopular with the colorado party and its sympathizers on account of his part in the Quinteros affair. It was true that his energy had crushed out almost instantly the Diaz rebellion, and put revolutions out of fashion, so that no other was attempted for seven years afterwards, and the country, instead of being cursed again with civil war, enjoyed, until the time of the Flores invasion, a degree of prosperity unexampled in South American history. If he was to be readmitted into the councils of the government, it was very certain that Flores and his gauchos would have some hard fighting to do, instead of the diversions of freebooters. This, it was said at the time, had the effect to hasten the action of the Brazilian commissioners, Saraiva and Bastos, to commence reprisals, hoping that Flores, with the assistance of the Brazilian troops, would be able to drive out the legitimate government before Carreras could bring any effective resistance against them.

Carreras, on being called into the councils, offered to proceed at once to Paraguay, and if President Lopez could be induced to take up arms in defence of the Oriental independence, he would then return to take the entire management of home affairs. But he would be the government, and not subject to any cabinet councils or superior dictation. On the 28th of August he returned from his mission, and was immediately made Minister of Foreign Relations, Minister of Finance, and Minister of War and Marine. He had not been able to draw Paraguay into an alliance, though he took with him assurances that Lopez would resist the encroachments of Brazil and had seen that he was preparing for war, and was determined to make war on somebody, and show the world that it still had a great warrior, though Napoleon was dead. Soon after his departure, therefore, the Minister for Foreign Relations, José Berges, addressed a note, in accordance with the programme previously agreed upon, to the Oriental Minister resident, Vasquez Sagastume, in which the alliance previously proposed was declined. But though declining an alliance, Paraguay would by independent action endeavor to maintain the equilibrium of the Plata, and thus reach the same general result.

On the same day, August 30, 1864, Señor Berges addressed a note to Vianna de Lima, the Brazilian Minister. This note was in the form of a protest, in which, referring to the ultimatum of Commissioner Saraiva, threatening reprisals and occupation of the Oriental territory in case his demands were not satisfied, it was ambiguously stated that Paraguay would regard such a proceeding as a just cause of war. As very much depends on the construction put on this note in forming a judgment on the events that followed, a literal extract and translation of the material part of it are here given: —

'His Excellency, the President of the Republic, has ordered the undersigned to declare to your Excellency, as the representative of his Majesty the Emperor of Brazil, that the government of the Republic of Paraguay will regard any occupation of the Oriental territory by Imperial forces, for the reasons alleged in the *ultimatum* of the 4th instant, which was addressed to the Oriental government by the Emperor's minister plenipotentiary charged with a special mission near that government, as infringing the equilibrium of the states of the Plata, which concerns the Republic of Paraguay as a guaranty of its security, peace, and prosperity ; and that it protests against such an act in the most solemn manner, disclaiming from the present time all responsibility for the ulterior consequences of the present declaration." *

This was understood by the Brazilian government, as by everybody else, to be but a strong protest, and was taken as an intimation that Paraguay might declare war in case that Brazil carried her threat of reprisals and occupation of the Banda Oriental into execution. No one, however, understood it as a declaration of war, nor as an intimation that without further notice hostilities would be commenced, if Brazil should begin war against the Republic of the Uruguay. The alliance with the latter had been declined by President Lopez, and therefore an invasion of its territory could not be regarded as an act of war against Paraguay. It was not considered, even in Paraguay, that war with Brazil would commence without further notice ; and there is good reason for believing that Lopez himself did not intend it at the time, and it is certain that he had information of the hostile proceedings of Brazil against Uruguay for some days before he did any act indicating that war had begun. A short time previously he had sent a note to the Argentine government of similar import and tenor to the protest of the 30th of August. Yet the Argentines had not desisted from their course by reason of this threat of Lopez, but they continued to do just what he protested against, and yet he did not follow up his protest by any overt act of war against the Argentine Republic. It was not war

* "S. E. el Sr. Presidente de la Republica ha ordenado al abajo firmado declare á V. E. como Representante de S. M. el Emperador del Brasil ; que el Gobierno de la Republica del Paraguay considerará cualquiera ocupacion del territorio Oriental por fuerzas imperiales por los motivos consignados en el *ultimatum* del 4 de este mes, intimado al Gobierno Oriental por el Ministro Plenipotenciaro del Emperador en mision especial cerca de aquel Gobierno, como atentatorio al equilibrio de los Estados del Plata que interesa á la Republica como garantia de su seguridad, paz y prosperidad, que protesta de la manera mas solemne contra tal acto, descargándose desde luego de toda la responsibilidad de las ulterioridades de la presente declaracion."

then which followed, and no one could suppose that so different a construction would be put on the two protests so exactly alike in character. The attempt to capture the Villa del Salto took place on the 26th of August, 1864, and the Brazilian troops entered the Oriental state as early as the 16th of October. Of both of these acts President Lopez was promptly informed. But he made no intimation that war had already commenced, not even to the Oriental Minister, with whom he was in almost daily consultation. Had the war been commenced by Brazil, as was afterwards alleged, by acts of overt hostility against Uruguay, then it was clearly the duty of the government to notify the Brazilian Minister of the fact, and send him his passports. But that was not done, and there was no intention of doing anything of the kind, as it had not at that time occurred to any one, not even to Lopez, that Brazil had begun war on Paraguay.

To the protest of the 30th of August, Vianna de Lima made an immediate reply, — a reply evincing his confidence in the capacity of his own government at will to wipe Paraguay out of existence. He declared that his government would not for any consideration be diverted from its purpose of securing indemnification from the Republic of Uruguay.

It was about six weeks after the interchange of these notes that the Brazilian troops entered the Oriental territory and commenced what were called reprisals. The Brazilian government, however, declared it was not making war. It had only taken this course to collect its debts. Soon after taking this step, that certainly looked like an act of war though called by another name, the Brazilian government sent a large squadron to Montevideo to establish a blockade such as was never heard of or imagined before. The object of this was to blockade vessels bearing the national flag of the port, and leave all other flags free. A regular blockade could only exist during time of war, and therefore it was given out, that, without making war, Oriental vessels might be captured as reprisals. The Oriental vessels had previously been employed, to a greater or less extent, in conveying troops and munitions of war to different points on the river Uruguay, where they were required. To put a stop to this, the Brazilian admiral established his new kind of blockade. As the troops and arms carried by these vessels had always been employed against Flores and his gang, this lawless proceeding was evidently for his benefit, and was generally so understood. Yet there had been no declaration of war, and Brazil, like the Argentine Republic, professed to observe the strictest neutrality in the Oriental strife. It afterwards occurred to the stupid admiral, who enjoyed the title of the Baron de Tamandaré, but whose proper title would be the "Genius of Imbecility," that neutral vessels, as well as those bearing the white and blue stripes, might be employed by the Oriental government in conveying munitions of war. He therefore addressed a circular letter to the different foreign ministers in Montevideo, advising them of the kind of blockade he had established, and requesting them to give the necessary orders to all vessels under their respective flags, that they should not receive aboard either troops or munitions of war, and thus maintain the perfect neutrality incumbent on them at that juncture. But in case they did not observe that perfect neutrality, then, he said, he would be obliged to exercise over them a constant vigilance and seize whatever he found aboard contraband of war.

To this arrogant and foolish circular the ministers all immediately responded with wonderful unanimity. They all protested that there could be no such thing as neutrality, as there were no recognized belligerents. There had been no declaration of war on the part of Brazil, and therefore all commerce, whether of warlike stores and arms or general merchandise, was alike legitimate, and would be protected by their respective governments. The English *Chargé d'Affaires*, William G. Lettsom, expressed the general import of the replies of all in the following terms: "There are no belligerents in the contest now going on, inasmuch as the military chief who has thought proper to raise the standard of rebellion against the government of his country cannot be regarded by me in the character of a belligerent. He is simply a rebel; and, there being no belligerents, there are no neutrals."

After this unanimous response to his bombastic circular, the gallant admiral subsided, and made no more threats of searching neutral vessels in time of peace. He was, however, left in command of the squadron for more than two years, during which time it absolutely did nothing but disgrace itself, and spend millions on millions of money. The scintillations of his genius for doing nothing will be found to illuminate greatly the period when he was in authority.

The first overt act of hostility on the part of Brazil took place on the 26th of August, four days before the date of the Paraguayan protest. This fact was known in Asuncion by the 12th of September, if not earlier. No notice, however, was given to the Brazilian Minister that war had commenced. On the contrary, when he was asked for explanations in regard to it, he replied he had none to give, as he had no official information in regard to the matter. On the 14th of October, the invasion of the Banda Oriental by the Brazilian troops took place. This was known in Asuncion a few days later, but no one there thought of war as being at hand, nor did President Lopez at that time consider that the friendly relations with Brazil had been broken off. Vianna de Lima continued to reside at Asuncion, and held occasional interviews with the Minister for Foreign Affairs, and was treated in all things as though there had been no interruption of former relations. The Paraguayan packet steamers came and went as usual, passing the Brazilian gunboats in the river, whose commanders never suspected that they were the vessels of an enemy.

Thus affairs stood on the 9th of November, 1864, when the Brazilian packet steamer Marques de Olinda arrived at Humaita on its way, as usual, to Matto Grosso. This steamer belonged to a company that was subsidized by the government to make eight round trips a year between Rio de Janeiro and the upper waters of the Paraguay. The service was performed by an ocean packet from Rio to Montevideo, from Montevideo to Corumba in the province of Matto Grosso by the Marques de Olinda, and from Corumba to Cuyuba, a distance of some six hundred miles, in steamers of lighter draught. It had started on its regular trip, and nothing of danger was suspected, as two months had passed since the publication of the protest of the 30th of August, and no steps had been taken by Paraguay to indicate that it was at war with Brazil. On the contrary, the letters of the Brazilian Minister in Asuncion to his colleague in Buenos Aires, written after the news of the occupation of the Oriental territory by the imperial troops had reached Paraguay, made no allusion to any change in his relations with the government of Paraguay. And when the steamer reached the fortifications at Humaita she made her customary salute to the fort, which was returned as ever before, and the steamer proceeded on her way to Asuncion, where she arrived early on the morning of the 11th of November. Suspecting nothing, she brought the letters of all who chose to send their correspondence by her instead of waiting for the Paraguayan packet. The letters were promptly delivered without suspicion, the necessary coal and provisions were taken aboard, and about one o'clock the same day the steamer started again on her voyage.

Here it becomes necessary to allude to what had been transpiring elsewhere. We have seen that in the month of the preceding August Dr. Carreras had left Paraguay, bearing assurances from President Lopez that he would take a part in the war that was impending over the Republic of the Uruguay. He had a large army well organized and armed, and he had promised to employ it against those who were seeking to overthrow the Oriental independence. Returning with such assurances, Carreras was constituted *the government* of Montevideo, the three most important departments being all confided to his hands. Yet for some time Lopez made no sign. He had indeed put forth the protest of the 30th of August, but it was followed by no decided action. He had months before made a similar protest against the Argentine Republic, but he did nothing afterwards; and perhaps, on this occasion, he was only seeking to frighten by the terror of proclamations, instead of venturing into actual war. The minister resident at Asuncion, Vasquez Sagastume, was a man of most courtly manners and persuasive eloquence. His object, and that of Carreras, was to draw Lopez into some act of overt hostility so that he would be compelled to bring his large forces into the field, and thus draw off the attention of the enemies of the Oriental Republic. They cared little how he commenced his operations if he would only begin, as they owed neither respect nor good-will to the Brazilians or Argentines, who had both been making a dishonest and treacherous warfare on the legitimate government of their country, in defiance of every principle of morality and good faith. Sagastume knew the weakness of Lopez, and knew that no flattery was too gross for his ears. He told him that he was a great warrior, as had been established when he was but a boy in the campaign of Corrientes, where, though his enemies said no fighting had been done by his troops, and he had not been near enough to a battle-field to hear the whistling of a bullet, yet had his masterly dispositions so confounded the enemy that they were glad to make terms. And then with his army all armed and disciplined he could throw a large force into Brazilian territory, take possession of several important towns, and so distract and harass the Empire that his Majesty would be glad to treat for peace on any terms that the conqueror might demand. Then what a name and fame he would have!

Yet all these flattering illusions were as nothing to those that Lopez cherished in his own mind. In convivial and unguarded moments he sometimes showed that he entertained projects so vast, fanciful, and ridiculous that the revery at Alnaschar was in comparison but a reasonable calculation. But he was not yet ready to begin his grand enterprise. He had heard of the revolution in naval warfare caused by the monitors and iron-clads of the United States, and he knew that neither Brazil nor the Argentine Republic had any vessels of the kind, nor had they bespoken any. His plan was therefore to obtain one, two, or three of these invulnerable steamers before his designs were suspected by his neighbors. For this purpose he ordered his Congress to authorize a loan of $ 25,000,000, which he believed could be negotiated in Europe on such terms as would supply the funds necessary for such a fleet. Once provided with vessels of this class, then his way was clear. He would sweep down like Napoleon from the Alps on unprotected Buenos Aires and Montevideo. He would have the valley of the Plata at his feet, and then, while all the world trembled at the terror of his name, he would sweep round to Rio de Janeiro and dictate to it terms of surrender; and then, while the Yankees were paralyzed at his audacity, he would enter the harbor of New York and demand satisfaction for the insult and wrongs suffered by his country in the affair of the Water Witch.

But affairs seemed to be culminating in the Banda Oriental, and that in contempt of his protest and his promise to preserve the equilibrium. He wanted time, if not time sufficient to make his loan and build or buy iron-clads, at least till a large quantity of arms already ordered, and many of them on the way, should be safe above Humaita. The Oriental government, impatient of delay, sent several agents in a semi-official capacity to urge immediate action, and to see and report if Lopez was really preparing for war. Among these was a colonel in the Oriental army, named Laguna, and a man by the name of Juan J. Soto, who formerly having been a merchant in Asuncion had known Lopez intimately, and had ever since kept up a correspondence with him. The former, it will be seen, remained too long, and to his great sorrow. Soto, however, returned and reported the attitude of Lopez as doubtful and undecided. But he soon devised a way to make him break cover.

The Marques de Olinda was to start on her regular trip for Matto Grosso, and it was reported that the Brazilian war steamer Amazonas was to accompany her. It was surmised that the two were to take up a large quantity of arms, and it was known that an eminent military engineer and a new

Governor or President for the province of Matto Grosso were to go up at the same time. It was also known that a valuable cargo would be taken, besides a large sum of money. Soto, being informed of all this, wrote to President Lopez, giving him a full account of all he had learned, and advised him by all means to seize the steamers. The letter he sent by the Marques de Olinda, whose capture he advised. The intention of sending the Amazonas was for some reason abandoned, and the Marques de Olinda started alone, and nothing occurred to her till after she had left Asuncion on the 11th of November.

President Lopez was at the time in the encampment at Cerro Leon, thirty-five miles from the capital. The correspondence brought by the steamer was taken out to him in the morning, and until he received it the state was at peace. In the afternoon, however, some hours after the Marques had left the port, an order was sent in, as fast as the engine detached from the train could bring it, for the Paraguayan steamer Tacuari to pursue the Marques de Olinda and order her to return to Asuncion, and if she did not comply to capture her by force. As soon as the fires could be lighted the Tacuari started, and being a faster vessel than the other, and crowding on all the steam she could make, she overtook the Marques the next day before she had passed the Paraguayan frontier; and the next night the two were anchored side by side in the harbor of Asuncion, and communication between all persons on board and the shore was strictly prohibited.

On learning, through common report, of these facts, the Brazilian Minister immediately addressed a note to the government, asking explanations; and the next day, the 14th, received an answer, together with another note dated two days earlier, in which the Foreign Minister, Berges, formally declares that the friendly relations hitherto existing between Brazil and Paraguay had, by the conduct of the former in its invasion of the Oriental Republic, been broken. This note evidently was not written till after the taking of the Marques de Olinda, and at the time of its date Paraguay did not consider itself at war.

The seizure of the steamer was an afterthought, and the note to Vianna de Lima, dated two days before it was written or delivered to him, was only a stupid and characteristic attempt to give a form of regularity to a most atrocious and unlawful proceeding. The new President of Matto Grosso was kept a close prisoner, and so was the military engineer and the commander and crew of the steamer. Not one of them was destined to see his friends or country again. Thus ensnared, they were to rot in prison. The Minister was not allowed to hold any communication with them. After a few days' detention on board the vessel, they were all, with the exception of the engineers, who were Englishmen, and some other passengers who were foreigners, transferred to some barracks near the bank of the river, and a few weeks after were sent into the interior, since when little more is known of them than that for a long time they were held close prisoners and given Paraguayan treatment, under which they dragged out some a shorter and some a longer period of misery, till they all died of starvation and torture.

To give the further appearance of regularity to the seizure of the Marques de Olinda, an admiralty court was improvised to decide on the legality of her capture. The proceedings of this admiralty court have never been published; and of the members who composed it, it is safe to say not a single one had the least idea before then what an admiralty court was. The accused party was not represented; neither officers, crew, nor passengers were allowed to be present or to give their testimony, nor was it ever known, except to the government, who composed the court. All that is known is, that what purported to be the judgment of a court, signed by Don Andres Gill, the chief-justice of Paraguay, condemning the vessel as a prize of war, was published in the *Semanario*. By the organic law of Paraguay, all cases whatever are subject to appeal to the President, so that the farce of a trial is but a roundabout way of recording his opinion or determination. In this case it is very sure that every step taken was according to his direct orders, and that if any member of the court had offered an opinion questioning the legality of the proceeding, he would have passed the next night in prison heavily loaded with fetters.

The seizure of the Marques de Olinda in the manner and under the circumstances in which she was taken was not so much a crime on the part of Lopez as a mistake. It was the commencement of a war in a manner so unexpected and so insulting that it left no middle ground for treaty or for arranging terms of peace. From that moment Brazil could never treat with Lopez without incurring the contempt and derision of the whole world. Brazil was a great empire, the largest in extent, with one exception, in the world. It had a population of some nine or ten millions, or more than ten times as many as Paraguay; and yet the latter had, without notice or previous declaration of war, seized a Brazilian steamer, made prisoners of her passengers and crew, and then defiantly waited for the Brazilians to come and get satisfaction. Brazil had large provinces, half as large as Europe, to the north of Paraguay, that were scarcely accessible except by the route that the Marques de Olinda was pursuing at the time she was captured. Lopez, without previous notice, had seized this steamer, in violation of all rules of modern warfare, and insisted he had a right to do so. If he had such right, then he would have the right to do it again, and Brazil would be virtually cut off from her northwestern provinces, for another steamer would never venture within his grasp. If he had no right to do it, he had shown he was not amenable to the laws of nations, and therefore was a common enemy. Besides, the defiant attitude he had taken rendered it certain that any offers of compromise or arrangement would have been met with insult, and that in his arrogance he would have demanded terms to which Brazil could not possibly accede. For a great power like Brazil to have proposed to treat under such circumstances would have shown such conscious weakness as would have endangered the integrity of the nation.

There had been, as we have previously seen, elements of insubordination and discontent for many years threatening the rupture of the Empire. But this indignity to the flag served to hush all discord, and the sentiment was universal that no terms should be made with the author of it. A proposal to arrange the affair through mediation or by any peaceable means would have been met by a general storm of indignation, — a storm that would in all probability have left the Empire a wreck from which would have arisen several republics of the South American type. The life of the Empire was at stake; and so, throughout the whole war that followed, the Brazilian government felt and acknowledged it must make an end of Lopez, or else see the nation dismembered.

Lopez had thus, by his seizure of the steamer, commenced a war with a nation apparently ten times as strong as his own, the end of which must be his own destruction or that of the Brazilian Empire. There was no middle ground on which terms of peace could be made, leaving him still in power. It was a crime thus to seize an innocent merchant vessel and make prisoners of her passengers and crew; and it was a blunder to stake all on the hazard of the die when the odds were so greatly against him.

Immediately on the seizure of the Marques de Olinda, orders were given that no vessel should leave the port, and that no person who might reveal the news should be permitted to pass the frontier. A confidential agent of the government, however, was sent to notify the Paraguayan agent in Buenos Aires of what had occurred, that he might take the necessary precautions in regard to any vessels in the river having arms or merchandise for Paraguay. This messenger also carried the money taken from the Marques de Olinda, two hundred thousand dollars in Brazilian currency, at that time at par. This money it was intended should have an additional signature to it before passing into circulation, and, had the news of its capture by Lopez reached Buenos Aires before the money itself, notice would have been given cautioning the public that all money wanting such signature would not be redeemed. But several days passed after the agent of Paraguay received the money before a word was known by the public of the important events that had transpired up river. During this time the bills had all passed into the hands of unsuspecting third parties, and were redeemed by the bank without question.

The unexpected seizure of the steamer and the harsh treatment of all on board of her naturally caused not only indignation, but alarm, to the Minister, Vianna de Lima. On receiving the letter of Señor Berges advising him that the friendly relations of the two governments had ceased, he immediately sent a note protesting against the detention of the Marques de Olinda, and asking passports for himself, family, and suite, that he might leave the country on the said steamer. The passports were sent the same day, but nothing was said of the means by which the Minister was to depart. The ports were closed, and for him and his family to leave the country in any way, except by the river, was next to impossible.

In this extremity, as his own relations with the government had ceased, the Minister must apply to the representative of another nation to interpose in his behalf and obtain such means of conveyance from the country as were consistent with the dignity of his position and the comfort and health of his family. And here the course of the narrative compels me to intrude the part that, as dean or senior member of the diplomatic body, I had to act in aid of the nonplussed Minister.

The President was still at Cerro Leon, and, hoping to arrange the affair without any formal correspondence, I sought an interview with the Minister for Foreign Affairs, Berges. I found him guarded and non-committal, and from the fact that he suggested it would be well for me to confer personally with the President on the matter I inferred he had not been instructed for such a contingency. The next morning, therefore, I took the train and went out to the camp. It was situate in a beautiful place, at the foot of two considerable hills, that, uniting bases with a third in the rear, made a watershed of sufficient extent to afford a copious stream of water, that, after supplying the troops, was collected into an artificial pond or reservoir that gave them all opportunities for bathing. The camp was located on an inclined plain that was of sufficient extent both for barracks and for field exercises. As I always found, before and since, whenever I had the honor to visit his Excellency, there was a funereal silence prevailing all around; no rude play, no light jesting among the soldiers, no listlessness, no shouts, laughter, or even smiles, but all with a serious, sad, anxious look, as if afraid of some dire and immediate calamity.

Directly on my arrival at the camp I was shown into the presence of his Excellency. After the usual commonplaces, I told him of the object of my visit, and expressed my surprise at the course of his government in detaining the Marques de Olinda, — for, up to that time, I could not believe he would be so foolhardy as to refuse to let her go. I told him that such a proceeding in time of peace was unprecedented in modern times; and that, as there had been no declaration of war, and the Brazilians had not suspected such action, there could be no justification of such a proceeding. He replied that war already existed, and therefore he was justified in seizing the Marques de Olinda and making prisoners of her officers and crew, and all others aboard of her who were in the service of the Brazilian government. I dissented entirely from his views, and told him that beginning the war in that way would compel Brazil to make a more energetic war upon him than it would or could have done, had he commenced after giving due notice. He said he had intimated what would be his course in the protest of the 30th of August. "But," said I, "that was not a declaration of war, nor even a declaration that there would be war; and the party most concerned, the Brazilians, never understood that war with Paraguay would necessarily follow a disregard of that protest." Certainly, he said, Brazil could not have put the same construction on the protest as he had done, else it would not have sent the steamer above Humaita. He then went on with more candor than discretion to say that the situation of Paraguay was such that only by a war could the attention and respect of the world be secured to her. Isolated as she was, and scarcely known beyond the South American states, so would she remain till by her feats of arms she could compel other nations to treat her with more consideration. Paraguay was a small power, he admitted, in comparison with Brazil; but she had advantages of position that gave her an equality of strength with any of her neighbors. Every soldier that Brazil might send against Paraguay must be brought thousand of miles and at great expense, whereas the Paraguayan troops were on their own territory, and their services would cost comparatively nothing. Besides they would be already fortified and intrenched before the Brazilians could arrive in any considerable numbers, and then, having shown the world their strength, and demonstrated to Brazil that they were not to be conquered except at ruinous cost and sacrifice, the Imperial government would be glad to treat for peace on terms highly advantageous to Paraguay; the old questions of boundaries would then be settled, and Paraguay would afterwards be recognized as a nation whose friendship was to be sought. The war could not last but a few months, for Brazil was not in a condition to engage in a long struggle, and, after the shedding of blood enough to show that Paraguay had the force necessary to protect herself, it would be easy to make peace.

I combated these ideas by saying that Brazil would not send a small force to Paraguay; that the government of the Emperor was well aware of his advantages of position and the number of his troops, and that he had no standing army sufficient to venture it near Paraguay until it was at least doubled or trebled in number; that Brazil being a very large and sparsely settled country, it would take six months at least before it could raise, equip, and call together an army large enough to send against Paraguay; that the troops would probably be sent by way of the ocean and the river, and that undoubtedly the Brazilian navy would be reenforced with iron-clads and monitors as soon as money could effect it, and I was greatly mistaken if any considerable force were ready to attack Paraguay in less than a year. But my reasoning, though but the plainest common sense, had no effect. He was bent on war, and he could not realize that, beginning it in that way, Brazil never could, never would, and never ought to treat with him.

I then said, that, supposing war was indeed begun, what was to be done with the Minister. His rights and immunities were not affected by it, and he was entitled to leave the country as freely as he had entered it. Lopez said that he had got his passports, and might leave as soon as he pleased. But how was he to get away? No vessel was allowed to leave the port. True, he said, the ports were temporarily closed, but he was not bound to open them for the departure of an enemy's ambassador when it might work great loss to the country. He could go by land if he liked, and if he did n't he could stay till the river was again free. I told him the idea that the Minister, his wife, sister, three children, secretary of legation, and servants could go by land was preposterous. The distance from Asuncion to Corrientes, the first town beyond the confines of Paraguay, was about two hundred and fifty miles. The roads were very bad, crossed by innumerable streams, some of which were scarcely fordable, while there were many broad *esteros*, or marshes, so that the route was, in that season of high water, difficult and wearisome, even for men accustomed to exposure and the saddle. To refuse them all other means of leaving the country except by land was therefore tantamount to a flat refusal for them to leave the country at all. He said that was their misfortune, but no fault of his; and I then began to realize that he probably intended to keep them all in the country as prisoners or hostages. I then said, that, whatever fault he might have to find with the Brazilian government or with its minister to Paraguay, he could have none against the passengers or crew of the steamer. Of course, they could not have had any idea that there was war existing, or else they would never have ventured into the country; and as their detention could not be of any service to Paraguay, but a source of care and expense rather, it was not only just, but expedient, that they should be allowed to depart. He was, however, disinclined to discuss that question then, and said it would receive due consideration after the case of the Minister was disposed of. Regarding that, I said, there was no occasion for any discussion, for, as dean of the diplomatic body, I was obliged to insist on the rights of legation; that I considered the Brazilian Minister had an unquestionable right to leave the country without any unnecessary delay; and that his detention would be an infringement of the immunities to which all duly accredited diplomatic persons were entitled, and if such a violation of the established laws, recognized by the governments of all civilized nations as binding and sacred, might be practised towards one minister, it might be towards all; therefore, in this case, it would be my duty, if the Brazilian Minister and his suite were not speedily provided with means for leaving the country, to protest, and I certainly should protest, against the act as unlawful; and then, if my protest were disregarded, I must ask for my own passports.

It was this threat, as I have always supposed, that secured the escape of Vianna de Lima and his family; for though the President had no reason to care anything for me personally, yet he did care to have an American minister in the country, for the only minister besides myself then left there was the Oriental, Sagastume, whose government was already tottering to its fall. His Excellency, however, showed no signs of yielding, and at the time I considered that my term of diplomatic service was near its close. Had he remained firm in the purpose that he then entertained of keeping them as prisoners in Paraguay, there was but one course for me to pursue: first, to protest against the act; and, next, to demand my passports, and leave the country if I could.

Our conversation lasted for two or three hours, and at the close it seemed as though it was Lopez's intention to detain the Minister and his family in the country. But having told him that such a course would be followed by a demand for my own passports, I took leave of him for a short time to call on the Surgeon-General, Dr. William Stewart, having first accepted his invitation to return and dine with him at a later hour.

The dinner is worthy of description, if for nothing else

for the number of courses. Everything was cooked in Paraguayan fashion. Soups, stews, forced meats, asado, vermicelli in a pottage with eggs, rice in the same way, and a variety of dishes I have never seen elsewhere than in Paraguay, were brought on, one after another, till it seemed that the dinner would not end until somebody died of repletion. To the credit of the President's stomach, it must be admitted that no dish was dishonored by his neglect. He partook of all with apparently a keen, if not a discriminating relish.

At the dinner were present two others who had the honor of generally dining at the same table with the President. These were Dr. Stewart and General Wenceslao Robles. The fortunes and fate of them both will be alluded to in their proper place.

After the dinner, at which the wine was not spared, we fell to discussing again the question that had brought me to the camp. By this time it seemed the President had reconsidered his previous resolution; at least, he assumed a more moderate tone. He said that it was of the first importance that the news of what had occurred should not pass the frontiers of Paraguay until several vessels, including the packet steamer Paraguayri had passed Humaita, or were safely beyond the reach of any Brazilian gunboats. That difficulty, I observed, would be obviated by the Minister, who, doubtless, would give all necessary assurances, in behalf of his government, that no advantage should be taken of any information that might be conveyed by the vessel taking him out of the country, and that the said vessel should be allowed to return to Paraguay without let or hindrance on the part of any Brazilian gunboat. To this it was objected, that, after what had occurred, Brazil might not consider herself bound to respect the pledge given by her minister. To meet this difficulty, I suggested that, however little inclined it might be to respect a promise made to Paraguay, it would be slow to break one made to a government much stronger than itself, and that I did not doubt Vianna de Lima would, in the name of his government, pledge himself in terms as strong as language could make them, both to Brazil and to the United States, to observe the condition, that in no form or manner would the former take advantage of any information that might be carried by the steamer that went to take him away.

After an infinite amount of quibbling and prevarication, at length we agreed to arrange the affair on this basis: I was to return to the capital and address a formal note to the Minister for Foreign Relations, which he was to answer, setting forth the difficulties and dangers in the way; and then I was to write again, sending Vianna de Lima's guaranty to Paraguay, and a copy of the one to me, that the terms agreed on should be strictly observed by all Brazilian authorities. With this understanding I returned the same night to the capital, and the next morning, having first seen Vianna de Lima, who assented to the terms I had agreed upon, — and would have gladly assented to harder ones to secure his egress from the country,—I addressed a note, on the 17th of November, to Señor Berges. The Minister, however, went to Cerro Leon the next day; and from what followed it would seem that the President had repented of his after-dinner concessions. On the 19th I received an answer to mine of the 17th, but it in no respect conformed to what had been agreed upon between the President and myself. After reciting the events that had occurred by which the two countries had been brought into hostilities, the Foreign Secretary says that the ports have for urgent reasons been temporarily closed, but that it is probable they will soon be opened again, so that the Brazilian Minister may leave by way of the river, but that, if he is in too great haste to await that time, he is at liberty to leave by land whenever he likes. From this I inferred that it was the intention of the President to recede from the verbal promise he had given me, and I therefore resolved to make it a question of fact, veracity, and good faith between us, and then, if he should deny my statements or refuse to execute his promise, I should have no course left but to demand my passports.

In my next note, therefore, I alluded to the circumstances of my interview with the President, and stated that Señor Vianna de Lima was prepared to give all the assurances for the safe return of the steamer, and that no advantage should be taken of any information conveyed by it. This intimation that I waited for the President to fulfil his promise greatly annoyed him, and the next note to me was carping and captious. It was evident that the President still hesitated whether to allow the Brazilians to depart or to detain them in the country. At length, however, a steamer was promised, and, as agreed upon, the Minister gave a pledge in the name of his government, in clear and precise language, both to Paraguay and the United States, that the conditions agreed upon should be observed. Still Lopez was not satisfied, and in the next note of his Foreign Secretary he said that he had supposed I was to give a similar pledge on the part of the United States. To this I replied I never promised anything of the kind. I had no authority to pledge my government to a course that would involve it in war and make it an ally of Paraguay in case Brazil did not observe the compact made by her minister. It would be for the President of the United States, with the approbation of Congress, to decide on the course it would adopt towards Brazil for any breach of contract or violation of faith. The powers of ministers did not go quite so far as to permit them to involve governments in war without their knowledge or consent.

This was construed to be an intimation that they did not know anything about the duties of foreign ministers, and, I learned indirectly, gave great offence, as from the time of Francia any suggestion that wisdom would not die with the head of the existing government was always a mortal affront. But as they had shown their ignorance by asking me to do an act that they ought to have known would have exceeded my powers, they wisely concluded to say no more on that subject, but try and catch me tripping on something else. The only occasion that offered was this: the Paraguayan packet steamer that arrived after the seizure of the Marques de Olinda had brought, all unconscious of danger, a special bearer of despatches for the Brazilian legation. He arrived after the Minister had received his passports, and, of course, wished to leave with him. I accordingly wrote a brief note to Señor Berges, advising him of the arrival of this bearer of despatches, and asking for a passport for him as a member of the legation who was entitled to the same privileges and immunities as the Minister. At this stage the deliberation was long and hesitating. Could they not reply to my note that it was disrespectful and insulting to the government? What right had I to tell them that a bearer of despatches had any peculiar rights? Did n't they know it before? and was it not insolent in me to tell them so, and thus assume that I knew more about such affairs than they did? After mature deliberation, however, they concluded that, much as they wanted to detain Vianna de Lima and his family, they had better let him go than have a rupture with me; and at last, after going through an infinite amount of circumlocution, and making a still longer delay, a little steamer was put in readiness, and on the last day of the month, three weeks after the taking of the Marques de Olinda, to my great delight, I saw them all on board. Until almost the last moment I had feared that some excuse or pretext for detaining them would be found; and though I then did not so fully realize the danger they were in as I had reason to afterwards, I may yet say I have seldom passed the same length of time in such anxiety. In the very limited amount of good society in Asuncion, we had welcomed these people as a great accession to the little circle; and though I have not often seen a family in which all the members were so agreeable, intelligent, and interesting, I may say I had never at that time heard sound so sweet as that made by the departing paddles of the little Parana that carried them away.

The despatches sent by the Brazilian government, which were considered so important that a special messenger had come to deliver them, were, of course, too late to be of any service. Señor Vianna de Lima, by answering the protest of the 30th of August so hastily, and without waiting for further instructions, had given the provocation of the violent and unlawful seizure of the Marques de Olinda. Had he awaited the arrival of further orders from home, it is probable the Marques would not have been seized at the time she was, and if war had followed afterwards it would have been commenced in a manner that would not have rendered impossible a subsequent arrangement of terms of peace. So far was the Emperor of Brazil from meditating war with Paraguay, or suspecting it already existed, that the bearer of despatches, whose arrival came near to being so fatal to the Minister, had come to bring the official letters of the Emperor to his "great and good friend," President Lopez, announcing the contract of marriage of his two daughters with European princes. It was because he had foreseen that, in disregard of his own overtures, such letters would be received, he had begun the war; and before they reached Paraguay he had provoked a death-struggle in which he or the Emperor must fall, never to rise again.

END OF VOL. I.

Cambridge: Electrotyped and Printed by Welch, Bigelow, & Co.

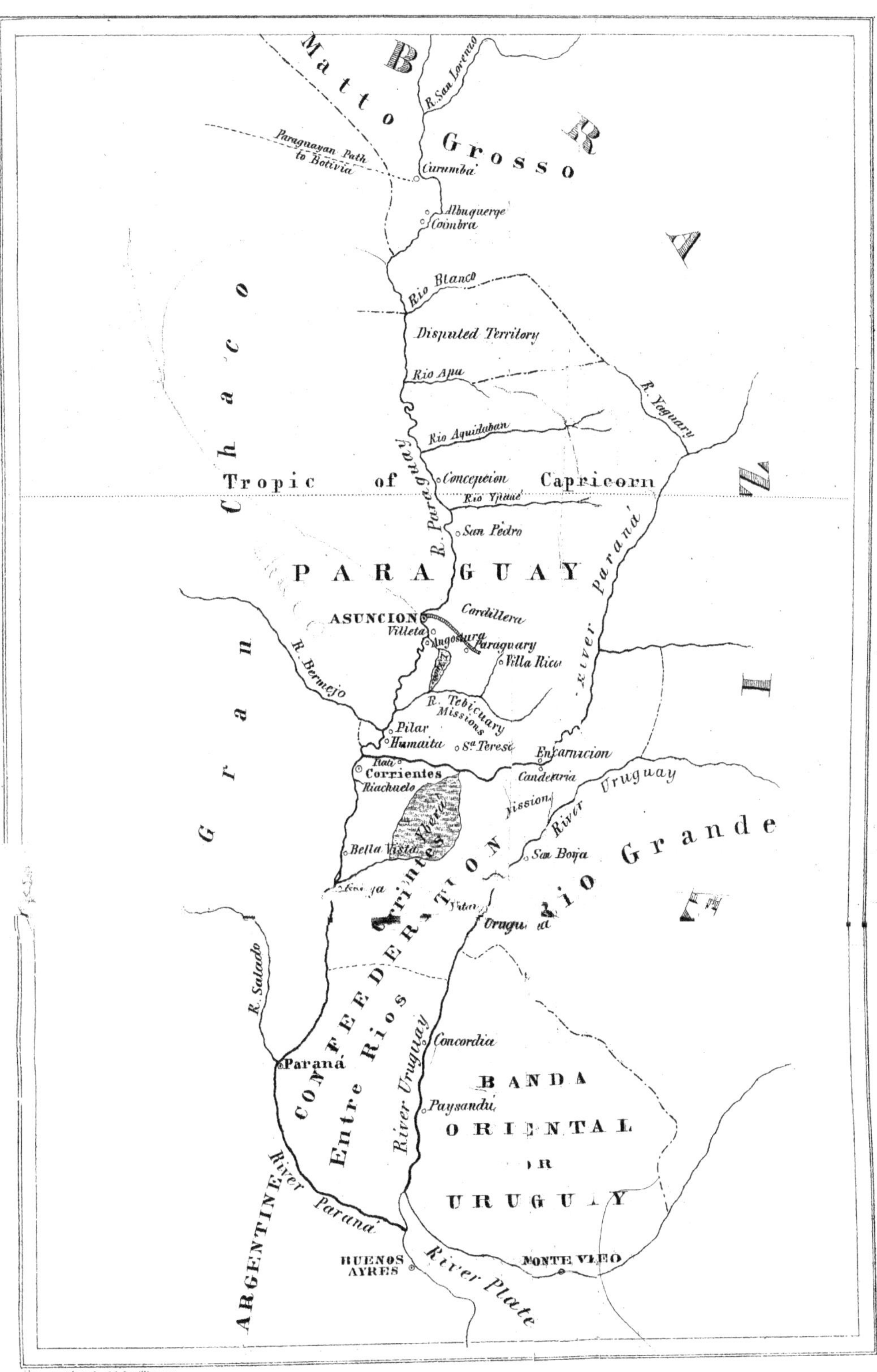

From Drawings by Col. Geo. Thompson.

www.ingramcontent.com/pod-product-compliance
Lightning Source LLC
LaVergne TN
LVHW021224110826
845150LV00002B/240

* 9 7 8 1 4 2 5 5 6 4 4 0 7 *